D0378781

HAUNTED CITY

HAUNTED CITY
NUREMBERG
AND THE NAZI PAST

NEIL GREGOR

YALE UNIVERSITY PRESS
NEW HAVEN AND LONDON

Copyright © 2008 Neil Gregor

All rights reserved. This book may not be reproduced in whole or in part, in any form (beyond that copying permitted by Sections 107 and 108 of the U.S. Copyright Law and except by reviewers for the public press) without written permission from the publishers.

For information about this and other Yale University Press publications, please contact:
U.S. Office: sales.press@yale.edu   www.yalebooks.com
Europe Office: sales @yaleup.co.uk   www.yaleup.co.uk

Set in Minion by IDSUK (DataConnection) Ltd.
Printed in Great Britain by TJ International, Padstow, Cornwall

Library of Congress Cataloging-in-Publication Data

Gregor, Neil, 1969–
    Haunted city: Nuremberg and the Nazi past/Neil Gregor.
      p.m.
    Includes bibliographical references and index.
    ISBN 978–0–300–10107–2 (ci: alk. paper)
    1. Nuremberg (Germany)—History—20th century. 2.   National socialism—Psychological aspects. 3.   Collective memory—Germany—Nuremberg. 4.   Reconstruction (1939–1951)—Germany—Nuremberg.
5.   Nuremberg War Crime Trials, Nuremberg, Germany, 1946–1949. I. Title.
    DD901.N92G74, 2008
    943'.324087—dc22

2008026762

A catalogue record for this book is available from the British Library.
10 9 8 7 6 5 4 3 2 1

For Alison

Contents

Illustrations

Unless otherwise acknowledged photographs are the author's own.

Acknowledgements

As is the case with many studies, the impulses which led to the writing of this book were a mixture of the personal and the intellectual. My first memories of hearing about the past are of my godparents, Hans and Anni Aumüller, telling me of their experiences of the allied air raids on Nuremberg; our shared walks through the landscapes of the rebuilt city provided many childhood vignettes. Their modest humanity taught me the presence of alternative political traditions in German history, and to make the necessary distinctions; their displeasure when they saw that I had spent their gift of 50 DM on a recording of Wagner's *Meistersinger* was an unbeatable introduction to the local politics of culture.

It took others to make me see scholarly possibilities in such personal reminiscences. The late Tim Reuter – an outstanding medievalist with a wonderfully intuitive understanding of modern Germany – first encouraged me to develop tentative comments expressed in an informal conversation into a substantial research project. The University of Southampton, the German Academic Exchange Service and, above all, the Humboldt Foundation provided generous financial support, enabling me to spend lengthy periods of time in Germany conducting archive work. With its commitment to academic freedom and its understanding of the open-endedness and unpredictability of scholarly research, the Humboldt Foundation provides a marvellous model which funding councils in my own country would do well to learn from. Norbert Frei kindly provided an institutional base at the University of Bochum. Beyond this, his encouragement, support and advice have been invaluable. Similarly, I should like to thank Richard Bessel, Svenja Goltermann, Hans Mommsen, Sharon Macdonald, Jeremy Noakes and Jill Stephenson for their support at various points along the way, and conference or seminar audiences in Bochum, Portsmouth, Exeter, London, Winchester, Edinburgh, Sheffield, Nuremberg, Southampton, Jena and Oxford for their helpful suggestions and comments. Latterly I have been most grateful for the award of a senior research fellowship from the British Academy. This enabled me to break the back of the writing. I should especially like to thank Ken Emond for his enthusiastic encouragement and the interest he has shown in the project. It is also a pleasure to be able to renew my thanks to Robert Baldock, Heather McCallum and their colleagues at Yale University Press – it is impossible to imagine a better publisher.

This book is based on much hitherto unused, and often uncatalogued, local archive material. I was largely unsuccessful in my efforts to gain access to the papers of various nongovernmental organisations in Nuremberg: some of those who publicly demand a more open confrontation of the city's past were among the most unhelpful when it came to unlocking their own cupboards. I am therefore all the more grateful for the support of the many archivists in the city who helped me to locate material and made it available even when it was not, as yet, formally in use. A special word of thanks in this respect is due to the staff of the Stadtarchiv in Nuremberg and, in particular, to Gerhard Jochem, who mentored much of my archive work. Their enthusiastic help and advice has gone far beyond that which one could reasonably expect. Similarly, the picture archivists at the *Nürnberger Nachrichten* were exceptionally helpful regarding my efforts to locate suitable images for the book, and I am very grateful for their permission to reproduce images from their archives here.

Closer to home – but still at work – professional debts start to become indistinguishable from personal ones. I owe thanks to many past and present members of the Department of History at the University of Southampton for their engaged criticism, suggestions or help with various aspects of the project, whether in the form of comments on a draft chapter, observations on a seminar paper, or – often most importantly – insights offered over refreshment of one kind or another. In this respect I should particularly like to thank George Bernard, Tobias Brinkmann, David Cesarani, Mark Cornwall, Peter Gray, Matthew Kelly, Tony Kushner, John Oldfield, Kendrick Oliver, Nils Roemer, Mark Roseman, Kevin Sharpe, Mark Stoyle and Joan Tumblety. As I worked on this book I have also had the pleasure of supervising a number of excellent PhD theses on issues of memory in twentieth-century Germany. I have benefited from being able to follow the progress of studies by Jörg Arnold, Tim Grady and Caroline Sharples in particular, and owe them thanks for the stimulus which their outstanding work has provided.

During my many visits to Nuremberg I have enjoyed the convivial hospitality of Walter and Doris Höchtl, for which I have always been immensely grateful; in moments of low enthusiasm the pleasant distractions of many friendships developed in Germany over the years have offered perfect respite. At home, my debts to Dusty and Ella Ayres, the last dowager duchesses of Bassett, are similarly great. Their unique typing skills have been a particular help.

Finally, my debts to Alison are enormous. Not only did she endure with good humour the disruption caused by my lengthy trips to Germany, she even feigned interest when dragged around Bavarian cemeteries in the rain. I can only hope that the *Spargel* and the *Bratwürste* were some compensation. Anyhow, her love and friendship mean everything to me.

Southampton, January 2008

Abbreviations

APO	Extra-Parliamentary Opposition
BDK	League of German War Victims (formerly BDKK)
BDKK	League of German War-Disabled and Surviving Dependants
BdM	League of German Girls
CDU	Christian Democratic Union of Germany
CSU	Christian Social Union
DDP	German Democratic Party
DGB	German Trade Union Federation
DP	Displaced Person
EEC	European Economic Community
EHIK	Protestant Aid Service for Internees and Prisoners of War
FDP	Free Democratic Party
GDR	German Democratic Republic
ID	Infantry Division
IKG	*Israelitische Kultusgemeinde*
IR	Infantry Regiment
KPD	Communist Party of Germany
KZ	(*Konzentrationslager*) Concentration Camp
MAN	*Maschinenfabrik Augsburg-Nürnberg*
NATO	North Atlantic Treaty Organisation
NPD	National Democratic Party of Germany
NSDAP	National Socialist German Workers' Party
NSKK	National Socialist Motorised Corps
POW	Prisoner of War
SA	(*Sturmabteilung*) Storm Detachment
SD	(*Sicherheitsdienst*) Security Service
SED	Socialist Unity Party of Germany

SPD	Social Democratic Party of Germany
SS	(*Schutzstaffel*) Protection Squad
VdH	Association of Former Prisoners of War
VVN	Association of Persecutees of the Nazi Regime
Waffen-SS	Armed SS
ZSL	Central Office of State Justice Departments

Introduction

In the mid-1950s a simple memorial was erected in the Gartenstadt suburb of Nuremberg. Taking the form of a fountain, it consisted of a low, circular basin to collect and hold the water, and a pillar from which the water flowed. The pillar was inscribed on three sides; on top of the pillar stood a small sculpted dove.[1]

The inscription read:

Vorbei sind die langen Tage u. Nächte tiefster Beklemmung während des Bombenhagels
The long days and nights of deepest trepidation during the hail of bombs are over
Behoben sind die durch den Zweiten Weltkrieg verursachten Zerstörungen in unserer Gartenstadt
The destruction caused by the Second World War to our Gartenstadt has been overcome
Bleiben soll die Erinnerung an die grosse Leistung des Wiederaufbaues 1945–1953
What should remain is the memory of the great achievement of reconstruction 1945–1953

As would have been obvious to a contemporary, the memorial referred to the immense destruction caused by the ever-intensifying air raids on German cities towards the end of the Second World War, and to the subsequent

---

[1] The original dove was removed in 1989. Elke Masa, *Freiplastiken in Nürnberg. Plastik, Denkmale und Brunnen im öffentlichen Raum der Stadt* (Nuremberg, 1994), 323.

1. Memorial to the bombing and reconstruction of Gartenstadt suburb (mid-1950s).

process of reconstruction. As the dove reminded, it stood in a city whose strong Social Democratic traditions responded to this experience with a deeply anti-militarist memory of the war. Yet the imagined community which the 'we' of the memorial both reflected and served to constitute – the 'we' whose consensual acceptance of the text was assumed at the very same time that this 'we' was being proclaimed – was not even that of the city, but was more local than that. After all, while the 'great achievement of reconstruction' may have been brought to a close by 1953 in this particular suburb, other parts of town would bear the obvious physical traces of wartime destruction for a further ten years.

It was not only in its close focus on a highly localised space that the memorial eschewed the making of wider connections. Entirely absent was any reference to the wider dynamic of the war, and above all to the fact that the bombing had come in the wake of a campaign of imperialist aggression initiated from within Germany itself; equally absent was any reference to the particular political and ideological impulses which had given rise to this war. Instead, the authors of the text had reached for the metaphor of natural catastrophe – the 'hail of bombs' – in order to make sense of the unprecedented destructiveness of the air war. In this way, local citizens were permitted to imagine themselves as innocent victims of a war not of their making, rather than enjoined to reflect upon their possible responsibilities as perpetrators or accomplices in an act of genocidal annihilation; neither were they encouraged to make connections between the suffering they had endured and the untold continent-wide suffering meted out by them, with their sanction, or on their behalf.

Nonetheless, the stories told in the memorial were not merely imaginative fictions invented to facilitate the reintegration of the mass of the compromised and the guilty into post-war society. The 'deepest trepidation' referred to in the inscription reflected the fact that the bombing had been a terrifying experience; the resulting destruction had bequeathed landscapes of rubble in which 300–400,000 Nuremberg citizens lived in conditions of often appalling hardship for several years after the war. In talking about the bombing, ordinary Germans were not inventing their suffering; rather, they were struggling to order it into amenable narratives capable of commanding consensus, and to fashion positive meanings around it. In reaching for the language of natural catastrophe they were not only avoiding guilt, but were also seeking to make sense of an unprecedented set of experiences which no obvious language existed to describe.

What was most striking about the memorial, however, was the underlying tension between the invocation to remember and the urge to forget. The first two lines of the inscription emphasised the past status of the experiences as much as the experiences themselves; they emphasised not so much the damage done but the fact that it had been overcome. Indeed, in its exhortation to remember something else – the achievements of the rebuilding – the inscription clearly implied that the memorial's ostensible focus – the experience of the bombing – should actually be forgotten.

In resisting the possibility of connecting stories of local suffering even to those of the wider community the memorial betrayed the inherent self-centredness of post-war West German memory cultures. In its unresolved tension between remembering and forgetting it typified how the acknowledgement of one experience often went hand in hand with the glossing over of another; at the same time, it illustrated the search for meaning in an experience from which German society wished to move on, but from which it could not easily escape. In its elision of perpetrators and victims it reflected the workings of a culture unable or unwilling to address its responsibility for its own suffering, still less that of others. If its sparse iconography bespoke the difficulties of finding an appropriate visual idiom to describe the events of the Second World War, its symbolic use of the dove showed that politics and ideology were in operation; at the same time, its recollection of intense fear reminded that memory was rooted in shocking experience, and that the logic which underpinned the memory culture was an emotional as well as a political one. Partial, evasive and narcissistic, and yet at the same time manifesting a need to make sense of horrifying experiences in a manner agreeable to all, this memorial is a microcosm of the memory culture which forms the subject of this book.

The past was always present in post-war West Germany.[2] Far from being driven to the margins of public concern by a population whose shared desire to forget constituted an act of collective amnesia, it resonated through post-war political, social and cultural life in many different ways.[3] War crimes trials[4] and denazification,[5] scandals over former Nazis in high places, arguments over the amnestying and reintegration of party members,[6] negotiations for restitution, pensions entitlement or compensation were debated across the many forums of West German public life;[7] the causes and consequences, together with the attendant political and moral burdens, of Nazism, war, genocide and defeat, were addressed – sometimes explicitly, sometimes

[2] The literature in this field is now immense. General studies which have informed this book include Ulrich Herbert and Olaf Groehler, *Zweierlei Bewältigung. Vier Beiträge über den Umgang mit der NS-Vergangenheit in beiden deutschen Staaten* (Hamburg, 1992); Jürgen Danyel (ed.), *Das geteilte Vergangenheit. Zum Umgang mit Nationalsozialismus und Widerstand in beiden deutschen Staaten* (Berlin, 1995); Mary Fulbrook, *German National Identity after the Holocaust* (Cambridge, 1999); Aleida Assmann and Ute Frevert, *Geschichtsvergessenheit, Geschichtsversessenheit. Vom Umgang mit deutschen Vergangenheiten nach 1945* (Stuttgart, 1999); Peter Reichel, *Vergangenheitsbewältigung in Deutschland. Die Auseinandersetzung mit der Diktatur von 1945 bis heute* (Munich, 2001); Harold Marcuse, *Legacies of Dachau. The Uses and Abuses of a Concentration Camp, 1933–2001* (Cambridge, 2001); Alon Confino and Peter Fritzsche (eds), *The Work of Memory. New Directions in the Study of German Society and Culture* (Urbana, IL, 2002); Helmut König, *Die Zukunft der Vergangenheit. Der Nationalsozialismus im politischen Bewußtsein der Bundesrepublik* (Frankfurt/Main, 2003); Jeffrey K. Olick, *In the House of the Hangman. The Agonies of German Defeat, 1943–1949* (Chicago, 2005).

[3] Perhaps the best known, and polemical, formulation of the amnesia argument is Ralph Giordano, *Die Zweite Schuld oder von der Last ein Deutscher zu sein* (Hamburg, 1987). See also Wolfgang Benz, 'Nachkriegsgesellschaft und Nationalsozialismus. Erinnerung, Amnesie, Abwehr' in *Dachauer Hefte* 6 (1990), 12–24.

[4] Of the older literature see Adalbert Rückerl, *NS-Verbrechen vor Gericht. Versuch einer Vergangenheitsbewältigung* (Heidelberg, 1982); Jürgen Weber and Peter Steinbach (eds), *Vergangenheitsbewältigung durch Strafverfahren? NS-Prozesse in der Bundesrepublik* (Munich, 1984); of more recent scholarship see on the Nuremberg trials Donald Bloxham, *Genocide on Trial. War Crimes Trials and the Formation of Holocaust History and Memory* (Oxford, 2001); on the trials of the 1960s see Rebecca Wittmann, *Beyond Justice. The Auschwitz Trial* (Boston, MA, 2005); Devin Pendas, *The Frankfurt Auschwitz Trial, 1963–1965. Genocide, History and the Limits of the Law* (Cambridge, 2006); also Dick de Mildt, *In the Name of the People: Perpetrators of Genocide in the Reflection of their Post-war Prosecution in West Germany. The 'Euthanasia' and 'Aktion Reinhard' Trial Cases* (The Hague, 1996).

[5] Klaus-Dietmar Henke, *Politische Säuberung unter französischer Besatzung. Die Entnazifizierung in Württemberg-Hohenzollern* (Munich, 1981); Lutz Niethammer, *Die Mitläuferfabrik. Die Entnazifizierung am Beispiel Bayerns* (Bonn, 1982); Klaus-Dietmar Henke and Hans Woller (eds), *Politische Säuberung in Europa. Die Abrechnung mit Faschismus und Kollaboration nach dem zweiten Weltkrieg* (Munich, 1991).

[6] On the question of amnesty and reintegration see Norbert Frei, *Vergangenheitspolitik. Die Anfänge der Bundesrepublik und die NS-Vergangenheit* (Munich, 1996).

[7] On compensation debates see Christian Pross, *Wiedergutmachung. Der Kleinkrieg gegen die Opfer* (Frankfurt/Main, 1988); Ludolf Herbst and Constantin Goschler (eds), *Wiedergutmachung in der Bundesrepublik* (Munich, 1989); Hans Günter Hockerts and Christiana Kuller (eds), *Nach der Verfolgung. Wiedergutmachung nationalsozialistischen Unrechts in Deutschland* (Göttingen, 2003); on the distribution of the material costs of war within West Germany see Michael L. Hughes, *Shouldering the Burdens of Defeat. West Germany and the Reconstruction of Social Justice* (Chapel Hill, NC, 1999).

implicitly – in media as diverse as newspapers,[8] radio,[9] architecture,[10] land-scape,[11] television[12] and film[13] as well as through the political process itself; through acts ranging from constitution-writing to commemoration and memorialisation, the diverse actors of West German public life not only dealt with the practical legacies of the past but engaged in a complex process of contesting and imparting meaning to an experience of fascist dictatorship which had contained not one but a multitude of interlocking histories of aggression, persecution, violence, murder, destruction and suffering.

As time went on, some of these experiences were acknowledged in public memory while others were marginalised. German civilian victims of the war were honoured in war memorials in the 1950s, but former forced foreign workers were not. *Wehrmacht* soldiers were depicted as the ordinary casualties of an ordinary military conflagration, their deaths described in the customary language of an older, inherited national pathos.[14] The role that many of them had played in mass murder was passed over. When the Nazi regime was mentioned, and thus the peculiar political context of the war addressed, it was to emphasise that the German people themselves, rather than the foreign victims of the occupation of Europe, had been innocent victims of a uniquely tyrannical system. By contrast, the experiences of the real victims of Nazi racism, above all the Jews, were all but ignored in a dominant memory culture which saw the imperialist and genocidal dimensions of Nazi warfare, and ordinary Germans' complicity in these, largely written out of the script. Rather, in memorials, museums, commemorations and all manner of literary and popular representations, ordinary Germans were permitted, indeed encouraged, to imagine themselves as having been victims with no moral burdens to bear.

One prominent strand of scholarly writing on the post-war memory cultures of western Germany has offered an explanation for what are seen, in

---

[8] J. Wilke, B.Schenk, A.A. Cohen, T. Zemach, *Holocaust und NS-Prozesse. Die Presseberichterstattung in Israel und Deutschland zwischen Aneignung und Abwehr* (Cologne, 1995); Heiko Buschke, *Deutsche Presse, Rechtsextremismus und nationalsozialistische Vergangenheit in der Ära Adenauer* (Frankfurt/Main, 2003).

[9] René Wolf, ' "Mass Deception without Deceivers"? The Holocaust on East and West German Radio in the 1960s' in *Journal of Contemporary History* 41/4 (2006), 741–55.

[10] Gavriel D. Rosenfeld, *Munich and Memory. Architecture, Monuments and the Legacy of the Third Reich* (Berkeley, CA, 2000); also Rudy Koshar, *Germany's Transient Pasts. Preservation and National Memory in the Twentieth Century* (Chapel Hill, NC, 1998).

[11] Peter Reichel, *Politik mit der Erinnerung. Gedächtnisorte im Streite um die nationalsozialistische Vergangenheit* (Munich, 1995); Detlef Hoffmann (ed.), *Das Gedächtnis der Dinge. KZ-Relikte und KZ-Denkmäler 1945–1995* (Frankfurt/Main, 1998); Petra Frank and Stefan Hördler (eds), *Der Nationalsozialismus im Spiegel des öffentlichen Gedächtnisses. Formen der Aufarbeitung und des Gedenkens* (Berlin, 2005).

[12] Christoph Classen, *Bilder der Vergangenheit. Die Zeit des Nationalsozialismus im Fernsehen der Bundesrepublik Deutschland 1955–1965* (Cologne, 1999).

[13] Heide Fehrenbach, *Cinema in Democratizing Germany. Reconstructing National Identity after Hitler* (Chapel Hill, NC, 1995).

[14] George Mosse, *Fallen Soldiers. Reshaping the Memory of Two World Wars* (Oxford, 1990).

essence, as cultural distortions which is largely political. On the one hand, the political and ideological exigencies of the east–west divide made it inexpedient for both the new West German government and its former enemies in the west to place the crimes of Nazism at the centre of the Federal Republic's memory culture immediately after 1949.[15] Focusing on the crimes of a former enemy was not compatible with building it up militarily and economically against a new one – the Soviet Union. On the other hand, domestic political continuities in the Federal Republic itself also militated against an open 'confrontation of the past': the return of powerful figures to leading positions in the bureaucracy, judiciary, economy and indeed politics itself following the hiatus of denazification created a situation in which 'raking over the past' was incompatible with the restoration of the power, influence and legitimacy of old elites.[16] When the Holocaust was acknowledged, it was only as a foil for relativising comparisons with moments of German suffering, such as the expulsions from the east in 1945 and 1946. In the virulently anti-Communist context of West Germany in the 1950s, this history lent itself to the reconfiguration of ordinary Germans from having been the agents of Nazism to the victims of the Soviet Union.[17] Conversely, the easing of Cold War tensions in the 1960s, combined with the onset of the social–liberal climate in domestic West German politics made a more (self-)critical memory culture possible in that decade.

Much of what such scholarship has discovered about the memory culture of the Federal Republic in the 1950s and the 1960s at a general level also manifested itself in local communities, spaces and cultures. In Nuremberg, as elsewhere, the outlines of the 'victim discourse', as it has come to be known, are immediately discernible. As this book will show, the 1950s witnessed the establishment in the city of monuments to dead and missing soldiers and to casualties of the air raids, but none to the murdered Jews; it saw the holding of annual ritual commemorations in which German suffering was foregrounded while the Holocaust was marginalised; meanwhile, in the 1960s, a set of tangible changes occurred which led locally to the challenging of this discourse, and to the emergence of voices demanding a more open, confrontational engagement with the genocidal past.

---

[15] See, for example, Ulrich Brochhagen, *Nach Nürnberg. Vergangenheitsbewältigung und Westintegration in der Ära Adenauer* (Hamburg, 1994).
[16] Ernst Klee, *Was sie taten – was sie wurden. Ärzte, Juristen und andere Beteiligte am Kranken- oder Judenmord* (Frankfurt/Main, 1986); Ingo Müller, *Furchtbare Juristen. Die unbewältigte Vergangenheit unserer Justiz* (Munich, 1987); Jörg Friedrich, *Die kalte Amnestie. NS-Täter in der Bundesrepublik* (Munich, 2nd edn, 1994); Ernst Klee, *Deutsche Medizin im Dritten Reich. Karrieren vor und nach 1945* (Frankfurt/Main, 2001).
[17] The pre-eminent advocate of an argument which privileges the shaping power of the Cold War in its explanatory model is Robert Moeller: see, most importantly, his key study, *War Stories. The Search for a Usable Past in the Federal Republic of Germany* (Berkeley, CA, 2001); for a more recent iteration see Moeller, 'Germans as Victims? Thoughts on a Post-Cold War History of World War II's Legacies' in *History and Memory* 17, 1–2 (2005), 147–94.

Yet it is precisely at the local level – in the examination of histories played out in ordinary communities – that the limits of many pre-existing studies become apparent. While the shaping of narratives in the context provided by Cold War, western integration and the early history of the Federal Republic has been extensively examined, it is only recently that scholars have begun to consider the thorny questions: what made these stories so compelling? Why did they gain traction with ordinary Germans? All too often, the scholarly literature has contented itself either with the assumption that ordinary members of West German society simply internalised the apologetic narratives made available through the dominant culture, accepting them as their own, or embraced them for largely self-serving, instrumentalist ends.

The answers to these questions, however, lie in connecting the study of such representations of Nazism, war and genocide to the study of the wider social and cultural contexts through which those representations moved and of which they were part.[18] For a moment's consideration of the rubble landscapes against which background these stories were told reminds us that Germany was not just a Cold War society, nor just a post-Nazi society, but also a post-war society, in which millions of people who had suffered in multiple, varied and often unprecedented ways were struggling to make sense of their past experiences, their present situation and the connections between the two.[19] The rubble landscapes were inhabited by those rendered homeless by allied air raids, by soldiers returning from the violence of war and from captivity, by refugees and expellees who had fled or been driven from their homes at war's end or shortly thereafter, and by millions of relatives seeking news of missing loved ones. They were also, of course, inhabited by many former party members who, for a brief but significant while, faced a highly uncertain future.

All of these groups, moreover, moved in and through spaces in which a large number of other histories had recently been played out – on the one hand, the massive mobilisation of German society in the pursuit of conquest and war, on the other, the persecution of political opponents of Nazism, the exclusion and killing of many types of social outsider, the discrimination, deportation and murder of local Jews, and the brutal exploitation of foreign forced workers. This was, in other words, a society whose members had seen, or had knowledge of, appalling criminal acts, even if they had not been to the

[18] Iwona Irwin-Zarecka, *Frames of Remembrance. The Dynamics of Collective Memory* (New Brunswick, 1994), 14–15.
[19] Hans-Peter Schwarz, 'Die ausgebliebene Katastrophe. Eine Problemskizze zur Geschichte der Bundesrepublik' in Hermann Rudolph (ed.), *Den Staat denken. Theodor Eschenburg zum Fünfundachtzigsten* (Berlin, 1990), 152; more generally Klaus Naumann (ed.), *Nachkrieg in Deutschland* (Hamburg, 2001); Vera Neumann, *Nicht der Rede Wert. Die Privatisierung der Kriegsfolgen in der frühen Bundesrepublik* (Münster, 1997); for interesting comparative perspectives see Richard Bessel and Dirk Schumann (eds), *Life after Death. Approaches to a Cultural and Social History of Europe During the 1940s and 1950s* (Cambridge, 2003).

front or to the occupied territories. Indeed, those who now considered them-selves to be victims had, in very many cases, only shortly before been the perpetrators of the many acts of destruction pursued by the Third Reich.[20]

Taking the city of Nuremberg as its focus, this study examines the forma-tion and workings of an urban memory culture in the context of the wider post-war social history of the community. Nuremberg was, in some respects, an unusual example. After all, its associations with the Nuremberg party rallies, the Nuremberg Laws and the vicious anti-Semitic newspaper of its notorious Gauleiter Julius Streicher, *Der Stürmer*, gave the city a particular image problem after the war.[21] Few, if any, German cities were as closely asso-ciated with the hubris of the Nazi regime by 1945. Not for nothing did the victorious allies hold their trials of leading members of the Nazi regime at the International Military Tribunal in Nuremberg, providing a further set of unwelcome associations for the city to deal with. Indeed, one dimension of the local story of post-war memory formation lies precisely in the contorted efforts of the city's new Social Democratic powerholders to reassert the city's progressive credentials in the face of these unwanted associations, and to connect with alternative cultural traditions in the city which the Nazis had suppressed, distorted or appropriated for their own ends.

In other respects, however, Nuremberg was a quite typical city, and it would be misleading to imply that attempts to deal with these peculiar legacies consti-tuted the main focus of post-war memory work. As a major industrial centre the sociology and politics of local engagement with Nazism had not been radi-cally dissimilar from many other cities; neither had the experience of the city during the war been unusual. As a movement, the Nazi party had mobilised voters from across the city's population, but disproportionately from within its nationalist-inclined middle classes. Despite the strong Social Democratic tradi-tions of the city, the Nazis had gained much support; the bitterly divided poli-tics of the city in the early 1930s ensured that once the Nazis had gained power the suppression of the Left was brutal, as it was elsewhere. The city's bourgeois, professional and administrative elites had proceeded to collaborate with the Nazi regime in the implementation of terroristic justice, the administration of Nazi racial persecution and expropriation, and the exploitation of forced labour in local factories; more generally, broad sections of the city's population had offered plebiscitary support to the charismatic regime. Many of its young

---

[20] Moeller, 'Germans as Victims?', 176–7.
[21] In recent years these associations have been the subject of local debate which has given rise to several excellent publications. See Centrum Industriekultur Nürnberg (ed.), *Kulissen der Gewalt. Das Reichsparteitagsgelände in Nürnberg* (Nuremberg, 1992); Bernd Ogan and Wolfgang Weiß (eds), *Faszination und Gewalt. Zur politischen Ästhetik des Nationalsozialismus* (Nuremberg, 1992); Geschichte für Alle e.V., *Geländebegehung. Das Reichsparteitagsgelände in Nürnberg* (Nuremberg, 2nd edn, 1995).

men had fought in the *Wehrmacht* or served in the police in the occupied areas; some had served in the SS. A minority of its population had resisted or suffered in the concentration camps; others had been persecuted on racial or ideological grounds. The city was bombed extensively and suffered heavy damage.

The post-war history of the city was in many respects quite typical too. After the war, it experienced an influx of refugees, although its heavily damaged state ensured that this was initially limited. It also had to integrate the mass of demobilising soldiers, most of whom returned within two or three years of the end of war, but some of whom remained in captivity well into the 1950s. It faced shrill demands for housing not only from the tens of thousands of homeless evacuees, many of whom were forced to live in outlying areas for years after the war, but also from a population obliged to live in intensely cramped, often highly unsanitary, conditions. Only as the 'economic miracle' gradually gained purchase during the 1950s did the hardship of the immediate post-war years abate; even then, the consequences of the war ensured that many citizens lived in very limiting circumstances well into the 1960s.

Though wrestling with its own peculiar burdens Nuremberg was thus in many respects quite representative. However, this study seeks to do more than just confirm the tedious truism that some elements of a broader study find confirmation at the local level while others demand qualification or reveal peculiarities. Rather, it proceeds from the assumption that local political cultures have their own logic and their own rules – their own modes of operation – which cannot be assumed from the workings of a wider culture. It argues that in order to make historical sense of the various victim narratives of the post-war years one has to study their formation, circulation and operation within their specific social and cultural context.[22] Individual urban cultures, as 'meaningful social spaces and cultural interfaces of whole social processes, discursive (self-) understandings, communicative interactions and subjective appropriations' lend themselves ideally to this.[23] It is at the level of the local, in the post-war histories

---

[22] In this sense the approach offered in this book owes much to the insights in Alon Confino and Peter Fritzsche, 'Introduction: Noises of the Past' in Confino and Fritzsche, *The Work of Memory*, 1–21.
[23] Adelheid von Saldern, 'Einleitung' in Adelheid von Saldern (ed.), *Inszenierter Stolz. Stadträpresentationen in drei deutschen Gesellschaften (1935–1975)* (Stuttgart, 2005), 24–5; for reflections on the spatially bounded qualities of memory cultures see Sabine Damir-Geilsdorf and Béatrice Hendrich, 'Orientierungsleistungen räumlicher Strukturen und Erinnerung. Heuristische Potenziale einer Verknüpfung der Konzepte Raum, mental maps und Erinnerung' in Sabine Damir-Geilsdorf, Angelika Hartmann, Béatrice Hendrich (eds), *Mental Maps-Raum-Erinnerung. Kulturwissenschaftliche Zugänge zum Verhältnis von Raum und Erinnerung* (Münster, 2005), 25–48; on the city as memory space see Peter Reichel (ed.), *Das Gedächtnis der Stadt. Hamburg im Umgang mit seiner nationalsozialistischen Vergangenheit* (Hamburg, 1997); also Sven Keller, *Günzburg und der Fall Josef Mengele. Die Heimatstadt und die Jagd nach dem NS-Verbrecher* (Munich, 2003); Marcuse, *Legacies of Dachau.*

of ordinary communities, that the multitude of representations of Nazism and war can best be connected to the experiences to which they related and to the contexts which produced them.[24] It is here where their varying purchase can be studied – here they can be examined not simply as so many endless representations which might as well be selected at random, to be discussed for their fictional qualities but not for the meanings they gained only once embedded in these social and cultural contexts. It is on the level of the local, in other words, where the links between experience and memory are best approached.[25]

In connecting the evolution of an urban memory culture to the multiple histories of wartime violence and post-war hardship in the community which that memory culture addressed, this study seeks to explore the emotional, as well as the political, logics in operation, and thus to acknowledge the more affective, visceral qualities of such memory cultures. Above all, it proceeds from the standpoint that for all the insights a functionalist approach to memory, one which stresses the political utility of certain narratives, gives us, we can only make sense of post-war memory cultures if we take seriously the connections (however indirect) between the discourse of victimhood which grew up around the experience of war, defeat and occupation, and the real presence of massive suffering which those experiences entailed. In emphasising what the generation of Germans who lived through the war *did* choose to remember (or at least to articulate publicly) as well as what they did *not* remember, it argues that civic memory politics were driven not only (and perhaps not even primarily) by an instrumentalist desire to suppress awkward truths about murdered others, but also by the need to address people who were trying to make sense of their own experiences of suffering.[26] It starts from the premise that, for the generation with first-hand experience of the war, the logic of local memory cultures demanded a focus on imparting meaning to the shocking, disorientating experiences of those present, not those absent. The consequence of this was, of course, the marginalisation of the Holocaust and the associated crimes in the memory culture of the post-war era. But if this was a direct consequence of the way in which such cultures operated, the operations of that culture were not necessarily driven only by the pursuit of this outcome.

Clearly politics *were* in operation in the formation of a memory culture, which was anything but a politics-free space. However, this book argues that the relationship between politics and memory was more indirect, and more complex, than has sometimes been assumed. Studies of post-war West German memory have tended to fall into two groups. On the one hand, there

---

[24] Malte Thießen, 'Das Gedächtnis der Stadt. Hamburgs Gedenken an Luftkrieg und Kriegsende 1943 bis 2005', PhD, University of Hamburg, 2006, 1–20.

[25] Irwin-Zarecka, *Frames of Remembrance*, 17.

[26] On this point see Anthony D. Kauders, *Democratization and the Jews. Munich, 1945–1965* (Lincoln, NE, 2004), 22.

have been those who have overemphasised the consensual qualities of the 1950s. Robert Moeller's pioneering study is perhaps the pre-eminent example of an argument which explores how an apparently homogenous West German society embraced the stories of victimhood offered by the experiences of homecoming prisoners of war and expellees and co-opted them into the service of a victim narrative adopted by the nation as a whole.[27] Sometimes explicit, sometimes implicit, in this line of argument is the suggestion that the 'People's Community' engineered by the Nazis – based on the integration of the majority through the exclusion of the persecuted minority – survived essentially intact through collapse and defeat, refashioning itself first (in the late stages of the war) as a 'Community of Fate' (*Schicksalsgemeinschaft*) and then (in the post-war years) as a 'Community of Victims' (*Opfergemeinschaft*), in which the sufferings of the majority perpetrator society were articulated and those of the minority of victims suppressed.[28]

This fault-line – between the majority of the guilty, tainted and compromised and the minority of the real victims – was very much there in post-war West Germany and, as this book will demonstrate, also reproduced itself locally in Nuremberg. Yet arguably this characterisation, when taken alone, overstates the degree of homogeneity of the post-war majority society, which was itself bitterly divided, full of fissures and riven with conflict – between former Nazis and non-Nazis, between indigenous inhabitants and refugees, between those who had lost their homes to bombing and those who had not, between city-dwellers and rural population, and so on. In the situation of extreme shortage which the immediate post-war years represented this played itself out in the form of intense distributional conflict (for housing, for food, for clothing, for shoes) against which background the evolution of the city's memory politics must be read.

Yet those who have foregrounded the divided nature of post-war German society and have sought, as a result, to emphasise the contested nature of memory have often, in turn, taken an overly reductionist view of the relationship between politics and narratives of Nazism and war, in that they read Social Democratic accounts of Nazism for their Social Democratic ideological content, conservatives' accounts for their conservative ideological content, and so on.[29] In this way, the past becomes merely another site on which the politics of the present are being played out, the diverse stories told a reflection of the competing forces in a pluralistic, democratic political culture.

---

[27] Moeller, *War Stories*.
[28] This is the clear implication of Sabine Behrenbeck, 'Between Pain and Silence: Remembering the Victims of Violence in Germany after 1949' in Bessel and Schumann, *Life After Death*, 37–64, here 63, for example.
[29] The best example of this approach is the similarly pioneering study by Jeffrey Herf: *Divided Memory. The Nazi Past in the Two Germanys* (Boston, MA, 1997).

On one level, clearly, this was true: in the case of Nuremberg, too, a Social Democrat-dominated city produced a set of dominant narratives which, in their pacifist rhetoric, betrayed the political preferences of its elected leadership. However, as Alon Confino has argued, a characteristic feature of memory cultures is precisely their ability to give a sense of shared experience to groups with conflicting positions – they function, in other words, not so much to *reflect* as to *overcome* divisions within a community, insofar as they manage 'to represent, for a broad section of the population, a common destiny that overcomes symbolically real social and political conflicts in order to give the illusion of a community to people who in fact have very different interests. People construct representations of the nation that conceal through symbols real friction in their society.'[30] What holds true for the nation holds true, in this sense, for local communities too.[31] For, in addition to the fault line described above – that between a majority 'perpetrator society' and a minority of surviving victims – there were at least two other kinds of fissure running through the politics of post-war Nuremberg. The first, which was naturally strongest in the immediate post-war years, but remained highly tangible into the late 1950s, was that which existed between the different social groups created by war and the circumstances of defeat – the returning soldiers, the relatives of the missing, the refugees, the former party members, the evacuees, the homeless, and the small, but significant, group of the victims of fascism. As the tensions to which these divisions gave rise slowly faded, another fissure resurfaced – the deep division in German political culture between bourgeoisie and working class, a division which constituted the central fault line in urban society in the early and mid-twentieth-century period, and which returned as a distinctive feature of Nuremberg politics in the post-war era once the chaos of the collapse had been stabilised.

It was precisely against this background of multilayered division that official narratives of Nazism and war capable of commanding consensus had to be fashioned. This book explores, then, how the forging of mutually agreeable stories of victimhood within a particular community, or on its behalf, reflected not the workings of a society characterised by strongly consensual social and political ties – the residual ties of the *Volksgemeinschaft* – but an attempt on the part of civic leaders to *re-forge*, through the promotion of shared memory, a

---

[30] Alon Confino, 'Collective Memory and Cultural History: Problems of Method' in *American Historical Review* 102 (1997), 1386–1403, here 1400. The notion that memory cultures serve to constitute, rather than reflect, the nation, is echoed in Insa Eschebach, *Öffentliches Gedenken. Deutsche Erinnerungskulturen seit der Weimarer Republik* (Frankfurt/Main, 2005), 69; on the political utility of vagueness within the remembering community see also Peter Fritzsche, 'Cities Forget, Nations Remember: Berlin and Germany and the Shock of Modernity' in Greg Eghigian and Paul Betts (eds), *Pain and Prosperity. Reconsidering Twentieth Century Germany* (Stanford, 2003), 35–60, here 59.

[31] For the implications of work which has begun to be carried out on other local spaces, see Thießen, 'Das Gedächtnis der Stadt', 181.

minimum degree of civic consensus in a community wrenched apart by the divisive experience of war, collapse, defeat and the associated chaos. In this case, an overarching narrative of German victimhood became the means by which a shattered, divided, conflict-ridden society re-established itself as a functioning community with a renewed sense of civic identity.

Such an argument has implications, in turn, for how historians understand the much-vaunted silences which characterised post-war West German memory. If such language does violence to the fact that there was, sometimes, a surprising amount of noise surrounding the genocidal dimensions of the recent past in the 1950s, it captures nonetheless the fact that the Holocaust was still, at most, a highly marginal part of most public narratives in the first fifteen years after the war.[32] The fundamental nebulousness of such narratives – with their, at best, evasive, tortuous allusions to mass murder – has usually been taken simply to reflect a shared understanding within a majority society of former perpetrators that the fact of the Holocaust should remain unspoken. However, this book argues that such nebulousness was not only a product of the asymmetry between a majority of former perpetrators and a minority of victims, but also of the need to bridge deep-seated divisions within the majority German community: that only vague, nebulous narratives were capable of commanding consensus in the divided society described above. In this sense Hermann Lübbe's controversial suggestion that a 'certain silence' was necessary to allow the integration of former Nazis into West German society and their emergence as citizens of the Federal Republic has a clear logic. A critical, confrontational memory politics was not compatible with the reconstitution of a functioning civil society; conversely, only once this civil society had been re-established, as it had been by the late 1950s, could the possibility of a more critical discussion be entertained.[33]

It is also, however, when one examines post-war memory in its social context that the limits of any reading of the 'silences' which focuses solely on the political become apparent. In seeking to create consensual, shared narratives of Nazism and war, ordinary people and their representatives were trying to make sense of unprecedented experiences of violence and brutality. In some

[32] On the nature of the 'silence' and the problematic usages of the term, see Confino and Fritzsche, 'Introduction: Noises of the Past', *The Work of Memory*, 14.

[33] Hermann Lübbe, 'Der Nationalsozialismus im deutschen Nachkriegsbewußtsein' in *Historische Zeitschrift* 236 (1983), 579–99. Where Lübbe's argument becomes problematic is in his critique of subsequent attempts to foster a critical memory culture rather than accept the advisability of 'letting sleeping dogs lie'. There are strong echoes of Lübbe's argument concerning the immediate post-war period in Herf, *Divided Memory*; more critically Wilfried Loth and Bernd-A. Rusinek (eds), *Verwandlungspolitik. Ns-Eliten in der westdeutschen Nachkriegsgesellschaft* (Frankfurt/Main, 1998). On the pursuit of consensus as a dominant structural feature of post-war democracy-building see Christina von Hodenberg, *Konsens und Krise. Eine Geschichte der westdeutschen Medienöffentlichkeit 1945–1973* (Göttingen, 2006).

cases, a ready-made language existed, as in the case of soldiers' deaths, for example, which, like those of previous cohorts of soldiers, could be constructed as 'heroes' deaths' suffered by those who 'fell for the fatherland'.[34] For others, however, there was no such ready-made verbal or visual idiom. Neither those acts of suffering which Germans had visited upon others – most obviously the genocide – nor some of those endured themselves – such as the bombing – lent themselves easily to representation within a received repertoire of images. There was, in other words, not always an immediately obvious language in which to frame a meaningful response to the events of the war. Sometimes the silences were clearly the product of simple expediency. But such silences also contained something less obviously self-serving: a mixture of sorrow, shame and remorse. The multi-dimensional shock which aspects of the war had caused to German society, and the shock it caused to millions of individuals, had sometimes rendered them, quite literally, speechless.[35]

How does one model the evolution of a memory culture? What vocabularies exist to describe it? Given the extreme nature of the shock that the experience of war and defeat administered to Germany, it is unsurprising that many scholars have reached for the language of trauma.[36] Yet while such terminology functions adequately as a general metaphor for the catastrophic rupture of war and its physical and psychological after-effects, it quickly breaks down in the application. For one thing, the description of a perpetrating society as traumatised by its own actions raises obvious, if ultimately not insurmountable, political and ethical concerns.[37] For another, it is entirely unclear that either the social psychology of remembering and forgetting or the relationship between knowledge and its public articulation work according to the same mechanisms as those in operation in individuals. The language of repression, for example, with its implication that the 'silences' regarding the Holocaust reflected a forcing of the genocide into the collective unconsciousness, fundamentally mistakes the nature of that silence, which contained an ever-present, and potentially speakable, knowledge.[38] When, in the 1960s,

---

[34] Mosse, *Fallen Soldiers, passim.*
[35] Lutz Niethammer, 'Diesseits des "Floating Gap". Das kollektive Gedächtnis und die Konstruktion von Identität im wissenschaftlichen Diskurs' in Kristin Platt and Mihran Dabag (eds), *Generation und Gedächtnis. Erinnerung und kollektive Identitäten* (Opladen, 1995), 25–50, here 28.
[36] Dominick LaCapra, *History and Memory after Auschwitz* (Ithaca, 1998); Wolfgang Schivelbusch, *The Culture of Defeat. On National Trauma, Mourning and Recovery* (London, 2003); Jenny Edkins, *Trauma and the Memory of Politics* (Cambridge, 2003); for sensitive and nuanced discussions see Kerwin Lee Klein, 'On the Emergence of Memory in Historical Discourse' in *Representations* 69 (Winter 2000), 127–50; Peter Gray and Kendrick Oliver, 'Introduction' in id., (eds), *The Memory of Catastrophe* (Manchester, 2004), 1–18.
[37] LaCapra, *History and Memory after Auschwitz,* 8–9; 41–2.
[38] Kauders, *Democratization,* 17.

some began to speak more openly about the Holocaust, this was not so much the 'return of the repressed' as the product of a renegotiation of the compromise between speaking and keeping quiet, itself made possible by a complex set of transitions in the political culture of West Germany, not the workings of a West German psyche.[39]

At the same time, the notion of trauma reminds us that the language of memory, when applied to societies, is in itself highly metaphorical: 'memory' is no more, and no less, than a metaphor for the ways in which, through their narrativisation, experiences become rendered as stories which circulate through, within and around a society, or sections of it, becoming part of that society's 'shared cultural knowledge', knowledge expressed in memorials, exhibitions and commemorations, but also in daily conversation.[40] At times, this knowledge is part of the common sense of a community; at other times it becomes the stuff of active debate, dispute and contestation. It is, in fact, precisely that process of contestation that gives memory cultures their inherently unstable quality, or at least potential, and which ensures that even following a period of (relatively) stable memory politics new challenges can emerge, and new configurations be forced, as happened in West Germany in the late 1950s and early 1960s.

Clearly, the memory culture of post-war Nuremberg was neither entirely disordered nor completely contingent. Relations of power, ideological climates and material conditions, and above all, perhaps, demographic realities – the presence of large numbers of former soldiers or air-raid victims against that of a tiny number of Holocaust survivors – combined to make it likely that one set of narratives would emerge over another at any given juncture. However, the workings of such cultures cannot be reduced to an expression of such things. Only an emphasis on the independently dynamic, contested, unstable and, at times, downright unpredictable nature of memory can enable the historian to trace the crucial changes which took place from the 1950s through to the 1960s against the background of wider political, economic, social and cultural change, while at the same time remaining cognisant of the thoroughly non-determined nature of the transitions that were taking place.[41]

Moreover, understanding these shifts demands focus not only on the changing overall context – the easing of the Cold War, the impact of dynamic economic growth, the fading presence of old elites and the emergence of a younger

---

[39] Ido de Hahn, 'Paths of Normalisation after the Persecution of the Jews. The Netherlands, France and West Germany in the 1950s' in Bessel and Schumann, *Life after Death*, 65–92, here 69.

[40] On memory as 'shared cultural knowledge' see Confino, 'Collective Memory and Cultural History', 1386; see also the helpful discussion in Christoph Cornelißen, 'Was heißt Erinnerungskultur? Begriff – Methoden – Perspektiven' in *Geschichte in Wissenschaft und Unterricht* 54 (2003), 548–63.

[41] Jeffrey K. Olick, *In the House of the Hangman*, 19–21; Assmann and Frevert, *Geschichtsvergessenheit, Geschichtsversessenheit*, 12; Astrid Erll, *Kollektives Gedächtnis und Erinnerungskultur* (Stuttgart, 2005), 13.

generation – but also on the active agency of individuals and social actors such as pressure groups, trade unions or churches. In other historical contexts such individuals might be referred to as 'movement intellectuals': it would, indeed, be legitimate to describe some of these activists, such as Hermann Glaser, the head of the city's Schools and Culture Office from 1964 onwards, in such terms.[42] However, as this study emphasises, the range of actors which drove these shifts was much broader and came from across many diverse sectors of civil society; for the most part, these actors neither identified themselves as intellectuals nor spoke in overtly intellectualised terms. Rather, their understanding of their activism was political and moral – the sensibility which informed their campaigning agendas was political and ethical, rather than narrowly intellectual. Either way, if the comparative study of the memory of genocide and colonial atrocity tells us anything it is that the increasing engagement with the Holocaust in the 1960s was anything but pre-programmed – if anything, it was the exception – and that it demanded the campaigning intervention of engaged activists who were pressing against considerable resistance.[43]

It is on the level of the local that both the nature of the activism and the resistances to it become clear; it is on this level that the limits of the transition of the 1960s become most apparent. It is also, however, here that the dangers in defining the decade as the decisive turning point in a teleological master narrative of West German *Vergangenheitspolitik* – one which traces its evolution from initial post-war evasiveness to the contemporary embrace of a globalised culture of Holocaust remembrance as if the outcome was at every stage a given – become obvious. For one thing, many aspects of memory politics in the 1960s, such as the local embrace of the refugee and expellee histories, owed their occurrence to a quite different dynamic to that which produced the growing sensitivity towards the Holocaust. For another, the narratives produced by the early manifestations of Holocaust pedagogy were themselves highly problematic, evincing, for example, a considerable evasiveness concerning the identity of the perpetrators or the wider structures of institutional complicity and popular consensus underpinning the Nazi regime. Perhaps most significant, it was precisely the ethical and political challenges of the nascent culture of Holocaust awareness that prompted a reformulation of earlier apologetic myths which translated, in turn, into

---

[42] On the role of intellectuals in framing the changing discourse on the Nazi past, see Olick, *In the House of the Hangman*; Dirk Moses, *German Intellectuals and the Nazi Past* (Cambridge, 2007); Hodenberg, *Konsens und Krise*.

[43] See, for example, Volkhard Knigge and Norbert Frei (eds), *Verbrechen erinnern. Die Auseinandersetzung mit Holocaust und Völkermord* (Munich, 2002). In formulating the approaches adopted in this book I have benefited from the comparative insights afforded by a number of volumes, including Jay Winter and Emmanuel Sivan (eds), *War and Remembrance in the Twentieth Century* (Cambridge, 1999); Timothy G. Ashplant, Graham Dawson and Michael Roper (eds), *Commemorating War. The Politics of Memory* (London, 2000); Gray and Oliver, *Memory of Catastrophe*.

substantial continuities in civic memory culture. When the local journalist Fritz Nadler published his 1969 volume *A City in the Shadow of Streicher* he was not referring to the peculiar burden bequeathed to the post-war city by its historic associations with the regime, but was implying, instead, that the city of Nuremberg had been uniquely victimised by the peculiarly tyrannical local manifestation of the Nazi regime embodied in the notorious Gauleiter of Franconia, Julius Streicher.[44] It was, indeed, in the 1960s that the idea coalesced that 'the city' – an inherently nebulous, but all-the-more powerful marker of local identity – had constituted the actual victim of Nazism and the war. Such ideas enjoyed great longevity in the memory culture of the city.[45]

This book is divided into four sections. The first offers a social history of the city from occupation through the early years of reconstruction. Focusing on the different 'victim' groups of the wartime and post-war years (the refugees, the evacuees, the returning soldiers, the 'relatives of the missing', the victims of fascism and the self-styled 'victims of denazification', in other words, ex-Nazis) and on their relationships to one another, it explores the nature of the Federal Republic as a post-war society in which the widespread, overlapping experiences of different kinds of suffering precluded an ability to think critically about the crimes committed against others. At the same time the many divisions bequeathed to this society by the experiences of Nazism, war and defeat provided an extreme challenge for those seeking to build a post-Nazi, post-war democratic consensus. With the return of the last prisoners of war in 1956, the closure of most of the refugee camps and the completion of the first phase of reconstruction in the late 1950s, this immediate post war period may be said to have ended at this time – as the book argues, this was one important precondition for the emergence of more critical voices in the late 1950s and early 1960s.

In invoking the social as a key dimension of the analysis, my purpose is not, again, to insist on the determining primacy of some form of underlying structure. This book argues that in two respects – the presence of social categories created by the specific circumstances of war and defeat, and the more deep-seated presence of divisions between working class and bourgeois traditions within the city – the material conditions mattered in shaping what could and could not be said at any given juncture. It was, conversely, the radical dynamism of the post-war economic boom which gave the memory culture under discussion much of its unstable, fluid quality. Nonetheless, the book emphasises the social more because it wishes to connect the representational aspects of memory to their experiential aspects. Put another way, it is

---

[44] Fritz Nadler, *Eine Stadt im Schatten Streichers* (Nuremberg, 1969).
[45] On underlying continuities in local post-war memory which extended to the end of the twentieth century, see Neil Gregor, ' "The Illusion of Remembrance": The Karl Diehl Affair and the Memory of Nazism in Nuremberg, 1945–1999' in *Journal of Modern History* 75 No. 3 (2003), 590–633.

interested in the ways in which evolving conditions and the attendant experiences encouraged, without ever determining, the production of particular shared knowledge about the recent past. Put at its simplest, it sees the social history of the immediate post-war years as key to why some memories were initially rather more likely to become dominant than others.[46]

The second section connects the emergence and operation of the memory culture of the 1950s both to the ideological and political climates of the period and to the social context described in the first section. It examines how the actors of civil society interacted with the institutions of local government to produce a local memory culture, and how that memory culture served to bridge the divisions of post-war society in the pursuit of renewed civic peace. It examines the rich associational life of the city – through consideration of veterans' leagues, refugee associations and the like; it examines the establishment of war memorials and discusses their meanings; it examines the significance of large public commemorations such as the 'Day of National Mourning' and the annual ceremonies for the victims of allied air raids; it also examines the representations of national history in the Germanic National Museum, whose construction of Germanness in the 1950s was intended, among other things, to maintain a claim to the lost lands of the east and to integrate the expellees. In this way, the evolution of a dominant local discourse on the past between the collapse of Nazism and the erection of the Berlin Wall is outlined.

The third section traces the emergence of a more self-critical dialogue concerning the Nazi past from the late 1950s onwards. Considering the local media reception of impulses which came from outside of the city – the most obvious of which were trials of Nazi-era crimes, such as the 1958 Ulm *Einsatzgruppen* trial, the capture and trial of Adolf Eichmann in 1960 to 1961, and the Frankfurt Auschwitz trial of 1963 to 1965 – it explores how these dovetailed with impulses emanating from within the community itself to produce a shift towards discussing the genocide. These local impulses included an exhibition on the history of the Jews of Nuremberg in 1965, educational work in local schools, the forging of links with former Jewish residents of the city now living in Israel, and the staging of the Nuremberg Conversations, in which national and international figures from academia, the media and other spheres of public life participated in round-table discussions on the Federal Republic and the Nazi past.

As the nascent attempts by civic leaders to endow the genocide with meaning in this era showed, however, the nature of local society continued to place strong limits on what could be said. While the immediate social divisions of the post-war period which the initial 'victim discourse' had served to

---

[46] See Geoff Eley and Keith Nield, *The Future of Class in History. What's Left of the Social?* (Ann Arbor, MI, 2007).

bridge had faded, older, deeper-seated divisions remained. As a result key speakers of the new sensibility – such as mayor Andreas Urschlechter or Hermann Glaser – had to enunciate narratives which could appeal across the political traditions of the city. It was in this context that the idea of 'the city' itself as victim – a notion which was calculated to reach beyond the Social Democratic constituency of the city's powerholders and gain traction with broad sections of the local bourgeoisie – came to the fore. Such narratives served to contain the new challenges Holocaust memory posed even as the fact of genocide was ostensibly confronted.

In any case, as the fourth section argues, while the responses of the 1950s were no longer new, they were still very much there. Many sections of society continued to see the Second World War as an ordinary war in which they, as the losers, had been victims. It also emphasises that, while a dialogue between 'remembering' and 'forgetting' became more prevalent in the 1960s, it was not always concerned with remembering the Holocaust. Rather, it was prompted by the war generation's insistence that young people should not forget the sacrifices their seniors had made for the nation. Moreover, the building of the Berlin Wall gave renewed impetus to the anti-Communist rhetoric which had shaped the 1950s, a rhetoric which was deployed by the expellee interest groups which emerged as a major force in the city in the 1960s. Examination of the city's handling of the presence of the former party rally grounds also shows that local politicians still struggled to grasp the moral implications of the past, or to comprehend correctly the nature of the city's position in relation to past crimes: indeed, in its forceful opposition to the neo-nationalist National Democratic Party's (NPD) attempts to occupy symbolically the rally ground space in the 1960s it again revealed the continued presence of a mentality which saw the city as the victim of Nazism, rather than part of the society which had produced fascist fanaticism in the first place. Meanwhile, the languages used to describe the past at key moments of public commemoration did not differ substantially from those of the 1950s. At all points the liberalising impulses of the 1960s remained contested and their purchase limited.

The source base for this book is unapologetically diverse and eclectic. At its core are the voluminous files of the city council from 1945 to 1968, along with the surviving records of the many associations and interest groups which operated in the city. Beyond this, it ranges across popular literary representations, memorials and their inscriptions, epitaphs and cemetery landscapes, murals on apartment blocks, parish newsletters, tourist office brochures, museum and exhibition catalogues, journalistic references and more.[47] In

---

[47] In doing so it embraces Christoph Corneliβen's laudably expansive definition of the range of texts which may usefully be interrogated as elements of a memory culture (Corneliβen, 'Was heiβt Erinnerungskultur?', 558).

doing so it seeks to explore 'the variety of mnemonic processes, practices and outcomes and . . . their interrelations' which, together, constituted a memory culture.[48] Conversely, in exploring these interrelations it remains cognisant of the limits to which all elements of a memory culture neatly 'fit together', and thus aware of the need to balance the ordering proclivities of both theory and narrative with a firm sense of the 'irreducible ambivalences and ambiguities' inherent in the object of study.[49] Mindful of the importance of religious as well as secular narratives, and of the role religion continued to play in imparting meaning to loss, suffering and shame in mid-twentieth-century Germany, the book also draws extensively on material gathered in the Protestant Church archives.[50] At times its use of archival material is strategic, based on the conviction that certain forms and acts of representation were central to the creation of meaning in the period under discussion. At other times its usage is pragmatic, interrogating archival traces in the knowledge that the same story could probably be examined with similar sets of traces produced in parallel spheres. In other words, it seeks to work empirically while avoiding the empiricist conceit that what is in the archive equates simplistically to what actually 'was'.

The most locally focused, empirically saturated study cannot, ultimately, resolve the central tension of all studies of the relationship between public representa-tions of the past and the contents of 'collective memory'. It is a standard, and entirely legitimate, refrain of critics of such studies that examination of the production of any kind of text, the meanings assumed or the messages intended by its author, tells us nothing about the consumption of that text, its reception or reading. Quite clearly, neither the meanings ascribed by individuals nor those ascribed by groups to locally produced and circulated representations of the past can be read from the representations themselves, any more than they can be for those produced and circulated on a national scale.[51]

Nonetheless, the relatively small size of the different groupings discussed in this study, their clearly visible character as interpretative communities bound together by shared understandings of past and present, the intimacy of their relations to one another and to the local organs of power, together with the often striking confluence of languages, narratives and idioms across a wide

---

[48] Jeffrey Olick, 'Collective Memory: The Two Cultures' in *Sociological Theory* 17/3 (1999) 333–48, here 346.

[49] Gerald Sider and Gavin Smith, 'Introduction' in id. (eds), *Between History and Histories: The Making of Silences and Commemorations* (Toronto, 1997), 10.

[50] This point is also emphasised by Thieβen, 'Das Gedächtnis der Stadt', *passim*.

[51] See the discussion contained in Wulf Kansteiner, 'Finding Meaning in Memory: A Methodological Critique of Collective Memory Studies' in *History and Theory*, 41 (May 2002), 179–97; also Irwin-Zarecka, *Frames of Remembrance*, 140.

variety of different texts which circulated through adjacent and overlapping social spaces render the gap sufficiently narrow for operable assumptions to be made about the existence of shared memories and shared mentalities in local communities. Moreover, the often protracted negotiations between associations, bureaucracies, community politicians and engaged individuals – not to mention the varied histories of sponsorship, competition, design approval, commission and production – that characterised the creation of material artefacts such as memorials render the very notion of authorship problematic; the subsequent participation of many of the same activists, administrators, politicians and members of the public in ritual acts of remembrance performed before the same memorials was such that many of those who collaborated in the process of producing a memorial became that memorial's consumers also. In the often highly intimate operations of such local cultures the clear distinction between author and reader, producer and consumer thus begins to break down, or at least to lose in definition.

Yet again, studying the mechanics of a memory culture demands recognition that in the social and political world through which its actors moved, distinctions of office, role and function remained, and that the utterances of one actor cannot simply be substituted or equated with another as interchangeable expressions of a broader discourse on the past, or as cumulative confirmations of shared mentality. In examining the operations of an urban memory culture this study works with a loosely tripartite model of local society which distinguishes between the official (in the sense of the activities and pronunciations of the city council and its attendant bureaucracies), the civil (the activities of the institutions, agencies, pressure groups, parties of a pluralist civil society) and the social (in the sense of the wider histories lived out by ordinary people in the community). At the same time it seeks to connect the operations of this public culture to the experiences, interventions and attitudes of individuals, drawing on the many and varied letters of ordinary citizens to the city council or other organisations, and other forms of personal manuscript, to do so. It attempts to trace the effects of Nazism and war across the social, cultural and mental landscapes of post-war society in a manner which assumes the porousness of the boundaries between all three.[52]

Sometimes the interfaces between the different levels – between the official, the civil and the social, or between the public and the private – were smooth. The attendant silences reflected consensus, and the ability of individuals to find meaning in their own experiences through the representations available in the

---

[52] In this sense the work is informed by the same understanding as Olick, 'Collective Memory', particularly 336; also Alon Confino, 'Telling about Germany: Narratives of Memory and Culture' in *Journal of Modern History* 76/2 (2004), 389–416, here 407; see also the summary in Erll, *Kollektives Gedächtnis* 97–8.

public culture. At other times official pronunciations, or the claims of one group, clashed with the views, demands or expectations of the public or other sections of it, producing a conflict which left its archival traces. At other times, however, these interfaces did not, in fact, interface at all, but missed completely, as when narratives of heroism, sacrifice or adventure offered stories which did not begin to address individuals' experiences of violence or give them meaning.

In other words, these imperfect interfaces created sparks, but they also left black holes – black holes of memory whose content cannot be known. There were always gaps between some individuals' personal memories and public practices and articulations.[53] But for all their unknowability, it is precisely in the very local, in the unspectacular, quotidian utterances of ordinary people that the faint echoes of such individuals' experiences of violence are occasionally discernible, the slight traces of appalling events and terrible acts which resisted verbalisation. It is precisely here that we can begin to recognise the complexity of the silences, which reflected the fact that some things were not simply unsayable, or even unspeakable, but for ordinary people often defied narration. Again, then, it is in the local that we can approach the visceral qualities of memory cultures too often reduced to a set of instrumentalised, politically convenient sounds and silences.

[53] Klaus Naumann, 'Agenda 1945 – Das Jahr des Kriegsendes im aktuellen Geschichtsdiskurs' in Bernd-A. Rusinek (ed.), *Kriegsende 1945. Verbrechen, Katastrophen, Befreiung in nationaler und internationaler Perspektive* (Göttingen, 2004), 248; more generally Lutz Niethammer, 'Diesseits des "Floating Gap" ', 27.

I

A Society of Victims?
The Post-War Years, 1945 to 1957

I.1

Lives in Ruins?
Nuremberg from Rubble to Reconstruction

Much of the physical substance of Nuremberg was destroyed in the war.[1] In over 40 air raids of ever-increasing intensity and frequency, one half of its housing stock had been either destroyed or heavily damaged; only 10 per cent of homes had survived unscathed. Over 6,000 of its citizens had been killed. The city's population, which had stood at 420,000 on the eve of war, had already fallen under the impact of the bombing to 270,000 by December 1944; a series of devastating raids in 1945 had then razed large parts of the city to the ground and caused approximately 100,000 more to flee.[2] On 2 January 1945, 900 British bombers had destroyed almost the entire historic city centre in the course of less than an hour, killing around 1,800 people; further large-scale attacks in February 1945 had killed a further 1,390 people, while the last major raid before the ground battle for Nuremberg, on 16 March, had claimed 597 lives.[3] The city had been so heavily damaged that, in the words of an account of a small raid in March 1945, 'the majority of the bombs fell on fields of ruins'.[4] The city authorities' own official chronicle observed that 'the destruction of the old city along with parts of the suburbs is such that it is

---

[1] On the impact of the air war on Nuremberg society see Neil Gregor, 'A *Schicksalsgemeinschaft*? Allied Bombing, Civilian Morale, and Social Dissolution in Nuremberg, 1942–1945' in *Historical Journal* 43, 4 (2000), 1051–70; on the major raid of 2 January 1945 see Michael Diefenbacher and Wiltrud Fischer-Pache (eds), *Der Luftkrieg gegen Nürnberg. Der Angriff am 2. Januar 1945 und die zerstörte Stadt* (Quellen und Forschungen zur Geschichte und Kultur der Stadt Nürnberg 33) (Nuremberg, 2004).
[2] On the development of the city's population during the war see Gregor, '*Schicksalsgemeinschaft*?', 1068–70.
[3] For casualty figures and assessments of the physical damage see Diefenbacher and Fischer-Pache. *Der Luftkrieg gegen Nürnberg*, 517–18.
[4] StadtAN F 5/491, Abschlussmeldung über die Einzel- und Störangriffe auf den BdO-Bereich in der Zeit vom 17 März mit 19 März 1945, 22.3.45.

2. Aerial view of Nuremberg city centre (1945).

easier to report which historical buildings are still standing, even in damaged form'.[5]

When American troops occupied Nuremberg on 20 April 1945 they found a city in which little resembling communal life was discernible.[6] The local Nazi power apparatus had dissolved. When the city's residents surfaced from the bunkers and cellars in which they had sat out the last weeks of the war, or returned from the outlying quarters in which they had sought refuge, they found that the water, gas and electricity supply was not functioning. The transport network was out of action. The economy had also largely ground to a halt.

For the American occupying forces, the immediate priority was to secure military control, public order and the wider authority of their writ in the shattered city. The focus of their initial relief effort was on specific sections of the population, such as displaced persons (DPs), rather than on the German population at large. Practical responsibility for the welfare of the ordinary population, meanwhile, was placed swiftly into the hands of the local administrative elites. While the city's administrative apparatus had all but ceased functioning in the final few weeks of the war, mirroring the wider disintegration of civil society under the impact of the bombing, its swift re-emergence as the de facto coordinator of

[5] StadtAN F 2/48, Stadtchronik 1945, 41.
[6] For an account of the battle for Nuremberg, see Karl Kunze, *Kriegsende in Franken und der Kampf um Nürnberg im April 1945* (Nuremberg, 1995).

crisis management at a local level was such that it constituted a thin, but crucial line of bureaucratic continuity during the transition from dictatorship to military occupation. The first post-war mayor to be appointed by the Americans, Julius Rühm (1882–1960), a career civil servant, symbolised this bureaucratic continuity; his replacement in July 1945 by the Social Democrat Martin Treu (1871–1952) marked the transfer of political authority to a democratic party which swiftly reclaimed its historic status as the dominant force in the local political culture. The pattern for the exercise of political and administrative authority during the occupation years was thus largely established by July 1945. A succession of Social Democratic Party (SPD) mayors and deputy mayors directed the activities of a local administrative elite – albeit one in a state of extreme flux during the years of denazification – which had been shaped by bureaucratic cultures stretching back to the Wilhelmine era; these local political and administrative elites were themselves supervised under the increasingly distant and detached regime of the American military government, which soon largely confined itself to the position of watchful observer of day-to-day affairs.[7]

The immediate tasks of the city authorities were determined by the nature of the crisis; the administration's temporal horizons were set by the challenge of the coming winter. In August 1945 mayor Treu defined the most pressing tasks as: the provisional repair of 12,000 moderately damaged apartments, which would provide temporary accommodation for 40–50,000 citizens; the procurement of fuel 'to protect the population from freezing to death'; the securing of the food supply; the restoration of transport capacity in order to allow building materials, fuel and food into the city; the prevention of contagious diseases and epidemics; and the maintenance of law and order.[8] Crucial to all of this, as well as to preparing the city for the eventual work of reconstruction, was the removal of fields of rubble which stretched as far as the eye could see.

The scale of the devastation wreaked by the bombing made the clearance of rubble a phenomenal task. The volumes to be moved defied the imagination. Estimates of the total amount ranged from ten million to twelve million cubic metres, or approximately 23 cubic metres per head of the population.[9] The

---

[7] From 1946–8 a 'third mayor' was also in office (Adam Geier, CSU). An excellent examination of the re-establishment of democratic politics in Nuremberg is offered by Wolfgang Eckart, *Amerikanische Reformpolitik und deutsche Tradition. Nürnberg 1945–1949. Nachkriegspolitik im Spannungsfeld zwischen Neuordnungsvorstellungen, Notlage und pragmatischer Krisenbewältigung* (Nuremberg, 1988); more generally John Gimbel, *The American Occupation of Germany* (Stanford, 1968); Conrad F. Latour and Thilo Vogelsang, *Okkupation und Wiederaufbau. Die Tätigkeit der Militärregierung in der amerikanischen Besatzungszone Deutschlands 1944–1947* (Stuttgart, 1973); Wolfgang Benz (ed.), *Neuanfang in Bayern 1945–1949. Politik und Gesellschaft in der Nachkriegszeit* (Munich, 1988).

[8] StadtAN C 29/160, Bürgermeister Treu an die Militärregierung Nürnberg, 11.8.45.

[9] StadtAN C 29/283, Referat Oberbaudirektor Dr Erdmannsdörfer vor dem Beirat am 30 Januar 1946; Jeffry M. Diefendorf, *In the Wake of War. The Reconstruction of German Cities after World War II* (Oxford, 1993), 15.

first head of the city's building authorities after the war put it graphically: 'If a timescale of ten years is assumed for its complete removal, then every year 1.2 million cbm of rubble must be moved and about 4,000 cbm of rubble every day, that is a tower of rubble ten metres wide by ten metres long and 40 metres high must be transported out of the city day after day.'[10] Similarly, it was assumed that just to make good the damage to existing buildings that were not beyond repair – never mind build new ones – would take ten years if all the currently available building workers were put to this task. The city authorities underlined in July 1945 that 'many thousands of apartments are soaked through each time it rains, as lack of material and labour means that damage to the roof has still not been made good; the windows and doors in these apartments are destroyed or heavily damaged so that they are just about inhabitable in the summer months but impossible to live in however in the autumn and winter'.[11]

With American help city officials were able to organise the clearance of the main traffic arteries. With mechanical transport the process of conveying rubble out of the city centre to collecting dumps was begun. However, the shortage of building workers meant that progress was very slow. Volunteers for organised rubble clearance were few; the legal basis for insisting on obligatory participation was unclear; forcing former Nazi party members to engage in extra rubble work as penance was not rigorously implemented. Rubble clearing was, in any case, only one of a number of pressing immediate priorities for the population. Another was food. Even before the end of the war the food supply, which had held up well under the strict regulation of the Nazi regime, had started to falter. The breakdown of regional economic ties as a result of military action, the accelerated collapse of the transport system under the impact of bombing, and the momentary dissolution of civil authority at the end of the war meant that the food supply all but ground to a halt in April and May 1945. In May 1945 the city's Food Office was observing that 'the transportation of milk is occurring only very slowly, and in practice the farmers are forced either to process the goods or dispose of them themselves. This is facilitated by the fact that, as a consequence of the unregulated situation, an endless stream of foragers flows out into the countryside, starting first thing in the morning and ending late in the evening.'[12] As a result, the authorities estimated that 50 per cent of fats were being lost from regular distribution channels. Black market animal slaughter, similarly, accounted for

[10] StadtAN C 29/283, Referat Oberbaudirektor Dr Erdmannsdörfer vor dem Beirat am 30 Januar 1946.
[11] StadtAN C 29/424, Monatsbericht des Oberbürgermeisters der Stadt Nürnberg für Juli 1945.
[12] StadtAN C 28/163, Ernährungsamt/Aktennotiz betr. Schwarzer Markt, 8.5.45.

one third of all slaughtering. This set the pattern for many months to come. In October 1945, for example, the military government reported that 'the food situation throughout the month was critical. Pork and veal collections were practically negligible.'[13]

The collapse of the Nazi regime thus ushered in a period of intense welfare crisis. Extreme hunger and physical hardship were the dominant experiences of a population whose immediate struggle for survival took precedence over all else. Whatever space existed for emotional reflection was focused on establishing the whereabouts of family members. Reflection on wider issues of politics was a luxury few could afford. While the core of the old organised working class reconstituted itself into a coherent, engaged political movement, for the broader public political sentiment oscillated between apathy, resentment and anti-American ersatz nationalism. In opposition to the Social Democrats the Christian Social Union (CSU), Free Democratic Party (FDP) and, for a time, the Economic Reconstruction Association (WAV) sought – alongside a number of more ephemeral protest groupings – with limited success to mobilise political commitment among a disorientated bourgeoisie, but for most the only politics that mattered – with the exception of denazification – were those of resource allocation.[14]

It is, ultimately, impossible to separate convincingly the development of the extreme post-war crisis from the increasingly shrill and plaintiff rhetoric which surrounded it. Whether the high point of the city administration's complaints to higher offices marked the nadir of the crisis, or merely the most intense manifestations of the rhetoric itself, is unclear. Claims concerning the unique suffering of the city's population during the crisis years also represented an early rehearsal of claims to unique victimhood during the war itself that would surface later in the city's memory culture. Neither did references to the inadequate rations available to workers in the city's pleas for relief always reflect accurately the actual calorific intake of the population, or capture the differing ways in which different groups of the population were able to navigate the crisis.[15] This was determined, largely, by an individual's access to the black market, which, in turn, was conditioned by whether or not one had goods available to barter. Those whose homes had been destroyed in the bombing were thus

[13] StadtAN F 6/2, OMG Kreis Nürnberg, Regierungsbezirk Oberfranken und Mittelfranken, Monthly Historical Report from 1.10.45–31.10.45. On the black market see Willi A. Boelcke, *Der Schwarzmarkt 1945–1948. Vom Überleben nach dem Kriege* (Braunschweig, 1986); Paul Erker, *Ernährungskrise und Nachkriegsgesellschaft. Bauern und Arbeiterschaft in Bayern 1943–1953* (Stuttgart, 1990), 23–230.

[14] On the CSU see Thomas Schlemmer, *Aufbruch, Krise und Erneuerung. Die Christlich-Soziale Union 1945 bis 1955* (Munich, 1998); on the WAV see Hans Woller, *Die Loritz-Partei. Geschichte, Struktur und Politik der Wirtschaftlichen Aufbau-Vereinigung (WAV) 1945–1955* (Stuttgart, 1982).

[15] For an overview of the development of official rations levels see Eckart, *Amerikanische Reformpolitik*, 189–91.

disadvantaged compared to those whose apartments had survived at least partially intact. Access to food also depended on informal connections to other networks of supply – those provided by the presence of family and friends who worked in professions which gave them access to food, or who lived in outlying rural areas. Here, indigenous citizens were at an advantage over refugees, for example. The precise functioning of these networks was undoubtedly often more mundane than caricatures of the black market implied. Much procurement of food took the form of straightforward theft from the fields. Images of twilight characters working out of the rubble captured a truth of sorts, but they often betrayed the anti-modern gaze on the metropolis of their conservative authors, not to mention the lingering racist neuroses of the Nazis' anti-urban imagination. Penetrating the languages of officialdom or the embittered complaints of the population to examine in detail the unfolding of the post-war food crisis in the city is, in this respect, very difficult too.

Nonetheless, the crisis rhetoric of the years 1946 to 1948 represented anything but the exaggerated outbursts of an administrative apparatus predisposed to unnecessary polemical excess. The very fact that the agents of a bureaucratic system culturally given to sober administration were tempted into increasingly sharp expressions of criticism and emotive pleading was itself eloquent testimony to the depths of the crisis. While the crisis affected different sections of the population in different ways at different points, 1947 marked a particularly difficult period for virtually all.[16] In December 1946, the Economics Office of the city warned that 'the general situation is rapidly heading towards a low point, the extent of which cannot yet be seen'.[17] By the summer of 1947, the Americans' local weekly intelligence report was recording that 'it is reported by Nürnberg city officials that the food situation of Nürnberg will soon end in a catastrophe, if transportation facilities are not improved immediately'.[18] In November 1947, the city authorities were pleading that 'housewives really don't know what they are supposed to cook any more'.[19] A month later, the same offices remarked that 'as was to be foreseen, the main market . . . came almost to a standstill. Of the limited available vegetable produce the ever-increasing part does not get distributed via the open market, as exchange and barter suck up the supplies.'[20] As the reservoir

---

[16] On the development of the food crisis see Erker, *Ernährungskrise*; Günter J. Trittel, *Hunger und Politik. Die Ernährungskrise in der Bizone (1945–1949)* (Frankfurt/Main, 1990).

[17] StadtAN C 28/25, Monatlicher Tätigkeits- und Lagebericht des Wirtschaftsamtes Nürnberg-Stadt zum 20 Dezember 1946.

[18] StadtAN F 6/79, Weekly Intelligence Report, 3.–10.7.47.

[19] StadtAN C 29/428, Monatsbericht des Stadtrats zu Nürnberg für die Zeit vom 20 Oktober 1947 bis 19 November 1947.

[20] StadtAN C 29/428, Monatsbericht des Stadtrats zu Nürnberg für die Zeit vom 20 November 1947 bis 19 Dezember 1947.

of still available superlatives failed, they simply noted in the following January that 'the food situation is getting ever more critical'.[21] Reduced by the absence of goods to distribute to playing the role of commentator on the deepening crisis, the Economics Office summarised that 'the wasting away of the economy has reached its final stage and in some sectors has already become a direct, indeed deadly threat to broad sections of consumers'.[22]

The essential truths which such assessments contained, polemically loaded as they undoubtedly were, were confirmed by the more sober data collected by health officials. According to a survey of schoolchildren's health carried out over the winter of 1945 to 1946, 'the close examination of a few 1,000 children ... showed that only 3–6 per cent of all children were still really well-nourished'.[23] Monthly surveys of the average weights of adults told a similar story. The average weight of a man in his thirties, for example, fell from 59.2 kg in July 1946 to 55.2 kg in July 1947, reaching 52.4 kg in February 1948.[24]

The catastrophic food situation naturally had a highly negative impact, in turn, on ordinary citizens' ability to work. The city authorities pleaded on behalf of their own employees that 'the recent reductions in rations have led to ever more visible signs of tiredness amongst large parts of the workforce in the city administration'; while they understood fully that manual workers needed adequate food to perform physical labour, 'one is deluding oneself if one assumes that desk workers can work responsibly for nine hours and more each day on 900 calories.'[25] By 1947, the food crisis was leading to protest strikes.[26] In July 1947, for example, a deputation of factory council representatives from the MAN factory and the Vereinigte Deutsche Metallwerke announced to the mayor that 'the workers cannot work on for weakness and hunger. The hunger rations on offer hitherto have completely used up their nerves and strength. The planned further reductions make it impossible to work on.'[27] As a result, the workers had ceased working. The hunger and other

[21] StadtAN C 29/428, Monatsbericht des Stadtrats zu Nürnberg für die Zeit vom 20 Dezember 1947 bis 19 Januar 1948.
[22] StadtAN C 28/24, Monatsbericht des Wirtschaftsamtes der Stadt Nürnberg vom 21.11.–20.12.47.
[23] StadtAN F 6/89, Bericht aus der Nürnberger Jugendhilfe: Schulärztlicher Dienst seit 1945, 20.5.48.
[24] StadtAN F 6/79, Weekly Intelligence Report, 17.–24.7.47; StadtAN C 29/428, Monatsbericht des Stadtrats zu Nürnberg für die Zeit vom 20 November 1947 bis 19 Dezember 1947; C 29/428, Monatsbericht des Stadtrats zu Nürnberg für die Zeit vom 20 Februar 1948 bis 19 März 1948.
[25] StadtAN C 29/427, Monatsbericht des Stadtrats zu Nürnberg für die Zeit vom 20.4.1947 bis 19.5.1947.
[26] Paul Erker, 'Solidarität und Selbsthilfe. Die Arbeiterschaft in der Ernährungskrise' in Benz, *Neuanfang in Bayern*, 82–102, here 93ff.; Erker, *Ernährungskrise*, 196–221; Trittel, *Hunger und Politik*, 254ff.
[27] StadtAN C 29/446, Oberbürgermeister Ziegler an Ministerpräsident Ehard, 14.7.47; see also StadtAN C 29/428, Monatsbericht des Stadtrats zu Nürnberg für die Zeit vom 20 Dezember 1947 bis 19 Januar 1948; Eckart, *Amerikanische Reformpolitik*, 206–7.

shortages also led increasingly to strident behaviour towards the city authorities themselves. In October 1946 the shortage of goods was causing the
'attitude of applicants to become ever more aggressive'.[28] Following ration
cuts in the spring of 1947, the authorities noted in their monthly report that
'the dissatisfaction among the population is exceptionally great and the Food
Office is on the receiving end of heavy reproaches, even though it has no
influence on the setting of rations'.[29] By October 1947, the Economics Office
was warning that the department responsible for distributing allocations of
shoes, among others, was having to call in police protection on a regular
basis.[30]

In a situation in which the production of goods, the channels of distribution and a functioning administration recovered only slowly and unevenly
from the chaos of defeat and collapse, it was often the case that goods and
the ration coupons to match them did not reach the same place at the same
time. While in the immediate aftermath of war this could be put down to the
inherent difficulties of the situation, the reports of the city authorities suggest
that the population sensed increasingly that goods were being withheld from
circulation intentionally, either by higher authorities wishing to ensure an
adequate supply of goods to protect the stability of a new currency the introduction of which was widely anticipated, or by producers and traders who saw
holding goods of fixed value as their best chance of negotiating the vicissitudes of the post-war crisis successfully. In October 1947 the Economics
Office observed that 'the shoe traders complain about the limited sales opportunities but it can be assumed that in view of the possibility of a currency
reform some traders are not unhappy at this stockpiling of material goods'.[31]
As the economy spluttered into life, this discrepancy became more and more
apparent. In April 1948, the economic authorities of the district government
of Middle Franconia reported that 'ordinary consumers in the Bizone can feel
no tangible progress in the supply of everyday consumer goods as of this
point. This stands in contrast to the announcements and statistics of increases
in production in the most diverse areas.'[32] As a result, the public was
expressing mistrust of the figures and questioning how goods were being

[28] StadtAN C 29/426, Monatsbericht des Stadtrats zu Nürnberg für die Zeit vom 20 September
bis 19 Oktober 1946.
[29] StadtAN C 29/427, Monatsbericht des Stadtrats zu Nürnberg für die Zeit vom 20 März bis 19
April 1947.
[30] StadtAN C 28/25, Monatlicher Tätigkeits- und Lagebericht des Wirtschaftsamtes Nürnberg-
Stadt zum 20 Oktober 1947.
[31] StadtAN C 28/25, Monatlicher Tätigkeits- und Lagebericht des Wirtschaftsamtes Nürnberg-
Stadt zum 20 Oktober 1947.
[32] StadtAN F 6/91, Regierung Mittelfranken/Regierungswirtschaftsamt an Bayerisches
Staatsministerium für Wirtschaft, Monatlicher Bericht über die wirtschaftliche Lage für April
1948.

distributed. The years 1946 to 1947 marked a low point, but life remained exceptionally harsh throughout the first three years after the war.

If the currency reform of June 1948 marked a decisive moment in the process of recovery on a macroeconomic level, and a key pre-condition for successful reconstruction in the longer term, it did little to alleviate the immediate sense or experience of crisis.[33] It changed the nature of the difficulties and redistributed the brunt of the hardship between different sectors of the population some-what, but in its short-term impact it was not the panacea of subsequent mythology. The flow of goods into the city remained very uneven, and certainly inadequate to meet the massive ongoing demand for basic items caused by the destruction of the war. Prices began to rise strongly. The population, for its part, hurried to turn a currency which had yet to prove its stability into tangible goods before prices rose even further. An element of inflation psychosis born of the memory of developments after the First World War was partly to blame.[34] In September 1948, two months after the currency reform, it was observed that 'the population does not contemplate saving but quickly converts its income into consumer goods. The instability of the price structure may contribute considerably to a continuous propensity to spend, to which must be added the fact that demand remains exceptionally high and still cannot be completely satisfied.'[35] A month later, the district government of Middle Franconia was warning that the price spiral was leading to social tensions and that the standard of living of wage earners was 'constantly declining'.[36]

While those in paid employment could hope that their wages might keep pace, at least in part, with prices, the inflationary spiral hit those on fixed incomes – pensions, rents and, most of all, savings – particularly hard. Such groups figured very prominently in the new wave of claimants registered by the city's welfare authorities.[37] In the first three months after the currency reform the city Welfare Office registered nearly 2,300 new claimants, of whom 'almost half are old people incapable of work who have no pension and previously lived primarily from their savings'; a further quarter were disabled war veterans and relatives of killed soldiers whose pensions had not yet been fixed and who were also living off their own reserves.[38] In the majority of cases it was thus those who war, defeat and collapse had left incapable of work for one

[33] Erker, *Ernährungskrise*, 256–62.

[34] StadtAN C 28/24, Monatsbericht des Wirtschaftsamtes der Stadt Nürnberg vom 1.–31.8.48.

[35] StadtAN C 28/25, Monatlicher Tätigkeits- und Lagebericht des Wirtschaftsamtes Nürnberg-Stadt zum 20 September 1948.

[36] StadtAN F 6/93, Monatsbericht der Regierung Mittelfranken, Oktober 1948.

[37] See Erker, *Ernährungskrise*, 263ff.; more generally Hans-Günter Hockerts, 'Integration in der Gesellschaft. Gründungskrise und Sozialpolitik in der frühen Bundesrepublik' in *Zeitschrift für Sozialreform* 32 (1986), 25–41.

[38] StadtAN F 6/93, Wochenbericht der Regierung Mittelfranken, 9.–15.9.48.

reason or another who were most affected by the post-currency reform welfare crisis. While average weights had risen again substantially by June 1949, suggesting that the worst period of the hunger crisis had passed, for those unable to work the situation remained acute. Twelve months after the currency reform the number of cases being handled by the welfare agencies had risen by two-thirds, while the 'state of need of those who have lost their livelihoods and stand before the abyss as a result of war damage has now reached unbearable levels and demands immediate help'.[39] Pensioners, widows and orphans were among those suffering most from a crisis in which the authorities feared that 'the need has reached a scale which greatly favours radicalisation'.

The post-currency reform economic adjustment took place in a city in which the pace of reconstruction work remained slow. By the end of 1949, a little over one quarter of the rubble had been removed from the town. In his annual end-of-year report for 1949 mayor Otto Ziebill (1896–1978; mayor 1948–51) underlined for his audience the city's planning horizons when he asserted that 'the incredible damage of the last war will not be overcome in years, but in decades, and not by one, but by several generations'.[40] A year later, on the same occasion, Ziebill warned that despite widespread building activity the city had reached only 57 per cent of the pre-war number of apartments, while the population had already recovered to 86 per cent of its 1939 level.[41] The absence of a Bavarian reconstruction law meant an ongoing legal vacuum concerning questions of ownership which hampered progress. An expert curatorium was established in 1948 to address fundamental issues of planning and urban development; a basic plan for the reconstruction of the old city was only adopted in 1950. The straitened circumstances of the city authorities, meanwhile, whose finances were deeply affected by the currency reform, placed limits on the volume of building which could be financed in the early reconstruction period.[42]

As the economy recovered in the early 1950s, however, the reconstruction effort gathered pace. The old city was rebuilt along recognisably the same lines, insofar as medieval walls and major monuments were rebuilt or restored, and major markers of local cultural identity were re-established; at the same time an extensive modernisation of the inner city's street network,

---

[39] StadtAN C 29/430, Monatsbericht des Stadtrats zu Nürnberg für die Zeit vom 1 bis 30 Juni 1949.

[40] StadtAN C 29/518, Rede des Bürgermeisters, (undated, December 1949).

[41] StadtAN C 29/519, Jahresschlussansprache des Oberbürgermeisters Dr Otto Ziebill, 20.12.50.

[42] For references together with overviews of reconstruction and planning issues see the *Verwaltungsberichte der Stadt Nürnberg* for the 1950s; more generally Diefendorf, *In the Wake of War*; Günther Schulz, *Wiederaufbau in Deutschland. Die Wohnungsbaupolitik in den Westzonen und der Bundesrepublik von 1945–1957* (Düsseldorf, 1994).

and a reduction in the number of buildings and resident population of what gradually evolved into a new central business district meant that rebuilding did not take the form of a direct reconstruction of the old city. Instead, the city planners moved a large part of the population out to rebuilt or newly developed suburbs over the 1950s and 1960s.[43]

Assessing when the rebuilding of war damage merged into a more general process of economic transformation is a forlorn task; from the outset reconstruction occurred alongside and within a more general process of modernisation.[44] However, by 1956 the city's population had regained its pre-war level; it was also in 1956 that the number of residential apartments in the city reached the level of 1939.[45] This re-establishment of the pre-war equilibrium of population and housing did not mean that the pressure on accommodation was no longer acute. If nothing else, the channelling of building capacity into rearmament in the 1930s had meant that there had been a great shortage of homes by the outbreak of war. The migration of refugees from outlying rural areas into the cities in the 1950s and 1960s was but one component of a wider process of rural–urban migration in the post-war period which meant that demand for housing in the city remained intense into the 1960s. The restoration of this equilibrium did, however, mark a milestone in the reconstruction process insofar as it signified that some form of normality was gradually returning. It was also in the mid- to late 1950s that the wider, tangible legacies of war started to fade. The last refugee and displaced persons' camps were mostly closed down in this period; the return of the last prisoners of war from Soviet captivity in 1956 marked for many a symbolic end to the post-war era.[46]

Yet as such references suggest, the social history of the legacies of the war is only very inadequately described if one restricts oneself to a general overview of housing and welfare conditions for the population in the post-war era. Within this overall picture there was a great variety of different groups, their

---

[43] An overview of the reconstruction of the old city – albeit one offered from a highly subjective position regarding the merits of some architectural agendas over others – can be found in Erich Mulzer, *Der Wiederaufbau der Altstadt von Nürnberg* (Erlangen, 1972). For an analysis of how debates over reconstruction were infused with conflicting narratives of the German past see Rosenfeld, *Munich and Memory*.

[44] The general context of the reconstruction boom is well outlined in Werner Abelshauser, *Die Langen Fünfziger Jahre. Wirtschaft und Gesellschaft der Bundesrepublik Deutschland 1949–1966* (Düsseldorf, 1987); Axel Schildt and Arnold Sywottek (eds), *Modernisierung im Wiederaufbau. Die Westdeutsche Gesellschaft der 50er Jahre* (Bonn, 1993); for its attendant effects see also Axel Schildt, *Moderne Zeiten. Freizeit, Massenmedien und Zeitgeist in der Bundesrepublik der 50er Jahre* (Hamburg, 1995); for thoughtful reflections on the relationship between reconstruction and modernisation in the 1950s see Mark Roseman, 'Reconstruction and Modernization. The Federal Republic and the Fifties' in *Bulletin of the German Historical Institute London*, 19,1 (1997), 5–16.

[45] StadtAN C 29/537, Jahresabschlussansprache (undated, December 1956).

[46] Robert Moeller, ' "The Last Soldiers of the Great War" and Tales of Family Reunions in the Federal Republic of Germany' in *Signs: Journal of Women in Culture and Society* 24/1 (1998), 129–45.

differing fates conditioned by their various positions and experiences during the Nazi era and war itself. To understand the circumstances in which a post-war memory culture emerged, and to understand something of what gave its dominant narratives such strong purchase, a more differentiated examination of post-war Nuremberg society is needed.

The following chapters therefore examine, in turn, the experiences of the various categories of 'victim' thrown up by the circumstances of war and defeat. Clearly, the separate categories deployed for the purposes of historical explication are, in some respects, artificial. There were, after all, no clear boundaries between former party members, homeless victims of the bombing and returning prisoners of war: in reality, one Nuremberg citizen might have joined the Nazi party in 1937, been called up to the *Wehrmacht* in 1942, and returned from captivity in 1947 to find his home in ruins, while another might have been mobilised into the army in his home town of Dresden, made his way westwards upon release, only to find that his wife and family had been killed in an air raid. In this sense categories such as 'Refugee', 'Air Raid Victim', 'Surviving Dependant' or 'Homecomer' were both crude bureaucratic conveniences and ideal-types of post-war popular culture as much as accurate descriptors of real people's lives.

Nonetheless, these labels were not just simplistic fictions. For one thing, such bureaucratic categories carried with them entitlements – at least on paper – to goods and services, and thus created real social effects which impacted significantly upon lived experience. For another, the moral discourse which grew up around each ideal type of victim was central to the wider contest for scarce economic resource in the post-war years – the claims to material redress on the part of each group depended on the receptiveness of the authorities, and indeed society at large, to the uniqueness of that group's suffering. Most importantly, these categories were not merely a reflection of bureaucratic labelling processes; they were central to the labelling of the self in the post-war years. In defining people to themselves, moreover, they did not just become markers of individual identity, but spurs to organisational mobilisation, and thus determinants of the contours of post-war civil society. In this way, they decisively shaped the environment in which a post-war memory culture would form.

I.2

'Victims of Bolshevism'?
The Refugees and Expellees between Assimilation and Self-Assertion

Into the chaotic and highly fluid situation of post-war Germany, and into this disorientated, shocked and often desperate community of indigenous citizens came millions of refugees and expellees from East Europe. Some had already begun to flee as the Red Army advanced on Germany: anti-Bolshevik propaganda, anti-Slav prejudice and awareness of what Germans themselves had done during the barbaric occupation of the east had led them to fear the worst; such fears were confirmed by initial experiences of Red Army brutality in 1945.[1] To the initial refugee influx was added a much larger number of expellees, in the form of ethnic Germans forced out of former German territories east of the Oder-Neisse line – East Prussia, Pomerania and Silesia – or driven from countries in which they had previously lived as minority ethnic groups: Hungary, Yugoslavia, Poland and Czechoslovakia. In these cases, the desire for revenge for the brutalities of German occupation compounded memories of the fractious ethnic politics of the interwar years, during which time the presence of often troublesome German minorities had provided the pretext for Nazi interference and invasion.[2] Between 1944 and 1950 an estimated twelve million people were forced westwards into the reduced boundaries of post-war Germany in campaigns of expulsion which were often

[1] Norman Naimark, *The Russians in Germany. A History of the Soviet Zone of Occupation 1945–1949* (Cambridge, MA, 1995), 69–140; Atina Grossmann, 'A Question of Silence: The Rape of German Women by Occupation Soldiers' in Robert G. Moeller (ed.), *West Germany under Construction. Politics, Society and Culture in the Adenauer Era* (Ann Arbor, MI, 1997), 33–52.
[2] On the legacies of interwar ethnic politics for 1945 see Norbert Krekeler, 'Die deutsche Minderheit in Polen und die Revisionspolitik des Deutschen Reiches 1919–1933'; and Rudolf Jaworski, 'Die Sudetendeutschen als Minderheit in der Tschechoslowakei 1918–1938' in Wolfgang Benz (ed.), *Die Vertreibung der Deutschen aus dem Osten. Ursachen, Ereignisse, Folgen* (Frankfurt/Main, 1995), 16–32; 33–44.

highly violent.[3] As the main wave of expulsions subsided after 1946, a steady stream of German 'illegals' fleeing the Soviet occupation zone ensured that the refugee flow remained continuous; it was only when the Berlin Wall was built in 1961 that the influx was largely halted.[4]

Even before the end of the war, this unprecedented population movement had begun to make its mark on Nuremberg. By the end of June, the American military occupiers were reporting that 'refugees arrive daily by train with no advance notice' and that 'increasing numbers of trains are coming into Nuremberg carrying many DPs and refugees but no food; many of the passengers are hungry and ill'.[5] In September, the railway charity mission was processing 'hundreds of refugees daily' alongside German former prisoners of war trying to make their various ways home.[6] For the authorities in such a heavily damaged city, struggling already to cope with extreme housing shortages, the problem of where to put them was indeed acute. Not for the last time, the answer was partly found in pragmatic use of the physical residues of the Nazi era. The urban landscape of Nuremberg was littered with large-scale wooden barrack enclosures which had been used to house tens of thousands of foreign forced workers in the city from 1940 to 1945. Their chronic state of disrepair in 1945 was such that most were soon pulled down; a few functioned briefly as displaced persons' camps.[7] The intense pressures created by the uncontrolled influx of refugees and expellees was such that some, however, were swiftly rededicated as refugee camps. Two large camps were created 'literally overnight' in the Schafhof district of the town and in the *Witschelstrasse*; further accommodation was found in the former air-raid shelters that likewise littered the landscape in 1945; an additional camp was later opened in Buchenbühl.[8]

By November 1945, the refugee population of Nuremberg stood at approximately 6,100.[9] While the city took proportionately few refugees in the immediate post-war years – in common with many heavily damaged cities it succeeded in having a formal ban placed on refugees moving to the city – the gradual process of reuniting refugee family members and recruiting skilled

[3] Dierk Hoffmann, Marita Kraus, Michael Schwartz, 'Einleitung' in id. (eds), *Vertriebene in Deutschland. Interdisziplinäre Ergebnisse und Forschungsperspektiven* (Munich, 2000), 9–25, here 9.
[4] An excellent overview of refugee politics in Bavaria is provided by Franz J. Bauer, *Flüchtlinge und Flüchtlingspolitik in Bayern 1945–1950* (Stuttgart, 1982); for comparison see Sylvia Schraut, *Flüchtlingsaufnahme in Württemberg-Baden, 1945–1949. Amerikanische Besatzungsziele und demokratischer Wiederaufbau im Konflikt* (Munich, 1995).
[5] StadtAN F 6/151, Semi-Weekly Report, HQ, Det. F1B3, 26.–28.6.45.
[6] StadtAN C 29/424, Monatsbericht des Oberbürgermeisters der Stadt Nürnberg für den Monat September 1945.
[7] On the experience of the displaced persons in 1945 see below, Chapter I.7.
[8] StadtAN C 29/424, Monatsbericht des Oberbürgermeisters der Stadt Nürnberg für Juli 1945; see also F 6/90, Aufstellung der Wohn- und Massenlager, undated (1949).
[9] 'Nürnberg und sein Heimatkreis', *Nürnberger Nachrichten*, 29.11.45.

3. *Witschelstrasse* Refugee Camp (mid-1950s).

refugee workers for reconstruction work meant that their numbers steadily increased. As refugees were drawn into the reconstruction workforce, additional private barracks were opened by large employers to accommodate them. Although the brunt of the immediate refugee crisis of the late 1940s was borne by less heavily damaged rural areas, over 27,000 refugees were living in the city by 1951.[10]

Beneath the homogenizing terminology of 'refugee' and 'expellee' lay a highly diverse group, whose historical experiences, cultural backgrounds and prior relationships to broader notions of 'Germany' and 'Germanness' were varied in the extreme. In their own homelands they had been stratified by the same divisions of class and gender, profession and confession, generation and political preference as the indigenous population into whose midst they had now been propelled. Something of this diversity was captured by the characterisation of refugee-camp life in the *Nürnberger Nachrichten*: 'the most different of dialects resonate in one's ear. Here an industrialist, whose factory stood in upper Silesia, there a farmer, who ploughed in Transylvania.'[11] If, however, such distinctions of origin and outlook ensured that their experience of integration or assimilation would be quite varied over subsequent years, in

[10] LKAN DW 1384, Statistik des Bayerischen Staatsministerium des Innern: Heimatvertriebene und Wohndichte, 1.1.51; on the geographical distribution of the refugees and expellees in Bavaria, see Bauer, *Flüchtlinge und Flüchtlingspolitik*, 161–82.
[11] 'Nürnberg und sein Heimatkreis', *Nürnberger Nachrichten*, 29.11.45.

the short term their fate was largely determined by the shared circumstances of their arrival. 'Refugees' remained a prominent administrative category within the overarching welfare crisis of the post-war years for a good decade after the defeat; the label 'refugee' remained a catch-all marker of difference, of otherness relative to the indigenous population, for considerably longer than that. For host authorities and host population at large, the multiple distinctions which divided the refugee and expellee population internally held comparatively little interest.

For some years after the war life in refugee camps was at best spartan and at worst appalling.[12] In the first place, the barracks themselves were often in a desperate state of repair, a reflection not only of the extreme shortages of the post-war years themselves but also of the fact that immediately prior to their occupation by the refugees they had been used to house the 'racial enemies' of the Nazi regime. In the autumn of 1945 the city authorities were warning that the Schafhof and *Witschelstrasse* camps would not be inhabitable in the seasonally deteriorating weather, and that the barracks were in an 'exceptionally inadequate state'. Many camp inhabitants were already demanding that they be returned to the bunkers where they were originally housed, 'as the cold nights in the barracks are unbearable, especially for children'.[13] By the following, particularly harsh, winter little seemed to have improved, the Refugee Commissioner for the city reporting that 'the cold period has made clear the unfortunate situation in the camps'; the negligible amounts of heating fuel allocated were such that the situation amounted to a 'serious crisis'.[14] A month later, he described the situation in the Schafhof camp as 'unbearable'.[15]

Not only did the refugees in the camps suffer from a particular lack of sound accommodation and heating, they were also even less well catered for than most in terms of warm clothing. Having arrived with few, if any, possessions, they were reliant upon handouts from supplies confiscated from former party members or donated by charitable organisations. In November 1946, as the winter approached, the Refugee Commissioner warned that 'warm winter clothing and work clothing are missing above all';[16] over a year later, in early 1948, officials were still complaining that 'the provision of refugees with textiles ... is very inadequate'; the points-based ration system in operation

---

[12] Bauer, *Flüchtlinge und Flüchtlingspolitik*, 182–201; also Jutta Neupert, 'Vom Heimatvertriebenen zum Neubürger. Flüchtlingspolitik und Selbsthilfe auf dem Weg zur Integration' in Benz, *Neuanfang in Bayern*, 103–20, here 113–14.
[13] StadtAN C 29/424, Monatsbericht der Stadt Nürnberg für den Monat September 1945.
[14] StadtAN C 40 Abg. 73/9, Tätigkeitsbericht des Flüchtlingskommissars Nürnberg-Stadt, 1.–31.12.46.
[15] StadtAN C 40 Abg. 73/9, Tätigkeitsbericht des Flüchtlingskommissars Nürnberg-Stadt, 1.–31.1.47.
[16] StadtAN C 40 Abg. 73/9, Tätigkeitsbericht des Flüchtlingskommissars Nürnberg-Stadt für die Zeit vom 1.–30.11.46.

was unable to cover even the most immediate of essential needs, and 'many camp refugees have not been able to get even a single item of the necessary textiles in this way'.[17]

The stresses caused by the wholly inadequate living conditions of the majority of refugees were compounded by the desperate food situation, in which most refugees were at a disadvantage even compared to the hungry mass of the indigenous population. Unlike many of the city's long-standing residents, they had no extended network of friends or relatives with connections or access to goods, especially in the outlying rural areas; having arrived with little more than the clothes on their back they had next to nothing to barter; they had no accessible savings on which to draw in order to meet the demands of the black market.[18] While the *Nürnberger Nachrichten* could claim in November 1945 that 'the state of health of the refugees is generally satisfactory', the authorities were, unsurprisingly, soon registering a different picture.[19] In March 1946, the military government of the city recorded that 'cases of undernourishment are still very frequent'.[20] By May, the city authorities were commenting that 'the majority of refugees are undernourished, and there are increasing cases of exhaustion, fainting and dizziness attacks as well as hypotension'.[21]

Living under these dreadful conditions the health of the refugees declined markedly. As early as March 1946, a survey of the health of schoolchildren in the city concluded that the refugee children in the camps were 'significantly shorter and underweight in comparison to the Nuremberg children . . .'[22] In the winter of 1946, the Refugee Commissioner observed that 'the generally reduced health and strength levels necessarily leads to an increased susceptibility to cold and flu infections'; in cases these were leading to broncho-pneumonial lung infections which were causing 'serious cases of illness especially among children'.[23] If, by the following April, the same official was able to opine that 'the onset of Spring has finally made camp life tolerable', it remained the case that 'the danger to health as a result of the food shortages is still relatively present'.[24] In any case, warmer weather brought its own problems. A year earlier, the monthly report of

[17] StadtAN C 40 Abg. 73/9, Tätigkeitsbericht des Kreisbeauftragten für das Flüchtlingswesen Nürnberg-Stadt, 1.–31.1.48.
[18] Bauer, *Flüchtlinge und Flüchtlingspolitik*, 234.
[19] 'Nürnberg und sein Heimatkreis', *Nürnberger Nachrichten*, 29.11.45.
[20] StadtAN F 6/2, OMG Kreis Nürnberg, Regierungsbezirk Oberfranken und Mittelfranken: Monthly Historical Report from 1.–31.3.46.
[21] StadtAN C 29/425, Monatsbericht des Oberbürgermeisters der Stadt Nürnberg für die Zeit vom 19 April 1946 bis 20 Mai 1946.
[22] StadtAN F 6/89, Bericht aus der Nürnberger Jugendhilfe: Schulärztlicher Dienst seit 1945, 20.5.48.
[23] StadtAN C 40 Abg. 73/9, Tätigkeitsbericht des Flüchtlingskommissars Nürnberg-Stadt, 1.–31.12.46; see also C 40 Abg. 73/9, Tätigkeitsbericht des Flüchtlingskommissars Nürnberg-Stadt, 1.–28.2.47.
[24] StadtAN C 40 Abg. 73/9, Tätigkeitsbericht des Flüchtlingskommissars Nürnberg-Stadt, 1.–30.4.47.

the Schafhof camp observed that 'with the onset of the warm weather an increase in the number of bugs is observable . . . there is a constant battle against mice and rats'.[25]

Generalising about encounters between the refugees and the citizenry at large is very difficult.[26] The preoccupation of the city authorities with the mass camps in their care was such that relatively little written record exists of inter-actions between officialdom and those refugees who lived in private accommo-dation, or of interactions between the refugees and other city dwellers. There were, clearly, incidences of conflict between locals and newcomers, particularly where the former rented accommodation to the latter, but how much these reflected the general stresses of living in the cramped and unhealthy conditions of the city in the early post-war years as opposed to tensions specifically between refugees and the indigenous population is not always clear. The rela-tively limited number of refugees in the city compared to the population as a whole may partially account for the fact that recorded incidences of conflict are limited; the fact that most refugees housed in private accommodation were economically active workers contributing their skills to the reconstruction effort undoubtedly eased relationships. Certainly relationships were less fraught than in outlying rural areas, where the much higher proportion of refugees placed greater strains on an often rudimentary infrastructure, where the absence of employment opportunities caused the refugees to be seen more as an unwelcome burden on the local economy and where cultural differ-ence was often more acutely felt.[27] Nonetheless, the dominant attitudes were those of resentment, hostility or, at best, indifference: solidarity was certainly rare.[28]

For the refugees themselves, the main initial concern of many was to find news of friends or relatives from whom they had become separated in the trek westwards; as with the rest of the population, ascertaining the whereabouts of family members last heard of at the front was a

---

[25] StadtAN C 40 Abg. 73/5, Tätigkeitsbericht für das Flüchtlingslager Schafhof für Mai 1946; see also Tätigkeitsbericht für das Flüchtlingslager Schafhof für den Monat Oktober 1946. For a similar account of refugee hardship from 1948 see StadtAN C 40 Abg. 73/9, Tätigkeitsbericht des Kreisbeauftragten für das Flüchtlingswesen Nürnberg-Stadt, 1.–31.1.48.

[26] For an account of the tensions between indigenous citizens and newcomers, see Bauer, *Flüchtlinge und Flüchtlingspolitik*, 235–8.

[27] For an excellent overview of refugee politics in the surrounding area, see Paul Erker, *Vom Heimatvertriebenen zum Neubürger. Sozialgeschichte der Flüchtlinge in einer agrarischen Region Mittelfrankens 1945–1955* (Wiesbaden, 1988); on refugees' and expellees' difficulties in the labour market see Bauer, *Flüchtlinge und Flüchtlingspolitik*, 201–19.

[28] Cf. Michael Schwartz,' "Zwangsheimat Deutschland". Vertriebene und Kernbevölkerung zwis-chen Gesellschaftskonflikt und Integrationspolitik' in Naumann, *Nachkrieg in Deutschland*, 114–48, here 120.

priority.[29] In the fluid situation of 1945 rumours concerning the possibility of an imminent return home were also rife. In July 1945, shortly before the Potsdam Conference, the rumour circulated that the Americans and Russians had reached an agreement concerning the repatriation of refugees from the former German eastern territories, so that the city authorities evidently began to consider preparations for a return of the Silesian refugees in particular.[30] Such rumours surfaced periodically for some time after the war.[31]

The limited, and often contradictory, observations in the surviving written record which concern the morale of the refugees suggest only that it varied and that it fluctuated. Despite the onset of winter, the Refugee Commissioner for Nuremberg expressed the optimistic view in November 1946 that the refugees 'are pulling themselves together again, starting to show interest in events and have the desire to engage in life, and in the economy, once more. The urge towards economic independence is a pleasing phenomenon among most refugees.'[32] However, the ongoing problems of housing, hygiene and health to which the refugees were subjected clearly took their toll. Half a year later the same official was bemoaning the 'mental and social isolation of the mass barrack';[33] shortly thereafter the relevant local refugee official observed of the camps that it was noticeable how the 'well-known unfavourable living conditions inhibit the desire for life and self-preservation, and generate an indifference among some camp families which will become a danger to society if the miserable housing situation lasts considerably longer'. Urging support for those refugees who had become 'tired of life' he expressed the fear that 'some families cannot be freed from their state of torpor without outside help'.[34]

Ironically, the very welfare activities fostered by the city authorities – and indeed the refugees themselves – to overcome the negative features of life in the mass barracks acted, if anything, to reinforce the sense of separation from the broader community which gave rise to feelings of isolation. What began as a pragmatic relief effort designed to provide for the social, material and spiritual needs of the refugees led, in time, to the emergence of a largely self-contained camp infrastructure which generated its own community life largely detached from that of the indigenous population.

[29] See, for example, StadtAN C 40 Abg. 73/11, Bekanntmachung, 20.6.45; C 40 Abg. 73/9, Tätigkeitsbericht des Flüchtlingskommissars Nürnberg-Stadt, 1.–30.6.47; on the culture of searching and news exchange in general see below, Chapter I.5.

[30] StadtAN C 40 Abg. 73/11, Niederschrift über die Besprechung mit den Obleuten am 3.7.45.

[31] See, for example, StadtAN F 6/79, Weekly Intelligence Report, 21.–28.8.47.

[32] StadtAN C 40 Abg. 73/9, Tätigkeitsbericht des Flüchtlingskommissars Nürnberg-Stadt für die Zeit vom 1.–30.11.46.

[33] StadtAN C 40 Abg. 73/9, Tätigkeitsbericht des Flüchtlingskommissars Nürnberg-Stadt, 1.–30.6.47.

[34] StadtAN C 40 Abg. 73/9, Tätigkeitsbericht des Kreisbeauftragten für das Flüchtlingswesen Nürnberg-Stadt, 1.–31.10.47.

As early as 1945, a separate school had been established in the Schafhof camp, for example.[35] Unsurprisingly, conditions were far from ideal. Initially, classes were held in the barracks, with their thin walls and poor light; thereafter, they were held in the virtually unheated main camp building. There were about 75 pupils per teacher; the very diverse intake of the school, the pupils of which came from 'East Prussia, Berlin, the Sudetenland, Hungary, Poland, Russia and especially from Silesia' made teaching difficult since all had very different reservoirs of prior learning. Moreover, 'many children are poorly clothed, underfed and often ill. As a result, school attendance is often especially poor during periods of poor weather.' Nonetheless, the camp school was able to offer rudimentary instruction in German, arithmetic and religion, and by December 1946 was initiating evening classes for adults. These were organised by the Leisure Association (*Feierabendwerk*) of the camp, an agency of 'cultural self help' created by the refugees themselves and founded in September 1946 'with the goal of drawing together all the intellectual forces of the camp to work in unity with and for each other for the purposes of knowledge and education and to strengthen the personality'.[36] By 1948, the association was offering courses and study groups in English, Russian, geography and shorthand, along with activities such as dance, poetry, art history and music, and was organising lectures and cultural events.

Such secular educational and cultural activities were paralleled in the development of religious life in the camps, for which purpose institutions separate to the local churches also emerged.[37] While the church authorities charged with caring for the refugees' spiritual needs did make some efforts to foster integration with the local community – encouraging members of its flock to invite refugees to family meals, for example – the main focus of church work was similarly inside the camps, and consisted of the provision of clothes, contributions to education work and the care of the elderly. Religious worship took place largely inside the main Schafhof camp, which had its own church choir, held its own bible classes and – in a further indication of the ways in which cultural differences were defended and fostered inside the camps – followed the distinctive 'Silesian' liturgy.[38]

---

[35] StadtAN C 40 Abg. 73/1, Bericht über die Flüchtlingsschule Schafhoflager in Nürnberg, 13.12.46.
[36] StadtAN C 40 Abg. 73/9, Tätigkeitsbericht des Kreisbeauftragten für das Flüchtlingswesen Nürnberg-Stadt, 1.–31.1.48; see also C 40 Abg. 73/9, Tätigkeitsbericht des Flüchtlingskommissars Nürnberg-Stadt, 1.–31.12.46.
[37] LKAN Kd Nbg 291, Richtlinien für die kirchliche Versorgung der Flüchtlinge, 25.7.46; see also Hartmut Rudolph, *Evangelische Kirche und Vertriebene 1945 bis 1972* (2 vols, Göttingen, 1984–5) which, despite its tendency to overemphasise the harmonious aspects of the encounter, contains much interesting material.
[38] LKAN Kd Nbg 291, Übersicht über die Kirchliche Arbeit im Flüchtlingslager Schafhof vom 1. April bis zum 15 September 1947; for a similar assessment of developments in outlying rural areas see Erker, *Vom Heimatvertriebenen zum Neubürger*, 38. On the responses of the Roman Catholic Church see Frank Buscher, 'The Great Fear: The Catholic Church and the Anticipated Radicalization of Expellees and Refugees in Post-War Germany' in *German History* 21/2 (2003), 204–24.

Furnished with their own welfare, educational and spiritual infrastructure, and governed by their own routines of work, channels of food and clothing distribution and patterns of leisure activity, the refugee camps gradually became the focal points of a self-contained, substitute community life. Their only limited connections to the wider city community fostered the emergence of a largely autonomous refugee subculture the members' of which shared sense of living in an unfamiliar environment and enforced close proximity to one another encouraged the formation of strong networks. In the long run, such ties formed the basis for the creation of more institutionalised, politically focused refugee organisations – the more familiar refugee cultural organs of the 1950s often had their origins in rudimentary forerunners in the camps. In the short term, they provided important support upon which refugees relied to negotiate the multiple hazards of life in an alien environment.

Despite the spartan conditions, therefore, many refugees were reluctant to leave the camps even when alternative accommodation was on offer.[39] In December 1947, over 400 refugees who were still being housed in air-raid bunkers and who were scheduled to be re-housed in camps in Lower Franconia protested against these plans, insisting that 'they were not willing to leave their present quarters in mid-winter'.[40] Shortly thereafter, one senior district official was forced to acknowledge that 'the refugees mostly refuse to leave the camps, however miserable they are' and suggested that police force might be necessary to remove them.[41] The resistance of the refugees to transfer outwards was partly due to the fact that employment opportunities were considerably worse in outlying rural areas, especially in the aftermath of the currency reform. However, the refugee authorities were forced to accept that resistance also stemmed from the refugees' 'links to the asylum location of Nuremberg' and from their unwillingness to break the bonds which had developed with other camp families.[42] Similarly, the seemingly belligerent demands of the Buchenbühl camp residents' committee in 1950 that permanent housing be built for its inhabitants on the site of the current barracks, and its rejection of proposals that would have seen the dispersal of its residents to various new building projects in the city, suggest that the initial camp experience was at the core of the formation of a distinct refugee subculture and identity within the wider city community in the longer term.

---

[39] Bauer, *Flüchtlinge und Flüchtlingspolitik*, 196.
[40] StadtAN F 6/79, Weekly Intelligence Report, 27.11.–4.12.47.
[41] LKAN DW 1382, Protokoll über die 2. Arbeitstagung des Beirates beim Regierungsbeauftragten für das Flüchtlingswesen, 13.1.48.
[42] StadtAN C 40 Abg. 73/9, Tätigkeitsbericht des Kreisbeauftragten für das Flüchtlingswesen Nürnberg-Stadt, 1.–31.8.48.

The refugees were also hard hit by the currency reform of June 1948.[43] The sharp shock the currency reform administered to the city's tight finances meant that work on improving living conditions in the camps had to be suspended for lack of resources.[44] Refugees were particularly affected by the subsequent high unemployment, causing a substantial increase in the number of refugees who were reliant upon the welfare agencies of the city.[45] During this period, the refugees appear to have constituted a reservoir of considerable protest potential.[46]

However, once the post-currency reform crisis subsided, and the process of reconstruction gathered pace, the refugees were slowly transferred out of the camps and into new residential housing. The Buchenbühl camp was eventually closed in 1952;[47] the closure of the *Witschelstrasse* camp followed in 1955 to 1956;[48] the Schafhof camp, which still housed nearly 2,000 refugees in the mid-1950s, was not closed until 1959.[49]

Despite this, the absorption of refugees into the general housing stock of the city did not immediately lead to a dissolution of refugee community identities. Issues of cultural habit, religious observance or ongoing differences of dialect aside, the widespread official practice of allocating particular claimant groups to housing projects earmarked under specific programmes meant that many new housing estates, both large and small, continued to provide almost exclusively for refugees in the 1950s and beyond. In particular, the development of the south-eastern corner of the former party rally grounds into refugee housing projects after 1949 ensured that in the cultural geography of the city refugees continued to be associated with specific urban spaces for decades after the war. The naming of streets in the nascent suburb of Langwasser, as it was to become, after towns in Germany's lost eastern territories – *Breslauerstrasse, Oppelnerstrasse, Gleiwitzerstrasse* – perpetuated the association, while in 1963 the two primary schools built to serve the expanding suburb were named after Adalbert Stifter and Gerhart Hauptmann, reflecting the cultural identities of Sudeten and Silesian German refugees respectively.[50]

---

[43] Ian Connor, 'The Refugees and the Currency Reform' in Ian D. Turner (ed.), *Reconstruction in Post-War Germany. British Occupation Policy and the Western Zones 1945–1955* (Oxford, 1989), 301–26; Bauer, *Flüchtlinge und Flüchtlingspolitik*, 212–17; Buscher, 'The Great Fear', 211–12.

[44] StadtAN C 40 Abg. 73/6, Flüchtlingsvertrauensleute der Lager Schafhof an Regierungsbeauftragten für das Flüchtlingswesen bei der Regierung Mittel- und Oberfranken, 9.7.48.

[45] StadtAN F 6/5, Regierung Mittelfranken, Wochenbericht für die Zeit vom 24 Februar mit 31 März 1949; Connor, 'Refugees', 310–26.

[46] Connor, 'Refugees', 321–3.

[47] *Verwaltungsbericht der Stadt Nürnberg 1952*, 219.

[48] *Verwaltungsbericht der Stadt Nürnberg 1954*, 236; *Verwaltungsbericht der Stadt Nürnberg 1955*, 235.

[49] *Verwaltungsbericht der Stadt Nürnberg 1958/9*, 208.

[50] StadtAN C 85 III/33, Beschluss des Stadtrates, 18.9.63.

The embryonic housing projects for German refugees were not the only refugee complexes to emerge in Langwasser in the 1950s. Rather, the evolving outlines of the 'Langwasser settlement' and other reconstruction projects in the area formed part of a broader, fluid landscape of successive temporary barrack and compound arrangements, dotted among the archaeological and architectural ruins of the Nazi era, which housed a diverse, multi-ethnic and polyglot population of migrants, refugees, stateless persons and former Nazi collaborators from across eastern Europe. Despite the vehement protests of the city council, which wished to use the capacity created by the closure in 1949 of the internment camp for former Nazis to accommodate some of the German refugees already housed in the city, the state government of Bavaria imposed the creation of an additional camp with a separate purpose.[51]

Even before the decision of the Bavarian government, the so-called Valka Camp – named after a border town between Estonia and Latvia – already housed a large number of Estonian and Latvian former Nazi collaborators.[52] Then, from 1949 onwards, the camp became home to up to 4,500 anti-Communist Czechs who had left their homeland in the wake of the Communist takeover in 1948. In 1950, as most other Bavarian displaced persons' camps were closed down, it became a collecting point for many of the remaining DPs in the state: in October 1951 it housed twenty-eight nationalities. To these were added the residents of an additional camp for foreigners in neighbouring Schwabach, which was dissolved in May 1952: in this way, former SS collaborators from Yugoslavia and Hungary joined its diverse array of occupants. In 1954 it was transformed into a Federal Collection Camp for Homeless Foreigners, surrounded by concrete walls and barbed wire; it was finally closed in 1960.[53]

Relations between the German population and the many foreign nationalities resident in the camp, and indeed between the various ethnic groups themselves, were often fraught; in addition to inter-ethnic clashes the domestic politics of various countries were also played out in exile in the camp. In December 1949, for example, the military government intelligence report recorded 'growing tension between Czech and Sudeten German refugees' which had quickly

[51] On the conflict between the city council and the state government of Bavaria, see StadtAN C 40 Abg. 73/4, Stadtrat zu Nürnberg: Entschliessung, 16.2.49 and Beschluß des Stadtrats zu Nürnberg, 16.1.49; Abschrift: Bayerisches Staatssekretariat des Innern/Staatssekretär für das Flüchtlingswesen: Protokoll über die Besprechung im Landtag am 24.2.49 mit Herrn Stadtrat Schönleben und den Abgeordneten Haas, Euerl, Donsberger, Albert, Dr Linnert, Emmer, 24.2.49; Notizen von der Dienststellenleiterbesprechung am 10.3.49 im Referat VIII.

[52] On the presence of Estonians, Latvians and Lithuanians in post-war West Germany, see Wolfgang Jacobmeyer, Von Zwangsarbeiter zum Heimatlosen Ausländer. Die Displaced Persons in Westdeutschland 1945–1951 (Göttingen, 1985), 79–82.

[53] For an excellent overview of the development of the camp and its changing population see Geschichte für Alle (eds), Nürnberg-Langwasser. Geschichte eines Stadtteils (Nuremberg, 1995), upon which this section is partly based.

developed after 800 Czech nationalists were housed in barracks adjacent to the new Langwasser settlement for refugee Germans. In the words of the report, 'Nuremberg police chief Leo Stahl told the undersigned that some hotheads among the Sudeten Germans had threatened to set camp Valka afire when advance notice of the arrival of Czechs reached Nuremberg'; despite a considerable police presence there were 'bodily clashes on Saturday afternoon when some Czechs visited the German camp shops to make purchases'.[54] Such tensions were compounded by internal disputes among the Czech inhabitants. According to the intelligence report, 'The inmates have now organised themselves in four groups which fight each other vehemently . . . A horse-mounted detachment of the Nuremberg city police had to be sent to the camp on December 20 1949, in order to maintain peace.' Shortly after, in March 1950, clashes between followers of different political groupings inside Czechoslovakia were such that a state of emergency was declared in the camp, 'the inhabitants of which are in possession of all types of fighting instruments short of firearms'.[55]

Penetrating the highly subjective lenses through which the various organs of officialdom saw the camp to reconstruct something of the daily reality of life in Valka for its multitude of different occupants is virtually impossible; the limited surviving testimony of individual residents offers only fragmentary glimpses into the experience of thousands of people whose transmigrant status was such that they were often only very briefly in the camp.[56] Nuremberg city officials lost no time in constructing the camp as a hotbed of crime, the police chief complaining that 'the Valka camp has become the collecting point for refugees from all satellite states. This trail westwards does not however always occur for idealist reasons, but also to a considerable extent out of criminal motives'. He was thus able to draw upon an entrenched vocabulary which associated both 'the foreigner' and 'the camp' with criminality.[57] The democratically elected representatives of the city were scarcely more sympathetic. In 1953 the then deputy mayor, Social Democrat Julius Lossmann (1888–1957; deputy mayor 1949–57), complained to the Bavarian Interior Minister Wilhelm Hoegner, that 'Nuremberg is a tourist city and we are dependent on tourism. The city of Nuremberg has gained a very poor reputation abroad because of the Valka camp.'[58] His KPD (Communist

---

[54] StadtAN F 6/145, Bi-Weekly Intelligence Report, Nuremberg Field Office, 1.12.49.
[55] StadtAN F 6/146, Nuremberg Field Office, Bi-Weekly Report, 29.3.50; on the various political groupings in the camp see StadtAN C 29/307, Regierungslager A 'Valka' Nürnberg an Regierung von Mittelfranken, 8.5.50.
[56] Cf. however the testimonies in Geschichte für Alle (eds), *Nürnberg-Langwasser*, 97–104.
[57] StadtAN C 29/448, Polizeipräsidium Nürnberg an Regierung Mittelfranken, Regierungsbeauftragte für das Flüchtlingswesen Lütke, 3.10.50.
[58] StadtAN C 7 IX/714, Niederschrift über die Aussprache mit Staatsminister Dr Hoegner betr. Valka-Lager, 9.6.53.

Party) colleague Councillor Wagner observed that 'the great majority of the Nuremberg population rejects the inhabitants of the camp and regards this camp as the source of all crimes which have been committed in recent years. The West German taxpayer has to put his hand in his pocket for these people.' If his comment that 'there are still people there who fought for Hitler in 1942' indicated that some hostility to the Valka camp was rooted in an anti-fascist awareness of the collaborationist past of some of its residents, his remarks also suggested that the far-left traditions of communal politics were far from immune from associating foreigners with criminality.

Even those whose task it was to assist the occupants of the camp with their basic welfare needs were not always entirely sympathetic. The monthly reports of successive Protestant welfare workers in the camp, for example, betray a strong sense of frustration with residents who, in the eyes of the aid workers, were excessively dependent upon charity handouts, guilty of selling clothes which had just been distributed to them, and given to drinking their modest camp allowance. In October 1952 the then Protestant welfare worker complained that 'the constant handing out of things without demanding anything in return is having a calamitous effect on the character of those being cared for. They think they have to do nothing to look after themselves any more ... the only help for those camp inmates capable of work is, in my view, normal work, and not the constant dispensing of alms.'[59] In her constant distinctions between the deserving and the undeserving, between the orderly and the 'asocial', or the diligent and the workshy, her reports betrayed the gaze of the Protestant missionary social work ethic as much as they described the situation in the camp itself. Similarly, it is unclear how far her distinctions between the mostly industrious women of the camp and a male population given to alcohol abuse reflected the realities of camp life, the highly gendered gaze of the woman concerned or a more general stereotyping of eastern European camp inmates. Either way, such reports offer only the most distorted of views on people with unknown histories of persecution, violence, expulsion and murder – some as perpetrators, others as victims, and many, most likely, as first one then the other – whose subsequent emigration to mostly new-world destinations similarly dispersed the memory of their experiences.

Overall, the experience of the refugees and expellees who came to Nuremberg was as diverse, indeed more so, than the wartime and post-war experiences of the population into whose midst they were thrust. Compared to the situation in post-war Germany as a whole, relatively few German refugees and expellees found their way to the city immediately in 1945 to 1946; in the immediate post-war years, the history of the refugees was largely

<hr/>

[59] LKAN DW 1527, Else Frese an Regierung von Mittelfranken betr. Fürsorgebericht für die Monate September und Oktober 1952.

one which was played out in rural areas, with the refugees moving to the cities in greater numbers during the 1950s. Of those who did arrive in the city in 1945 to 1946, we are far better informed about the camp refugees than about the silent (eventual) majority who lived in private accommodation. These camp refugees lived in considerable isolation from the rest of the community: it was, however, precisely the alternative infrastructure developed within the camps that laid the foundations of the refugees' organisational strength, and thus growing agency within the local memory culture in the later 1950s and, above all, the 1960s.

The slow integration of the ethnic German refugees into Nuremberg society in the 1950s and 1960s, and the corresponding embrace of their experiences within the memory culture of the city, meanwhile, masked the social and cultural marginalisation of the thousands of foreign refugees who passed through the city, whose histories were never acknowledged and whose fate illicited little sympathy from the German population. Traditions of ethnic arrogance towards national groups always regarded as inferior in German political culture, combined, perhaps, with shame at the presence of former collaborators in crimes of which the population did not wish to be reminded. The city authorities regarded them only as disruptive sources of crime and an illegitimate burden on the city's stretched resources. When the Valka camp closed, its occupants were either transferred, melted anonymously into the community, or emigrated, as had countless camp inhabitants over the course of the 1950s. As a result, the experiences of camp residents such as the 80 or so Russian émigrés who had fled their homeland following the Bolshevik revolution, and had lived for twenty or so years in Serbia, Bulgaria or Romania before fleeing again in 1944 to 1945, faded swiftly into oblivion as far as the local memory culture was concerned.[60]

[60] LKAN DW 1527, Else Frese an Regierung von Mittelfranken betr. Fürsorgebericht für den Monat Dezember 1952.

I.3

'The First Expellees of the War'?

The Evacuees as 'External Citizens'

Far greater pressure on what remained of the city's housing stock was placed by the many tens of thousands of evacuees who flooded back to Nuremberg in the months following the end of the war. From 1941 onwards residents of the city – primarily women and children – had been evacuated by the regime to outlying rural areas.[1] As the air war had intensified and the destruction of the city gathered pace, this process was accelerated; finally, towards the end of the war increasing numbers of citizens simply left of their own accord, their movements unregulated by a local government apparatus now in an advanced state of collapse.[2] Relations between evacuated city-dwellers and their host communities during the war were often fraught and, unsurprisingly, when the hostilities ceased, many of the city's inhabitants did not wait for official approval before returning to what remained of their homes. As early as July 1945 the city council was complaining that, in addition to coping with the influx of refugees and released prisoners of war 'an equally not insignificant number of women and old people who found shelter in rural areas because of the air war are now streaming back – without the permission of the Housing Office – partly of their own accord and partly on the orders of the mayors and county prefects of the evacuation zones'.[3]

With large parts of the city economy having come to an effective standstill, and no question in the immediate post-war era of initiating long-term reconstruction work, there was nowhere for the evacuees to go. Reflecting on the

---

[1] On the history of evacuation in and to Bavaria during the war, see Katja Klee, *Im 'Luftschutzkeller des Reiches'. Evakuierte in Bayern 1939–1953: Politik, Soziale Lage, Erfahrungen*, (Munich, 1999).

[2] On Nuremberg citizens fleeing the city towards the end of the war, see Gregor, '*Schicksalsgemeinschaft?*', 1065ff.

[3] StadtAN C 29/424, Monatsbericht des Oberbürgermeisters der Stadt Nürnberg für Juli 1945.

process of returning evacuees to the city from the vantage point of 1956, the authorities noted that while 180,000 Nuremberg citizens had come back to the city by 1948 – effectively doubling the population of the city as it had stood in May 1945 – only an additional 7,800 apartments had been built by that time.[4] The great bulk had been forced to live together in highly cramped, unhealthy and often completely unsafe quarters which had been patched up with only temporary repairs. While this had provided a short-term solution during the summer months of 1945, the lack of building materials for proper repairs meant that it had been impossible to make much damaged accommodation sufficiently habitable for its occupants to remain during the winter. The authorities also feared that extreme overcrowding in the city could lead to political unrest.[5] As a result, the city was effectively re-evacuated in the autumn of 1945.[6]

In June 1949, one year after the currency reform, a total of 43,571 Nuremberg citizens, or over 10 per cent of the 1939 population, were registered as still evacuated.[7] The great majority of these had found temporary homes in the outlying towns and villages of Middle Franconia, but Nuremberg evacuees were distributed across the whole of Bavaria. From the outset, the evacuees represented a substantial burden on the city's welfare authorities, who, in the face of their host communities' refusal to help, were forced to assume the task of supporting them.[8] While the gradual process of economic recovery and ongoing repairs to buildings slowly increased the amount of available room to house returnees, for those who were forced to remain outside the city life remained harsh. Evacuees suffered disproportionately from unemployment; those who had work in Nuremberg were forced to undertake long daily journeys to and from the city, with all the additional cost and exhaustion that this entailed; others were billeted in such remote villages that they were forced to pay for additional accommodation in Nuremberg during the week, adding both additional expense and the emotional burden of separation from their families. In some cases, every member of a family was forced to live in a separate rented room for lack of suitable housing.[9]

[4] StadtAN C 29/324, Obmännertagung der Nürnberger Evakuiertenausschüsse in Bayern, 26.5.56.
[5] StadtAN C 29/304, Aktennotiz betr. Nürnberger-Hilfe, 4.9.45.
[6] On the re-evacuation of German cities in 1945 see also Michael Krause, *Flucht vor dem Bombenkrieg. 'Umquartierungen' im Zweiten Weltkrieg und die Wiedereingliederung der Evakuierten in Deutschland, 1943–1963* (Düsseldorf, 1997), 190–8.
[7] StadtAN C 29/430, Monatsbericht der Stadt Nürnberg für die Zeit vom 1 bis 30 Juni 1949.
[8] StadtAN C 29/424, Monatsbericht des Oberbürgermeisters der Stadt Nürnberg für die Zeit vom 20 Dezember bis 19 Januar 1946. For the refusal to help C 29/308, Niederschrift über die Tagung der Obmänner der Evakuiertenausschüsse am 23.2.50.
[9] StadtAN C 7 IX/703, Bericht über die Evakuiertenfürsorge, 31.3.49; see also C 29/430, Monatsbericht der Stadt Nürnberg für die Zeit vom 1 bis 31 August 1949.

While it is clear that the city's reports on the situation of evacuees tended to stress the most spectacular cases of hardship, in order to underline the pressing need for additional rebuilding resources, it is also evident that the social situation of the evacuees was often extremely difficult. By 1949 it was mostly the 'socially weaker' circles of the population who remained outside of the city, as the better off had generally found ways and means of getting back into Nuremberg.[10] In other words, the bourgeois circles from which the Nazis had drawn disproportionate support were also those least likely to suffer the long-term effects of evacuation. Not only did they often have the best networks of contacts and influence to ensure favourable treatment, they were also most able to find the resources to contribute towards house-building projects which was sometimes necessary in order to be allocated new homes; given that the early practice of compensation of bomb-damage tended towards a restoration of the status quo ante in terms of property distribution, it also seems likely that ex-Nazis were likely to suffer the long-term consequences of bombing less than their non-Nazi counterparts.

The economic effects of the currency reform, in particular, led both to a worsening of the evacuees' economic position and to a heightening of tension between them and the indigenous populations of the evacuation zones. In its report on the welfare of evacuees of March 1949, for example, the Evacuees Office observed that 'our experiences have made us certain that more so than after the capitulation the evacuee is regarded as an alien body [*Fremdkörper*] in their current place of residence, and that both the indigenous population and local organs for the most part do not voluntarily wish to take the measures on behalf of the evacuees which are absolutely necessary'.[11] It continued that 'the social struggle of the evacuees is practically focused on the basic necessities of survival: housing, food and clothing along with household goods are problems which are of fundamental significance for all evacuees'. In part, their problems reflected cultural differences and differing living standards between town and country. In part, however, they were clearly rooted in distributional conflict and the exceptionally desperate conditions in which many were forced to live: 'poor homes, in many cases storerooms which would normally never be used for housing, serve as accommodation; the health of adults and children is daily put at great risk by this poor accommodation . . . Living next to people who have lost next to nothing due to the war and who cannot understand the situation of the evacuees leads to constant mental and social conflicts.'

[10] That it was generally the socially marginal who constituted the residual evacuee population in the 1950s is suggested by Krause, *Flucht vor dem Bombenkrieg*, 200–5; 316–19.
[11] StadtAN C 7 IX/703, Bericht über die Evakuiertenfürsorge, 31.3.49.

Neither did the evacuees find it easy to get work. According to the Evacuees Office, 'the evacuees cannot always be put to work in the farmers' work processes because they are either not physically in a state to do so or because they cannot find suitable work locally'. The currency reform had clearly intensified their problems, as they had lost the remaining savings on which they had been living since 1945, while previous sources of income in their temporary homes had been lost as employers responded to economic difficulties by doing the work themselves or by favouring their long-term employees when deciding whom to dismiss first.

Some county prefects responded to the heightened tensions and distributional conflicts by renewing their demands that the evacuees leave, or, indeed, by taking matters into their own hands. At a meeting of the mayors and county prefects of Middle Franconia held in December 1948, for example, the city's head of housing and reconstruction, Karl Schönleben, complained to his audience of largely rural officials that 'six county prefects are constantly moaning at me and demanding the return of the Nuremberg citizens resident in their counties. If that were to happen there would be a debacle, for where are we supposed to find the space for these people?'[12] Similarly, addressing the same forum in 1950, the president of the regional government of Middle Franconia complained that 'in May this year Nuremberg evacuees from some communes in which Nuremberg evacuees are housed appeared in Nuremberg with their luggage and belongings and announced that their mayors had told them that they only need go to Nuremberg and they would get accommodation ... it has actually occurred that one such family appeared with all their baggage and belongings in Nuremberg, had themselves dropped at the town hall and waited for someone to look after them'.[13]

Even before the currency reform, however, the city council had realised that its evacuated citizens were in need of particular aid, and moved in February 1948 to create a dedicated office charged specifically with dealing with their needs. On the one hand, the Evacuees Office aided Nuremberg evacuees who turned to the city for help or advice, providing small amounts of financial aid or familiarising evacuees with their rights. On the other, it acted as the focal point for liaison with evacuees' representatives in the individual towns and villages. In each area containing more than 500 Nuremberg evacuees an 'Evacuee Committee' was formed, the members of which were to distribute information or directives to the evacuees in their area.[14] By 1951, the city

[12] StadtAN C 29/411, Niederschrift über die Tagung der Oberbürgermeister und Landräte des Regierungsbezirks Mittelfranken in Eichstätt, 13.12.48; more generally Klee, Im 'Luftschutzkeller des Reiches', 212ff.
[13] StadtAN C 29/411, Niederschrift über die Tagung der Oberbürgermeister und Landräte in Greding, 14.9.50.
[14] StadtAN C 7 IX/703, Bericht über die Evakuiertenfürsorge, 31.3.49.

maintained such committees in 52 outlying communes. City representatives travelled to each in turn, explaining the progress the city was making and listening to the evacuees' concerns;[15] conversely, periodic meetings between the city authorities and evacuee representatives were held in Nuremberg itself.

At successive meetings with the evacuees the mayor and city authorities sought to placate their frustrated 'external citizens', claiming that they were doing everything they could to prioritise evacuees in the allocation of new housing as it became available, offering explanations as to why some evacuees seemed to be privileged over others in the distribution of accommodation, and offering the promise of renewed efforts in the coming years.[16] However, while the city could use its limited powers to try to ensure that as great a proportion of the apartments built under state-financed programmes went to evacuees as possible, it was ultimately limited by the inadequate pace of recon-struction relative to the scale of the demand.[17] In 1950, for example, the city was able to return around 5,500 – according to the mayor the return process would take approximately another ten years.[18]

Unlike the refugees, the evacuees also lacked recourse to specific legislative provision in the immediate post-war years: in the litany of evacuee groups' complaints in post-war West Germany, the absence of a dedicated evacuee law to match the legislation aimed at refugees was a constant refrain. When, in 1953, a Federal Evacuee Law was finally enacted, it enshrined a legal right to return to one's home city for those who wanted it, but the absence of a fixed timescale – the return was merely to happen as resources permitted – and the lack of prov-ision of dedicated resources for building homes specifically for evacuees, meant that the law had little more than symbolic status.[19] Moreover, the provisions of the Federal Housing Distribution Law, which also came into effect in 1953, greatly reduced the city's ability to determine who should be allowed into private rented accommodation when it became available. The law, which repre-sented a considerable step towards the liberalisation of a hitherto highly regu-lated sphere, shifted decision-making rights concerning the choice of tenant towards the homeowner. The consequence of this, according to SPD councillor and later mayor Andreas Urschlechter, was that 'less will be able to be done specifically for the Nuremberg evacuees than last year'.[20] The result was that in

[15] StadtAN C 29/311, Bericht über die Tätigkeit der Evakuiertenfürsorge im Jahre 1951.

[16] StadtAN C 29/308, Niederschrift über die Tagung der Obmänner der Evakuierten-Ausschüsse am 23.2.50.

[17] See on this point StadtAN C 29/314, Niederschrift betr. Tagesordnungspunkt 3 der Jahrestagung der Obmänner der Evakuierten am 20.4.53.

[18] StadtAN C 29/308, Niederschrift über die Tagung der Obmänner der Evakuierten-Ausschüsse am 23.2.50.

[19] Krause, *Flucht vor dem Bombenkrieg*, 252ff; Klee, *Im 'Luftschutzkeller des Reiches'*, 273ff.

[20] StadtAN C 29/314, Niederschrift betr. Tagesordnungspunkt 3 der Jahrestagung der Obmänner der Evakuierten am 20.4.53. See also StadtAN C 29/319, Niederschrift betr. Tagesordnungspunkt 3 der Tagung der Nürnberger Evakuiertenausschüsse am 29.5.54.

1953 to 1954 only approximately 2,500 evacuees were returned, less than half the achievement of 1950. In effect, the conservative Federal government was addressing the needs of the middle-class property owners which formed its core constituency, while the housing needs of the economically much weaker evacuees took second place. Indeed, in May 1956, eleven years after the end of the war, over 22,000 citizens were still registered as wishing to return to the city.[21]

While the city could insist on its good intentions, evacuee representatives were quick to distinguish between concrete achievements and mere 'words of consolation';[22] while the city claimed that cooperation between it, the host communities' authorities and evacuee representatives was good, the evacuees themselves became increasingly frustrated at the slow progress towards their return.[23] Who, however, did the evacuees blame for their continued plight? An examination of their often bitter recriminations sheds light on the evasions which characterised the 'victim discourse' of the immediate post-war years – but also on the fissures which ran through the society that generated it.[24]

In isolated cases, those who had suffered bomb-damage – evacuees and those living in Nuremberg alike – focused their anger on former Nazis. In one instance, a widow guesthouse and café proprietor whose premises were destroyed on 2 January 1945 complained to the mayor that while former Nazis were officially to be removed from the economy this was not occurring in practice. Having heard 'that party comrades are supposed to disappear from economic life as well as from the civil service', she had gone to the Chamber of Industry and Commerce to apply for one of the business premises which she assumed would be vacated as a result. There, she had been informed that former party members only had to make their business over to their wives, sons or daughters for the military government's demands to have been fulfilled. When she complained that this represented nothing but a 'camouflage', she was told that the military government required merely for the former party member not to appear in the shop, leading her to the conclusion that 'we non-party comrades, who lost our existences, homes and entire possessions through enemy attack and now have to start again from the beginning, are the fools in this story if economic life continues in this way'.[25]

---

[21] StadtAN C 29/324, Obmännertagung der Nürnberger Evakuiertenausschüsse in Bayern, 26.5.56.
[22] StadtAN C 29/308, Niederschrift über die Tagung der Obmänner der Evakuierten-Ausschüsse am 23.2.50.
[23] On post-war evacuee protest politics in a local context see Thießen, 'Das Gedächtnis der Stadt', 145–7.
[24] Compare, in addition to the works already cited, Randolf Hillebrand, 'Migrantenpolitik der Stadt Köln 1950–1961. Vertriebene und Flüchtlinge versus Evakuierte' in Jost Dülffer (ed.), *Köln in den 50er Jahren. Zwischen Tradition und Modernisierung* (Cologne, 2001), 89–99, esp. 95–6.
[25] StadtAN C 29/303, K.K. an Oberbürgermeister Treu, 10.9.45.

Yet as this example showed, the woman involved was as concerned to use the denazification stipulations to her advantage when trying to re-establish her business as to express a moral opinion per se. In any case, her sentiments were not typical of the views of the evacuees, who were interested less in apportioning blame for the destruction than simply in denying the claims of other groups to whatever housing remained. Rather than blame those who had supported the regime and its war for the current housing crisis – and rather, even, than blame the allies who had bombed the city – the evacuees thus focused their anger on the refugees. In 1948, for example, the mayor received a letter from those Nuremberg evacuees currently living in Emskirchen, announcing that they had together passed a resolution to the effect that 'we bombed-out Nurembergers reject the fact that in decrees and other announcements of Nuremberg city council the refugees are always spoken of before the bombed-out Nurembergers and still rank above us bombed-out citizens although we became homeless and property-less years before the refugees in some cases and were mostly able to rescue far less of our property than was possible for the majority of refugees'. Rehearsing a demand common among evacuees, they pointed to the 'exemplary stance of the mayor of Berlin, who refused to take in refugees with the remark that that which is rebuilt must first go to bombed-out and evacuated Berliners', and demanded both that Nuremberg be closed to 'outsiders' and that the influence of refugee representatives on decisions relating to residency be sidelined.[26]

This resolution, the timing of whose dispatch again indicates the heightening of tensions brought about by the currency reform, was mirrored in discussions at evacuee meetings in Nuremberg itself. Complaints concerning the alleged disadvantaging of the evacuees compared to the refugees appear like a running refrain in the records of the meetings between the city council and its 'external citizens'. In February 1950, for example, representative after representative lined up to complain that 'we are literally being overrun by the refugees', that 'the promises made to us have only been fulfilled for the refugees and the bombed-out have all come away empty-handed', or that when new apartments were built refugees received more than their fair share, as evacuee families could not afford the necessary building subvention.[27] Top of a list of seven demands presented in a confrontational manner to the city authorities was 'equality of status of the totally bombed-out evacuees with the expellees

---

[26] StadtAN C 29/454, letter from Nuremberg Evacuees in Emskirchen to Ziebill, 12.12.48; see also the letter of Hans Joachim B. to the Evacuees Office of 24.1.50, reproduced in Nicole Kramer, 'Kinderlandverschickung, Evakuierung und Rückführung', in Diefenbacher and Fischer-Pache, *Luftkrieg gegen Nürnberg*, 476.

[27] StadtAN C 29/308, Niederschrift über die Tagung der Obmänner der Evakuierten-Ausschüsse am 23.2.50.

in all material legal decrees'. A particular complaint was the alleged privileging of refugees in the distribution of emergency relief money under the auspices of the Emergency Aid Law (*Soforthilfegesetz*). In January 1950 the city council acknowledged that 'at the moment Emergency Aid is the worry-child of the evacuees: they feel disadvantaged compared to the refugees';[28] typical in their polemical tone were the comments of one evacuee representative when he remarked caustically that 'whatever their fortunes the bomb-damaged get 200 DM. The refugees get unlimited sums. The refugees register huge claims for damages. No-one can check them out. I am just waiting for one of them to say he lost a "castle".'[29]

At the same time that they were denying the refugees' claims to privileged treatment, the evacuees were busy appropriating their vocabulary. Exhibiting an acute awareness of the need to legitimate material claims with a compelling rhetoric of victimhood, they started to describe themselves, too, as 'expellees'.[30] Likewise, the city authorities began to use the language of expulsion to describe the plight of their evacuated citizens. In 1949, when resisting the attempts of the Bavarian government to convert parts of the Langwasser camp to refugee housing rather than use them to house evacuees as it wished, the city council reminded the state authorities that '70,000 Nuremberg citizens who were once expelled by the violence of the events of the war still find themselves in the six county districts around Nuremberg';[31] in a formulation which resonated with acute silences concerning the fate of the Jews deported from Nuremberg and murdered during the war, it justified another intervention with the Bavarian state authorities on the grounds that 'the evacuated Nurembergers were actually the first who had to leave their home city as a result of the unfortunate war . . .'[32] Similarly, in 1956 it asserted that the evacuees 'were once upon a time the first refugees and surely deserve the same federal aid as the other expellees'.[33] More generally, demands for improved resources to expedite the return of the evacuees were underpinned with a vocabulary of *Heimat* (homeland) very similar to that used by the refugees. In 1954, for example, councillor Urschlechter insisted that the case of the evacuees represented more than a mere issue of numbers and building programmes: 'Behind all the sober

---

[28] StadtAN C 29/430, Monatsbericht der Stadt Nürnberg für die Zeit vom 1 bis 31 Januar 1950.
[29] StadtAN C 29/308, Niederschrift über die Tagung der Obmänner der Evakuierten-Ausschüsse am 23.2.50. On tensions between refugees and evacuees in Bavaria, see Klee, *Im 'Luftschutzkeller des Reiches'*, 222ff.
[30] StadtAN C 29/308, Niederschrift über die Tagung der Obmänner der Evakuierten-Ausschüsse am 23.2.50.
[31] StadtAN C 40 Abg. 73/4, Stadtrat zu Nürnberg: Entschliessung, 16.2.49.
[32] StadtAN C 29/314, Niederschrift betr. Tagesordnungspunkt 3 der Jahrestagung der Obmänner der Evakuierten am 20.4.53.
[33] StadtAN C 29/322, Obmännertagung der Nürnberger Evakuiertenausschüsse in Bayern, 26.5.56.

numbers lies the harsh fate of those who have been forced to live away from their home town (*Heimatstadt*) for nearly a decade, a hometown which was once the centre of their relationships and their existence.'[34] Even in 1959 – by which time the first echoes of a new sensibility regarding the persecution of the Jews were audible in West Germany society – the city was able to claim in its official gazette that the evacuees had been 'the "first refugees" of the last war'.[35]

Why did the city council place so much emphasis on the interests and needs of the evacuees? One explanation lies in the affinity the Social-Democratic-dominated council felt with a section of the population disproportionately comprised of the socially disadvantaged; another may lie in the strong sense of community identity shared by council and evacuees alike. The desire to demonstrate the ongoing links between the city and its evacuees certainly provided the official justification for the organisation of annual 'Evacuee Days' for its citizens from 1951 onwards. On these occasions, elderly or needy evacuees were invited to spend a day in the city as the guest of the council. The railway authorities provided free travel; the Germanic National Museum, the city zoo and local cinemas gave away free tickets; guesthouses and restaurants offered reduced-price meals to the visiting evacuees.[36] Even if partly born of the desire to be favoured by the council in future business, such widespread support bespoke a strong sense of sympathy for the evacuees. In 1951, around 1,000 evacuees from the western parts of Middle Franconia were invited; in 1952, the Evacuee Day was open to those living in Upper Franconia, *Oberpfalz* and the southern part of Middle Franconia.[37] In 1959, the city council was able to record that all evacuees over the age of fifty had enjoyed one such visit; those who lived further afield had been invited several times.[38]

By this point, however, the number of evacuees taking advantage of the invitation each year had fallen considerably, suggesting either fading interest on the part of evacuees, or fading ability to attend.[39] The fact that the city council insisted on holding such annual events for the evacuees even as their interest waned indicated, in turn, that more than mere sympathy for their

[34] StadtAN C 29/319, Betr. Tagesordnungspunkt 3 der Tagung der Nürnberger Evakuiertenausschüsse am 29.5.54.

[35] 'Evakuiertentag 1959', *Amtsblatt der Stadt Nürnberg*, 3.6.59. The persistence of such imagery in the popular culture of the city is demonstrated further, for example, by repeated references to *Bombenflüchtlinge* [Refugees from Bombing] in the well-known account of wartime events based on the diary extracts of local journalist Fritz Nadler, published in 1969: cf. Nadler, *Eine Stadt im Schatten Streichers*, e.g. 154.

[36] See, for example, the material in StadtAN C 40 Abg. 77/3 (i).

[37] StadtAN C 29/311, Bericht über die Tätigkeit der Evakuiertenfürsorge im Jahre 1951.

[38] StadtAN C 40 Abg. 77/3 (iv), Aktennotiz betr. Abhaltung eines Evakuiertentreffens im Juli 1960, 3.3.60.

[39] On declining attendances see StadtAN C 40 Abg. 77/3 (iv), Stadtrat Nürnberg/Sonderfürsorge an Referat V., 6.3.59; Aktennotiz betr. Evakuiertenbetreuung, 28.6.65.

plight was at stake. Reflecting in 1959 that the previous year's experience showed that elderly Nuremberg evacuees living at a distance found it difficult to attend, the office responsible for organising the Evacuee Days opined that as a result of their gradually returning to the city over the 1950s, deciding to move elsewhere or stay put in the locations where they had now put down roots – alongside the fact that many had died in the interim – the number of evacuees had dwindled to a residual amount. In a remark which underlined that, by the late 1950s, the city attached more importance to the occasion than did the evacuees, it reminded that the Evacuees Office had already been forced in the previous year to invite older evacuees from less than forty kilometres away in order to give the event some sense of size and occasion; even so, only half those invited had bothered to come. Accordingly, it suggested that it was time to draw a line under such events.[40] The reply, however, made clear that the mayor wished for the occasion to be held one more time in the same form as previously; in particular, prior to the usual event in the Opera House, an additional meeting was to be held 'with the participation of the press' at which the mayor would speak. The reason for this was clear: 'It is to be assumed that by that point certain efforts will be handled before the legislature and that particular resonance for this event can be counted upon in this connection.' The city's official gazette made the point in even more obvious fashion when it underlined that 'with the array of other demands the evacuees should not be forgotten. This meeting, in particular, should clearly place anew the evacuee question foremost in the minds of all those in positions of responsibility.'[41] The city council was, in other words, instrumentalising the plight of the evacuees to highlight to the state and Federal governments the ongoing need for resources to continue the process of rebuilding.

The correspondence files of the Evacuees Office show that a small residual group remained outside of the city, notionally registered as wishing to return, well into the 1960s.[42] Yet despite the original size of the group – there were still many more Nuremberg evacuees than there were refugees living in the city in 1950, for example[43] – and despite their persistence as a sociological phenomenon, the evacuees faded in the 1960s as an object of broader concern and, thereafter, of popular memory. Although the city council saw utility in perpetuating awareness of their plight, it did not come to occupy a place in the memory culture of the city.

One explanation for this lies in the demographic composition and physical distribution of the evacuees. The city council's practice of privileging the

[40] StadtAN C 40 Abg. 77/3 (iv), Stadtrat Nürnberg/Sonderfürsorge an Referat V., 6.3.59.
[41] 'Evakuiertentag 1959', *Amtsblatt der Stadt Nürnberg*, 3.6.59.
[42] See, for example, the *Verwaltungsberichte der Stadt Nürnberg* for the early 1960s.
[43] *Verwaltungsbericht der Stadt Nürnberg*, 1950, 173–8.

economically active and independent when choosing whom to allow back to the city meant that, from an early stage, a disproportionately large element of the evacuees consisted of the elderly.[44] Moreover, an increasingly dispropor- tionate number of the remaining evacuees in the 1950s were women. As early as March 1949 the Evacuees Office was noting that, in addition to the elderly, a particular problem was posed by 'women with children, whose husbands fell or have not yet returned from captivity and who are not in a position to work. These are completely reliant on public support following the loss of their savings after the currency [reform].'[45] The practicalities of childcare rendered it impossible for such women to work; without the necessary income, however, they were unable to afford to move back to Nuremberg.[46] By 1955, 60 per cent of remaining evacuees were female; in the age group 20 to 65, in particular, twice as many evacuees were women as men. The majority of these were widows with children.[47]

Unsurprisingly, therefore, most of the evacuees lived in considerable poverty. In 1955 70 per cent were either unemployed, 'dependants without work' or pensions and welfare recipients. In the view of the city's welfare authorities, the general failure of the evacuees to take up the offer of financial aid to start a new existence in their temporary place of residence lay in the fact that most evacuees were those no longer in a position to help themselves.[48] Poor, elderly, or struggling to survive alone with young children, they were found by the Evacuees Office often to be unaware of their basic rights, let alone able to mobilise politically.[49] In the view of the Evacuees Office many lived a withdrawn life, ashamed of their poverty.[50] Dispersed throughout northern Bavaria, lacking economic resource, and consisting of a dwindling number of the socially marginal, the evacuees had few starting points for fixing their plight permanently in the wider public consciousness. In this they stood in stark contrast to the refugees, whose growing weight in the city measured against the population as a whole made them an increasingly significant constituency – albeit one which was still relatively minor in the 1950s – and whose concentration in a barrack environment had created the possibility of

---

[44] On this point see also Krause, *Flucht vor dem Bombenkrieg*, 233.

[45] StadtAN C 7 IX/703, Bericht über die Evakuiertenfürsorge, 31.3.49.

[46] StadtAN C 29/311, Bericht über die Tätigkeit der Evakuiertenfürsorge im Jahre 1951.

[47] StadtAN C 29/322, Fürsorge für Evakuierte der Stadt Nürnberg im Jahre 1954, 1.6.55; see also Kramer, 'Kinderlandverschickung', 481–2.

[48] StadtAN C 29/430, Monatsbericht der Stadt Nürnberg für die Zeit vom 1 bis 30 September 1950.

[49] StadtAN C 29/311, Bericht über die Tätigkeit der Evakuiertenfürsorge im Jahre 1951.

[50] On the inability of the evacuees to organise effectively, see Klee, *Im 'Luftschutzkeller des Reiches'*, 245–7; on the weakness of the evacuees within the Central League of the Victims of Air-Raids, the Evacuees and the Victims of Currency Reform (ZVF), see also Krause, *Flucht vor dem Bombenkrieg*, 233–40.

shared activity. The bonds engendered by a sense of shared origin and cultural difference in an alien environment further fostered collective organisation, unlike the evacuees, for whom no comparable bonds existed.

Yet as the attempts of the evacuees to appropriate the language of expulsion implied, there were more than just issues of demography or sociology at stake. Women, after all, also figured disproportionately in the refugee population, so that gender composition per se offers only a partial explanation for the marginalisation of the evacuees. Just as importantly, the refugees, with their distinctive war-time experiences, were able to draw on a peculiar narrative of victimhood when pressing their claims. The evacuees could draw on no such narratives, for the experience of bombing was hardly unique to them. It had been a near-universal experience for the city's population, or at least for those who had lived through the war in the city and, by the late 1950s, had certainly been reworked into a universal experience in the memory culture of the city.[51] As the experience of bombing was appropriated for all, the ability of the evacuees to ground a peculiar claim to victimhood was correspondingly eroded: as a result, they faded into the shadows as the 'economic miracle' took hold.

---

[51] On the appropriation of gendered experiences as universal experiences in the 1950s, see Elizabeth Heineman, 'The Hour of the Women: Memories of Germany's "Crisis Years" and West German National Identity', *American Historical Review*, 101/2 (1996), 354–95. On the centrality of the experience of bombing to the memory culture of the city in the late 1950s and 1960s, see sections II and IV below.

I.4

The Veteran as Victim
The *Heimkehrer* between War and Peace

In addition to the refugees and returning evacuees the city authorities faced the challenge of another influx: the war veterans, or *Heimkehrer* ('home-comers'), who returned from the violence of war and the trials of internment to confront civilian life in their now ruined city. Exactly how many former soldiers returned to Nuremberg after the war is not clear. Given, however, that at least eight million Germans were held as military captives by the allies at the end of the war – one in ten of the population – a rough estimate would be 30–40,000 men.[1]

Three-quarters of prisoners of war taken by the allies had fallen into western captivity; the majority of these were released during the first twelve months after the war, and by the end of 1948 all those prisoners held in the west had returned home.[2] Of the approximately two million held in the east, some were also released relatively promptly, and most had been released by 1950; small numbers of releases continued in successive waves into the 1950s, however, and it was only in 1956 that the final few prisoners of war returned from Soviet captivity. Not only the length, but also the experience of captivity varied greatly: while camp experiences in the west had usually been

---

[1] On the number of German prisoners of war see the overviews in Arthur L. Smith, *Heimkehr aus dem Zweiten Weltkrieg. Die Entlassung der Deutschen Kriegsgefangenen* (Stuttgart, 1985), 11ff.; Wolfgang Benz, 'Einleitung: Leben hinter Stacheldraht' in Wolfgang Benz and Angelika Schardt (eds), *Deutsche Kriegsgefangene im Zweiten Weltkrieg. Erinnerungen* (Frankfurt/Main, 1995), 7–33; see also Albrecht Lehmann, *Gefangenschaft und Heimkehr. Deutsche Kriegsgefangene in der Sowjetunion* (Munich, 1986).
[2] Benz, 'Einleitung', 12.

tolerable, conditions in prisoner of war camps in the eastern bloc were often terrible.[3]

The same was true of the soldiers' actual wartime experiences. Some had been conscripted in the 1930s, surviving military campaigns in both west and east; some had spent the war in Africa or mostly as occupation troops somewhere in the west while others had experienced the brutality and barbarism of the eastern front; some had not experienced the victories of the early part of the war but had only known a long, increasingly desperate war of defence and retreat; many of the youngest had been called up only in the last phase of the war, their experience of fighting relatively brief. Some, moreover, had survived the war physically intact; others had sustained injuries from which they would recover; others were permanently maimed. Beneath the often two-dimensional images of the *Heimkehrer* which circulated in post-war West German culture thus lay a diverse group bound together only in most general terms by the shared experience of violence, aggression and fear.[4] However, if not all men had fought in the war – and if not all those who had served in the armed forces or experienced post-war captivity had been men either – the *Heimkehrer* nonetheless constituted a body of millions of men whose experience of the front underlay one of the major gendered fault lines which ran through post-war society.

In many respects the challenge of readjustment to life in post-war Nuremberg was the same for the *Heimkehrer* as it was for others, and the problems they faced – the constant struggle for clothing, the ongoing competition for improved housing and the continual presence of hunger – were those faced by the rest of the community. Both state and private agencies, and both secular and religious organisations, created an extensive network of initial relief for a group of men who often arrived in Nuremberg with only the clothes they were standing in. As well as the city welfare offices the Red Cross, the 'Workers' Welfare' agency, the Protestant Inner Mission and the Roman Catholic Caritas attempted to help with basic clothing, with money and with advice concerning welfare and legal entitlements, and with finding housing, work and training. A wide range of literature was distributed to prisoners upon their release – who were returning not only to destroyed homes but also to a community whose political structures, administrative procedures and

---

[3] On the POW camp experience in the western zones see Christof Strauß, *Kriegsgefangenschaft und Internierung. Die Lager in Heilbronn-Böckingen 1945–1947* (Heilbronn, 1998); on the camps in the Soviet Union see Stefan Karner, *Im Archipel GUPVI. Kriegsgefangenschaft und Internierung in der Sowjetunion 1941–1956* (Munich, 1995); Klaus-Dieter Müller et al. (eds), *Die Tragödie der Gefangenschaft in Deutschland und in der Sowjetunion 1941–1956* (Cologne, 1996); Andreas Hilger, *Deutsche Kriegsgefangene in der Sowjetunion, 1941–1956. Kriegsgefangenenpolitik, Lageralltag und Erinnerung* (Essen, 2000).
[4] On images of the *Heimkehrer* in post-war West Germany see Habbo Knoch, *Die Tat als Bild. Fotographien des Holocaust in der deutschen Erinnerungskultur* (Hamburg, 2001), 314–23.

legal frameworks had radically altered since they had last lived in the city, and in which they were in need of considerable orientation.

As ever, the gap between paper entitlements and the reality of the *Heimkehrer*'s experiences remained great. While legislative or administrative measures shaped the general context in which veterans sought to re-establish themselves, their paper provisions give at best highly imperfect insight into individual *Heimkehrer*'s lives. In the American zone, for example, prisoners returning in 1948 received a brochure from the authorities informing them that 'in cases of particular hardship *Heimkehrer* who have no possessions receive the most necessary items of clothing and footwear in the release camps. At the place of release [their home town] they receive a limited amount of textile coupons together with their first ration cards. In justified cases the Economics Office gives out coupons for clothes and footwear', while *Heimkehrer* from the eastern bloc were entitled to further allocations beyond the basic.[5] However, in 1947, during which time the large numbers of *Heimkehrer* formed a focal point of the welfare agencies' work, only a small minority could hope to receive aid of any meaningful kind. In November the city council complained that 'one of the greatest needs among the *Heimkehrer* is the lack of clothing. Many *Heimkehrer* returned to find damaged, bombed-out homes. Their former clothing had got lost or burned. Since all of our reserves of clothing are used up, we tried to get a special allocation from the authorities, but all attempts were in vain.'[6]

Of particular concern were those repatriated from the Soviet Union.[7] Conditions in Soviet prisoner of war camps had been especially appalling in the immediate post-war years, and many German soldiers had not survived captivity; those who returned in the 1940s were often in a very poor state of health. In April 1947 the military authorities in Nuremberg noted that 'during the last days German Prisoners of War have returned from Russia to various communities in the *Landkreis* of Nürnberg. They are all in a very bad state of health and have either to get medical treatment or to be hospitalised';[8] a year later it was still recording that 'most of the PWs returned from Russia are undernourished and in rather poor health. Only few of them are able to take up work immediately on their return.'[9] As a result, both civil and religious

---

[5] Landesarbeitsgemeinschaften für Kriegsgefangene in der amerikanischen Besatzungszone (ed.), *Informationen für Heimkehrer* (Stuttgart, 1948), 27.
[6] StadtAN C 29/428, Monatsbericht des Stadtrats zu Nürnberg für die Zeit vom 20 Oktober bis 19 November 1947. See also StadtAN C 28/25, Monatlicher Tätigkeits- und Lagebericht des Wirtschaftsamtes Nürnberg-Stadt zum 20 Oktober 1947.
[7] See, for example, StadtAN C 29/428, Monatsbericht des Stadtrats zu Nürnberg für die Zeit vom 20 Januar bis 19 Februar 1948.
[8] StadtAN F 6/79, Weekly Intelligence Report, 17.–24.4.47.
[9] StadtAN F 6/26, OMGBY/FOD Area Nuremberg, Intelligence Report, 30.6.48; also C 29/428, Monatsbericht der Stadt Nürnberg für die Zeit vom 1 bis 30 April 1948.

authorities were forced to organise 'recovery homes' in peaceful rural surroundings, where particularly ill or exhausted *Heimkehrer* could convalesce before returning fully to civil society.[10] Only a minority of *Heimkehrer* were afforded the opportunity of such convalescence; even those who were only stayed for a matter of weeks. The Bavarian Protestant Aid Association, for example, had provided 2,800 veterans with residential stays of four to six weeks by 1949.[11]

Thereafter much depended on their ability to find work and to pick up the threads of their former lives, assuming they were old enough to have had a working life of any significance prior to their conscription. How the veterans integrated into the community in the mid- and longer term, and how they gave meaning to their wartime experiences in the process is, in many respects, a matter for conjecture.[12] Some soldiers moved into and within a broad network of regimental associations and organisations campaigning on behalf of veterans. These practised, with varying degrees of emphasis, the fostering of shared sociability within a community of sentiment based on notions of 'comradeship' and the 'preservation of tradition' (*Traditionspflege*), the maintenance of charitable welfare provision for veterans who were disabled or in need of financial support, and the pursuit of improved conditions for ex-soldiers through the political process. They were informed, for the most part, by a culture of unreflective national-patriotic sentiment in which shared understandings of soldierly bravery, sacrifice and victimhood offered comforting narratives into which those veterans who were drawn to this milieu could order their experiences.[13]

Despite the national-conservative, patriotic rhetoric of these groups, however, there is little to suggest that the mass of *Heimkehrer* ever constituted a reservoir of anti-democratic protest potential in any serious sense. There is evidence that the neo-Nazi Socialist Reich Party sought to mobilise *Heimkehrer* for its extreme right-wing politics (organising, for example, a benefit concert for veterans in 1952);[14] in the mayoral correspondence one also finds extreme anti-Semitic pamphleting purporting to convey the opinions of the so-called 'International Committee of Prisoners of War for the Solution of the Guilt Question'.[15] However, the occasional incidence of such extremist literature in the archival record is not evidence of the widespread prevalence of such views among

[10] LKAN DW 2349, Heimkehrerfürsorge des Evangelischen Hilfswerks Bayern, Hauptbüro Nürnberg, 9.1.50; StadtAN C 29/428, Monatsbericht des Stadtrats zu Nürnberg für die Zeit vom 20 Januar bis 19 Februar 1948.

[11] 'Kirchliche Rundschau', *Nürnberger Evangelisches Gemeindeblatt*, 23.1.49.

[12] See the perceptive comments in Hilger, *Deutsche Kriegsgefangene in der Sowjetunion*, 370–6.

[13] Thomas Kühne, *Kameradschaft. Die Soldaten des nationalsozialistischen Krieges und das 20 Jahrhundert* (Göttingen, 2006); see below, Chapter II.1.

[14] StadtAN C 29/312, Eberhard Engelhardt (Rechtsanwalt) an Amtsgericht Nürnberg, 4.8.52.

[15] StadtAN C 29/469, Abschrift: 'Wir deutschen Kriegsgefangenen'/Internationaler Kriegsgefangenen-Ausschuss zur Lösung der Schuldfrage (undated, November 1948).

veterans, or indeed the population as a whole: a significant element of the mayor's correspondence on many issues expressed the unrepresentative views of an obsessive minority. The American military authorities were of the view that 'the returning POWs show little interest in politics but are primarily concerned with problems of their personal welfare' and that they tended to join a political party only if they had belonged to the same party before; in their assessment 'of all the PWs becoming members of a political party 75 per cent are believed to join the SPD, the rest CSU and FDP'.[16] The SPD itself was of the view that it enjoyed a particular degree of support among *Heimkehrer* from the east, who, whatever their different views on many other issues, were regarded as being almost uniformly anti-Communist as a result of their experiences of captivity.[17]

Only rarely, in fact, do the voices of individual *Heimkehrer* find their way into the archival record of the city. For the most part, one is reliant upon the reports of those agencies and institutions who now had to deal with them in various ways – the occupation forces, the German civilian authorities, the medical profession, the churches and other welfare agencies; otherwise, their voices were usually mediated by the regimental and war victim associations which claimed a mandate to speak on their behalf. Each of these institutions saw the *Heimkehrer* through a particular lens; each had a highly homogenising gaze on to a group whose essential feature was its diversity.[18] For the Church, for example, 'homecoming' was imagined in both literal and metaphorical terms: veterans were returning from war zones to their families and communities, but also from the clutches of godless totalitarianism to the embrace of the Church and from the temptations of wartime immorality to the possibility of a Christian lifestyle.[19] Yet however they saw the *Heimkehrer* – as former agents of a militarist regime in need of democratic reorientation, as endangered souls in need of spiritual succour, as victims of violence in need of rehabilitation, or merely as one of many competing groups of claimants on stretched welfare resources – certain themes repeated themselves in the observations of those concerned: worries over both physical and mental health, marital problems, difficulties in readjusting to civilian routines, bitterness at 'missing out' on being able to enjoy the prime years of youth in circumstances of peace, disappointment and disillusionment after the initial joy of return. Typical was

---

[16] StadtAN F 6/26, OMGBY/FOD Area Nuremberg, Intelligence Report, 30.6.48.

[17] On SPD views of electoral politics in 1949 see StadtAN C 29/299, SPD Bezirk Franken – Rundschreiben Nr 4, 5.9.49.

[18] On the various ways in which the *Heimkehrer* were constructed in West Germany in the post-war years see Frank Biess, 'Survivors of Totalitarianism: Returning POWs and the Reconstruction of Masculine Citizenship in West Germany, 1945–1955' in Hanna Schissler (ed.), *The Miracle Years. A Cultural History of West Germany, 1945–1968* (Princeton, NJ, 2001), 57–82; Moeller, *War Stories, passim.*

[19] See, for example, LKAN DW 2351, Heimkehrer-Genesungsheim der Inneren Mission, Schloss Craheim, Jahresbericht 1949, 6.3.50.

the guidance given by the Protestant Church deanery to all parish priests in its area on how to handle veterans: 'The *Heimkehrer* finds his homeland destroyed, perhaps including that part which belonged to him. His house, his business, his family – a ruin – the family scattered, maybe dead. And where he does find his family, his wife and child have perhaps become strangers to him. The situation is particularly difficult in the case of war marriages, which were entered into in a fit of passion and now struggle to withstand the trials of daily life. Often he finds the children bad-mannered and impertinent. Not seldom the marriage has been destroyed by the unfaithfulness of the wife.'[20]

Such an image betrayed a host of conservative anxieties widespread in the immediate post-war era – about the impact of war on the nuclear family of Christian convention, about temptation and moral licentiousness during the occupation years, and so on – and captured only a truth of sorts, about some *Heimkehrer* at best. Yet it described problems recognisable and familiar, at least in outline, to many families.[21] The Schloss Craheim recovery home, meanwhile, observed in 1949 that while the physical state of returning soldiers had improved compared to the immediate post-war period, mental pressures were now taking an increased toll. Fears and uncertainties concerning when they would be released were compounded by 'the multiple disappointments experienced by the *Heimkehrer* in the completely changed circumstances of the homeland'. Stressing that this was not only a problem for refugee veterans struggling to adjust to a new, unfamiliar home, it bemoaned the fact that for indigenous *Heimkehrer* too 'once dear family members have been changed by the climate of the times', while some public and private bodies treated them with bureaucratic indifference or commercial cold-heartedness.[22]

Particular problems of adjustment were faced, of course, by war veterans who had been permanently disabled by their injuries.[23] As official classifications of war-related disabilities, which were widely reproduced in veterans' literature, attest, the nature and extent of injuries varied incredibly widely.

[20] LKAN Kd Nbg 332, Evang.-Luth. Kreisdekan Nürnberg an alle Pfarrämter im Kirchenkreis Nürnberg, 31.7.45.
[21] On aspects of family and marital problems among *Heimkehrer,* see Sibylle Meyer and Eva Schulze, *Von Liebe sprach damals Keiner. Familienalltag in der Nachkriegszeit* (Munich, 1985); Lehmann, *Gefangenschaft und Heimkehr,* 140ff.; see also the relevant essays in Annette Kaminsky (ed.), *Heimkehr 1948. Geschichte und Schicksale deutscher Kriegsgefangener* (Munich, 1998); Elizabeth D. Heineman, *What Difference does a Husband Make? Women and Marital Status in Nazi and Postwar Germany* (Berkeley, CA, 1999), 108ff.
[22] LKAN DW 2351, Heimkehrer-Genesungsheim der Inneren Mission, Schloss Craheim, Jahresbericht 1949, 6.3.50.
[23] The Protestant parish newsletter for Nuremberg recorded in 1950 that of 100 men born in 1924, 23 had been killed or were missing in action, two were still held prisoner in the Soviet Union, 31 had been heavily wounded and a further five wounded mildly, while two others were incapable of work due to accident or illness. In 1947 only 37 out of every 100 men in this age cohort enjoyed full health. 'Kirchliche Rundschau', *Nürnberger Evangelisches Gemeindeblatt,* 22.1.50

The medical and insurance authorities' practice of defining inability to work in standardised percentage terms based on the type of injury sustained (with minor disabilities categorised as causing 10 to 20 per cent reduced work capacity, and major disabilities 80 to 100 per cent incapacity) offered at best a highly crude method of assessing how much an individual had been damaged by his or her experience of war. This was especially the case given that such classificatory systems focused almost exclusively on physical injuries, and paid scant regard to psychological problems, the symptoms of which were treated as arising from brain damage rather than mental health effects.[24] However, as the endless articles in the veterans' associational literature, or the many letters from organisations of the war-disabled to the city authorities, or pieces in the local press in the 1950s indicate, the city's *Heimkehrer* suffered from the full range of war wounds, from amputation to blindness. Similarly, the prevalence of advertisements in veterans' newspapers for prosthetic limbs, together with essays detailing improvements in artificial limb technology or the development of disabled sports activities bear witness to the daily trials of many *Heimkehrer* struggling to cope with their broken bodies.[25]

While seeking to make sense of what had happened to them, and while learning in many cases to live with the daily practical consequences of this, former soldiers also had to contend with the memory of what they had witnessed – and the knowledge of what they had done. Ordinary soldiers had both enacted and faced violence, dismemberment and death on an enormous scale, the experience of which was not captured by the sanitised, heroicised or trivialised narratives of strategic manoeuvre, daring adventure or humorous escapade which circulated widely in post-war society.[26] In the post-war years,

---

[24] See, for example, 'Einschätzungstabelle aus den Anhaltspunkten für die ärztliche Gutachtertätigkeit im Versorgungswesen', *Kriegsopferjahrbuch* (1954), 76ff.

[25] For subtle readings of the ways in which some *Heimkehrer* verbalised their war experiences and interpreted their injuries, see the series of articles by Svenja Goltermann: 'Verletzte Körper oder "Building National Bodies". Kriegsheimkehrer, "Krankheit" und Psychiatrie in der westdeutschen Nachkriegsgesellschaft, 1945–1955', *Werkstattgeschichte*, 24 (1999), 83–98; 'Die Beherrschung der Männlichkeit. Zur Deutung der psychischen Leiden bei den Heimkehrern des Zweiten Weltkriegs 1945–1956', *Feministische Studien* (2000), 2, 7–19; 'Im Wahn der Gewalt. Massentod, Opferdiskurs und Psychiatrie 1945–1956' in Naumann, *Nachkrieg in Deutschland*, 343–63.

[26] On the centrality of immediate violence to the experience of war, see Michael Geyer, 'Eine Kriegsgeschichte, die von Tod spricht' in Thomas Lindenberger and Alf Lüdtke (eds), *Physische Gewalt. Studien zur Geschichte der Neuzeit* (Frankfurt/Main, 1995), 136–61; Michael Geyer, 'Das Stigma der Gewalt und das Problem der nationalen Identität in Deutschland' in Christian Jansen, Lutz Niethammer, Bernd Weisbrod (eds), *Von der Aufgabe der Freiheit. Politische Verantwortung und bürgerliche Gesellschaft im 19. und 20. Jahrhundert'* (Berlin, 1995), 673–98; on post-war representations of military experience see Michael Schornstheimer, *Die leuchtenden Augen der Frontsoldaten. Nationalsozialismus und Krieg in den Illustriertenromanen der fünfziger Jahre* (Berlin, 1995); on the gap between soldiers' individual experiences and public narratives of war, see Assmann and Frevert, *Geschichtsvergessenheit, Geschichtsversessenheit*, 47.

an untold number of young and middle-aged men walked around with the awareness of having killed. A significant minority of these lived with the knowledge that they had murdered innocents in acts which could not be excused by reference to the fact that they had been committed while Germany had been in a state of war. It is not difficult to detect in the constant assertions of post-war politicians and veterans' leaders that the *Wehrmacht* had fought a 'decent' war the recognition, deep down, that this had been anything but an honourable campaign. Whatever moral frameworks they subscribed to as individual citizens, it seems likely that most, if perhaps not all, *Heimkehrer* who had fought in the east were, on some level, aware of this too. Ideological commitment, or at least an entrenched mentality of ethnic arrogance, had encouraged the participation of many in the murder of Jews or other Soviet civilians. For others, however, the pressures of the killing moment had been more complex; alternatively, the hostile, brutal environment of the east had forced them to do things – in order to survive – which they would not have countenanced doing in peacetime. They now lived with the knowledge of being murderers.

Locating the precise impact of the experience of war on soldiers – of the multiple, overlapping experiences of aggression and fear, of killing and seeking to avoid death, of perpetrating acts which were by turn criminal, brutal or simply desperate – and seeking to make meaningful generalisations from rare accounts by individuals who clearly struggled to verbalise the images they carried with them is nearly impossible. Outside of therapeutic environments few spoke.[27] However, there were occasional exceptions. Some insight into the memories ordinary soldiers had of the violence which had been at the core of their experience of war is afforded by the typescript of an amateur divisional history produced by a member of the Association of the Former 98th Infantry Division, which was raised in Franconia and the Sudetenland. The division saw military action in France, Russia and Italy; the typescript covered the 'Deployment in Russia from July 1941 to February 1942'.

Describing the billeting of his company in Rowno at the beginning of the campaign, the author recounted how 'suddenly, far below us in the valley, we heard the crack of salvoes, which made everyone think. As it shortly turned out, many innocent people, no matter what nation or religion they belonged to, died as a result of this non-stop machine-gun and machine-pistol fire. SS special units gave them a short trial; they were then finished off! What a sad, mendacious, despicable world!'[28] Its mixture of honesty and evasiveness, of acknowledgement and careful distancing notwithstanding, such an account

---

[27] One exception was provided in the form of soldiers who later became writers: see, for example, Elizabeth Snyder Hook, 'Awakening from War: History, Trauma and Testimony in Heinrich Böll' in Confino and Fritzsche, *The Work of Memory*, 136–53.
[28] StadtAN E 6/1180 I, MS (unpublished), W.H., 'Einsatz in Russland, Juli 1941–Februar 1942', 5.

admitted that ordinary soldiers had at least been aware of the mass shootings, mostly of Jews, which accompanied the attack on the Soviet Union in 1941. The absence of grammatical agency in the description of the killing event, which was recounted in the passive voice – the SS was only directly described as holding the 'trial' – left much space for things to be left unsaid about precisely who had done what. Whether or not it was an allusion to more direct participation on the part of the regular troops, carefully coded to deny active involvement, or whether it was an act of psychological displacement on the part of one unable to admit his own participation in the killings is unclear. The awkwardness of description may, however, suggest not just evasiveness but the fundamental difficulty of speaking on a subject for which no publicly sanctioned vocabulary was available.

If the narrator was willing only to concede to having played the role of bystander to the murder of Jews, he acknowledged that beneath the convenient stories of legitimate and necessary 'anti-partisan' warfare there had also been a more complicated, considerably less edifying, story: 'In Makarova a conflict arises between us and Lieutenant K. concerning the burning in the villages. Our opinion was "the civilians have done nothing to us, why should we proceed harshly against them?" It made us think of what would then happen if that was our home? Three years later it had reached that point at home!'[29] Again, embedded in carefully constructed protestations of individual decency was simultaneous recognition of the brutality which had been visited by the German army upon Soviet civilians, and an awareness that the dreadful violence experienced by Germans at the hands of the Red Army in 1945 was not entirely without antecedent.[30] Finally, as the narrator implied, the brutality of the physical environment, as well as the nature of the war being waged, had fostered a climate in which soldiers were forced to be merciless in order just to survive. Recounting his company's experiences of the Russian winter, the narrator observed that 'we had no snow vests, but the Soviets did . . . So what did we do? If a Russian had fallen, one undressed him down to his shirt. If a Russian was wounded, one took off his felt boots, took his snow vest and his fur hat. There were privates who took off everything. These awful acts of heroism were carried out by the Soviets against us too. Thus the war was fought ever more brutally, ever more mercilessly.'[31]

Even this one account – which ends as the war ended for the narrator, when he lost a leg in action – suggests forcefully that *Heimkehrer* lived with a complex, sometimes vivid, set of mental images and fragments which were

[29] W.H., 'Einsatz in Russland'.
[30] On the nature of 'anti-partisan' warfare on the eastern front see Christian Gerlach, *Kalkulierte Morde. Die deutsche Wirtschafts- und Vernichtungspolitik in Weißrussland 1941 bis 1944* (Hamburg, 1999), 859–1055.
[31] W.H., 'Einsatz in Russland'.

not remotely captured by the dominant narratives of post-war political and popular culture. Moreover, it was not just returning soldiers who had witnessed the barbarism of war and occupation in the east, and who lived with mental images of violence and murder. In the 1960s, the Central Office of State Justice Departments (ZSL), which was set up in 1958 to investigate war crimes, examined the activities of a company of regular and reservist policemen which had been raised in Nuremberg and which, during the war, had been stationed in Brest-Litovsk and Mokrany, among other places. During this time the unit, which had consisted of between 100 and 120 men, had participated in the massacre of Jews and 'anti-partisan' warfare; it had also been involved in the clearing of the Brest-Litovsk ghetto.[32]

From the interrogation records it appears that the investigation was triggered by a former member of the unit writing to the mayor to inform him that 'in Russia, thousands of women, children and old people had been murdered, in sometimes bestial fashion, by the Police Company "Nuremberg".'[33] In the subsequent interrogations of other former members of the unit, some claimed never to have seen executions of Jews; others claimed never even to have heard of them. Others, however, blamed the SS and the SD, implying that while they themselves were not guilty they were well aware that such things had been going on; still others placed so much emphasis in their statements on their having personally fulfilled the roles of chef or secretary to the company – and thus having not participated in the mobile activities of the unit – for their accounts to constitute a tacit acknowledgement that the company had indeed been directly involved in murder. Moreover, while most of those questioned about the unit's activities at Brest-Litovsk admitted only to having played a subsidiary role in guarding the ghetto as it was cleared by the SD, one claimed that 'when it is put to me that various former members of my police company have said that they were not deployed inside the ghetto but only outside of it to seal it off, I cannot understand this. I believe that I remember concretely that my whole company moved in close formation into the ghetto and was then dispatched by E., partly to comb through the houses and partly to seal off the ghetto from inside.' This testimony was no more inherently reliable than anyone else's, but in the circumstances of a judicial inquiry it was hardly in the interviewee's interests to overemphasise the unit's role. He also admitted that

---

[32] For these and the following details see the files contained in StadtAN F 5/930 and F 5/931, which contain copies of Zentrale Stelle der Landesjustizverwaltungen (ZSL) 204 AR Z 334/59, and ZSL 204 AR Z 334/59 IV. On the challenge of reading such sources see Christopher R. Browning, *Ordinary Men. Reserve Police Battalion 101 and the Final Solution in Poland* (New York, 1992); on post-war legal process and the crimes of police battalions see Stefan Klemp, *'Nicht ermittelt'. Polizeibataillone und die Nachkriegsjustiz – Ein Handbuch* (Essen, 2005).
[33] StadtAN F 5/930, Vernehmung E.W., 12.4.60.

'of course the experiences of the day were discussed amongst one another in the evenings, especially under the influence of alcohol'.[34]

If a sense of shame, if not outright guilt, was thus rarely acknowledged, it was not entirely absent, and the sometimes contorted, sometimes evasive, accounts of wartime experiences which circulated beneath the surface of more public discourses suggest the presence of an awareness that the war had been characterised by deep wrongdoing. Yet while efforts to raise the subject of guilt in more public forums were similarly very rare, they were also not completely non-existent. In the immediate post-war period the Protestant Church was willing to entertain the notion that some *Heimkehrer* had incurred guilt – or, in its language, committed sins – and to acknowledge that some of them might have something on their conscience.[35] In its guidelines to parish priests on how to deal with the *Heimkehrer* circulated in July 1945, for example, the deanery of Nuremberg emphasised the importance of engaging each individual *Heimkehrer* in a one-to-one conversation: while 'the conversation must not be allowed to dwell on recriminations concerning the past', the guidance insisted that 'no-one should be allowed to go without asking the question (even if it is only first posed at the point of departure): do you come home sound not only in body but also of soul?'[36]

There again, the sins to which the Church referred on this occasion did not include participation in genocide. The emphasis on the sixth and seventh commandments ('you shall not commit adultery', 'you shall not steal') implied clearly that it was shame over wartime breaches of the legal and ethical codes of civilian life, such as marital infidelity while stationed abroad, and not participation in barbaric acts of mass murder, which were at the head of the Church's lists of concerns. Overall, the Protestant Church preached at best an ambiguous message in this regard. Its language reflected deep-seated theological traditions of discussing general issues of authority, obedience, repentance and forgiveness rather than a desire, or ability, to engage with the peculiar moral and political challenge posed by participation in genocide.[37] Any such attempts to address issues of guilt, or sin, faded very quickly as the immense hardships of 1946 and 1947 further encouraged both the population and the church which ministered to its needs to focus not on their past misdeeds but on their own present suffering.

In any case, it is unlikely that most *Heimkehrer* found a simple message of guilt compelling or appealing, any more than it is likely that the clear

[34] StadtAN F 5/930, Interview J.P., 11.11.61.
[35] Martin Greschat, 'Zwischen Aufbruch und Beharrung. Die evangelische Kirche nach dem Zweiten Weltkrieg' in V. Conzemius et al. (eds), *Die Zeit nach 1945 als Thema kirchlicher Zeitgeschichte* (Göttingen, 1988), 99–126, here 114–15.
[36] LKAN Kd Nbg 332, Evang.-Luth. Kreisdekan Nürnberg an alle Pfarrämter im Kirchenkreis Nürnberg, 31.7.45.
[37] D. Althaus, 'Luther und das öffentliche Leben', *Nürnberger Evangelisches Gemeindeblatt*, 10.3.46; 'Zum Bußtag 1946', *Nürnberger Evangelisches Gemeindeblatt*, 10.3.46.

narratives of adventure, heroism and sacrifice which circulated in post-war popular culture captured or reflected the complex, contradictory, fragmentary images of war that they carried in the post-war era.[38] A faint glimpse of this is offered by the Protestant parish newsletter which, for all its peculiar take on the world, was adept at reading the concerns, anxieties and problems of its flock. In 1954, under the heading, 'Is the last war forgotten?' it used the occasion of a workshop on the memory of the war for Protestant workers to contrast the typical stories told in public with the reality of individuals' responses. Noting that 'no, the last war is not forgotten. The question is merely what it actually is that one retains in the memory', the piece suggested that there were two standard ways of narrating: 'One is of the war as adventure, with anecdotes of how one "sorted things out" and "had luck", one of comic situations and friendly arabesques. The other side is of the war as strategy. It is the revelation of that which the private did not know, the war from the perspective of the leaders, with their hidden power struggles, their grand deliberations and their great mistakes.' It went on to ask: 'But is that all? One notices at a conference if one has to take a subject to the listeners, to force it on them so to speak, or whether one just needs to touch upon it lightly for it to be there. At the discussion of the war, which did not focus on strategy and anecdotes, the second was the case. It was as if for the participants – and it is not the case just with these – the war as an experience still sits just under the skin.' The article observed that a French war film, shown at the workshop, brought flooding back to the author the sensations of extreme fear, danger and the proximity of death: 'this feeling which was part of us for years'. It concluded that 'to put it directly, many of us are not ready to work through these experiences. They push them away, shut the war years out, make them into "lost years", render them silent and think that if they do not think about them then they also did not happen.'[39]

Such accounts no more captured an unmediated reality or universal experience of soldiering than the adventure stories they dismissed. Yet in their own way they were highly perceptive. They suggest that the relative absence of individual *Heimkehrer* voices in the public culture of the post-war era testifies not so much to the lack of political radicalism or protest activism among a population of veterans who returned home with little more than the desire to pick up the threads of their civilian existences and lead quiet lives in peace, as to the absence for many of an adequate language with which to narrate their experiences in public, and indeed to verbalise at all the fragmented images of violence, terror and fear with which they now lived.[40]

---

[38] Michael Schornstheimer, *Die leuchtenden Augen der Frontsoldaten*.

[39] 'Ist der letzte Krieg vergessen?', *Nürnberger Evangelisches Gemeindeblatt*, 14.3.54.

[40] Hook, 'Awakening from War', 143–4; Hilger, *Deutsche Kriegsgefangene in der Sowjetunion*, 370–6.

I.5

Loss, Absence and Remembrance
The Relatives of the Missing

For each family able to greet its *Heimkehrer* at the city railway station upon his return there were many more standing in the background at the official celebration gathering. They stood holding photographs of soldiers either registered as missing in action or believed to have been taken into captivity at the end of the war. To judge by newspaper images of those who held such photographs, they were disproportionately middle-aged women. Some were seeking news of their husbands; perhaps the larger part were mothers seeking news of their sons. The presence of such women reminds us that for many years after the war, the 'missing' were an object of popular acute concern whose presence – in the form of absence – was at the core of the impact the war had on German families of all political persuasions.

The immediate post-war period was dominated for millions of families by the search for loved ones. The search gave rise to a ubiquitous culture of news exchange in the immediate post-war period which manifested itself in numerous ways. Newspaper columns contained advertisements from families trying to make contact with relatives; churches and welfare associations circulated lists of names of those believed to be, or have been, in the area; railway stations were filled with noticeboards with pictures of captured or missing soldiers placed by family members in the hope that a returning soldier from the same unit might recognise them and bring news.[1] Similarly, the city cemetery authorities in Nuremberg engaged in extensive correspondence with relatives seeking to find out whether missing persons were known to have

---

[1] See, in addition to the collection of essays and images in Kaminsky, *Heimkehr 1948*, Deutsches Historisches Museum (ed.), *Kriegsgefangenen* (Berlin, 1990), 151–5; on the process of searching see Lehmann, *Gefangenschaft und Heimkehr*, 115–17; for individual examples see the case studies in Sybille Meyer and Eva Schulze, *Wie wir das alles geschafft haben. Alleinstehende Frauen berichten über ihr Leben nach 1945* (Munich, undated) and Meyer and Schulze, *Von Liebe sprach damals Keiner.*

4. Red Cross Missing Soldiers Search List (undated).

been killed, or buried, in the area. These approaches were usually born of the fact that the family's last news of the relative concerned was that their unit had been fighting in or around Nuremberg towards the end of the war; often they were more speculative even than this, and most had to be answered with the brief remark that the cemetery authorities had no knowledge of the death or resting place of the person concerned.[2]

---

[2] See, for example, the extensive correspondence between the local cemetery authorities and individual families in StadtAN C 7 I/12188 and C 7 I/12189.

If the claims of the Protestant parish newsletter are to be believed, indeed, the relatives of the missing went to unusual lengths in their search for news. In July 1947 the newsletter published a short news item detailing – and clearly bemoaning – the supposed spread of fortune-tellers in post-war Germany. It asserted that:

> In Berlin there is one *fortune-teller* for every 100 people. 99 per cent of their customers are women who wish to learn something of the uncertain fate of their relatives. One fortune-teller in Neukölln has a daily income of 5,000 RM and was forced to employ 4 assistants in order to deal with the queue in front of his house each day.[3]

It would be foolish, of course, to take such stories at face value. The parish newsletter in which it appeared served to encourage religious observance in a world of temptation and false belief, and the column in which these observations appeared often contained anecdotes recording the 'strangeness' of the world, the clear aim of which was to warn against idolatry or godless behaviour in an increasingly secular and materialistic society. Neither were such references to the sufferings of ordinary Germans in 1947 always devoid of political resonance or separate from unspoken rhetorical agendas on the part of the Protestant Church. References to the tribulations of those with relatives missing or presumed dead were situated in a broader national-conservative discourse on the past in which ordinary German 'victims' of war and defeat were privileged over the non-German victims of Nazism more generally.

But if the genre of the publication in which this item appeared, its placing within a specific column and the fact that it was authored on behalf of an institution which projected an essentially national-conservative memory of the war in the late 1940s and early 1950s give rise to some scepticism as to whether women did actually visit mediums, then the mere decision to publish such an item also tells its own story. The Church's understanding of its mission, and above all of its role as an agent of consolation, was such that its focus on the sufferings and anxieties of the bereaved was central to its ministry in the immediate post-war years. Apocryphal or not, such stories thus betrayed in their own way the Church's awareness of the desperation of its flock.

It is also clear that there were many who were willing to exploit the desperation of relatives by charging extortionate fees to conduct spurious searches which had little, if any, prospect of success. In 1945 to 1946 there was a thriving industry of such unregulated search services, demanding substantial sums of money for the translation of letters to the occupation authorities, for interpretation services

---

[3] 'Kirchliche Rundschau', *Nürnberger Evangelisches Gemeindeblatt*, 20.7.47.

and for carrying out individual searches for missing people.[4] The press, for its part, fuelled rumours concerning the possibility of finding relatives in this fashion by publishing details of organisations allegedly able to provide information. In January 1946, for example, the Protestant Aid Service for Internees and Prisoners of War (*Evangelisches Hilfswerk für Internierten und Kriegsgefangenen* – EHIK) warned in its circular to the parish priesthood of Bavaria that 'the Russian Colonel Mamenko in Berlin was recently named in the press as the head of a Russian Prisoner of War Information Office. Many people are trying to approach it directly. It is unclear, however, if this office is even functioning.'[5] One month later, the EHIK circulated parish churches once more with the news that 'our suspicion that the *Mamenko-Aktion* is a failure has been fully confirmed.'[6] Similarly, it asked parishes to point out that the 'League of Friends of the Soviet Union', which was demanding a fee of 13 RM to conduct a search for prisoners of war in Russian captivity, had absolutely no dispensation to do so: 'Even the Communist Party declares officially that it regards this office with great mistrust and has no connection to it.' Insisting that there were 'no reliable means of searching for German soldiers in Russian captivity at the moment', it stressed that 'all search services on a private basis have no prospect of success and simply serve the purpose of eliciting fees of sometimes unacceptable size'.[7]

In recognition of the unscrupulous exploitation that was taking place, the Bavarian Ministry of the Interior banned such private search services in February 1946. Henceforth the main civilian search services were organised by the Red Cross in collaboration with the EHIK and Caritas, operating through two main offices, Hamburg in the north and Munich in the south.[8] By January 1946 this agency had been able to bring together 200,000 people in Bavaria alone. For missing members of the *Wehrmacht*, meanwhile, the EHIK could only forward lists of soldiers to the International Red Cross in Geneva. Otherwise, the churches and other involved agencies were limited to acts such as the circulation of lists of soldiers killed in action on German territory for relatives to examine. The League for the Care of German War Graves

---

[4] Lehmann, *Gefangenschaft und Heimkehr*, 120.
[5] LKAN Kd Nbg 332, Evangelisches Hilfswerk für Internierte und Kriegsgefangene, Erlangen an alle Pfarrämter der Evang.-Luth. Landeskirche Bayerns, Jan. 46.
[6] LKAN Kd Nbg 332, EHIK Rundschreiben Nr.2 an die Pfarrämter der Ev.-Luth. Landeskirche Bayerns, Feb. 1946.
[7] LKAN Kd Nbg 292, Ev.-Luth Landeskirchenrat an sämtliche Dekanate der Landeskirche und an sämtliche Pfarrämter der Dekanate in Ingolstadt, Regensburg, Rosenheim betr. Nachforschungen nach deutschen Kriegsgefangenen in russischer Gefangenschaft, 23.2.46.
[8] For the evolving mechanics of the search activities of the EHIK and the Red Cross, see LKAN Kd Nbg 332, Evangelisches Hilfswerk für Internierte und Kriegsgefangene an die Freunde und Förderer des Evangelischen Hilfswerkes für Internierte und Kriegsgefangene, 10.9.45; LKAN Kd Nbg 332, Evangelisches Hilfswerk für Internierte und Kriegsgefangene, Erlangen an alle Pfarrämter der Evang.-Luth. Landeskirche Bayerns, Jan. 46; 'Suchdienst in allen Zonen', *Nürnberger Evangelisches Gemeindeblatt*, 24.8.47.

(*Volksbund Deutscher Kriegsgräberfürsorge*) began circulating such lists in 1946.[9] Likewise, in 1948 the Aid Service for Prisoners of War and the Missing in Stuttgart, a joint organisation of the churches and the Red Cross, distributed a list of 30,000 military field post numbers in the hope that somebody who had been in the same unit as a missing person might be able to shed light on their fate or whereabouts.[10]

Most difficult of all was the search for prisoners of war and news of those missing in the east. The EHIK maintained a branch of its organisation in Berlin, which sought through various channels to find news of the whereabouts and conditions of German prisoners. Beyond this, however, it was limited in 1945 to drawing people's attention to the fact that Moscow Radio broadcast lists of prisoners of war held in Russian captivity each day, along with messages from civilians in the Soviet Zone of Occupation. In the longer term, the churches continued to distribute whatever news they could on the situation of prisoners in various countries and on the likelihood of impending releases. In its parish newsletter of 31 August 1947, for example, the Nuremberg Protestant Church reported that the Czech Foreign Ministry had indicated that 'German Prisoners of War currently held in the CSR cannot as yet be released from captivity as they are needed to remove the consequences of the German occupation and repair the damage caused by German soldiers on our territory'; noting that the Moscow Conference had agreed that all German prisoners of war should be released by the end of 1948 it stated that the only exceptions would be invalids, priests and trained medics, along with prisoners 'who could prove that they had participated in the struggle against Nazism'.[11] Similarly, in September 1948 it surveyed the numbers of prisoners of war remaining in captivity, informing readers that there were still approximately 70,000 in Yugoslavia, whose condition was in general good, whereas 'there are no exact figures for the numbers of prisoners of war still held in Russia, but the releases are continuing'. All prisoners had been released from Britain by this stage, while those in Egypt and the Middle East were slowly being returned; finally, there were still approximately 100,000 prisoners and 150,000 voluntary workers in France, and 35,000 prisoners in Poland 'of whom, however, very little news reaches us'.[12]

---

[9] LKAN Kd Nbg 332, EHIK Rundschreiben Nr.2 an die Pfarrämter der Ev.-Luth. Landeskirche Bayerns, Feb. 1946.
[10] 'Kirchliche Rundschau: Hilfe bei der Suche nach Vermißten!', *Nürnberger Evangelisches Gemeindeblatt*, 5.12.48.
[11] 'Kirchliche Rundschau', *Nürnberger Evangelisches Gemeindeblatt*, 31.8.47.
[12] 'Kirchliche Rundschau', *Nürnberger Evangelisches Gemeindeblatt*, 5.9.48. Such independent searches continued on a widespread basis well into the early 1950s. See, for example, LKAN Kd Nbg 334, Ev.-Luth. Landeskirchenrat an sämtliche Evang-Luth. Dekanate der Landeskirche betr. nicht zurückgekehrte Kriegsgefangene, 21.3.50; 'Kirchliche Rundschau', *Nürnberger Evangelisches Gemeindeblatt*, 27.1.52.

The Church not only acted as a clearing agent for searching relatives or as a disseminator of information concerning possible releases, however. Underlining the centrality of bereavement, grieving and desperate hoping for safe return of the missing to local communities, church readings, prayers and sermons in the post-war years were replete with biblical references to absence and loss, to searching and finding. The guidelines distributed for the September 1947 prayer week for the activities of the Innere Mission, one of the Protestant Church's charitable works, for example, stipulated that one evening of prayer should be dedicated to 'the imprisoned and the missing'.[13] In the same vein, church bells were rung regularly throughout the late 1940s and early 1950s to express sympathy for the missing and their relatives, and the parish newsletter regularly published songs, hymns and prayers to the same end.[14]

Neither did the Church confine itself to offering consolation, to endowing death with meaning or to giving expression to anguished hope. It also played a key role in the mobilisation and articulation of public opinion, for which return of the prisoners of war was a central demand. In November 1946 the Council of the Protestant Church in Germany announced that it had been sending private envoys and requests to various foreign offices for months with a view to improving the lot of the prisoners and gaining their release, but that 'the Council does not now wish to refuse the requests from our parishes to intervene for our prisoners of war in public as well'.[15] During Advent 1946 a national petition was organised. Demands were to be sent to the governments of the states holding German prisoners, to the Allied Control Council, to the International Red Cross, to the World Council of Churches, and to the churches of all states holding prisoners; in addition to submitting the results at national level, individual deans were to send the locally collected petitions to the local military commander with a standard covering letter.

The petition, which was organised in Nuremberg amidst great publicity, generated an enormous response. The *Emmauskirche* reported that 'the request resonated strongly with the population, with some parishioners still coming in the late evening hours in order to give their signature';[16] the parish of Laufamholz-Hammer likewise recorded 'two very well-attended services' on the day the petition was initiated.[17] Overall, in a city of some 220,000

---

[13] LKAN Kd Nbg 61, Ev.-Luth. Kreisdekan Nürnberg an alle Pfarrer im Kirchenkreis Nürnberg betr. Gebetswoche der Inneren Mission, Sept. 1947.

[14] See, for example, 'Gedächtnisläuten für die Gefallenen, Gefangenen und Vermißten', *Nürnberger Evangelisches Gemeindeblatt*, 1.2.48.

[15] LKAN Kd Nbg 332, Aufruf des Rates der EKD an die Gemeinden, (undated, November 1946).

[16] LKAN Kd Nbg 334, Ev.-Luth. Pfarramt Emmauskirche an Kreisdekan Nürnberg, 27.12.46.

[17] LKAN Kd Nbg 334, Protokoll, 26.12.46.

Protestant inhabitants, 81,600 citizens signed the petition, while in Bavaria as a whole some 750,000 signatures were collected.[18]

By the end of 1948, most of the remaining prisoners of war had been released. In June 1947 there had been 7,337 Nuremberg soldiers registered as prisoners;[19] by 1950 there were 251.[20] By November 1953 there were only 83 remaining Nuremberg soldiers still registered as being in captivity.[21] The issue continued to arouse strong passions, however, and indeed in some ways gained in intensity, as the number of remaining prisoners fell rapidly in the 1950s. At the same time, clearly, the desperation grew of those who had either not heard of their missing relatives since the war, or who knew that they had been taken captive but had not heard of them for some time. In 1950 the EHIK consoled those families whose loved ones were not among those who had recently returned with the news that 'many prisoners of war in the east have been held back from release and taken to so-called interrogation camps', and initiated a renewed campaign to list those still yet to return.[22] According to Bishop D. Theodor Heckel, the head of the EHIK, in a speech delivered in Frankfurt in March 1950 and reported upon in the Protestant parish newsletter in Nuremberg there were still thousands of prisoners in Spain and Albania, in Poland and Yugoslavia, and 'especially in Russia', including women and children 'whose fate is unknown'.[23]

What meanings were attached to the issue of the prisoners of war in the east? In the first place, pressure to release the prisoners was clearly expressed in a language which was replete with political and ideological inflection. The prisoners of war held in Soviet captivity were co-opted into a relativising narrative of the Second World War which sought to equate any crimes committed by Germans with those committed by Germany's enemies, and were appropriated by conservative forces to underpin a renewed climate of anti-Communism which drew on sentiments expressed, mobilised and reinforced by Nazi

---

[18] LKAN Kd Nbg 332, Ev.-Luth. Kreisdekan in Nürnberg an die Militärregierung Nürnberg (undated, Christmas 1946). It appears that at least one further petition was organised in 1952 as part of that year's Prisoner of War Remembrance Week: see 'Kriegsgefangenengedenkwoche – Veranstaltung der evangelischen Kirche in Nürnberg', *Nürnberger Evangelisches Gemeindeblatt*, 19.10.52.
[19] StadtAN C 29/428, Statistische Nachrichten der Stadt Nürnberg: Die Ergebnisse der Kriegsgefangenen- und Vermißten-Registrierung, 27.10.47.
[20] LKAN Kd Nbg 334, Vermisste und Kriegsgefangene: Aktennotiz, (undated, 1950).
[21] StadtAN C 7 I/1661, Fürsorgeamt: Opfer der beiden Weltkriege in bzw. von Nürnberg, 13.11.53.
[22] 'Nicht entlassene Kriegsgefangene melden!', *Nürnberger Evangelisches Gemeindeblatt*, 5.2.50; on the campaign, which, as with all other campaigns for the release of the remaining POWs, was given great prominence by the Church, see also LKAN Kd Nbg 62, Ev.-Luth. Dekanat an alle Pfarrer, 27.2.50.
[23] 'Gebt unsere Kriegsgefangenen frei!', *Nürnberger Evangelisches Gemeindeblatt*, 26.3.50.

propaganda itself.[24] The 'missing' were deployed rhetorically in a critique of the occupation authorities which, in alluding subtly to similarities between the criminality of the Nazi regime and the supposedly arbitrary and harsh policies of the allies, betrayed a blindness on the part of the Protestant Church towards the murderous barbarism of the Third Reich.[25]

And yet the ringing of church bells, the collection of petitions, the placing of advertisements and the circulation of photographs, the prayers said, readings given and sermons delivered in the ten years after the Second World War tell an additional story the meaning of which is not primarily understood by reference to the emerging Cold War context in which these took place. Neither is the constant inflation of the number of remaining prisoners in captivity to be understood solely in terms of anti-Communist polemical excess, although this played a part.[26] The massive public interest in the issue of the prisoners of war, especially when measured against the relatively limited numbers of prisoners remaining in Soviet captivity by the 1950s, was, rather, a reflection of the fact that for hundreds of thousands of families in post-war Germany, the continued presence of prisoners of war in the Soviet Union offered a glimmer of hope that a loved one registered missing at the front might still be alive.

In 1952, for example, on the occasion of the Day of National Mourning, the parish newsletter reminded its parishioners that 'there is hardly a house in our city in which either a fallen soldier, or soldier who died in captivity, or a missing soldier, is not absent', but that 'here it should not be forgotten that all those who are still waiting for a missing person are in the worst position. For common sense considerations say that the missing person is no longer alive. But as long as there is not complete clarity, hope clings to every possibility.'[27] Such hopes were sustained not just by the absence of definite news in itself, but by the widespread belief, nurtured by the generally poor communications between prisoners and their families at home, in the existence of so-called *Schweigelager*, or 'silent camps'.[28] The West German press was full of rumours

[24] Moeller, *War Stories*, 1018–19; Biess, 'Survivors of Totalitarianism', 63.
[25] 'Ein Wort an die Evangelischen Christen im Ausland', *Nürnberger Evangelisches Gemeindeblatt* 27.7.47; for similar relativising rhetoric on the part of senior Protestant churchmen see the words of Bishop Dibelius of Berlin, which were read from the pulpit of all Bavarian churches in April 1949: LKAN Kd Nbg 332, Ev.-Luth. Landeskirchenrat an allen Evang.-Luth. Pfarrämter und exponierten Vikariate betr. Kanzelverlesung am Sonntag 3.4.49, 25.3.49.
[26] For two of many such examples see Karl Hoppe (ed.), *Das Schicksal der kriegsgefangenen Soldaten und Frauen in Russland* (undated, c. 1948), which claims that 'more than 2,000,000 German prisoners of war must still be on Russian soil' (5) and the material in Dieter Riesenberger, *Das Deutsche Rote Kreuz, Konrad Adenauer und das Kriegsgefangenenproblem. Die Rückführung der Deutschen Kriegsgefangenen aus der Sowjetunion (1952–1955)* (Bremen, 1994), 120–4.
[27] 'Das Kreuz bleibt stehen. Zum Volkstrauertag 1952', *Nürnberger Evangelisches Gemeindeblatt*, 16.11.52.
[28] Lehmann, *Gefangenschaft und Heimkehr*, 119–21; Moeller, *War Stories*, 40.

of punishment camps in which large numbers of prisoners had been detained, but from which they were not allowed to write home.[29] Again, parish newsletters were suggestive. In November 1951, for example, in the parish newsletter dedicated to remembrance of the dead, the following words of consolation were offered:

Today we must remember with especial love those who, six years after the end of the war, still do not know what has become of their missing son, husband or father; they have only the last army postcard in their hands, and from then on there is no trace. In Nuremberg, too, many families are still waiting in vain. . . . Time and again the torturous question arises: is he still alive, or long since dead? On the one hand clear reason says that at that time, the time of collapse, thousands of soldiers were killed and hundreds of thousands died afterwards in the early period of captivity, and that all those still missing are long since dead. But then one hears another unverifiable piece of news concerning silent camps, or one gets told that somewhere a man has come home who had not written at all after the end of the war. And if mostly the rumour turns out to be of little substance once it has been more closely checked, the old hopes are awakened once more. And how could it be different?[30]

How many people did all of this affect? In June 1947, the state-wide registration of all prisoners of war and missing soldiers and civilians recorded 7,337 prisoners of war, 7,721 missing soldiers and 522 missing civilians from the city.[31] Expressed as a proportion of the population, 2.3 per cent of Nuremberg's citizens were still held in captivity and 2.5 per cent were registered as missing. A further official registration carried out in March 1950 revealed that, while the number of prisoners of war from the city had fallen to a residual 251, 6,932 soldiers, and now 405 civilians, were still listed as missing.[32] Of the 800 soldiers no longer registered as missing it is unclear how many had since returned: undoubtedly many families had been sufficiently realistic to have their missing husband, son or father declared dead. The fact

[29] For a particularly good example, because of its suggestive title, 'Tote kehren aus Russland heim', *Nürnberger Nachrichten*, 29.12.53.

[30] 'Vermißt! Ein Trostwort für Wartende', *Nürnberger Evangelisches Gemeindeblatt*, 25.11.51; see also 'Sieben Jahre und sieben Monate in russischer Kriegsgefangenschaft', *Nürnberger Evangelisches Gemeindeblatt*, 26.10.52; 'Das Problem der Schweigelager in Rußland. Bischof Heckel antwortete dem Gemeindeblatt', *Nürnberger Evangelisches Gemeindeblatt*, 28.12.52; for additional material on the problem of the 'silent camps' see Neil Gregor, ' "Is he still alive or long since dead?": Loss, Absence and Remembrance in Nuremberg, 1945–1956' in *German History*, 21/2 (2003), 183–203.

[31] StadtAN C 29/428, Statistische Nachrichten der Stadt Nürnberg: Die Ergebnisse der Kriegsgefangenen- und Vermißten-Registrierung, 27.10.47.

[32] LKAN Kd Nbg 334, Vermisste und Kriegsgefangene: Aktennotiz (undated, 1950).

that having a missing person declared dead was a precondition for the receipt of a pension will clearly have played a significant role here.[33] Expressed as a percentage of the population, the numbers of missing may not appear high at first sight. But when placed in the context of a network of family, friends and colleagues it is clear that there will have been few people who were not at least aware of a prisoner of war or missing person.[34]

It should also be remembered, of course, that the 15,000 or so prisoners of war and missing persons were in addition to the 10,811 soldiers from Nuremberg and 5,297 Nuremberg civilians killed in the war.[35] Even before the war had ended, bereaved relatives had faced the task of making sense of their losses. Others began to do so in the immediate post-war years. With the release of the final prisoners of war from the Soviet Union in 1956, all but a few were forced to concede that the missing relative for whose safe return they had hoped was now dead. Such searching for meaning continued well into the post-war years. As State Bishop Dr Lilje of Hanover stated in his address on the Day of National Mourning in 1955, which was reprinted in the Protestant parish newsletter, 'there is still much pain of death among our people which has yet to be overcome. I include in this the sorrow for the death of dear people which the bereaved have still not understood, accepted and overcome inside.'[36] Various narratives were available, depending on the world view or convictions of the bereaved individual. Some told a story of the heroic 'soldier's death' defending the fatherland against Bolshevism, drawing on the masculine and martial myths which had been central to the Nazis' own nationalist cult of the dead; others consoled themselves with the idea that their father, husband, brother or son had died doing his duty in defence of his *Heimat* or his community; non-Nazis knew simply that their family member had been conscripted, sent to the front and had been killed. Among surviving soldiers, the widespread language of comradeship bespoke the belief – or the desire to believe – that those killed had given their lives not in pursuit of an illegitimate political cause but in sacrifice for each other.

---

[33] That the number of soldiers registered as missing in a later survey in 1953 had risen to 7,205 is to be explained in terms of the rapidly rising population of a city in which the extent of bombing had been such that the number of inhabitants had halved during the war: as the city was rebuilt, the evacuees returned, and as they returned, they brought their missing to the city's statistics. On the post-war struggles over welfare and benefits see Hughes, *Shouldering the Burdens of Defeat*.

[34] In 1955 an opinion poll suggested that 27 per cent of West Germans had a relative missing in action in the east or actually held in a camp; a further 15 per cent said that they had such a personal acquaintance. Moeller, 'The Last Soldiers of the Great War', 130.

[35] StadtAN C 7 I/1661, Fürsorgeamt: Opfer der beiden Weltkriege in bzw. von Nürnberg, 13.11.53; see also 'Betet für den Frieden! Zahlen des Grauens aus der Bilanz des letzten Krieges', *Nürnberger Evangelisches Gemeindeblatt*, 30.12.51.

[36] 'Der christliche Sinn eines Volkstrauertages', *Nürnberger Evangelisches Gemeindeblatt*, 13.11.55.

The presence of such secular narratives should not, however, divert attention from other, still very widespread, ways of seeing which offered quite different stories of death and dying. Their relative purchase may be hard to surmise, but their prevalence in quite mainstream spaces suggests that these had an equal purchase within at least some sections of the community. The Protestant parish newsletter of 20 December 1945, for example, contained the following 'Intercession for a Missing Person':

Lord, our heart seeks him whom we love and do not know where we should find him. But you know where he is. If he is still alive, show him that you are close to him. We cannot speak to him, but you can, and your word is stronger than ours. We cannot show him that we love him, but you can, and your love is more than ours. We cannot console him, but you can and you are the God of all consolation and know how to console him in his loneliness and need . . . If it be your holy will, unite us again. If you have decided differently, take him into your heavenly kingdom; give him eternal peace and show him the eternal light. Console us, however, with the hope that all those who have died with Christ awake with him to life in the next world.[37]

For those with strong Christian conviction, biblical truth told a clear story concerning the transience of earthly flesh, the passage of the soul and the impending Last Judgement. Yet what is equally striking is the extent to which such theologically robust narratives, offered by authoritative voices in spaces with apparently obvious meanings, and to an audience accustomed to their claims to absolute truth, became interwoven with more overtly secular vocabularies, such as those of duty and obedience, or with stories of sacrifice and laying down one's life for others which could simultaneously have both religious and secular meanings or echoes. Christian religious language fused, moreover, with a vocabulary of fate and destiny which had its obvious antecedents in the political rhetoric of the Nazi regime itself, but which also suggested a more inchoate, inarticulate religiosity the theological grasp of which exhausted itself in a much more nebulous sense of the sad mystery of the world.

A large proportion of dead German soldiers had been killed and buried in foreign countries. The absence of peace treaties or bilateral agreements in the immediate post-war era meant that the repatriation of bodies even from former enemy territory in the west could not occur until the 1950s. A lucky few were able to make use of this possibility eventually. But for many more there was no body to repatriate. The need for a physical space in which to mourn a lost body was such that many families simply added the name of their lost individual to their established family graves. Indeed, the cemeteries

---

[37] 'Fürbitte für einen Vermißten', *Nürnberger Evangelisches Gemeindeblatt*, 30.12.45.

of Nuremberg contained not only epitaphs mourning those killed in air raids, or those killed in action near the city and thus buried in a marked grave, but numerous examples of gravestones erected in memory of those who had not been officially recorded as dead but who were listed as missing in action – many contained epitaphs such 'Fritz H., missing in East Prussia, Jan. 1945', or 'Heinz B., lost in the East, 1944'.

If the references to time and place in such epitaphs betrayed the fact that the deaths of loved ones were being ordered into some kind of narrative, the meanings of these narratives for individual families remain unclear. 'The East' was, in itself, a complex marker of space the various and evolving meanings of which reflected the vicissitudes of German nationalism in the modern era. In the traditional power politics of the nineteenth century it had signified the home of the Tsarist empire; in the German nationalist imagination it had been the home of inferior Slavic peoples; in colonialist discourse it had represented fertile lands and a space ripe for colonisation; to the Nazis it had also been the home of Jewish Bolshevism and thus the locus of the great ideological enemy. After 1945 the meanings ascribed to it were reshaped, once again, in the light of Cold War politics. In the post-war era, however, it had taken on an additional meaning for many families. It was now simply a vast, boundless space, the site of an

5(a–b). Epitaphs, Nuremberg city cemeteries.

unfathomable war; it was a space above all into which family members had vanished, and a place in which a missing family member still 'was'.

Moreover, if such epitaphs testify to the centrality of loss to the experience of the war at the level of the family, they are often equally striking for the absence of narrative they offer. Increasingly, epitaphs eschewed all reference to time and place of death in favour of noting only that the person concerned was 'missing' (*vermisst*) or 'vanished' (*verschollen*). In some cases, this was undoubtedly simply because the grieving relatives knew no more. Nonetheless, such references simultaneously betray the presence of a grief to which the various cultural and political narratives of military death on offer in the late 1940s and 1950s were unable to connect: like the silences of the *Heimkehrer*, they suggest that for many bereaved families the shock of war was such that there was, for a long time, nothing meaningful to say. A family member, once 'there', was now 'gone', leaving a numbness which simply resisted articulation.

I.6

Rehabilitation and Reintegration

The 'Victims of Denazification'

Few Germans were given as much opportunity to contemplate the causes of their suffering, and to reflect upon their responsibility for it, as the citizens of Nuremberg. The city's symbolic associations with the Nazi regime made it a natural location for the victorious allies to stage their post-war trials of the Nazi leadership. The International Military Tribunal was intended simultaneously to punish the crimes, to establish the historical record and to have a wider educational effect. The majority of the twenty-two defendants, including the former Gauleiter of Franconia, Julius Streicher, were found guilty and executed; some received lengthy prison sentences; a few were acquitted. Then, in twelve subsequent proceedings which lasted until 1949, the Nuremberg Military Tribunals prosecuted 185 members of the political, functional and economic elites of the Third Reich – SS and Nazi party figures, civil servants, military men, leading figures from the worlds of business and medicine, whose trials were intended to symbolise the wider complicity of Germany's institutions and professions in the crimes of the Nazi regime. Many were imprisoned; most were then released early as the Cold War climate of the 1950s led to the reversal of a policy for which enthusiasm had long since been waning.[1]

Both the foreign press and the local media reported the trials extensively. The focus of the world media's gaze on the trials was such that it would be easy to assume that they had a pervasive educational effect. Contemporary observers, however, discerned a more ambiguous response: acknowledgement, however reluctant, competed with defensiveness or refusal; a moment of reflection for some became merely an early opportunity to rehearse

---

[1] On the release campaigns of the early 1950s see Frei, *Vergangenheitspolitik*, 133–306.

convenient fictions for others; for every individual who was provoked by the trials to consider his or her own guilt there were others for whom proceedings against the perpetrator elite served only to confirm their own sense of injured innocence.[2]

To many outsiders, in fact, the citizens of Nuremberg distinguished themselves by their absolute lack of interest in the trials. Reporting for *Newsweek*, for example, James O'Donnell concluded as early as 10 December 1945 that 'there is probably no city its size in the world where this trial is less discussed by the man in the street than Nuremberg, no country in the world where less is known about it than Germany'.[3] The *Nürnberger Nachrichten* also acknowledged the general impression gained by visitors to the city that 'the citizen of Nuremberg, at least, shows little interest in the world events taking place inside his ruined city walls'.[4]

However, the *Nürnberger Nachrichten* was also at pains to point out that foreign journalists often had unrealistic expectations of how civilians should react. It continued: 'Of course, the people of Nuremberg do not congregate in huge, impatient crowds in front of the court building, waiting tensely for the latest facts from the courtroom. Of course, they do not prey like a wild horde before the prison, wanting to lynch the accused.' It was indeed the case that 'in the ruined home of the Nuremberger the search for a pound of plaster for the most urgent repairs is indeed much more pressing than curiosity over the latest from the trial in newspaper or radio reports'. It defended the population, however, arguing that this would be the case anywhere, and that it was wrong to see it as a sign of lack of interest: 'The interest of a people expresses itself differently: in thinking about things in principle, in honest acceptance, in an impatient desire to know (which even so-called trial opponents do not deny), in occasional engagement with the basic questions.'

Overall, indeed, the *Nürnberger Nachrichten* sought to maintain a balance between promoting the just cause of the allied trials while avoiding a tone of excessive accusation which it knew would do little to foster reflection. Yet even as it defended the necessity of the trials to a population which was far from unanimously in support of them, the *Nürnberger Nachrichten* also indulged in the rehearsal of arguments which prefigured the apologetics of subsequent years. Speaking of the apparent ignorance of Germans – albeit in this case

---

[2] For an overview of ordinary Germans' responses as gauged by contemporary observers, see Anneke de Rudder, ' "Warum das ganze Theater?" Der Nürnberger Prozeß in den Augen der Zeitgenossen' in *Jahrbuch für Antisemitismusforschung* 6 (1997), 218–42; specifically on Nuremberg see Heike Kröscher, 'Nürnberg und kein Interesse? Der Prozeß gegen die Hauptkriegsverbrecher 1945/46 und die Nürnberger Nachkriegsöffentlichkeit', *Mitteilungen des Vereins für Geschichte der Stadt Nürnberg* 93 (2006) 299–317.

[3] James O'Donnell, 'German on der Strasse: What War Guilt Trials?', *Newsweek*, 10.12.45.

[4] 'Wie reagieren die Deutschen auf den Nürnberger Prozeß?', *Nürnberger Nachrichten*, 27.2.46.

Germans who had been interned in Switzerland – it opined that 'we do not have the slightest reason to doubt this ignorance and the honesty of the astonishment at the reports. This ignorance will have to be taken into account when addressing the question of German collective responsibility.'[5] Others, including James O'Donnell, picked up on the cries of innocence, relating the alleged words of a former shopkeeper: 'those KZs [. . .]! Terrible! You must realise that we common people did not know anything about that.'[6]

Intertwined with these myths of ignorance, moreover, were early rehearsals of the narrative which acknowledged the crimes of the Nazi leadership only to reinforce the belief that German society, and the physical substance of German cities, had been their main victims. O'Donnell offered the words of a former soldier who, in his account, had fought in Poland, France and Russia: 'I look at my home town of Nuremberg – the ruined churches and museums, the shattered house of Albrecht Dürer – at this crime the twentieth century has committed against the fifteenth. And I look at the prostrate fatherland, not forgetting what I have seen of want and desolation in many lands. And then I say if these men had five pfennigs' worth of honesty or character they would stand up before the world and shout Guilty! Guilty! Guilty!'[7]

If the period of the trials marked a brief 'interregnum' before the marginalisation of the Holocaust in the memory culture of the 1950s, therefore, the extent to which it witnessed an honest, self-critical engagement on the part of the ordinary population of the city may be regarded as open to question.[8] Insofar as the Nazi regime was acknowledged as having been criminal, its main victims were felt by the population to have been Germans; insofar as the sufferings of others were acknowledged they were deemed merely to be on a par with the tribulations of the Germans themselves; insofar as the dimensions of foreign victims' suffering were recognised to have been different, the crimes which had caused this were deemed to have been committed by a few, not by the many, whose supposed ignorance of the very presence of the camps itself testified, logically, to the fact that they could not have been guilty on account of them. Echoing through local responses to the trials, therefore, were already many of the refrains which would characterise the memory culture of the 1950s.

---

[5] 'Die Deutschen müßen die Kriegsverbrechen erfahren', *Nürnberger Nachrichten*, 20.10.45; for a summary of the literature concerning Germans' participation in, and awareness of Nazi crimes during and after, the war see Neil Gregor, 'Nazism – A Political Religion? Rethinking the Voluntarist Turn' in id. (ed.), *Nazism, War and Genocide. Essays in Honour of Jeremy Noakes* (Exeter, 2005), 1–21.
[6] O'Donnell, 'German on der Strasse'.
[7] Ibid. For a similarly phrased account by a local resident see also StadtAN F 5/488, MS (unpublished), Marie S., 16.12.45.
[8] For this argument see Herf, *Divided Memory*, esp. 206–8; for a more sceptical account see the persuasive study by Bloxham: *Genocide on Trial*.

The political and moral reckoning which exercised the minds of most citizens was not the major showpiece trial programme but denazification. A process which went through several phases, first under American and then German jurisdiction, this improvised and highly contentious attempt to remove the influence of Nazism from public life first took the form of a crude purge of Germany's political, administrative and commercial institutions; as measures rooted in a structural understanding of how the Nazi regime operated gave way to a process rooted in reforming the individual 'Nazi', however, and as emerging Cold War imperatives encouraged the occupation powers to move towards the rebuilding of their respective zones, a set of practices geared initially towards punishment evolved inexorably into a machinery of rehabilitation.[9] Yet while the vast majority of former Nazi party members had been rehabilitated and reintegrated within two years of the end of the war, receiving at most token punishments, the denazification process was the cause of exceptional resentment: indeed, it proved to be a highly charged issue which defined one key fault line of local political culture in the immediate post-war period.

The initial framework for denazification was laid down by the American directive of 7 July 1945, which provided for the automatic dismissal of a wide range of individuals, including: all members of the Nazi party who had joined before 1 May 1937, all functionaries of the Nazi party and its associated formations, all SS men and officers of the *Waffen-SS*; in addition, all senior government and administrative personnel, together with prominent military and business persons if they had actively partipated in the regime, were to be removed. The persons affected were to fill in a questionnaire – not until they had demonstrated that they had only been a nominal Nazi would they be allowed to return to senior positions.[10]

Even before the directive of 7 July, over 800 city employees had been removed from their posts.[11] Further dismissals followed throughout the summer and autumn of 1945. By August, eight of the twelve main departments of the city administration were without a director.[12] By December, approximately one-third of the city's employees had been sacked.[13] Some parts of the local state

---

[9] The standard work on denazification in the American zone remains Niethammer, *Mitläuferfabrik*. For an overview of developments in Nuremberg see Eckart, *Amerikanische Reformpolitik*, 238–78; for other local and regional studies of the process as it occurred in Franconia see Hans Woller, *Gesellschaft und Politik in der amerikanischen Besatzungszone. Die Region Ansbach und Fürth* (Munich, 1986), 95–165; Jutta Beyer, *Demokratie als Lernprozeß. Politische Kultur und lokale Politik nach 1945 am Beispiel der Städte Forchheim und Schwabach* (Nuremberg, 1989), 63–90; for a wider overview see Cornelia Rauh-Kühne, 'Die Entnazifizierung und die deutsche Gesellschaft' in *Archiv für Sozialgeschichte* 35 (1995), 35–70.

[10] On the directive of 7 July 1945 see Niethammer, *Mitläuferfabrik*, 150ff.

[11] StadtAN C 29/424, Monatsbericht des Oberbürgermeisters der Stadt Nürnberg für Juni 1945.

[12] StadtAN C 29/160, Bürgermeister Treu an Militärregierung Nürnberg, 11.8.45.

[13] For figures see StadtAN C 29/424, Monatsbericht des Oberbürgermeisters der Stadt Nürnberg für die Zeit vom 20 November bis 19 Dezember 1945; see also Niethammer, *Mitläuferfabrik*, 181.

apparatus, such as the courts and schools, were hardly able to function; many others were left with only a skeletal staff.[14]

The dismissals were greeted with howls of protest. The first mayor appointed by the Americans – the career civil servant Julius Rühm – complained that the dismissals were bound to lead to a 'collapse of anything approaching an adequate administrative process'.[15] Rühm, who had himself been a nominal member of the Nazi Party, retained by the military government only to ensure the minimum level of bureaucratic continuity necessary to master the immediate crisis, was soon dismissed.[16] He was replaced by two SPD men: Martin Treu (who had been deputy mayor in the 1920s) became mayor; Hans Ziegler (1877–1957; deputy mayor 1945; mayor 1945–48) was appointed as his deputy. Yet this transfer of administrative responsibility from a conservative bureaucrat into the hands of more stridently anti-Nazi figures did not translate into a much greater desire to cooperate in the denazification process. Treu, no less than his predecessor Rühm, saw the dismissals as merely an impediment to the restoration of a functioning city apparatus; his interventions with the military government conveyed no greater recognition of denazification as a moral or political necessity. In August, the city authorities complained in their monthly report that 'the dismissals by the American military government, which cannot be reconciled with German law, continued and naturally led to a gradual dissolution of the once so orderly administration of the city of Nuremberg' and that 'the purely mechanical dismissals conflict not only with all civil service and employment law but also with the general sense of right and wrong'.[17] Such belated sensitivity towards the dictates of fairness sat in stark contrast to the activities during the Third Reich of many of those now dismissed, but officials were apparently blind to the possibility that they might be accused of demanding standards of treatment which they had themselves willingly breached only very recently. Moreover, in tones not dissimilar to those of conservative critics of denazification, Treu warned of the 'political consequences which occur when hundreds and thousands have to be dismissed who in their inner convictions were never Nazis and who thus regard their dismissal as a real injustice. In this way, all these people get turned into Nazis and thus branded enemies of the state. But in no way will such people be won over to democracy by such draconian and schematic actions.'[18]

---

[14] See also Niethammer, *Mitläuferfabrik*, 182.

[15] StadtAN C 29/424, Monatsbericht des Oberbürgermeisters der Stadt Nürnberg für Juni 1945.

[16] On Rühm's career see Eckart, *Amerikanische Reformpolitik*, 225–9.

[17] StadtAN C 29/424, Monatsbericht des Oberbürgermeisters der Stadt Nürnberg für den Monat August 1945.

[18] StadtAN C 29/161, Aktennotiz über die Besprechung bei Herrn Ministerpräsidenten Dr Hoegner in München am Freitag, den 16. Nov 1945.

However self-serving they were, Treu's comments pointed to the dilemma the ex-Nazis posed – to the necessity of removing them from positions of influence, and of giving them cause to reflect, and yet at the same time offering them the possibility of integration into a new democratic system. His criticisms of the schematic nature of early denazification practice chimed with the beliefs of many non-Nazis as well as ex-party members, and did not fall on entirely deaf ears within the military government itself.[19] Nonetheless, his perceived obstructionism made him increasingly unpopular with the military government. Eventually the local military government removed him, too, and replaced him as mayor with his deputy Hans Ziegler.[20]

The dismissals of 1945 were the most obvious means by which former party members were given to understand that they were 'out in the cold' in the immediate aftermath of the regime's collapse. Not only did they lose their official employment and the associated rights – they were entitled to perform only menial or manual labour – they were subject to a range of material and symbolic penalties designed both to humiliate and to force them to bear a disproportionate share of the general burdens of defeat. Former party members were obliged to perform additional rubble-clearing work.[21] Then in January 1946 the city council published details of a decree whereby prominent party members, SS members and the leadership cadres of SA and *Waffen-SS*, the National Socialist Motor Corps (NSKK) and the Hitler Youth were obliged to register their residences with a view to their being confiscated for the use of other residents in need.[22] As a result, nearly 1,700 apartments were seized.[23] The housing authorities were also instructed to force on party members to live in more cramped conditions to help alleviate housing shortages; party members were also subject to the confiscation of clothes or furniture to help provide for the refugees or, most pointedly, the victims of fascism.

How former party members responded varied. One wrote to mayor Ziegler in September 1946 acknowledging the rightness of the obligatory rubble work and donating the money he had been paid towards rebuilding the city.[24] Such gestures were, however, rare: evasion was a more common response. In April 1946 the Intelligence section of the military government recorded that it had

---

[19] See, for example, the self-critical comments by the Americans in StadtAN F 6/104, MG Det. E1B3, Memo – Policy Matters, 13.8.45.
[20] StadtAN F 6/2, OMG Kreis Nürnberg, Regierungsbezirk Oberfranken und Mittelfranken: Monthly Historical Report from 1.–31.12.45.
[21] StadtAN F 6/2, Annual Historical Report 21 April 1945 to 20 June 1946; StadtAN F 6/152, Det F1B3, Weekly Report, 21.–27.7.45.
[22] StadtAN C 29/424, Monatsbericht des Oberbürgermeisters der Stadt Nürnberg für die Zeit vom 20 Dezember 1945 bis 19 Januar 1946.
[23] StadtAN C 29/425, Monatsbericht des Oberbürgermeisters der Stadt Nürnberg für die Zeit vom 20 Januar bis 19 Februar 1946.
[24] StadtAN C 29/444, H.B. an Oberbürgermeister Ziegler, 5.9.46.

heard complaints concerning 'the alleged and obvious lack of initiative on the part of local Labour Office officials against proven active Nazis and active militarists. This complaint originates particularly within the ranks of reliable anti-Nazis but is frequently heard from so-called "little Nazis" and asserts that the type of active Nazis and former professional officers is most successful in dodging their labour duties by means of "medical certificates" and by a well-organised clique system'.[25] The second deputy mayor, Adam Geier, of the CSU – who was in charge of denazification in the city once it had been turned over to the Germans – argued against the practice of punishment labour, claiming that 'the summoning of members of the party as a punishment . . . may have the drawback that the whole additional work bears the character of a punishment and thus the desire to work will be weakened in the beginning'.[26] Geier's argument that other cities had had negative experiences of such forced clearance work may or may not have been true; this notwithstanding, his intervention against the programme fitted a general pattern of interceding on behalf of former party members which bespoke a clear lack of commitment towards enforcing such measures rigorously. Similarly, complaints were widespread that many ex-Nazis were finding it possible to avoid the seizure of their apartments.[27]

Complaints such as these formed but a tiny fraction of a mass of correspondence in 1945 in which former party members pleaded innocence, begged clemency or sought to shift the blame, while non-party members complained that former Nazis were still in positions of authority, were exploiting connections to gain favourable treatment or were not being adequately punished. Former party members bombarded the authorities with letters claiming that they had been forced to join the Nazi party, that they had joined only to protect their families or that they had joined to resist from the inside. Those who had joined the party early on claimed that they had done so out of idealism, and would never have done so had they known how the regime would develop; those who joined after 1937 argued that they had done so only for conformity's sake, rather than out of zeal. For the former, the blame clearly lay with those who had joined later, even after it became clear what the Nazi party was really like; for the latter, it fell on the early activists – without them, the movement would never have come to power in the first place. Whatever the truth of individual claims, their common rhetorical thrust was to establish that it had all been someone else's fault.

Common to both ex-Nazis and anti-Nazis, however, was the widespread conviction that party membership in itself was not a watertight criterion for judging guilt: both former party members and opponents pointed to the fact

[25] StadtAN F 6/163, ICD Intelligence Section, Nbg. Detachment, Political Affairs Report, 13.4.46.
[26] StadtAN F 6/50, Stadtverwaltung/Hochbauamt an MG Nuremberg, 28.5.46.
[27] StadtAN F 6/77, Office of US Chief of Counsel to Lt. Col. Carl Kleiss, MG Nuremberg, 6.2.46.

that many figures in elite circles in particular had been active in sustaining the regime in power or facilitating its criminal acts. For ex-party members, this reinforced the self-pitying belief that denazification was focusing excessively on the 'little man', rather than on the regime's more powerful backers; for anti-Nazis the point was not that such elite figures should be punished instead of ordinary party members, but rather that they should be punished as well. It was also commonly held that those in state employment were being treated more harshly than those in the private sector, firstly because they were more likely to have been pressed into joining the party in the first place and, second, because in the private sector it was easier to avoid the stipulations of the denazification directive. Within the working class, in particular, a powerful anti-fascist impulse focused its anger on the many members of the business elites – whether party members or not – who were believed to have slipped through the net.[28]

It was partly in response to the widely held sense that the business sector had not been subject to the same relatively rigorous early denazification process as the public sector that the so-called Law No. 8 was introduced on 29 September 1945.[29] A German law rather than an American directive, it marked an attempt to redress the balance by intensifying the denazification of the economy. Former Nazis were not allowed to perform managerial or supervisory roles until they had proven that they had been no more than nominal party members; companies employing ex-party members in more than menial positions faced sanction and possible closure; meanwhile, in an additional measure aimed at denazifying the private sector, companies owned by politically tainted individuals were to be put into the hands of trustees, so that the influence of Nazis in the economy could be curtailed without underlying property rights being affected.[30]

If the presence of an appeals process – which was, predictably, invoked by large numbers of aggrieved former party members – marked an attempt to make the system appear fairer, its operation by Germans prefigured some of the structural problems which attended the later denazification tribunals instituted in March 1946. The numerous appeal boards, established for each branch of industry, commerce and the professions, were comprised of four representatives of the economic sector concerned, together with two neutral

---

[28] See, for example, the various examples contained in StadtAN F 6/150, Dept E1B3, Interoffice Memorandum: Complaint of Workers that Nazis Retained in the Factories, 28.6.45; StadtAN C 29/444, Betriebsvertretung der Strassenbahn-Hauptwerkstätte Muggenhof, Gleisbau und Kraftwagenpark an Oberbürgermeister der Stadt Nürnberg, 22.8.45; StadtAN F 6/152, HQ MG Nuremberg, Weekly Report, 6.–12.10.45; StadtAN C 29/444, Arbeitsgemeinschaft der Betriebsratsvorsitzenden Nürnbergs an den Herrn Oberbürgermeister der Stadt Nürnberg, 12.8.45.

[29] On Law No. 8 See Niethammer, *Mitläuferfabrik*, 240ff.; Woller, *Gesellschaft und Politik*, 245–9.

[30] On the trustee system and its operation see Woller, *Gesellschaft und Politik*, 249–56.

advisers.[31] The principle behind this, according to the military government, was not only to 'put the main burden of denazification upon the Germans (and thus to make them realise a new democratic responsibility)', but also to 'leave a way open, by way of the Boards of Appeal, to those Nazi elements which the community regarded as capable of being re-educated'. In practice, this meant that responsibility for denazification of a key stratum of society which had disproportionately supported and collaborated with the Nazi regime was placed into the hands of a self-regulating community: unsurprisingly, the great majority of appeals were successful. Widespread exemptions were available to those working in essential industries, such as food production and sale;[32] the trustee system was also open to abuse.[33] Overall, Law No. 8 was not a great success.[34]

Of considerably greater significance was the Law for the Liberation from National Socialism and Militarism of March 1946. The Law determined denazification practice in the American zone for the remainder of the occupation period and defined the terms on which the overwhelming majority of former Nazis were reintegrated into society. Legalistic in its formulations, but political in its purpose, it instituted a quasi-judicial process through which local communities could impose strict punishment on radical Nazis while rehabilitating the mass of ordinary party members. While drawing on elements of denazification practice as it had developed over 1945, the new law sought to move away from schematic dismissals on the basis of function or position towards a system whereby each party member was assessed according to his or her behaviour during the Nazi era.

Every adult was obliged to fill in a questionnaire, detailing membership of Nazi organisations, their employment and income. All were subject to a preliminary assessment. Those deemed to be affected by the law were barred from all but menial labour pending their appearance before a tribunal. Officials allocated them into one of five categories: Main Guilty Party, Guilty/Incriminated, Moderately Guilty/Incriminated, Fellow Traveller, Not Incriminated. These assessments formed the basis for the tribunal hearings, usually conducted by local representatives of the main political parties, appointed by the Ministry for Special Tasks which oversaw denazification; at these, the classification of the defendant was either confirmed or altered and

---

[31] StadtAN F 6/2, OMG Kreis Nürnberg, Regierungsbezirk Oberfranken und Mittelfranken: Monthly Historical Report from 1.–31.10.45
[32] StadtAN C 29/424, Monatsbericht des Oberbürgermeisters der Stadt Nürnberg für die Zeit vom 20 Oktober bis 19 November 1945.
[33] See, for example, StadtAN F 6/163, ICD Intelligence Section, Political Affairs Report, 3.5.46.
[34] For similar assessments see Niethammer, *Mitläuferfabrik*, 245; Woller, *Gesellschaft und Politik*, 249.

the relevant punishment dispensed. For those classified in the first two categories – this turned out to be a tiny minority – the penalties included imprisonment, forced labour, confiscation of assets and the surrender of civil rights; for those deemed to be Fellow Travellers – the great majority – the punishment consisted merely of a token fine: thereafter the defendant was permitted to return to civil society, his or her political rehabilitation complete. For the majority, therefore, the period of punishment was actually that prior to the tribunal; it was not the tribunal but the waiting for it that constituted the disadvantage.

The immediate consequence of the Liberation Law was to generate an enormous amount of paperwork. The city authorities were responsible for collecting approximately 280,000 questionnaires, each of which had to be assessed before the tribunal process could begin. This process alone took three or four months.[35] Around 60,000 cases fell under the law and went forward for consideration by the tribunals.[36] At the same time, the city authorities were bombarded with a new wave of letters and requests from affected individuals for prioritised treatment, which threatened to overwhelm the offices concerned.[37] The first tribunal, which consisted of one representative each of the city council, the SPD, CSU, KPD and DDP (German Democratic Party), together with two trade union members, was not sworn in until June; at least two of the five tribunals did not begin their activities until August.[38] By the time officials had collected and sorted the late returns – some 30,000 citizens had sent in their questionnaires late, clearly sensing the merits of delay in a climate which was becoming less and less enthusiastic about the whole idea – the law had been passed for nearly half a year.

From the outset, there were accusations of unfairness. In order to facilitate the re-establishment of the city's justice and education system, the tribunals prioritised the denazification of unspectacular cases of judges and teachers who had been party members. The city council's emphasis on re-establishing such institutions rather than fostering fair process resonated through its complaint that the first two tribunals had denazified 'a considerable number of housewives and other unimportant persons' before the first teacher had been processed.[39] The arbitrariness of such criteria meant that the accident of

[35] StadtAN C 29/425, Monatsbericht des Oberbürgermeisters der Stadt Nürnberg für die Zeit vom 19 April 1946 bis 20 Mai 1946; Monatsbericht des Oberbürgermeisters der Stadt Nürnberg für die Zeit vom 20 Mai 1946 bis 19 Juni 1946; C 29/426, Monatsbericht des Oberbürgermeisters der Stadt Nürnberg für die Zeit vom 20 Juni 1946 bis 19 Juli 1946.
[36] For figures see StadtAN F 6/79, Weekly Intelligence Report, 18.–25.9.47.
[37] StadtAN C 29/425, Monatsbericht des Oberbürgermeisters der Stadt Nürnberg für die Zeit vom 20 Mai 1946 bis 19 Juni 1946.
[38] StadtAN C 29/426, Monatsbericht des Stadtrats zu Nürnberg für die Zeit vom 20 Juli 1946 bis 19 August 1946.
[39] StadtAN C 29/426, Monatsbericht des Stadtrats zu Nürnberg für die Zeit vom 20 August 1946 bis 19 September 1946.

occupation, rather than an individual's degree of guilt, partly determined who was processed quickly and who was made to wait; as a result, some were able to return to work relatively swiftly, while others faced continued restriction of employment. On the other hand, the fact that the tribunals became more lenient as time went on meant that those processed first felt that they were treated with unfair harshness. In this way, the reputation of the process was further undermined.

There were also accusations of political interference. A military government intelligence report noted that second deputy mayor Geier, who was in charge of denazification, 'is often reputed to have "pulled his weight and rank" in order to help well-known local Nazis whom he pictured as harmless. It is generally said in this city that his voice can be heard in favour of locally well-known personalities with "big money bags" but never in favour of little followers.'[40] Such behaviour fitted the pattern of CSU policy on denazification generally: the same office recorded 'general amazement over the unconcealed courting for former Nazis on the part of this party in order to strengthen and increase its followship [*sic*]. Informants pointed to various instances where CSU agents promised "mild treatment" by CSU members of denazification courts.'[41] Such denunciations were born of a climate in which self-interested parties sought to discredit opponents before the eyes of the military government; their precise truth contents are thus open to question. However, the open intercession of the CSU on behalf of former Nazis who faced the requisitioning of their apartments suggests that the accusations were not entirely unfounded.[42]

The FDP, as a party of the Protestant middle classes, was no less active in pressing for leniency towards former Nazis, which, given that its constituency was precisely that from which Nazism had drawn the core of its support, was unsurprising.[43] Such interventions went hand in hand with attempts to limit the influence of former victims of the Nazi regime, who were represented as 'biased' and thus unsuited to presiding over the fate of former Nazis. The FDP openly acknowledged the link between the marginalisation of former concentration camp inmates and the pursuit of milder treatment of ex-Nazis in its request to the military government that former camp inmates be prevented from sitting on tribunals, arguing that 'a tribunal which consists of a majority of radical former inmates will pass harsher judgements than will be the case with a tribunal consisting of more moderate people'.[44]

---

[40] StadtAN F 6/163, Intelligence Section, Nuremberg, Weekly Political Affairs Report, 20.7.46.
[41] StadtAN F 6/163, Intelligence Section, Nuremberg Detachment, Political Affairs Report, 10.6.46.
[42] StadtAN F 6/163, CSU Nürnberg an Military Government Nürnberg, Wochenbericht, 6.8.46.
[43] Jay Howard Geller, *Jews in Post-Holocaust Germany, 1945–1953* (Cambridge, 2005), 146–52.
[44] StadtAN F 6/163, FDP an Military Government Nürnberg, Wochenbericht, 31.7.46.

It was not just the bourgeois parties, however, who advocated leniency towards the mass of ordinary former Nazi party members: the SPD and KPD did so too. Here, the desire to solicit votes from party members from modest backgrounds interacted with an ideological predisposition to see Nazism as the creation of reactionary elites rather than as an expression of mass desire. Both electoral exigencies and the political imagination of most on the Left thus encouraged the working-class parties to embrace narratives of the Nazi past agreeable to the compromised majority. If, initially, both SPD and KPD placed themselves at the head of the anti-fascist impulses of their working-class constituencies, calling for widescale purges and reform, by 1946 they too were each drawing clear distinctions between 'the real Nazis' and 'the little man'.[45]

To the secular political consensus in favour of rehabilitating the mass of former party members was added the voice of the churches. The Protestant Church, which, as the dominant church in Nuremberg, had a particularly influential voice, positioned itself from the outset as the champion of the former Nazis. Support for its middle-class flock, residual nationalist and authoritarian sentiments – which were at the root of a corresponding moral blindness towards the crimes of the Third Reich on the part of the first generation of post-war church leaders – together with fears of the influence of the Left, underpinned a rhetoric of clemency and forgiveness which betrayed a set of distinctly political concerns.[46] In July 1945 the Protestant dean of Nuremberg, Julius Schieder, wrote to the military government expressing his view that 'in the interests of justice a difference must be made between "party comrades" and "party comrades". '[47] He rehearsed familiar arguments concerning the idealism of party members, the pressures individuals faced and the dangers of driving desperate former party members into the hands of Bolshevism. In doing so, he was part of a broad campaign pursued by the Protestant Church on behalf of those affected which argued constantly for mercy. As with the returning prisoners of war, it argued that whatever sins former Nazis had committed, they were to be judged by God; the human

[45] StadtAN C 29/390, Die Sozialdemokratische Partei in Nürnberg ruft! (undated, 1945/6); on the Communists compare C 29/390, Aufruf der KPD 1945 with F 6/163, Der Neue Weg. Mitteilungsblatt der Kommunistischen Partei, Nürnberg, 28.3.46; see also the responses of prominent local left-wingers to the Christmas Amnesty of 1946: F 6/165, ICD Nuremberg, Bericht/Comments of leading Nuremberg Personalities on current affairs in Bavaria and Germany, 10.1.47.
[46] Clemens Vollnhals, *Evangelische Kirche und Entnazifizierung 1945–1949. Die Last der national-sozialistischen Vergangenheit* (Munich, 1989) remains the standard work on the Protestant Church's response to the Nazi past in the immediate post-war years. See also Greschat, 'Zwischen Aufbruch und Beharrung', 109–10; Michael Renner, *Nachkriegsprotestantismus in Bayern. Untersuchungen zur politischen und sozialen Orientierung der Evangelisch-Lutherischen Kirche Bayerns und ihres Landesbischofs Hans Meiser in den Jahren 1945–1955* (Munich, 1991), 117–47.
[47] LKAN Kd Nbg 139, Schieder an Militärregierung Nürnberg, 11.7.45.

weaknesses which had led many to join the party were regrettable but did not constitute a crime.[48] Moreover, in formulations which revealed both the partiality of the Church's interventions and its ongoing predisposition towards authoritarian values, Schieder argued that church members who had supported the party deserved more, not less sympathy. It was regrettable, he concurred, that Christians had not resisted more, but 'why did Christians not show this open resistance? Because their conscience, as bound by God's word, demanded that they remain *silent*, if they did not have exact knowledge of the misdeeds of the National Socialists; conscience demanded that they did not form judgements on the basis of unsubstantiated rumours.' Similarly, the tribunals should take account of Lutheran traditions of obedience to secular authority, which made resistance harder precisely for his Protestant flock.

The Church played a leading role in pleading on behalf of individual tribunal defendants, and was prominent in the issuing of so-called *Persilscheine* – 'white-washing' references written on behalf of the accused by colleagues, friends or figures of authority which sought to make the case for generous treatment. Widely resented among non-Nazis, who believed that such testimonies were a means by which a climate of excessive leniency was being fostered, and among ordinary ex-Nazis who believed that those with connections had privileged access to such *Persilscheine*, the statements stressed the personal qualities of the defendants over their political proclivities; they stressed the excellent professional or technical skills of their subjects and thus their indispensability to the reconstruction effort; they emphasised unduly those aspects of their behaviour during the Third Reich which might qualify them as resisters – or at least non-Nazis – while glossing over perhaps greater evidence that the person concerned had been a compliant and willing member of the 'People's Community'.[49] In Julius Schieder's case, *Persilscheine* were apparently written for any church member who had supported the Confessing Church over the German Christians, and who had therefore proven their 'anti-Nazi' credentials in the eyes of the Bavarian church leadership, even though commitment to the Confessing Church under Schieder had been perfectly compatible with belief in nationalism, anti-Bolshevism, support for the war and indeed anti-Semitism. In their tendency to write moments of conflict with specific aspects of the regime as acts of fundamental opposition to Nazism, the biographical narratives circulated via the ubiquitous *Persilscheine* thus revealed again how strongly the discourse surrounding denazification prefigured the memory culture of the 1950s.

By the second half of 1946, the growing calls for leniency, and indeed amnesty, were not falling on deaf ears. The American military government,

---

[48] LKAN Kd Nbg 25, Ev.-Luth. Kreisdekan Nürnberg an das Ministerium für Sonderaufgaben, 19.1.47.
[49] Marcuse, *Legacies of Dachau*, 91–2.

whose policies began to betray the preoccupations of the emerging Cold War, slowly moderated its commitment to a firm line against the majority. The harshness of daily life in the post-war years further fostered short memories concerning how widespread support for Nazism had been among a population that the members of which were increasingly inclined to see themselves as victims of the regime. Even before the tribunal system had got under way a Youth Amnesty – by which all those born after 1919 and not placed in categories I and II were pardoned – was announced, in July 1946.[50] In this way, 16,000 out of about 60,000 files were effectively closed little over one year after the end of the war.[51] Then, in December 1946, the Americans announced the Christmas Amnesty, whereby all defendants on modest incomes or with physical disabilities were similarly let off en masse.[52] In this way, nearly 16,000 more people were amnestied in Nuremberg without ever having to appear before a tribunal.[53] Overall, half of former party members in Nuremberg thus benefited from these amnesties.[54]

The implementation of the Christmas Amnesty occupied the energies of the denazification authorities throughout the spring of 1947 – it was not until mid-1947 that the focus returned fully to the remaining incriminated party members. By this point, however, enthusiasm for the process had waned further; disillusionment was great, even among its supporters; the inconsistencies and inadequacies of the system meant that it was widely discredited. The widespread desire to bring the process to a swift conclusion led to procedural revisions which speeded the tribunal judgements up; as a result, many defendants received notice of their classification by writing, and were not obliged to appear in person. An increasingly mechanistic and perfunctory approach was thus adopted at precisely the moment when many of the worst offenders were considered by the system; many who a year or two earlier would have been classified as serious offenders were rehabilitated as 'fellow travellers'.[55]

A few months later, in August 1948, only 1,000 cases remained. Most of these, the local military government confirmed, were heavily incriminated offenders, making it difficult to speed the process up further. In anticipation

---

[50] Niethammer, *Mitläuferfabrik*, 354.

[51] StadtAN F 6/79, Weekly Intelligence Report, 8.–15.4.48.

[52] Niethammer, *Mitläuferfabrik*, 436–41.

[53] StadtAN F 6/79, Weekly Intelligence Report, 8.–15.4.48.

[54] For the welcoming response of the Trade Unions see StadtAN F 6/165, ICD Nuremberg, Bericht/Comments of leading Nuremberg personalities on current affairs in Bavaria and Germany, 10.1.47; for the Protestant Church's comments see LKAN Kd Nbg 25, Ev.-Luth. Kreisdekan Nürnberg an das Ministerium für Sonderaufgaben, 19.1.47. According to Harold Marcuse, amnesties reduced the overall workload of the tribunals by 70 per cent: Marcuse, *Legacies of Dachau*, 92.

[55] For the tendency towards increased leniency see, for example, StadtAN F 6/79, Weekly Intelligence Report (undated, April 1948).

of an imminent end to the denazification process, however, tribunal personnel were given notice of their dismissal from the end of September.[56] The fact that 1,000 difficult cases could be dealt with in a month or so demonstrated in itself how perfunctory the procedure had become, even when committed former Nazis were concerned. While the closure of the tribunals marked the end of the period of official discrimination against former Nazis, for the tribunal employees – who had become increasingly resented and marginalised by broad sections of the public – the ending of denazification forced them out on to the labour market at precisely the point when the currency reform was causing unemployment.

The disillusionment felt by wide sections of the non-Nazi population with the modalities of denazification should not be mistaken for the dissipation of an anti-fascist ethos overall. This still existed, and had powerful mobilising potential, as was demonstrated by the events of January and February 1947, when a series of bombs was thrown into buildings which housed the tribunals or which were otherwise symbolically associated with the denazification process.[57] In response to the first, the trade unions organised a brief general strike; in response to the second a longer strike was organised. At the MAN plant the factory council also responded by demanding the removal of four managers regarded as Nazis, refusing to sanction a return to work until this occurred; despite trade union attempts to mediate, workers at the factory occupied the administrative buildings amid tumultuous scenes, and were persuaded to return to work only once the offending four had been removed.[58] Neither was the reinstatement of former Nazis uncontroversial. As the impact of the currency reform began to bite, such issues became acute. In February 1949, for example, the factory council of the Municipal Insurance Office in Nuremberg wrote to the deputy mayor to complain about plans of the Bavarian Ministry for Work and Social Welfare to enforce the re-employment of former party members. Since the number of positions in the office was fixed by formula, this re-employment would inevitably be at the expense of those who had replaced them. The factory council had been promised by the ministry that only incompetent workers would be dismissed but was not reassured, for it knew that 'if there are too many people for the available posts then incompetent people will be looked for and will be found!'[59]

The occasional traces of such conflict in the late 1940s suggest that while former Nazis had largely been rehabilitated by this point, tensions between

---

[56] StadtAN F 6/79, MG Nürnberg FOD an OMG Bavaria FOD, 30.8.48.
[57] StadtAN C 29/427, Monatsbericht des Stadtrats zu Nürnberg für die Zeit vom 20.1.1947 bis 19.2.1947; C 29/446, Oberbürgermeister Ziegler an Innenminister Seifried, Munich, 26.2.47.
[58] StadtAN C 29/446, Niederschrift über die Ereignisse bei der MAN Werk Nürnberg am 3. u. 4.2.47.
[59] StadtAN F 6/86, Betriebsrat der Allgemeinen Ortskrankenkasse Mittelfranken, Nürnberg, an Bürgermeister Landgraf, Nürnberg, 14.2.49.

them and their non-Nazi antagonists in the workplace and community did not die away overnight. Only as unemployment fell again in the 1950s did such conflicts lose some of their potency; even then, knowledge of who had been a Nazi did not simply evaporate, even if it was rarely voiced. Yet the great majority of former party members were, ultimately, readmitted to the community with relative equanimity. In one sense, their very number offered little alternative: they had to be reintegrated. Beyond this, what facilitated the pragmatic reintegration of most was their willingness to accept defeat and its consequences, and to adapt to the realities of a new democratic system. In this sense, the 'return of yesterday's men' to which concerned commentators pointed in the 1950s was only very inaccurately described as a 'renazification'. Even if this captured polemically the fact that many tainted figures in the economic and functional elites returned to civil society with their reputations undeservedly intact, it did not do justice to the process of democratisation that was under way – a democratisation which was slow and hesitant, but nonetheless there.

That former Nazis accepted defeat and its consequences for the nation did not, however, mean that they acknowledged their personal complicity in the nation's catastrophe. In insisting that they had only been doing their jobs many refused to question the role they had played in the wider machinery of persecution and brutality; in assuring each other that they had remained 'decent' they were attesting only that they had conformed to the shared norms of a society in which it had been deemed acceptable to exclude, isolate and enrich oneself at the expense of outsiders. In a society in which exclusionary rhetoric was regarded not only as tolerable but as normal it was easy to tell oneself and others that one had 'done nothing wrong' as long as one had not actually physically mistreated someone.

There was thus a considerable moral blindness at the heart of popular responses to the denazification process. Above all, rejection of the legitimacy of mass denazification was rooted in the fact that the attempt to confront ordinary party members or supporters with the issue of their own complicity in the crimes of the Third Reich collided fundamentally with the widespread popular desire to believe that Germans themselves had been victims of a regime whose terroristic nature had left them no alternative, and that Nazi exclusion, persecution and murder had been the fault not of the many, but of a few. Even as they were being reintegrated into civil society, ex-Nazis were thus telling themselves that they had been innocent 'victims of denazification'.

I.7

Re-marginalising the Marginalised
The 'Victims of Fascism'

What of the real victims – the victims of political repression, racial persecution and genocidal barbarism? As the post-war cemetery landscapes of the city powerfully attested, many were dead. Nearly 4,000 Soviet prisoners of war and civilian deportees, victims of the murderous wartime programme of forced labour, were buried in the South Cemetery, alongside hundreds of other military and civilian coerced workers from most countries in Europe.[1] Both the West and South cemeteries also held urns containing the ashes of concentration camp victims. In the former, a collective tomb held the remains of 541 victims of Flossenbürg and Hersbruck, whose bodies had been sent to the city for cremation.[2] The South Cemetery held a further 340 such urns. After the war, the city authorities were unable to ascertain the identities of these victims, since 'records of the nationalities of the persons contained in the KZ urn graves are not available', and were forced to deduce the likely nationality of each victim from his or her name.[3]

While a small number of Nuremberg's Jewish community who had fallen victim to the Nazi regime were buried in the city's Jewish cemetery, most of the city's murdered Jews had no graves.[4] At least 2,373 Nuremberg Jews died in the Nazi genocide: the majority of these perished on successive transports from Nuremberg to Riga, Izbica (Lublin) and Theresienstadt in 1941 and

---

[1] Statistical evidence on the graves of foreigners in Nuremberg can be found in StadtAN C 36 I/322, Bericht über die im Südfriedhof bestatteten ausländischen Soldaten und Zivilarbeiter, 6.5.49; StadtAN C 7 I/8045, Aktennotiz: Bestand an Soldaten-, Luftopfer und Ausländer-Gräber bei Bestattungsamt Süd, 23.11.53.
[2] StadtAN C 7 I/8045, Aktennotiz betr. Kriegsgräberfürsorge 1939/1945, hier Friedhöfe der Juden, KZ-Häftlinge und Ausländer (Fremdarbeiter) – Kostentragung, 13.12.46.
[3] StadtAN C 7 I/8045, Stadtrat Nürnberg, Bericht an die Regierung von Mittelfranken, 4.9.53.
[4] On the transfer of the bodies of Nuremberg Jews from Dachau to Nuremberg, see Arnd Müller, *Geschichte der Juden in Nürnberg 1146–1945* (Nuremberg, 1968).

1942.[5] An unknown number of non-Jewish Nuremberg citizens also died in the concentration camps and prisons of the 'Third Reich', having been incarcerated as 'community aliens' – an elastic concept which covered everything from political opponents to homosexuals, priests and the 'workshy', or merely those who had been unlucky enough to voice dissent in the wrong place at the wrong time. Many more survived Nazi persecution only by going into exile.

Of those victims of Nazism who survived to witness the end of the war in Nuremberg itself, by far the largest group comprised foreign forced workers, now categorised by the occupation forces and relief agencies as 'Displaced Persons', or DPs.[6] At the point of liberation, there were between 30,000 and 40,000 DPs in Nuremberg. The declining food situation in the final months of the Nazi regime, and the increasingly chaotic circumstances of the last few weeks of the war, had compounded the already dreadful suffering of people who had, in some cases, endured years of malnourishment, exploitation and terror. Many were in an appalling state of health. They had been living in squalid, sometimes inhumane, conditions. When the American occupiers moved to install newly arrived refugees in the barracks hitherto lived in by Russian forced workers, they found them to be in an 'undignified state. There was vermin, faeces and knee-deep rubbish; windows and all items of furniture were missing.'[7] The DPs became the focus of an immediate relief effort: all were repeatedly dusted with DDT to combat the spread of infection;[8] those in urgent need of medical attention were hospitalised;[9] the local German authorities were ordered to provide essential clothing, blankets and footwear from existing civilian stocks with the proviso that the DPs were to have priority where supplies were inadequate – which, in 1945, they always were.[10]

Summarising the situation in August 1945, by which time the great majority of DPs had already been repatriated, the occupation authorities observed that 'the 20 nationalities have been obliged to live together in a crowded camp, eat the same food and undergo the same lack of privacy, absence of essential sanitary facilities and severely curtailed freedom, but with a considerable increase in the number of wild rumours expected to be found in such a group. In spite of these handicaps calculated to create further tension

---

[5] Comprehensive details are provided in Gerhard Jochem and Ulrike Kettner (eds), *Gedenkbuch für die Nürnberger Opfer der Schoa* (2 vols, Nuremberg, 1998–2002).

[6] The standard overview of the history of forced labour during the 'Third Reich' is Ulrich Herbert, *Hitler's Foreign Workers: Enforced Foreign Labor in Germany under the Third Reich* (Cambridge, 1997).

[7] StadtAN C 36 I/322, Aktennotiz betr. Betreuung der Kriegsgefangenen, Flüchtlinge und ehem. Konzentrationslagerhäftlingen (undated, summer 1945).

[8] StadtAN F 6/44, Daily Report, Utilities Section, 24–25.5.45.

[9] StadtAN F 6/151, Semi-Weekly Report, HQ, Det. F1B3, 3.–5.7.45.

[10] StadtAN F 6/28, Supply Status Report, 12.6.45.

among people whose nerves already were frayed, they have lived together with surprisingly little evidence of misunderstanding.'[11] If, however, the initial relief effort had brought a degree of stability and respite to a group of long-suffering people, then – as the comments of the American occupiers indicate – they were not seen by the authorities merely as survivors of brutality waiting patiently for their turn to return home. The 'severely curtailed freedom' to which they were subjected reflected the fact that from the outset the DPs were regarded not simply as victims in need of care, but as a significant problem of law and order.

The state of near-starvation in which many survivors of forced labour found themselves in April and May 1945 was such that many resorted to plundering food and other goods at war's end.[12] Although ordinary German citizens were also involved in such acts, they immediately became associated in both official and popular discourse with the DPs. By mid-1946, the authorities were focusing in particular on Poles, who comprised around half of the remaining DP population at this point. Their offences were apparently 'in many cases of a serious nature, such as looting, robbery, breaking into houses by threatening the inhabitants, unlawful possession of firearms, and murder. Poles were involved with 60 per cent of all cases dealing with illegal possession of weapons . . . If repatriation of Poles had taken place on a larger scale, many problems concerning public safety and security would have been avoided.'[13] It was largely for this reason that DPs were concentrated into two main camps in 1945, where their behaviour and movements could be policed more effectively.[14]

There was a reality outside of these reports in which DPs did engage in plunder, operate on the burgeoning black market, and – no doubt – participate in various low-level criminal acts, of a kind similar to those committed by ordinary Germans faced with little choice if they wished to survive the desperate conditions of the immediate post-war years. Yet in the case of the German civilian authorities in particular, it is clear that whatever links were made between 'foreigners' and 'crime' (or, similarly, 'foreigners' and 'disease') were explained not in terms of the extreme suffering of the DPs prior to their liberation, or of their highly precarious position on the margins of post-war German society, but by drawing on older refrains that constructed outsiders as criminals or bearers of disease by virtue of their national origins or alleged genetic predisposition. It was all the more tempting to reach for such language

---

[11] StadtAN F 6/47, HQ Det F-211, DP Section, Summary of 3 Months' DP work, 10.8.45.

[12] StadtAN F 6/14, HQ Infantry Division, Military Government Section, Public Safety Report, 27.4.45.

[13] StadtAN F 6/2, Annual Historical Report, 21.4.45–20.6.46; on the popular association of DPs, especially Jews, with the black market, see Eva Kolinsky, *After the Holocaust. Jewish Survivors in Germany after 1945* (London, 2004), 200–11.

[14] StadtAN F 6/47, HQ Det F-211, DP Section, Summary of 3 Months' DP work, 10.8.45.

when it served the purpose of removing unwanted foreigners in a situation in which housing was in desperately short supply. In June 1946, for example, the Housing Office wrote to the military government authorities complaining that a Polish couple was occupying a two-bedroomed apartment above a guest-house 'while the family of the owners of the guesthouse have in total only 11m² at their disposal'. Asserting that 'this Polish couple will not allow officials of the housing authorities into the flat' and that 'neither partner works', the Housing Office stated without any apparent evidence that 'we suspect that black-market operations are being carried on there or that stolen goods are being stored' and requested that the Poles in question be transferred to a camp.[15] Similarly, the Housing Office complained to the military government in December 1948 of a house, supposedly inhabited by Poles without the requisite official permis-sion, in which undefined forms of immoral behaviour were allegedly occur-ring. Repeating the familiar accusation that 'they could not prove to have an employment' [*sic*] and thus drawing on older associations of east Europeans and laziness which were the common currency of German ethnic prejudice, it again observed that 'we should be glad if these Polands [*sic*] and the female persons living there could be moved into the camp provided for them. In this case we could obtain about 20 living rooms for people looking for same.'[16] When the military government investigated the allegations it discovered that the occupants were in fact Ukrainians, in possession of all the necessary papers; that they were living in clean and tidy, if basic, quarters; and that 'although the three single girls probably entertain soldier guests from time to time, it is the opinion of the undersigned that the families have behaved as well as any family in Nürnberg today and that the immoral practices are no greater here than in any other similar type of home in Nürnberg.'[17]

The xenophobic neuroses which resonated through these bureaucratic constructions of the 'foreigner' as 'criminal' betrayed both a continuation of the racist mentalities which had underpinned the Nazi regime and a strong sense of powerlessness vis-à-vis groups over whom the local authorities had but recently presided to brutal effect. They were compounded by a more general popular hostility which drew its force from the depth of the distribu-tional crises of the immediate post-war years.[18] When, for example, ration

---

[15] StadtAN F 6/77, Oberbürgermeister der Stadt Nürnberg/Wohnungsamt an Herrn Stadt-kommandant von Nürnberg, 3.6.46.
[16] StadtAN F 6/66, Stadtrat Nürnberg/Hauptwohnungsamt an MG Nürnberg, 24.12.48.
[17] StadtAN F 6/66, Nuremberg FOD to Mr Emerich, MGO Nuremberg, 19.1.49. For a similar example of bureaucratic racism, this time from the regional government, see F 6/5, Regierung Mittelfranken, Wochenbericht für die Zeit vom 24.2 mit 31.3.49.
[18] For comparison see Sybille Steinbacher, ' "... daß ich mit der Totenklage auch die Klage um unsere Stadt verbinde". Die Verbrechen von Dachau in der Wahrnehmung der frühen Nachkriegszeit' in Norbert Frei and Sybille Steinbacher (eds), *Beschweigen und Bekennen. Die deutsche Nachkriegsgesellschaft und der Holocaust* (Göttingen, 2001), 11–33, here 19–20.

cuts began to cause labour unrest and wildcat strikes, the metalworkers' section of the regional trade union held a shop stewards' meeting in January 1948. The American intelligence report recorded the following: 'Mention of DPs by the speaker roused a wave of discontent in the audience because of the special allocations they get. Exclamations were heard to the effect that they should get the same rations as the German population or otherwise leave the country.' At a subsequent meeting between local military authorities and Nuremberg city officials, a union representative voiced fear that 'food shops would be looted if the situation should worsen. Particularly endangered are the store houses in which provisions for DPs are stored.'[19]

If no overtly Nazi ideological residues were apparent in these comments as such, the more diffuse ethnic resentments they expressed nonetheless betrayed the presence of a moral economy among post-war Germans in which DPs had no legitimate prior claim to resources in scarce supply. The relatively few DPs who had not departed Germany shortly after war's end thus found themselves marginalised by the indigenous population, who placed them outside the circle of those whose suffering was mutually acknowledged as creating a right to resources, restitution or, indeed, a basic level of human sympathy. In the shadow of the overarching welfare crisis they merged quietly into the broader, diverse population of foreigners in the city, whose reason for being there the German residents quickly forgot.

Of the German concentration camp survivors who returned to Nuremberg in 1945, meanwhile, the largest group consisted of political opponents of Nazism – Social Democrats and, above all, Communists.[20] The precise number of former political persecutees who returned to Nuremberg after the war is unclear. In June 1945 the Economics Office of the city administration claimed to have processed about 2,800 cases;[21] by October 1946, the city authorities were speaking of approximately 3,500 registered persecutees.[22] Either way, former political victims accounted for somewhere in the region of 1 per cent of the population, and thus similarly constituted a minority constituency in a city overwhelmed by competing claims to both resources and sympathy.

As with the DPs, a simultaneous policy of aid and control characterised the occupation power's initial stance towards political persecutees. In August 1945 the military government ordered that a committee to help 'persons who were held prisoner in German concentration camps for other than criminal

[19] StadtAN F 6/79, Weekly Intelligence Report, 8.–15.1.48.
[20] StadtAN C 29/410, Tagung der Oberbürgermeistern und Landräten des Regierungsbezirks Ober- und Mittelfranken am 13.1.47.
[21] StadtAN C 29/424, Monatsbericht des Oberbürgermeisters der Stadt Nürnberg für Juni 1945.
[22] StadtAN C 29/410, Besprechung des Regierungspräsidenten mit den Oberbürgermeistern und Landräten des Regierungsbezirks Ober- und Mittelfranken am 7.10.46.

reasons' be established under the direct supervision of the mayor. At the same time, 'all other committees and societies other than those permitted by this letter must be immediately dissolved'.[23] This link between welfare and control was openly acknowledged within the military government, an internal report on a more limited forerunner of the committee observing that 'a board has been organised to protect the interests of liberated political prisoners. This is intended to prevent their being discriminated against and to discourage the formation of illegal anti-Nazi groups'.[24] How far this was merely part of the broader process of imposing order on a still chaotic situation, how far it represented nascent Cold War mistrust of a group whom the military government doubtless knew to be disproportionately composed of Communists, and how far it demonstrated awareness that encounters between spontaneously organised political victims and those who had supported the Nazi regime could prove potentially explosive is unclear. However, the military government's insistence in September 1945 that a planned demonstration on the part of concentration camp victims and the 'victims of the Nuremberg Laws' (as Jewish survivors were euphemistically called) be cancelled on the assumption that 'the city police is as yet not strong enough to suppress any counter-demonstrations which may occur' suggests that the latter possibility played at least some role.[25]

In 1946, the city reorganised its welfare provision for the victims into two parallel offices: the 'Help and Advice Centre for Former Political Concentration Camp Inmates' and the almost identical 'Help and Advice Centre for the Victims of the Nuremberg Laws'.[26] Both were supervised by committees that consisted at least in part of former victims; both had a full-time staff and apparatus. The committees were responsible for assessing the welfare needs of individual applicants, and could make one-off grants of small sums; larger sums, or the payment of ongoing financial support, demanded the additional agreement of the mayor.[27] Later, when the initial relief effort had enabled some sort of physical stabilisation for the majority of survivors, and preliminary

[23] StadtAN C 29/336, Abschrift: Aktennotiz, Militärregierung Nürnberg an Oberbürgermeister Nürnberg betr. Ausschuss zur Hilfe für ehemalige Insassen deutscher Konzentrationslager, 3.8.45.
[24] StadtAN F 6/151, Semi-Weekly Report, HQ, Det. F1B3, 29.6.–2.7.45.
[25] StadtAN C 29/160, Niederschrift über die Besprechung bei Herrn Oberst Andrews, 8.9.45.
[26] StadtAN C 29/336, Hilfs- und Beratungsstelle für ehemalige politische KZ-Häftlinge an den Herrn Bürgermeister der Stadt Nürnberg, 16.8.45; Hilfs- und Beratungsstelle für Opfer der Nürnberger Gesetze an den Herrn Bürgermeister der Stadt Nürnberg, 16.8.45. Some material indicates that the Advice Centre for the Jewish victims was in existence as an autonomous organisation considerably earlier: see C 36 I/322, Hilfs- und Beratungsstelle für Opfer der Nürnberger Gesetze an Stadtarchiv Nürnberg, 18.1.46, in which it appears that the centre was created as early as May 1945.
[27] StadtAN C 29/336, Betreuung ehemaliger Konzentrationslager-Häftlinge und aus den Nürnberg Gesetzen Geschädigter, Nürnberg, 13.8.45.

legislation concerning restitution had been adopted in Bavaria, the city's aid offices focused their work more on the administration of pension, restitution and compensation claims.[28]

It was soon clear, however, that the 'Help and Advice Centres' were functioning in a far from ideal way, and were capable of providing only limited support for people, many of whom were in extreme need.[29] Above all, the limited volume of goods made available to help the victims of fascism was insufficient to meet even the most basic needs of individuals who had in many cases returned from years of incarceration.[30] Similar problems existed concerning the provision of housing for persecutees, who might have returned from years of incarceration to find their home reduced to rubble. Although the city housing authorities had the right to confiscate the property of former Nazi party members and allocate the vacant space to the regime's victims – and indeed made use of this right – there were still around 400 political and racial persecutees in need of somewhere adequate to live in August 1946.[31] Indeed, in the chaotic circumstances of the immediate post-war period it was not unknown for the military occupation forces to make use of their powers of requisition to take over houses owned or lived in by the victims of Nazi persecution.[32]

Neither were relations between different groups of political persecutees always harmonious. Far from fostering a sense of shared purpose based on the shared experiences of incarceration, the political and moral legitimacy conferred by internment in the concentration camps became increasingly disputed property between the SPD and KPD. The intelligence reports of the military government noted in August 1947, for example, that 'the controversies between SPD and KPD have been intensified by a leaflet several copies of which recently circulated in a number of Nürnberg factories'.[33] The growing

---

[28] See, for example, StadtAN C 29/428, Monatsbericht des Stadtrats zu Nürnberg für die Zeit vom 20 Oktober bis 19 November 1947; Monatsbericht des Stadtrats zu Nürnberg für die Zeit vom 20 November bis 19 Dezember 1947; Monatsbericht des Stadrats zu Nürnberg für die Zeit vom 20 Januar bis 19 Februar 1948; on the development of compensation legislation in Bavaria and the American zone see Hans-Dieter Kreikamp, 'Zur Entstehung des Entschädigungsgesetzes der amerikanischen Besatzungszone' in Herbst and Goschler, *Wiedergutmachung in der Bundesrepublik* 61–75.

[29] StadtAN C 29/444, Ziegler an den Staatskommissar für die Juden in Bayern, 15.1.46.

[30] StadtAN C 29/410, Besprechung des Regierungspräsidenten mit den Oberbürgermeistern und Landräten des Regierungsbezirks Ober- und Mittelfranken am 7.10.46.

[31] StadtAN C 29/426, Monatsbericht des Oberbürgermeisters der Stadt Nürnberg für die Zeit vom 20 Juni bis 19 Juli 1946; Monatsbericht des Stadtrats zu Nürnberg für die Zeit vom 20 Juli bis 19 August 1946.

[32] StadtAN F 6/123, OMG Bavaria an Direktor, OMG Bavaria, 4.4.46. For an expression of bitterness on the part of survivors see StadtAN C 29/336, Die ehemaligen politischen Gefangenen aus den Konzentrationslagern, Zuchthäusern und Gefängnissen von 1933–1945, die Opfer der Nürnberger Gesetze und deren Betreuung in Nürnberg (undated, 1945/6).

[33] StadtAN F 6/79, Weekly Intelligence Report, 14.–21.8.47.

rift between the SPD and KPD reached its logical conclusion when the SPD banned its members from belonging to the Association of Persecutees of the Nazi Regime (VVN) in the summer of 1948: by now, the VVN was regarded as a Communist-dominated organisation controlled by the eastern German Socialist Unity Party (SED).[34] The prevalence of Communists among the political victims of Nazism ensured that the concentration camp survivors were condemned to growing isolation.

If this rift bore witness to the growing tensions within the Left created by the intensifying Cold War, then responses to the political persecutees from within non-working class circles testified to the fact that many had never seen internment in a concentration camp as conferring any political status or legitimising any moral claims, and, indeed, continued to see former political prisoners in much the same light as they had seen them during the Nazi era itself. For a population which had grown accustomed during the Nazi years to having both politics and crime defined in biological terms, the distinction between political and criminal inmates was clearly sometimes at best ambiguous, particularly in bourgeois circles.[35] In the outlying rural and small town areas of Franconia, the political cultures of which were distinctly more conservative and nationalist-inflected that that of Nuremberg itself, hostility to the former concentration camp inmates was particularly pronounced; those who emerged from the camps to seek office in the new democratic structures were widely regarded as political adventurers who were up to no good.[36] In Nuremberg itself, the concentration camp survivors met with more sympathy in some circles. Many victims had come from within its strong working-class subcultures; at least some evidence exists to suggest that money was collected in support of the political persecutees from within the city community.[37] However, even the political culture of a Social Democrat-dominated industrial city such as Nuremberg was far from immune to hostile rhetoric, and the sympathy victims enjoyed in sections of the working-class milieu should not

[34] For a local statement of the incompatibility of membership in the SPD and the VVN see StadtAN C 29/299, SPD Bezirk Franken, Rundschreiben Nr. 34 (undated, Nov/Dec. 1948); Geller, *Jews in Post-Holocaust Germany*, 154.

[35] On popular support for the concentration camp system during the Nazi era, see Robert Gellately, *Backing Hitler. Consent and Coercion in Nazi Germany* (Oxford, 2001); on elements of continuity into the post-war years, and on the particular isolation of non-political victims, see the excellent overview in Constantin Goschler, 'Nachkriegsdeutschland und die Verfolgten des Nationalsozialismus' in Hans-Erich Volkmann (ed.), *Ende des Dritten Reiches – Ende des Zweiten Weltkrieges. Eine Perspektivische Rückschau* (Munich, 1995), 317–42, here 332.

[36] See, for example, the tenor of the discussion in StadtAN C 29/410, Besprechung des Regierungspräsidenten mit den Oberbürgermeistern und Landräten des Regierungsbezirks Ober- und Mittelfranken am 7.10.46.

[37] StadtAN C 29/336, Die ehemaligen politischen Gefangenen aus den Konzentrationslagern, Zuchthäusern und Gefängnissen von 1933–1945, die Opfer der Nürnberger Gesetze und deren Betreuung in Nürnberg (undated, 1945/6); see also C 29/336, Appeal for the Collection of Money and Objects for the Victims of the Hitler Regime (undated, c. August 1945).

detract from the fact that they were mistrusted elsewhere. According to the military government's intelligence report for April 1946, for example, 'inter-party complaints consist of accusing the KPD of shielding criminal elements in the ranks of KZ victims'.[38]

For their part, both the SPD and KPD responded by emphasising at all times that they were the parties of the politically persecuted, rather than the persecu-tees per se, and laid claim to the legacies of the political resistance only. There was a deeply unfortunate irony here: the more the SPD and KPD emphasised their commitment to political persecutees, the more those Germans who had been incarcerated as 'non-political' prisoners were marginalised. As a result, while the recognition of the political persecutees' suffering within both the KPD and SPD provided some solace for the indifference and hostility with which they were regarded by the wider population, and informed the observa-tion of a commemorative cult of anti-fascism within restricted circles until the early 1950s, the non-political victims of the concentration camps were isolated even more. Bereft of organisational support, social sympathy and sometimes, as in the case of homosexuals, still criminalised, they fell into a black hole of memory from which their voices emerged only decades later.

If the former political persecutees represented only a very small fraction of the total population of the city, the number of Jewish survivors was tiny even in comparison to that. Approximately 40 Jews survived the war in the city as partners in mixed marriages.[39] Others survived because they had been cate-gorised as *Mischlinge* – the offspring of mixed parentage – by the regime, or lived as converts to Christianity who remained Jews in the eyes of the Nazis. The Protestant Church registered the existence of some 300 families of Protestant racial persecutees in North Bavaria after the war, a significant number of whom were in Nuremberg.[40] All had experienced extreme hard-ship, persecution and stress during the Nazi era; those in mixed marriages were saved from deportation only by subterfuge and administrative break-down towards the end of the war.[41]

A second group of Jewish survivors consisted of the tiny minority who had survived deportation. Seventeen of those transported to Riga lived to see the end of the war; 35 returned from Theresienstadt; twenty survived other camps

[38] StadtAN F 6/94, Political Intelligence Report, 27.4.46; Marcuse, *Legacies of Dachau*, 127–57.
[39] Müller, *Geschichte der Juden*, 292.
[40] LKAN DW 1384, Nora Schüller an Pfarrer Majer-Leonhard, 18.10.49 (Bericht über die Lage der evangelischen, ehemals rassisch verfolgten Familien Nordbayerns); see also in the same file 'Aus einem Bericht über meine Arbeit gehalten in der Mitarbeiterzusammenkunft der Nürnberger Stadtmission am 10. Juni 1952' (Nora Schüller). Nora Schüller was charged by the Aid Association of the Protestant Church with the care of Protestant racial victims in northern Bavaria.
[41] Müller, *Geschichte der Juden*, 293.

and deportations.[42] Finally, an untold number of foreign Jews found themselves in or passing through the city in 1945, and others came shortly after, fleeing renewed persecution in eastern Europe. Many foreign Jews returned home, or emigrated, but some of these also eventually settled in Nuremberg.[43]

The Jewish survivors, out of whom a new community gradually emerged, thus constituted a socially and culturally very diverse group in 1945.[44] All, however, were in extreme need; all had to contend not only with their own suffering but with the fact that many of their close family and friends had been murdered.[45] Expropriated, expelled and subjected to years of brutal mistreatment, returning Jews were not only completely reliant on the distribution of aid, they were also the least likely to be able to source help and goods through informal social networks of support. There is little evidence that they enjoyed much sympathy from their fellow citizens.[46] In March 1947 a bomb was even thrown through the window of the local offices of the Bavarian Aid Association for the Victims of the Nuremberg Laws. The military government intelligence report recorded that 'the Nürnberg population unanimously condemns such acts of violence, but it is significant that nevertheless frequently anti-Jewish remarks are overheard when the bombing incident is discussed'.[47]

The military government linked such resentments to the fact that Jewish survivors had been allocated a temporary increase in their meat rations for the Easter period, unlike the rest of the population: a week later, it reported that 'to counteract the ill-will aroused by the extra allocation of 2,500 grams of meat to Jews, the Jewish community unanimously agreed not to avail themselves of this privilege'.[48] Such a response fitted into a policy on the part of the

[42] Ibid., 295.
[43] On Polish Jews in Nuremberg in 1945 see StadtAN F 6/37, Daily DP Office Report, 23.7.45; for Romanian Jewish survivors of Belsen who stayed briefly in the city see F 6/45, Fiscal Section Daily Report, 21.12.45; for reference to east European Jews in the city see Müller, *Geschichte der Juden*, 297.
[44] On the general situation of Jews in Germany in 1945 see Eva Kolinsky, *After the Holocaust*; Geller, *Jews in Post-Holocaust Germany*, 17–39; Michael Brenner, *After the Holocaust. Rebuilding Jewish Lives in Postwar Germany* (Princeton, 1997); Jael Geis, *'Übrig sein – Leben danach'. Juden deutscher Herkunft in der britischen und amerikanischen Besatzungszone Deutschlands 1945–1949* (Berlin, 1999), 157–63.
[45] See, for example, the account of Arno Hamburger, later to become chairman of the local Jewish community, in Michael Brenner, *After the Holocaust*, 117–19.
[46] For post-war attitudes towards Jews see Constantin Goschler, 'The Attitude towards Jews in Bavaria after the Second World War' in *Leo Baeck Institute Yearbook* 36 (1991), 443–58; Frank Stern, *The Whitewashing of the Yellow Badge, Antisemitism and Philosemitism in Postwar Germany* (Oxford, 1992); Kolinsky, *After the Holocaust*, 187–211; Geller, *Jews in Post-Holocaust Germany, passim.*
[47] StadtAN F 6/79, Det B 211 Stadtkreis/Landkreis Nürnberg, Weekly Intelligence Report, 20.–27.3.47.
[48] StadtAN F 6/79, Det B 211 Stadtkreis/Landkreis Nürnberg, Weekly Intelligence Report, 27.3–3.4.47.

Jewish community of keeping as low a profile as possible among the ordinary German population. The Bavarian Aid Association was entitled, for example, to carry out an annual street collection on behalf of the Jewish survivors, but refrained from doing so for the first four years after the war. It first did so only in 1949, and then only out of desperation, 'because our reserves are exhausted, above all due to the currency reform, and it is hardly possible for us to support our circle of people in need adequately despite the limited state subsidies we receive'.[49] Even then, it chose to solicit donations discreetly from other bodies and organisations rather than appeal directly to the public. Such reticence betrayed a clear nervousness about seeking support from a population whose reservoirs of sympathy were regarded as strictly limited.

A second, highly important, focus of aid work and community life was the *Israelitische Kultusgemeinde* (IKG), which was reformed in December 1945.[50] Unlike many Jewish communities in post-war western Germany, which had to form themselves from completely new personnel, the leadership of the IKG in Nuremberg after the war consisted mainly of members of long-standing Nuremberg Jewish families who had been prominent in community life for some years. Under its first post-war chairman, Dr Julius Nürnberger – who had survived the war performing forced labour at one of the Jewish cemeteries in Nuremberg – its focus was on the re-establishment of a rudimentary religious and cultural life, the restitution of property formerly owned by the community or by its individual members, and the ongoing welfare needs of fragile, often elderly, survivors. In order to house the returning survivors of Theresienstadt, the nascent community secured the return of a former Jewish nurses' home, which had been used by the SS during the war. Damaged by bombing, it was repaired to form a Jewish old people's home, caring for around 35 people. By September 1945 the residents had recovered physically to the extent that most were in a 'relatively satisfactory' state of health, but the mayor acknowledged that 'care must be taken to ensure that the consequences of years of undernourishment and mental strain are compensated for to some extent'.[51]

Of particular concern to the IKG was the repair of its two cemeteries, which had been heavily damaged by both the Nazis and the effects of war.[52] The first, in the *Bärenschanzstrasse*, had been established in 1870 and was in use until 1930; in October 1945 a Jewish citizen complained to the military government

[49] StadtAN C 29/454, Bayerisches Hilfswerk für die durch die Nürnberger Gesetze Betroffenen (Munich) an Oberbürgermeister der Stadt Nürnberg, September 1949.

[50] StadtAN C 7 I/9272, Vorstand der Israelitischen Kultusgemeinde Nürnberg an Oberbürgermeister der Stadt Nürnberg, 21.12.45.

[51] StadtAN C 29/424, Monatsbericht des Oberbürgermeisters der Stadt Nürnberg für den Monat September 1945.

[52] On the significance of cemeteries in the re-establishment of Jewish communities after the war, see Geis, '*Übrig sein – Leben danach*', 157–63.

that it was 'totally dilapidated – the fence is broken away, the residents throw rubbish and debris on the graves, the gravestones are stolen and so on'.[53] In the second, established in 1910 and still in use during the Nazi years, many graves had been destroyed or damaged and needed replacing; as with the old cemetery, a large number of bronze epitaph plaques had been removed forcibly by the regime; the buildings in both cemeteries had also been damaged by wartime bombing.[54]

Although the city council made labour available for immediate tidying and repair, it was unable or unwilling to attach priority to extensive restoration work immediately after the war, and drew spurious distinctions between the different forms of damage that had occurred. In 1946, when the IKG requested 50,000 RM to cover the cost of renewing the bronze epitaphs, the city council's Building Committee decided that 'this project will have to be postponed due to shortages of material and labour';[55] when the IKG submitted a repeat request to the effect that 'the city should bear the costs of damage caused by war as well as political damages', the Senior Council insisted that money could be made available 'only to repair damage caused by political actions and not that caused by the war as well', as if a meaningful distinction could be made.[56] In the mid-1950s repairs of Nazi-era damage were still far from complete.[57] Only after 1956, when the Federal government assumed formal responsibility for the care of Jewish cemeteries as an act of material and moral restitution did the necessary change in emphasis occur.[58]

During the 1950s the IKG continued to keep a low profile. Its tiny size – by 1961 the Jewish population had reached only 195 – meant that meaningful social exchange with the majority Christian community did not develop.[59] However, the gradual growth of the Jewish community was such that by the mid-1950s the IKG felt it necessary to approach the city council for help with the building of a larger prayer facility at its *Wielandstrasse* centre. As the

---

[53] StadtAN C 7 I/12188, Aktennotiz Treu, 24.10.45.

[54] StadtAN C 7 I/8045, Oberbürgermeister Bärnreuther an Bayerisches Landesentschädigungsamt, 7.8.52; Oberbürgermeister Bärnreuther an Bayerisches Landesentschädigungsamt, 23.12.54; on the damage to the cemeteries during the Nazi era see also *Juden in Nürnberg. Geschichte der Jüdischen Mitbürger vom Mittelalter bis zur Gegenwart* (Nuremberg, 1993), 60.

[55] StadtAN C 7 IX/1269, Niederschrift über die Sitzung des Bauausschusses, 10.7.46.

[56] StadtAN C 7 IX/1251, Niederschrift über die Sitzung des Ältestenausschusses, 13.12.46; Beschluss des Ältestenausschusses, 13.12.46; on the background, including disputes over who bore responsibility for financing repairs and upkeep, see Andreas Wirsching, 'Jüdische Friedhöfe in Deutschland 1933–1957' in *Vierteljahrshefte für Zeitgeschichte* 50/1 (2002), 1–40, esp. 31ff.

[57] StadtAN C 7 I/8045, Oberbürgermeister Bärnreuther an Bayerisches Landesentschädigungsamt, 7.8.52; Oberbürgermeister Bärnreuther an Bayerisches Landesentschädigungsamt, 23.12.54; Bayerisches Landesentschädigungsamt an Oberbürgermeister Bärnreuther, 7.1.55.

[58] 'Jüdische Friedhöfe betreut', *Nürnberger Nachrichten*, 5.9.56. Technically the responsibility was assumed in 1957 (Wirsching, 'Jüdische Friedhöfe', 39–40).

[59] This figure comes from StadtAN C 85 I Abg. 94/A 48, Oberverwaltungsrat Sebastian an Zeev Falk, Jerusalem, 5.1.68.

Senior Council's discussions demonstrated, the democratically elected city leaders, at least, were aware of the peculiar sensitivities involved. As one – Dr Pirkl – remarked, 'Nuremberg and the Jews is a specific issue. We have a past behind us which is not the nicest, even if the individual Nuremberg citizen can do nothing about it.' Others concurred that the money would have to be found; a subsidy amounting to half the total cost of the new prayer room was granted.[60]

Yet as Pirkl's comment demonstrated, gestures born of moral acknowledgement could – and usually did – occur alongside exculpatory insistence on the innocence of local people for the Jews' suffering. Such apologetic refrains were in equal, indeed in greater evidence in the responses of the city's administrative apparatus to individual Jewish citizens: here, bureaucratic indifference and insensitivity bordering on hostility routinely greeted those who sought compensation and restitution, or merely wanted information from the city authorities which would enable them to make progress with a case being pursued elsewhere.

In 1948, for example, a Jewish family sought restitution of a property they claimed to have sold under duress to a German in 1936, by which time the practice of 'aryanisation' had been fully established.[61] The Nuremberg Higher State Court (*Oberlandesgericht*) refused the claim on the grounds that the sale price gave no reason to suspect that the property had been sold 'due to force and threat', as had to be demonstrated to justify restitution; it also opined that 'neither does the timing of the sale – 30.4.1936 – suggest the role of force or threat, as at that point the practices of November 1938 were not yet usual'.[62] Such responses both drew on and reinforced pervasive fictions concerning the absence of persecution in the early years of the regime, and denied the often insidious nature of the discrimination and terror which had forced many Jews to opt for emigration in the 1930s.

In the same year, the sister-in-law of three members of a Jewish family contacted the mayor on behalf of the inheritors of their apartment and effects. Noting that 'the furniture was auctioned and the resulting sums taken by the city', she wished to register her claim against the local authorities.[63] When the mayor circulated her letter within the city administration, the Residents Office, which registered all arriving and departing citizens, wrote back merely with the disingenuous confirmation that 'according to the records they departed on 24.3.42 to an unknown address'. The Economics Office showed

[60] StadtAN C 7 IX/1379, Niederschrift über die Sitzung des Ältestenrats am 21.10.55; C 7 IX/1378, Niederschrift über die Sitzung des Ältestenrats am 20.1.56.
[61] Avraham Barkai, *Vom Boykott zur 'Entjudung'. Der wirtschaftliche Existenzkampf der Juden im Dritten Reich 1933–1943* (Frankfurt/Main, 1987).
[62] StadtAN F 6/173, Oberlandesgerichtspräsident Nürnberg an Nuremberg Detachment, OMGB, Legal Division, German Courts Branch, 21.8.48.
[63] StadtAN C 7 I/9272, J.M. an Oberbürgermeister der Stadt Nürnberg, 23.11.48.

little more sensitivity, informing only that some such furniture had been given to 'people of modest means' (implying that it had been taken for wholly legitimate purposes), that 'nothing was known in this office of the origins of the furniture' and that much of it had been destroyed during the war. On this basis, the relevant city official repeated to the sister-in-law the points concerning the distribution of the furniture to the needy and the claims of ignorance of its origins, emphasised that the proceeds had been passed on 'in accordance with the regulations' to the finance authorities, and also informed her that much of the furniture had not survived the war. Insisting on the absence of local knowledge concerning the issue, he concluded that 'this is hardly surprising, since the regrettable actions to which your letter refers were all carried out by the Reich authorities, not by offices of the city'.[64] This version of events conveniently sidestepped the central role played by numerous local and regional offices in all aspects of the persecution of the Jews during the Nazi era.[65]

Perhaps the most telling insight into the problems faced by survivors of persecution seeking to rebuild their shattered lives in the city, however, is afforded by an exchange between the father of a so-called *Mischling* and Julius Schieder, the Protestant dean of Nuremberg, eighteen months after the war. The father – a Protestant married to a Jew – recounted how in 1938 his priest in the parish of St Jobst, a pastor Beck, had refused further confirmation lessons to his daughter on the grounds that she was a *Mischling*, that he was experiencing problems with this, and that the other children refused to have her in the class. In the course of his discussions with the priest the father gained the impression that 'due to his National Socialist attitudes he could not or would not give me any advice'. The father continued: 'Today I wanted to attend the service in St Jobst with my daughter and we found to our horror that Herr Beck was the presiding priest. The service was spoiled for us.' While he accepted that the priest may have been denazified in the meantime, he argued that it was unnecessary for him 'to be preaching the word of God today at the same place and on the same spot where he previously engaged himself in word and deed for National Socialism'.[66]

Schieder's reply assured the father that the priest had been retired and had merely been standing in for the regular pastor who had been ill.[67] The case, however, was highly indicative of a much broader phenomenon, which manifested itself in countless small encounters in everyday life in the workplace, the

[64] StadtAN C 7 I/9272, Stadt Nürnberg/Thieme an J.M., 15.12.48.
[65] For an additional example of bureaucratic indifference and absent moral reflex – this time concerning attempts to locate the graves of Jewish former residents – see StadtAN C 7 I/8015, Israelitische Kultusgemeinde an Stadtrat Nürnberg, 17.1.55; Stadtrat Nürnberg an Vorstand der Israelitischen Kultusgemeinde, 17.1.55.
[66] LKAN Kd Nbg 273, E.D. an Oberkirchenrat Julius Schieder, 15.12.46.
[67] LKAN Kd Nbg 273, Oberkirchenrat Schieder an E.D., 20.12.46.

guesthouse or the street in the post-war years – encounters between a small minority of victims and fellow citizens who, in their equally countless small daily acts, had sustained the machinery and climate of oppression and persecution and who now seemed, on the surface at least, to have re-established a degree of normality and stability in their lives which the victims would take years to attain.

The victims of Nazism thus underwent a threefold process of marginalisation in the post-war years. Most of the victims of Nazi persecution in Nuremberg, as in the Third Reich as a whole, were foreign. After the war, the prompt departure of the majority of survivors amounted to a spatial marginalisation which was only compounded by the onset of the Cold War. The same Cold War climate also contributed to the political marginalisation of most German survivors: in the viciously anti-Communist climate of the post-war years concentration camp survivors were increasingly regarded as subversives, not victims. Finally, Jewish survivors endured renewed isolation in a society which made little effort in the immediate post-war years to engage with the remnants of a community which had been all but destroyed. Ignorance, indifference, mistrust and hostility greeted those who embodied an unwanted mirror to the shame which German society had brought upon itself.

I.8

Politics, Ideology, Sympathy, Empathy
Voicing Suffering in the Post-War Era

What kind of a memory culture would emerge in this shattered, divided, disorientated city? What forces – ideological, political, social, psychological, emotional – would shape the ways in which stories of the past would be told? What means existed to enable a population which had suffered in unprecedented ways to make sense of their past experiences, their present situation and the connections between the two? How might positive meanings be fashioned out of these many diverse experiences of aggression, violence, destruction, suffering and sorrow? What vocabularies were available, and who or what would determine the uses to which they were put?

The next section of this book examines in detail the evolution of the memory culture of the 1950s and its operations. Taking four key manifestations of civic memory politics – the activities of war-related victims' associations, the creation of war memorials, the development of ritual commemorative practices and the negotiation of the awkward legacies of the past in the permanent and temporary exhibitions of the Germanic National Museum – it seeks to discern common elements of a dominant discourse on the past across these different fields of action and speech while remaining cognisant of the distinctions and differences which remained. Examining memory formation against the background of post-war social conflict and integration it shows how the fostering of consensus in the field of memory politics was central to the reconstitution of a democratic polity out of the wreckage of Nazism after 1945. Conversely, in stressing the limits of that process of integration and the ongoing presence of memory disputes and conflicts it emphasises that a key function of the nebulous 'victim' consensus was to gloss over the existence of significant material and political fissures in a society that remained far from harmonious. It was precisely the fragility of the memory consensus of the 1950s that made it so open to sustained challenge from the late 1950s onwards.

Before examining the operations of this memory culture and its manifestation in successive formal, official or institutional memory acts, however, it is important to recognise that it sat on top of, and was embedded in, a post-war society in which the experiences of the past were narrated much more widely – in public, in private, and in the many indeterminate places, encounters and utterances on the boundaries between the two. This final chapter of the first section examines how the everyday speech and actions of local parties, agencies, institutions and people echoed with memories which were inflected with politics and ideology: according to context or purpose, narrative accounts of the Nazi past could either embody partisan political postures or resonate with the wider ideological conflict of the Cold War. At the same time, it underlines that such speech acts, even those enunciated by party-political figures, were also meaningful both to their speakers and their audiences on a more visceral, emotional level: the politics of the past were partly so powerful, indeed, precisely because they were so emotive.

In examining occasions when speakers misjudged their audiences when talking about the past, provoking anger and hostility in doing so, it emphasises that for narratives to become part of the shared understanding of a community they had to chime with the sentiments of the speaker's audience (that is, in the case of the civic memory culture, ultimately the population as a whole). Similarly, for a civic dignitary's speech to gain purchase among both his literal and his figurative extended audience, the experiences of suffering to which he alluded had to coincide with the communities of sentiment and empathy present among those to whom (and for whom) he spoke. Conversely, it suggests that the sense of imagined community invoked in formal speech acts by civic dignitaries reflected the affective bonds of those who saw themselves as having endured a shared experience of suffering, and that the narratives projected on such occasions figured as more than mere fictional representations – rather, they gained meaning within the memory culture because they reflected more widely held understandings of past experience present in the community. The memory culture of the city was so powerful, in other words, because it did more than rehearse convenient fictions in a politically expedient language; rather, it connected with, and helped to make sense of, wartime experiences as remembered by the population.

The nascent institutional structures of post-war western Germany, fixed in their essential outlines by the creation of the Federal Republic in 1949, provided a framework within which memory could be preserved, fostered, challenged or silenced as a conscious political act.[1] The consolidation of

---

[1] On the Bavarian political context within which Nuremberg's memory culture unfolded after 1945, see Edgar Wolfrum, 'Geschichtspolitik in Bayern. Traditionsvermittlung, Vergangenheitsbearbeitung und populäres Geschichtsbewußtsein nach 1945' in Thomas Schlemmer and Hans Woller (eds), *Politik und Kultur im föderativen Staat 1949 bis 1973* (Munich, 2004), 349–410.

Chancellor Adenauer's power at Federal level and the gradual emergence of the CSU as the dominant force at Bavarian state level were key in shaping which kinds of public memory would be actively promoted, even if liberal and Social Democratic voices offered constant alternatives; the return of senior figures to leading positions in conservatively inclined professions and institutions in the aftermath of denazification also placed strong limits on the possibilities of a critical memory culture, even if their dominance was never complete.[2]

That this conservative control of the regional state apparatus translated into mechanisms of repression which were not psychological but determinedly political is suggested by the circular sent down from the Bavarian Ministry of the Interior to district and local government officials, and evidently circulated as far down as local cemetery offices, concerning a proposed brochure on concentration camp graves. The Bavarian state authorities had been approached by a woman allegedly acting on behalf of the State Compensation Office (*Landesentschädigungsamt*) – one of the few institutions in which victims of Nazism had meaningful presence – which apparently intended to produce a brochure not only documenting the presence of concentration camp graves in Bavaria but also 'the behaviour of the population towards the prisoners'. Both the district government of Lower Bavaria and the Bavarian Ministry of the Interior had expressed their opposition to the idea; the Bavarian Ministry of Finance, whose views were also relayed, was of the opinion that 'it could be detrimental to German interests if the distressing events of those times are constantly presented to the outside world'. For these reasons the Finance Ministry had asked that the contract be cancelled; the Ministry of the Interior also ordered that local officials 'make no contribution to the planned brochure on concentration camp graves in Bavaria'.[3]

Such political repression was strongly shaped by the emerging Cold War climate of the 1950s and the cultures of anti-Communism to which this gave rise.[4] This manifested itself most obviously in the hounding and subsequent banning of numerous groups deemed to be front organisations of the KPD or otherwise engaged in unconstitutional extreme left-wing behaviour. In 1951, for example, the Bavarian Ministry of the Interior elected to adopt the decision of the Federal Interior Ministry to blacklist all companies which were suspected of supporting or dealing with 'organisations hostile to the constitution', including

---

[2] Detlef Garbe, 'Äußerliche Abkehr. Erinnerungsverweigerung und "Vergangenheitsbewältigung": Der Umgang mit dem Nationalsozialismus in der frühen Bundesrepublik' in Schildt and Sywottek, *Modernisierung im Wiederaufbau*, 693–716, esp. 700–1; on the significance of personnel continuities for the development of memory politics see Loth and Rusinek, *Verwandlungspolitik.*
[3] StadtAN C 7 I/12189, Bayerisches Staatsministerium des Innern an Regierung von Niederbayern, Regensburg, 27.6.51.
[4] On anti-Communism see Patrick Major, *The Death of the KPD. Communism and Anti-Communism in West Germany, 1945–1956* (Oxford, 1997).

the KPD 'and all its suborganisations', Social Democratic Action, the Free German Youth, the Society for German-Soviet Friendship, the Democratic Women's League and several other groups, including right-wing extremists too.[5]

This persecution manifested itself directly at the local level where, by the 1950s, police harassment of Communist activities was widespread.[6] In October 1950 a planned 100,000-strong demonstration of the Free German Youth in Nuremberg was banned by the Bavarian Ministry of the Interior; a surrogate demonstration in neighbouring Fürth was met with police suppression.[7] Meanwhile, in August 1952, Nuremberg police president Leo Stahl wrote to a local female activist proscribing a meeting of the Democratic Women's League of Germany on the grounds that 'despite its apparently unpolitical character in reality it serves political propaganda purposes which are opposed to the principles of the Federal Republic'. The distribution of posters and leaflets was forbidden, while 'any substitute meeting may be prevented by police means'.[8] Neither was the suppression of the activities of the Democratic Women's League confined to the deskbound issuing of bans. In an incident which tellingly suggested the presence of a memory of bereavement that was at least partially gendered, and a corresponding impetus towards female peace activism in the post-war era, Nuremberg mothers had apparently demonstrated against the sale of war toys at the 1950 Nuremberg toy fair. According to the Democratic Women's League's version of events, the Nuremberg police had 'physically attacked the women who were carrying placards and, despite their resistance, had ripped the cardboard posters in pieces from their bodies'; for their part, the police had 'claimed in some cases to be acting "on higher orders" '.[9]

The memory culture that was to emerge in the post-war city thus evolved in a context in which power was distributed unevenly and in which state agency was used to suppress awkward, critical voices. Nonetheless, in a nascent democracy it was no longer possible for one guardian of memory – the state – to silence violently those who wished to challenge its preferred

---

[5] StadtAN C 29/330, Bayerisches Staatsministerium des Innern an die dem Staatsministerium des Innern unmittelbar unterstellten Behörden und Stellen, 24.4.51.

[6] On the state persecution of Communists see Alexander von Brünneck, *Politische Justiz gegen Kommunisten in der Bundesrepublik Deutschland 1949–1968* (Frankfurt/Main, 1978), esp. 52–70; Rolf Gössner, *Die vergessenen Justizopfer des kalten Krieges. Über den unterschiedlichen Umgang mit der deutschen Geschichte in Ost und West* (Hamburg, 1994).

[7] StadtAN C 29/430, Monatsbericht der Stadt Nürnberg für die Zeit vom 1 bis 31 Oktober 1950.

[8] StadtAN C 29/312, Polizeipräsident Stahl an Frau A., Nürnberg, 28.8.52.

[9] StadtAN C 29/454, Demokratischer Frauenbund Deutschlands/Gruppe Nürnberg an Otto Ziebill, 16.5.50; for comparable developments in Munich see Anna Giebel, 'Trauer und Erinnerung in München 1945–1955', MA Dissertation, Ludwig-Maximilians-Universität Munich, 2006, 80–3; on female peace activism after 1945 see Irene Stoehr, 'Kriegsbewältigung und Wiederaufbaugemeinschaft. Friedensorientierte Frauenpolitik im Nachkriegsdeutschland, 1945–1952' in Karen Hagemann and Stefanie Schüler-Springorum (eds), *Heimat-Front. Militär und Geschlechterverhältnisse im Zeitalter der Weltkriege* (Frankfurt/Main, 2002), 326–44.

narratives of the past. Indeed, the diversity of ideologically inflected narratives which emerged after 1945 reflected the diversity of the party-political spectrum in post-war Nuremberg.[10] More generally, the competition between different voices reflected the workings of a civil society comprised of many social and institutional forces. The restabilisation of capitalist property relations was accompanied by the projection of accounts of the Third Reich which cast business as its victim and were silent on local companies' close involvement in the racial barbarism of the Nazi regime;[11] the return of compromised elites to the bureaucracy fostered stories in which the complicity of local and regional administrative organs in the crimes of Nazism was glossed over;[12] the resurgent influence of the churches demanded the circulation of histories which cast Christianity as the victim of godless atheism.[13] The Protestant Church, in particular, drew on its history of institutional conflict with the regime as a result of the activities of the Confessing Church to claim that it had been in fundamental resistance to the Third Reich, glossing over the substantial areas of ideological affinity – anti-Communism, anti-Socialism and, indeed, anti-Semitism – which had made its relationship to Nazism somewhat more problematic in retrospect than its own accounts would allow.[14]

The KPD, whose strong local base prior to 1933 had been weakened but not entirely destroyed by Nazi terror, experienced a brief but substantial resurgence in the immediate aftermath of war. The effects of political repression, Stalinisation and self-marginalisation were compounded both by the impact of working-class commitment to political unity, which favoured the SPD, and by social changes which made the party's collectivist politics appear increasingly anachronistic by the mid-1950s. However, prior to this the KPD represented an important voice in local politics, advancing a narrative of Nazism, terror and war which placed blame on the crises of capitalism, on divisions in the working-class movement and on reactionary elites whose material interests it saw Nazism as having served. Its political programme, informed by this

[10] On party-political constructions of the recent past in the immediate post-war period in western Germany see Eike Wolgast, *Die Wahrnehmung des Dritten Reiches in der unmittelbaren Nachkriegszeit (1945/6)* (Heidelberg, 2001), 112–67.

[11] For local examples of the erasure of business complicity in the crimes of the Third Reich see Karl Seiler (ed.), *Nürnberger Wirtschaftsleben 1950. 900 Jahre Nürnberger Wirtschaft 1050–1950* (no place, 1950); Walter Gerlach (ed.), *Das Buch mit alten Firmen der Stadt Nürnberg im Jahre 1959* (Prien am Chiemsee, 1959); more generally S. Jonathan Wiesen, *West German Industry and the Challenge of the Nazi Past, 1945–1955* (Chapel Hill, 2001).

[12] See, for example, StadtAN F 6/49, Memorandum on Removal of Administrative and Teaching Personnel/J.Raab, Superintendent of City Schools, 19.7.45.

[13] For early iterations of this narrative see LKAN Kd Nbg 32, Übersicht über den Kirchenkampf, 17.5.45; Kd Nbg 147, 'Was war die "Bekennende Kirche" oder "Bekenntnisfront" in den Jahren 1934–1945', 10.12.46; also Martin Greschat, 'Zwischen Aufbruch und Beharrung', 110–11; Wolgast, *Wahrnehmung*, 179–284.

[14] Greschat, 'Zwischen Aufbruch und Beharrung', 104; 106.

ideologically coloured memory of the Third Reich, called for widespread nationalisation of industry and agriculture, working-class unity and an end to 'Prussian militarism'.[15] In doing so it was drawing not only on hostility within organised working-class circles to cultures of authoritarianism and imperialism, but also on a strong tendency in the region to construct Nazism as having come from northern Germany.

At the other end of the spectrum, various formations of the far Right voiced a narrative which actively denied or radically downplayed the fact of Nazi genocide and was silent on the fate of the regime's victims.[16] The Christian Social Union, meanwhile, which emerged from the fluid milieu of post-war non-Nazi bourgeois politics to become the main mouthpiece of the moderate Right, lost no time in mocking the claims of the Left that they were the inheritors of the moral mantle of resistance, and appealed to the feelings of those who resented opponents of Nazism who had fled or chosen to go into exile.[17] Speaking at a CSU rally in March 1947, for example, the leading CSU politician Dr Josef Müller emphasised the credentials afforded to him on account of his having been held by the Gestapo while stressing that 'the German people should reflect on the men ... who were able to flee in time and on those who had to withstand all the pressures of the 12 years ... those who stayed in Germany comprised a community of fate and we are not ashamed of this'.[18] The observer of the meeting recorded repeated applause for this reworking of the history of the Third Reich, a reworking in which the Nazis' own propaganda rhetoric was appropriated in the service of myths of bourgeois resistance to a regime which most from that milieu had, in fact, avidly supported. Such narratives sat perfectly with the CSU's coalescence into a party of anti-Communist integration and Christian conservatism.[19]

Of greatest significance in terms of party-political constructions of the past was the stance of the Social Democratic party. The party had been the dominant force in the local politics of what was a highly industrialised city with a large working-class population since the late nineteenth century. Its local elder

[15] See, for example, StadtAN C 29/390, Aufruf der KPD 1945; C 29/445, Kommunistische Partei Deutschlands, Bezirksleitung Nordbayern an den Oberbürgermeister der Stadt Nürnberg, 27.12.45.
[16] See, for example, the comments attributed to the local leader of the far right-wing Deutsche Block, August Hacker, in StadtAN F 6/97, Bi-Weekly Report of Civil Administration Team no. 3 for Regierungsbezirk Ober- und Mittelfranken, 3.–13.5.49.
[17] On the CSU's attitudes towards anti-Semitism and the Holocaust see Geller, *Jews in Post-Holocaust Germany*, 143–6.
[18] StadtAN F 6/164, Bericht über CSU/Kundgebung Dr Josef Müller am 22.3.47, 24.3.47.
[19] See also Thomas Schlemmer, 'Grenzen der Integration. Die CSU und der Umgang mit der nationalsozialistischen Vergangenheit – Der Fall Dr Max Frauendorfer' in *Vierteljahrshefte für Zeitgeschichte* 48/4 (2000), 675–742; on conservative interpretations more generally see Jean Solchany, 'Vom Antimodernismus zum Antitotalitarismus. Konservative Interpretationen des Nationalsozialismus in Deutschland 1945–1949' in *Vierteljahrshefte für Zeitgeschichte* 44/3 (1996), 373–94.

statesman, left-wing trade unionist Josef Simon, lost little time in informing the American military occupiers that 'if all wards would have voted like Nuremberg or Franken, where the Social Democrats were leading against the Nazis, Hitler would never have got into power'.[20] In its first programmatic statements after the war it could similarly claim that locally the electorate of the SPD had been the main bulwark of anti-fascist support, its vote having been the only one apart from that of the Nazis to rise strongly from November 1932 to March 1933.[21] In implying the relative softness of the vote of its main rival – the KPD – such claims denied the impact of the Nazis' massive terror campaign on the Communists in the wake of the Reichstag fire. However, there was some merit in the SPD's self-image as the locus of mainstream opposition to Nazism prior to 1933; in insisting immediately after the war that 'Social Democracy needs to change neither its name nor its programme', it powerfully asserted the claim to renewed political hegemony of a city whose political culture it had profoundly shaped.

Competing claims to martyrdom, victimhood and leadership of the working class notwithstanding, the similarities between the Social Democrats' construction of the Nazi past in the early post-war years and that of the KPD were greater than the differences. Both represented Nazism as the creation of reactionary elites, privileged critiques of imperialism over denunciations of genocide in their accounts of Nazi barbarism, and emphasised the lead role played by the working class in resistance to the regime; both drew their anti-fascist credentials and claims to post-war moral authority from histories of brutal persecution. There was much more to the Social Democrats' accounts, however, and indeed to those of some of their bourgeois opponents, than merely present-centred myths legitimating contemporary political positions.[22] The past was, rather, the repository of experiences which had been in turn horrific, confusing, disorientating and shameful, and for which the population now sought some kind of meaning. When the first post-war generation of Social Democratic mayors mobilised images of concentration camp martyrs in their peace rhetoric, they were not simply the mouthpieces for a wider set of political myths which were being spoken through them: as often as not they were drawing on painful experiences etched on to their own bodies in the concentration camps in which they themselves had been interned. Julius Lossmann, for example, Social Democratic deputy mayor in the 1950s, had been interned in Dachau from 1933 to 1944.[23]

---

[20] StadtAN F 6/29, Josef Simon an MG Nuremberg, 7.9.45.
[21] StadtAN C 29/390, Die Sozialdemokratische Partei in Nürnberg ruft! (undated, 1945/6).
[22] Alon Confino, 'Collective Memory and Cultural History', 1386.
[23] Walter Bauer and Elke Mahlert, *Kennen Sie das andere Nürnberg? Eine antifaschistischer Stadtführer* (Nuremberg, 1994), 59. Likewise Franz Haas, deputy mayor in the 1960s, had been held in Dachau ('Er genießt Achtung und Ansehen', *Nürnberger Nachrichten*, 16.1.64).

Conversely, in enunciating narratives of the past to a wider public, local civic leaders, both secular and religious, did not have free rein. The mayor speaking at a commemorative ceremony, the parish priest seeking to give solace to his bereaved flock, the politician trying to garner votes – all had to offer meaningful accounts of the experience of war, chaos and collapse which connected with the knowledge of those who had delegated them to speak or invested their words with authority. While all manner of political and ideological scripts resonated through the multitude of representations of the past that circulated through post-war society, only some narratives gained purchase with the population, or wide sections of it. Others did not. Only those that did acquired valency within the city's memory culture, taking on meanings in the community which made them part of the city's shared cultural knowledge, and helping to shape civic identity among the population: the others remained insignificant fictions.

Of what social attitudes were civic leaders most acutely aware, and which popular sentiments did they ignore – or resist – at their peril? Responses to the shock of war, defeat and post-war hardship were diverse, reflecting both the diversity of war experiences themselves and the various perspectives of those seeking to make sense of them. However, some refrains surface with sufficient regularity in the surviving written record for one to be able to suggest that they constituted, if only on a very general level, a form of shared currency in the post-war years, circulated, exchanged and accepted amongst civilians as legitimate and valid responses to both past and present.

The crisis years were informed by a widespread insistence that the situation of misery in which ordinary Germans found themselves was the fault of anybody but the German people. In January 1949, for example, the military government and the county prefect of the outlying Nuremberg rural district organised a meeting for local women to air their grievances. In the words of the subsequent military government report, the significant moment in the meeting came when 'the county prefect asked the simple question whether the people understood why Germany was in such a miserable condition'. According to the observer, 'several people shouted "black market" '. When the county prefect responded that responsibility lay not with black-market operators but with the Nazis, who had prepared, fought and lost a great war, and then suggested that 'Germany cannot help but be poor and unfortunately we must suffer', the audience reacted badly. There was, in the words of the report, 'not a single "yes", but on the other hand a definite feeling of antagonism'.[24] Such anecdotal evidence was confirmed by more general observations by the Americans, who a year earlier had concluded that 'voices blaming military government for being partly responsible for the deterioration in food situation [*sic*] are steadily

[24] StadtAN F 6/85, Special Report on Women's Meeting at Leinburg, 21.1.49.

increasing. Many people in the street express the opinion that German export is purposely kept at a very low level' and that 'proceeds for a normal export [*sic*] could easily balance the necessary food imports'.[25]

Such a climate of resentment made it all too easy to slip into relativising comparisons of the current experience of ordinary Germans and the suffering endured by others during the Nazi era. In a protest demonstration against hunger attended by an estimated 30,000 people in January 1948, for example, one KPD representative was recorded as having said 'we have been blamed for not protesting against crimes against humanity committed in Germany. Now again crimes against humanity are committed and we shall not be blamed a second time for having been silent.'[26] From here it was but a small step to relativising acts of aggression and barbarism during the war itself in a manner which suggested limited desire or ability to comprehend the enormity of the crimes committed under Nazi rule. In one meeting, held as part of the Americans' re-education programmes, a group of listeners responded to a speaker who opined that the Germans were guilty of 'a certain kind of arrogance' with regard to 'the happenings of the past' by being 'most outspoken. They attempted to make comparative analysis of atrocities, for example air raids by the allies, the inadequate feeding and housing of the Germans at the present time.'[27]

Resentment over the difficult food supply was one element of a wider anti-Americanism which functioned as a form of ersatz nationalism during the occupation era. The political and emotional charge of this sentiment drew on reservoirs of hostility which were often diffuse. Its strong anchoring within sections of the working class as well as middle class suggests that widespread bitterness over the current situation was fostering a renewed articulation of a populist anti-capitalism in which America functioned as a convenient signifier of exploitation and inequality as much as of national humiliation. But while outbursts of anti-American invective during the occupation years were, for the most part, not to be understood simply as a continuation of the quite differently inflected radical nationalism of the previous years, there was also often more to such outbursts than ill-focused protest over hunger and hardship. Indeed, some expressions of nationalist sentiment suggested that the effects and attractions of the radical mobilisation of the immediate previous period had not vanished entirely.[28]

---

[25] StadtAN F 6/79, Weekly Intelligence Report, 15.–22.1.48; in general Josef Foschepoth, 'German Reactions to Defeat and Occupation' in Moeller, *West Germany under Reconstruction*, 73–89.
[26] StadtAN F 6/79, Weekly Intelligence Report, 15.–22.1.48.
[27] StadtAN F 6/403, Narrative Supplement to Weekly Report of Amerika-Haus, 1.–7.12.48. On American re-education attempts see Harald Leder, 'Americans and German Youth, 1945–1960: A Study in Politics and Culture', PhD, Louisiana State University, 1997.
[28] Bernd Weisbrod (ed.), *Rechtsradikalismus in der politischen Kultur der Nachkriegszeit. Die verzögerte Normalisierung* (Hanover, 1995).

On the one hand, expressions of Nazi or anti-Semitic attitudes in anonymous letters to the mayor suggested the bitterness of disempowered individuals who, through the very act of writing anonymously, acknowledged that
their ideological positions no longer constituted permitted discourse; the
failure of extreme right-wing groupings to move beyond the political fringe in
the late 1940s and early 1950s in Nuremberg indicated that their neo-Nazi and
radical nationalist visions no longer held mass appeal. On the other hand, the
late 1940s witnessed an apparent resurgence of a nationalism at once more
unreflective and diffuse but at the same time not entirely free of the aesthetic
trappings of its more ideologically focused antecedents. Military government, left-wing politicians and representatives of the victims of Nazism all
registered this with concern.

In one incident at the Nuremberg 'People's Festival' in August 1949, for
example, the brass band in one of the beer tents was reported to have 'enthu-
siastically performed fascist and military marches' including the well-known
Badenweiler March, the associations of which with the Nazi regime would
have been well known to the audience.[29] If such incidents are not to be taken
in simplistic fashion as evidence of neo-Nazi sentiment, they do indicate the
presence of a nationalist nostalgia which – if the bandmaster's decision to play
the marches had accurately judged the desires of his audience – held some
kind of appeal. This, in turn, fed into wider assertions about the conduct of
the war which were rooted in the insistence – on the surface at least – that it
had been fought with legitimate means. Again, the ways in which this was
expressed varied in form, tone and content; the motives for their expression
were probably not always as simple or as obvious as might appear. While at
times uncompromising voices insisted without irony that the war had been
fought in the rightful pursuit of living space or as an act of anti-Bolshevik self-
defence, other occasions suggested the simultaneous presence of, on the one
hand, awareness that the war had been fought in a wrong cause with, on the
other, an unwillingness or inability to accept that individual soldiers had died
for ignoble reasons, still less had done anything wrong.

The sensitivities of this were revealed with remarkable clarity at a meeting of
the *Bayernpartei* – a political manifestation of resurgent monarchist, separatist
and anti-refugee tendencies which played a significant role in Bavaria in
the 1950s before fading into insignificance[30] – at which ex-minister Josef
Baumgartner had asked in an unguarded moment, 'What were the last thoughts
of our dying soldiers?' When someone in the audience shouted back 'Germany!'
the American intelligence report in which the meeting was discussed recorded
that Baumgartner had retorted, 'No, God and our Homeland . . . If somebody

[29] StadtAN F 6/157, Intelligence Division Report, 29.8.49; C 29/457, VVN Bezirksstelle
Nürnberg an Otto Ziebill, 1.9.49.
[30] Ilse Unger, *Die Bayernpartei. Geschichte und Struktur 1945–1957* (Stuttgart, 1979).

thought of Germany he was surely a Nazi.' According to the report 'this remark caused violent reaction and the scene in the circus became tumultuous for more than twenty minutes. Baumgartner tried in vain to resume his speech, but every attempt was drowned in shouting and whistling.' Control of the meeting was lost as members of the audience climbed on to the rostrum to try to address the audience; a disabled veteran allegedly tried to assault Baumgartner, whose gathering closed in chaos.[31]

Such incidents are suggestive for the light they shed upon the relationship between speaker and audience, between political leader and civil society. The occasions when speakers got it wrong – as in the case of Baumgartner – remind us that what speakers were able to say was heavily dependent upon what those who listened were willing to hear. What held true for the dynamics of a public meeting had a wider logic too: the logic of democratic politics demanded, ultimately, that political leaders address and articulate the concerns of the majority.

In the case of post-war Nuremberg this meant, first and foremost, addressing the concerns of the many tens of thousands who had been rendered homeless; it meant addressing the demands of thousands of returning soldiers for housing and welfare provision commensurate with the sacrifices they believed they had made; it meant addressing the demands of refugees for accommodation, work and parity of treatment with the indigenous population. The pragmatic imperative of integrating many thousands of former Nazi party members and sympathisers also condemned politicians of liberal and socialist persuasion, and not just conservatives, to speak up for the 'little man', who had been foolishly seduced by the Nazis but who was in no way to blame for their crimes and who thus now deserved leniency. This translated into welfare promises in the political parties' programmes which reflected the needs and demands of the majority, and not the minority of victims whose concerns faded from the agendas of all parties as the initial anti-fascist impulse of 1945 to 1946 receded. The same dynamic underpinned the evolution of civic memory politics in the post-war era: in addresses to the assembled representatives of civil society at moments of ritualised commemoration, or in considering requests for the establishment of memorials to various groups claiming war victim status, the city authorities had to speak or act in a manner which acknowledged, and rearticulated, the shared understandings present in the community they purported to represent or face swift marginalisation and eventual political oblivion.

Yet again, there was much more in the making of a memory culture than a simple political logic flowing from the asymmetrical relationship between a majority of former perpetrators, collaborators and compromised bystanders – now reconfigured as 'victims' – on the one hand and a minority of former 'real'

---

[31] StadtAN F 6/79, Weekly Intelligence Report, 18.–25.3.48.

victims on the other, whose small number made them an irrelevant constituency for civic leaders voicing popular concerns. There was also an emotional logic in operation, rooted in the ways in which many tens of thousands of people had experienced, in various permutations, the terrifying horrors of bombing, the atrocious violence of combat, the ruthlessness of expulsion and the numbing pain of bereavement.

Something of this echoed through an article in a Protestant parish newsletter of November 1952, published to coincide with the Day of National Mourning. Entitled 'Letters of Consolation from a 20-Year-Old to his Mother', it reminded its readers that 'in these days, as the German population mourns the memory of the victims of the last war, letters are once more dug out in many lonely homes – the last signs of life of those who did not return'. It reproduced the letters of one local woman's son who had been called up, captured in Russia in 1944, and who had died in captivity in the Urals. In the letters he consoled her over the death in 1943 of her husband and his father, offering words of Christian solace. The piece, which closed with the contents of a last letter written by a comrade in which he detailed the son's last days, assured the reader that 'the letters . . . are here in our hands', and described how 'they have already been read with motherly love so often that they are crumpled and falling apart'.[32] In its use of the Day of National Mourning to promote Christian understandings of death the newsletter was clearly making use of the letters for its own evangelising purposes; the general air of pathos, made possible only by ignoring the wider causes and context of the war, was also unmistakable. However, such articles intimated awareness of the presence of pain and the search for meaning which manifested themselves elsewhere too. In 1948, for example, the parish priest of the outlying community of Altdorf wrote to dean Julius Schieder seeking reinstatement of a national day of commemoration on the grounds that 'the search for the meaning of this great death moves most people and only the fewest find an answer . . .'; he had been prompted to write in particular by the experience of a home visit to a woman 'who said bitterly how much it always pained her when the Americans honour their dead but no-one finds words for our fallen'.[33]

Such claims of indifference to the memory of dead German soldiers notwithstanding, awareness of shared pain underpinned circles – both large and small – of mutually acknowledged sorrow, of communally understandable grief which was recognised as embodying a legitimate claim on sympathy and support. Collection practices offer a key indicator of where sympathy within the wider community lay. In December 1949, for example, the factory council

---

[32] 'Trostbriefe eines Zwanzigjährigen an seine Mutter. Im Februar 1945 in Russland verhungert', *Nürnberger Evangelisches Gemeindeblatt*, 16.11.52.
[33] LKAN Kd Nbg 221, Ev.-Luth. Pfarrstelle Altdorf bei Nürnberg an Julius Schieder, 7.2.48.

of the city's public transport works organised a voluntary collection to provide Christmas gifts for the children of colleagues killed in the war or still in captivity. Claims implying the unique victimhood of 'the poorest of the poor ... those whose breadwinner is absent' sidestepped, as ever, the welfare needs of the Nazi regime's surviving victims; the 'moral obligation' of which the factory council spoke did not extend to such persecutees. The invocation to 'please put yourself in their position and imagine what feelings you would have' underlines that emotional empathy – in this case for the families of colleagues killed in action – and was what gave cultures of memory their cement and fostered group identification among those directly affected.[34] Similar sympathies informed the widespread practices, often organised by the churches, of sending parcels to prisoners of war and internees, including war criminals, or the collection of money for the League for the Care of German War Graves, which not only made possible the establishment of orderly war cemeteries in Germany and abroad and the ongoing identification of the dead, but also subsidised bereaved relatives' visits to their loved ones' graves.[35]

Perhaps the clearest suggestion of the reach of this community of acknowledged suffering and the boundaries of social sympathy for those affected in one way or another by Nazism and war was offered by the Easter message of the State Bishop of Bavaria, which was read from all Protestant pulpits over Easter 1947, and which – its more conservative emphases and its manifest sympathy for former Nazis notwithstanding – anticipated clearly the contours of the dominant memory culture of the 1950s developed under the auspices of the SPD:

We remember the great mass of those living in miserable quarters and bitterest poverty who, expelled from their homeland or bombed out of their homes, are in danger of going under physically and spiritually. We remember the thousands who lost their homes and often all their possessions through housing confiscation after the war. We remember the millions of German prisoners of war who, two years after the end of hostilities, still do not know when they will be allowed to return home, and are consumed with yearning for their loved ones. We remember the thousands upon thousands who sit in prisoner of war and internment camps without interrogation or judgement, awaiting due process ... among them are those with

[34] StadtAN C 29/299, Städtische Werke Nürnberg/Verkehrsbetriebe – Betriebsrat (undated, December 1949).
[35] For references to such activities see, for example, 'Zur 1. Hilfswerk-Sammlung dieses Winters', *Nürnberger Evangelisches Gemeindeblatt.* 9.11.47; 'Kirchliche Rundschau', *Nürnberger Evangelisches Gemeindeblatt*, 19.12.48; LKAN Kd Nbg 62, Ev.-Luth. Dekanat Nürnberg an alle Pfarrer im Dekanat Nürnberg, 4.10.50; LKAN Kd Nbg 63, Ev.-Luth. Dekanat Nürnberg an alle Pfarrer im Dekanat Nürnberg, 30.4.51; 'Vergeßt die Kriegsgräber nicht!', *Nürnberger Evangelisches Gemeindeblatt*, 14.6.53.

amputated legs, the seriously ill, the elderly . . . we remember the enormous army of those who, through no particular fault of their own, have been forced out of their positions and are indispensable for the establishment of our economic and spiritual life . . . we remember the families who are in desperate need because the breadwinner is missing or cannot find work.[36]

It would, however, be too easy to read this all-embracing account of German suffering as the reflection of a homogeneous community of victims of war and defeat whose willingness to recognise each other's suffering formed the basis of a shared language of victimhood from which only the persecutees of Nazism were excluded. If the constant rhetoric of suffering fed into evolving narratives of collective victimhood which characterised the nascent memory culture of the 1950s, it should be remembered that the language of shared experience that came to dominate on the cultural plane masked a situation in the material and social sphere which was characterised by division, conflict and, often enough, hatred. As subsequent chapters argue, the civic memory culture of post-war Nuremberg was characterised by many competing claims to victimhood *within* the majority society of ordinary Germans: official stories thus had to contain accounts that reached *across* the multiple political and social divisions of post-war society and could command support among most, if not all, of the population *despite* their divisions. In this sense the inherent vagueness of the major narratives of the 1950s enunciated by local political elites represented not so much an intentional avoidance of reference to specific crimes born of a shared desire to repress guilty truths as the necessary recourse to a vocabulary of lowest common denominators which alone might make possible a minimum degree of civic consensus in a highly divided society. Not mentioning certain things, or only talking about them in a certain way, was the precondition for the re-establishment of a functioning civil society, with a sense of shared civic identity, in which – the conflicts of a pluralist culture notwithstanding – all were willing to play a part.

[36] LKAN Kd Nbg 42, Evang.-Luth. Landeskirchenrat an alle Pfarrämter betr. Wort des Landesbischofs an die Gemeinden der Evang.-Luth Kirche in Bayern zum Osterfest 1947, 20.3.47.

II

The Making of a Memory Culture
Manufacturing Civic Consensus, 1945 to 1961

II.1

Mobilising Memory Communities

Associational Life and the Contestation of the Past

The post-war years saw the emergence of a wide variety of associations which sought to organise and represent the major social groupings which had been created as a result of Nazism, war and defeat. Refugees and expellees, returning prisoners of war, disabled servicemen and their dependants, the 'relatives of the missing' and the bereaved all mobilised to press for material and moral recognition of their suffering. The re-emerging civil society of the late 1940s and 1950s was one in which the legacies of war played a key role in shaping both the city's associational life and its political culture more generally. The mobilisation by diverse associations of the campaigning and protest potential present within each group of 'victims', rooted as it was in a sense of having experienced suffering which was both peculiar to the group and uniquely undeserved, played a key role in fostering the growth of communities of remembrance which defined themselves on the basis of shared narratives of mutually acknowledged wartime suffering.[1] If members of the group knew implicitly that only they themselves could ever really understand the suffering each other had experienced – this was the unspoken knowledge which provided the emotional cement for the group – they continued nonetheless to press their claims to unique victimhood within the wider community, knowing that material redress depended upon the successful projection of such 'victim narratives' within society at large.[2]

[1] On communities of remembrance see Irwin-Zarecka, *Frames of Remembrance*, 47–65; Jeffrey Olick, 'Collective Memory', 342.
[2] On the competition between these 'memory communities' for acknowledgement of their suffering and the barrier to the reconstitution of a functioning civil society this represented, see Klaus Naumann, 'Institutionalisierte Ambivalenz. Deutsche Erinnerungspolitik und Gedenkkultur nach 1945', *Mittelweg* 36 (April/May 2004), 64–75, here 66; the relationship between claims to victimhood and the pursuit of material redress is underlined also by Thießen, 'Das Gedächtnis der Stadt', 146.

6. Protest rally of war victims' association (undated, 1950s).

Some of these groups were large, some small. Some existed for a long time, some for only a very brief period. Indeed, the regularity with which organisations with similar sounding names and apparently similar remits appeared and disappeared, or the overall number of such organisations which left at least limited traces in the archive, may too easily be taken for an extensive public presence: the rate at which they were founded and refounded, and their capacity to generate splinter groupings, may just as easily be taken as evidence of the difficulties of getting such an organisation off the ground, and of sustaining its activities and internal harmony once it was established. Some formed part of a wider milieu with connections to other associations and campaign groups, their boundaries permeable and their memberships reproducing each other; some competed with each other, their fields of activity the sites of rival groups. Those whose activities left archive traces did so as much because their work brought them into contact with city authorities as because they were particularly energetic; other, perhaps equally active, organisations left fewer traces because their self-contained cultures made correspondence with city offices largely unnecessary.

Even the best organised of the various associations did not represent all members of the interest group concerned, or even the majority of them. A minority of activists – often only a handful – stood at the apex of organisations the memberships of which were generally more passive or disinclined to time-consuming involvement; behind these stood an even greater mass of individuals who showed no interest in defining themselves publicly through their past experiences, but who preferred, rather, to get on with rebuilding their lives. On the other hand, civic leaders saw in such organisations the mouthpieces of the wider community of suffering from which they had emerged, drawing on their advice and comment when formulating policy, and seeing in them agencies the voices of which represented the views of the communities for whom they claimed to speak. In the political culture of the city their size and vocal presence were taken as indicative of the social and political power of the interest group more generally; the logic of democratic politics ensured that their demands were listened to in corresponding fashion. Moreover, their widespread activities in the public sphere made them not just the officially acknowledged faces of the wider interest group but key determinants of how that group was perceived in society at large. This was all the more the case for the fact that their activities were not only witnessed directly by those who shared their presence at commemorative acts or ceremonies, or who saw their processions, concerts, social gatherings and protest rallies at the moment in which they occurred, but were also seen within wider society via extensive newspaper or radio reporting of their events. They acted as key mediators between political elites and society, and indeed between different sections of society itself.

One of the best organised and most active associations to emerge in Nuremberg was the League of German War-Disabled and Surviving Dependants (*Bund Deutscher Kriegsbeschädigter und Kriegshinterbliebener –* BDKK). Formed in 1949, its regional and national headquarters were located in Nuremberg. While it did not develop into one of the major national war victims associations, it did develop a strong, highly visible, presence within the city.[3] From 1953 onwards it published the 'War Victims' Yearbook'; later, it published the monthly newspaper, the 'War Victims' Review' (*Kriegsopfer-Rundschau*). Its local membership was over 2,000-strong in 1955; its regular meetings usually attracted between 100 and 200 people in the 1950s.[4] Its meetings were used to update members on the progress of campaigns to revise relevant laws, of ongoing negotiations with the Federal government, or of improvements to pension and welfare provisions introduced over the 1950s. Locally, it provided legal support and practical advice, helping members to

---

[3] See Diehl, *The Thanks of the Fatherland. German Veterans after the Second World War* (Chapel Hill, NC, 1993) 89–90.
[4] StadtAN E 6/601/217, Minute Book of Ortsgruppe Nürnberg 1955–1967, Generalversammlung am 19.10.57.

deal with the state bureaucracy and welfare apparatus; a dedicated social worker and dependants' worker held regular surgeries; a women's group also held monthly meetings.

Remembrance was not, in itself, the focus of the League's activities, which were aimed at gaining practical improvements to the current lot of its membership. However, members' meetings always began with a solemn silence in honour of the dead. The sense of mutual obligation which informed the internal culture of the organisation was born of a strong, shared understanding of the sacrifice made by dead or missing soldiers and the corresponding suffering endured by their surviving relatives. Moreover, the campaigning activities of the League drew strongly on stories of the war which were understood as conferring unique legitimacy on the League's struggle. Resonating through these stories was a national-conservative memory of conflict which deployed, by turns and according to need, a vocabulary of innocence, of sacrifice, of selflessness and of victimhood in which any reference to the murderous violence in which some of its members had participated was conspicuous by its absence.[5]

Central to the culture of the League was the assertion that individual members had been forced to participate in the war against their will and thus had a moral and legal right to compensation in principle rather than to welfare handouts based on individual need. In its first yearbook, for example, it published an opening programmatic statement which argued that 'the right of war victims to support is based on a legal claim for compensation as the state, through an act of sovereignty, forced the war-disabled and the dependants' providers into dangerous situations which regularly led to permanent disability and death . . . loss of health and of the provider is thus a particular sacrifice which the state has forced on to a certain number of people'.[6] The innocence of the victims had, in the view of the League, been impugned by the Allied Control Council's suspension of all hitherto existing German military pension provision in August 1946, an act allegedly informed by the then widespread 'defamation of the German *Wehrmacht*' which had wrongly held sway in the immediate aftermath of war. In the view of the BDKK, however, the judgement of the International Military Tribunal at Nuremberg in October 1946 had represented an abandonment of this 'false doctrine'. With this judgement, 'all moral justification for the suspension of military and war victim provision was removed'.

---

[5] The archaeology of the relationship between rhetorics of sacrifice and claims to welfare entitlement is explored in Greg Eghigian, 'Injury, Fate, Resentment, and Sacrifice in German Political Culture, 1914–1939' in Greg Eghigian and Matthew Paul Berg (eds), *Sacrifice and National Belonging in Twentieth Century Germany* (Arlington, TX, 2002), 90–117.
[6] Hermann Albrecht Steneberg, 'Warum reiner deutscher Kriegsopferverband?', *Deutsches Kriegsopferjahrbuch*, 1953, 4.

The focus of the BDKK's campaigning zeal, indeed, was the fact that, denied access to military pensions, its members had been forced to rely on general welfare handouts alongside the broader mass of those suffering from the consequences of the war, in a manner which denied their peculiar moral claim to support. Refusing vehemently to join with other categories of disadvantaged citizens or to admit them into its ranks, its rhetoric of sacrifice for the greater good underpinned an insistence that its members had a higher claim to redress; its relations with other organisations were correspondingly fraught.[7]

If the language of selfless sacrifice – with its implications of voluntary surrender to the greater needs of the whole – sat in tension with the image of compulsion by the all-powerful state which informed the League's claims to victimhood, it also lent itself ideally to the dissociation of individual soldiers' deaths from the cause for which they had fought. Such dissociation of German soldiers from the wider political and ideological context in which they had fought and died was part of a wider reworking of the history of the Second World War among veteran communities in the post-war era which sought to separate the Nazi regime from its wider anchoring in German society. Indeed, it was precisely in such forceful assertions of the distinction between 'Nazism' and 'Germany' that the illegitimate nature of what had been a criminal war was implicitly acknowledged. Resonating through the publications of the League was the constant insistence that, instead, 'wherever German soldiers stood, they fought with the holy conviction in their heart to stand their ground for people and fatherland, homeland and family'. In telling the soldiers' deaths as a story of 'sacrifice for the protection of the Christian Occident' Germany's prior act of aggression was written out of narratives of the conflict which cast it as a war of defence against the Bolshevik east, suiting the ideological exigencies of the 1950s down to the ground.[8]

Such stories also fitted with a practice of redescribing the Second World War as a normal war whose story could be told within a continuum of national defence stretching back to the nineteenth century. What was perhaps most striking about the BDKK's construction of the Second World War as a 'normal' war, indeed, was not so much the distorting impact of the Cold War rhetoric which ran through it as the propensity of the organisation's literature to draw on much older nationalist vocabularies of self-defence. In a piece published in 1955, leading BDKK functionary Carl Langfritz emphasised the unifying impact of mobilisation in a manner which recalled the 'Burgfrieden' of 1914. Reminding readers of the heroic willingness to fight on the part of soldiers who had no thoughts of personal danger, he insisted that 'the call to

---

[7] See, for example, 'Die historische Schuld der Mischverbände', *Deutsches Kriegsopferjahrbuch*, 1954, 5; further Diehl, *The Thanks of the Fatherland*, 89–90.
[8] See Carl Langfritz, 'Wir blicken nach Bonn. Reminiszenzen und Aspekte zur Bundestagswahl 1953', *Deutsches Kriegsopferjahrbuch*, 1955, 36.

arms does not ask after party loyalties nor after confession . . . the phrases of an Internationale, of a world brotherhood are scattered in the firestorm of the conflict of nations'.[9]

If such phrases recalled the mythical moment of unity in 1914, in which domestic political strife was supposedly suspended in the rush to defend the fatherland, the use of archaisms such as 'Dear Fatherland, be calm . . .' ('*Lieb Vaterland, magst ruhig sein . . .*') to evoke assurances given to civilians by the troops – which came from Max Schneckenburger's nationalist song 'The Watch on the Rhine' of 1840 – or the use of phrases such as 'the fatherland is in danger, and all who love it come to defend it' – which had echoes of an earlier mythical mobilisation in 1813 – saw the BDKK drawing on a nationalist idiom that went back to the early nineteenth century. The inscription of the Second World War within this decidedly traditional narrative of national self-defence was rooted, in part, in the fact that many leading functionaries of the BDKK in the 1950s were in their seventies; some had been active in the nationalist associational life of war veterans and the war-disabled in the interwar years; it would seem likely that this had been rooted in the experience of soldiering during the First World War itself. The presence in descriptions of the Second World War of imagery more appropriate to the First World War thus represented more than the merely disingenuous conflation of the two conflicts in a manner designed to erase the barbaric peculiarities of the latter – even if this was, in part, its effect. It was also the expression of the nationalist mentalities and memories of an older cohort which had survived the Nazi era and briefly re-established itself before fading in the following decade.[10]

Similarly complex continuities were in evidence in the forms, symbols and ritual practices of the BDKK's internal activities. The appellation of 'comrade', which was shared between members, both male and female, or the letterhead of the association – an iron cross embedded with a steel helmet – suggested the dominance of a conservative, national-patriotic ethos which drew on nationalist soldierly values reminiscent of interwar right-wing veterans' politics. The continued use of terms such as *Heldengedenktag* to describe the Day of National Mourning, the consecration of sacred banners or – most strikingly, the use of the terms *Ortsgruppe* and *Ortsgruppenleiter* to describe local chapters and their leaders – suggested, at first sight, a more overtly Nazi continuum. Yet while strongly right-wing attitudes were certainly present, such continuities in the forms and practices of local associational life testified,

---

[9] See, for example, Carl H. Langfritz, 'Der Dank des Vaterlandes', *Deutsches Kriegsopferjahrbuch*, 1955, 28. On the survival of national rhetoric from the wars of liberation see Karin Hausen, 'The "Day of National Mourning" in Germany' in Sider and Smith, *Between History and Histories*, 128.
[10] The stubborn longevity of this national-conservative idiom is the key assertion of Eghigian and Berg, *Sacrifice and National Belonging*; on the residual presence of 'Wilhelmine' modes of thinking in the 1950s see also Hodenberg, *Konsens und Krise*.

if anything, to the persistence of unbroken traditions into which the Nazis themselves had successfully inserted their style of activism and mobilisation. These traditions manifested themselves most obviously in the reverential attitude of local functionaries to the minute-book, the agenda, the treasurer's report, the lapel pin and the table pennant.

It would therefore be easy to overestimate the presence of specifically Nazi mental continuities in organisations such as the BDKK. But its national patriotic ethos translated into an attitude towards democracy which was lukewarm, and into a preference for martial ways of seeing which sat uneasily with the slowly emerging pluralist culture of the Federal Republic. Above all, the bonds which joined the membership of the BDKK in peacetime were deemed to draw their strength from the 'comradely front spirit' of an imagined community of wartime sacrifice which formed the basis for a higher moral community in the post-war era.[11] Its notions of peacetime activism were correspondingly replete with military metaphors. Its 1954 yearbook argued, for example, that the organisation's successes were based on 'four years shaped by struggle, years of hardest and most selfless engagement [*Einsatz*] by each one of us – years of true comradeship in the fight for the right and unity of the German war-disabled and survivors' dependants.'[12] Only as the economic recovery was consolidated throughout the 1950s and gradual improvements to provision for the war-disabled and dependants were introduced did the organisation become more reconciled to democracy; even then it remained firmly on the Right.

There was, in any case, more to the BDKK than campaigning for improved pensions on the basis of national conservative representations of the war. The affective bonds which linked the members of the group to one another went deeper, and worked on a level whose meanings were not primarily ideological. The BDKK's activities suggested the presence of a moral and emotional community tied together by more than the self-interested desire for improved welfare provision: the ties were also those of shared grief and mutual sympathy for recognisably similar experiences of the pain engendered by war. The organisation of children's parties at Christmas, made possible by house-to-house collections carried out by members, attested to sympathy with the orphaned offspring of dead German soldiers. Similarly, the distribution of small sums to the mothers of dead soldiers was informed by the belief that the elderly parents of those whose children were not there to provide for them were among those suffering the greatest hardship as a consequence of the war.[13] Most striking,

---

[11] Thomas Kühne, ' "Kameradschaft – das beste im Leben eines Mannes". Die deutschen Soldaten des Zweiten Weltkrieges in erfahrungs- und geschlechtergeschichtlicher Perspektive' in *Geschichte und Gesellschaft* 22 (1996), 504–29, esp. 523ff.

[12] Carl H. Langfritz, '4 Jahre BDKK', *Deutsches Kriegsopferjahrbuch*, 1954, 4.

[13] On the gendered qualities of the practice of comradeship after the war, see Kühne, ' "Kameradschaft" ', 526–8.

however, was the great significance attached by the League to Mother's Day, on which occasion it always organised a social event for the mothers of dead soldiers.[14] Such events indicate, again, that even if the issue of the missing prisoners of war faded from the public agenda after 1956, the bereavement caused by war retained its central place in the communities of remembrance to which the war had given rise, and that the tone of activities within associations such as the BDKK was shaped by such sentiments long after the immediate political agenda had moved on to other things.

A similar foregrounding of the vocabulary of 'victimhood' and 'sacrifice' on behalf of the wider community, and a similar emphasis on the innocence of those whose suffering was not their own fault, but that of the force of world politics, informed the campaigning rhetoric of the Association of Former Prisoners of War (*Verband der Heimkehrer* – VdH), which had a highly visible presence in the city in the 1950s. Formed as a national organisation in 1950 out of various local and regional groups which had emerged in the late 1940s to press the interests of former prisoners of war in the difficult aftermath of the currency reform, it lobbied for legislation to improve the lot of the *Heimkehrer* and for work and welfare programmes to help reintegrate them into civilian life. Later, once the 1950 Federal Prisoner of War Law had been passed, it moved on to campaigning for compensation for *Heimkehrer* who had performed forced labour in captivity, arguing that this had been a form of reparations carried out on behalf of the whole nation, and that the nation should therefore compensate the *Heimkehrer* in return.[15]

Like the BDKK, the VdH argued that the particular experiences of its members gave its claims higher moral status than those of others. In the words of one of its annual yearbooks, 'Each individual who spent years of his life in captivity as a prisoner of war through no fault of his own, and each individual who still finds himself in captivity, has made a sacrifice before and on behalf of all Germans which the German population as a whole cannot deny recognising and socially acknowledging.'[16] It also claimed that the unique experience of captivity in prisoner of war camps created a barrier between the *Heimkehrer* and the wider population which it was the task of the association to overcome. In the same yearbook's words, 'It is a peculiar realisation that neither after the First nor after the Second World War was the returning prisoner of war really understood by his homeland' and 'because it is so difficult for those who have not lived through it to understand this special experience

---

[14] StadtAN E 6/601/217, Minute, 8.5.59.
[15] Diehl, *The Thanks of the Fatherland*, 171ff.
[16] Harald Boldt, 'Werden und Wesen des VdH', *Wir Mahnen die Welt. VdH Jahrbuch* (undated, Hanover *c.* 1952), 73.

the *Heimkehrer* are forced to join together.'[17] If the VdH claimed to be motivated by the higher values of 'humanity' and 'reconciliation', its campaigning
activities reinforced the relativising rhetoric of those who refused to acknowledge either the agency of the *Wehrmacht* in the crimes of the Nazi era or the
unique nature of the racial persecutees' suffering during the Third Reich. The
organisation's symbol – a triangle of barbed wire representing the camp
environment – and its widespread use of images of emaciated prisoners
performing forced labour or searching for food also had unmistakeable
echoes of the concentration camp experience of the Third Reich.[18]

Locally, the VdH engaged in a range of activities. In the first place, it inter-
ceded with city authorities on behalf of individual members whom it regarded
as particularly deserving of priority treatment in the allocation of housing or
welfare aid; individual *Heimkehrer* clearly saw the local VdH as an agency
which might intercede effectively on their behalf.[19] As the *Heimkehrer* were
gradually absorbed into the economy and otherwise merged back into the
wider community, the VdH focused increasingly on the fate of those still
missing. It was a leading force behind the establishment of the city's first
prominent war memorial, erected on the wall of the *Nassauer Haus* in 1952 to
remember the fate of the prisoners of war and the missing.[20] It was also the
lead agency in the organisation of the 'Prisoner of War Remembrance Weeks'
held annually in the early 1950s to press for the remaining prisoners' release.[21]

Therein, however, lay the seeds of the VdH's own gradual marginalisation. As
the immediate welfare needs of the returned prisoners of war were gradually
met, and as economic recovery fostered their integration into the community,
the field of activity of the VdH became more limited; the return of the final prisoners from Soviet captivity in 1956 meant that, whatever search services the
Heimkehrer community organised in private, their public resonance – and thus
the VdH's prominence – also faded. With this the organisational activities of
war veterans at a local level began to shift.

Those former soldiers who had suffered neither disabling injury nor lengthy
post-war captivity represented a highly diverse array of veterans whose wartime
experiences had been shaped by the history of their regimental deployments
in specific theatres as much as by the development of the war as a whole. The

---

[17] W. Freiherr von Lessing, 'Die inneren Motive des Zusammenschlusses der deutschen
Kriegsgefangenen', *Wir Mahnen die Welt*, 74; 78.
[18] See, for example, the illustrations and articles in *Wir Mahnen die Welt*.
[19] See, for example, StadtAN C 29/473, Verband der Heimkehrer, Kriegsgefangenen- und
Vermißtenangehörigen Deutschlands e.V. Kreisverband Nürnberg-Stadt an Oberbürgermeister
Bärnreuther, 14.8.53 and the enclosed Paul Büttner an die Kreisgeschäftsstelle des Verbandes der
Heimkehrer, Nürnberg, 5.8.53.
[20] See below, Chapter II.2
[21] See below, Chapter II.3.

affective bonds of 'comradeship' were also based on a memory of particular shared experiences with other individual soldiers – the costly attack, the retreat under fire, the pleasures of leave while stationed as occupation troops – as much as on a sense of camaraderie within the armed forces more generally. Individual regiments, rather than the armed forces as a whole, thus increasingly provided the imagined communities within which individuals ordered their experiences; regimental associations correspondingly became key homes for communities of remembrance based on shared stories of soldiering.[22] The ability of each of these regimental associations to construct amenable narratives of war was dependent not least upon the wartime experiences of the regiments themselves. Unsurprisingly, those that had fought in eastern Europe had by far the most problematic task in this respect; equally unsurprisingly, it was these regimental associations which tended to propagate the most evasive and contorted narratives, and whose protestations of innocence or ignorance of wartime atrocities were the most shrill.

The Nuremberg branch of the Afrika-Korps Association, for example, was striking for its exclusive focus on wartime events in the North African theatre.[23] Announcing as its mission the 'fostering of comradeship', membership was open only to 'those former members of the *Wehrmacht* whose units were deployed in and for North Africa between El Alamein and Tunis, along with the relatives of their fallen, missing and dead comrades'.[24] In line with the assumption, central to the ways in which the association represented the war experiences of its members, that the campaign in North Africa had been fought in a decent manner and with respect for the enemy, it sought to foster 'the maintenance of the spirit of chivalry', along with that of sacrifice and 'love for the German people and fatherland'. Beyond this, nationalist overtones or authoritarian proclivities were largely absent, although the strong identification of the associational rank-and-file with the former commanding generals of the Afrika-Korps, manifest in hefty applause for such figures at gatherings, suggested an unwillingness to acknowledge the complicity of some such figures in genocide. The appointment of the convicted war criminal former Field Marshal Albert Kesselring as honorary chairman of the association in 1952, following his release from Werl prison, certainly did not suggest

[22] Thomas Kühne, 'Zwischen Vernichtungskrieg und Freizeitgesellschaft. Die Veteranenkultur der Bundesrepublik (1945–1995)' in Naumann, *Nachkrieg in Deutschland*, 90–113; also Jörg Echternkamp, 'Mit dem Krieg seinen Frieden schließen – Wehrmacht und Weltkrieg in der Veteranenkultur 1945–1960' in Thomas Kühne (ed.), *Von der Kriegskultur zur Friedenskultur? Zum Mentalitätswandel in Deutschland seit 1945* (Hamburg, 2000), 78–93.
[23] StadtAN E 6/580/1, Kreiskameradschaft Nürnberg des Verbandes ehemaliger Angehöriger des Deutschen Afrikakorps e.V.: Protokoll über Gründungssammlung des Kreiskameradschaft am 10 Juni 1953 in Nürnberg.
[24] StadtAN E 6/580/1, Satzung des Verbandes Deutsches Afrikakorps e.V. (1972). This describes accurately the focus of the association in the earlier period too.

widespread acknowledgement within the Afrika-Korps of the criminal behaviour of the *Wehrmacht*.[25] The strong connections of the association to the name Rommel – after whom the association's social fund for members fallen on hard times was named – were, nonetheless, highly conducive to distancing the history of the Korps from that of the campaign of genocide, given that Rommel himself was widely remembered as the archetypal 'decent' officer who had, through his resistance connections, become a 'victim' of the regime.

Most meetings of the local chapter, whose membership numbered at most a few dozen, were social and convivial, and centred on *Fasching*, Father's Day or Christmas; alongside monthly meetings the chapter undertook occasional outings to meet with comrades from Augsburg or Würzburg.[26] The shared experience underpinning the association's cultures of sociability, self-support and commemoration was not that of the war, or of membership of the *Wehrmacht*, still less that of having fought a war of imperialist aggression – the Nazi regime itself was rarely, if ever, mentioned in its literature – but of having fought with the Afrika-Korps in the particular environment of North Africa. The literature of the association, especially its newsletter 'The Oasis' (Die Oase), contained articles devoted almost entirely to military engagements in that theatre, which propagated overwhelmingly positive images of the soldierly virtues of bravery, comradeship and sacrifice, and images of a decent war fought according to the rules in a desert environment whose challenges were met with great inventiveness. Such representations of war were informed by a sense of pride in superior weaponry which oscillated between the fondness reserved for an old friend on the one hand and a fascination with the capacities of military technologies – their range, their accuracy, their reliability, their speed of fire – on the other. Although respect for the memory of the dead was central to the culture of the group, as it was for all other military associations, and although a search service and grave location service acknowledged the emotional effects of loss among its membership, the language of victimhood was largely absent from its literature. For the Afrika-Korps Association, the soldier's life was heroic, his cause had been honourable and his death a proud sacrifice.

The geographical deployment of the Afrika-Korps made it relatively easy to dissociate its activities from the wider history of the Nazi regime. Other, larger, groups of *Wehrmacht* veterans faced a harder task. Included in these were the regimental associations of Infantry Regiment 21 (IR 21) and its 'daughter' regiments IR 213 and 351/480. These regiments had largely been raised in Bavaria;

---

[25] StadtAN E 6/580/1, Chronik des Verbandes Deutsches Afrikakorps e.V., 1951–1980; on Kesselring in the post-war era see Kerstin von Lingen, *Kesselrings letzte Schlacht. Kriegsverbrecherprozesse, Vergangenheitspolitik und Wiederbewaffnung: Der Fall Kesselring* (Paderborn, 2004), esp. 321–39.
[26] StadtAN E 6/580/1, Veranstaltungschronik der Kreiskameradschaft Nürnberg/Verband Deutsches Afrikakorps 1953–1983.

their regimental associations regularly converged on Nuremberg for reunions. Their histories were often considerably more problematic than that of the Afrika-Korps. Following service in Poland and France, the IR 21 had participated in Operation Barbarossa, taking many prisoners at a time when the treatment of such captives was murderously brutal. IR 213 had taken part in 'cleansing activities' in Poland at the outbreak of war;[27] it had seen action in France, in the campaigns in south-eastern Europe and in the Soviet Union, where it had fought in the Ukraine and the Crimea; later, it had transferred to Warsaw, where, in the regimental association's words, 'it had experienced the Polish Uprising'. IR 351, meanwhile, had also fought in France and had served as occupation troops in Czechoslovakia, before moving on to Yugoslavia. Here, according to the regimental association's account, it took part in 'cleansing actions in the inaccessible mountain ranges of Bosnia'.[28] As IR 480 it had participated in Operation Barbarossa, where it had been deployed in the Pripjet Marshes and had participated in the Moscow Offensive; for a time during the winter of 1941 to 1942 it had been deployed under the command of an SS-battalion. Later, it experienced the retreat and collapse of the Army Group Centre, its remaining soldiers falling into captivity in July 1944.[29]

In many respects the culture and activities of these regimental associations mirrored those of the Afrika-Korps Association. At their regimental reunion of 1955, for example, the first evening of the two-day event included an open-air brass-band concert on the main market place, followed by a wreath-laying ceremony at the *Nassauer Haus* memorial to remember those missing and still – in the minds of the participants – held in captivity. This was then followed by a 'grand reunion and convivial gathering' in an inn, accompanied by more live music. On the following day a similar mix of solemn commemoration, reminiscence and conviviality was evident. The veterans held a further ceremony at the *Luitpoldhain* memorial at the former party rally grounds in honour of the dead, at which both former divisional chaplains spoke; in the afternoon another 'comradely gathering' in an inn was accompanied by a search action on the part of the Red Cross, where attending veterans were asked to help clarify the fate of missing comrades.[30]

---

[27] On army atrocities in Poland, see Alexander B. Rossino, *Hitler Strikes Poland. Blitzkrieg, Ideology and Atrocity* (Lawrence, KS, 2003).

[28] On the role of the German army in Yugoslavia during the war, see Walter Manoschek, *'Serbien ist Judenfrei'. Militärische Besatzungspolitik und Judenvernichtung in Serbien, 1941/42* (Munich, 1993).

[29] These summaries are taken from the regimental associations' own accounts in StadtAN C 29/489, Kameradentreffen des Infanterie Regiments 21 1945–1955; C 29/497, Kameradentreffen der Nürnberger Infanterie, 16.–17.11.57: Infanterie Regiment 21, Infanterie Regiment 213, Infanterie Regiment 351.

[30] The centrality of searching to veterans' culture is underlined by Karsten Wilke, 'Organisierte Veteranen der Waffen-SS zwischen Systemopposition und Integration: Die Hilfsgemeinschaft auf Gegenseitigkeit der Angehörigen der ehemaligen Waffen-SS (HIAG) in der frühen Bundesrepublik' in *Zeitschrift für Geschichtswissenschaft* 51/1 (2005) 149–66, here 161–3.

Underpinning their gatherings was a sense of community rooted in an intense feeling of shared experience rather than in the self-interested pursuit of pensions provision. In the words of IR 21's former regimental commander, 'shared experience creates bonds and unites'.[31] Similarly, the programme of the major reunion of 1957 argued that 'what soldered us front soldiers together was comradeship, born of blood and death! . . . Only the inner urge to prove himself at the place in which he was deployed drove [the soldier] on and led him to fulfil his duty'.[32] If such assertions were wrapped up in specious claims of moral probity and innocence they were more than convenient fictions: notions of comradeship within the imagined community of the regiment embodied something highly real for those who subscribed to them. As with other groups, the shared values learned and inherited from military experience provided orientation for the post-war era; as with other groups, military vocabularies offered a means to describe the challenges of the present.

Precisely what forms of reminiscence such gatherings prompted is unclear; how far the boundaries of permitted discourse extended even within a close community of sentiment such as this cannot be ascertained; whether the abundant presence of alcohol on these occasions prompted the expression – as the evening wore on – of things known but otherwise unspoken can only be speculated upon. Whatever allusions to shared knowledge of criminal acts took place in the confines of a closed reunion, the official literature of the IR 21's regimental association remained stridently committed to a version of history which not only cast the *Wehrmacht* as an honourable army but sometimes even implied that other combatant nations had failed to live up to its high standards.

The foregrounding of notions of comradeship within the regimental associations notwithstanding, relations between their constituent elements could be fractious. In the late 1950s, internal conflicts led, for example, to the emergence of two rival IR 21 regimental associations. Whether political differences were to blame is unclear: it is just as likely that the slowly declining organisational strength and size of such groups from the late 1950s onwards gave their internal power struggles a more personal character, and that, as such, these disputes testified to their slow marginalisation within the city's wider associational life as the years wore on. The presence of political and ideological fissures, as opposed to merely personal differences, beneath the surface of the pervasive victim discourse of Nuremberg society in the 1950s was all the more apparent, however, in the often ambivalent and sometimes deeply hostile relationship between the regimental associations and the SPD-dominated city council.

---

[31] StadtAN C 29/489, Foreword to 'Kameradentreffen des Infanterie Regiments 21 1945–1955'.
[32] StadtAN C 29/497, Kameradentreffen der Nürnberger Infanterie, 16.–17.11.57: Infanterie Regiment 21, Infanterie Regiment 213, Infanterie Regiment 351.

Successive SPD mayors and council representatives showed themselves willing to support the fostering of convivial ties among former soldiers, and to aid the organisations' attempts to help their members reintegrate into civil society. To this end, the city council provided the VdH with rent-free offices and facilities.[33] Neither did SPD councillors question the integrity of individual ex-soldiers, on whose possible participation in acts of genocidal murder they remained silent. Rather, ordinary veterans who sought to return to civilian life were treated by the SPD as innocent victims of war with legitimate welfare claims. In the words of one SPD city councillor, councillor Widmayer, in 1958, 'people's deaths on the battlefield were often all too human. But they acted in good faith and did their duty. The SPD declared its support for these soldiers in the First and Second World Wars and we declare our support for the victims too.'[34] Such comments reflected simultaneously a pervasive narrative which saw Nazism as a creation of reactionary elites for which ordinary citizens – the 'little man' championed by the SPD – had not been responsible, a commitment to providing for the socially disadvantaged and a pragmatic desire to reintegrate a large number of former soldiers who had come, in many cases, from the SPD's own traditional milieu.

At the same time, the SPD's response to the veterans' associations reflected the deep-seated hostility to militarism which had been an integral part of the party's traditions since its foundation and which had gained renewed impetus from the experience of Nazism. This manifested itself in clear suspicion of some associations, and a corresponding desire to keep a firm distance from anything that suggested nationalist, militarist or anti-democratic activism on the part of such groups. In his welcome to the 17 ID's reunion in October 1958, for example, mayor Urschlechter (b. 1919; mayor 1957–87) emphasised that the meeting should primarily be about the renewal of acquaintances, the memory of the fallen and the search for news of the missing, and pointed out to members that, as a location for their reunion, 'Nuremberg reminds all participants in the war so vividly of what the madness of war destroyed and what peaceful construction work can achieve.'[35] Commitment to peaceful, humane politics and a rejection of militarism also underlay the SPD council fraction's distance from the League of Stalingrad Fighters, whose national reunion the mayor conspicuously failed to attend. In the ensuing city council debate, in which the CSU admonished the mayor for the council's failure to send a representative, SPD councillor Widmayer retorted that 'one can only support these meetings if they are genuinely informed by a commitment to peace and if the survivors take on the task of ensuring that a further world war

---

[33] StadtAN C 7 IX/1378, Niederschrift über die Sitzung des Ältestenrates am 20.1.56.
[34] StadtAN C 7 IX/741, Niederschrift über die 43. Sitzung des Stadtrats am 22.10.58.
[35] StadtAN C 85 I Abg. 94/A211, Geleitwort zum Treffen der 17 ID in Nürnberg, Oktober 1958.

is prevented'. Without wishing to blame the participants of that particular meeting, Widmayer complained that a German soldiers' newspaper had recently declared that 'the attack must be fostered once more', giving rise to concern that the veterans' milieu was the home of revanchist thinking.[36]

The greatest hostility, however, was reserved for those right-wing soldiers' associations that drew on the paramilitary traditions, paraphernalia and imagery of the interwar years. Here, bitter memories within the local cadres of the SPD of the divided and violent politics of the late 1920s and early 1930s were in full evidence. When, in 1956, the Nuremberg chapter of the *Stahlhelm* sought permission from mayor Otto Bärnreuther (1908–57; mayor 1952–57) to include the city's coat of arms on part of its banner, Bärnreuther was unequivocal in his insistence that 'the *Stahlhelm* is an association directly opposed to the Republican ethos'.[37] In subsequent discussion he repeated that 'it is an association of the old marchers – they can march without our city arms'; underlining how memories of interwar political strife informed his judgement he argued that 'in 1933 to 1934 many people who wanted nothing to do with the Nazis tried to find a niche there and were then betrayed. Today it is still the same association.'[38] The bitterness of Bärnreuther's attack on the *Stahlhelm* reminds that, at a local level, disputes surrounding memory were not merely issues of political utility or ideological conflict: the antagonisms, and the experiences which underlay them, were personally felt, and the sentiments they provoked highly visceral.

Similar nervousness on the part of the SPD-dominated council towards associations suspected of fostering revanchist cultures and indulging in intemperate nationalist rhetoric informed relations with the refugee and expellee associations, of which there had emerged a large number by the early 1950s. Initially, the main focus of refugee organisational activity had been in the outlying rural areas, reflecting their geographical distribution in the early post-war years. There, they constituted part of a wider amorphous protest potential which the occupying powers and German authorities struggled to contain.[39] As the refugee population gradually moved into the cities in greater numbers, however, and as the particular cultural aspirations of the refugees within the city took shape, associations began to emerge in Nuremberg too.

---

[36] StadtAN C 7 IX/741, Niederschrift über die 43. Sitzung des Stadtrats am 22.10.58.
[37] StadtAN C 7 IX/1378, Niederschrift über die 76. Sitzung des Ältestenrats am 2.3.56.
[38] StadtAN C 7 IX/1378, Niederschrift über die Ältestenratssitzung am 15.4.56.
[39] See, for example, StadtAN F 6/2, Quarterly Historical Report covering the period from 1 October to 31 December 1947; for a study of relations between expellee groups and authorities in the early post-war years which focuses on these problems, see York R. Winkler, *Flüchtlingsorganisationen in Hessen 1945–1954. BHE – Flüchtlingsverbände – Landsmannschaften* (Wiesbaden, 1998).

As already discussed, a rudimentary form of cultural self-mobilisation had begun to take place in the refugee camps in the 1940s. In the early 1950s, however, the organisational base of this refugee activism was consolidated and strengthened considerably. The main focal points of refugee political, social and cultural activism were the 'homeland associations' (*Landsmannschaften*), which organised the refugees and expellees on the basis of their lands of origin.[40] They cooperated with each other on matters of shared interest through umbrella organisations such as the League of Expellees (*Bund der Vertriebenen*) but otherwise maintained a distinct, individual identity. As with the veterans' associations, they functioned both as interest group organisations defending material interests and as communities of sentiment rooted in shared experience – and, in this case, a shared affective bond to the lost homeland, its landscape and cultural traditions. If shared affection for the lost lands of 'the East' created a general sense of unity, the diverse origins of the expellees, their diverse histories and diverse traditions gave rise to a wide variety of sentimental longings whose points of focus – topographical, cultural, emotional – were correspondingly also varied.[41]

The agendas of the individual homeland associations also varied. The Homeland League of Breslau, for example – which, to judge by the list of signatories at its founding meeting, was born in the Schafhof refugee camp – claimed as its tasks 'the maintenance of the traditions of the homeland' and the offering of 'advice and help on economic issues within the limits of the available possibilities' suggesting a focus on self-reliance and self-help rather than active lobbying. Its commitment to 'social events and cultural exchange with the indigenous population with the aim of mutual understanding' and its emphasis on its democratic foundations implied a moderate organisation aimed at fostering integration within the wider community. Indeed, its stated aims specifically excluded the pursuit of foreign policy agendas.[42] The Homeland Association of East and West Prussians in Nuremberg similarly took as its goals the 'maintenance and care of our native cultural traditions through lectures, homeland evenings and so on, along with the preservation of writings and other traditional lore' but also claimed a firm role in 'promoting the social demands and the representations of all the interests of all its members vis-à-vis the authorities, the economy and the public',

[40] On the *Landsmannschaften* see most recently Pertti Ahonen, *After the Expulsion. West Germany and Eastern Europe 1945–1990* (Oxford, 2003), 24–53.

[41] Michael von Engelhardt, 'Generation und historisch-biographische Erfahrung – Die Bewältigung von Flucht und Vertreibung im Generationenvergleich' in Hoffmann, Kraus and Schwartz, *Vertriebene in Deutschland*, here 340; on the place of the expulsions and the lost *Heimat* in the expellees' cultural imagination in the post-war era, see Elke Mehnert (ed.), *Landschaften der Erinnerung. Flucht und Vertreibung aus deutscher, polnischer und tschechischer Sicht* (Frankfurt/Main, 2001).

[42] StadtAN C 22 VI/1614, Satzung des Heimatbundes Breslau (undated, 1948).

suggesting a more stridently campaigning agenda.[43] The apparent existence of a rival 'Community of the Expellees of East and West Prussia in Nuremberg', which focused even more closely on the 'representation of the interests of its members, especially in relation to the creation of housing and work and in respect of the Equalisation of Burdens Law', reminds us that divisions and competitive rivalries existed not only within the expellee milieu as a whole but inside its constituent groups.[44] The largest of these homeland associations quickly emerged as well-organised groupings with strong regional and national infrastructures – in February 1949 the founding membership of the Sudeten German Homeland Association's Nuremberg chapter was sufficiently large for it to be subdivided into sections for Nuremberg-North, -South, -East and -West.[45]

By the early 1950s the homeland associations constituted an established presence in the associational landscape of the city, although the relatively small number of refugees in the city meant that their significance was less than it was later to become.[46] A focal point for all was the organisation of annual 'Homeland Days' (*Tag der Heimat*) as part of events held across the Federal Republic to mark the ongoing bonds of the expellees with their former home territories and to assert their agenda of return. These large-scale events, which were attended not only by expellees and refugees but also by West German homeland associations and representatives of officialdom, the churches, welfare organisations and the press, were accompanied by the flagging of buildings, the holding of church services, processions in traditional costume and demonstrations which mixed folk song performance with speeches by expellee leaders.[47] Alongside these collective Homeland Days individual associations organised periodic regional and national conventions of their own which followed a similar pattern and which could attract thousands of visitors. In 1957, for example, the Pomeranian association held a state-wide gathering in Nuremberg, with the financial support of the city

[43] StadtAN C 22 VI/1617, Satzung der Landsmannschaft der Ost- und Westpreussen in Nürnberg, 4.10.52.
[44] StadtAN C 22 VI/1618, Satzung der Gemeinschaft der Heimatvertriebenen Ost- und Westpreussen in Nürnberg (undated, 1952).
[45] StadtAN C 22 VI/1615, Protokoll über die Gründungssammlung der Sudetendeutschen Landsmannschaft, Landesverband Bayern, Kreisverband Nürnberg-Stadtkreis, 19.2.49; see also Sudetendeutsche Landsmannschaft, Landesverband Bayern, Kreisverband Nürnberg-Stadt an Polizeidirektion Nürnberg, 6.3.49.
[46] In 1952 the League of Expelled Germans in Nuremberg listed as members expellee groups representing Germans from Danzig, Carpathian Germans, East and West Prussians, Pomeranians, Transylvanian Germans, Sudeten Germans, 'Danube Swabians' (*Donauschwaben*) and Germans from the Weichsel and Warthegau regions; the League of Silesians constituted a large additional group outside of the League of Expellees. See StadtAN C 29/462, Bund Vertriebener Deutscher Nürnberg an Oberbürgermeister Bärnreuther, 26.6.52.
[47] See, for example, the general guidelines in StadtAN C 29/476, Verband der Landsmannschaften, Rundschreiben, 3.6.53.

council;[48] in 1955, the Sudeten German Homeland Association held such a gathering on the site of the former party rally grounds, its leadership using the crumbling ruins of the Zeppelin Tribune for a podium. Despite the unmistakeably irredentist symbolism of this use of the rally ground landscape, the city council not only permitted the event, but also found considerable sums of money for the repairs necessary to make it possible.[49]

Such myopic pragmatism – which was typical of the council's disavowal of the city's historic associations with the Nazi regime in this period – was all the more surprising for the fact that fears of chauvinist activism on the part of the expellee groups were widespread within the forces of the Left which dominated political life in the city. The SPD emphasised from the outset that its commitment to the expellees was based solely on social welfare concerns and the desire to integrate them into the community as equal citizens. At its 1948 party congress, which was held in Nuremberg, it reiterated that 'the Social Democratic party has always felt solidarity with all those in need of help. For this reason it has taken up the cause of the expellees and the bombed-out as its own and fights with them for the achievement of social justice in all areas of public and private life.' It emphasised that 'as a return to their old homeland is not currently possible for the expellees, the most important task of Social Democratic politics remains the achievement of the integration of the refugees in the economic, political and social life of their new homeland'.[50]

The city council was nervous, however, of being seen to support any association which voiced revisionist aspirations in its foreign policy demands. When, for example, the Silesian Homeland Association requested that the city adopt the role of patron of all Silesians from Hirschberg – with a view to it becoming a surrogate home city on which the Hirschbergers could centre their cultural activities – city councillor Staudt insisted that 'care must be taken that nothing like an irredentist movement emerges. It must not appear as if we want to foster things which prevent the refugees from being calm.'[51] The KPD – which regarded the expellee organisations simply as agents of anti-Communist agitation – was downright hostile, councillor Wagner arguing that rather than acting as cultural patron 'our task should be to overcome unemployment and housing shortages among these people. The thing is

---

[48] StadtAN C 85 I Abg. 94/A211, Pommersche Landsmannschaft Landesgruppe Bayern an Oberbürgermeister Bärnreuther, 29.1.57; Oberbürgermeister Bärnreuther an Pommersche Landsmannschaft, 21.2.57.

[49] StadtAN C 7 IX/1350, Niederschrift über die Sitzung des Bauausschusses, 21.2.55; see also Geschichte für Alle e.V., *Geländebegehung. Das Reichsparteitagsgelände in Nürnberg* (Nuremberg, 1995), 153.

[50] StadtAN C 29/299, Sozialdemokratische Partei Deutschlands, Bezirk Franken, Rundschreiben Nr 34 (undated, November/December 1948).

[51] StadtAN C 7 IX/1256, Niederschrift über die Sitzung des Ältestenrats am 16.5.52.

geared generally towards the promotion of chauvinism.'[52] When, despite these concerns, mayor Bärnreuther agreed to assume the role of patron of this group of Silesian refugees, it was under the strict condition that 'the patronage . . . has no political significance' and that 'the Hirschbergers therefore expect from the patronage no support for political aspirations within its ranks now or in the future'.[53]

More generally, the city council's nervousness of forging too close links with the expellee associations was born of the fear that they would bring obligations which would place excessive burdens on the stretched housing, welfare and financial resources of the heavily damaged city. When the head of the Germanic National Museum, Ludwig Grote, wrote to mayor Bärnreuther in 1952 to pass on the request of the Transylvanian Saxon Homeland Association that Nuremberg assume the role of patron of this group, arguing that it fitted well with the Germanic National Museum's agenda of 'making Nuremberg the spiritual centre of all expellees', the city council declined. Bärnreuther replied that 'we neither wish nor are we able to take on such an obligation'.[54] Practical reasoning and recent experience argued against promoting such a profile. When considering the Sudeten German Homeland Association's request to hold its 1955 gathering in Nuremberg, the city's police chief, Leo Stahl, argued that 'for us the experience of the former party rallies was sufficient. The major part of the participants will come into the city. If one erects beer tents for 30,000 people that will have consequences, for the people will obviously drink.'[55]

While a similar request had been rejected on such grounds in 1953 – because, as deputy mayor Lossmann put it, 'Nuremberg was still not in a position to manage such a mass throng of people' – the city's recovery had now reached a point where such a meeting might bring benefits. In Lossmann's words, 'Such a concentration of people for one to two days in Nuremberg would bring increased revenues for the Nuremberg business community from which the city would also benefit through increased tax revenues.' This spoke not only in favour of allowing the meeting but of following the practice of other cities which offered the homeland associations subventions to hold their meetings there. Despite the objections of KPD deputy Finger, who argued that 'these congresses of the home-land associations no longer have the character of fostering personal or family ties, but are increasingly becoming political demonstrations', that 'the speeches – especially those of Mr Lodgman von Auen [the chairman of the Sudeten German Homeland Association] – leave nothing to be desired in their clarity and

---

[52] StadtAN C 7 IX/1256, Niederschrift über die Sitzung des Ältestenrats am 23.5.52.
[53] StadtAN C 7 IX/1256, Entwurf: Oberbürgermeister Bärnreuther an Landsmannschaft Schlesien / Alfred Hoehne, Forchheim (undated, May 1952).
[54] StadtAN C 29/235, Ludwig Grote an Oberbürgermeister Bärnreuther, 18.9.52; C 7 IX/1256, Niederschrift über die Sitzung des Ältestenrats am 3.10.52.
[55] StadtAN C 7 IX/1341, Niederschrift über die Sitzung des Ältestenrats am 17.12.54.

aggressiveness' and that 'the city should not declare its solidarity with such a stance by playing the role of host', economic pragmatism triumphed.

The growing presence of expellees in the city, their slow but steady economic and social integration and their ongoing desire to maintain their cultural distinctiveness gave their organisations an increased prominence which stood in contrast to the veterans' associations, whose significance reached its high point in the 1950s. Common to both, however, was a relationship to the city council governed by the latter's desire to balance concern for the social welfare of the constituencies concerned with a rejection of openly irredentist or militarist demands. The rejection of aggressive nationalism implicit in this stance made it surprising, then, that the city council adopted a conciliatory stance to a group generally associated with former Nazi party members – the 'Interest Group of those Damaged by the Occupation' (*Interessensgemeinschaft der durch Besatzungsmassnahmen Geschädigten*).

The group was one of a number of organisations formed disproportionately of ex-Nazi party members which sought to redefine as 'victims' those who felt that they had been unfairly disadvantaged by the American occupation. Formed in Nuremberg in October 1948, it pressed for the return of property confiscated by the American troops and for compensation for any damage incurred as a result.[56] The group quickly developed a well-organised and highly visible local, regional and zone-wide structure which, in addition to giving legal advice to its individual members, campaigned vociferously at all levels of government. The group's willingness to organise, among other things, protest rallies in public suggests that, rather than regard confiscation of one's house as a source of shame or indicator of political guilt, its membership felt able to press its demands openly in a climate of opinion it believed would be sympathetic.[57] From a founding membership of 30 it grew locally into a pressure group of which the membership fluctuated between 300 and 400 in the early 1950s, representing the owners of some of the more than 2,500 apartments originally confiscated by the US troops.[58]

The locations of the suburbs in which it held its initial meetings suggest that its membership was drawn disproportionately from the middle-class sections of Nuremberg society.[59] In part, this reflected the fact that the Americans had

[56] StadtAN C 22 VI/1605, Karl Balling an Polizeidirektion Nürnberg, 11.10.48; Nürnberger Interessensgemeinschaft der durch Besatzungsmaßnahmen Geschädigten: Satzung (undated, 1948).
[57] See, for example, StadtAN E 6/884/1, Interessensgemeinschaft der Besatzungsgeschädigten – Protestversammlung (undated, September 1949).
[58] By 1955 the group numbered 378 members: StadtAN E 6/884/3, Rundschreiben Nr 32 der Interessensgemeinschaft der Besatzungsgeschädigten Nürnberg, 1.3.55.
[59] StadtAN E 6/884/1, Interessensgemeinschaft der durch Besatzungsmaßnahmen Geschädigten, Rundschreiben Nr 1., January 1949.

tended to confiscate good houses in the less damaged outlying suburbs which were home to the city's middle classes; in part, however, it reflected the fact that confiscations had been visited disproportionately on former members of the Nazi party, for whom such seizures were intended as symbolic punishment. The group was, indeed, acutely aware of the widespread assumption that it was an organisation which primarily represented the interests of well-heeled former Nazis, and that this attitude was in danger of compromising what it saw as the moral legitimacy of its members' claims to redress. With this in mind it emphasised the results of a questionnaire it had sent to its members, the results of which were intended to undermine the suggestion that 'allegedly only the houses of "Nazis" were confiscated'.[60] According to its findings, of those who had returned the questionnaire, over half had been classified as 'not affected' by the denazification law. This, of course, still left nearly 50 per cent of the total who had been either amnestied or classified as 'Fellow Travellers', to say nothing of those who had not thought it helpful to their cause to return the question-naire at all.

As the ironic punctuation of the term 'Nazis' implied, the group did not regard classification as 'Fellow Traveller' as evidence that an individual had been in any way morally or politically responsible for the Nazi regime. It certainly did not disqualify such individuals from inclusion in the wider imag-ined community of victims created by the war. The submission in 1949 of the Bavarian regional section of the Interest Group to the Bavarian *Landtag* demanding a law to safeguard its constituents' rights was typical in its inclu-sion of the 'victims of occupation' in the wider category of 'victims of war'. As it argued, 'people know of the need of the refugees, the bombed-out and the political persecutees and have tried to meliorate and overcome their hard fate. But do people know . . . the difficult lot and the intolerable situation of thou-sands of families damaged by occupation measures and [do] they dare to intervene for their rights and their demands?'[61]

In common with other groups, however, it went further, implying that the lot of its members gave them a special claim to sympathy: in arguing that the occupation measures were the 'saddest consequences of the post-war era' it claimed unambiguously that its members had suffered more than any others. While the organisation's rhetoric was generally free of nationalist or radical polemic, such remarks betrayed the all-too-familiar obsession with one's own woes, an unwillingness to consider the broader context in which the confisca-tions had taken place and an inability to accept the presence of materially more pressing or morally more compelling claims. When the wider context

---

[60] StadtAN E 6/884/1, Statistische Erhebungen, 30.4.49.
[61] StadtAN E 6/884/1, Landesverband der Besatzungsgeschädigten in Bayern: Eingabe über Verhandlungen mit der Besatzungsmacht und Antrag zur Schaffung eines Gesetzes zum Schutze der Rechte der Besatzungsgeschädigten an den Bayerischen Landtag, 19.3.49.

was, occasionally, acknowledged, it was to suggest that this supported the group's claims rather than undermined them. In 1954, for example, its local chairman, Georg Leidel, argued that 'when people – above all from the German side – repeatedly tell us that we Germans did, of course, lose the war and that the confiscations were also a consequence of this war, I would like to counter by saying that we victims of the occupation were neither the only ones to want the war nor the only ones to lose it, and we refuse to bear the weight of all post-war burdens on our shoulders'.[62] The group's campaigning rhetoric was certainly informed by a strong note of moral equivalence, enabling it to demand without a hint of irony 'the inclusion of the victims of occupation in the top priority category of those seeking housing, on a par with the treatment of the political, racial and religious persecutees'.[63]

However, the group's rhetoric also contained an element of anti-American occupation sentiment which made it not unattractive to sections of the SPD also. Indeed, while complaints on the part of the 'victims of occupation' that city council representatives were not attending its gatherings imply a sense of frustrated marginalisation, the SPD and the city council did back the group's demands.[64] In 1955, by which time most confiscated properties had, in fact, been released, deputy mayor Lossmann expressed his regret in a city council meeting 'that Nuremberg citizens have had to go without their property for ten years' and that 'houses have stood empty for a whole year without our having the possibility of making use of them'.[65] Shortly thereafter, another senior SPD councillor, August Meier, backed the renewed protests of the group, arguing – with the group itself – that the recent return of West German sovereignty should be the occasion of the release of the remaining confiscated properties.[66]

Such language did not imply undue sympathy for former Nazis on the part of the SPD. Rather, ongoing housing shortages predisposed a civic leadership still seeking to overcome the effects of the destruction of the city to demand the return of all available housing to civilian use. Similarly, the willingness of the city administration in the mid-1950s to compensate former Nazis for the confiscation of clothing and other domestic effects during the occupation years suggested not recognition of the validity of their claims to having been mistreated, but rather pragmatic desire to avoid potentially far more costly legal disputes. Above all, the SPD's accommodating stance towards the group betrayed a preference for political reintegration over the exclusion of former

[62] StadtAN E 6/884/12, Bericht über die 6. Mitgliederhauptversammlung am 27.1.54.
[63] StadtAN E 6/884/1, Landesverband der Besatzungsgeschädigten in Bayern: Eingabe über Verhandlungen mit der Besatzungsmacht und Antrag zur Schaffung eines Gesetzes zum Schutze der Rechte der Besatzungsgeschädigten an den Bayerischen Landtag, 19.3.49.
[64] See, for example, StadtAN E 6/884/5, Protokoll über die Verwaltungssitzung am 5.3.49.
[65] StadtAN C 7 IX/725, Niederschrift über die Sitzung des Stadtrates am 11.5.55.
[66] StadtAN C 7 IX/729, Niederschrift über die Sitzung des Stadtrates am 22.2.56.

Nazis: in return for renouncing radical invective the SPD was willing to readmit former Nazis to civil society and to acknowledge their claims to redress.

Something of the same pragmatism informed the city council's response to the occasional presence of another contentious group – veterans of the elite tank division *Grossdeutschland*. Although not a *Waffen-SS* division it had fought alongside the *Waffen-SS* on many occasions and was closely associated by opponents with the Nazi regime.[67] In 1955, for example, the Association of the Persecutors of the Nazi Regime (VVN) wrote to the mayor expressing its anger that the regimental association was planning to hold a reunion in the city. Mobilising the full force of its anti-fascist rhetoric in an appeal to Social Democratic memories of the experience of Nazism in the city, it pointed out to the mayor that 'you, as head of the city of Nuremberg, know only too well from your own experience that the current organisers of this soldiers' amusement were already marching through your beautiful city with Hitler's brown marching columns when Hitler had not yet usurped power. They terrorised the Nuremberg population in their brownshirts before 1933 and were the driving force behind the brutal persecution of the democratically inclined Nuremberg citizens between 1933 and 1945.' Reminding him that 'thousands of Nuremberg citizens had to pay for their democratic attitudes with death or years of dungeon or concentration camp internment' and that 'Nuremberg was and is a democratically inclined city', it pleaded with the mayor to 'look at the war cripples, think of the victims of fascism and visit the ruins of the last war which are still standing in Nuremberg. You will then surely put an end to the games of the old brown marchers before it is too late.'[68] Despite this powerful intervention by surviving victims of fascism, the city administration elected to allow the gathering to go ahead. Its annotation of the VVN's letter observed that 'Herr Dir B [deputy mayor Lossmann] is in the picture regarding the event. It is taking place on a very small scale. Herr Dir. B. has directed us not to answer the letter.'

With such letters the VVN attempted to draw attention to neo-Nazi, radical nationalist or anti-democratic activities while preserving the memory of the murdered victims of the regime. Other groups were similarly motivated. These included the League of German Victims and Surviving Dependants of Persecution under National Socialism for Freedom, Human Rights and Dignity, and the Association of Democratic Resistance Fighters and Persecutees' Organisations of North Bavaria; they also included the Camp Association of Dachau which, as its name suggests, sought to organise survivors of the first major concentration camp – whose name resonated strongly within the

---

[67] James Lucas, *Germany's Elite Panzer Force: Grossdeutschland* (London, 1979).
[68] StadtAN C 29/489, VVN Landesverband Bayern an Oberbürgermeister der Stadt Nürnberg, 30.8.55.

Bavarian working class as a symbol of persecution.[69] They were generally on the Left, reflecting the main focus of Nazi terror towards the German population between 1933 and 1945. If their overwhelmingly German membership and their emphasis on the preservation of resistance traditions predisposed them to advocacy of the rights of political, rather than racial, persecutees of the Third Reich, and if their sometimes diffuse, emotive anti-fascism lent itself only indirectly to fostering reflection on the mechanics of Nazi genocide, they represented a small, but crucial, repository of counter-memory in the first fifteen years after the war.

As the decision of the city administration not to answer the VVN's letter regarding the tank division reunion indicates, however, the city authorities maintained a cautious distance to organisations representing the victims of fascism. Despite the fact that many SPD members had experienced the concentration camps first-hand, the SPD-led administration remained hostile to what were generally regarded as Communist-dominated organisations. When, for example, the Camp Association of Dachau wrote to the mayor asking for a subvention to allow poorer members, surviving relatives and orphans to attend its annual commemoration of the liberation of the camp in 1956, the request was referred to the police and to the Bavarian Ministry of the Interior. The local police chief, having checked with the State Office for the Protection of the Constitution, replied that the issue was 'highly suspect'; a Bavarian Ministry of the Interior official offered the advice that 'while the organisation is not forbidden, you should refrain from making a contribution'. Such responses typified the ways in which Cold War hostility to Communism hampered attempts by surviving victims of the concentration camps to commemorate their suffering and gain wider acknowledgement of it.

In summary, the landscape of associational life in the city experienced the emergence in the late 1940s and 1950s of a wide variety of organisations that functioned as communities of remembrance based on shared experiences of wartime suffering and violence. On the one hand, these were political communities, held together by the pursuit of shared agendas aimed at compensation, improved welfare provision or restitution, in a climate of shortage in which various groups competed for redress on the basis of claims to unique victimhood. On the other, they were also emotional communities, whose internal bonds were as much affective as political, and whose self-centred focus on their

---

[69] StadtAN C 22 VI/1612, Amtsgericht Nürnberg, Aktennotiz, 10.9.63; C 22 VI/1610, Satzung des Verbandes demokratischer Widerstandskämpfer und Verfolgtenorganisationen Nordbayern, Sitz Nürnberg (VDWV Nordbayern e.V.), 17.5.58; Protokoll über die am Sonntag, den 27 April 1958 ab 10 Uhr in Nürnberg, Gaststätte 'Straßenbahnzentrale', Fürtherstrasse 152, abgehaltene Gründungsversammlung; C 29/493, H. R., Lagergemeinschaft Dachau an Oberbürgermeister Bärnreuther, 19.4.56.

own peculiar experience of suffering – the loss of *Heimat*, the loss of limbs, the loss of family members or the loss of property – underpinned a strong sense in each case that they had a prior claim to moral recognition which only they could understand. Notably, few of these associations included or built bridges to other victim groups – *Heimkehrer* made little reference to the sufferings of expellees, victims of bombing showed no interest in the relatives of the missing. Indeed, while collectively the presence of these various associations represented an organisational expression of the wider 'victim discourse' that characterised the memory culture of the 1950s, what is perhaps most striking about these groups is how their competing rhetorical claims reflected the material fissures and tensions running through a divided post-war society.

Relations with the city council varied. In general, the city administration, driven as it was by a Social Democratic welfare ethos, showed itself willing to acknowledge the welfare needs of each claimant group and to provide material support within the limits of its ability, but hostile to any manifestations of extreme right-wing, nationalist or revanchist language. In the case of the expellees, the caution of city councillors reflected both attitudes to outsiders which were widespread and a fear of overburdening the city's stretched material resources, as well as dislike of the expellee associations' more strident revisionist claims. In the case of veterans' associations, antipathy towards militarism combined, on occasion, with hostility to representatives of a milieu whose members had been on the opposing side of the political conflicts of the 1920s and early 1930s.

Most marginal of all were the groups representing the victims of fascism. Numerically, they were too small to constitute a constituency in need of courting; ideologically, they fell foul of a Cold War political climate in which their mere existence provoked suspicions of Communist subversion. But the victim rhetoric of much larger, more powerful, constituencies also fostered their marginalisation. Soldiers' claims of heroism and sacrifice embodied a denial of the murderous barbarism that had occurred on the eastern front; expellee claims to have been victims of totalitarian violence undermined awareness of the unique suffering experienced by survivors of Nazi persecution. The organisations of victims of Nazism were greeted, at best, with indifference by society at large.

II.2

Marking Suffering, Masking Schism

The Inscription of Memory on the Urban
Landscape, 1945 to 1961

A key terrain on which the commemorative agendas of various victim groups
were pursued, and the competing interests of each played out, was the process
of memorialisation in the form of plaques, reliefs, statues and monuments. As
emotional communities such groups sought meaningful sites at which to
share the expression of grief; as interest groups they sought to inscribe such
monuments with texts that validated their campaigns for restitution or their
expressions of injured protest; as political groups they sought monuments
which provided ideological orientation. Above them, mediating and intervening as both broker and positioned actor, stood the secular and religious
authorities upon whose assent the creation of such memorials rested. Their
dispensations were, in turn, shaped by deep political, ideological, cultural or
theological traditions, and reflected long-standing preferences for certain
forms, idioms, vocabularies and iconographies.[1]

The human and institutional agency that led to the establishment of individual memorials varied. Some owed their creation to individual requests from
within the community; others were driven by the strident demands of pressure
groups claiming to represent a wider constituency; in other cases, the initiative
appeared to come from city or religious authorities themselves. In some cases
the memorials were funded by public collections, in others by the authorities.
In some cases – mostly those erected in secular spaces – the memorials were the
product of competitions, the outcome reflecting the aesthetic choices of prize
committees formed of civic dignitaries; in other cases – mainly memorials
established on sacred ground – they reflected strict guidelines laid down by the
ecclesiastical authorities.

---

[1] Reinhart Koselleck, 'War Memorials: Identity Formations of the Survivors' in id., *The Practice
of Conceptual History. Timing History, Spacing Concepts* (Stanford, 2002), 285–326.

Institutional strictures notwithstanding, the memorials established in Nuremberg in the 1950s varied considerably in form and focus. In some respects they betrayed a striking continuity in cultural habit from the post-1918 era, taking as they did largely traditional forms – from the individual grave to the plaque, relief or sculpture to the renaming of the street or square – and being placed in familiar spaces – the church, the cemetery, the prominent public building – where they became the sites of familiar rituals. In church spaces, in particular, monuments also deployed an understandably familiar visual vocabulary which drew on the iconographic core of Christian tradition, reminding us that, in the context of social crisis, moral disorientation and emotional anguish brought about by the war, one response was to reach for the old, the familiar and therefore, perhaps, the comforting.[2] In other respects, however, the memorial aesthetic of the post-war era betrayed the difficulty of finding a visual language appropriate to this particular war, or capable of endowing with acceptable meaning experiences and events the public acknowledgement or articulation of which were not permissible in the 1950s. Indeed, what was perhaps most striking about memorials established in the 1950s – and indeed beyond – was the general absence of figurative representations of war or warriors, suggesting an unspoken but shared awareness of what this war had involved, and the sense of shame this knowledge generated.[3]

If unspoken knowledge of the nature of the war made a certain visual idiom appear unacceptable, the political and ideological context of the Cold War and western integration gave its own impetus to the need to give this illegitimate, criminal war agreeable meanings around which a cohesive community memory could, on the surface at least, coalesce. The image of the German as 'victim', misled and terrorised by the Nazis, forced to fight a war against his or her wishes and to suffer the horrors of the front or of allied bombing lent itself perfectly to this. Indeed, the essential characteristic of the memorial landscape of the 1950s lay in its expression of the minimum social consensus that Germans had, collectively, been innocent victims of war, and that the suffering endured by others at their hands was only that which war inevitably brings to all. Yet while this overarching 'victim' discourse is not difficult to discern in the

---

[2] In this sense Sabine Behrenbeck's assertion that 'following World War II it was impossible to continue older traditions of public commemoration in Germany because the war had lacked moral justification' is, perhaps, a little one-sided (Behrenbeck, 'Between Pain and Silence', 42). On formal continuities in memorials within the western cultural tradition, see also Reinhart Koselleck, 'Einleitung', in Reinhart Koselleck and Michael Jeismann, (eds), Der Politische Totenkult. Kriegerdenkmäler in der Moderne (Munich, 1994), 1–20, although Koselleck likewise emphasises that significant changes did occur after the Second World War.

[3] On the abandonment of the heroic idiom after 1945 see Simone Derix, 'Der Umgang mit dem Nationalsozialismus in Kölner Mahnmalen der fünfziger Jahre' in Dülffer, Köln in den 50er Jahren, 261–76, here 261; on the difficulties of finding a visual idiom see Koselleck, 'War Memorials', 321–4.

dense material culture of monuments, plaques and memorial places to which the experience of war gave rise, the cohesiveness and coherence of this discourse was always fragile. Only slightly beneath the surface lay a more complex, fragmented and contested memory culture in constant evolution, the memorials of which may collectively have told back to the community a story of universal suffering but which, individually, hid more fractious stories of division and dispute, the tensions of which could only be resolved consensually at the level of a vague minimum assertion of shared victimhood.

The first sites on which the authorities and interested agencies sought to memorialise the experiences of war and to endow them with agreeable, non-Nazi meanings were the city's cemeteries. In 1945 their desolate state reflected the hubris and nemesis of the Third Reich and the legacies of its inhumane racist utopianism. Nazi insignia on SA and SS graves reflected the movement's heroicising cult of the fallen; mass graves for victims of the allied air raids – described as the 'air war fallen' (*Luftkriegsgefallenen*) – bore witness to the blurring of military and civilian casualties in the pursuit of total war by the 'People's Community'; the visiting of military violence on the city was evident not just in the graves of air-raid victims but in those of the many soldiers killed in defence of the city; the chaotic circumstances of defeat were such that many soldiers lay where they had been hastily buried in civilians' gardens or at the roadside. Meanwhile, the presence of the remains of thousands of prisoners of war, deported civilian labourers and concentration camp inmates testified to the enactment of Nazi racial barbarism in the immediate environs of the city itself between 1933 and 1945. Victims and perpetrators alike now lay in shattered cemeteries which bore all the hallmarks of allied bombing in the form of destroyed buildings, bomb craters and damaged graves.

The first five years after the war witnessed a massive programme of reburial through which the imprint left by the Third Reich on the cemetery landscapes of the city underwent a substantial process of erasure. Firstly, the large numbers of individual soldiers buried provisionally in the last weeks of the war were exhumed and their remains transferred to the city's South Cemetery.[4] Meanwhile, air-raid victims who had been buried in mass Nazi ceremonies were exhumed from the 'cemetery of honour' (*Ehrenfriedhof*) in which they had been originally interred and transferred to individual graves.[5] By early 1948, the final remains in the Nazi official air-raid graves had been exhumed and the section was dissolved.[6] Similarly, the insignia on SA, SS and

---

[4] StadtAN C 29/424, Monatsbericht des Oberbürgermeisters der Stadt Nürnberg für Juli 1945.
[5] StadtAN C 29/424, Monatsbericht des Oberbürgermeisters der Stadt Nürnberg für die Zeit vom 20 November bis 19 Dezember 1945.
[6] StadtAN C 29/428, Monatsbericht des Stadtrats zu Nürnberg für die Zeit vom 20 Februar bis 19 März 1948.

soldiers' graves were removed as part of a wider campaign to remove the visual traces of Nazi rule from the urban landscape.[7]

At the same time, the city initiated discussions with the League for the Care of German War Graves concerning the re-landscaping of those sections of the South Cemetery that contained the remains of many of the military and civilian casualties of the war. Two options emerged. In the League's favoured plan – for which it was willing to contribute the bulk of the cost – the military casualties would be kept separate from the civilian casualties in two reconfigured burial groves.[8] In the second, devised within the city administration itself, the existing distribution of graves would be broadly retained, so that military and civilian casualties would remain buried alongside one another in various sections of the cemetery. This option was cheaper overall, but the League would be unwilling to contribute, so that the bill for the city would be higher.[9]

In the pre-currency reform situation, in which absence of labour and materials was a considerably greater hindrance than lack of financial resources, issues of cost were secondary. Faced with the League's option, which sat recognisably within a national-conservative tradition of marking as distinct the heroic sacrifice of the soldier, and the locally preferred alternative, which de-emphasised the military character of the soldiers' death, the city council opted for the latter. Arguing that the large-scale exhumations demanded by the League's plans were unacceptable 'for reasons of piety', it decided instead that 'the war victims should, rather, be left in their current places of rest as far as possible, without drawing a distinction between soldiers and civilians'.[10] If such choices reflected an understandable desire within Social Democratic circles to create a cemetery landscape clearly distinct from the militaristic burial practices of their Nazi predecessors, their blurring of the differences between civilian and military casualties both prefigured the erasure of distinctions that characterised the memory culture of the 1950s and ironically mirrored the Nazis' own such blurring; whereas for the Nazis the demands of 'total war' had turned civilians into 'soldiers of the home front', their deaths to be acknowledged in correspondingly martial fashion, Social Democratic hostility to militarism led to a civilianising construction of soldiers in which their participation in aggressive military violence was downplayed.

However, the debilitating impact of the currency reform on communal finances removed the earlier luxury of choice, placing the city authorities in a much weaker position when it came to rejecting the League's plans. Revisiting

[7] StadtAN C 7 I/8015, Aus der Niederschrift über die Sitzung des Verwaltungs- und Polizeisenats am 24.9.46 (Abschrift).
[8] See also Mosse, *Fallen Soldiers*, 214–16.
[9] StadtAN C 7 IX/699, Niederschrift über die Sitzung des Stadtrats am 21.5.47.
[10] StadtAN C 7 IX/700, Beschluss des Stadtrats, 16.7.47.

7. Memorial sarcophagus, Grove of Honour, South Cemetery, Nuremberg (1952).

the issue in 1950, by which point nothing had been done, the council reversed its opposition to working with the League, and adopted the latter's proposals.[11]

In any case, the League's plans had by now been modified to the extent that the grave of honour (*Ehrenhain*), as finally completed in 1952, now included both fallen soldiers and some civilian victims. More generally the grove, its design and the ceremonial surrounding its inauguration reflected a set of aesthetic and political compromises between Social Democratic and conservative conceptualisations of the dead and of wartime sacrifice, and between Christian, heathen and secular iconographies and inscriptions. Each individual grave was marked by the same basic stone, on which the name of the occupant was engraved. Interspersed between the individual rows of graves were granite crosses, giving an overtly Christian tone to the grove. At its centre stood a sarcophagus – a form pre-dating Christian practice – on which was inscribed, on one side, the words 'Here lie German Soldiers and Air War Victims from the War of 1939–1945. Men, Women and Children' and, on the other side, 'Your sacrifice, our sorrow / be dedicated to the Lord of the World / Dark paths – who understands / A People grows from its sacrifice'. In comparison to the nearby First World War monument to the military dead (established in 1925), on which a very masculine, martial figure in military steel helmet lay floored but ready to rise again, embodying a clear message of nationalist revanchism, the sarcophagus, with its inclusion of men, women and children in the same

---

[11] StadtAN C 7 IX/1255, Niederschrift über die Sitzung des Ältestenrats, 24.2.50; C 7 IX/705, Niederschrift über die Sitzung des Stadtrats, 1.3.50.

8. First World War memorial, South Cemetery, Nuremberg (1925).

inscription, struck a decidedly unmilitary, unaggressive tone, while the questioning reference to 'dark paths – who understands' spoke to a culture which, in 1952, was still struggling to fathom the meanings of the war.[12]

The inauguration of the grove reflected the same compromises. Senior figures from both churches were prominent at the occasion, where 'the Catholic representative emphasised approvingly that the sarcophagus in the middle was decorated almost exclusively with Christian symbols'.[13] Meanwhile, the presence of Minister President Hans Ehard ensured that a secular, if similarly conservative, voice of authority was heard. The accompanying music offered a blend of the religious and secular, with pieces by J.S. Bach and Bruckner alongside the vernacular melody the 'Song of the Good Comrade' (*Das Lied vom Guten Kameraden*).[14]

It was, indeed, in such music that the continuities and compromises that fed into the creation of monuments such as the *Ehrenhain* found their most subtle expression. Since at least the First World War, the 'Song of the Good Comrade' had played a key role in the folk nationalist canon of marching songs, and had also occupied a central place in the Nazi musical repertoire. Yet the song itself was the setting of a poem written by Ludwig Uhland during the Napoleonic Wars: in singing it, local choirs and dignitaries were thus not so much rehearsing

[12] Masa, *Freiplastiken*, 325–7.
[13] 'Ehrenfriedhof für Kriegsopfer in Nürnberg', *Nürnberger Evangelisches Gemeindeblatt*, 26.10.52.
[14] LKAN Kd Nbg 352, Einweihung des Ehrenfriedhofs im Südfriedhof, 19.10.52.

the radical nationalist excesses of the immediately preceding years as connecting to a much older national-patriotic continuum into which Nazism had success-fully inserted itself. Moreover, while attending veterans could, if they wished, hear in it reaffirmation of the easy fiction that their experience of soldiering had sat within a decent tradition of military action rather than figure as a specifically Nazi act, progressively minded participants could also hear a song favoured by sections of the Left during the Spanish Civil War. Music, in other words, did not merely endow the ritual with one fixed meaning: it permitted, but simulta-neously masked, the ascription of a variety of such meanings.

What, meanwhile, of the thousands of foreign victims of the Third Reich buried in Nuremberg's cemeteries by the end of the war? During the years of military occupation, the presence of allied authority ensured that they were kept in reasonable repair.[15] If the repeated circulation of military government directives concerning the maintenance of such graves implied a belief within higher circles that they were not being followed as strictly as they might, the city leadership was agreed that 'of course all graves of foreigners who died in Nuremberg during the war must also be carefully tended'.[16] It complained that 'repair work causes exceptional difficulties because the necessary building material – including wood – is very hard to procure' but was, nonetheless, sufficiently diligent to have wooden crosses made for dead prisoners of war, small gravestones for foreign workers and 'temporary wooden plaques' for the Russian prisoners of war in 1946.[17]

The presence in 1945 of such graves testified to the murderous violence of Nazi labour and racial policy.[18] However, the evolving diplomatic constellation

[15] StadtAN C 7 I/8045, Bayerisches Staatsministerium des Innern an die Regierungspräsidenten, 3.9.46; C 7 I/8045, Mission Militaire Française de Liaison auprès de la 3ème Armée Americaine, Regierungsbezirk Ober- et Mittelfranken to Dr Schregle, Regierungspräsident Ober- und Mittelfranken, 24.1.46.

[16] StadtAN C 29/425, Monatsbericht des Oberbürgermeisters der Stadt Nürnberg für die Zeit vom 20 Januar 1946 bis 19 Februar 1946.

[17] StadtAN C 29/425, Monatsbericht des Oberbürgermeisters der Stadt Nürnberg für die Zeit vom 20 Mai 1946 bis 19 Juni 1946. See also StadtAN C 7 I/8045, Nachweisung über den Bedarf an Mitteln für die Instandsetzung und Pflege der Gräber der Angehörigen der Wehrmacht, die während des jetzigen Krieges gestorben sind und nicht auf reichs- oder heereseigenen Friedhöfen ruhen und der Gräber der Luftkriegsopfer sowie der Gräber der Kriegsgefangenen und der ausländischen Zivilarbeiter (undated, 1946).

[18] The history of forced labour in Nuremberg during the war is comparatively under-researched. See, however, Gerhard Jochem, 'Der Einsatz ausländischer Arbeitskräfte während des Zweiten Weltkriegs am Beispiel der Stadtverwaltung Nürnberg' in Barbara Ostyn, Die steinerne Rose. Erinnerungen einer polnischen Fremdarbeiterin in Deutschland 1942–1943 (Nuremberg, 2003), 39–78; Gerhard Jochem, 'Feind bleibt Feind! Kriegsgefangene in Nürnberg 1939–1945' in Mitteilungen des Vereins für Geschichte der Stadt Nürnberg 93 (2006), 228–98; Gerhard Jochem, 'Bedingungen und Umfeld des Einsatzes der ungarischen Sklavenarbeiterinnen in Nürnberg' in Michael Diefenbacher and Gerhard Jochem (eds), 'Solange ich lebe, hoffe ich'. Die Aufzeichungen des ungarischen KZ-Häftlings Ágnes Rósza 1944/45 in Nürnberg und Holleischen (Nuremberg, 2006), 63–93.

of the late 1940s and early 1950s was highly conducive to the remodelling of the cemeteries in ways which could erase such unwelcome reminders. From 1949 to 1950, mirroring the gradual normalisation of Franco-West German relations, extensive exhumations of the hundreds of French prisoners of war and civilians buried in the city were carried out by French commissions charged with repatriating the remains.[19] Shortly thereafter a smaller number of Dutch graves were exhumed and the remains repatriated in the same way.[20]

The existence of a KPD fraction on the city council, meanwhile, ensured the presence of voices willing to speak on behalf of commemorating the dead of other countries in a dignified fashion. However, even before the end of the occupation there was a tangible tendency towards the neglect of Soviet graves. In July 1947, for example, one KPD councillor, Schirmer, was forced to complain about the 'undignified interment of the Russian dead compared to other prisoners of war'.[21] He was clearly fighting a losing battle. The onset of the Cold War, the withdrawal of allied supervision and the impact of the currency reform on communal finances combined to foster the accelerated onset of a culture of neglect in the early 1950s to which the Soviet graves swiftly fell victim.

Yet it would be wrong to see in this neglect merely the consequences-in-reverse of the same international political constellation that led to the repatriation of western victims' remains. As the apparent neglect of the graves of Italian victims in the 1950s suggests, post-war reconciliation was no safeguard against the absence of piety when it collided with different national or cultural attitudes on the ground.[22] The widespread resentment on the part of Germans of former allies who they felt had betrayed them had led to terrible mistreatment of Italian military internees during the war, sometimes on a par with that meted out to Soviet workers; the continuing effects of such resentments, dovetailing as they did with a deeper seated cultural arrogance towards Italians, operated to ensure that their graves, too, were neglected.[23] In this sense, the patterns of care and neglect for graves in the post-war years reflected not just the vagaries of post-war international relations but the residual presence of the mental structures of Nazi racism: neglect of Soviet graves reflected not just Cold War expediency but lingering ethnic arrogance towards people widely regarded as inferior.

---

[19] See, for example, StadtAN C 29/430, Monatsbericht der Stadtrat Nürnberg für die Zeit vom 1 bis 31 August 1949; Monatsbericht der Stadt Nürnberg für die Zeit vom 1 bis 31 Januar 1950; Monatsbericht der Stadt Nürnberg für die Zeit vom 1 bis 31 August 1950; on the modern practice of separating the dead of different nations, see Koselleck, 'War Memorials', 313–14.

[20] StadtAN C 29/430, Monatsbericht der Stadtrat Nürnberg für die Zeit vom 1 bis 31 Dezember 1950.

[21] StadtAN C 7 IX/700, Niederschrift über die Sitzung des Stadtrats am 16.7.47. See also StadtAN C 7 IX/705, Niederschrift über die Sitzung des Stadtrats am 1.3.50.

[22] On the neglect of Italian graves see StadtAN C 7 I/8039, Bestattungsamt an Volksbund Deutscher Kriegsgräberfürsorge, 8.8.51.

[23] Gerhard Schreiber, *Die italienischen Militärinternierten im deutschen Machtbereich 1943 bis 1945. Verraten – Verachtet – Vergessen* (Munich, 1990), esp. 339ff.

By the mid-1950s, any sense of moral obligation to tend the graves of foreign victims of Nazism had faded. The sections of cemeteries in which foreign victims remained had become, figuratively speaking, dead spaces, neither acknowledged nor claimed by any individuals or group. In 1955 the cemetery authorities wrote to the League for the Care of German War Graves asking if it were possible to transfer the remaining foreign graves – with the exception of Italian, French and Belgian ones – to another cemetery in Neumarkt (apparently without success).[24] In 1957 the remaining 450 Italian graves were exhumed and reburied in an official cemetery in Frankfurt, including the remains of former inmates of Flossenbürg, Hersbruck and the Langwasser camp.[25] By this time, a cemetery landscape which, in 1945, had reflected the history of Nazism's violent destructiveness, had been largely reordered into a space in which the ordinary German dead could appear to any passing visitor to have been the ordinary victims of an ordinary war, the victims of Nazi racial imperialism having been removed or neglected for reasons of political expediency, ethnic arrogance and moral indifference.

In the early 1950s, the focus of memorialisation activity in the city was firmly on the German soldiers of the Second World War. Reflecting the centrality of the issue of the missing and the unreleased prisoners of war to the mental and emotional landscapes of the population, the first prominent memorial to German soldiers to be unveiled was not to the dead but to those believed still to be alive. The initiative came from the Association of Former Prisoners of War, which in early 1952 proposed that a plaque or memorial book be created in which the names of all those yet to return be listed. The number of former soldiers from the city listed as missing was such that this was impossible, but the city council – the great majority of the members of which bought into the popular consensus that the missing soldiers were alive and the innocent victims of arbitrary Soviet justice – was willing to establish a plaque on the prominent *Nassauer Haus*, opposite the central, iconic *Lorenzkirche*.

The plaque was conceived specifically as an exhortation on a live issue, rather than as a memorial to losses past. As deputy mayor Lossmann put it, 'it should not be a memorial plaque, but one of admonition, to remind the people that many thousands of people still live behind barbed wire and that everything should be done to free them again'.[26] The fact that all prisoners in the west – a few major war criminals aside – had been released by this point

[24] StadtAN C 7 I/8045, Bestattungsamt Nürnberg an Volksbund Deutscher Kriegsgräberfürsorge e.V., 26.2.55; Volksbund Deutscher Kriegsgräberfürsorge e.V., Landesverband Bayern an Stadtrat Nürnberg/Bestattungsamt, 16.3.55.

[25] 'Gefallene Italiener werden umgebettet – Exhumierungen auf dem Südfriedhof in aller Stille', *Fränkische Tagespost*, 24.4.57.

[26] StadtAN C 7 IX/709, Niederschrift über die Sitzung des Stadtrats am 13.2.52.

made the political focus of the admonition obvious: the Cold War climate of the early 1950s made it easy for local politicians, Social Democrats included, to co-opt the missing prisoners of war into a wider anti-Soviet rhetoric. It was, therefore, unsurprisingly, the KPD who spoke against the plaque, councillor Schwab accusing the city council of using the issue to foster a new climate of militarism in support of West German rearmament. Pointing to the fact that all those still retained in captivity were convicted war criminals, she argued that the other parties should focus instead on pursuing more peaceful relations with the east. The SPD's response was to reassert the innocence of the remaining prisoners, deputy mayor Lossmann insisting that 'I must decisively reject the representation of the issue from the east which treats it as one of condemned war criminals'. Denying wholesale the legitimacy of Soviet justice, Lossmann continued that 'even if one tries to brand them as war criminals we know how such judgements are formed'. Despite the opposition of the KPD the motion to erect the plaque was passed; the consensus underpinning its creation was such that it was ready to unveil only three months later, in May 1952, at a demonstration organised by the Association of Former Prisoners of War.[27] A simple plaque, inscribed with the words 'We remember our as yet unreturned prisoners of war and our missing. The City of Nuremberg 1952', the work eschewed any visual representation of the prisoners or the missing. During the early 1950s it became the focal point of numerous vigils, demonstrations and protest marches.[28]

There was a small but significant coda to the creation of the plaque in the form of a subsequent request in February 1956 on the part of the Association of Former Prisoners of War to establish an additional memorial to the missing on the walls of Nuremberg's castle.[29] Coming as it did in the wake of the return of the final prisoners from Soviet captivity in the winter of 1955 to 1956, its timing suggests an upsurge of anguish on the part of those anxious relatives whose hopes had rested on Adenauer's visit to Moscow; the association's present tense description of the need for an additional memorial for 'the thousands of those being held back, the missing, deported and disappeared, who are waiting in hope for a lifetime for a faraway family member' indicated that many had yet to reconcile themselves to the truth.[30] The additional memorial was never established, but the fact and the timing of the request remind us, again, that there was always more than Cold War rhetoric at stake in the memorialisation process, both for city authorities, pressure groups and

---

[27] StadtAN C 7 IX/1256, Niederschrift über die Sitzung des Ältestenrats am 16.5.52.
[28] See below, Chapter II.3.
[29] StadtAN C 7 IX/1378, Niederschrift über die Sitzung des Ältestenrats am 2.3.56; see also Niederschrift über die Sitzung des Ältestenrats am 8.6.56.
[30] StadtAN C 7 IX/1378, Verband der Heimkehrer / Kreisverband Nürnberg an Oberbürgermeister Bärnreuther, 27.2.56.

9. Memorial plaque to the prisoners of war and the missing, *Nassauer Haus*, Nuremberg (1952).

the public at large, and that sites such as the *Nassauer Haus* plaque addressed the anxieties of a population whose fears, hopes and sentimental reflexes were not reduceable to a set of political resentments, even if the expression of those anxieties was often inflected with political overtones.

Thousands of other families lived with the certain knowledge that their loved ones had been killed in action. During the early 1950s it was the churches which took the leading role in establishing memorial plaques, on which the names of the dead were listed, in each parish church. For the Protestant Church, the first was erected in the *Erlöserkirche* (Church of the Redeemer) in Leyh in July 1952; further plaques followed in the *Friedenskirche* (Church of Peace) in June 1953, and in the parish church of St Jobst in November 1954.[31] Reflecting the strict control exercised over them by the church authorities, they largely conformed to a standard pattern, yet their simple inscriptions and iconography told much about the impact made by the war on local communities and the meanings that grew up around it.

The example in St Jobst was typical in its simple listing of the names of the dead by the year of their death. Framing the names were a crucifix and the simple inscription 'Thy Will Be Done: In Memory of the Victims of 1939–45'. Such

---

[31] 'Erste Gefallenen-Gedenktafel in Nürnberg enthüllt', *Nürnberger Evangelisches Gemeindeblatt*, 27.7.52; 'Einweihung von zwei Gefallenengedenktafeln in der Friedenskirche', *Nürnberger Evangelisches Gemeindeblatt*, 21.6.53; 'St Jobst: Einweihung der Gefallenen-Gedenktafel', *Nürnberger Evangelisches Gemeindeblatt*, 21.11.54.

10. Memorial to the victims of the Second World War, St Jobst Parish Church (1954).

Christian language and imagery lent itself to Cold War constructions of German soldiers as defenders of western Christendom against hostile Bolshevik atheism, but the iconography and inscription also reflected mental dispositions that predated 1945. As the Protestant Church authorities argued, the symbolism of the cross offered the one true meaning of death to those who sought it.[32] Only one name was listed for 1940, reflecting the limited demographic impact of the 'Blitzkrieg' years. From 1941 onwards, however, the list of names expanded substantially for each remaining year of the war. Despite the fact that it ended after less than five months of 1945 had passed, the largest number of casualties was recorded for that year, reflecting the huge losses caused by the collapse of the German armies in the east in the preceding winter. Even more telling, the list of the 'missing', appended to the list of the military dead, was twice as long as the list of those killed in 1945. The majority of those missing had also, of course, been killed in the final months of the war, again underlining how by far the most intense military losses hit the community precisely at the time when it was suffering the terrifying climax of the bombing campaign, administering a demographic and emotional shock to the community which resonated for years.

Appended to the list of those killed in action or missing were the names of those who were known to have died in Soviet captivity – one in 1946 and one

---

[32] 'Das Kreuz bleibt stehen. Zum Volkstrauertag 1952', *Nürnberger Evangelisches Gemeindeblatt*, 16.11.52.

in 1948. Finally, in seamless continuity from the military casualties came a list of the civilian casualties of the war. Here, the occasional presence of more than one name from the same family reflected the impact the bombing had on unfortunate individual households. The listing of the names of military and civilian casualties together on the memorials again attested to the desires of a community that wished to imagine soldiers as innocent civilians-in-uniform rather than as agents of imperialist aggression, and to an environment in which the assertion of an overarching shared victimhood functioned as a means to refashion a shared community identity, whatever other sharp material, social or political divisions pertained.

The same multilayered continuities in operation in the creation of the *Ehrenhain* in the South Cemetery were evident in the city's remodelling of its main monument to the dead soldiers of the First World War. Originally inaugurated in 1930, the *Luitpoldhain* monument consisted of a classical arcade, inscribed inside with the names of battles in which Nuremberg regiments had fought, and flanked on either side by a series of flame-bearing pylons. This formed three sides of a square which could be used for commemorative ceremonies. During the Nazi era, the monument became the focal point of the massive *Luitpoldarena*, in which the SA, SS and other Nazi formations paraded and the movement's martyrs of 1923 were honoured; the *Luitpoldarena* became, in turn, an integral part of the party rally ground complex.[33] In 1945 the arena stood as one of many embarrassing archaeological relics with which the city had to contend.[34]

As the evolution of the city's plans for the monument in the post-war era show, the Social Democrats' proclivity to conflate different categories of wartime experience did not stop at the blurring of the identities of the military and civilian casualties of the Second World War. It extended, firstly, to the elision of the soldier victims of the First World War with the military casualties of the later conflagration – placing the experience of the latter in a continuum with the former which eroded the distinctions between each. Moreover, in drawing the victims of fascism into the same memorial site as the military casualties of the war, it imparted the same status of victimhood to the perpetrators as to those they had murdered.

Originally the SPD-led council had planned to commemorate the 'victims of fascism' at the *Wodansplatz*, which was renamed the *Platz der Opfer des Faschismus* (Square of the Victims of Fascism) in 1946.[35] Initially, it was intended to establish a memorial specifically to the victims of fascism

[33] Geschichte für Alle e.V., *Geländebegehung. Das Reichsparteitagsgelände in Nürnberg* (Nuremberg, 1995), 13–15.
[34] See below, Chapter IV.4.
[35] StadtAN C 7 IX/1251, Niederschrift über die Sitzung des Ältestenausschusses, 22.3.46.

11. *Luitpoldhain* memorial (re-dedicated 1953).

there too.[36] Yet it was not long before the council was rowing back on this decision: in 1947 the original decision to establish a memorial was reduced to the commitment to provide a suitable space.[37] By the time the VVN approached the council in 1949 to request that the city establish the monument as well as provide the space, with the apparent justification that 'similar such memorials have been established in most large cities and specifically Nuremberg, as the former city of the Reich party rallies, should not be behind on this', the enthusiasm had waned further.[38] While SPD councillor Otto Bärnreuther spoke in support, another council member, councillor Eduard Brenner (SPD) remarked, in an unfortunate choice of words, that while in favour in principle, he thought that 'it is wrong, however, to spend so much money today on a dead cause'. In the course of the discussions, SPD councillor Lossmann proposed to solve the issue in connection with the repair of the war damage to the *Luitpoldhain*, with the implicit advantage of saving the expense of a separate memorial.[39]

---

[36] StadtAN C 7 IX/698, Niederschrift über die Sitzung des Beirats der Stadt Nürnberg, 24.4.46; C 7 IX/1251, Niederschrift über die Sitzung des Ältestenausschusses, 12.12.47; StadtAN C 7 IX/1410, Niederschrift über die Sitzung des Ältestenrates am 11.1.57.

[37] StadtAN C 7 IX/1252, Niederschrift über die Sitzung des Ältestenausschusses, 12.12.47.

[38] See the discussion in StadtAN C 7 IX/1254, Niederschrift über die Sitzung des Ältestenrates, 22.4.49.

[39] According to Masa the separate memorial at the *Platz der Opfer des Faschismus* was nonetheless erected between 1950 and 1955 (*Freiplastiken*, 240), but there is no evidence to say when exactly this occurred.

Herein lay the basis for the decision, finally taken in 1953, to remodel the 'hall of honour' for the First World War soldiers at the *Luitpoldhain* into a 'memorial to the victims of both world wars and National Socialist tyranny'.[40] The hall was restored, its original inscriptions erased, and a new one added which read 'To the Victims of the Wars of 1914 to 1918 and 1939 to 1945 and of Violent Tyranny [*Gewaltherrschaft*] 1933 to 1945. The City of Nuremberg'.

The reworking of a major Nazi shrine into a site of intended democratic remembrance implied, perhaps, a degree of aesthetic insensitivity – especially as much of the rest of the Nazis' *Luitpoldarena* remained intact at this point. It would be wrong again, however, to see in this reuse of the original *Ehrenhalle* the workings of an uncritical continuity in Nazi mentalities. The remodelling of the *Ehrenhalle* was, if anything, an act of re-appropriation of a site created prior to the Nazi era, when the city was in the hands of democratic politicians. Yet the remembrance culture of the 1920s embodied in the *Ehrenhalle* – with its glorification of military engagements – had itself been far from unproblematic; as the masculine, martial First World War memorial at the South Cemetery also showed, the city's pre-1933 memory culture had been far from free of revanchist nationalist inflection.

Moreover, as subsequent discussions of the *Luitpoldhain*'s rededicated purpose again showed, the SPD enjoyed an ambivalent relationship with the former perpetrators of Nazi violence. On the one hand, the city council's refusal to countenance the establishment of individual regimental memorials on the monument showed its familiar dislike of anything reminiscent of militarist tradition.[41] On the other hand, the nebulous characterisation of Nazism as 'violent tyranny' reflected an underlying unwillingness, or inability, to challenge openly or name clearly those institutions, agencies or interest groups which Social Democratic tradition knew to have been disproportionately complicit in the local enactment of Nazi politics – namely elite groups in the judiciary, big business, the civil service as well as the military; the very vague allusions to those who had suffered bespoke a similar inability to acknowledge the Europe-wide dimensions of the Holocaust or the Jewish and/or foreign identity of the majority of the Nazi regime's victims.

Again, then, the overarching formulations of universal victimhood reflected in deputy mayor Lossmann's insistence that 'the city of Nuremberg's memorial was created for all victims of both wars and the tyrannical rule of National Socialism' indicated how the pragmatic necessity of reintegrating former political enemies militated against a forthright insistence on historical truth, and how vagueness was the essential precondition for the acceptability of narratives

---

[40] StadtAN C 7 IX/1314, Niederschrift über die nicht-öffentliche Sitzung des Bauausschusses, 20.4.53; C 7 IX/1330, Niederschrift über die Sitzung des Ältestenrats am 11.12.53.
[41] See, for example, StadtAN C 7 IX/1351, Niederschrift über die nicht-öffentliche Bauausschusssitzung, 21.3.55.

around which a cohesive communal memory could form. At the same time, the reuse of the *Luitpoldhain* for commemorative rituals in the post-war era ensured that, while the dominant Social Democratic political classes could express their democratic sentiment there, right-wing veterans' groups and conservative politicians could simultaneously imagine themselves to be re-entering a nationalist tradition of remembrance which they had never accepted as problematic in the first place.[42]

If the memory culture of the 1950s focused primarily on soldier casualties, the mid-1950s witnessed something of a shift towards the commemoration of civilian losses, above all those killed in air raids. This was a partial, rather than a complete, shift. The conflation of military and civilian losses in the early 1950s ensured that air-raid victims were acknowledged in some form from an early stage; conversely, commemoration of soldierly sacrifice continued well beyond the mid-1950s. Yet there was a tangible shift of emphasis, which culminated in the inauguration of a large monumental tower to the memory of the air-raid victims in the South Cemetery in January 1959.

In comparison to the early focus on soldiers, this desire to commemorate the bombing had coalesced only slowly. In 1951 an FDP motion to the city council to the effect that a central monument to the destruction of the medieval city be erected went round the committees but got nowhere;[43] as the Gartenstadt memorial with which this book opened suggested, attitudes continued to oscillate uneasily between a desire to remember and an urge to forget. In the mid-1950s this had started to change. This was not confined to official memorialisation and commemoration, as is shown by the publication in 1957 of the local journalist Fritz Nadler's diary extracts entitled *I Saw the Downfall of Nuremberg*, which chronicled life in the city in 1945 and quickly became a widely read text.[44]

Several factors combined to encourage this shift. Part of the timing of this new commemorative focus, perhaps, reflected the difficulties inherent in settling on an agreeable idiom in which to express mourning for a new kind of wartime suffering. The fact that prior traditions of commemorating military death existed made soldierly sacrifice an easier starting point in the search for meaning after the Second World War – once again, soldiers could be constructed as falling in defence of the eternal nation – while the absence of commemorative traditions in the case of civilian casualties meant that there was

---

[42] On the use of the *Luitpoldhain* for the Day of National Mourning, see below, Chapter II.3.

[43] StadtAN C 7 IX/1257, Antrag der FDP Stadtratsfraktion (undated, June 1951); C 7 IX/1257, Niederschrift über die Sitzung des Ältestenrates am 29.6.51; C 51/294, Fortsetzung der Niederschrift über die Sitzung des Schul- und Kulturausschusses, 10.12.54; C 51/294, Aktennotiz betr. Errichtung einer Gedenkstätte anstelle der früheren Hauptwache, 13.12.54.

[44] Fritz Nadler, *Ich sah wie Nürnberg unterging* (Nuremberg, 1957).

no such ready-made language for which to reach. The closure of the prisoner of war issue – after the initial upsurge of anguish – marked, perhaps, the point at which the emotional focus on the military dead became less intense, making space for other forms of mourning; the successes of the reconstruction era may, conversely, have prompted growing reflection on the destruction of 1945, especially given the centrality of Nuremberg's iconic medieval skyline to the civic identity of the city. Finally, it is possible that the shift of focus towards commemorating civilian casualties responded – consciously or not – to the first stirrings of a more critical memory of the war and the Holocaust, which made the uniformed agents of the regime less compelling victim figures than before.[45]

The initiative to establish a memorial to the city's air-raid victims went back to December 1955, when the city council announced a competition in which local artists and stonemasons were invited to tender proposals.[46] The winning design foresaw the creation of an artificial mound of rubble at the end of one of the main arterial paths in the cemetery, crowned with a concrete block on which would be mounted crucifixes.[47] But while this, and a number of other proposals, were regarded as worthy entries all were regarded as problematic for either aesthetic or practical reasons.[48]

Instead, the city's Construction Office settled on the creation of a bell-tower whose bells would evoke the air-raid warnings of the war while serving the practical need for bells for burials at the cemetery.[49] As the protracted discussions of the appropriate forms of wording for the monument showed, however, divided memories of the social impact of the bombing made a consensual formulation hard to achieve. Moreover, the material used to build the tower itself was not without deeply awkward symbolism. Indeed, even as the council pondered the necessity of acknowledging the origins of the stones it revealed how commemorating the ordinary German dead went hand in hand in the mid-1950s with the widespread desire to bury – figuratively and literally – awareness of the crimes of the past.

The creation of the monument was accompanied by lengthy discussions concerning the most appropriate inscription for the three planned bells. These revealed that the fault lines that ran beneath the surface of the overarching victim discourse were also gendered ones. The city official in charge of the project, councillor Schmeissner, initially proposed that the bells be inscribed, from smallest to largest, with the words 'remember the children, victims of the air war 1941–1945', 'remember the women, victims of the air war 1941–1945'

[45] See below, Chapter III.1.
[46] StadtAN C 29/323, Ideenwettbewerb zur Erreichung von Entwürfen für ein Mahnmal im Südfriedhof zur Erinnerung an die Luftkriegsopfer der Jahre 1939–1945, 5.12.55.
[47] StadtAN C 29/324, Niederschrift über die Sitzung des Preisgerichtes für den Ideenwettbewerb für ein Mahnmal im Südfriedhof zur Erinnerung an die Luftkriegsopfer der Jahre 1939–1945, 9.3.56.
[48] StadtAN C 7 IX/1367, Niederschrift über die Sitzung des Schul- und Kulturausschusses, 28.9.56.
[49] StadtAN C 51/297, Niederschrift über die Sitzung des Schul- und Kulturausschusses am 21.6.57.

and 'remember the men, victims of the air war 1941–1945'.[50] The suggestion provoked councillor Vogel to respond with the question, 'Why should men be remembered on the largest bell? The women and children are more significant here. After all, the air war affected precisely women and children.' However, if this intervention reflected the reality of life in the city in the second half of the war, which had been characterised by a gender imbalance that caused women to endure the horrors of the bombing to a correspondingly greater degree, subsequent researches revealed that more men than women or children had still been killed in the air raids.[51] It was only when it was pointed out that no-one would see the bells, because they would be at the top of the tower, that the argument was defused; the final decision to inscribe them all with the same line, 'to the memory of the victims of the bombing war 1941–1945', demonstrated again that, in respect of gender too, a memory culture capable of forging consensus at the level of visual representation was possible only if the distinctions of experience during the war were glossed over in a more general appeal to shared victimhood.

During the course of discussions of the planned monument, it also emerged that the city's Construction Office intended to use the surviving stones of the former synagogue on the *Hans-Sachs-Platz*, which had been destroyed by local Nazis in 1938. A member of the Society for Christian-Jewish Cooperation had contacted the chairman of the Schools and Culture Committee, deputy mayor Franz Haas (1904–89; deputy mayor 1957–72) to question the propriety of the use of the stones. The matter was the subject of brief clarification: some of the stones were being used in building work for the zoo, some for the new town hall, and some indeed were being used for the air-raid monument. Having also clarified that the city had the legal right to dispose over the stones, the committee was reassured. Certainly no-one questioned the difficult symbolism inherent in taking the material relics of a minority community that had all but been destroyed in the Nazi era and using them to commemorate citizens who, as members of the perpetrator community had, in some cases, joined the Nazi party, supported it and even, perhaps, participated directly in its murderous policies. Quite the reverse: chairman Haas concluded the discussion with the assertion that 'the proposal of the Construction Office is a really dignified one with which the Jewish citizens will be totally satisfied too'.[52]

The extent to which voices from within bourgeois sections of the community supported the marginalisation of the persecution of the Jews within the broader memory culture of the city was underlined four months later when

[50] StadtAN C 7 IX/1410, Niederschrift über die Sitzung des Ältestenrats am 18.10.57.
[51] StadtAN C 7 IX/1410, Niederschrift über die 26. Sitzung des Ältestenrats am 1.11.57.
[52] StadtAN C 51/297, Niederschrift über die Sitzung des Schul- und Kulturausschusses am 21.6.57.

deputy mayor Haas again raised the question of whether the origins of the stones might not be indicated in an inscription on the tower. Stating that 'the affair of the synagogue is not a page of glory for the city', councillor von Loeffelholz (FDP) counselled against such an acknowledgement, suggesting instead that 'maybe it would be appropriate to record this fact in the foundation stone document'.[53] The suggestion was adopted: the acknowledgement of the stones' origins, together with a record of the dedication of the monument, was deposited into a copper container which was then built into the base of the tower.[54] The outside of the monument, meanwhile, was adorned near the base with the inscription 'As a Reminder and in Memory of the 6621 Men, Women and Children, Victims of the Bombing War and of the Fighting in the Homeland, 1941–1945. Erected 1957–8.' All external reference to the destruction of the synagogue in 1938 was absent: following its mention at the inauguration of the tower on 2 January 1959 the connection between the tower and the persecution of the city's Jews was once again not acknowledged. In this case, commemoration of German citizens as victims went hand in hand with burial of the memory of racial persecution in the city.

In many other respects, mayor Urschlechter's speech at the inauguration of the monument – 2 January 1959, the fourteenth anniversary of the destruction of the old city – typified the discourse which had grown up locally surrounding the wartime destruction of the city.[55] For one, in treating the raids within a self-contained narrative of ever-increasing attacks on the city, the air war was radically decontextualised. Rather than place it within the broader history of the Second World War, and thus within a dynamic of attack and defence in which Germany had figured as the aggressor, the mayor's account began in the middle of the war; rather than mention the political context provided by the Nazi regime, and thus connect the suffering of the city to the fascist activism of sectors of its own population, the civilian casualties figured only as passive objects of military attack.

Furthermore, the account of the air-raids, which had lasted for four years, was focused almost entirely on the events of 2 January, into which all raids were telescoped, despite the fact that the great majority of deaths had occurred in other raids, and despite the fact that almost half of the population had already left the city by the beginning of 1945. The reason for this, undoubtedly, lay in the fact that the historic old city had been destroyed in that raid, offering a focal point for all of the city's citizens in a manner in which other raids could not. In this way, 2 January 1945 lent itself to being constructed as an act of cultural vandalism, in which the physical substance of

[53] StadtAN C 7 IX/1410, Niederschrift über die Sitzung des Ältestenrates am 18.10.57.
[54] StadtAN C 7 IX/1410, Niederschrift über die Sitzung des Ältestenrates am 11.12.57.
[55] For the text of the speech see 'Glockenturm feierlich seiner Bestimmung übergeben', *Amtsblatt der Stadt Nürnberg*, 7.1.59.

the city, rather than the Nazi regime – or its plebiscitary support base – figured as the target.[56] As mayor Urschlechter emphasised, 'As the bombers ended their wretched action they left behind them the torso of a blazing city, built up through the development of centuries by the industriousness of her citizens and destroyed in the few minutes of the bombing attack.' Finally, reflecting both the preference for integration over accusation which ran through the Social Democratic memory agenda of the 1950s, and the strong pacifist conclusions which the Left had drawn from the war, he insisted that questions of guilt were less significant than a commitment to reconstruction in peace: 'Just as each one of us can overcome the harsh blows of fate neither just through asking after guilt, innocence or partial guilt nor through hate, so life demands of us the following: the sacrifice of our air-war dead must place on us, who were permitted to survive the horrors of this war and to lift our hands for the reconstruction of our city, a great and inalienable obligation: constantly to work and to contribute to the peaceful reconstruction of our town, our state and our Federal Republic . . . and to dedicate all our energies together with all those of good will to ensuring throughout the world that a bombing war may never again rage over the towns of our country or the world, and that freedom and human dignity remain unharmed.'[57]

What was perhaps most striking of all about Urschlechter's speech, however, was its intensively local focus. Urschlechter's conclusions – 'we bow before the sacrifice of these men, women and children of our town in humility. This bell-tower . . . should always remind the population of our town of the sacrifice of these 457 children, 2,631 women and 2,997 men, but also oblige us to devote all our strength to ensure that a bombing war does not come to our city again' – typified a speech whose focus only once went beyond Nuremberg to mention Germany as a whole, let alone other nations or peoples. The persistent presence of such civic narcissism in the city's memory culture was a key barrier to the making of connections between the suffering endured in the city and the much wider suffering engendered by the war; in setting the spatial boundaries of those entitled to commemorative mention so narrowly, such speeches set a framework which even the more critical memory agenda of the 1960s would struggle to break out of. For what in the 1950s discouraged local citizens from contemplating adequately the connections between their suffering and that of soldiers or civilians from other countries eventually also served to focus reflection on Jews who had been deported from Nuremberg, rather than on the millions murdered across Europe. This

[56] On the 'telescoping' of multiple air-raids into a single site of memory, see Jörg Arnold, ' "In Quiet Remembrance"? The Allied Air War and Urban Memory Cultures in Kassel and Magdeburg, 1940–1995', PhD, University of Southampton, 2006, 29ff.
[57] 'Glockenturm feierlich seiner Bestimmung übergeben', Amtsblatt der Stadt Nurnberg, 7.1.79.

ensured that whatever shifts towards greater openness gradually occurred, it would take considerably longer for the enormity of the genocide in the east, or for the continent-wide range of the killing terrain, to be acknowledged.

More broadly, the coalescence of a local memory culture surrounding the bombing and the emergence, in particular, of a discourse surrounding the war in which 'the city' figured as victim, marked a crucial development which did much to shape the terms (and limits) of the transition to the more critical culture of the 1960s. For, while the overarching rhetoric of German victim-hood began to lose its integrative purchase once the intense suffering of the post-war period had been overcome, the ongoing prominence of older divisions in the political culture of the city – those between its bourgeois and Social Democratic traditions – made the need for narratives capable of bridging schism as strong as ever. In the face of the direct challenges to the carefully crafted consensus of the 1950s represented by new attempts to engage the history of the Holocaust, the notion of 'the city' as victim would lend itself ideally to this.

Outside the community of survivor groups and the wider milieu of left-wing sentiment with memories of active participation in the political struggles of the 1920s and 1930s, few showed any willingness in the 1950s to commemorate the regime's victims from the local community, let alone Europe as a whole. There was a brief discussion of the possibility of establishing a memorial on the site of the destroyed synagogue on the *Hans-Sachs-Platz* in 1946.[58] The initiative, however, came from an American officer stationed in the city, rather than from within the community, and the fact that the site was currently in use as a dumping ground for rubble made it impossible; the lack of clarity concerning ownership of the site provided an additional excuse to postpone the discussion again in 1949.[59] The issue was first revisited nearly ten years later, in November 1958, when the Society for Christian–Jewish Cooperation proposed the establishment of plaques on the sites of both the city's main former synagogues to mark the occasion of the twentieth anniversary of the Night of the Glass in November 1938.[60] The main political parties were all open to the suggestion in principle: the Jewish community leadership, however, 'advised strongly against placing a plaque in an openly accessible space, because the slightest defilement of the plaques would go round the world press and damage Nuremberg greatly'.[61]

[58] StadtAN C 7 IX/1251, Niederschrift über die Sitzung des Ältesten-Ausschusses, 14.10.46; Beschluss des Ältesten-Ausschusses, 14.10.46.
[59] StadtAN C 7 IX/1271, Niederschrift über die Sitzung des Bauausschusses, 14.11.49.
[60] StadtAN C 85 III/388, Niederschrift über die 41. Sitzung des Ältestenrats am 21.11.58.
[61] StadtAN C 85 III/389, Niederschrift über die 45. Sitzung des Ältestenrats, 13.2.59; Niederschrift über die Sitzung des Ältestenrats, 10.7.59.

12. Mural depicting allied air raids, *Platz der Opfer des Faschismus*, Nuremberg (1953).

Such responses demonstrated the proclivity of the Jewish community to maintain a low profile and the attachment of its long-standing, assimilated community leadership to the city; the desire on the part of the city council to restore a civic reputation it regarded as unjustly sullied by its associations with the Third Reich was, in many respects, shared by the Jewish community leadership. It also, however, reflected awareness that, within some sections of the population at least, an ongoing hostility to the Jewish community, or at least refusal to accept that the Jews had a legitimate claim to commemorative attention, made attempts at such public memorialisation premature.

The fear of opposition was well founded: that the legitimacy of the victims' claims to commemoration was widely contested had been demonstrated, for example, on the *Platz der Opfer des Faschismus*. In a move which gained its rhetorical force precisely from the physical location of the act, the owners or architects of the new apartment blocks created on the square in 1953 had chosen to adorn the wall of one block with a prominent mural in three parts. The existence of the mural was not in itself remarkable, but the choice of images was. The first showed industrious burghers, going about their business in a scene of harmonious innocence. The second moved to a scene of destruction, in which planes wreaked havoc on a flaming city and terrorised defenceless citizens. The third, which showed a woman holding the fruits of her labours between the dates 1945 and 1953, symbolised the achievements of reconstruction. Resonating with all the silences familiar from other accounts, this visual narrative issued a clear riposte to those who wished to place the victims of fascism above the suffering of ordinary Germans.

It would be wrong, again, however, to see in such responses the attitudes of a majority community whose memory culture was entirely consensual. The memory of military sacrifice was itself sometimes contested, especially where local knowledge was aware of the histories of some of those killed in the war. Perhaps the most telling example of this was the war memorial in the outlying suburb of Reichelsdorf. Begun in the interwar period as a memorial for the fallen soldiers of the First World War, it had not been finished; in 1957 a citizens' group had formed to press for its completion.[62]

Completed sometime thereafter, the memorial, a large, square granite structure, was sculpted on one side with an inlaid relief depicting a family grieving over the soldier's grave of their loved one. A wife and child alluded to the experience of widow- and orphanhood; the central figure of the father, alongside whom stood the mother, attested to the widespread presence within the community of grieving parents.

Around the other three sides were listed the names of the dead of the two world wars. The dead of the First World War took up one third of one side. In common with the church memorials of the early 1950s, the dead of the Second World War were listed by the year in which they were killed. None was listed for 1939; only four had been killed in 1940; from 1941 the list grew significantly until, like the St Jobst memorial described above, 1945 registered the greatest losses. On the final side was a list of the missing of the Second World War – larger than any single year of confirmed losses, and larger than the losses from the entire First World War.

Included in the names of the dead for 1945 was one Michael Fick. In common with standard practice, his forename and surname had been reversed; his fore-name had been abbreviated to 'Mich', so that he appeared listed, in alphabetical order, between 'Euerl Ludwig' (Ludwig Euerl) and 'Flasch Albert' (Albert Flasch), as 'Fick Mich'. 'Fick Mich' is German for 'fuck me'. Was this an accident? Or merely a tasteless impiety? The former is unlikely, the latter possible. A more probable interpretation, however, resides in the identity of Michael Fick himself, whom locals knew to have been a member of a prominent local Nazi family that ran a guesthouse frequented by brownshirts in the 1930s.[63] It seems likely,

[62] StadtAN C 22 VI/385, Auszug aus der Satzung der Interessensgemeinschaft zur Fertigstellung des Kriegerdenkmals in Reichelsdorf (undated, March 1957).
[63] 'Der Flaneur von Nürnberg', *Plärrer. Das Stadtmagazin* 24/8 (2000), 18.

13(a–b). Reichelsdorf war memorial (late 1950s).

therefore, that a left-leaning stonemason, familiar with the history of the community and the place of certain families within it, had chosen to subvert the mixture of pathos and heroicisation inherent in listing the names of the 'fallen' in an anti-fascist gesture of contempt for the individual, whose right to pious commemoration he disputed. It showed, then, that the contestation of such sites and their meanings, and the associated conflicts over the legitimacy of claims to victimhood and sympathy, occurred not just between majority 'perpetrator community' and the minority of persecutees, but within the dominant community too, along the fault lines provided by the city's multiple political traditions.

The presence of this anti-fascist ethos – which drew on strong memories of political persecution within the powerful tradition of working-class politics in the city – was one important element of the preservation of a critical counter-memory of the Nazi past. Yet in its own way, it compounded the difficulties of addressing adequately the conflicting political, psychological, emotional and moral challenges posed by the experience of dictatorship and war, and by the knowledge of genocide. The dilemmas and hindrances facing those charged with finding an acceptable mode of narration for the events of the Third Reich were encapsulated precisely in SPD mayor Otto Ziebill's speech at the unveiling of the memorial to the murdered Jews established by the Jewish community in the New Jewish Cemetery in August 1949.[64] For, even in this Jewish space, at a moment dedicated to the memory of the murdered Jews, mayor Ziebill showed himself unable to address the Jewish dimensions of the experience of persecution, or indeed even to mention the Jewishness of the Holocaust's main victims.

Unlike the later inauguration of the air-raid monument by the then mayor, Andreas Urschlechter, Ziebill did at least attempt to connect the suffering of local victims to a wider history, opening his speech with the declaration, 'We have gathered here in sombre mood to honour the millions of victims, above all the 1,621 Nuremberg victims of fascism.' Yet in going on to seek the connections between the suffering of some of Nuremberg's citizens and that of millions of others he did not reach for the overarching explanation of the genocide, nor did he link the fate of Nuremberg's 'victims of fascism' to the continent-wide experience of terror, persecution and murder: the 'millions' he had in mind were not the millions of Jews murdered by the Nazi regime, but the millions of people killed in the war. Again, then, the 'victims of fascism' were simply being subsumed into wider ranks of the war dead. As he continued: 'It seems appropriate to reflect for at least a moment on the fact that the victims of that tyranny comprised a much higher, untold number of

---

[64] StadtAN C 29/511, Errichtung eines Mahnmals auf dem israelitischen Friedhof (undated, 1949); for a description of the monument see Masa, *Freiplastiken*, 447.

millions . . . for to name the victims of this regime in the broadest sense one would have to invoke the spirits of all the soldiers, who themselves were not supporters of National Socialism but now lie buried all over the world . . . we may also not forget the countless civilians, women and children who fell victim to the air war and must remember the many, many relatives who suffer the heartache of the loss of their loved ones.' When, moreover, Ziebill did return to the ostensible theme of his speech – the 'victims of fascism' – he quickly ordered them into a hierarchy which, in its privileging of the political martyrs of the resistance, relegated the Jews to the status of secondary victims. Listing the 'direct victims of National Socialist tyranny' he counted 'the racial persecutees, who perished simply because of their membership of a race disliked by the dominant caste; the religious persecutees, who sealed their courageous faith with death; and above all the political persecutees, who, because of the strength of character with which they held to their political principles and ideals, were robbed of their freedom and suffered martyrdom and death.'[65]

For a Social Democrat such as Ziebill, revenge was not the answer: the answer lay in the creation of a democratic, anti-fascist state into which the former perpetrators could be safely reintegrated. Dressing a pragmatic political necessity as a superior moral act, he argued that 'we should have the moral strength to say a firm no to all of our feelings of anger and revenge'.[66] Political leadership must pass to committed anti-fascists, but former Fellow Travellers must be allowed the possibility of repentance and rehabilitation: 'He who for years followed a wrong flag should now follow ours, if he is convinced of the opposite of his former views, and should work with us on the removal of the rubble left behind and on reconstruction.' In justification of this argument Ziebill had already reached for the mythologies which were to become standard weapons in the arsenal of exculpatory rhetoric of the 1950s: 'Most people had been seduced. Only a relatively small caste was actually criminal in the real sense.'

The very ineptitude of the mayor's attempts to rise to the challenge posed by the memory of the genocide bore clearest witness to the difficulty, if not impossibility, of finding a language so soon after the war that was capable of addressing adequately the multiple legacies of Nazi repression, war and racial barbarism. But at the same time, they reflected the mindset of a generation of Social Democratic activists who had, in many cases, paid a heavy price for their brave opposition to Nazism. Words such as Ziebill's drew their inspiration and force not from abstract ideological constructions, but from shared experience: again, one irony was that the memory of the victims of racial persecution was

[65] On the construction of ordinary German casualties of the war as 'victims of fascism' see Arnold, ' "In Quiet Remembrance"?', 101–2.
[66] StadtAN C 29/511, Errichtung eines Mahnmals auf dem israelitischen Friedhof (undated, 1949).

marginalised not only by the indifference of a majority population who felt no obligation to remember, but also by the more powerful, competing claims of political cadres whose renewed influence in working-class cities such as Nuremberg in the post-war years gave their voices much greater strength. However angry or bitter they were, the Social Democratic cadres who had actively opposed Nazism knew that in a society in which the bulk of the population had supported Nazism in one way or another, a confrontational memory politics was largely impossible.

Collectively, then, the memorials erected to the suffering of the Second World War were calculated to address, validate and reinforce the sense of victimhood that was widespread among the ordinary German population. The suffering of the regime's real victims, by contrast, was barely acknowledged. When it was, it was in spaces invisible to the majority population, or through nebulous formulations referring merely to the 'victims of tyranny', soon dissolving into competing claims to victimhood between political and racial persecutees in which the former, operating as they were in a political culture dominated by the Social Democratic tradition, usually prevailed. Yet if the nebulousness meant that the identities of neither the victims nor the agents who killed them were openly acknowledged, it did not follow that the knowledge was not there. On the contrary: violently conflicting views of the meaning of that knowledge were what made a more confrontational, open memory culture impossible in the 1950s. The nebulousness, again, was the precondition for refashioning a cohesive society capable of functioning as a political community despite the divisions, hatreds and bitterness bequeathed by Nazism and the war.

II.3

Rehearsing Sorrow, Re-forging Society

Rituals of Remembrance between Mourning and Politics

Even before the experiences of the war had been marked in the form of official monuments, residents of the city gathered at key pre-existing sites of memory to remember the war and its losses; even before the city council had inaugurated a formal calendar of civic remembrance in the shape of events marking key anniversaries or moments of destruction, the various communities of remembrance gathered to remember their dead in shared ritual acts. In doing so they reached instinctively for sites already invested locally with commemorative meaning by the population of the city. Again, they used a largely familiar vocabulary of words, gestures and highly choreographed acts.[1] At times these drew on a repertoire of speech, action and location which predated the Nazi era, and represented attempts to reassert an older memorial idiom which the preceding regime had sought to suppress – most obviously one infused with Christian symbolism. At other times such commemorative acts revealed the lingering presence of a ritual culture learned in the Nazi era itself. Often both were simultaneously in evidence in one and the same act. As an official ritual culture coalesced over the course of the 1950s – manifested first in remembrance weeks for the missing prisoners of war, then in the annual Day of National Mourning held in November each year, and finally in the annual commemorations of the destruction of the old city in January 1945 – the same formal continuities were still evident, most notably in the use of the physical space of the *Luitpoldhain* as the site on which the Day of National

---

[1] Again, in respect of commemorative rituals, Sabine Behrenbeck's argument that 'following World War II it was impossible to continue older traditions of public commemoration in Germany because the war had lacked moral justification' does not do adequate justice to the blend of continuities and shifts that characterise the memory cultures of the early post-war years. See Behrenbeck, 'Between Pain and Silence', 42. For a differentiated account of the various continuities and discontinuities, see Eschebach, *Öffentliches Gedenken*.

Mourning was held, even as the Social Democratic city leadership sought to use such commemorative events to assert an anti-militarist memory of the violence of Nazism and war.

On one level, the practice of gathering for shared ritual occasions, and the widespread emphasis on participation in a shared repertoire of symbolic gestures – the silent procession, the lighting of candles, the solemn laying of wreathes – marked the embrace of acts of remembrance which both responded to and engendered a sense of community among their participants born of imagined common suffering. It bespoke, again, the operations of an apparently homogeneous memory culture in which the mutual acknowl-edgement of shared experiences underlay the strong purchase of a dominant discourse of collective victimhood; its emphasis on certain categories of suffering and its silence over others betrayed, accordingly, an apparently shared desire on the part of those who wished above all to gloss over issues of mutual embarrassment, shame and guilt. In another sense the emphasis in such ritual moments on the performance or observation of non-verbal acts bespoke in the immediate aftermath of war, again, an emotional numbness which, at points, defied verbal articulation. On another level, however, the prominence of the non-verbal elements of the ritual, together with the often highly nebulous content of the verbal elements, testified to the ways in which a society greatly divided by the war and its effects had to develop a ritual culture on to which different sections of the community could project divergent memories, and to which they could ascribe very different meanings.[2]

This, once more, reflected the workings of a memory culture in which the meanings of Nazism and war were in fact strongly disputed – between, at the very least, the left-wing political leadership of the city and its working-class, trade union base on the one hand, and the wider network of largely conserva-tive, sometimes nationalist associational groupings together with their allies in the CSU on the other. It also reflected the very diverse experiences of war and violence which had given rise to this associational landscape in the first place, and which now competed for acknowledgement as part of the wider competi-tion for political capital and material resource.[3] It was precisely in this context of memory contestation, underpinned by sentiments which often extended to vitriolic antagonism, that civic leaders – most obviously successive Social

---

[2] On the capacity of ritual to reveal the differences within as well as the underlying coherence of cultures, see Gerald Sider and Gavin Smith, 'Introduction', in id., *Between History and Histories*, 3–28.

[3] Sabine Behrenbeck's argument that 'public ritual ... did not serve to integrate the former Volksfremde but indeed reaffirmed the social ties of the Nazi Volksgemeinschaft' does not do justice to the multiple social and political fissures evident on such occasions: Behrenbeck, 'Between Pain and Silence', 63.

Democratic mayors of the city – had to enunciate a narrative of Nazism and war that found common assent among the diverse constituencies who assembled for such rituals. The silences were thus not merely disingenuous attempts to deny crimes that everyone knew had occurred, but the necessary price for the sufficient integration into a workable democratic polity of political opposites whose knowledge of the recent past must otherwise incline them to mutual, paralysing hatred.[4]

Underlining the fact that the various associations of war victims, veterans or the disabled were not only pressure groups seeking material redress, but also communities of sentiment, the affective bonds of which rested on a shared memory of 'their' dead, a wide range of associations gathered at local sites of memory from, at least, the early 1950s onwards. In many respects their activities set the tone for the culture of official commemoration that emerged in their wake.[5] In the first place, they often congregated at sites dedicated to the memory of the dead of the First World War. In July 1950, for example, the German League of the Disabled (*Deutsche Versehrtenbund*) held a wreath-laying ceremony at the First World War memorial in the South Cemetery.[6] In part, of course, this reflected pragmatic choices made in a period before memorials dedicated specifically to the dead of the Second World War had been inaugurated. However, the use of First World War memorials also reflected the instinctive tendency of an organisation whose activist leadership was drawn from the veterans' generation of the First, rather than the Second World War, to place the soldierly sacrifice of the latter conflagration into a historical continuum with that of the former. Indeed, the ongoing preference of some veterans' associations for the First World War memorial over the newly inaugurated *Ehrenhain* in the early 1950s suggested that for conservative-inclined soldiers' groups, at least, the martial, masculine idiom of the earlier monument continued to have a far greater resonance than the later one with its emphasis on the civilian status of the dead soldiers.[7]

Second, they reflected a highly self-centred memory culture in which the sacrifice of dead comrades was dissociated not only from the experience of war as a whole, but even from that of the wider German war dead. From the early 1950s, for example, the local chapter of the League of Former German

---

[4] On the unity-endowing dimensions of such commemorations, see Eschebach, *Öffentliches Gedenken*, 9–18.

[5] On the importance of local acts of commemoration to the coalescence of a memory culture in the immediate post-war years, see Behrenbeck, 'Between Pain and Silence', 41.

[6] StadtAN C 7 I/8048, Deutsche Versehrten-Bund, Geschäftsstelle Franken, an Städtische Fried-hofverwaltung, 27.6.50.

[7] StadtAN C 7 I/8048, Verband der Heimkehrer, Kriegsgefangenen und Vermißtenangehörigen, Bezirksverband Mittelfranken an Bestattungsamt, 21.10.53.

Parachutists held its annual 'Crete Remembrance Day' in May, with wreath-laying ceremonies attended by thirty to forty people at which the dead and missing parachutists from the Crete campaign were remembered.[8] This wide-spread habit of such regimental associations of remembering the dead and missing of their own campaigns at the expense of a wider commemoration of the war dead betrayed, again, an unspoken desire to focus on the decency and heroism of their particular war histories, whatever the crimes of the wider war; the simultaneous presence on such occasions of the Red Cross search services emphasised, again, that the close affective bonds within such communities of remembrance were born of the shared experience of violence and loss, and not just present-centred material expediency.

The first commemorative acts supported by the city council were not for dead German soldiers, however, but for the 'victims of fascism'.[9] The brief efflorescence of a cult of anti-fascism in the two to three years after the war witnessed the SPD-led city council back a number of ceremonies organised by the VVN at both the *Platz der Opfer des Faschismus* and the city's opera house, to which the city council, leading civic dignitaries and the population at large were invited.[10] In 1948, at least, the Bavarian state-wide Day of the Victims of Fascism was accompanied by small remembrance ceremonies in the region's schools.[11]

Against the background of the harsh conditions of the immediate post-war situation, however, and the culture of self-pity to which they gave rise, all efforts on the part of the Social Democratic political elites, trade union groups and the surviving victims themselves to foster a wider anti-fascist remembrance culture within the public life of the city were doomed to failure. Although significant anti-fascist impulses existed within the working class and its political formations, these did not, evidently, translate into a widespread desire to participate in the ritualised commemoration of the dead immediately after the war. While sporadic evidence exists to suggest the continuation into the 1950s of commemorative ceremonies at the remains of the former

---

[8] StadtAN C 7 I/8048, Bund Deutscher Fallschirmjäger Kameradschaft Nürnberg-Fürth an Amt für Friedhofsverwaltung Nürnberg, 15.5.52; Bund ehemaliger deutsche Fallschirmjäger Kameradschaft Nürnberg-Fürth an Bestattungsamt Nürnberg, 13.3.53; see also 'Kreta-Tag wird begangen – Durch den Bund ehemaliger Fallschirmjäger', *Nürnberger Nachrichten*, 16.5.52.

[9] On the background to this see Gilad Margalit, 'Gedenk- und Trauerkultur im Nachkriegs-deutschland. Anmerkungen zur Architektur', *Mittelweg* 36 (April/May 2004), 76–92, here 82–3.

[10] See, for example, LKAN Kd Nbg 139, Dr Levié an Schieder. 4.3.46; StadtAN C 29/446, VVN Bezirksstelle Nürnberg an Ziegler, 17.4.47; C 7 IX/700, Niederschrift über die Sitzung des Stadtrats, 10.9.47.

[11] StadtAN F 6/93, Monatsbericht der Regierung Mittelfranken, September 1948. See also the *Nürnberger Nachrichten*'s caustic account of the population's indifference to the Day for the Victims of Fascism in 1947: 'Trauer und Beschämung', 17.9.47.

14. Demonstration on the *Hauptmarkt*, Prisoner of War Remembrance Week (early 1950s).

concentration camp inmates at the South Cemetery, these clearly generated little interest outside a small circle of Social Democratic officials, survivors and relatives of the regime's victims.[12]

In the late 1940s and early 1950s the sentiments of the population were focused on a quite different group of victims – the remaining prisoners of war held in the east and those believed to be missing in action. Correspondingly, it was the missing prisoners of war who formed the focal point of the first major commemorative acts held annually in the city after the Second World War. With the support of the Federal government the Association of Former Prisoners of War organised in the early 1950s annual Prisoner of War Remembrance Weeks (*Kriegsgefangenengedenkwochen*), involving not only veterans' and relatives' associations, but also the churches, political parties, local authorities and the public at large.[13] From 1950 onwards memorial silences in the *Bundestag* and state parliaments, together with public radio addresses delivered by prominent figures, complemented a week of local events that included symbolic gestures

[12] On the holding of such ceremonies see, for example, StadtAN C 29/487, H.R. an Oberbürgermeister Bärnreuther betr. Tag der Opfer des Faschismus, 6.9.55; Programm zur Gedenkfeier, 11.9.55.
[13] Frank Biess, 'Survivors of Totalitarianism', 64.

such as the two-minute-long sounding of sirens, the ringing of church bells, the observance of work stoppages and traffic stoppages, followed in the evenings by vigils, silent processions and the lighting of beacons around borders and on high ground.[14]

These events varied somewhat from year to year, but the essential format and tone remained the same. The programme for the week-long event in 1952, for example, contained an opening demonstration for the Monday addressed by one of the mayors, by the head of the local veterans' association and by a lawyer acting for imprisoned war criminals; this was followed on the Tuesday by a concert in the central *Lorenzkirche* at which music composed by dead and missing soldiers was performed. On the following day a special commemorative meeting of the city council was held, followed in the evening by a demonstration of women organised by the Housewives' League. On the Thursday a benefit concert was organised to provide money for food parcels to be sent to those in captivity, while on the following day a performance of Beethoven's *Fidelio*, whose theme of liberation from tyranny would not have been lost on the audience, was dedicated to the prisoners. The weekend saw a further concert and demonstrations, culminating in a large rally on the main market place followed by a silent march by torchlight to the commemorative plaque dedicated to the missing at the *Nassauer Haus*.[15] In 1954, at least, the innocent victimhood of those who suffered most as a result of the failure to return the supposedly remaining prisoners was underlined by the order of the procession, the *Nürnberger Zeitung* communicating to its readership that 'women and children should go first, with the men forming the second part of the procession, to symbolise the fact that they stand as comrades behind the mothers, wives and children of those who have yet to return'.[16]

For the entire week two large banners were hung at the main railway station and the market place – one invoking the citizens of Nuremberg to 'fight for our Prisoners of War and our Missing!', the other demanding 'Freedom and Justice for our Prisoners of War, Loyalty to our Missing and their Relatives!'[17] Meanwhile, all public buildings were to fly their flags at half mast for the week, until the final day when the flags were to be raised to full mast 'as a sign of hope'. During the same event for 1953, at least, this was accompanied by the

[14] See, for example, LKAN Kd Nbg 334, Bundesverband der Heimkehrer, Kriegsgefangenen- und Vermisstenangehörigen e.V., Landesverband Bayern/Sonderrundschreiben zur Ausgestaltung der Treue- und Protestkundgebung am 4.5.51.

[15] StadtAN C 7 I/1106, Bundesverband der Heimkehrer, Kriegsgefangenen- und Vermisstenangehörigen e.V. Bayern, Kreisverband Nürnberg an Bürgermeister Lossmann, 8.10.52.

[16] 'Nürnberg gedenkt der Kriegsgefangenen – Brennende Kerzen am 23 und 24 Oktober an den Fenstern – Schweigemarsch', *Nürnberger Zeitung*, 20.10.54.

[17] StadtAN C 7 I/1106, Aktennotiz betr. Kriegsgefangenen-Gedenkwoche/Transparente, 15.10.52.

invocation to 'light a candle for the prisoners of war', when the population was encouraged to show its solidarity according to a custom of prayer for missing fishermen.[18] The 1953 events also included the release of balloons as a symbol of hope.[19] Through the cumulative impact of such highly visible symbolic acts and gestures and their widespread reporting in the local press the remembrance weeks attained a high degree of presence in the life of the city for the week which went much beyond the range of people who actively participated in them. While the events were clearly designed, on one level, to remind those sectors of the population who had moved on to other things of the continued plight of those in Soviet captivity, the large attendances and public interest generated by such events suggest that they served to fill a deep-seated emotional need, the intensity of which reflected the desperate desire of thousands of families to believe that their missing loved one was still alive and might yet return.

With the release of the final prisoners of war from the Soviet Union the Prisoner of War Remembrance Weeks lost their purpose: from this point, ritual public acts could no longer articulate the hope that the missing soldiers were alive, they could only serve to express grief at their deaths. Even before the resolution of this issue, however, those Nuremberg citizens who knew that their loved one had died gathered for formal ritual acts of remembrance of the dead. Here it was the churches that played the key role in re-establishing a memorial calendar which drew on the traditions of previous eras. While in most other respects the Protestant Church, rooted as it was in the bourgeois milieu, embraced a national-conservative memory culture that contained substantial residues from the Nazi era itself, in this case the churches' policy embodied a strong rejection of the Nazi cult of the fallen and a desire to reconnect instead with non-Nazi, non-military traditions. From 1945 onwards the Protestant Church reverted to its traditional 'Day of the Dead' (*Totensonntag*), which took place in November, as its occasion for remembering the fallen, avoiding the Nazis' 'Heroes Remembrance Day' (*Heldengedenktag*) which had been held in March; likewise, the Roman Catholic Church reverted to All Souls' Day as its main day of commemoration.[20] In this way the traditional period of Christian reflection upon the transience of earthly flesh superseded a springtime ceremony the

---

[18] 'Zündet die Kerze für die Kriegsgefangenen an', *Nürnberger Zeitung*, 24.10.53; Moeller, *War Stories*, 41.
[19] StadtAN C 7 I/1106, Verband der Heimkehrer, Kriegsgefangenen- und Vermisstenangehörigen Deutschlands e.V., Kreisverband Nürnberg Stadt, an den Stadtrat Nürnberg, 8.10.53.
[20] On the theological and political meanings of these dates in the Christian calendar for Germans, see Karin Hausen, 'The "Day of National Mourning" in Germany', 131–3.

seasonal associations of which with rebirth and renewal suited the Nazis' agendas better.[21]

Such moves did not pass without contradiction: in the nascent memory culture of the post-1945 era, disputes over the commemorative calendar formed an integral part of the wider contestation of the war's meaning.[22] Both within the lower ranks of the Protestant Church and within the wider conservative associational milieu of the city there were those who wished, instead, to draw on the ritual calendar of the immediately preceding regime.[23] There were, moreover, state institutions and war associations keen to embrace a third possibility, namely the 'Day of the Victims of War', fixed by the Bavarian Ministry of the Interior for celebration on the first Sunday of September to commemorate the anniversary of the outbreak of the war. In 1950, at least, such a ceremony was held in Nuremberg 'in memory of the dead, the missing and the prisoners of war', and to express 'the solidarity of the whole people with the living victims of the war, the wounded, the parents, the widows and the orphans'.[24] However, in the face of church refusals to acknowledge this date, it did not become established in the memorial calendar of the city. In the protracted discussions between West German religious, secular and associational leaders it was, rather, the church leadership's preferences which prevailed: neither March nor September, but November, was chosen for the reinstitution of the Day of National Mourning on a Federal level in 1952.[25]

From 1952 onwards the reinstated Day of National Mourning was staged at the restored *Luitpoldhain* monument on the former party rally grounds. Despite its dedication to the 'victims of both world wars and National Socialist tyranny' it remained firmly focused on remembrance of the German dead, a moment at which the rehearsal of the victim discourse of post-war West Germany was enacted most powerfully. If both the location of the ceremony and the basic components of the ritual – music, speech, wreath-laying – suggested certain formal continuities with the ritual acts of the Nazi era, then

---

[21] See, for example, StadtAN C 29/424, Monatsbericht des Oberbürgermeisters der Stadt Nürnberg für die Zeit vom 20 November bis 19 Dezember 1945; C 29/426, Monatsbericht des Stadtrats zu Nürnberg für die Zeit vom 20.10.46 bis 19.11.46; C 29/428, Monatsbericht des Stadtrats zu Nürnberg für die Zeit vom 20.10.47 bis 19.11.47; C 29/428, Monatsbericht des Stadtrats zu Nürnberg für die Zeit vom 20.11.47 bis 19.12.47; LKAN Kd Nbg 61, Ev.-Luth. Dekanat Nürnberg an alle Pfarrämter im Dekanat Nürnberg, 9.11.48; LKAN Kd Nbg 62, Ev.-Luth. Dekanat Nürnberg an alle Pfarrämter im Dekanat Nürnberg, 10.11.49; LKAN Kd Nbg 62, Ev.-Luth. Dekanat Nürnberg an all Pfarrämter im Dekanat Nürnberg, 16.11.50; StadtAN C 29/430, Monatsbericht der Stadt Nürnberg für die Zeit vom 1 bis 30 November 1950.
[22] On the background see also Margalit, 'Gedenk- und Trauerkultur', 83–6.
[23] LKAN Kd Nbg 221, Ev.-Luth. Pfarrstelle Altdorf bei Nürnberg an Schieder, 7.2.48; LKAN Kd Nbg 62, Ev.-Luth. Dekanat, Nürnberg an alle Pfarrämter im Dekanat Nürnberg, 14.3.49; 'Gedenket eurer Kriegstoten!', *Nürnberger Evangelisches Gemeindeblatt*, 27.3.49.
[24] LKAN Kd Nbg 61, Verband der Kriegsbeschädigten, -Hinterbliebenen und Sozialrentner Deutschlands, Landesverband Bayern, an das Ev.-Luth. Kreisdekanat Nürnberg, 22.8.50.
[25] Hausen, 'The "Day of National Mourning" in Germany', 140.

these were again indicative of the extent to which the Nazis themselves had appropriated and adapted central features of the civic culture and calendar; the continuities with which the architects of the Day of National Mourning were reconnecting for the most part ran deeper than any links to the immediately preceding regime. Moreover, both the musical and spoken elements of the rituals of the 1950s defined themselves in overt opposition to those mostly favoured in the Nazi era; the absence of martial effect – at least in the early 1950s – was, similarly, evidence of a desire amongst local civic leaders to develop a consciously non-Nazi commemorative style. Musically, the occasions stood out for their strong preferment of sacred over profane music: the 1952 event, for example, opened with religious music by Mozart and Beethoven and closed with similar music by Schubert and Nicolò Jommelli. In addition to the mayor's speech, addresses were given by both Protestant and Roman Catholic churchmen.[26] This also stood in stark contrast to the heathen emphases of Nazi ritual.[27] Although the post-war events drew on a mostly German repertoire of classical and romantic music, and thus operated within a recognisably national idiom, it was only during the wreath-laying ceremony itself, in which the 'Song of the Good Comrade' was played, that the audience was offered the possibility of placing the ceremony within an overtly nationalist tradition. Again, however, the use of this song at the Day for the Victims of Fascism in the mid-1950s reminds us that the meanings attached even to this piece were more varied than might immediately be assumed.[28] Once more, music facilitated the masking of differences as much as the projection of consensus.

Invitations went to all city councillors, city officials, to the city's *Bundestag* and *Landtag* deputies, and to local dignitaries or authorities such as church representatives, doctors, leading figures from industry and commerce, and public servants from the spheres of education, justice and administration. Meanwhile, the various war associations were invited to attend as official delegations and – in some years – to lay additional wreaths. In 1952, this list was dominated by groups claiming to represent the injured, bereaved or otherwise damaged victims of war: deputations were invited from the League of War-Disabled and Surviving Dependants, from the rival Reich League of War-Disabled and Surviving Dependants, from the League of War-Disabled, Surviving Dependants and Social Pensioners of Germany, from the League for the Care of German War Graves, from the Association of Former Prisoners of

---

[26] StadtAN C 7 I/1661, Einladungskarte, Volkstrauertag 1952 (undated, November 1952).
[27] On the music of Nazi commemorative rituals see Volker Ackermann, *Nationale Totenfeiern in Deutschland. Von Wilhelm I bis Franz Josef Strauß. Eine Studie zur politischen Semiotik* (Stuttgart, 1990), 260–8.
[28] StadtAN C 29/487, Programm zum Gedenkfeier, 11.9.55; on song and commemorations see Eschebach, *Öffentliches Gedenken*, 83–8.

War and from the Association of the Bavarian War Blind.[29] Despite the osten-sible focus of the day on the 'victims of National Socialist tyranny', the local Jewish community was not invited to lay a wreath; between 1952 and 1955 the VVN was also deliberately not invited.[30] Indeed, the practice of laying a wreath at the remains of the concentration camp victims at the South Cemetery on a different occasion underlines the fact that the victims of fascism were far from fully integrated into the community of those being remembered in the manner that the memorial's dedication to 'the victims of violent tyranny' implied.[31]

Over the course of the 1950s the list of invited groups expanded consider-ably. By 1957 it included, in addition to the original groups, deputations from the regimental associations for IR 21, IR 213 and IR 351, a deputation from the *Stahlhelm*, from the Mountain Troops' Association and from the *Traditionsgemeinschaft* of the *Grossdeutschland* Panzer Corps. In part, this reflected the proliferation of regimental groups within the wider associational landscape of the 1950s; in part, however, it reflected the renewed acceptability of military service in a political culture adapting to the reality of West German rearmament in the mid-1950s. Finally the greater part of the participants was made up of ordinary members of the public. In 1952, the police planned for an attendance of 3–4,000; in 1956, the city authorities expected 2–3,000, so that these were sizeable gatherings.[32]

The speeches of successive mayors, which also displayed a substantial degree of continuity of content from year to year, were tailor-made for the great majority of the audience, whose wartime and post-war suffering they addressed, reflected and interpreted back to the audience themselves, before didactically offering their listeners a view of the correct political conclusions to be drawn. In 1958, for example, mayor Urschlechter began by connecting the gathering at which he was speaking to the gatherings being held simulta-neously across West Germany, invoking a wider imagined community of participants commemorating German suffering of which the local gathering was merely a part: 'Today hundreds of thousands of people are gathered alongside us before memorials in many towns and communities in Germany to mark the Day of National Mourning.'[33] It was, indeed, not just the dead of Nuremberg, but the dead of both world wars on which the mayor sought to focus the minds of his audience: 'We remember thus the millions of people

---

[29] StadtAN C 7 I/1661, Aktennotiz, Tag der Opfer des Krieges: an Polizeipräsidenten Stahl, 8.11.52.
[30] In 1952 the VVN was initially included on the list of intended invitees but was later scored out: see StadtAN C 7 I/1661, Einladungsliste anläßlich des Volkstrauertages am 16.11.52.
[31] StadtAN C 7 I/1661, Aktennotiz, Volkstrauertag 1955 am 13 November 1955.
[32] StadtAN C 7 I/1661, Aktennotiz betr. Volkstrauertag 1956, 5.11.56.
[33] 'Zur Totengedenkfeier der Stadt Nürnberg', *Amtsblatt der Stadt Nürnberg*, 20.11.58.

who were carried off by the madness of the wars, especially the Second World War, at the fronts, be that in far-off lands or in their own country.' He continued: 'In their thousands they marched out of a feeling of duty and sense of responsibility, in their thousands they did not return, but fell in the field, be it in the First World War, be it in the bitter fighting on foreign soil in the Second World War or on home ground in the last phases of the Second World War.' Reflecting perhaps the fading purchase of the residual nationalist rhetoric that had accompanied such events in the early 1950s, and the passage of moves towards reconciliation embodied in western integration, mayor Urschlechter also made a passing attempt to connect the sacrifice of the German soldiers to that of others, reminding his audience that 'at this hour we must also remember those who died for their homeland on the other side, in that they gave their lives in the disastrous wars, which after all have two fronts'.

Yet the connections the mayor was most interested in making were not those between German military losses and the dead of other nations, but those between different kinds of German suffering. As he emphasised, German military losses were accompanied by civilian suffering: 'In the Second World War there was not only a front to the outside, but also a front in the homeland, in that in our towns, but also in our villages, many people gave their lives as a result of the events of the air war.' Describing the civilian losses in terms both more graphic and emotive that the violence experienced by soldiers, he evoked images of 'people suddenly and abruptly wrenched from their everyday existences and purposeful lives in collapsing buildings or phosphorous flames' and emphasised that these were innocent victims: 'Hardworking people, mothers, children, infants, old people relinquished their lives in the homeland in this way, their wearied hopes for an imminent end to the war abruptly dashed.' The rhetorical effect was swiftly to draw the audience's focus away from the suffering endured by others and back to that visited upon their own community.

In keeping with the Social Democratic traditions of the political leadership of the city, the mayor did move on to address the issue of the victims of fascism. Yet, again in keeping with Social Democratic habits of remembrance, it was the political victims, rather than the victims of Nazi racism, whose suffering was foregrounded – those who 'were executed in the concentration camps, in the penitentiaries and in the prisons', but not those murdered in the extermination camps; those who were persecuted 'because they had a different world view, a better conscience' than the Nazis, but not those of different religious, cultural, national or ethnic backgrounds. In any case, again, such passing comment was swiftly followed by the refocusing of the audience's attention on the greater suffering of the (German) living: 'I think above all of those left behind, of the mothers and fathers whose sons did not return from the war . . . I think of the widows, whose husbands did not return from the war and tore an irreplaceable hole in the shared life of the family. I think of the war orphans, who have to make their way in life without the protection of their parents.' As a Social Democrat, finally, the meaning with which the death and suffering of the war should be endowed was clear: in an era of renewed rearmament and the development of destructive military technology the legacy of the war dead, 'who may be physically dead but are inwardly with us', demanded that 'with all our strength we try to ensure that humanity does not live in conflict any more, but joins together in common work for peace and for life'.

The silences in such a speech are clear. Beyond the nebulous general allusions to Nazi terror there was, most obviously, no mention of the Jews – neither the Jews of Germany nor the many more Jews murdered in the innumerable killing fields of occupied Europe. Still less was there any mention of the non-Jewish victims of the wider war of racial annihilation – of the victims of Nazi euthanasia, of foreign prisoners of war or foreign forced workers. Neither was there any attempt to consider Germans as perpetrators of terrible crimes. The victims of Nazism had been killed by 'National Socialist tyranny', not by a collaborative project involving the cadres of the Nazi party and Germany's military, bureaucratic and industrial elites and its professional classes more widely, or by hundreds of thousands of individual Germans. Instead, the military dead were constructed only as having been on the wrong end of wartime violence: their role in an ideological war in which they had figured as agents of destruction went uncommented, and, insofar as their motives for participation in the war were described, these were those of 'a feeling of duty' and 'awareness of their responsibility'. Likewise, the innocence of the civilian casualties of the air war was stressed: the fact that many of those killed had been party members, party supporters, admirers of Hitler and indeed agents of his genocidal vision both at home and abroad was glossed over.

In this sense, the mayor's speech on successive Days of National Mourning sat squarely within a 'victim discourse' in which a nebulous narrative of wartime suffering was offered to a community of former perpetrators who wished only to deny the historical fact of Nazi crimes and their collective position in relation to them, and to re-imagine themselves as a society of victims whose wartime suffering deserved sympathy and redress. As mayor Urschlechter explicitly stated in his address of 1958, 'At this hour we do not wish to ask after the cause or after guilt for things past. This line of questioning would not bring us any further.' Yet if this nebulous narrative enjoyed the support of the great majority of attendees – and by implication the wider community of the city – then this, again, should not be taken without further ado as evidence of the operation of an entirely consensual memory culture. There were, for one thing, other silences in the mayor's speech which cannot be explained by reference to the asymmetrical relationship between the presence of a majority community of former supporters of Nazism and the absence of a minority of opponents or foreign victims of Nazi persecution and genocide. The mayor made no mention, for example, of the millions of German refugees and expellees driven from their homes in 1945 to 1946. This reminds that in the competition for moral acknowledgement some German groups had yet to gain a sympathetic audience for their voice, and that there were other fissures in the memory culture across which the mayor had to project his voice on such occasions.

Most of all, the meanings of the mayor's speech on such an occasion can be understood not simply through consideration of the words themselves, but in terms of their function in the specific context of the ritual gathering, and in terms of their performance to the wider – diverse – audience which he was addressing. If the desire to respond to the emotional needs of the audience, which, on one level, governed such occasions, demanded that the mayor articulate the sorrows and suffering of those present, not those absent, the logic of democratic politics, whose operations determined, on another level, the relationship between the speaker and those being addressed, demanded that the suffering of each constituency be given its mention in turn. And, as closer examination of those attending suggests, the relationships within and between the different constituent elements of the audience reflected the wider fissures in the political culture and traditions of the city, both before, during and after the war.

In the first place, the deputations of the various groups were representatives of the very organisations which, in the post-war struggle for political and financial resource, existed in a competitive relationship to one another; the wider audience also contained members of the variety of communities of suffering to which the war had given rise – victims of bombing, relatives of the missing, disabled *Wehrmacht* veterans, and so on. In offering his reflections on the war and the Nazi past, the mayor had above all to project a narrative which could command minimal consensus among an audience composed of people who had been positioned in diverse, and often diametrically opposed, ways in relation to the crimes of the Nazi era, and who now came face to face with one another at the ceremony. Far from speaking to an audience whose sense of shared suffering engendered solidarities which dissolved all other differences, the mayor was addressing an audience whose membership had existed in relationships to one another during the Third Reich which had left a legacy of bitterness.

The Day of National Mourning marked, after all, a moment at which perpetrators met victims across the solemn pieties of a wreath-laying ceremony. In 1956, for example, the list of invitees shows wartime exploiters of forced labour, such as the prominent local industrialist Karl Diehl, attending alongside survivors of forced labour in the form of the VVN; it shows those who had survived the horrors of the extermination camps – members of the *Israelitische Kultusgemeinde* – coming face to face with representatives of those who had transported them there (the state railways) or those who had administered the property stolen from them at the point of deportation (the finance authorities).[34] The exchange of local administrative elites that took place in 1945 was such that the position was, it is true, often only structural, insofar as the figures representing compromised institutions in the post-war era had not always been personally complicit in the administration of genocide. The size of the city also meant that the relationship between those with good reason to hate each other was often anonymous. Yet the city, and above all its individual suburbs, were also small enough for such encounters sometimes to be personal. This was, perhaps, above all the case when representatives of the Social Democratic elected political elites met the rehabilitated representatives of institutions such as the police or the justice system, which had enforced locally the apparatus of terror, or members of militarist groupings such as the *Stahlhelm*, against whom they had fought in the street battles of the early 1930s. In this sense, again, the audience reflected not only the asymmetrical division between a majority of former perpetrators and a minority of former victims, but, even more so, the major fault line in the political culture of the city which ran between working class and bourgeoisie. This fault line reproduced itself in the tensions between a Social Democratic elected leadership caste and the conservative, sometimes nationalistically inclined culture of the city bureaucracy, business community and wider associational life of the city, that is, those institutions and people that had been part of the fascist consensus and, sometimes, agents of the regime's barbaric crimes.

Such divisions manifested themselves, moreover, in attempts on the part of the nationalist associations to inject a military tone into the occasion. In 1954, for example, a representative of the local *Stahlhelm* – who described himself as the temporary *Ortsgruppenleiter* standing in for the group's absent *Führer* – wrote to mayor Bärnreuther to ask if the group could lay a wreath embellished with the black-white-red ribbons of national-conservative tradition and with the image of the iron cross. Further, he sought permission for the group's delegation to parade with the old 'Reich War Flag' (*Reichskriegsflagge*), arguing that 'the parading of the flag could no longer be seen as a provocation, as it was in earlier years'.[35] The request was met with a polite but firm refusal, mayor Bärnreuther replying that 'in order to preserve the neutral character of this occasion the participating associations do not carry flags'; the request to

[34] StadtAN C 7 I/1661, Einladungsliste für die Totengedenkfeier am 18.11.56.
[35] StadtAN C 7 I/1661, Stahlhelm e.V. Bund der Frontsoldaten Ortsgruppe Nürnberg/Ortsgruppenleiter (stellv.) Wittig an Stadtverwaltung Nürnberg/Amt für Öffentliche Verwaltung, 2.11.54.

lay a wreath was met with the remark that only the mayor was to lay one that year.[36] Behind such a move undoubtedly lay the attempt to restrict the visual impact of the growing presence of military and regimental associations at the occasion. Likewise, deputy mayor Haas's unenthusiastic response to the *Bundeswehr*'s request to send a deputation to the 1957 event – 'I am of the view that we cannot refuse the participation of the *Bundeswehr*' – betrayed the strongly anti-militarist ethos of an SPD which was highly sensitive to any suggestion of the creeping return of the trappings of militarism.[37]

It is only when seen in this light that the silences which echoed through the mayor's speech on such occasions reveal their full meaning. If a sense of guilt, or at least shame, partly underlay the failure to mention adequately the regime's victims, it also reflected in part the peculiar emotional logic of such events, which functioned to give solace to those in attendance at a time when the war was still fresh. Obliged to mention each suffering constituency in turn, the silences concerning foreign victims or Jews reflected not simply the shared desire among these different groups to forget the crimes, so much as the work-ings of a speech whose task it was to acknowledge the suffering of those present. The failure to mention the perpetrators by name, meanwhile, reflected the fact that, for a functioning community to be refashioned out of the ruins of a society whose recent fratricidal divisions still resonated powerfully through the political culture of the city, certain things *had* to remain unspoken if a degree of reconciliation between Left and Right sufficient to enable a restored democratic polity to work was to occur.

It is in this light, then, that the mayor's words, 'at this hour we do not wish to ask after the cause or after guilt for things past. This line of questioning would not bring us any further', are to be correctly understood. This was all the more the case when one recognises that the silences resonating through commemorations such as these in the 1950s did not serve primarily to shape ignorance or to promote denial. Rather, they contained very immediate and widespread knowledge. This was knowledge not only of the terror visited by some members of the community on others, but also knowledge of German society's open secret in the post-war era: the open secret of genocide. After all, just because things remained unspoken it did not mean that they were unknown.

It remains the case, nonetheless, that both the Social Democratic narratives of Nazism, with their privileging of political persecution and their invocation of anti-militarism, and the conservative-nationalist narratives of comrade-ship, heroism and sacrifice favoured in bourgeois circles, reflected the general tendency of the 1950s – visible across all the other manifestations of the

---

[36] StadtAN C 7 I/1661, Bärnreuther an Stahlhelm e.V./Herr Wittig, 9.11.54.
[37] StadtAN C 7 IX/1410, Niederschrift über die Sitzung des Ältestenrats am 18.10.57.

memory culture of the era – to push the genocidal dimensions of the war to the margins of people's concerns. In this they were aided by the churches, whose narratives of sacrifice and redemption offered equally few starting points for acknowledging the crimes perpetrated against the Jews. Yet as the publications of the Protestant Church on the occasion of the Day of National Mourning suggest, the logics conspiring to prevent adequate articulation in the immediate post-war decade or so of the fact of the genocide were also far from purely political, and had their roots in the massive shock administered by war and defeat to the German people themselves.

The Protestant Church did not fail, of course, to use the occasion to promote its views of life, death and the cosmos, and to remind its flock that the only meanings of the war were to be found in the revelation of biblical truth. In the edition of its newsletter which appeared nearest to the Day of National Mourning in 1954, for example, it observed that 'we seek after something that enables us to work through this mass death inside and overcome it, so that we are not left at the end standing in the darkness of doubt and inner turmoil, but may enter into the strong light of real consolation'.[38] It opined that 'we can recognise as the ultimate lesson of this last war and its terrible sacrifices the fact that we must recognise the error of our previous ways and make a decisive change. Away from a narrow nationalism and towards a humanity which unites all peoples! Away from a dishonest glorification of violence and of war and towards a passionate willingness to seek genuine understanding. And we can see precisely as the purpose of this Day of National Mourning that it becomes a day of true repentance and conversion.' It continued, however, that 'despite this a feeling of ultimate helplessness remains, from which we cannot escape'. The answer, naturally, lay in opening oneself to the word of God. For 'what does God let us do, when we stand helplessly at the graves and ask in vain on the Day of National Mourning after the ultimate meaning of this great death? . . . that we allow ourselves unassumingly and faithfully to receive the message which God has ready for us . . .'

For all its evangelising appropriation of the Day of National Mourning, however, the Protestant Church demonstrated a sensitivity to the enduring shock that the war had administered which went beyond the rehearsal of biblical piety. Taking as its reading for the Day of National Mourning in 1955 Psalm 73, verse 16, 'but when I tried to understand it, it was too painful for me', for example, it sought to acknowledge the ongoing difficulties many faced in making sense of the war. 'Understand? The mystery of the front, that let all life choke in blood and mud or freeze in snow and ice. Understand? That raging, which turned night time in our cities to day, and with its clouds of smoke darkened day into night. Understand? That slow death in the winter

---

[38] 'Volkstrauertag', *Nürnberger Evangelisches Gemeindeblatt*, 14.11.54.

cold during the refugee treks or the nameless extinction behind three-ply barbed wire!'[39] In its accounts of the fate of the soldiers, the air-raid victims, the refugees and the German prisoners of war it was, on one level, merely repeating the standard victim refrains of the post-war period. However, in its subsequent comments it suggested awareness of a more complex set of responses to the war, rooted in the ongoing presence in the here-and-now of images of the past which continued to haunt those who had survived, that underlay some of its flock's difficulties in overcoming the war. It continued: 'Of course, for many life goes on, as if nothing had happened in these last decades. But can we really pass over so lightly those who once stood next to us and fell? Do not those pale boyish figures accompany us, in which life unlived sought so yearningly after achievement and fulfilment? Do they not look at us questioningly, those family fathers who faced a dual demand – on the one hand that of the harsh orders of the front, and on the other that of duty to their loved ones at home?'

In voicing such issues it was alluding to the psychological and emotional challenges its flock was still facing ten years later in trying to find stable and usable meanings for the violence and for the bereavement to which it had given rise. Such writings remind us, again, that the workings of the post-war memory culture are not to be understood solely as those of a perpetrator community that had adjusted easily to the pleasures of peacetime reconstruction, suppressing through silence and the disingenuous assertion of its own victimhood the knowledge of its past misdeeds against others. They were an infinitely more multilayered set of processes by which a society shattered by the multi-dimensional experience of violence and its powerful aftershocks sought – with only slow, hesitant success – to give meaning to the experiences of its members.

It was also the Protestant Church that took the lead in organising remembrance of the destruction visited upon the city by the air war.[40] On 2 January 1946 it held a memorial service at the graves of victims of the allied air raids in the South Cemetery, thus marking the first anniversary of the destruction of the old city. According to the city council's report, this occurred 'with the keen participation of the population'.[41] The church authorities' emphasis on the fact that the victims had initially been buried 'without any kind of church blessing' showed, again, their desire to give retroactive Christian meaning to

---

[39] 'Ich dachte ihm nach . . .', *Nürnberger Evangelisches Gemeindeblatt*, 13.11.55.
[40] On the role of the Protestant Church in early post-war commemorations of bombing, compare Thießen, 'Das Gedächtnis der Stadt', 138–40.
[41] StadtAN C 29/424, Monatsbericht des Oberbürgermeisters der Stadt Nürnberg für die Zeit vom 20 Dezember bis 19 Januar 1946.

the deaths; in their words, 'This meets a strong desire within our parishes.'[42] If, again, the focus remained on the local destruction of 'our city' and on the deaths of 'very many residents of Nuremberg', this reflected not only the initial inability of a population still in shock to connect its suffering to the wider destructiveness of the war, but also the presence of a strong identification with the physical environs of the city, its familiar buildings, spaces, landscapes and horizons, and the integrative power commemoration of this aspect of the war could afford in the long run.

Some element of church-centred commemoration continued during the first ten years after the war, reflecting and drawing upon community identities that were sometimes even more localised than the level of the city. In August of every year, for example, the Protestant Church in the suburb of Wöhrd held a memorial service to commemorate the August 1943 destruction of much of the suburb along with its church.[43] For the first ten years after the war, however, the secular authorities of the city refrained from any kind of commemorative activity. Not until the approach of the tenth anniversary of the destruction of the old city did the city council consider the possibility of holding an event devoted specifically to this issue.[44]

A range of events to mark the tenth anniversary was, indeed, held on 2 January 1955. Drawing on patterns familiar from both the Prisoner of War Remembrance Weeks and the Day of National Mourning, the occasion was marked by numerous public symbolic gestures which gave the day a visual and aural prominence in the city reaching beyond those who attended its formal, orchestrated moments. Federal, state and city flags were flown at half mast to mark the occasion; at 18.43 – the time at which the warning sirens had begun on 2 January 1945 – the city's church bells were rung 'in remembrance and exhortation' and 'for contemplation'.[45] Both Protestant and Catholic churches held services to mark the day, which fell on a Sunday; in addition, the Protestant Church held ceremonies at the West, South and Johannis Cemeteries. At the South Cemetery alone 500 people attended.[46] At the core of the event was a commemoration ceremony held in the city opera house, led by mayor Bärnreuther. As with the Day of National Mourning, religious music predominated, the evening closing with a performance of Mozart's Requiem Mass. As with the Day of National Mourning, the central address was given by the mayor.

In many respects, mayor Bärnreuther's speech echoed the refrains uttered on the Day of National Mourning. Reflecting upon the capacity of both

---

[42] StadtAN C 7 I/8048, Evang.-Luth. Pfarramt, Emmauskirche an Städtische Bestattungsamt, 12.12.45.
[43] 'Kirchliche Rundschau', *Nürnberger Evangelisches Gemeindeblatt*, 22.8.54.
[44] StadtAN C 51/294, Niederschrift über die Sitzung des Schul- und Kulturausschusses, 17.9.54.
[45] 'Nürnberg gedachte seiner Bombenopfer', *Amtsblatt der Stadt Nürnberg*, 7.1.55.
[46] StadtAN C 7 I/8048, Ev.-Luth. Pfarramt Nürnberg-Lichtenhof an Bestattungsamt, 29.12.54.

nature and mankind to inflict disaster upon communities, he began by situ-
ating the air war not within the wider context of Nazism and the Second
World War as a whole, but within a longer-term narrative of catastrophes
visited periodically upon the town – floods, the plague and cholera, as well as
the Thirty Years War and the First World War. The bombing thus took its place
within an historical continuum in which tragedies were inflicted upon a
passive, innocent city from outside, not as the result of the behaviour or
choices of the residents themselves. As far as the history of Nazism was
concerned, the mayor's narrative was singularly selective, noting only that
'around ten years after the First World War a worldwide Depression brought
Germany, too, an army of unemployed. The ever-more threatening economic
downfall ultimately helped Nazism to power in Germany. The subsequent
apparent economic flourishing, which was only created by an immense arma-
ments boom, was followed by the unavoidable catastrophe in 1939.'[47]

As for the war, he opined, it was worse than any previous war, but what
made it most terrible was the air raids: 'That which in the entire events of
the war marked itself out to be particularly reprehensible were the air raids
targeted upon open cities with a hitherto unknown mercilessness and
brutality.' This, he emphasised, was pursued by all sides: 'At the start of the war
the highest authorities on both sides disputed the sad and inglorious status of
who had been first to commit the crime of the terror from the air against
innocent women and children and against defenceless old people'; as on the
Day of National Mourning, the question of guilt was sidestepped: 'It should
not and cannot be our task today to seek after those really guilty for initiating
such an inhumane pursuit of war . . . It is clear that it was a crime, whoever
started it.' As on the Day of National Mourning, he stressed that the war hit
the 'hardworking and peaceable citizens of our city of Nuremberg' and
claimed 'many innocent lives' as well as destroying the physical substance of
the city. He closed, similarly, with an interpretation of the meanings of these
deaths which, in its invocation of the need for world peace, sat squarely within
a mainstream Social Democratic discourse on the war and post-war era.

In many respects, then, the message reinforced that of the Day of National
Mourning, with its relativising assertions that crimes had been committed on
both sides, its rehearsal of spurious myths of civilian innocence and its refusal
to address the much greater crimes carried out as part of a war of racial annihilation unleashed by the Third Reich. Yet in other respects its emphasis was
different. Above all, its far greater focus on the local suffering visited by the air
war upon the local community, as opposed to Germany as a whole, emphasised even more resolutely that 'the city' itself had been the ultimate victim of
the war. Indeed, 'the city' was more than once the subject of personifying

---

[47] 'Nürnberg gedachte seiner Bombenopfer', *Amtsblatt der Stadt Nürnberg*, 7.1.55.

imagery. Mayor Bärnreuther described, for example, how three days after the attack, 'Nature herself' showed mercy: 'In the form of a snow blanket a great wide shroud was spread out over the still unburied dead people, over the rubble and over the remains of our city.' He continued with 'this catastrophe was to be far from the last blow that fell from the air in the further course of the war on to a Nuremberg which was bleeding from unspeakable wounds'.

By 1960, on the occasion of what became established as an annual event after the inauguration of the memorial to the victims of bombing at the South Cemetery in 1959, this tendency to focus on the local had, if anything, become even more pronounced; the invitation to identify with 'the city' as victim was even more explicit.[48] Indeed, the speech, now delivered by Bärnreuther's successor, mayor Urschlechter, made quite clear that 'the wreath which I have laid before the memorial in the name of the city council and thus of the entire citizenry of Nuremberg serves to remember the 6,621 men, women and children who here in Nuremberg fell victim to the bombing war and the fighting on home soil', while his speech was littered with references to 'we Nurembergers', to 'our city', to 'our home town' and to the loss of 'our fellow citizens'.[49] Even as moves within the wider culture to address the hitherto marginalised genocidal dimensions of the Second World War were beginning to emerge, Urschlechter emphasised that the imagined community of suffering whose fate was being acknowledged here was very much confined to the local population.

How does one account for the upsurge of commemorative noise surrounding the bombing war in the mid- and late 1950s? While the convention of commemorating round-number anniversaries provided one stimulus for a centring of increased attention on the destructiveness of the bombing, it seems unlikely that this was the only cause.[50] One clue, perhaps, lies in the unusually graphic accounts of the horrors of bombing which accompanied such ceremonial occasions, whose descriptions of death were otherwise bathed in gentle pathos. In 1955, for example, Bärnreuther urged his listeners not to delude themselves that the victims of the air raids had died a 'normal' death: 'In reality it was much less merciful. While many were buried alive by collapsing walls and had to fight against death for hours in dreadful circumstances before being released by it, others suffered the unspeakable martyrdom of being burned alive. Yet others suffered a horrible death through suffocation.'[51] As already noted, mayor Urschlechter dwelt particularly on the horrors of the air raids on

---

[48] On similar rituals in other cities in the 1950s see, for comparison, Arnold, ' "In Quiet Remembrance"?', 108ff.

[49] 'Gedenkfeier auf dem Südfriedhof', *Amtsblatt der Stadt Nürnberg*, 7.1.60.

[50] For a discussion of the comparable delay in commemoration of the bombing in Hamburg and the resurgence of interest in the 1950s, see Thießen, 'Das Gedächtnis der Stadt', 138ff.

[51] 'Nürnberg gedachte seiner Bombenopfer', *Amtsblatt der Stadt Nürnberg*, 7.1.55.

the Day of National Mourning in 1958, painting images of 'people suddenly and abruptly wrenched from their everyday existences and purposeful lives in collapsing buildings or phosphorous flames'.[52]

One may speculate, again, that such graphic images of horror testify to an experience both so awful and so novel that they could not be ordered into a meaningful, agreeable narrative immediately after the war by those who had suffered them;[53] at the same time such images were etched so firmly into the minds of those who had witnessed them that they returned and resonated for much longer. The much larger number of citizens who had experienced, or witnessed, the bombing of the city, and the greater similarity of their ordeals – compared to the more disparate memories of soldiers who had experienced the war all over Europe – combined with the greater immediacy of memories born of experiences endured in the familiar spaces in which they continued to live, ensured that, from the mid-1950s onwards it was the memory of the air raids that had the widest purchase and the greatest integrative effect.

As already argued in respect of war memorials, it also may be that it was precisely the gradual emergence from the late 1950s of a more critical discourse on the recent past, one which was gradually focusing more on the genocide, that was partially behind the upsurge of commemorative noise around the bombing. If the general suffering of the war and post-war era had given rise to narratives around which some form of renewed community could cohere over the 1950s, the nascent stirrings of a new, more critical discourse on the events of the war – above all the slow emergence of critical debate on the Holocaust – meant that the events of the wider war began to lose their integrative capacity. As the immediate effects of post-war suffering were overcome, a general 'victim' discourse was no longer sufficient to describe the events of a war whose meanings were once more becoming contested and divisive, but now in different ways. The martyrdom of 'the city', meanwhile – the destruction of its cultural monuments, historic buildings and treasured vistas – provided a focal point for the creation of a different narrative of victimhood still capable of gaining purchase within a population who, despite other divisions, identified strongly as Nurembergers with the familiar landscapes and skylines of the town. As argued, this particular configuration of the narrative of wartime suffering would be central to the containment of the new challenges which were to emerge in the 1960s.

[52] 'Zur Totengedenkfeier der Stadt Nürnberg', *Amtsblatt der Stadt Nürnberg*, 20.11.58.
[53] On the difficulty of finding a non-Nazi idiom of remembrance, see Arnold, ' "In Quiet Remembrance"?', 94–5.

II.4

Local Stories, National Stories
Exhibiting Memory at the Germanic National Museum

For both the Social Democratic political leadership and the bourgeois arbiters of the cultural life of the city, creating agreeable narratives of the experiences of Nazism and war meant more than just the fashioning of myths of victimhood on behalf of the population at large. It also demanded tackling the problematic legacy bequeathed by Nuremberg's historical associations with the Nazi regime. The Nuremberg rallies, the Nuremberg laws and the activities of the notorious Gauleiter Julius Streicher had generated – in some respects quite ironically, given the strongly Social Democratic political traditions of the modern city – an image, second to none, as a 'Nazi town'. In electing to hold their post-war trials of the Nazi leadership in the city most associated with the hubristic will to power of the regime the allies had underlined those connections further.

Attempts to forge consensual narratives surrounding the Nazi past were thus interwoven with moves to dissociate the city from its 'Nazi' connotations and to rebuild Nuremberg's image as a democratic town. The city's strong Social Democratic traditions gave such efforts some degree of historical legitimacy. However, in seeking to re-forge an alternative identity rooted in the city's progressive credentials the authorities reinforced, from a different direction, the convivial myth that Nazism had come from outside local society, and that the city itself had thus been the 'victim' of recent history. This final chapter on the emergence of the 'victim' myth of the 1950s explores how the city's cultural icons and institutions were pressed into the service of recreating the city's image. It explores how local sites were used to articulate national myths of victimhood, most notably those surrounding the expulsions and the division of Germany, and at the same time to project images of a specifically local victimhood – images that contributed to establishing a framework within which the new challenges of the late 1950s and early 1960s would be channelled and contained.

When emphasising the depth of the crisis facing the city, commentators easily linked the physical rubble left by the air war to the moral rubble left by the Nazi connections. In a discussion of the future prospects of the Germanic National Museum, for example, the American occupation newspaper, the *Neue Zeitung*, underlined that 'Nuremberg – the free city of the middle ages – belongs in the first tier of those cities whose face appeared irretrievably disfigured after the war. Germany's largest medieval settlement, the great city of the Renaissance, had become, as the "City of the Reich Party Rallies", the antiquated backdrop to mass parades. A Gothic Christianity ossified to stone and the magnificent bourgeois display of the Reformation era drowned in the colours of the swastika and the insignia of the twelve-year Reich.' The extent of the damage both to the substance and the reputation of the city was such that, according to the newspaper, it was considered after the war whether to move the collections of the Germanic National Museum to a 'less damaged and historically less compromised location'.[1] Most notably, Federal President Theodor Heuss, speaking in his capacity as chairman of the governing board of the Germanic National Museum on the occasion of its 100th anniversary celebrations in 1952, described 'the fate of recent past decades: Streicher and Hitler, the "City of the Reich Party Rallies" and the city of the "Nuremberg Laws", and then as a counter act the city of the "Nuremberg Trials" ', and thus how 'the honourable name of Noris was to be smeared by history and remain smeared! . . . I say these things quite calmly, for I see in them the historical task of cleansing the notion of "Nuremberg" and restoring to view its intellectual and cultural vitality not only in its own mind but before the world.'[2]

The first post-war director of the Germanic National Museum, E.G. Troche, when forwarding a copy of the *Neue Zeitung* piece to mayor Ziebill, opined in his covering letter that 'of course we as a museum are hardly delighted by the piece, and the city of Nuremberg will be even less so. But it shows precisely what we collectively have still to do.'[3] Restoring the reputation of the city was, indeed, central in ways both spoken and unspoken to cultural policy from 1945 onwards. Mayor Ziebill acknowledged as much to the mayor of Tel Aviv in October 1949 when he insisted that 'the city council, as the elected representative of the great majority of the population of Nuremberg, is trying seriously and from innermost conviction to prove that the ill spirit is overcome and that we will do everything to regain for Nuremberg a name as a city of humanity and culture'.[4] That sanitising the city's reputation, as much as meeting head-on the diverse moral challenges posed by past complicity in Nazism, was paramount was suggested by the internal response to acts of vandalism against the city's old

[1] 'Nürnberg und das Germanische Nationalmuseum', *Neue Zeitung*, 19.11.49.
[2] Theodor Heuss, 'Das Germanische Nationalmuseum', *Noris. 2 Reden* (Nuremberg, 1953), 24–5.
[3] StadtAN C 29/195, E.G. Troche an Oberbürgermeister Ziebill, 21.11.49.
[4] StadtAN C 29/448, Oberbürgermeister Ziebill an Oberbürgermeister der Stadt Tel Aviv, 13.10.49.

Jewish cemetery in 1952: 'Damage to Jewish cemeteries in particular could lead to exceptionally negative consequences for the city. Only through immediate personal intervention could we ensure that nothing of the recent events in the old Jewish cemetery appeared in the press. I am not willing to allow youthful pranks to place the reputation of Nuremberg in a bad light once again . . .'[5]

For Social Democrats in particular, restoring the city's reputation meant asserting repeatedly that the association of the town with the Nazi regime was undeserved. In 1948, for example, the then mayor Ziegler observed that 'Nuremberg still does not have an especially good reputation abroad because of the Reich party rallies, Nuremberg Laws, Military Tribunals et cetera, even if this is quite unjustified.'[6] Similarly, when addressing visiting senior occupation dignitaries, his successor, mayor Ziebill, emphasised that 'you know, ladies and gentleman, what role the city of Nuremberg played in the fateful years of the Nazi regime, a role which has nothing to do with the actual nature and tradition of the city'.[7] This meant not just asserting the city's status as a citadel of modern Social Democracy, but also enlisting older histories in the recreation of a non-Nazi image. Above all, the city's historical experiences as a flourishing centre of trade, craftwork and culture were drawn upon to project an image of open-ness, moderacy and quiet industriousness inimical to the values of the Third Reich – which, so the logic implied, had been an alien imposition on the town.[8]

In many respects liberal and conservative voices reproduced these positions in their writings on Nuremberg's past and present. One of the curators of the Germanic National Museum, for example, Ludwig Grote – who was to become its director in 1951 – insisted in 1947 that 'the reality of Nuremberg consisted at all times in the sober and clear calculation of its citizens, in its energetic inventive activity, in worldwide trade and the achievement of the highest refinements of craftsmanship under an exemplary city government, all in a uniquely stern warm-heartedness of specifically Nuremberg-Franconian stamp'; his argument that 'dreaming and flight from reality were never the Nuremberg way' marked an obvious attempt to contrast indigenous traditions to the intoxicating hysteria of the Nazi era.[9]

There were initially differences of emphasis. Social Democrat voices tended to foreground the destructiveness of the war in a manner which enabled them

---

[5] StadtAN C 29/313, Aktennotiz betr. Beschädigung von Grabmalen in Städtischen Friedhöfen, 29.9.52.

[6] StadtAN C 29/447, Ziegler an Herrn W.G., Nuremberg, 6.4.48.

[7] StadtAN C 29/511, Speech on the Occasion of the Visit of McCloy, October 1949.

[8] See, for example, StadtAN C 29/511, Eröffnung des Internationalen Kongresses am 5.9.49. See also Clemens Wachter, *Kultur in Nürnberg. Kulturpolitik, kulturelles Leben und Bild der Stadt zwischen dem Ende der NS-Diktatur und der Prosperität der fünfziger Jahre* (Nuremberg, 1999), 43–4; 332–5. See also below, Chapter IV.4.

[9] Ludwig Grote, 'Das Germanische National-Museum und Nürnberg', *Germanisches Nationalmuseum. Zweiundneunzigster Jahresbericht* (Nuremberg, 1947), 3–22, here 16.

to press the urgency of reconstruction and welfare aid: in doing so, they inevitably emphasised the creation of a *tabula rasa* and the possibilities the collapse of Nazism offered for a modernisation of the city's infrastructure, while allowing a recovery of more progressive cultural traditions. Bourgeois voices, by contrast, reached more explicitly for the reassurance of continuity. Even as they joined with the wider chorus of voices pressing the extensive damage caused by the war into the wider narrative of collective victimhood, they insisted on the widespread survival of positive topographical and cultural markers from the past. Thus, while mayor Ziebill emphasised at the opening of the 1949 Building Exhibition that 'Nuremberg stands, as is well known, in second place behind Dresden in the sad ranking list of the degree of destruction',[10] Grote was arguing as early as 1947 that 'it may on no account be overlooked that Nuremberg's old bearing points still stand firm. Belonging to these are the surrounding city walls, this shaping frame – still the best-preserved and most defiant of ramparts which the medieval era left in Europe. The castle of Nuremberg still is the towering feature of the cityscape, despite the odd ruinous silhouette.' Such survivals were not, moreover, limited to the fortifications: 'With the two great city churches, St Sebald and St Lorenz, both already on the way to re-establishment, the burghers' city stands as ever on firm supports on the banks of the Pegnitz. Most other monuments of old religiosity doubtless also look forward to their resurrection, as they need on no account be given up . . .' Moreover, the main markers of the city's earlier flourishing were allegedly still present too: 'In beautifully self-contained fashion the square at the *Tiergärtnertor*, with the house of Albrecht Dürer, remains, which will allow us to maintain the example of the gothic Nuremberg residential house, as will the still burned-out *Nassauer Haus* opposite St Lorenz with the rare type of high-medieval residential tower.'[11] Overall, Grote argued, the surviving outlines of extant streets and the façades of patrician houses meant that 'much more of the old Nuremberg can be rebuilt than it appears in the sea of rubble today . . .'[12]

It was this emphasis on the possibilities of reconnecting with older architectural and cultural traditions which gained sway in the first ten years after the war. If progressive voices reminded us that a full reconstruction of the city was both undesirable and impossible, and if the demands of modern sanitation, traffic management and commercial activity meant that the rebuilding process was the occasion of a substantial modernisation of the city's infrastructure, then the emphasis on preservation of much of the city's old street lines, the reconstruction of many historic monuments and above all the

[10] StadtAN C 29/511, Eröffnung des Internationalen Kongresses am 5.9.49.
[11] Grote, 'Das Germanische National-Museum und Nürnberg', 16–17.
[12] Ibid., 17.

attempt to preserve, as far as possible, the main features of the city's historic skyline embodied a clear cultural-political programme.[13]

The links between a reconstruction programme that prioritised the restoration of historic monuments and the rehabilitation of the city were explicitly acknowledged on the occasion of the reopening of the Albrecht Dürer House in August 1949, when mayor Ziebill observed that 'it is the task of us all to work to ensure that the name of this old German city is respected and held in regard in the world once more. I hope that we have taken a significant further step in these efforts as Germany and the world witness how much we honour the greatest son of the city, Albrecht Dürer, and when we mark this esteem visibly by once more opening to the public his house and the site of his activity.'[14] Although attempts to renew a more progressive cultural life in the city manifested themselves in occasional events such as the 1947 exhibition, 'Art with New Eyes' – a display of 146 paintings and sculptures from twentieth-century artists such as Franz Marc mounted by the Germanic National Museum – local political and cultural exigencies, compounded by the inherent conservatism of the regional political culture ensured that this focus on the medieval and early modern past predominated in the 1950s.[15] As early as 1948 such attitudes were also beginning to predominate in Social Democratic circles. In September 1948, for example, the mayor acknowledged the significance of Nuremberg's ancient historical flourishing for its contemporary attempts at cultural orientation when, opening an exhibition on 'Nuremberg Art of the Medieval Era', he suggested that 'we look not only with pride, but also reverent modesty on the great artistic achievements of our city in the past; maybe we do so with a little sadness, we, the somewhat unfortunate members of a tumultuous era of transition which nourishes itself from the inheritance of the past and lives in hope for the future'.[16]

As the 1950s progressed, the image of a city rebuilt in the spirit of its old traditions – with which it had established a degree of continuity sufficient to justify the epithet of an 'old city' – gained in strength, even, paradoxically, as the experience of bombing and the extent of the physical destruction this caused became more central to the wider victim myths in circulation.[17] The most

---

[13] On the balance between traditionalism and modernisation in the reconstruction plans for the city, see Wachter, *Kultur in Nürnberg*, 314–23; see also Rosenfeld, *Munich and Memory*; Koshar, *Germany's Transient Pasts*.

[14] StadtAN C 29/254, Speech of Mayor Ziebill at the reopening of the Albrecht Dürer House (undated, August 1949). See also Wachter, *Kultur in Nürnberg*, 323–5.

[15] On the exhibition 'Art with New Eyes' see *Germanisches Nationalmuseum. Zweiundneunzigster Jahresbericht*, 35.

[16] StadtAN C 29/511, Rede im Germanischen Museum am 11 September 1948.

[17] For a survey of this process see Wachter, *Kultur in Nürnberg*, 325–32. A striking example of the tension between the tropes of total destruction on the one hand and cultural continuity on the other is represented by the popular history by August Sieghardt: *Nürnberg. Wesen und Schicksal einer Stadt* (Nuremberg, 1950); for the 900-year celebrations, see Wachter, *Kultur in Nürnberg*, 352–9.

prominent location of this renewed emphasis on the city's medieval and early-modern historical inheritance was the Germanic National Museum. Founded in 1852, in the wake of the disappointment of liberal-national ambition in 1848 to 1849, it had acted since the nineteenth century as a key barometer of the vicissitudes of Germany's national making and remaking.[18] The essentialist constructions of Germany and Germanness that informed its collecting and exhibiting habits, as well as its scholarly output, predisposed it to function in the Cold War era not only as an agent of attempts within Nuremberg to foster an alternative, non-Nazi civic identity, but also as a site for projecting various myths of national victimhood in the wake of the Second World War.

The exhibitions, catalogues and other publications of the Germanic National Museum told at least three stories simultaneously in the first fifteen years after the war. The first was the story of the institution itself in the immediate past. Here, predictably, extensive surveys of air-raid damage enabled the museum to claim its own status as a victim of bombing, and thus as an innocent casualty of war, while acting as counterpoint to self-congratulatory accounts of the museum's reconstruction.[19] While the prompt transfer of the museum's collections to outlying depots for safekeeping during the war was such that relatively few works of art were destroyed by the bombing, a number were lost to plunder and fire at war's end, so that the collections themselves could also be represented as victims of the war.[20]

Meanwhile, accounts of the collecting and exhibiting practices of the museum during the Third Reich also stressed the museum's victimisation at the hands of a regime of philistine totalitarianism. These accounts focused on the confiscation by the Nazis of works of art rather than discussing the problematic circumstances of the museum's acquisition of works of art in occupied France or otherwise reflecting upon the possibly dubious provenance of its purchases in the 1930s.[21] The possibility that the museum – which had not had to struggle unduly to accommodate its celebration of greater German cultural tradition and its essentialist constructions of national identity to the demands

---

[18] Martin Prösler, 'Museums and Globalisation' in Sharon Macdonald and Gordon Fyfe (eds), *Theorising Museums* (Oxford, 1996), 21–44, here 33.

[19] See, for example, *Germanisches Nationalmuseum. Zweiundneunzigster Jahresbericht*, 36–40; *97 Jahresbericht des Germanischen Nationalmuseums (1951 bis 1954)* (Nuremberg, 1955), 6–7.

[20] *Jahresbericht des Germanischen Nationalmuseums 1949* (Nuremberg, 1949), 86–7 [list of works lost as a result of war/fire in 1945].

[21] On the acquisition of works in France see the material in GNM, Vertrauliche Korrespondenz. In the 1960s, the museum acknowledged that some works had been returned under post-war restitution programmes. Wolf Schadendorf, 'Zur Sammlungsgeschichte des Germanischen Nationalmuseums und der Städtischen Galerie Nürnberg: das erweiterte Sammlungsprogramm des Germanischen Nationalmuseums', *Anzeiger des Germanischen Nationalmuseums* (1966), 142–72, here 159. Nonetheless, it continued to display objects collected by leading Nazis during the war and retained by the Federal Republic as the legal successor to the Third Reich: 'Leihgaben fürs Germanische Museum: Bundesschatzminister Dollinger übergibt 18 Gemälde aus ehemaligem Reichsbesitz', *Süddeutsche Zeitung*, 25.10.66.

of the Third Reich – had in any way contributed to sustaining the ideological climate of the 'People's Community' was not entertained. The museum's collaboration in exhibitions such as 'Political Germany: the German People's Path of Fate' to chime with the Party Rally of 1936, or 'Nuremberg: the German City' – the catalogue of which had the subtitle 'From the City of the *Reichstage* to the City of the Reich Party Rallies' which emphasised the close identity of the city with the regime – was not mentioned.[22] Neither did the museum reflect upon the question of whether its 1939 exhibition, '700 Years of Germandom in the *Weichselbogen*', shown in October 1939 to mark the conquest of Poland, had represented a contribution to sustaining the Nazis' war of racial imperialism and its murderous programme of Germanisation in the east. Mirroring wider trends within the memory culture of the late 1940s and 1950s, the museum emphasised, through its ongoing focus on centuries-old Germanic folk culture, its status as guardian of a healthy national tradition entirely distinct from the corrupting influences of radical nationalism, rather than asking whether its curation of this imagined national heritage had contributed to a climate in which more radical visions of community could flourish.

The second story – told through the re-establishment of the standing displays, the installation of special exhibitions and the associated programmes of lectures and publications – foregrounded the city's centrality to the great flourishing of the German Renaissance, while openly claiming its most famous figures as products of a specifically Nuremberg, rather than wider German, heritage.[23] Above all, the reinstalled permanent collections embodied a narrative of German art history centred on the genius of Albrecht Dürer, who had lived and worked in the city for much of his life. The main exhibition areas of the ground floor were largely given over to 'Nuremberg painting and sculpture from the fourteenth century to the Age of Dürer'. Rooms were devoted, variously, to 'the School of Dürer', to 'the greatest German woodcarver of the age of Dürer' (Veit Stoss) or to 'the greatest work of painting from the time before Dürer', exhibiting all other works not for their own merit but in relation to the same focal point. According to the museum's annual report of 1955, 'The art and culture of the old Reich city are offered in such well-rounded fashion for the first time in the history of the Germanic National Museum. From the famous Marian Altar of *c.* 1400 and the Clay Apostles through the Master of the Tucher Altarpiece, Pleydenwurff, Wolgemut and Veit Stoss the visitor is led to Dürer as the high point of Nuremberg art.'[24]

---

[22] Hans-Ulrich Thamer, 'Geschichte und Propaganda. Kulturhistorische Ausstellungen in der NS-Zeit' in *Geschichte und Gesellschaft* 24/3 (1998), 349–81, here 357.
[23] On the place of medieval and early-modern culture in the civic identity of Nuremberg, see Anne G. Kosfeld, 'Nürnberg' in Etienne François and Hagen Schulze (eds), *Deutsche Erinnerungsorte* (Band 1) (Munich, 2001), 68–85; Stephen Brockmann, *Nuremberg: The Imaginary Capital* (London, 2006).
[24] *97 Jahresbericht des Germanischen Nationalmuseums (1951 bis 1954)*, 10.

To these were added a series of temporary exhibitions in the late 1940s and early 1950s which focused, similarly, on aspects of the Renaissance and its legacy or on the much older cultural traditions of the city of Nuremberg. In 1946 to 1947, the museum mounted the exhibition 'Peter Flötner and the Renaissance in Germany'. The connections between this focus on older traditions and the search for orientation in a time of crisis were again clear. As mayor Ziegler emphasised in his foreword to the catalogue, 'Nuremberg, the once so glorious and now so stricken city, has more occasion than ever before to reflect upon the great creative masters, whose skill contributed in great measure to the rise and reputation of Nuremberg.' The exhibition embodied, in his view, the reassertion of healthy traditions in dual fashion. Firstly, it connected with a long-standing tradition of marking significant cultural anniversaries with major exhibitions at the museum: 'In honouring Peter Flötner, who died 400 years ago, the city of Nuremberg and the Germanic National Museum which it hosts proudly within its walls continue the series of commemorative exhibitions which on the occasion of the 400th anniversary of the death of Albrecht Dürer in 1928 and of Veit Stoss in 1933 showed the works of the great masters who once gained Nuremberg a reputation as the "Eye and Ear of Germany"'. Second, it sat within the wider attempts of the city to reconnect with the positive cultural traditions of the past: 'At the same time this first great exhibition of German art in Nuremberg after the horrors of the war and rule of violence marks the laying of a foundation for the new significance of Nuremberg in the peaceful field of art and culture. It should serve as proof that the necessary rebuilding of this city will take place conscious of its old, so significant inheritance.'[25]

This was followed by the exhibitions '900 Years of Nuremberg' and 'Nuremberg's Great Art' in 1949, and 'The Dawn of the Modern Age' (*Aufgang der Neuzeit*), which focused on the period between Dürer's death and the Thirty Years War, in 1952.[26] In the latter case, the catalogue stepped gingerly through the minefield of problematic associations born of the fact that elements of the period – such as the *Meistersinger* tradition – had themselves recently been appropriated in the service of nationalist politics.[27] The 1961 exhibition on 'Masters around Albrecht Dürer' marked the culmination of the first post-war wave of exhibitions on this era.

Not all exhibitions in the city fitted this pattern. In addition to the 'Art with New Eyes' display of 1947, the city's 'Franconian Gallery' showed in December

---

[25] Hans Ziegler, 'Vorwort', *Peter Flötner und die Renaissance in Deutschland. Ausstellung anläβlich des 400 Todestages Peter Flötners* (catalogue) (Nuremberg, 1946).
[26] 'Die Sonderausstellungen' in Bernward Deneke and Rainer Kahsnitz (eds), *Das Germanische Nationalmuseum Nürnberg 1852–1977. Beiträge zu seiner Geschichte* (Munich, 1978), 1147–8.
[27] *Aufgang der Neuzeit. Deutsche Kunst und Kultur von Dürers Tod bis zum Dreissigjährigen Kriege 1530–1650* (catalogue) (Nuremberg, 1952).

1945 a small exhibition, entitled 'The Excluded', of twenty-two works by the former Bauhaus artist Richard Grune, who had been incarcerated in Lichtenburg and Sachsenhausen.[28] If the anti-fascist impulse reflected in the exhibition soon faded, attempts to draw succour from the democratic traditions of German politics also manifested themselves in exhibitions such as 'The German Freedom Movement of 1848', held in the Germanic National Museum to mark the hundredth anniversary of the 1848 revolution. Yet for the Germanic National Museum – by far the most significant cultural institution in the city – any such attempts to connect with democratic political traditions or to engage with the suffering of the victims of Nazism were of marginal significance compared to the imperative to represent the territorial and cultural integrity of the German nation itself as the ultimate victim of the war. This perspective formed the third narrative projected by the museum's activities.

From the outset, the collecting and exhibiting practices of the Germanic National Museum had been informed by an implicit understanding of Germanness based on the postulated unity of a series of related tribes (*Stämme*), each of which was rooted in a specific geographical space (Saxons in Saxony, Swabians in Swabia, and so on). The geographical conditions, historical trading patterns and associated influences had given rise to a series of distinctive territorial ethnicities, each with its own culture – evident not only in the art of the region, but also in costume, food, dialect, song and folk artefact – and each with its own temperament.[29] The nation and its constituent tribes existed as imagined constants irrespective of specific manifestations of political or territorial unity – or disunity – at any given historical moment; the emphasis on geography and temperament, and on the longevity of the cultural traditions, gave a strongly essentialist flavour to the notions of nationhood to which the museum subscribed. Certainly the inventedness of nationhood, its modernity or contingency, were not subjects for consideration. Rather, the past through which the nation and its tribes moved was seen as a politics-free space, or, at least, one in which an evolving but always ordered and harmonious polity dissolved difference and conflict. Similarly, the homogenising gaze of the museum and its specialists on to the geographical spaces it claimed as 'German' was such that their ethnic, linguistic or cultural diversity was mostly ignored. Where it was acknowledged, the violent clashes to which this sometimes gave rise were smoothed out in narratives of peaceful exchange between Germans and Czechs or Germans and Poles.

---

[28] StadtAN C 34/163, 'Die Ausgestossenen, 1945' – list of exhibited pictures (undated, 1945); Aktennotiz Dr E.G. Troche, 26.11.45; Biographical Sketch, Richard Grune (undated, 1945).
[29] See, for example, the descriptions of the display of folk dance and costume contained in *Hundertjahrfeier des Germanischen Nationalmuseums am 9. und 10. August 1952* (undated, Nuremberg, 1952).

It was in line with this tradition of imagining the ancient 'cultural nation' rather than narrating its troubled politics that the museum mounted in the 1950s a series of exhibitions displaying 'Documents of Culture from the Lake Constance Region' (1952), 'Documents of Culture from the Upper Palatine and Lower Bavaria' (1953) and 'Documents of Culture from Bavarian Swabia' (1954–55). In keeping with its refusal to restrict itself to focusing on the cultural traditions contained within the current state borders, the museum included in this series an exhibition of 'Documents of Culture from Hesse, Thuringia and Saxony' in 1958; the origins of the museum in the 'Greater German' intellectual and political traditions of the nineteenth century underlay the inclusion of a similar exhibition on Austria (1957–58).

Of particular significance in this respect were the exhibitions mounted in the 1950s on aspects of German culture in the east. In 1953 the museum mounted exhibitions of both Silesian and Upper Silesian art, timed to coincide with meetings of Silesian expellee associations in the city; in 1955 it showed an exhibition of 'Art and Culture in Bohemia, Moravia and Silesia' in close association with the Sudeten German Homeland Association, with whose gathering it chimed;[30] in 1958 the opening of the new Theodor-Heuss building was marked by an exhibition of the famous church vestments (*Paramentenschatz*) of Danzig and the treasures of the 'Blackheads of Riga', a fraternity of medieval German merchants in Latvia.[31] The tone of these exhibitions was typified by the foreword to the catalogue of the 1955 exhibition on Bohemia, Moravia and Silesia, which was penned by the chairman of the Sudeten German Homeland Association, Rudolf Lodgman von Auen. 'The cultural and intellectual life of the Occident cannot be imagined without the contribution made by the lands of Bohemia, Moravia and Silesia.' Stressing how in the areas of Sudeten German settlement 'there grew from the diversity of centuries of mutual cultural fertilisation, from the interplay of the multitude of cultural forces of the Occident that grandiose picture of timeless cultural achievements still in effect today', he stressed the exhibition's capacity to show 'how the great and immortal rises over the hardships of everyday life'.[32]

Most obviously, in their highly idealised postulation of a timeless German presence in the east, marked by centuries of peaceful cultural achievement embodied in the exquisite artefacts on display, such exhibitions glossed easily over a recent history of German activity in these spaces marked by imperialist aggression and genocide. The emphasis on 'mutual cultural fertilisation' in particular stood in stark contrast to a recent occupation of eastern Europe

---

[30] *Kunst und Kultur in Böhmen, Mähren und Schlesien. Ausstellung im Germanischen National-Museum zu Nürnberg vom 22. Mai bis September 1955* (catalogue) (Nuremberg, 1955).

[31] *Aus dem Danziger Paramentenschatz und dem Schatz der Schwarzhäupter zu Riga* (catalogue) (Nuremberg, 1958).

[32] Rudolf Lodgman von Auen, 'Zum Geleit' in *Kunst und Kultur in Böhmen, Mähren und Schlesien*.

which had set as its goal the eradication of the cultural life of 'sub-human' Slavs, while the narrative of Germany's civilising presence drew unmistakeably on older traditions of ethnic arrogance towards the east.

Beyond this, however, such exhibitions embodied a territorial claim. Informed by the presumption of eventual reunification, they were intended to project an image of the Germanness of the lost territories which underlined that their current political status was both provisional and illegitimate. That maintaining an active sense of the German histories of the eastern territories formed part of an ongoing political agenda, rather than merely the expression of nostalgia, was acknowledged in the foreword to the catalogue of the Danzig church vestments exhibition, penned by a former pastor of the Church of St Mary in Danzig, whose assertion that 'one of the great dangers that the catastrophe of 1945 has engendered, with the expulsion and arbitrary scattering of long-standing communities, the separation of lands and the dismemberment of the territory of our Reich is that we run the risk of losing our sense of history' implied that keeping this knowledge alive served the greater ambition of return.[33] The State Secretary of the Bavarian Ministry for Culture, which bore much of the burden of funding the museum in the post-war years, was even more explicit in his assertion of the political function of the museum's exhibitions, stating during a board discussion of how to raise funds for the museum in 1950 that 'we must make clear that we are in a propaganda war with the Communists [in the] eastern zone and that they are culturally very active there. Something impressive therefore needs to happen here as well . . .'[34] The museum was, indeed, successful in asserting its claim as the sole collector of the 'East German cultural heritage' – by which was meant not only the territories of the German Democratic Republic, but also the lands east of the Oder-Neisse line and the areas of former German settlement in south-east Europe – and received considerable funding from the Federal Ministry for Refugees for its exhibitions on that basis.[35]

The interaction of the Germanic National Museum and the homeland associations was not limited to the installation of occasional exhibitions on the culture of the east. From the early 1950s onwards the museum authorities sought to raise the profile of the regional cultures of the expulsion territories

[33] D. Gerhard Gulzow, 'Der Danziger Paramentenschatz', *Aus dem Danziger Paramentenschatz*, 6.
[34] StadtAN C 29/195, Niederschrift über die Sitzung des Verwaltungsrates des Germanischen Nationalmuseums Nürnbergs, 22.9.50. For evidence that the museum's activities were viewed as such in the eastern bloc, see GNM, Heimatgedenkstätten (i), Grote an Heuss, 12.1.56.
[35] StadtAN C 29/235, Anlage 1 zum Verwaltungsratsprotokoll der Sitzung vom 2.7.54: Verwaltungsbericht des Germanischen Nationalmuseums in Nürnberg über das Jahr 1953/54; GNM, Heimatgedenkstätten (i), Bundesministerium für Vertriebene, Flüchtlinge und Kriegsgeschädigte an Grote, 10.11.55.

within the museum and the city more generally. In part, this followed logically from its self-appointed mission to represent the history of the entire German 'cultural nation'. In part, the promotion of refugee culture lent itself to fostering the narratives of national victimhood which the museum projected.[36] In part, such moves also reflected the personal sympathies of the head of the Germanic National Museum from 1951 to 1962, Ludwig Grote, who had visited Germans in Transylvania as a restoration consultant in the interwar years and had developed strong bonds of affection for the region.[37] It was Grote who had approached mayor Bärnreuther in 1952 to request that Nuremberg take over the role as patron of the Transylvanian Saxons and to win him for the plan to make Nuremberg 'the spiritual centre of all expellees'.[38]

Grote was also behind the original proposal to establish *Heimatgedenkstätten* – memorial sites to the 'homeland' – in the Germanic National Museum. On the occasion of his inauguration as director in 1951 he called for 'the creation of memory sites for the ethnic German groups' in which 'the Transylvanians, East Prussians, Silesians and others can find a collection point for their costumes, their implements, their works of art and documents and establish a permanent memorial to their homeland'.[39] The proposal was adopted in October 1951, and a new department of the museum was created in which 'documents of German culture from the eastern territories' were brought together in discrete displays to function in shrine-like fashion as sites of memory.[40] One room comprised the *Heimatgedenkstätte* of the Transylvanian Saxons, displaying 'the church treasures of Bistritz, costumes and colourful ceramics'; another room displayed a loaned collection of the Danzig church vestments; beyond this, 'East and West Prussia, Silesia, Bohemia and Moravia can be found in the *Heimatgedenkstätten* with significant works of art.'

If President Heuss' pathos-laden words on the occasion of the 100th anniversary of the museum in 1952 were to be believed, the basis for these memorial displays lay in donations made by the expellees themselves. In his announcement of the creation of the *Heimatgedenkstätten* he promised an 'intricate collection of the cultural documents of those German homeland associations and tribes who today know their homeland to be under the tyranny of foreign domination. As they were forced into the miserable lot of expulsion many of them – those to whom the history of their homeland was dear – tried, and understood the need to bring things with them: sacred and secular items,

---

[36] See, for example, *Hundertjahrfeier des Germanischen Nationalmuseums am 9. und 10. August 1952.*
[37] For Grote's career see 'Hier bin ich ein Herr', *Süddeutsche Zeitung*, 2.11.62.
[38] StadtAN C 29/235, Ludwig Grote an Oberbürgermeister Bärnreuther, 18.9.52.
[39] StadtAN C 29/235, Einführungsrede von Herrn Dr Ludwig Grote anlässlich seiner Wahl zum Ersten Direktor (undated, 1951).
[40] *97 Jahresbericht des Germanischen Nationalmuseums (1951 bis 1954)*, 13.

archive pieces, exemplars of traditional household industry. Their current location is often arbitrary, the danger that they are lost or have to be sold off in the individual or group's situation of need is great. To these we wish to give a refuge and a home in newly created rooms.'[41] In this way, the museum would become 'the fortified keep [*Fluchtburg*] of the German soul'.

In reality, however, and despite subsequent calls by the museum for donations from the expellee communities, the majority of exhibits came from the standing collections of the institution itself.[42] These were, themselves, quite limited. Despite the claims that 'when the *Heimatgedenkstätten* were established in 1951 . . . we could start with a respectable foundation from our holdings' and that 'we attempted to expand this department systematically through the purchase of significant objects', the museum was aware that its collection of objects from the relevant areas was quite modest.[43] It continued to acquire exhibits throughout the 1950s – in 1955, for example, its list of purchases over the previous four years included a painting of women in traditional Danzig costume from 1510, a silver beaker from Stralsund, eighteenth-century carved bookbindings from Silesia and examples of traditional dress from Pomerania, the Banat region and Transylvania – but these remained modest in comparison to the overall buying practices of the museum;[44] despite subventions from the Federal Ministry for Refugees it struggled to purchase significant works of art.[45] In their composition the displays thus represented arbitrary arrangements of items whose provenance owed as much to chance and financial constraint as to scholarly judgement or desiderata; the aura of timeless authenticity invested in the semi-random assemblages of objects from each area of settlement could hardly disguise their relatively limited museal importance. Their significance lay less in their aesthetic or documentary value than in their symbolic function.

Even this, however, was complex: beyond the claim that the *Heimatgedenkstätten* were intended to maintain the memory of German cultural achievement in the east, a variety of assumptions informed their creation.[46] Whilst Heuss' public reference to homelands 'under the tyranny of foreign domination' fitted into the wider anti-Communist discourse of post-war West

---

[41] Heuss, 'Das Germanische Nationalmuseum', 23.
[42] See, for example, the 'Aufruf' circulated to expellee newspapers and newsletters in GNM, Heimatgedenkstätten (i).
[43] *Kunst und Kultur in Böhmen, Mähren und Schlesien*, 7.
[44] *97 Jahresbericht des Germanischen Nationalmuseums (1951 bis 1954)*, 23.
[45] See also Stephan Waetzoldt, 'Die Heimatgedenkstätten des Germanischen Nationalmuseums' in Stiftung Preussischer Kulturbesitz (ed.), *Deutsche Kunst aus dem Osten* (Würzburg, 1989), 9–12, here 10.
[46] For this straightforward claim see 'Vorwort', *Kunst und Kultur in Böhmen, Mähren und Schlesien*, 7.

Germany and the expellee communities in particular, he made clear in closed session his concern that these artefacts be treated 'not separately, in the spirit of an irredentist, but within the framework of all-German issues'.[47] His comments to Chancellor Adenauer indicate, indeed, that for Heuss the memorial displays formed part of a strategy not of pandering to refugee irredentism but rather of domesticating their radicalism; he argued that if the project were realised much valuable cultural material would be rescued not only from loss or damage in private hands, but also 'possibly from being used in a politically tactless manner'.[48] For the museum, meanwhile, the purpose of the displays oscillated between preserving memory on behalf of the expellees themselves and using them to generate understanding and sympathy among the indigenous population. In its call to the expellees to supply exhibits, for example, it claimed that the displays were intended not only to maintain the memories of the expellees and their children but also 'to make those Germans who retained hearth and home aware that not just cornfields and coalmines were lost but also monuments of German history and culture which belong among the most significant products of the creative genius of our people'.[49] Similarly, at least some sections of organised expellee opinion believed the indigenous population, rather than the expellees themselves, to be the proper target. A representative of the Associated East German Homeland Associations argued in 1952, for example, that the merits of the Germanic National Museum lay in its ability to present eastern German artefacts 'as an organic part of greater German cultural expression' thereby ensuring that 'they are also noticed by the West Germans much more than if they are isolated, and it is, after all, an issue of making this demonstration to the West German population'.[50]

The ambiguities in the underlying purpose of the *Heimatgedenkstätten* were reflected in responses from the public which were both limited and at best mixed. The official responses of the homeland associations were positive, but these tell nothing about the reactions of ordinary expellees.[51] According to Grote, 'The *Heimatgedenkstätten* continue to find now a great echo among the

---

[47] StadtAN C 29/235, Niederschrift über die Sitzung des Verwaltungsrats des Germanischen Nationalmuseums Nürnberg, 4.10.52.

[48] GNM Heimatgedenkstätten (i), Theodor Heuss an Konrad Adenauer, 29.11.51; as such, cultural policy was a key dimension of 'taming the expellee threat': see Pertti Ahonen, 'Taming the Expellee Threat in post-1945 Europe: Lessons from the Two Germanies and Finland' in *Contemporary European History* 14/1 (2005), 1–22.

[49] GNM Heimatgedenkstätten (i), 'Aufruf'.

[50] GNM Heimatgedenkstätten (i), Dr Adolphi/Vereinigte Ostdeutsche Landsmannschaften an Meyer-Heisig, GNM, 23.1.52.

[51] For an official response, see, for example, GNM Heimatgedenkstätten (i), Verband Mitteldeutscher Landsmannschaften an Grote, 24.8.53; also Hans Wühr, 'Treuhänder unserer Volkskunst. Das GNM in Nürnberg' in *Siebenbürgischer Zeitung* No. 2, 20.2.52; on the problem of viewer response see Sharon Macdonald, 'Introduction' in Macdonald and Fyfe, *Theorising Museums*, 1–18.

refugees. But we hear occasional remarks that their contents are still very sparse.'[52] He expressed similar views to the Ministry for Refugees when he observed that 'the content of the memorials has hitherto consisted for the most part of folk artefacts. Refugees have repeatedly spoken to us about this and exclaimed that they were not after all just peasants, but bearers of great German culture. For this reason everything must be done to get works of art into the *Heimatgedenkstätten*.'[53] Such claims were to be seen in the context of attempts to prise funds from the Federal government, but they mirrored claims made elsewhere and represented a plausible account of the impact of the displays. Neither can the willingness of expellees to sell artefacts to the museum be taken as an indicator of emotional identification with the *Heimatgedenkstätten* project. The exceptional poverty in which many lived was such that the sale of objects may well have reflected economic desperation rather than political or emotional identification with the museum.[54] Similarly, there is little, if any, evidence to suggest a resonance of any kind among the indigenous Nuremberg population.[55]

In the 1960s the *Heimatgedenkstätten* were removed. Question marks over their artistic value had never been overcome but, more importantly, the territorial and political claim – however ambiguous – they embodied had become inexpedient.[56] Similarly, the museum ceased holding exhibitions on the theme of German culture in the east which might be interpreted as a provocation to eastern bloc states. Yet if the museum's role in integrating the expellees on a local level was limited compared to the slow process of economic and social integration stimulated by the economic recovery, its displays of German art fitted very much into a wider discourse in the Federal Republic on the victimhood of both the German people and the German nation. Its collecting, cataloguing and exhibiting practices had cast both the museum and the dismembered nation as victims of Nazism and war, and the war itself as an unnatural interruption in the continuous unfolding of a cultural nation whose timeless achievements testified to the civilising presence of the German nation throughout European history.

In the museum's silences, too, it reflected the operations of this overarching victim discourse. For all of its stated ambition to be to the German people 'a mirror to the inner life of their ancestors, to their culture in all its branches,

---

[52] StadtAN C 29/235, Niederschrift über die Sitzung des Arbeitsausschusses des Verwaltungsrats des Germanischen Nationalmuseums, 11.5.53.
[53] GNM Heimatgedenkstätten (i), Dr Ludwig Grote an Ministerialdirigent Dr Kleeberg, Bundesministerium für Vertriebene, 29.10.53.
[54] See the correspondence between the museum and individual expellees in GNM Heimatgedenkstätten (ii).
[55] For the wariness of the city council see GNM Heimatgedenkstätten (i), Grote an Lossmann, 19.12.51; Stadt Nürnberg/Zitzmann an Grote, 10.1.52; Grote an Lossmann, 11.1.52.
[56] Waetzoldt, 'Die Heimatgedenkstätten', 11.

in which the people recognises itself and learns to love and understand its history' there was one gaping omission: that of the rich traditions of German–Jewish culture. Its ingrained habit of imagining the 'tribes' of Germany as inhabitants of distinctive regional territories contained no possibility of representing the culture of a segment of the population that had been distributed across the entire nation, even if sections of German–Jewish opinion had latterly asserted their status as members of a Jewish–German *Stamm* in their tortured attempts to prove that they had belonged.[57] Indeed, its self-appointed mission as a 'living' museum reflecting the cultural identities of those in the present necessarily rendered a focus on Jewish history irrelevant. It was none other than the President of the Federal Republic, Theodor Heuss, who, in a discussion of the question of how to raise funds for the purchase of the tenth-century Echternacher Codex in 1954, suggested that the museum generate income by selling off some of its collection of German Judaica. While he cautioned that 'a disposal of these for the purposes of purchasing the Echternacher Codex must be assessed for political and tactical purposes, so that no damage is caused', the insinuation that the museum – and, by implication, the nation – no longer had an innate interest in the German Jewish heritage was nonetheless clear.[58]

Over the course of the 1950s a multilayered memory culture had emerged out of the interplay of sectional associational interests, political elites, local bureaucracies and the diverse actors of civil society more broadly. At its core was the association of shared victimhood, articulated in diverse genres of text and enacted in a wide variety of situations, both formal and informal. In speaking myths of victimhood through the creation or display of material artefacts, the performance of ritual acts or through their rhetorical rehearsal in all manner of spoken or written script, the dominant actors of the city's memory culture repeated myths in wider circulation which helped the population to make sense of its wartime and post-war suffering while fostering a set of narratives in which the often sharp differences between various sectional interests could be dissolved. In doing so they provided a shared framework for understanding the past, forming the civic consensus upon which a workable post-war democratic political culture could successfully re-emerge. This consensus was always fragile, and always open to contestation: as the following section of this book demonstrates, such contestation occurred from the late

---

[57] Till van Rahden, 'Germans of the Jewish Stamm: Visions of Community between Nationalism and Particularism, 1850–1933' in Neil Gregor, Nils Roemer and Mark Roseman (eds), *German History from the Margins* (Bloomington, IN, 2006), 27–48.
[58] StadtAN C 29/235, Niederschrift über die Sitzung des Verwaltungsrats des Germanischen Nationalmuseums am 2.7.54.

1950s and especially the early 1960s onwards on an ever greater basis. At the same time, the 1950s witnessed the emergence of myths of a specifically local victimhood in which the city, as much as its population per se, figured as the victim: these myths would survive into the 1960s and serve as a key tool with which to contain the new, more critical, challenges of that decade and thus to preserve the necessary minimum of civic peace across the chasms of a divided, disputatious local political culture.

III

Challenging the Consensus, Containing the Challenge
New Impulses, 1958 to 1968

III.1

Impulses from Without, Impulses from Within

Liberalisation and the 'Confrontation of the Past'

In the late 1950s the possibilities of a shift in the ways in which West Germans – or at least some of them – imagined the past, and their individual positions in relation to it, began to signal themselves. This shift, which became more visible as the decade turned, was anything but inevitable. Neither can it be reduced to a simple set of causes. Although changes in international relations, shifts in domestic political climate and ongoing generational change created an evolving terrain on which the legacies of a genocidal past could be played out in new ways, none of the transitions visible in these spheres translated in obvious or necessary ways into particular changes in the manner in which the Nazi era was engaged, 'confronted' or disputed. Changing diplomatic, political, institutional or cultural contexts undoubtedly opened up new spaces for various challenges to the dominant representations, narratives and rhetorics of the 1950s, but how such spaces would be filled could not be predicted and was most certainly not predetermined in any way.

The erection of the Berlin Wall in 1961 and the onset of the era of détente, for example, were paralleled by changes in domestic ideological climate which offered an opportunity for additional perspectives on the past to emerge. Yet if the slow normalisation of east–west relations brought with it a decline in the more hysterical forms of anti-Communist rhetoric that had characterised the 1950s, giving certain narratives of the past less purchase, it was precisely the building of the Berlin Wall that gave such anti-Communist sentiment intensified emotional appeal in some sections of society. Among expellee organisations in particular, the fear provoked by the gradual normalisation of relations that the Federal Republic would renounce ambitions towards territorial revision led to an increasingly shrill tone.[1] Anti-Communism

[1] Ahonen, *After the Expulsion*, 155ff.

remained a constituent element of the political culture of the Federal Republic sufficiently for certain blind spots in its memory politics – particularly those relating to the sacrifice made by KPD supporters in the fight against Nazism – to remain. Likewise, the return of sovereignty to West Germany in 1955, and its membership of NATO and the EEC, marked a normalisation of relations between the Federal Republic and its western neighbours which might just as well have fostered ongoing quiescence over the Nazi past as a shift towards a more active, reflective mode.[2]

Neither is it obvious that changes in domestic politics – conceived narrowly in terms of the ongoing contest for power within defined constitutional and institutional structures – worked in obvious ways to encourage a linear shift in the manner in which ordinary Germans thought about Nazism, war and genocide. On the most general level, clearly, it is true that the era of conservative hegemony, which reached its zenith with Adenauer's electoral triumph of 1957, began to wane in the early 1960s, giving way to the changed priorities of the emerging social-liberal era. Yet the emergence of a more critical discourse signalled itself precisely at the point at which Adenauer's dominance was at its peak. Moreover, the transition was a very slow, drawn-out affair. It reached its logical conclusion only with the arrival of Willy Brandt as West Germany's first post-war Social Democratic chancellor in 1969, long after the key shifts towards more critical reflection upon the Nazi past had occurred. Brandt's appointment followed in the wake of the interlude of the Great Coalition of 1966 to 1969, an extended moment whose own peculiar dynamic produced a set of impulses quite distinct from the wider slow embrace of Social Democratic politics in the Federal Republic. During this era, SPD participation in a government deemed by its critics in the 'Extra-Parliamentary Opposition' to be inherently authoritarian ensured that the SPD's role in promoting a 'confrontation with the past' lay as much in it being regarded as part of a hypocritical political establishment, as in its own pursuit of critical agendas in the field of memory politics.

At regional level, meanwhile, the CSU – whose entrenched parochial conservatism translated into an ongoing refusal to countenance the merits of a more self-critical engagement with the past – further consolidated its position as the dominant force in Bavarian state politics, so that the environment in which Nuremberg's civic leaders addressed issues of memory was, in some respects, less conducive to openness than it had been in the 1950s. At the local level itself, finally, power remained in the hands of the SPD, whose

---

[2] For the interplay of diplomatic constellations and memory politics, see Brochhagen, *Nach Nürnberg*.

continuous domination of civic institutions translated into a strong element of continuity in the commemorative practices of the city. The SPD's guardianship of narratives which were now quite established meant that attempts at greater acknowledgement of the genocidal dimensions of the Nazi past would have to be woven into these existing stories, rather than supplant them, if they wished to have any chance of gaining traction within the civic culture of Nuremberg.

There were, in short, no simple connections between the shifting political constellations of the 1950s and 1960s and the slow emergence of a more critical discourse on the past. Equally complex, and equally capable of pulling memory politics in the opposite directions to those they eventually took, was the impact of generational change. By the late 1960s, clearly, a minority of middle-class students were one of the driving forces behind increasingly strident demands to tear down the hypocritical façades of a society which had reintegrated former Nazi party activists and allowed them to enjoy good careers unimpeded by the burdens of a compromised past. Informed by a vulgarised theory of fascism which saw excessive continuities between the Nazi and post-Nazi eras, such critiques eschewed contemplation of the slow process of democratisation of West Germany's political culture after 1945, basing their hyper-critical polemics instead on the assumption that anyone who had been a Nazi in 1941 was the same Nazi in 1968. The culture of revelation and denunciation, visible in Nuremberg as elsewhere, became a characteristic feature of the political culture which had been largely absent in the 1950s.[3]

In the long run, the change in political culture which the protest activism of this cohort came to symbolise was a decisive factor in enabling the historical fact of the genocide to move to the centre of the Federal Republic's political identity and pedagogical conscience.[4] In the short term, however, the accusatory posturing of some of the students of the late 1960s against leading politicians, judges, university rectors or businessmen with compromised pasts provoked defensiveness, and identification on the part of the majority with those they were accusing, rather than acceptance of the need for more openness.[5] The convictions which informed the student critiques of the hypocrisies of their elders were also based on understandings of the Third Reich which were at best partial and which ensured that the genocide was a

---

[3] See, for example, 'Verwischte Aspekte', *Nürnberger Nachrichten*, 22./23.1.66. On personnel continuities and their impact on the political culture of the early Federal Republic see Loth and Rusinek, *Verwandlungspolitik*.

[4] For the long-term impact see the relevant essays in Carole Fink, Philipp Gassert, Detlef Junker (eds), *1968. The World Transformed* (Cambridge, 1998).

[5] For a sceptical, but timely assertion of the limits to which the events of '1968' impacted upon local memory cultures in the short term see Thießen, 'Das Gedächtnis der Stadt', 261–6.

relatively marginal aspect of their concerns; the legacies of the Nazi past were in themselves only one of a large number of protest causes.[6]

Six or seven years earlier, in any case, intra-generational criticisms – including those centred on alleged indifference to the burdens bequeathed by the past – had flowed in the opposite direction: around 1960, it was left-liberal sections of opinion within the generation that had lived through the war as young adults who were concerned not just at what they took to be the shallow present-centredness of the young, but specifically at their lack of knowledge about the Nazi past.[7] It was the pedagogical impulses this conviction produced, in the form of exhibitions or schools events – alongside the Nazi-era crimes trials of the 1960s – that sensitised what became the student cohort of the late 1960s to the issues it later claimed to be discovering for itself. If there was a crucial younger generation of memory activists which drove the decisive shifts then it lay in the intermediate generation between the 'Nazi' generation and their youthful accusers.[8] In Nuremberg, this meant figures such as mayor Andreas Urschlechter (b.1919) or Hermann Glaser (b.1928) who, as the city's head of Schools and Cultural policy from 1964 onwards, became a key arbiter of memory politics at the local level in the coming years. Even this must be qualified, since efforts to engage with the issues were already in evidence under Glaser's predecessor, Andreas Staudt (b.1893), a member of a considerably older Social Democratic cohort.[9]

If there was a decisive generational shift which made a more critical examination of the recent past both possible and more likely, in fact, it probably lay less in the emergence of new voices unencumbered by shame than in the fading presence of older voices shaped disproportionately and irretrievably by suffering. Here, the key cohort was that born in the 1890s – the generation which moved into its sixties during the 1950s and its seventies during the 1960s. This generation had first encountered the violence of war in 1914 to 1918: for the men of this generation in particular, the shaping of their knowledge of military violence through the first-hand experience of the earlier conflagration was doubtless a major barrier to their ability to contemplate the boundless criminality of the altogether different campaigns of 1939 to 1945. This was a generation, moreover, that had been repeatedly burdened with

---

[6] Nick Thomas, *Protest Movements in 1960s West Germany. A Social History of Dissent and Democracy* (Oxford, 2003).

[7] See, for example, Detlef Siegfried, ' "Don't Trust Anyone Older than Thirty?" Voices of Conflict and Consensus in 1960s West Germany', *Journal of Contemporary History*, 40/4 (2005), 727–44, here 731–2.

[8] The significance of the '1945 generation', of which Glaser was a prime example, has been underlined by a number of scholars recently. See, most importantly, Hodenberg, *Konsens und Krise*; Moses, *German Intellectuals and the Nazi Past*.

[9] See below, Chapter III.3.

massive bereavement and the associated grief. For men and women of this generation alike, the loss of siblings and friends familiarised them with the emotional shocks brought by war – before the Second World War brought renewed loss as parents.

Whatever their position in the ideological politics of the interwar and Nazi years, it is unsurprising, given their biographical trajectories, that as middle-aged and elderly people living in the rubble environments of the late 1940s and 1950s they were unable to imagine a national history of aggressive imperialism and genocidal barbarism in a manner that focused critical attention on their own compromised place within a perpetrator society. This generation retired from the dominant positions in West German politics and institutions over the 1950s and 1960s. The highly conservative dean of the Protestant Church in Nuremberg, Julius Schieder, for example, who had seen service as a military parson in 1914 to 1915, and who epitomised the ambiguous histories of the national-conservative Protestant tradition in the first half of the twentieth century, retired in 1958 and died in 1964.[10] As this generation faded, the logic of democratic politics meant that the guardians of the city's cultural policy were less constrained by the need to verbalise histories which accorded with those of this particular cohort's imagination, and the possibilities for change – of some kind – correspondingly emerged.

The fading purchase of the 'victim' narrative also doubtless owed much to the rapidly evolving landscapes of post-war life. By the late 1950s all but a few refugee and displaced persons' camps had been closed down, their occupants having either found permanent housing or emigrated. The building boom which had provided this housing was both symptom and cause of an economic recovery which had transformed West German society with remarkable speed. Meanwhile, the return of the last prisoners of war from Soviet captivity at the beginning of 1956 marked a symbolic end to the disruption of the war and post-war years, even if it only affected a few families directly.[11] A culture of scarcity had given way to a culture of plenty, or at least one of sufficiency. The prosperity enjoyed by middle-class citizens rendered their claims to wartime victimhood considerably less persuasive; at the same time such prosperity gave accusations that they had made a comfortable transition into a post-war world of hypocritical denial more obvious appeal.

The overcoming of the immediate devastation of war and its attendant effects marked a necessary, but not sufficient, condition for the emergence of more critical reflection on the crimes of the past within sections of West German society. The emergence of a more critical climate was not, however,

---

[10] Matthias Eckert, *Julius Schieder 1888–1964. Regionalbischof und Prediger in schwerer Zeit* (Neuendettelsau, 2004), 59–62.
[11] Moeller, 'The Last Soldiers of the Great War', 129–45.

inevitable. Rather, it was the product of a set of contingent events the cumulative reverberations of which resonated increasingly in a society experiencing
a more diffuse set of changes in its political culture.[12]

The return of the remaining prisoners of war from the Soviet Union, for
example, not only marked a moment of closure, but also set off one such
chain of contingent events which would eventually force the events of the
Holocaust to the fore. It was the interrogation of some of the returnees,
who included some high-ranking war criminals in their number, which
gave decisive impetus to a renewed willingness to prosecute Nazi crimes. This
found its initial expression in the Ulm *Einsatzgruppen* trial of 1958.[13] The
subsequent founding of the *Zentrale Stelle der Landesjustizverwaltungen*
(Central Office of State Justice Departments) initiated a wave of further prosecutions during the 1960s, drawing much public interest. At the same time,
the protracted debates about the Statute of Limitations – the twenty-year
Statute of Limitations for murder posed a major potential barrier to the
successful prosecution of Nazi-era crimes – further sensitised public opinion
to the unresolved issues arising from the Nazi past; the extension, and eventual lifting, of the Statute of Limitations for murder ensured prosecutions
could continue.[14]

The Ulm trial, the Eichmann trial of 1961 in Jerusalem and the Frankfurt
Auschwitz trial of 1963 to 1965, along with countless other trials across West
Germany, became media events. The transmission of the legal process, its
findings and implications to the public, and its function in stimulating wider
debate, owed much to the new communication technologies – particularly
television – which were becoming commonplace in an the era of high
consumerism. Their impact was reinforced by other media events such as
the anti-Semitic desecration of the Cologne Synagogue in 1959, which led
to public outcry, or the discussion surrounding the controversial 1963 play

---

[12] On the 1960s as an epoch of 'fermentation' see Klaus Schönhoven, 'Aufbruch in die soziallib-
erale Ära. Zur Bedeutung der 60er Jahre in der Geschichte der Bundesrepublik' in *Geschichte und
Gesellschaft* 25 (1999), 123–45, here 128. The chance nature of the occurrences which led to
many high-profile prosecutions of former Nazis, for example, is emphasised in Fritz Bauer,
'Im Namen des Volkes. Die strafrechtliche Bewältigung der Vergangenheit' in Helmut
Hammerschmidt (ed.), *Zwanzig Jahre Danach. Eine Deutsche Bilanz 1945–1965* (Munich, 1965),
301–14, here 305; for the background to the Auschwitz trial see Werner Renz, 'Der 1.
Frankfurter-Auschwitzprozess. Zwei Vorgeschichten' in *Zeitschrift für Geschichtswissenschaft* 50
(2002), 622–41; Rebecca Elizabeth Wittmann, 'The Wheels of Justice Turn Slowly: The Pretrial
Investigation of the Frankfurt Auschwitz Trial 1963–1965' in *Central European History* 35 (2002),
345–78; Pendas, *The Frankfurt Auschwitz Trial.*
[13] On the connections between the returning POWs and the creation of the Central Office, see
Adalbert Rückerl, *Die Strafverfolgung von NS-Verbrechen 1945–1978. Eine Dokumentation*
(Heidelberg, 1979), 49–58.
[14] Helmut Dubiel, *Niemand ist frei von der Geschichte. Die nationalsozialistische Herrschaft in den
Debatten des Deutschen Bundestages* (Hamburg, 1999); Peter Reichel, *Vergangenheitsbewältigung
in Deutschland* (Munich, 2001), 182–98.

Der Stellvertreter (The Deputy) by Rolf Hochhuth, which criticised the papacy for its alleged wartime indifference and inaction over the murder of the Jews.[15]

Much as the prosecution of Nazi criminals owed to the efforts of a minority of liberally inclined figures in the political and judicial elites – among them a number of returned former émigrés from the Third Reich – so the critical reporting of these cases owed to the increased openness of liberal sections of the media. This legal activism and its open discussion in the media connected, in turn, with the concerns of a political culture which was also undergoing significant change.[16] It is important not to overstate the immediate extent of this change: the 1950s had, after all, had their fair share of debate, conflict and protest.[17] Nonetheless, its effects cannot be ignored. The residual vestiges of authoritarian conformity – learned in an earlier era but still visible under Adenauer's chancellorship in the 1950s – slowly gave way to something tangibly different during the 1960s. Whatever belief in the virtues of deference remained gave further ground to the champions of challenging that which was established. The essential merits of consensus were disputed by those who valued disagreement as a virtue in itself, and the perception of rigidities which had hitherto militated against democratic engagement underpinned the embrace of argument. The presence of authority demanded contradiction. In other words, it was not so much the renewed prominence of left-liberal politics in a narrower sense that permitted the shifts of memory culture in the 1960s as a much wider liberalisation of West German society that also extended to its hitherto more conservative institutions.[18] It was in this climate that those voices demanding that West Germans should reflect more directly upon the crimes of the past began to find a more willing audience.

It should not be overlooked, finally, that there had always been a counter-memory, composed of various distinct strands, which had sought since 1945

[15] On the cemetery attacks of 1959–1960 see Werner Bergmann, 'Antisemitismus als politisches Ereignis. Die antisemitische Schmierwelle im Winter 1959/60' in Werner Bergmann and Rainer Erb (eds), *Antisemitismus in der politischen Kultur seit 1945* (Opladen, 1990), 253–75; for surveys of the changing memory culture of the late 1950s and 1960s see Axel Schildt, 'Der Umgang mit der NS-Vergangenheit in der Öffentlichkeit der Nachkriegszeit' in Loth and Rusinek, *Verwandlungspolitik*, 19–54, esp. 45ff.; Harold Marcuse, 'The Revival of Holocaust Awareness in West Germany, Israel and the United States' in Fink, Gassert, Junker, *1968. The World Transformed*, 421–38; Detlef Siegfried, 'Zwischen Aufarbeitung und Schlußstrich. Der Umgang mit der NS-Vergangenheit in beiden deutschen Staaten 1958 bis 1969' in Axel Schildt, Detlef Siegfried and Karl Christian Lammers (eds), *Dynamische Zeiten. Die 60er Jahre in den beiden deutschen Gesellschaften* (Hamburg, 2000), 77–113; and the essays in Philipp Gassert and Alan E. Steinweis (eds), *Coping with the Nazi Past. West German Debates on Nazism and Generational Conflict 1955–1975* (Oxford, 2006).

[16] The relationship between the emergence of a critical media culture and the wider 'second democratisation' of the Federal Republic is explored in Hodenberg, *Konsens und Krise*.

[17] Ibid., 12–13.

[18] On the changing political culture of the 1960s see Schönhoven, 'Aufbruch'; Schildt, Siegfried, Lammers, *Dynamische Zeiten*; Ulrich Herbert (ed.), *Wandlungsprozesse in Westdeutschland. Belastung, Integration, Liberalisierung 1945–1980* (Göttingen, 2002).

to place recognition of the crimes of Nazism and acknowledgement of the sufferings of its victims at the centre of reflection. Indeed, one of the most important foundations for the transitions which took place locally in the 1960s lay in the presence of a working-class counter-memory of the experience of the Third Reich. As an industrial city with strong traditions of organised working-class politics it had witnessed considerable left-wing opposition to the Nazi seizure of power – both in the streets, where large-scale demonstrations had occurred in 1933, and in the chambers of the city council itself, where Social Democratic councillors had courageously opposed the Nazi takeover.[19] Both Social Democratic and Communist traditions had offered resistance and suffered persecution from 1933 onwards: by 1945, both could list large numbers of concentration camp martyrs. Despite the integrative appeal of the Nazi regime – to which sections of the working class had been far from immune – the underlying political sensibilities of the organised working class had remained sufficiently intact through the Nazi years for both the KPD and SPD to resurface immediately in 1945, along with the trade unions. The experiences of 1933 to 1945 provided a powerful reservoir of memories which informed the political activism of the first generation of post-war left-wing leaders, many of whom were veterans both of the pre-1933 struggle against Nazism and survivors of the concentration camps themselves.

It was the instinctive working-class anti-fascism learned in the years 1933 to 1945 which had found expression in factory-floor criticisms of the allegedly lenient treatment of managers during the denazification process; the dual experiences of urban bombing and bereavement had led working-class women to demonstrate against the sale of military toys in 1950; the same anti-war sensibility found renewed articulation in the campaigns against rearmament and military service of the early and mid 1950s. If this aversion to war was primarily rooted in memories of one's own suffering, rather than focused on the suffering of foreign victims or on the victims of the genocide, it still drew upon a political and ethical sensibility which provided a relatively receptive terrain for later calls to engage more directly with the history of the Holocaust. An institutionalised culture of anti-fascism had never established itself in the city after the war – the efforts of 1945 to 1946 had quickly petered out – but the city's dominant political forces were embedded in a milieu in which, for example, from the 1950s onwards, commemorative events were held at the former concentration camps of Dachau and Flossenbürg.[20]

Long before middle-class student groups began to 'discover' the crimes of the Third Reich, the youth sections of the West German trade union

---

[19] See the account in Gerhard Hirschmann, *Das Ende des demokratischen Stadtrates in Nürnberg 1933* (Nuremberg, 1983).
[20] See the overview in Marcuse, *Legacies of Dachau*, 203–6.

movement were at the forefront of such events, including representatives from Nuremberg.[21] If members of the trade union youth movement slotted concentration camp histories into politically inflected narratives imbibed within the working-class milieu, their attendance at such commemorations was unlikely to represent merely the formal rehearsal of political pieties or acts of youthful ideological posturing: such participation was doubtless prompted, at least in part, by direct family memories of the smashing of the Left in 1933, and of the subsequent impact of a terror which had led to the deaths of many Bavarian SPD and KPD members. And if such commemorations still focused primarily on the German Left's own victims, they clearly helped to sensitise sections of young working-class opinion to wider issues earlier than was the case for many others. In 1963, for example, the Society for Christian–Jewish Cooperation reported that fifty members of the youth branch of the Nuremberg office of the German Trade Union Federation (*Deutsche Gewerkschaftsbund*) had volunteered to undertake repair work at the old Jewish cemetery 'as an act of goodwill and in order to contribute to atonement for the wrongs perpetrated against the Jews by National Socialism'.[22]

A quite different strand of counter-memory activism was represented by the activities of the Society for Christian–Jewish Cooperation itself. The city's small Jewish community largely eschewed public acts of commemoration: its events were held in Jewish spaces, such as the Jewish cemetery, and generated little interest in the wider German community. Its initially ambiguous attitude to a process of remembrance which was almost too painful to countenance was manifested in a letter to the city council of 1955 in which it assured mayor Bärnreuther that 'we are trying to forget the heavy, fateful blows which we had to endure . . .'[23] Via the Society for Christian–Jewish Cooperation, however, some members of the Jewish community pursued 'Christian–Jewish dialogue' with the minority of members of the Protestant Church community who were willing from the outset to acknowledge the enormity of the crimes committed against the Jews and the challenges this posed to Protestant tradition.[24] The number of participants in regular meetings was usually small, but the annual 'Brotherhood Weeks' organised by local branches attracted large audiences; the reporting of such encounters in the Protestant media ensured

---

[21] For references to participation in these commemorations in the 1960s, see StadtAN C 73 I/482, Gesellschaft für Christlich-Jüdische Zusammenarbeit Nürnberg-Fürth e.V., Rundschreiben, 28.11.62; StadtAN E 6/825/1, Rundschreiben der Gesellschaft für Christlich-Jüdische Zusammenarbeit Nürnberg-Fürth e.V., 19.10.64. As both these sources make clear, the annual visits had been taking place for some time.

[22] StadtAN C 73 I/482, Gesellschaft für Christlich-Jüdische Zusammenarbeit Nürnberg-Fürth e.V., Rundschreiben, 11.6.63.

[23] StadtAN C 29/493, Israelitische Kultusgemeinde Nürnberg an Bärnreuther, 3.1.55.

[24] Josef Foschepoth, *Im Schatten der Vergangenheit. Die Anfänge der Gesellschaften für Christlich-Jüdische Zusammenarbeit* (Göttingen, 1993).

that awareness of them reached an even wider audience.[25] Reporting on a conference on 'Christianity and Jewry' held at the Protestant Church's conference centre at Tutzing in 1949, for example, the Nuremberg parish newsletter openly acknowledged that 'there was not a participant from the Jewish side who had not withstood many years of spiritual and physical suffering under constant threat of death in German concentration camps'.[26] The Society became a prominent voice warning against apparent manifestations of renewed nationalism and anti-Semitism during the 1950s. In 1954 it issued a statement criticising the increasing nationalist sentiments that were allegedly accompanying rearmament and warning that 'it would be catastrophic if significant elements of the German population fell back into racial mania and hatred of Jews'.[27] Whether such warnings reflected actual increases in nationalist and racist sentiment, or merely a heightened sensitivity towards expressions of such attitudes as the 1950s progressed cannot be ascertained: either way, through publication in the Protestant parish newsletter such warnings again reached a wider audience.

Even where there was no meaningful counter-memory within the wider community, or where highly conservative hierarchies, traditions and mental dispositions rendered institutions ill-equipped for an open confrontation of the moral legacies of the Third Reich, the knowledge was always very much there, and was occasionally articulated in public – sometimes in quite provocative ways. The Protestant Church hierarchy, for example, circulated in 1951 an internal exposé assessing the numbers of Jews murdered during the genocide, based on the estimates of the Central Council of the Jews in Germany and the Contemporary Jewish Documentation Centre in Paris, which was intended not for publication but to place individual churchmen 'in a position to answer as accurately as possible questions asked of them from within the parish'.[28] In 1954, meanwhile, the Protestant parish newsletter published an article on technical progress and moral decline which asked, 'Who, for example, would have dreamt in 1930 that in Germany of all places gas chambers would be established for the destruction of countless people, and that people – not a few of them – would come forward to make this impossibility possible?'[29] In 1956 it was similarly referring openly to 'those

---

[25] Ibid., 140–8.

[26] 'Christen und Juden in Tutzing', *Nürnberger Evangelisches Gemeindeblatt*, 11.12.49.

[27] 'Kirchliche Rundschau', *Nürnberger Evangelisches Gemeindeblatt*, 19.12.54; for further examples see 'Kirchliche Rundschau', *Nürnberger Evangelisches Gemeindeblatt*, 29.6.58; 'Brüderlichkeit. Mitteilungen der Gesellschaft für Christlich-Jüdische Zusammenarbeit Nürnberg-Fürth e.V.', undated (March 1960), copy in StadtAN C 73 I/831.

[28] LKAN Kd Nbg 348, Ev.-Luth. Landeskirchenrat an sämtliche Dekanate der Ev.-Luth. Kirche in Bayern, 21.9.51.

[29] ' "Fliegende Untertassen"? Technischer Fortschritt und moralischer Verfall', *Nürnberger Evangelisches Gemeindeblatt*, 15.8.54.

horrific orders, contrary to all international law, to liquidate captured Russian commissars or Jewish ethnic groups'.[30] If such general references offered little challenge to the individual conscience of the reader, others were more pointed. In the same year, for example, the newsletter printed a speech by the Protestant theologian Helmut Gollwitzer which told the story of a wartime encounter between the author and a sergeant who had laughingly recounted how he had discovered and handed over to the police a Jewish family in hiding in Poland: 'Maybe he now lives somewhere as a decent citizen in prosperity and respectability with his family, votes for a democratic party and goes to church now and again – and has long since forgotten that he is a murderer.'[31]

In the 1950s such accounts were always wrapped up in warnings of the dangers of turning away from God, embedded in calls for a renewal of missionary zeal towards the Jews, or accompanied by promises of redemption through the power of prayer or God's mercy; they often closed with calls for reconciliation which showed a complete absence of self-awareness of the church's relationship to the perpetrating community, and a corresponding inability to contemplate the question of whether the offer of reconciliation was in the church's gift. However, they demonstrate again that knowledge of the Holocaust – sometimes quite detailed – was widespread, even if it was rarely articulated, and that when institutions such as the churches began in the 1960s to speak more regularly and directly about the Holocaust there was no 'surfacing' of the 'repressed' involved, but a new willingness to speak of issues about which they had hitherto been for the most part – although clearly not entirely – silent.

Yet perhaps even more significant than the fact that the Protestant Church was willing to voice these issues more often was the changed manner in which it was willing to do so. In a piece in its parish newsletter in August 1963, for example, it not only remarked that 'the conscience of many Protestant Christians does not let them sleep when they think of how little their church undertook to prevent the liquidation of six million Jews' but also discussed openly the anti-Semitic comments of a leading Bishop during the time of the Third Reich; moreover, it demanded that acknowledgement of guilt be followed by engaged social action.[32] Rather than ponder the mysteries of God's world or offer nebulous reflections on guilt and punishment in the manner in which it had been prone to do in the 1950s, it also sought to draw contemporary political conclusions. Illustrating its piece with a picture of US

---

[30] 'Was verstehen wir unter "politischer Verantwortung"?', *Nürnberger Evangelisches Gemeindeblatt*, 18.3.56.
[31] 'Professor Gollwitzer: "Zwischen uns und der Zukunft – Eine Besinnung um Buße und Vergebung" ', *Nürnberger Evangelisches Gemeindeblatt*, 18.11.56.
[32] 'Christen und Juden', *Nürnberger Evangelisches Gemeindeblatt*, 18.8.63.

national guardsmen confronting black civil rights demonstrators, it warned that 'this scene, which, with other uniforms and other skin colours, could have happened here too 25 years ago, draws our attention to Cambridge in the American state of Maryland, where members of the national guard disperse a demonstration of coloured people with bayonets mounted'. Such pieces pointed to the fact that the changes in the political culture of the Federal Republic which made some citizens more receptive to politically engaged criticism and debate – and which made them more open to the desirability of reflecting upon the Holocaust – were not confined to the slowly ascendant Left, but were making themselves felt across the institutions of civil society.[33]

The changes occurring in civil society gradually manifested themselves in the local corridors of power too. The precise means by which encouragement from associational activists translated into action on the part of the city's political elites are impossible to pin down with any degree of accuracy. It appears, however, that the calls for pedagogical action to address alleged shortcomings in young people's knowledge, which came in the wake of the perceived increases in anti-Semitism in the late 1950s, were an important initial catalyst.[34] In November 1958, for example, the Society for Christian–Jewish Cooperation forwarded to councillor Andreas Staudt, the city official responsible for Schools and Cultural policy, copies of a new book entitled 'It began on 30 January' together with the collection of 'Documents on the Treatment of Jews by the Third Reich', recently edited by the *Allgemeine Wochenzeitung der Juden in Deutschland,* and a report on a recent educational conference in Frankfurt of the same month.[35] Shortly thereafter, the City's Schools and Culture Committee earmarked 10,000 DM for literature on 'contemporary history' for teachers' use, SPD committee member councillor Buchner emphasising that 'it is shocking how little young people know of the events of the last decades' and that 'as the city of the Reich party rallies Nuremberg has a particular obligation here'.[36]

In May 1960, meanwhile, apparently prompted by the Cologne Synagogue attacks and the attendant debates, Paul Baruch, one of the leading members of the local Jewish community, produced a report on 'the Fate of the Jews in Nuremberg from 1933–1945' which was circulated to all the city's schools 'for

[33] On the liberalisation of the Protestant Church in the 1960s, see Martin Greschat, 'Protestantismus und Evangelische Kirche in den 60er Jahren' in Schildt, Siegfried, Lammers, *Dynamische Zeiten,* 544–81.

[34] Falk Pingel, 'Nationalsozialismus und Holocaust in westdeutschen Schulbüchern' in Rolf Steininger (ed.), *Der Umgang mit dem Holocaust. Europa – USA – Israel* (Cologne, 1994), 221–32.

[35] StadtAN C 73 I/831, Gesellschaft für Christlich-Jüdische Zusammenarbeit Nürnberg-Fürth an Stadtrat Staudt, Schul- und Kulturreferent der Stadt Nürnberg, 27.11.58. The book in question was most likely Wolfgang Jäger et al., *Es Begann am 30 Januar* (Munich, 1958).

[36] StadtAN C 85 III/407, Niederschrift über die Sitzung des Schul- und Kulturausschusses am 3.6.60.

use as appropriate'.[37] The historical outline focused on the situation of the community and its institutions in 1933, on stories of persecution and emigration in the 1930s, on the destruction of the synagogues and other property in 1938, on attempts to maintain community life through religious observance and schooling in the face of intensified wartime persecution, and on the deportations to Riga, Izbica and Theresienstadt. Its narrative form and basic contents provided a structure which strongly shaped subsequent local treatments of the issue. In its firm focus on the Jews of Nuremberg, rather than on the wider histories of the European-wide programme of mass murder, it reproduced, ironically, central elements of the very discourse it sought to challenge – but its circulation represented an important advance nonetheless.

Initiatives such as these marked the onset of a range of pedagogical activities which unfolded over the 1960s, including exhibitions on the Warsaw Ghetto (1964), on Auschwitz and on the Jews of Nuremberg (both 1965) and the mounting of the annual Nuremberg Conversations from 1965 onwards.[38] These represented significant attempts on the part of the city authorities to foster critical discussion and awareness of the recent past and its legacies. If the cumulative impact of such activities on the wider community is difficult to assess, the mere fact of their occurrence marked a substantial change in the memory culture of the city compared with ten years earlier.

The slow shifts in official sensibilities concerning the Holocaust and its implications for civic cultural policy are best observed, however, not through rehearsal of the list of events mounted in the 1960s for public consumption, but through examination of the city council's evolving interactions with Jewish voices from abroad and its gradual embrace of youth restitution work and exchange programmes. The first signs of changing pressures from abroad to which the city would have to respond came in early 1962, when the Consulate of the Federal Republic of Germany in Lyon wrote to mayor Urschlechter seeking financial support for the rebuilding of a synagogue for the Jewish community of Villeurbanne, Lyon.[39] The project was organised by the Protestant youth group *Aktion Sühnezeichen* (Action Sign of Remorse). Formed in Berlin in 1958, the group arranged visits of small groups of young West Germans to foreign countries to make practical gestures of help which were simultaneously symbolic acts of restitution in the form of building hospitals, repairing cemeteries or acting as social workers.[40] Initially working

---

[37] StadtAN C 73 I/394, Schul- und Kulturreferat der Stadt Nürnberg an alle Schulen zur gelegentlichen Verwertung, 16.5.60.

[38] See below, Chapters III.3 and III.4.

[39] StadtAN C 85 I Abg. 94/A44, Konsulat der BRD Lyon an Oberbürgermeister Urschlechter, 12.1.62.

[40] Christian Staffa, 'Die "Aktion Sühnezeichen" – Eine protestantische Initiative zu einer besonderen Art der Wiedergutmachung' in Hockerts and Kuller, *Nach der Verfolgung*, 139–56.

largely in western Europe and in Israel, they spread their activities to eastern Europe as diplomatic relations improved; by 1964, approximately 500 young people had participated. As the consul explained about the Villeurbanne project, '95 per cent of the Israelite community consists of German emigrants who survived the horrific time of the National Socialist occupation of France.' Among these were four former residents of Nuremberg, including the president of the Villeurbanne Jewish community. A collection was under way among the cities of Hesse which had previously had a synagogue but which had not rebuilt it after the war; although not part of Hesse the consul felt it appropriate to ask Nuremberg to participate in the fundraising action 'because the Jewish population of Franconia was particularly numerous and had to suffer even more under the local Gauleiter than elsewhere'.

Aware of the diplomatic sensitivities of such issues – for the Federal Republic, but also, it seems, for the city – but clearly unenthusiastic about the suggestion that the city should contribute, Urschlechter checked with the West German Foreign Office. He emphasised that in Nuremberg's case the Jewish community itself had decided against rebuilding the synagogue, and that the council had instead given substantial subventions to help with the cost of community buildings or repairs to its cemeteries.[41] If his remarks were conceived as an invitation to the Foreign Office to confirm that Nuremberg did not fall into the category of those expected to contribute, they failed. The Foreign Office confirmed its awareness and support of the project, but made clear that 'a subvention for the purchase of the synagogue plot cannot be made from official [that is, foreign office] funds in view of the global sums made available to the Conference on Jewish Material Claims against Germany', and underlined that 'the Foreign Office would strongly greet support from private sources'.[42]

The city treasurer thereupon sought the opinion of the local Jewish community. His formulation of the issue was again calculated to suggest to the *Israelitische Kultusgemeinde* that the latter release it from any moral obligation to contribute: 'As according to the letter of the consul initially only those towns are being approached in which a synagogue was destroyed but not rebuilt, and where the towns have as such made no contribution, we would be grateful for your opinion on how the city of Nuremberg should respond to the request, especially as the fact of the donation already made to the *IKG* in Nuremberg is obviously unknown to the German consul in Lyon.'[43] The *IKG* similarly refrained from offering such a release: although it was willing to

[41] StadtAN C 85 I Abg. 94/A44, Urschlechter an Auswärtiges Amt, 25.1.62.
[42] StadtAN C 85 I Abg. 94/A44, Auswärtiges Amt an Urschlechter, 30.1.62.
[43] StadtAN C 85 I Abg. 94/A44, Ref.II/Zitzmann an Israelitische Kultusgemeinde Nürnberg, 1.3.62.

confirm for the city council that the latter had made the contributions as claimed, it stated that 'to build a synagogue we would have had to approach the city of Nuremberg for a much greater financial contribution. For this reason we believe that it would be appropriate if you would participate in the building of the synagogue in Villeurbanne with a corresponding sum.'[44]

The city council opted for inaction. Two further months passed before the German consul in Lyon wrote to request an answer to his original letter – now four months old – prompting a city administration which appears to have hoped that the issue would simply go away to discuss it before concluding that it was unable to support the project and advising the consul accordingly.[45] It was similarly unwilling to respond positively to a request from New York in 1963 from sponsors of a project to build a synagogue in Haifa, Israel, to be dedicated to the memory of the former orthodox synagogue in Nuremberg and to the memory of its former rabbi. Here, again, a small number of Jewish former citizens in the USA appear to have been involved, but according to the group's letter neither they, nor the somewhat larger number of former citizens of Nuremberg now living in Haifa, had the means to support the project on their own.[46] In the early 1960s, clearly, the city was unwilling to make donations to such causes.

How far this was born of ongoing indifference, how far it betrayed ignorance of the still difficult circumstances of some refugee communities, how far it was rooted in the insistence that such acts of implicit compensation were the proper task of the Federal Republic – both because the Federal Republic had assumed legal succession to the Nazi regime and because, in the evasive imagination of local politicians, the Nazi state, and not local government agency, had been responsible for the genocide – and how far the city council simply feared the establishment of a precedent which would open the floodgates cannot be ascertained. However, despite these refusals the contact fostered through the distribution of Paul Baruch's historical exposé of 1960 marked the start of a process whereby the city council began to establish links with some of its former Jewish citizens.[47] This three page exposé – which was also sent to many Jewish former residents now living abroad, many of whom, in turn, sent additional details, corrections, or requests for further information – became an important stimulant of research and a catalyst for the establishment of

[44] StadtAN C 85 I Abg. 94/A44, Israelitische Kultusgemeinde/Paul Baruch an Zitzmann, 3.3.62.
[45] StadtAN C 85 I Abg. 94/A44, Konsulat der BRD Lyon an Oberbürgermeister Urschlechter, 3.3.62; Beschluss des Ältestenrats, 11.5.62; Urschlechter an Konsulat der BRD Lyon, 17.5.62.
[46] StadtAN C 85 I Abg. 94/A44, Chisuk Torah Inc., New York an Stadtgemeinde Nürnberg, 29.11.63; Urschlechter an Chisuk Torah Inc., New York, 12.3.64.
[47] The impulse for this also came, in part, from a private individual: see StadtAN C 85 I Abg. 94/A44, E.L. an Urschlechter, 18.9.63 and C 85 I Abg. 94/A45 Urschlechter an E.L., 23.9.63, in which Urschlechter claimed that such efforts had been under way for three years.

additional contacts. By the beginning of 1964 the city council was considering inviting a number of former Jewish citizens to visit Nuremberg at the council's expense. Requests from abroad for financial assistance thus clearly contributed to a sense of the need to acknowledge the shifting cultural sensibilities with practical measures of some kind. Recognition of the particular problems posed by Nuremberg's historical associations with the Nazi regime – underlined by the rhetorical strategies of figures such as the Federal consul in Lyon – not only reinforced this but shaped the terms on which such practical measures were undertaken. In the case of the planned invitation of former Jewish residents, for example, the internal memorandum in which it was mooted proposed a rolling programme of small group visits, partly in order to spread the cost, but also because 'a continuous, annually repeated action promises a greater public echo', and emphasised the benefits of what would be 'an advertisement for the modern Nuremberg'.[48] Here again it was improving the city's reputation, as much as fostering critical thought, that was on the administration's mind.

What appears to have given such efforts decisive impetus, however, was mayor Urschlechter's visit to Israel in June 1964. During the trip, the main purpose of which was to attend a town-planning conference, Urschlechter met a number of Jewish former citizens of Nuremberg to hear their views and to solicit their aid in further expanding the city's list of contacts.[49] In the extensive report delivered to the council on his return, he emphasised that 'no-one expresses a wish to return to Nuremberg or to other German cities', but that 'there is, however, a real love for Nuremberg, which repeatedly came to the surface in many serious conversations. Pictures of old Nuremberg in individual apartments, or the many questions asked about the reconstruction of Nuremberg prove that they like to think back to the good times of their life in Nuremberg, albeit always overshadowed by the tangible pain of not being able to live there anymore . . .'[50] On one level, such a summary of former Jewish citizens' attitudes betrayed a clear desire on the part of the mayor to ground positive civic identity in the imagined nostalgia of those once persecuted and driven abroad. Assertions of refugees' positive memories of the city contained an implied subtext pertaining to the oft-posited decency of the population's behaviour during the Nazi era, which was not entirely free

---

[48] StadtAN C 85 I Abg. 94/44, Aktennotiz betr. Einladung älterer jüdischer Bürger Nürnbergs zu einem Besuch der Stadt, 20.1.64.
[49] See, for example, StadtAN C 85 I Abg. 94/A45, Urschlechter an Dr Vorchheimer, Tel Aviv, 24.4.64; Vorchheimer an Urschlechter, 14.5.64; Urschlechter an Vorchheimer, 12.10.64; Vorchheimer an Urschlechter, 26.11.64; Dora Strauss, Haifa, an Urschlechter, 28.12.64. The latter contained the addresses of over 100 former Nuremberg citizens now mostly in Haifa and Tel Aviv.
[50] StadtAN C 85 I Abg. 94/A45, Bericht über die Israel-Reise des Oberbürgermeisters Dr Urschlechter, 30.6.64.

of exculpatory overtones. Nonetheless, the encounters clearly sharpened Urschlechter's sensitivity to the Holocaust and its impact. His visit to Yad Vashem, meanwhile, underlined once more the peculiar challenge left to the city by its history. As he recounted in his report:

> I visited the memorial for the victims of the concentration camps in Jerusalem. Here memory is kept alive for ever in one monumental memorial to the concentration camps, whose names are individually listed. Many Israelis come day and night to this place of commemoration to pray for their dead relatives. Next to this there is a remembrance museum, which begins with an exhibition of originals of the *Stürmer* newspaper edited by Julius Streicher, whereby the name of Nuremberg stands in big letters in the foreground. The 'Nuremberg Laws' are displayed in large text on one wall, so that the name of Nuremberg is emphasised once more. Thus the exhibition constantly makes connections with Nuremberg, which without a doubt unleashed great concern and uneasiness during my visit.

The delivery of this report, which came during the time of the Auschwitz trial, and which marked the first meaningful discussion of Israel in the city's main political forum, appears to have occasioned a significant shift in the manner in which the city authorities dealt with issues relating to the Holocaust. In 1965, for example, in marked contrast to its earlier refusals to make such donations, the city council gave 10,000 DM in support of the Hebrew University of Jerusalem.[51] Such engagement was given further encouragement with the arrival of Hermann Glaser as head of Schools and Cultural policy in 1964. It was Glaser who conceived and organised the Nuremberg Conversations; it was also Glaser who built upon the city's initial exchange efforts.[52] In 1965, a group of seventeen young Israelis visited Nuremberg as part of a broader trip to West Germany organised by the Protestant youth organisation, and were hosted at an official reception.[53] Glaser himself visited Israel to make contact with educationalists there and to foster further links.[54] He also sought to integrate Nuremberg into the *Aktion Sühnezeichen* project – which had been treated with scepticism a few years earlier and which had made little progress in Bavaria outside Munich – ensuring that a project group of fifteen young people who were renovating a boarding school for blind children in Israel departed from the city and gave

---

[51] StadtAN C 85 I Abg. 94/A44, Dr Hans Lamm, Munich, an Urschlechter, 4.3.65; Beschluss des Ältestenrats von 25.3.65.
[52] StadtAN C 73 I/394, Glaser an Urschlechter, 3.6.64. On the Nuremberg Conversations see below, Chapter III.4.
[53] StadtAN C 73 I/394, Aktennotiz an Herrn Langenberger, Presseamt, 30.9.65.
[54] StadtAN C 73 I/394, Aktennotiz Glaser, 10.11.66.

an account of their time on their return.[55] By the early 1970s, the city was finally realising its project of inviting Jewish former citizens to visit the city.[56] Such visits and exchanges naturally only involved a tiny fraction of the city's own population or of its former Jewish residents. However, the prominence accorded to them in the local media ensured a wider echo; the fact that the *Aktion Sühnezeichen* activists visited Nuremberg high schools on their return from Israel to relate and discuss their experiences points to the multiplying effect such programmes had, even if the reactions among school audiences cannot be assumed.

Equally, if the historical fact of the Holocaust loomed large over such encounters, and if an implicit desire to acknowledge guilt and overcome mistrust underlay exchange activities, they did not in themselves constitute a direct engagement with the historical issues. Moreover, even when the Holocaust was explicitly acknowledged – such as on the Day of National Mourning in the 1960s – or formed the direct focus of an initiative – such as the Auschwitz exhibition – considerable blind spots remained. Many issues were still evaded or not addressed; where they were raised, they became the occasion of a reformulation and restatement of older exculpatory myths. It was, after all, possible to acknowledge the historical fact of Jewish persecution while insisting on one's ignorance; one could accept that millions had been murdered but repeat the mantra that totalitarian domination had forced participation and made resistance impossible; conversely, one could acknowledge the regime's barbaric violence but insist on one's own resistance credentials. The open, regretful acknowledgement of the murder of the Jews also went hand in hand with ongoing silences on the fate of other victims of persecution and murder, such as the Sinti and Roma or homosexuals, for example. Whether they focused mainly on German sites of persecution – on concentration camps such as Dachau or Buchenwald – or focused their treatment of the Holocaust exclusively on Auschwitz, the enormity of the space in the east in which the genocide was perpetrated, and the endless variety of killing fields on which it was enacted, was not discussed.

Most striking, perhaps, were the nebulous and evasive formulations used to describe the perpetrators themselves – who were either described simply as 'the Nazis' or represented as a highly hazy 'mob' the essential characteristic of which lay in its outsider relationship to the respectable community which provided the point of identification for the ordinary citizen. That mass crimes had been committed was not in meaningful dispute. That they had been

---

[55] StadtAN C 73 I/394, Kutzner/Aktion Sühnezeichen an Glaser, 4.11.64; see the account of the group's return in 'Verständliche Skepsis in Israel', *Amtsblatt der Stadt Nürnberg*, 29.9.65.
[56] *Juden in Nürnberg. Geschichte der jüdischen Mitbürger vom Mittelalter bis zur Gegenwart* (Nuremberg, 1993), 64.

committed through mass participation remained largely unspoken. For all the attempts being made by liberal opinion-forming circles to foster critical reflection on the past, the possibilities for evasion and denial remained ample.

The following chapters explore in more detail the local manifestations of the new sensibility concerning the past which emerged in some quarters during the 1960s. As exploration of the local reception of Nazi-era crimes trials, the staging of exhibitions on the Holocaust and the mounting of the Nuremberg Conversations will show, the 1960s were characterised both by honest attempts to engage with certain issues and by the simultaneous rearticulation of inherited myths of victimhood. Indeed, it was precisely through such ostensible engagement that these myths were reworked and re-expressed. For the city's elites, in particular, the key challenge was to find ways of talking about the genocidal dimensions of the past which could find acceptance across its social and political divides. Even as the memory culture took a liberal turn, this placed strong limits on what could be said.

III.2

Indicting the Perpetrators, Exonerating the People

Trials and their Reportage in the Local Media

One clear manifestation of the new prominence of Nazi genocide in West German public discourse was the renewed wave of judicial prosecution of Nazi-era crimes from the late 1950s onwards. In courts across West Germany increasing numbers of individuals and groups were put on trial, variously, for their participation in *Einsatzgruppen* killings, for crimes committed in concentration and extermination camps, for political murders or for participation in the 'euthanasia' programme.[1] Their widespread reportage across the West German media contributed greatly to ensuring that details of many criminal acts were publicised and debated regularly, repeatedly and simultaneously through very mainstream, widely accessible channels, including not just print media and the radio but also, increasingly, television. The trials generated much discussion not just about the crimes themselves and the necessity or otherwise of prosecuting them, but also about the inadequacies of the judicial confrontation of the past pursued hitherto and the possible reasons for this. In this way, the trials acted as a catalyst not only for a more thoroughgoing confrontation of the past but also for a growing critique of the deficits of contemporary political culture which fed into the wider processes of democratisation of the Federal Republic in the 1960s.

If the trials did much to galvanise debate about the crimes of the past, the knowledge of the Holocaust that they generated was mediated to a wider public in at least two ways.[2] The first of these resided in the legal process itself.

---

[1] For a lengthy, but not comprehensive, catalogue of trials carried out above all between 1958 and 1963, see Hermann Langbein, *Im Namen des deutschen Volkes. Zwischenbilanz der Prozesse wegen nationalsozialistischer Verbrechen* (Vienna, 1963), 147–97.

[2] On the mediation of the crimes to the public see Devin Pendas, ' "I didn't know what Auschwitz was": The Frankfurt Auschwitz Trial and the German Press, 1963–1965' in *Yale Journal of Law and the Humanities* 12 (2000), 101–50.

The peculiarities of German legal tradition shaped both the decisions as to which criminal acts would be prosecuted and the subsequent courtroom discussion of those acts. The German criminal code of 1871, which formed the basis on which crimes committed as part of the Third Reich's programmes of mass killing were tried in post-war West Germany, was neither designed for nor suited to prosecuting acts of genocide.[3] Its insistence on demonstrating individual complicity in the individual murder of each individual victim was, in particular, ill-suited to prosecuting participation in group acts of mass murder where the identity of individual victims was unknown; it also demanded a level of proof which the historical circumstances of the Holocaust and its attendant crimes often made it impossible to satisfy.

Moreover, the criminal code's insistence on the need to prove subjective motivation, individual initiative and an awareness of the wrongness of the acts at the time at which they occurred in order to achieve a conviction for murder made it almost impossible to convict those who were – self-evidently – operating as part of a wider project of mass killing which they could not be said, in any meaningful legal sense, to have initiated. As a result, defendants were often found guilty of having been accomplices to murder, of having aided and abetted murder, or of having committed manslaughter, rather than murder, even when they had personally pulled the trigger. Such verdicts – which carried much lower sentences – not only struck liberal opinion as obtuse, but also raised the suspicion that a judiciary with historically strong sympathies for the Nazi regime was using the fine distinctions of legal tradition to pronounce judgements that were wilfully lenient.[4]

The distinction between murder and manslaughter was all the more crucial, meanwhile, for the fact that the Statute of Limitations as it operated during the late 1950s and early 1960s placed a time limit of twenty years for the prosecution of murder and only fifteen for manslaughter. After 1960, those who could successfully argue manslaughter rather than murder did not need to deny the act in order to walk free – they were safe in the knowledge that the time limit for prosecuting such crimes had passed. When defendants and their lawyers argued the presence of higher orders, or insisted that they had been reluctant killers unable to avoid the pressures of the situation, they were thus not merely invoking myths of totalitarianism in pursuit of moral exculpation but were playing on crucial legal distinctions on which the likelihood of their incarceration or release often turned.

In this way, the peculiarities of German legal tradition actively promoted the rearticulation of apologetic narratives which already had considerable

---

[3] For clear expositions of these issues see Wittmann, *Beyond Justice*, 36–41; 44–53; Pendas, *The Frankfurt Auschwitz Trial*, 53–79.

[4] See, for example, Langbein, *Im Namen des Deutschen Volkes*, 11.

purchase in the wider population. They also, however, led to distortions in the kinds of criminal participant state prosecutors felt it possible or worthwhile to prosecute. The need to demonstrate 'base motives' in order to gain a murder conviction led prosecutors to focus on the 'excess perpetrator' – the figure who had pursued his tasks with evident zeal and commitment, performing acts of sadism and 'unnecessary' brutality – rather than on the ordinary or typical SS guard, however obviously criminal the acts of the latter had been. Over time, the courtrooms thus tended to produce a distorted image of the concentration and extermination camps in which individual acts of 'excessive' brutality were focused upon while the systematic, organised, mass persecution and murder of the Nazi regime functioned, at best, as background. Both the need to prove individual participation in individual murders, and the need to demonstrate subjective intent, encouraged a focus on the particularly sadistic individual rather than on the bureaucratically organised, shared acts of murder enacted within the hierarchies of command, habits of conformity and cultures of shared understanding which had been at the centre of the European-wide genocide of the Jews. The result was that even for a camp such as Auschwitz, where the vast majority of victims had been murdered within hours of their arrival through the routinised operation of the gas chambers, the acts of mass extermination did not form the central focus of the judicial process.

On occasion, independent voices within the liberal media were able to find sufficient distance to critique the effects of legal protocol on the pursuit of justice. In April 1965, for example, the *Nürnberger Nachrichten* reported how survivors of the Treblinka extermination camp had put themselves through the pain of recollection at a trial of some of the camp guards: 'and so they took the witness stand and reported: on the conditions in the camp at the time, on the death trains, on the gas chambers, on the satanic torturing by some SS men'. The general history of the camp, clearly, was not in dispute. 'However', the report continued, 'the court chairman – bound by German penal law and the definitions of the criminal act in Murder Paragraph 211 [the section of the penal code which defined murder] – very soon threw some witnesses off their stride. He wants and has to know details. Blanket murder does not count. The law demands individual details of individual murders.' In response to court demands to name individual guards, individual victims, and the dates, times and locations of individual murders, the witnesses, according to the paper, 'shrug their shoulders in helpless miscomprehension. "How am I supposed to know the names of the SS men? They did not exactly introduce themselves to us," answered the sawplant manager Samuel Rajzmann from Montreal in a quietly agitated tone, for example.'[5] In such reports the sympathy of the liberal

---

[5] 'Schwere Prozeßführung', *Nürnberger Nachrichten*, 27.4.65; Pendas, *The Frankfurt Auschwitz Trial*, 161–8.

press for the testifying survivors and its scepticism towards the legal system was evident.

More often that not, however, in recounting daily events in the courtroom newspapers such as the *Nürnberger Nachrichten* simply reproduced and transmitted the distortions generated by the modalities of the legal system: when the court tried individual perpetrators of individual crimes, that was what the papers reported – if they reported anything at all. Moreover, if the legal system generated one set of distortions the press contributed its own, adding a second layer. For the media also operated according to its own rules, its own assumptions and its own logic. The constant pursuit of a 'human interest' story, likely to appeal to a wider readership for the duration of the proceedings, encouraged a focus on trials with an unusual individual defendant rather than on trials involving a large number of less distinguishable culprits. In this way, the media also encouraged a focus on the sadistic 'excess perpetrator' rather than on the 'ordinary' SS defendant. The constant pursuit of a novel angle which governed the daily press conflicted with the increasingly drawn-out nature of the proceedings, which often went on for months. The demand for sensation was rarely satisfied by the repetitive nature of the court proceedings, with their daily routines of evidence gathering and witness interrogation. Indeed, the slow, cumulative process of evidence gathering, which was so central not only to the rigorous assessment of a defendant's guilt but also to the transmission of a broader historical picture, was precisely that which was rarely reported after the first week or two of a trial. The *Nürnberger Nachrichten* clearly believed its readers were interested in the court proceedings as drama as much as in the proceedings as history, and correspondingly focused on the courtroom theatre of major trials – the duals between celebrity attorneys, the suicides or sudden escapes of defendants, the emotional breakdowns of witnesses – in its reportage as much as on the courts' pursuit of historical truth. In general, the longer the trial was, the more sporadic the reporting, especially if the trial took place outside the Franconian area and thus had no relevance to the newspaper's regional remit.

In many respects the gaps and sins of omission visible in both the legal process and its media reportage reproduced the wider silences present in the narratives that circulated through the Federal Republic at the time. In their focus on the individual 'excess perpetrator' they neglected the wider involvement of a much larger number of Germans in state-sanctioned genocide; in their focus on specific murders they drew attention away from issues of the wider structural collusion of institutions and interest groups in the apparatus of persecution. Neither could the largely arbitrary nature of who was put on trial and who escaped justice, or the sporadic, episodic reportage of many of those trials that did occur, lend themselves to generating a full, comprehensive picture of the Holocaust. Yet they did, clearly, mark progress. Enough trials occurred for it to be clear that complicity had been widespread, and that many murderers were undoubtedly still at large; graphic accounts of *Einsatzgruppen* killings or of euthanasia were sufficiently regular, and recounted a sufficiently varied range of cases and events, for the systematic, rather than isolated, nature of the crimes to be obvious to all but the most wilfully ignorant.

Moreover, the silences in courtroom discourse and the reportage which surrounded it did not simply reproduce themselves as gaps in the knowledge of those who consumed the media reports in question. The relationship of media narratives to social knowledge of the Holocaust, which was the open secret of post-war society, was far more complex. For the young, such trials, no doubt, helped to shape the acquisition of a knowledge that had hitherto been absent. For the older generation, however, they connected with a knowledge that was already there, a knowledge which had often been gained, indeed, with themselves as witnesses and agents of the events. On the second of three occasions at which the former SS *Generalleutnant* Max Simon was acquitted of the murder of three German citizens in April 1945, for example, one reader wrote to the *Nürnberger Nachrichten* that 'the Simon trial has brought back in my memory the horrors which were perpetrated by the SS in Riga during the war. 250,000 Jews were shot, gassed and hanged there. I secretly took some pictures of these excesses [*Ausschreitungen*]. No-one wants to accept that now, even though the murderers are still among us.'[6] When newspapers did not give a full account they were thus not necessarily perpetuating ignorance: indeed, the perfunctory outlines of the wider context of individual criminal acts offered in their reportage may actually testify to precisely the opposite – to their assumption that the events of the Holocaust were already widespread, shared social knowledge, knowledge gained not so much *since* as *during* the years of genocide themselves, and thus not in need of rearticulation.

Throughout the 1950s, a small number of trials were held in Nuremberg that provided a thin, but still important strand of continuity in the judicidial confrontation of the past.[7] In 1952 the former Foreign Office official Franz Rademacher had been tried for aiding and abetting deportations and shootings of Jews and sentenced to three-and-a-half years' imprisonment for the manslaughter of 1,300 people; his conviction, however, was overturned and he fled before new proceedings could be initiated.[8] In the same year the SS guard

---

[6] *Nürnberger Nachrichten*, letters, 10./11.5.58.
[7] On trials of Nazi-era crimes in the 1950s see, in addition to works already cited, Alaric Searle, *Wehrmacht Generals, West German Society and the Debate on Rearmament 1949–1959* (Westpoint, CT, 2003), 231–75.
[8] Langbein, *Im Namen des Deutschen Volkes*, 170–1.

Jakob Fries, who had served in Dachau, Oranienburg, Flossenbürg and Auschwitz, was sentenced to fourteen years' imprisonment;[9] five years later, in 1957, the Sachsenhausen guard August Kolb was sentenced to four years and three months for aiding and abetting murder and for manslaughter.[10] Max Simon and five co-defendants, meanwhile, were tried (and repeatedly acquitted) in 1955, 1958 and 1960.[11]

In the early 1950s, however, popular interest in such trials was clearly limited.[12] When the former Nuremberg police chief Benno Martin made one of his periodic appearances before the Nuremberg courts in 1951 to face charges of involvement in the deportation of Jews in 1941, the *Nürnberger Zeitung* noted that 'the trials for transgressions during the Nazi era do not generate particular interest any more'. Comparing attendances at these proceedings to those one could expect for the trial of a crime of passion, it noted how in the case of the latter, 'the listeners tear the clothes from each others' bodies to get a good seat'; in this case, however, 'the public is represented by two thin rows of listeners. In part these are former police officers who have a personal interest in the outcome of the case. Broader sectors of the public are no longer interested in these stories.'[13]

Such sentiments did not necessarily mean that there was no popular support for trials. Although for many a refusal to contemplate the enormity of the crimes underpinned indifference to those few trials that were occurring, for others declining interest was rooted precisely in the embittered awareness that justice was rarely, if ever, served in such cases. There was, in other words, dismay among progressive circles at the perceived failings of the judiciary in the mid-1950s. Indeed, it was not so much knowledge derived through the publicising of the trials themselves that fed local counter-memories and the attendant activism in this period so much as anger at the pattern of repeated acquittals or inadequate sentencing. The *Nürnberger Nachrichten*'s report of the second acquittal of Max Simon in April 1958 resonated with disappointment and bitterness at the predictable failure to convict.[14] It was the wearied recognition that such proceedings rarely achieved the desired outcome, rather than a lack of commitment to justice per se, which fed the *Nürnberger Nachrichten*'s practice of not reporting most such trials in the mid- to late 1950s.

The reporting of the trial in Ulm in the summer of 1958 of a large number of members of *Einsatzgruppe* A for the murder of Lithuanian Jews in 1941 fitted this pattern. A brief, understated article in the *Nürnberger Nachrichten*

[9] Ibid., 186–7.
[10] Ibid., 184–5.
[11] Ibid., 190–1.
[12] Pendas, *The Frankfurt Auschwitz Trial*, 15–16.
[13] 'Dr Martin und das Wannsee-Protokoll', *Nürnberger Zeitung*, 17.5.51.
[14] 'Simon-Prozeß endete wieder mit Freisprüchen', *Nürnberger Nachrichten*, 24.4.58.

announced the opening of the trial, which focused on the killing of over 5,000 Jews by one *Einsatzkommando*.[15] Thereafter, the paper reported its proceedings only very rarely: only once did more than one report appear in any given week; often, a fortnight or more elapsed between reports. Other things were clearly deemed to be more newsworthy: indeed, in the first few weeks of the trial, it had to compete with crises in France and in Cyprus, the declaration of a Republic in Iraq, American intervention in the Lebanon and a crisis in east–west relations. Above all, in June 1958 it competed for prominence with the football World Cup, which West Germany entered as champions and in which popular interest was correspondingly high. If the paper knew its readers, then these issues were of much greater importance to the public, to judge by the comparative prominence and regularity of their reporting.[16]

It was not lack of awareness of the significance of the trial that led the paper to refrain from reporting it. Two weeks into the proceedings it explained in an editorial: 'We considered whether or not to report extensively on the Ulm trial. But it is not worth it. Everything proceeds according to a recipe which is too well known from far too many previous proceedings for it to be newsworthy . . . they are a waste of money and time. And the courts are an embarrassment.'[17] Here again, cynicism within progressive circles at the failings of a judiciary regarded not only as conservative but also as deeply suspect, rather than moral equivalence concerning the need for justice, was in play.

Even the sporadic reporting that the paper did provide offered unmistakeable vignettes of the killing campaigns which left no doubt as to their organised, mass character or to the brutality which accompanied them. In a report of June 1958, for example, it described how 'the victims were led to the shooting site in groups of ten. The group following on each occasion had to watch proceedings and then throw the victims into the burial trenches.'[18] Another report repeated witness descriptions of how 'many Jews who were locked in there were burned alive' as the Krottingen synagogue was burned down on the orders of the Tilsit Gestapo.[19] Others recounted the drunkenness of the SS men at the mass shootings, wanton acts of violence with iron bars, or the 'scenes of desperation' that accompanied the killings.[20] The newspaper also gave prominence to the affidavit of Dr Hans Günther Seraphim of the

[15] '5000fache Mordanklage', *Nürnberger Nachrichten*, 29.4.58.
[16] On the media coverage of the Ulm trial and the public's response, see Caroline Sharples, 'A Liberal Turn? War Crimes Trials and West German Public Opinion in the 1960s', PhD, University of Southampton, 2006, 77–115.
[17] 'Recht – Gerechtigkeit. Schonzeit für die Mörder von Gestern', *Nürnberger Nachrichten*, 15./16.5.58.
[18] 'Opfer mit Stöcken angetrieben', *Nürnberger Nachrichten*, 3.6.58.
[19] 'In ihrer Synagoge verbrannt', *Nürnberger Nachrichten*, 14./15.6.58.
[20] See, for example, 'Es gab Verzweiflungsszenen', *Nürnberger Nachrichten*, 7./8.6.58.

University of Göttingen on the issue of the refusal of orders. Countering the defence argument that it was impossible under conditions of totalitarian domination to refuse orders, the paper recorded Seraphim's explanation that 'ten years of research on the history of the SS had not revealed one case . . . where the refusal of a destruction order had endangered the body and soul of the person who had refused. Such a refusal of orders had led at most to exclusion from the SS or transfer to the front.'[21]

In electing to report such affidavits, the *Nürnberger Nachrichten* was implicitly challenging the apologetic consensus that continued to prevail in the late 1950s. However, this could not detract from the fact that the regular proceedings of the trial in themselves had insufficient novelty to sustain repeated coverage. By the middle of the trial, occasional reports were more likely to focus on the suicide of a defendant – there were three such suicides in total – than on the historical substance of the issue itself.[22] Those aspects of the trial which demonstrated to liberal opinion within the judicial and political elites the need for a more systematic legal reckoning with the crimes of the Third Reich, and which led to the creation of the Central Office of State Justice Departments – its comprehensive examination of the involvement of a large number of defendants in a lengthy, organised campaign of murder – were precisely those which made it unsuited to the needs of the daily press. The absence of particularly unusual defendants made it difficult to generate interest out of the individual perpetrators themselves (some were never mentioned by name in the reportage); there was relatively little courtroom drama in the actual proceedings; that which made the trial so comprehensive militated against its full reporting precisely because repeated days of evidence-gathering provided no novelty.

What ultimately displaced the Ulm trial as a focus of editorial concern at the *Nürnberger Nachrichten*, however (with the exception of the verdicts and sentences, which were reported at length), was the trial of the former Buchenwald guard Martin Sommer.[23] Unlike the Ulm trial, the geographical proximity of the proceedings, which were held in neighbouring Bayreuth, meant that they fell within the paper's regional remit. Buchenwald's status as a German concentration camp that had incarcerated large numbers of German prisoners also gave it a relevance and immediacy in Franconia – home to strong Social Democratic and former Communist traditions – which

---

[21] 'Ausschluß oder Versetzung', *Nürnberger Nachrichten*, 19./20.7.58.

[22] '2 Zeugen nahmen sich das Leben', *Nürnberger Nachrichten*, 10.7.58. A third had committed suicide during the pre-trial investigations.

[23] For the reports of the closing pleas, verdicts and sentences in the Ulm case, see 'Viermal lebenslang beantragt', *Nürnberger Nachrichten*, 4.8.58; 'Die Angeklagten geben sich reuig', *Nürnberger Nachrichten*, 19.8.58; 'Größter Prozeß der Nachkriegszeit zu Ende', *Nürnberger Nachrichten*, 30./31.8.58.

the Ulm trial, focused as it was on events deep in the former occupied territories, did not have.

The trial of Martin Sommer also offered the human interest comparatively lacking in the Ulm proceedings.[24] In place of a number of defendants there was just one. That defendant, Sommer, generated fascination on account of his own invalidity. He had been wounded very late in the war, and was brought by ambulance and stretcher to the court proceedings each day, a fact captured more than once by the accompanying photographs. Much attention also centred on his wife, a young blonde nurse who, as the *Nürnberger Nachrichten* evidently struggled to comprehend, 'had not, as we know, married in pursuit of a pension, but had even broken off another promising relationship in order to marry this cripple'.[25] Witnesses obliged the newspaper by fainting under the stress of having to give evidence in court, providing the easy headline 'KZ-witness fainted';[26] courtroom tumult caused by Sommer's provocative remarks towards witnesses provided further drama for the paper to report.[27]

Most of all, however, Sommer conformed ideally to the type of the 'excess perpetrator' who lent himself to easy demonisation, and thus, in turn, to the respectable reader's self-dissociation from events at Buchenwald.[28] In repeated reports the paper recounted the testimony of those who described how he beat prisoners to death, killed them through injections or otherwise visited unspeakable brutality upon them; according to one report, 'Not only former prisoners of the concentration camp Buchenwald, who had to suffer indescribable torture in the arrest cells at the hands of former SS *Hauptsturmführer* and arrest administrator Martin Sommer, are currently accusing Sommer before the Bayreuth court of being a brutal beater and multiple murderer: his former colleagues from the ranks of the SS are also distancing themselves from him in horror.'[29] When Sommer received his conviction for twenty-five murders and a sentence of life-long imprisonment, the *Nürnberger Nachrichten* closed its final report by describing how, outside the court, as the gathered crowds adopted a threatening demeanour towards the departing Sommer, 'he pulled his face into a smile. "Is that still a human at all?", observers asked themselves'.[30] As in other spheres, the reportage thus mixed enlightenment and distortion, simultaneously offering the reader both the possibility of critical engagement and that of self-distancing; even as it expressed its horror of Sommer's crimes it drew on

[24] On the press coverage of the Sommer trial see Sharples, 'A Liberal Turn?', 116–54.
[25] 'Das Grauen weht durch den Gerichtssaal', *Nürnberger Nachrichten*, 25.6.58.
[26] 'KZ-Zeuge wurde ohnmächtig', *Nürnberger Nachrichten*, 19.6.58.
[27] 'Tumult um grünen Winkel', *Nürnberger Nachrichten*, 21./22.6.58.
[28] On the construction of perpetrator-types through the trials of Nazi-era crimes, see Ulrike Weckel and Edgar Wolfrum (eds), *'Bestien' und 'Befehlsempfänger'. Frauen und Männer in Ns-Prozessen nach 1945* (Göttingen, 2003).
[29] 'Sommer gibt ein Mordgeständnis von 1943 zu', *Nürnberger Nachrichten*, 26.6.58.
[30] 'Lebenslänglich für Sommer', *Nürnberger Nachrichten*, 4.7.58.

tropes which obviated the need for a focus on the wider complicity of ordinary Germans in the appalling crimes of the past.

The trials of the late 1950s did act as a catalyst for the emergence of a critical debate, at least within those sections of civil society where the moral burden of the Holocaust was already acknowledged. The local branch of the Society for Christian–Jewish Cooperation, for example, made reference to the recent trials, along with the wave of anti-Semitic attacks in its circular of 1959, when arguing that open confrontation of the past was an essential precondition for the renewal of society.[31] If there was one moment, however, at which the trial medium could be said to have forced the issue of Nazi genocide firmly into media prominence in Nuremberg, it was the Eichmann trial. Held in Jerusalem from April to August 1961, the trial generated worldwide interest. If the numerous reports carried by the *Nürnberger Nachrichten* prior to the trial are an accurate indicator it was awaited, indeed, with anticipation.

Numerous factors combined to make the trial particularly interesting. In part, the interest stemmed from the simple fact that Eichmann was the most senior figure involved in the Holocaust to be put on trial since the immediate post-war period. In part, the anticipation reflected interest generated by the dramatic circumstances of Eichmann's kidnap and transfer to Israel. In part, the fascination of the trial also lay in its visual quality – in the image of Eichmann enclosed in his bullet-proof cage, an image which the new medium of television did much to circulate. Its resonance in West Germany also lay in the fact that both courtroom rhetoric and media representation constructed Eichmann as a recognisable type – the deskbound perpetrator – which chimed with a nascent critique of capitalism, the state bureaucracy and its absent democratic reflexes. This in turn fed the political and intellectual ferment that underpinned the protest cultures of later in the decade.[32] The *Nürnberger Nachrichten* often reported how Israeli attorney general Hausner deployed commercial metaphors to describe Eichmann, repeating his references to Eichmann's 'business' or his descriptions of Eichmann as the 'bookkeeper of death'. The newspaper itself also described Eichmann in such terms: 'With his bald head and dark hornrimmed glasses the defendant appears like a middle-manager.'[33]

Meanwhile, the fact that Chancellor Adenauer himself made a television

[31] 'Nicht zu hassen, zu lieben sind wir da', *Brüderlichkeit. Mitteilungen der Gesellschaft für christlich-jüdische Zusammenarbeit Nürnberg-Fürth* (undated, 1959); a copy can be found in StadtAN C 73 I/831.
[32] See Knoch, *Die Tat als Bild*, 651–85; also Peter Krause, *Der Eichmann-Prozess in der deutschen Presse* (Frankfurt/Main, 2002), 170–89.
[33] 'Eichmann Prozeß eröffnet', *Nürnberger Nachrichten*, 12.4.61; 'Sein "Geschäft": Mord an Unschuldigen', *Nürnberger Nachrichten*, 19.4.61.

address on the opening day of the trial – an address reported by the *Nürnberger Nachrichten* – and that many other prominent figures offered public comment signalled to the readership of the newspaper that this was a trial of unusual significance and should thus command the readers' attention.[34] While the words of *Bundestagspräsident* Gerstenmaier to the effect that no-one could understand how the Holocaust had happened 'who had not experienced the terrible power and the seduction techniques of a totalitarian police state' revealed how such moments could serve as the occasion for the rearticulation of existing exculpatory narratives, comments of other prominent figures from conservative institutions showed how attitudes were beginning to shift across West German society. The Protestant bishop of Berlin, Dibelius, was reported in the *Nürnberger Nachrichten* to have rejected the defensive argument 'that it had only been a handful of German people who, in their megalomania, had forgotten all God's commands'; he insisted instead that 'it was people from our midst, of our blood, of our type, of our people'.[35] The continued tendency to think in biological notions of nationhood jarred, but such comments nevertheless marked a substantial departure from those proffered by the Protestant Church in the early 1950s, when it had been at the forefront of national-conservative mythmaking, and were again evidence of how the liberalisation of West German society was making itself felt across the political spectrum.

Like the Ulm trial, the Eichmann proceedings faced much competition in terms of their relative newsworthiness. In the first week of the trial it was swiftly knocked off the front page by Yuri Gagarin's first manned space flight; the closing days of the main proceedings were accompanied in August by the building of the Berlin Wall. However, unlike the Ulm trial, the Eichmann trial was reported in great depth in all but the phase during which Eichmann himself was interrogated, during which time his repetitive responses provided little for the newspaper to comment upon. Reproducing as they did the general progress of the courtroom argument, the cumulative reports offered a far more detailed account of the Holocaust than that which had emerged from the reportage of previous trials.

This, in turn, reflected the peculiarities of the Eichmann trial itself. Unlike the West German trials and their reportage, which tended to isolate the crimes and their perpetrators from the wider context that had given rise to them, the architects of the Eichmann trial took considerable pains to set his role against the background of the European-wide murder of the Jews. Partly, this was to underline the centrality of Eichmann to the evolution of the Final Solution, and thus to counter his claims that he had been but a small, insignificant functionary in

---

[34] 'Gerechtigkeit und die volle Wahrheit', *Nürnberger Nachrichten*, 11.4.61
[35] 'Beobachter aus 40 Ländern', *Nürnberger Nachrichten*, 11.4.61.

a much larger apparatus. Partly, however, it was for reasons of historical pedagogy not specifically connected with Eichmann's role.[36]

In reportage quite distinct in its focus from the very narrow accounts of West German trials which the paper customarily offered its readership, the *Nürnberger Nachrichten* thus relayed how, in his opening speech, Hausner offered a 'careful analysis of the National Socialist path to power' in which he explained how 'Hitler used race hatred as a means to gain power. The SS, Security Service and the Gestapo were the main tools for the domination of Germany and for the establishment of the rule of terror over the occupied territories.'[37] Lest anyone be deluded into seeing in this a reaffirmation of the customary view that this had been the tyranny of the brutal minority over the mass of the innocent and victimised, the *Nürnberger Nachrichten* repeated courtroom claims that 'the overwhelming majority of the German people tried to accommodate themselves to the new regime and, according to Hausner, "watched the terrible events phlegmatically" '. In contrast to the image of the brutal 'excess perpetrator' whose character and actions were defined through their difference to the civilised society with which most ordinary Germans identified themselves, Hausner also, according to the *Nürnberger Nachrichten*, insisted that the accomplices of Eichmann 'were neither gangsters nor people from the underworld, but the leaders of a nation, including professors, dignitaries in robes with academic titles, men with broad horizons – the intelligentsia'.

Both the prosecution speeches and the witness testimony – all of which was reported extensively by the paper – emphasised the European-wide nature of the destruction process. On successive days, reports followed witness accounts of events following the German invasion of Czechoslovakia in 1939,[38] the murder of Polish Jews following invasion in the same year,[39] or conditions in the Lodz, Przemysl or Warsaw ghettos.[40] In these testimonies, as in others, the emphasis was on the range of participants: as the *Nürnberger Nachrichten* underlined, 'For Germans they were also particularly depressing because they gave a sense of what terrible acts were committed from 1941 onwards on Jewish men, women and children, especially in occupied Poland, not just by a few but by countless SS leaders and SS men.'[41] There followed reports of courtroom testimonies on the Holocaust in Lithuania,[42] graphic accounts of *Einsatzgruppen* killings,[43] accounts

[36] Krause, *Der Eichmann-Prozess*, 50–9.
[37] 'Eichmann – Der Schreibtisch-Mörder', *Nürnberger Nachrichten*, 18.4.61.
[38] 'Viel zu viel Dokumente', *Nürnberger Nachrichten*, 28.4.61.
[39] 'Anklage braucht 2 Monate', *Nürnberger Nachrichten*, 29./30.4.61.
[40] 'Servatius nennt 4 Zeugen', *Nürnberger Nachrichten*, 3.5.61; 'Eichmann blieb unbewegt', *Nürnberger Nachrichten*, 4.5.61.
[41] 'Servatius nennt 4 Zeugen', *Nürnberger Nachrichten*, 3.5.61.
[42] 'Hund namens Eichmann', *Nürnberger Nachrichten*, 5.5.61.
[43] 'Noch lebend in den Todesgraben', *Nürnberger Nachrichten*, 9.5.61.

of the deportations of German Jews,[44] of the Holocaust in Yugoslavia,[45] Romania[46] and Hungary,[47] of the death marches[48] and, finally, lengthy reports of testimony on the individual extermination camps.[49] A month into the trial, the *Nürnberger Nachrichten* remarked that the 'proceedings in the Eichmann trial hitherto have given the impression that the whole National Socialist system, rather than the defendant, is stood in the dock'.[50]

As the trial moved on, the proceedings, and with them the reports, began to focus more specifically on Eichmann's own role. Here, as in the West German trials, two competing images of the perpetrator were offered. On the one hand, the prosecutors insisted on the seniority of Eichmann, on his centrality to the process, and on the importance of anti-Semitic fervour in driving his involvement. By late May 1961 the *Nürnberger Nachrichten* could report that 'the prosecutor has presented concrete, comprehensive and unambiguous material which shows that the accused former SS-*Obersturmbannführer* personally did everything to expedite the eradication of the Jews'.[51] By the end of the gathering of the witness statements, it reported that 'the prosecution has doubtless managed in the proceedings thus far to refute the Eichmann version of events, namely that he was only charged with the organisation of the transports. The tasks of his office were doubtless much more extensive, even if the fundamental order to eradicate millions of Jews was not given by him'.[52]

Against this, Eichmann and his defence insisted that he had merely been the 'subordinate receiver of orders', that the jurisdiction of his office had been highly limited, and that he had not been an anti-Semite himself.[53] During the period of the trial devoted to the cross-examination of Eichmann himself the reporting became a little less frequent and the individual articles shorter, as his repetitive claims that he had only been a functionary following orders offered little scope for the novel angle sought by the press. It was, perhaps, for this reason that the reportage tended to fade in intensity towards the end of the trial. The fact that

---

[44] 'Juden-Deportationen aus Deutschland', *Nürnberger Nachrichten*, 13./14.5.61.

[45] 'Italiener machten nicht mit', *Nürnberger Nachrichten*, 20./22.5.61.

[46] 'Rumänien – 300,000 Juden getötet', *Nürnberger Nachrichten*, 24.5.61.

[47] '81 Lidice-Kinder mußten sterben', *Nürnberger Nachrichten*, 25.5.61.

[48] 'Todesmarsch Ende 1944', *Nürnberger Nachrichten*, 2.6.61.

[49] 'Nun die Vernichtungslager', *Nürnberger Nachrichten*, 3./4.6.61; 'Erschütternde Berichte', *Nürnberger Nachrichten*, 6.6.61.

[50] 'Eichmann war gnadenlos', *Nürnberger Nachrichten*, 10.5.61.

[51] 'Juden mußten ihren Tod bar bezahlen', *Nürnberger Nachrichten*, 18.5.61.

[52] 'Beweisaufnahme beendet', *Nürnberger Nachrichten*, 10./11.6.61.

[53] For the specific quote, see 'Eichmann in eigener Sache', *Nürnberger Nachrichten*, 21.6.61; of the many other such reports see 'Nichts mit Einsatzgruppen zu tun', *Nürnberger Nachrichten*, 24./25.6.61; 'Handel mit den Gebeinen eines Toten', *Nürnberger Nachrichten*, 29.6.61; '. . . moralisch schuldig', *Nürnberger Nachrichten*, 8./9.7.61; on Eichmann's defence strategies see Krause, *Der Eichmann-Prozess*, 59–67.

the outcome was clearly assumed to be a foregone conclusion also did little to encourage more extensive discussion: the sensation which had surrounded the kidnap was not in the verdict itself.[54]

Debate on the Eichmann trial and on the many others that were occurring in West Germany in the early 1960s manifested itself across the organs of local civil society. The Protestant parish newsletter, for one, printed substantial articles discussing war crimes trials in the early 1960s. Its acknowledgement of the growing sense within the community of 'a mismatch between some judgements over crimes from the Nazi era and crimes committed in our day' – rooted in an awareness of the comparative leniency of the former – testified to the changing sensibilities on these issues which fed, in turn, widespread public debate on the need for reform of the Statute of Limitations.[55]

If local media reportage is an indicator, however, trial fatigue soon set in. Its effects were most visible in the coverage of the Auschwitz trial, which was held in Frankfurt/Main from December 1963 to August 1965.[56] Like the Eichmann trial, it generated enormous international interest. Even if the camp had not, by this time, emerged as the iconic symbol of Nazi genocide that it was later to become, there was still widespread awareness that this had been one of the central killing sites. The scale of the event, in which 22 defendants were initially put on trial, and hundreds of witnesses either interviewed in pre-trial proceedings or cross-examined before the court, dwarfed all previous trials in West German court history.

[54] For the verdict itself, which was delivered in December 1961 following a four-month break in the trial, and the sentencing, see 'Eichmann hörte: schuldig', *Nürnberger Nachrichten*, 12.12.61; 'Schuld in allen 15 Punkten', *Nürnberger Nachrichten*, 13.12.61; 'Eichmanns Tod gefordert', *Nürnberger Nachrichten*, 14.12.61; 'Gericht verurteilte Eichmann zum Tode', *Nürnberger Nachrichten*, 16./17.12.61.

[55] 'Der Rat der EKD zu den NS-Verbrecherprozessen', *Nürnberger Evangelisches Gemeindeblatt*, 31.3.63. For local coverage of the debates on the Statute of Limitations between 1964 and 1965 see, for example, 'Kein Sondergesetz für NS Verbrecher', *Nürnberger Nachrichten*, 6.5.64; 'Verlängerte Verjährungsfrist?', *Nürnberger Nachrichten*, 30.9.64; 'Verjährung: Geschenk für Nazimörder?', *Nürnberger Nachrichten*, 17./18.10.64; 'Verjährungsfrist wird nicht verlängert', *Nürnberger Nachrichten*, 12.11.64; 'Bonn ersucht um Mithilfe', *Nürnberger Nachrichten*, 21./22.11.64; 'Der Bundestag soll entscheiden', *Nürnberger Nachrichten*, 23.11.64; 'Sollen NS-Morde doch nicht verjähren?', *Nürnberger Nachrichten*, 8.12.64; 'Jetzt die Justizbehörde an der Reihe', *Nürnberger Nachrichten*, 10.12.64; 'Lösung für NS-Verjährungsfrist?', *Nürnberger Nachrichten*, 20.1.65; 'Mit Mördern leben?', *Nürnberger Nachrichten*, 27.1.65; 'Immer neue Proteste gegen Verjährung', *Nürnberger Nachrichten*, 30./31.1.65; 'Regierungskrise um die Verjährung?', *Nürnberger Nachrichten*, 6./7.2.65; 'Bundesmehrheit gegen Verjährung', *Nürnberger Nachrichten*, 11.3.65; 'Verlängerung in Kraft', *Nürnberger Nachrichten*, 22.4.65. For the Protestant Church's own contributions see 'Mörder auf freiem Fuß? Zur Frage der Verjährungsfrist', *Nürnberger Evangelisches Gemeindeblatt*, 7.3.65; 'Verlängerung der Verjährungsfrist. Podium: Nein – Plenum: Ja', *Nürnberger Evangelisches Gemeindeblatt*, 18.4.65.

[56] For general histories of this trial see Irmtrud Wojak (ed.), *'Gerichtstag halten über uns selbst . . .' Geschichte und Wirkung des ersten Frankfurter Auschwitz-Prozesses* (Frankfurt/Main, 2001); Wittmann, *Beyond Justice*; Pendas, *The Frankfurt Auschwitz Trial*.

Compared to the Eichmann trial, however, it generated little press anticipation in Nuremberg. In December 1963 the *Nürnberger Nachrichten* carried
one of its periodic reports on the large number of trials of Nazi-era crimes
taking place across West Germany during this period, but in the days leading
up to the opening of the trial its attention was focused on the deaths of
Federal President Theodor Heuss and SPD chairman Erich Ollenhauer.[57] On
the day of the opening of the Auschwitz trial the paper's front page carried the
headline 'Farewell to Erich Ollenhauer', together with a large picture of his
state funeral.[58]

Inside, the paper reported the opening of the trial.[59] From the outset,
however, the *Nürnberger Nachrichten* limited its coverage, choosing not to
follow the fates of all of the defendants with equal depth (some, indeed, were
mentioned at most once or twice in the entire twenty months of the proceedings) but instead concentrating on a smaller number of more (in its terms)
interesting cases. Its illustration of the report on the opening of the trial had
already reduced the defendants to more manageable and memorable propor-
tions, captioning its pictures with the description of '5 of the 22 defendants in
the Auschwitz trial. From the left: Oswald Kaduk, Hans Stark, Stefan Baretski,
Victor Capesius and the most important of all, Wilhelm Boger, allegedly the
inventor of the gruesome and deadly "Boger-Swing" '. It was not long before
the *Nürnberger Nachrichten* reduced its focus further, concentrating primarily
on the defendants Boger and Kaduk; later, Capesius and an additional defendant, Josef Klehr, gained in prominence in the reportage.

The clear predilection to concentrate from the outset on a few, rather than
all, of the defendants was paralleled by an equally clear disinclination to use
the trial to discuss the wider history of the camp or its overarching function.
Its account of the reading of the summary of the prosecution case described
how 'the terrible range of the types of death revealed by the prosecutor varied
from shooting, gassing, hanging, drowning, trampling, beating to death and
burning alive to a deadly phenol injection to the heart'.[60] Even this relatively
rare mention of gassing – the main activity of Auschwitz – subsumed such
killings within a general catalogue of brutality which understated the essential
differences between Auschwitz and most other camps; far more typical, in
fact, was the report that made no mention of the gas chambers whatsoever.
Occasional, perfunctory reports on the expert testimony of historians from
the Institute for Contemporary History and the University of Bonn did little

[57] 'Kriminalrat unter Mordverdacht', *Nürnberger Nachrichten*, 5.12.63.
[58] 'Abschied von Erich Ollenhauer', *Nürnberger Nachrichten*, 20.12.63.
[59] 'Heute beginnt der Auschwitz Prozeß', *Nürnberger Nachrichten*, 20.12.63.
[60] 'Kaul als Nebenkläger zugelassen', *Nürnberger Nachrichten*, 8.1.64.

to provide adequate contextualisation.[61] In this way the pattern established in the reporting of earlier West German trials, which had been briefly interrupted during the Eichmann proceedings, was swiftly re-established.

The erosion of such distinctions, which characterised the reportage throughout, was exacerbated above all by the paper's emphasis on Boger and Kaduk.[62] The focus on Boger's notorious 'swing' – an instrument of appalling sadism on which Boger often beat prisoners to death – lent itself easily to allusions to medieval torture. Similarly, accounts of children being thrown into flames, or of plagues of rats pouring over piles of dead bodies or gnawing at the breasts of female prisoners conjured up images akin to medieval visions of hell rather than modern sites of organised mass murder.[63] Reference to the mass deportations and gassings surfaced only in disputes as to whether a given defendant had taken part in 'selections' on the 'ramp', a topographical feature whose significance was never described, but always assumed.[64] Moreover, insofar as the industrialised murder processes of the camp did occasionally move to the fore, it was highly striking that the histories under consideration began, with rare exceptions, with the arrival at the ramp itself. In complete contrast to the Eichmann trial and its reporting, the overriding impression offered in twenty months of reportage on the Auschwitz trial was of a camp with no connections to the outside world – either to Germany, to German society or to large numbers of German perpetrators.[65] This distancing construction of Auschwitz as a space separated from wider German society reached its climax with the reporting of the words of presiding judge Hans Hofmeyer at the reading of the final judgement in August 1965, when the *Nürnberger Nachrichten* reported him as saying, 'Behind the walls of the camp hell began.'[66]

---

[61] For examples of the reporting of expert affidavits, see 'Ich gab den normalen Schießbefehl', *Nürnberger Nachrichten*, 18.2.64; 'Im Gerichtssaal festgenommen', *Nürnberger Nachrichten*, 22./23.2.64; 'Wie Polens Intelligenz vergast wurde', *Nürnberger Nachrichten*, 29.2./1.3.64.

[62] For examples of the reports on Boger, in particular, see 'Schriftsteller Langbein klagt an', *Nürnberger Nachrichten*, 7./8.3.64; 'Boger – der "Teufel von Birkenau" ', *Nürnberger Nachrichten*, 14./15.3.64; 'Folterkammer im KZ Auschwitz', *Nürnberger Nachrichten*, 17.3.64; 'Ein Zeuge schrie: "Mörder" ', *Nürnberger Nachrichten*, 24.3.64; 'Neben Christbaum erhängt', *Nürnberger Nachrichten*, 4./5.4.64; 'SED-Anwalt Kaul reitet Attacke', *Nürnberger Nachrichten*, 11./12.4.64; 'Ein krankhafter Sadist', *Nürnberger Nachrichten*, 16.–18.5.64.

[63] See, for example, 'Kinder lebendig verbrannt', *Nürnberger Nachrichten*, 3.3.64; more generally Pendas, *The Frankfurt Auschwitz Trial*, 286–7.

[64] See, for example, 'Zuhörerin rief: Mörder', *Nürnberger Nachrichten*, 4./5.7.64; 'Lagerapotheker schwer belastet', *Nürnberger Nachrichten*, 28.8.64; 'Lucas legte Geständnis ab', *Nürnberger Nachrichten*, 12.3.65; 'Dr Lucas wurde schwer belastet', *Nürnberger Nachrichten*, 27./28.3.65.

[65] Pendas, *The Frankfurt Auschwitz Trial*, 301; for contrast Norbert Frei, 'Auschwitz and the Germans. History, Knowledge and Memory' in Gregor, *Nazism, War and Genocide*, 147–65.

[66] 'Auschwitz-Greuel fanden ihre Sühne', *Nürnberger Nachrichten*, 20.8.65.

In any case, much of the focus of the reports in the first two months or so of the trial was less the historical actions of the defendants than the appearance, character traits and courtroom performance of the individual defendants themselves. Successive reports relayed the profiles and self-projections of the characters in the dock as much as their careers in the SS or their roles in Auschwitz. Here, again, the figures of Boger and Kaduk lent themselves particularly to the style of reportage: on 21 December 1963, for example, the *Nürnberger Nachrichten* reported that, on the previous day, 'Seven defendants could be interrogated in person. The most striking statement came from the defendant Wilhelm Boger, who had been brought up from custody. He explained: "You will get no great joy from me in the cross-examination as I shall remain silent." '[67] Similarly, in January 1964 the paper reported how Kaduk had stated, ' "I refuse to make any comment." In the icy silence of the court he turned round a few moments later and marched back to his seat, his head held high.'[68]

This fitted with the pattern, already established with the reportage of previous trials, of focusing on the human interest elements of the proceedings over the events ostensibly under discussion. In addition to the usual accounts of fainting or sobbing witnesses, or of tumultuous courtroom scenes as audience members shouted abuse at the defendants, the paper was able to give vivid accounts of the ongoing verbal dual between the right-wing defence lawyer Hans Laternser and the SED lawyer Karl Friedrich Kaul;[69] in August 1964, by which time the *Nürnberger Nachrichten* was clearly struggling to sustain its interest at all, its first report for two weeks related how two childhood friends, both victims of the camp, met again in the courtroom after years of separation: 'They kissed each other and, overcome by the memory of shared experiences, gave their tears free rein.'[70] Here, any reportage of the actual proceedings, let alone description of the camp itself, was entirely absent: for the newspaper, courtroom had become theatre.

For the first two months of the trial, the paper's reportage was naturally shaped by the fact that the proceedings were taken up with the cross-examination of the defendants. Here, such emphasis as was placed on the courtroom argument itself focused on adumbrating the defence rhetorics of each individual – their recourse, variously, to arguments that they had only been following orders, that they had not personally harmed anyone, that their functions had solely involved paperwork, that they had been ignorant of any

[67] 'Anträge, Debatten, heftige Kontroversen', *Nürnberger Nachrichten*, 21./22.12.63.
[68] 'Gnadenschuß aus Mitleid', *Nürnberger Nachrichten*, 21.1.64.
[69] On the Kaul-Laternser dual see Pendas, *The Frankfurt Auschwitz Trial*, 92–5.
[70] 'Ein Wiedersehen im Gerichtssaal', *Nürnberger Nachrichten*, 1./2.8.64; on the theatrical quality of the reportage, see Pendas, *The Frankfurt Auschwitz Trial*, 258–64.

misdeeds at the camp, or that they had acted to alleviate suffering in whatever way possible. The general moral stance of the paper, evident in its ironic distance from the claims of the defendants, was not in doubt. Headlines such as 'Saw nothing, heard nothing' in respect of defendant Robert Mulka's claims of innocence and ignorance, or 'SS man with gaps in his memory' in relation to Josef Klehr's claims not to recall various events made the paper's own views on the truth of the matter clear.[71] Claims such as that of defendant Gerhard Neubert, whom the paper recorded as insisting that 'as a member of the SS he had suffered much more in the concentration camp than the inmates themselves' were met with biting sarcasm: 'Clearly he was referring to the pangs of conscience which constantly tortured him during the appalling events at the notorious and largest mass extermination camp of the National Socialist era.'[72]

In its critical self-distancing from the spurious, mendacious and pernicious claims of the defendants the paper reflected, in its own way, the extent to which the political and ethical norms of the Federal Republic had shifted towards a liberal, democratic value system defined through firm rejection of the historical experience of Nazism. Such sarcasm, however, simultaneously betrayed a wearied sense on the part of the newspaper that the arguments and comments had all been heard before, that the truth was obvious, and that nothing essentially new would come of such trials now. As early as January 1964 – less than one month into proceedings – its headline proclaimed 'Interest in the Auschwitz trial is declining: audience seating now only occupied to a limited extent' in a manner which implicitly sanctioned its readers' own right to disengage, and, moreover, legitimated its decision not to give the trial comprehensive coverage.[73]

A new wave of more intensive reportage began in late February 1964 with the onset of the witness cross-examination in the courtroom. For a while, considerably lengthier accounts of witnesses such as Otto Wolken, Ella Lingens or Hermann Langbein conveyed more graphic, detailed images of the horrors of the camp. In its sizeable report on the statement of the first witness, Otto Wolken, the paper relayed his comments to the effect that 'the murder machinery in Auschwitz could not have functioned unless tens of thousands had been willing to work it'.[74] In this way, the reports transmitted to the

[71] 'Sah nichts, hörte nichts', *Nürnberger Nachrichten*, 10.1.64; 'SS-Mann mit Gedächtnislücken', *Nürnberger Nachrichten*, 1./2.2.64.
[72] 'Ich litt mehr als die Opfer', *Nürnberger Nachrichten*, 4.2.64.
[73] 'KZ-Wächter verweigert Aussage', *Nürnberger Nachrichten*, 11./12.1.64. On Auschwitz 'trial fatigue' see René Wolf, ' "Mass Deception without Deceivers"? The Holocaust on East and West German Radio in the 1960s' in *Journal of Contemporary History* 41/4 (2006), 753; on popular reactions more generally see Pendas, *The Frankfurt Auschwitz Trial*, 252–87.
[74] 'Das war die Hölle auf Erden', *Nürnberger Nachrichten*, 25.2.64.

reader – if only sporadically – a counter-rhetoric to the individualising focus promoted by the trial and, even more so, the reporting practices of the paper itself; they also went some way towards contesting the trivialising representations conveyed in the paper's reports of the defendants' own accounts.

Yet within a month or so, the reports had again been scaled back in size and regularity. By the summer of 1964 they rarely appeared more than weekly; by the autumn the frequency had been reduced to nearer once a fortnight. In its search for novelty the paper preferred to report the opening of new trials, such as that of Himmler's adjutant Karl Wolff (which was reported extensively from July to September 1964); more to the point, topics such as the civil rights disturbances in the USA or that country's deepening involvement in Vietnam moved to the forefront of its reporting concern. The increasing habit of the paper of opening its sporadic reports with phrases such as 'the Auschwitz tribunal . . . experienced a day rich in surprise yesterday' or 'in the Auschwitz trial there was a sensation yesterday' underlined how the proceedings of an 'ordinary' day of evidence-gathering and testimony-hearing was regarded as lacking the necessary interest.[75]

Ultimately, the very partial focus of the trial and its reportage rendered supremely ironic the *Nürnberger Nachrichten*'s comments at its close to the effect that the trial 'had once more revealed in all depth the dreadful crimes of the National Socialist leadership caste and its accomplices'.[76] The limited nature of the reporting, the fact that it declined in frequency as the trial progressed and, above all, the fact that the historical events supposedly under scrutiny faded from the paper's concern, rather than moved to its centre as the trial itself slowly built an account of events at the camp, meant that nothing remotely approaching a comprehensive historical portrait of Auschwitz was created for the public as a direct result of local media engagement with the trial. The public record of the trial created by the *Nürnberger Nachrichten* thus did not, ultimately, provide the basis for the transmission of knowledge of the camp and its history in any obvious way.

At the same time, the sheer volume of trials reported by the paper from the late 1950s through the 1960s was such that a disjointed knowledge of the Holocaust and its many killings sites was made available through the cumulative reportage of the local press. It was probably also the volume of the trials, rather than the detailed findings of any one of them, that contributed to a growing sense of the number of perpetrators who had yet to be brought to justice. However, the relationship between individual trials, their media transmission and changing public sensibilities concerning the crimes of the past

[75] 'Zeuge im Gerichtssaal verhaftet', *Nürnberger Nachrichten*, 17.7.64; 'Zonenminister als Zeuge', *Nürnberger Nachrichten*, 5.2.65.
[76] 'Das Auschwitz-Urteil angekündigt', *Nürnberger Nachrichten*, 11.8.65.

was, in any case, at once more complex and more diffuse. Most importantly, the trials' function within the evolution of the memory cultures of the Federal Republic did not lie in the generation of narratives which, once made available through the local media, were simply internalised as 'knowledge' by a hitherto ignorant reading public. A substantial proportion of the public brought a certain kind of unspoken knowledge to the trials, knowledge either learned elsewhere – trials were not the only catalyst for discussion, after all – or, most importantly, present in the form of remembered experience of Nazism itself. The trials' significance lay less in their capacity to act directly as agents of historical pedagogy to a wider public, than in the activism they stimulated among local progressive elites in the spheres of education and cultural policy. In this way, the trials generated a wider set of pedagogical impulses which echoed more broadly through local civil society and contributed to a further deepening of the nascent critical discourse on the past. It is, indeed, precisely in the examination of such initiatives in education and cultural policy that the limits of an interpretation which moves directly from the prevalence of media representations to an account of memory cultures are most obvious. For, as the examination in the next chapter of the city's exhibitions on the Holocaust in the 1960s shows, if any one moment in a long, drawn-out process could be deemed in retrospect to have been pivotal, it was, in fact, the Auschwitz trial – the very trial whose local reporting was so partial and limited – which sent the most decisive and far-reaching impulses through civil society in Nuremberg.[77]

---

[77] For a discussion of the wider echoes of the trial through West German public life, see Marc von Miquel, ' "Wir müssen mit den Mördern zusammenleben!". NS-Prozesse und politische Öffentlichkeit in den sechziger Jahre' in Wojak, '*Gerichtstag halten über uns selbst . . .*', 97–116; Wittmann, *Beyond Justice*, 246–71; for its place in the development of scholarly research on Auschwitz in West Germany see Norbert Frei, 'Der Frankfurter Auschwitz-Prozeß und die deutsche Geschichtsschreibung' in Fritz Bauer Institut (ed.), *Auschwitz. Geschichte, Rezeption und Wirkung. Jahrbuch 1996 zur Geschichte und Wirkung des Holocaust* (Frankfurt/Main, 1996), 123–38.

III.3

Displaying Barbarism, Displacing Blame

Exhibitions on the Holocaust in the 1960s

The extent to which impulses from outside of the city stimulated and inter-acted with initiatives from within is shown particularly well by the series of exhibitions on the Holocaust that was mounted in Nuremberg during the 1960s. In 1964 the first exhibition on the Holocaust to be mounted since the war – with the exception of the 1945 exhibition of the paintings by concentra-tion camp survivor Richard Grune – was held on the subject 'Life, Struggle and Death in the Warsaw Ghetto'. This was followed in 1965 by simultaneous exhibitions on Auschwitz and on the fate of the Jews of Nuremberg in the modern era.

For the most part these exhibitions were initiated and created elsewhere. The 1964 exhibition on the Warsaw ghetto, for example, owed its inception to the Jewish community in Berlin, and was furnished with material supplied by the Jewish Historical Institute in Warsaw; it was also the initial contact made by the Berlin Jewish community, rather than the efforts of the city council itself, which led to the mounting of the exhibition in Nuremberg.[1] Similarly, the exten-sive Auschwitz exhibition had initially been shown in Frankfurt to coincide with the opening of the Auschwitz trial. This exhibition, which had been financed by the city authorities of Frankfurt, the Federal Office for Political Education, the state Offices for Political Education in Wiesbaden and Hanover, along with dona-tions from both trade unions and big business, owed its conceptualisation to the *Frankfurter Bund für Volksbildung*, and to the support of individuals such as the Attorney General for Hesse, Fritz Bauer.[2] Moreover, in both instances the

---

[1] See the correspondence in StadtAN C 34/265 between Itzchak Pruschnowski of the Jewish community in Berlin and the city authorities in 1963 and 1964.
[2] Cornelia Brink, 'Auschwitz in der Paulskirche'. Erinnerungspolitik in Fotoausstellungen der sechziger Jahre (Marburg, 2000), 18–19.

exhibitions travelled extensively through the Federal Republic: in the case of the Auschwitz exhibition, the planned itinerary included not only Frankfurt and Nuremberg but Stuttgart, Munich, Augsburg, Vienna and Berlin, along with various north-German cities.[3]

As such, both the Warsaw ghetto and Auschwitz exhibitions were part of a national, indeed international, discourse on the Nazi past rather than products of anything particular to Nuremberg. Yet the exhibitions did not come to Nuremberg of their own accord. Rather, it took active input from within and, particularly, the embrace of the idea by the city council – or, at least, the arbiters of its cultural policy – for the exhibitions to be shown. In the case of the Auschwitz exhibition the local leadership of the trade union movement was particularly active in ensuring that the exhibition came to Nuremberg. Further, local political traditions overtly shaped decisions concerning precisely which exhibitions were shown. The Warsaw ghetto exhibition, for example, for which the city council opted, represented an active choice in favour of an exhibition of east European origin over a similar exhibition supported by the Federal government which toured West Germany at the same time.[4]

The circumstances under which the Warsaw ghetto and Auschwitz exhibitions came to be mounted in Nuremberg are also significant in that they demonstrate how early local initiatives drew on a Social Democratic counter-memory to the dominant culture of the Federal Republic – a counter-memory rooted in the deep political traditions of the city – before merging seamlessly into the more general democratising agendas of the self-consciously critical political culture borne by a younger generation of activists as the 1960s progressed. The Warsaw ghetto exhibition was brought to Nuremberg by the 70-year-old Andreas Staudt (b.1893), who had not only been head of the city's Schools and Culture Office since 1953 but had also been a Social Democratic city councillor until the Nazi seizure of power in 1933.[5] Staudt was thus a member of the local Social Democratic leadership cadre with experience of the political conflicts of the interwar years, whose engagement in memory politics was rooted in a strong adult experience of Nazi rule. The Auschwitz exhibition, by contrast, owed its presence in the city largely to the considerably younger Hermann Glaser – Staudt's replacement in 1964 – who, if anything, represented the 'Hitler youth' generation of post-war politicians and cultural activists.

Clearly, then, local Social Democratic tradition influenced the terms on which a visual, as well as a verbal, public memory of the Holocaust evolved in

---

[3] See the material relating to the preparation of the exhibition in StadtAN C 73 I/394.
[4] Brink, '*Auschwitz in der Paulskirche*', 9; on the history of the two parallel exhibitions, see also Knoch, *Die Tat als Bild*, 797ff.
[5] 'Ein Erzieher aus Berufung', *Nürnberger Nachrichten*, 28.5.63.

the 1960s. Through its directives to schools and its distribution of exhibition literature, the city council was also influential, along with the local media, in driving the transmission of the exhibitions' contents to a wider public. Beyond this, assessing the impact of the exhibitions demands caution: the narratives they projected were no more imbibed passively by a wider audience than were those on offer in monuments, at commemorative rituals or in press reportage of trials. What is clear, though, is that the narratives on offer in such exhibitions fitted the patterns of a wider set of discourses, in that enlightenment mixed with distortion, engagement with avoidance, and slowly growing knowledge with widespread ongoing ignorance. Sometimes that ignorance simply reflected the limits of scholarly knowledge. At other times, it reflected a dissimulating evasiveness, the product of the fact that some questions – generally the more awkward ones – were not being asked. In particular, the speeches accompanying the local openings of these exhibitions, in which the displays were endowed with official meaning by the city's political and cultural elites, continued to reflect the workings of a local memory culture: for all the extent to which Social Democratic political traditions shaped the evolution of a local visual memory of Nazism, the clear choice on the part of officials to avoid the endowment of the exhibitions with an overtly socialist meaning, and their preference instead for a pedagogy of radical humanism (one which saw the Nazis as a product of the rejection of the Enlightenment) showed that in the 1960s there remained a need locally to construct the past in a manner that bridged the gulf between the city's bourgeois and proletarian political traditions. Here, again, the reworking of notions of 'the city' as the locus of traditions of decency lent itself ideally to negotiating the challenges that Holocaust memory posed to the consensual narratives so carefully crafted in the 1950s.

The first of the new wave of historical exhibitions to be held in Nuremberg in the 1960s had originally been created to mark the twentieth anniversary of the Warsaw ghetto uprising of April 1943. The material surrounding this exhibition is exceptionally sparse, and offers only the most limited of insights into the circumstances of its inception in Nuremberg, its contents and its reception. It was, however, a substantial exhibition, consisting of sixty display boards and a further thirty-five cabinets mounted on table-high legs.[6] Its three main sections examined, in turn, the creation of the ghetto in 1940, 'Life and Death in the Warsaw Ghetto' and the uprising of 1943.[7]

---

[6] StadtAN C 24/265, Jüdische Gemeinde zu Berlin/Itzchak Pruschnowski an Stadtverwaltung Nürnberg, 24.4.63 (Technische Einzelheiten der Ausstellung 'Leben, Kampf und Tod').
[7] StadtAN C 24/265, Anweisungen zum Aufbau der Ausstellung 'Leben, Kampf und Tod im Ghetto Warschau' (undated, c. 1963).

If the small accompanying brochure reflected accurately the contents of the exhibition, it appears that the display was loose and episodic in structure, but that it drew broadly on two narratives. The first, reflecting its origins in the Jewish communities of Berlin and Warsaw, was the 'lachrymose' narrative of Jewish suffering, which placed the ghetto experience within a long history of continuous persecution; this history was contrasted with the equally long traditions of cultural achievement in which Poland's status as a centre of Jewish intellectual life was stressed.[8] Unlike many early West German accounts, the history of this ghetto was placed firmly within the wider context of Nazi destruction; the variety of the Nazis' criminal sites and the extent of the regime's reach was clearly underlined. Much as the proceedings of the Eichmann trial had sought to place Eichmann's activities within the overall process of mass murder, the brochure underlined that 'in more than 560 concentration camps, work camps, ghettos and other extermination centres in the occupied territories of Europe, National Socialism celebrated its diabolical triumph, a triumph which exceeds the human being's emotional capacity to comprehend'.[9] Following this contextualisation, however, it focused clearly on the Jewish experience in the ghetto, particularly on figures such as Emanuel Ringelblum, on whose secret archive much of the exhibition account was based.

Secondly, however, in emphasising through its focus on the ghetto uprising the fact of Jewish resistance, the exhibition offered an implicit riposte to accusations of Jewish passivity in the face of Nazi persecution. It underlined how 'from the desperation of the masses emerged courage and decisiveness', and how 'they fought desperately for every breath and gave their lives for the highest prize of an honourable death'. This narrative of heroic struggle sat easily with the resistance-driven narratives of eastern European historiography and the forward-looking political pedagogy these underpinned. The brochure emphasised that the exhibition 'does not serve the revival of resentments, or feelings of hate. It should serve to oblige our own generation while acting as a warning for future generations. Beyond that it should contribute to the renewed assertion of humanity in our time, so that the suffering of the recent past can serve as the spur to the creation of a better future.'[10]

By the time the exhibition was described in the *Nürnberger Nachrichten*, however, a different set of meanings – along with an equally striking insistence on the absence of meaning – had been attached, meanings which drew upon the then dominant West German, rather than the eastern European, discourse on the Holocaust. By his own admission, the newspaper's reporter struggled

---

[8] On the Jewish Historical Institute of Warsaw's historical understanding in the 1960s, see Knoch, *Die Tat als Bild*, 798–803.

[9] *Leben, Kampf und Tod: Dokumentarausstellung* (no place, 1964), 1.

[10] Ibid., 1.

to verbalise his response to the images he had seen, claiming that 'after twenty-one years and after all that which has already been written it is not easy to report on such a documentation and the impression which it leaves'.[11] However, he quickly reached for the perpetrator images provided through the West German media reportage of recent war crimes trials: 'The torturing quality comes not only from these pictures of misery and sadism but also from the equally sinister and philistine bureaucratism of the National Socialists. . . .' In this way, an east European account of the Warsaw ghetto uprising was read through the pre-existing interpretative framework familiar from the West German response to trials of figures such as Martin Sommer and Adolf Eichmann.

No sooner had the reporter attempted an analysis, however, than he retreated into the safe confines of vagueness. Making a virtue of his inability to put words to the pictures, he offered instead reflections on the emotive power of images as opposed to the inadequate analyses of historians. Following a brief résumé of the historical context the journalist opined that 'these are sober historical facts on matters before which all historical writing must fail. Fail in the sense that it can only offer a schematic representation of what happened here. But there are more than words, there are these pictures. And what these pictures conjure up in the beholder, what sentiments or thoughts they awaken, each must deal with for himself. No-one and no historical analysis can gainsay this.' He concluded that the pictures spoke only as a reminder: 'a reminder of that of which human beings are capable'. The vagueness of such reflections, their universalising ascription of the causes of the genocide to the human condition or some such thing, and their corresponding resistance to all forms of political interpretation of the events of the Third Reich, were so non-committal as to be meaningless.

Shortly after the Warsaw ghetto exhibition preparations began for the hosting of the Auschwitz exhibition in Nuremberg. The initiative for this came from the local branch of the *Deutsche Gewerkschaftsbund* (DGB), which wrote to the new head of the Schools and Culture Office, Hermann Glaser, that 'both the Bavarian state office and the local Nuremberg office of the DGB wish the city of Nuremberg . . . to host the travelling Auschwitz exhibition', providing technical details and a copy of the historian Martin Broszat's affidavit on the exhibition in support.[12] At the next meeting of the trade union representatives and city officials the chairman of the local DGB, Karl-Heinz Hagin, renewed his request, to which both mayor Urschlechter and Glaser responded positively.[13]

---

[11] 'Leben, Kampf und Tod im Warschauer Ghetto', *Nürnberger Nachrichten*, 7./8.3.64.
[12] StadtAN C 73 I/394, DGB Kreis Nürnberg an Hermann Glaser, 29.12.64.
[13] StadtAN C 73 I/394, DGB Kreis Nürnberg, Niederschrift der Arbeitstagung zwischen Kreisvorstand und Stadtverwaltung am 18.1.65.

Preparations were made over the spring, and it appears that considerable effort was made to overcome problems of finding suitable space and adequate finance in order that the exhibition should come to Nuremberg. Not only to spread the cost, but also 'with an eye to the intended broad reach of the exhibition', the Schools and Culture Office sought to engage the support of as many of the institutions of local civil society as possible for the project.[14] As well as collaborating closely with the trade unions, the Schools and Culture Office tried to engage the political parties, the chamber of commerce, the churches, and both the Bavarian Ministry for Education and Culture and the Bavarian State Office for Political Education. As a mark of civic commitment to the event, as much as a practical solution to the space demands of the display, the exhibition was mounted in the town hall in April 1965.

The official opening of the exhibition took place before a substantial gathering of trade unionists, churchmen, city councillors and other guests. Here, speeches by Glaser, Urschlechter and Hagin offered official accounts of the motives for mounting the exhibition, of its purpose and meaning. Each speaker drew on a number of then current narratives circulating within the various, intersecting communities of which they were part.[15]

Of the three, Hagin, the trade union leader, came closest to incorporating Auschwitz into the customary narratives of the political Left, claiming that 'under the leadership of robbers and murderers a people was forced to rise up and conquer the world. The heroes and martyrs of that era, however, are those who died and were ruined behind fences and barbed wire solely for the honour of the German people.' Even this resistance narrative lacked political specificity, however. Moreover, although his position as a trade union leader allowed him the possibility of a more partisan account than that open to Urschlechter or Glaser, he too chose to avoid a divisive critique of the politics of the interwar years or of the institutions and interests which had sustained fascism in power locally, in favour of a more general account focusing on the loss of freedom, the rule of law, and humanity. In this way, Nazism could be represented as a rejection of the customary values of bourgeois politics rather than the product, among other things, of bourgeois reaction to those very values during the interwar crisis years – a perspective unlikely to command universal acclaim in the room.

Both Hagin and Urschlechter, meanwhile, focused on the role of the exhibition in instructing young people; the present- and future-orientated focus of the local initiators of the exhibition was typified in Glaser's assertion that the message of Auschwitz lay in the need to prevent such things in their

[14] StadtAN C 73 I/394, Aktennotiz Glaser/Ref.IV betr. Auschwitz-Ausstellung, 10.2.65.
[15] See the account of the official opening in 'Auschwitz darf sich nie wiederholen', *Amtsblatt der Stadt Nürnberg*, 14.4.65.

infancy: 'Prevent the beginnings is the moral of every moment after Auschwitz!' In keeping with the democratic didacticism inherent in this rhetoric, Glaser argued that individual visitors to the exhibition should start with themselves, in that the history of the 'implementation of the inhuman' conveyed in the images obliged individuals to encourage one another 'for the sake of themselves, for the present and the future not to close their minds to these pictures and facts'; he argued, further, that the exhibition should prompt viewers into 'cleansing ourselves from the resentments and emotions which often push us in apparently insignificant ways down false paths'. The moral, in other words, was to work instead for the 'unfolding and flourishing of humanity, even on the level of the small and insignificant'.

Hagin, likewise, emphasised that 'this exhibition draws attention to the quite elementary dangers which stem from those parts of our personal nature against which we must secure ourselves politically and technically as well as we can'. In this way, the political content of his speech was directed yet further away from an historical analysis of fascism, in favour of a present-centred politics which focused instead on the need to combat contemporary fascist potential. Such comments were undoubtedly to be read against the background of the recent emergence of the neo-nationalist NPD. For this reason, too, the speeches and the city's record of them focused less on the specifics of anti-Semitism, in either their historical or contemporary manifestations, than on a more generic anti-racist message.

If this anti-racist message reflected a well-intended desire to encourage visitors to think critically about themselves, its effect was also, however, to dilute the historical specificity of Auschwitz and to navigate away from an analysis of its causes. While Hagin had ventured to describe Auschwitz as a product of the rejection of the Enlightenment, offering a narrative which would find purchase not only with his constituency on the Left, but also within the progressive elements of the local bourgeoisie, Glaser explicitly refused to offer any kind of historical analysis at all, stating that he did not intend 'to give an historical interpretation of the National Socialist terror and its concentration and extermination camps'. Glaser, of course, had his views, and had expressed them in print on a number of occasions.[16] As such, his remarks testified, like Hagin's, to an awareness on the part of those charged with representing the interests of the population as a whole of the ongoing divisiveness of the Nazi past, and of its continued potential to exacerbate the schism between progressive and reactionary political traditions in the city.

---

[16] Hermann Glaser, *Das Dritte Reich. Anspruch und Wirklichkeit* (Freiburg, 1961); id., *Spießerideologie. Von der Zerstörung des deutschen Geistes im 19. und 20. Jahrhundert* (Freiburg, 1964).

How did ordinary citizens respond?[17] The *Nürnberger Nachrichten* reported 'lively interest' and 'great attention' from the population, and that 'above all young people visited the documentary exhibition, whose reports and photos illuminated their subject so clearly that observers only felt able to communicate in whispers'.[18] The public interest was such, indeed, that the exhibition, which was originally scheduled to run for three weeks, was extended for a further month.[19] Beyond this, judging what kinds of knowledge visitors took away from the exhibition demands closer examination of precisely what they were invited to see.[20] Most obviously, the particular narrative chains offered by the exhibition were a product of editorial choice on the part of the creators of the display. There again, the images did not, in themselves, impart meaning to the events they depicted. They captured the fact of their historical occurrence but provided no direct interpretation: this was, at best, implied by the overall sequencing of the documents and photographs.[21] This, in turn, had originally been shaped by the simultaneous staging of the Auschwitz trial – one intended function of the exhibition had, indeed, been to offer documentary support to the prosecution. The result was a highly personalised narrative, focused on individual perpetrators, and a narrative which, in historiographical terms, embodied a strongly intentionalist line on the Holocaust. This, in turn, reflected the legal imperative to prove a subjective commitment to killing on the part of individual perpetrators in order to secure a conviction for murder.[22]

The first three rooms were dedicated to the 'pre-history of Auschwitz'.[23] They focused on Nazi ideology, the creation of the 'People's Community' during the 1930s, the 'burning of the books' and the early boycotts of Jewish businesses, before offering an account of earlier concentration camps such as Dachau and Sachsenhausen, and concluded with the attack on Poland in 1939 and the brutal persecution of Polish civilians. The next section of the exhibition focused on Auschwitz itself. Firstly, the topography and structure of the camp – its towers, blocks, barbed wire and guard posts – were recreated. Then, it detailed the mistreatment of its first prisoners, including Polish civilians and Soviet prisoners of war; further rooms described the deportation of the Jews of Europe, the Wannsee Conference and the process of systematic murder by gassing. The following rooms showed the 'selection' of arriving prisoners for

[17] For the public controversy surrounding the exhibition see Pendas, *The Frankfurt Auschwitz Trial*, 182–7.
[18] 'Ostern in der Stadt: ein ruhiges und besinnliches Fest', *Nürnberger Nachrichten*, 20.4.65.
[19] StadtAN C 73 I/394, Aktenvermerk Glaser betr. Auschwitz-Ausstellung, 15.4.65.
[20] On the presence of Auschwitz in the visual culture of West Germany in the 1960s in general, see Knoch, *Die Tat als Bild*, 828–40.
[21] Brink, '*Auschwitz in der Paulskirche*', 28; 64–74.
[22] Ibid., 25;47.
[23] The following account is based on Brink, '*Auschwitz in der Paulskirche*', 38ff.

labour or immediate murder on the notorious ramp, and the utilisation of prisoners' possessions in the 'Canada' part of the camp: what remained of the murdered prisoners was represented in piles of objects such as shoes, glasses and human hair. In the words of a recent study of the exhibition, 'Finally, only brief mention was given to forced labour at the camp for German industrial firms, to the murder of "gypsies" and to medical experiments on children, before images of the liberation announced the end of the camp complex Auschwitz.'[24]

According to Martin Broszat, who produced an assessment of the exhibition at the time for the Federal Office for Political Education, the initiators managed to assemble 'an astonishingly broad, representative collection of sources . . . to be particularly greeted is the fact that alongside the visually and emotionally effective large-format photos and text boards numerous official documents from National Socialist offices and authorities are reproduced as facsimile copies in original size, so that the desire for information and an objective view is to a great extent fulfilled'.[25] In the sense that such documents conveyed a strong sense of authenticity which should persuade Holocaust deniers, or at least those disinclined to acknowledge the full reality of Nazi mass murder, Broszat was no doubt justified in referring to the exhibition's 'objectivity'; indeed, his assertion that 'the range of the diverse, authentic documentary material will also leave its mark precisely on those who perhaps still have doubts in relation to events at Auschwitz' suggest that this was what he had in mind.

However, the gaze of the exhibition on to its subject matter was – for precisely the reasons outlined in Broszat's account – anything but objective. For one thing, arguing as it did largely through Nazi source material, it recreated a Nazi perspective on the Holocaust: the images of the Jews in the exhibition either reproduced the visual constructions of Jewishness familiar from Nazi anti-Semitic propaganda or, in placing the viewer in the position of the observing (invariably German) photographer, offered him or her the perspective of the perpetrator. At the same time, the exhibition reproduced an image of Auschwitz familiar from the trials and their reportage: namely, the sense that its boundaries had marked the limits of a hermetically sealed space, separated physically, politically and ethically from wider German society.[26]

The exhibition thus 'ascribed all responsibility to a place clearly separated off from the everyday, for which stood names or organisations such as "Hitler", "the SS" or "the Gestapo", rather than confront the visitor with concrete examples of the widespread stances of not-wanting-to-exactly-know,

[24] Ibid., 41.
[25] StadtAN C 73 I/394, Gutachten zur Auschwitz-Ausstellung in Frankfurt, 14.12.64.
[26] Knoch, *Die Tat als Bild*, 837–40.

of contributing or of profiting, of looking away or disinterestedly looking on – which were equally constitutive of the murder in the ghettoes and concentration camps'.[27] Certainly, the focus on two specific kinds of perpetrator – either the elite perpetrator such as Hitler, Himmler or Rudolf Hoess, or the sadistic 'excess' perpetrator embodied in the particularly vicious camp guard – did little to address the issues of the very large numbers of Germans who saw active employment in Auschwitz and the hundreds of other camps during the war, the wider criminal involvement of government institutions, party agencies and commercial enterprises in the genocide, or the extensive popular knowledge of what was happening during the Holocaust within the society which had given rise to this genocidal regime in the first place.

In a city such as Nuremberg it was, indeed, the wider connections between Auschwitz and German society which proved most troubling. In his contribution to the opening of the exhibition, mayor Urschlechter was keen to ensure that Nuremberg's position in relation to the histories being represented in the display was properly understood. Contrasting the history of the Third Reich with indigenous traditions of openness and tolerance, he reminded the audience of the significance of the town hall, where, in peaceful times past, some of its citizens had been honoured 'without regard for their status, their class or their race'; from the medieval era down to 1933, he insisted, this hall had served 'the forging of contacts between Nuremberg and many friendly cities from all around the world and from every direction'.[28] Likewise, the city's official gazette argued that 'If it [the exhibition] is shown in Nuremberg for the first time in Bavaria then this is not the expression of a particular recognition of guilt on Nuremberg's part, whose name was often misused by the powerholders and rogues of the brown dictatorship without its own involvement . . .' Such comments reflected the fact that, as the city's elites knew only too well, the growing engagement across the Federal Republic with the historical burden of the Holocaust posed particular problems for a city with such a tainted reputation as Nuremberg.

The nature of the difficulties the local history of the Third Reich presented to the authorities of a city such as Nuremberg was shown by the second exhibition to be mounted in Nuremberg in April 1965, on 'the fate of Nuremberg's Jews from 1850 to 1945'. Timed to run in parallel both to the Auschwitz exhibition and the inaugural Nuremberg Conversation, the exhibition recounted the experiences of the local Jewish citizenry in the modern era. Here, again, the exhibition owed its existence to the collaboration of internal and external agencies: in addition to contributions from the State Archive in Nuremberg,

[27] Brink, 'Auschwitz in der Paulskirche', 48.
[28] 'Auschwitz darf sich nie wiederholen', Amtsblatt der Stadt Nürnberg, 14.4.65.

the university library of Erlangen-Nuremberg, the local Jewish community and various local administrative offices, the exhibition enjoyed the input of the Institute of Contemporary History in Munich and, most notably, the Wiener Library in London.[29] Former and current Jewish citizens were also invited, including Paul Baruch, who had survived the Nazi era in Nuremberg and had become chairman of the local community shortly thereafter, and Bernhard Kolb, the last pre-war secretary of the Nuremberg Jewish community, who had survived deportation to Theresienstadt and had emigrated to the USA shortly after the war. In order to underline the significance of the exhibition and its status as a supra-local creation, Caesar Aronsfeld of the Wiener Library presented one of the opening speeches.[30]

As with the Auschwitz exhibition, the opening speeches represented a moment at which local elites sought to insert the contents of the exhibition into an interpretative framework capable of commanding local support; in this case, in particular, the speeches marked the search for a means of interpreting the history of the Third Reich which sat agreeably with narratives of civic tradition and local identity already present in the culture of the city. While Aronsfeld mentioned the historical associations of Nuremberg with the Nazi regime, his main focus was on offering a historical overview of anti-Semitism and the origins of the Holocaust. It was thus left to mayor Urschlechter and to Hermann Glaser to address the particular issue of the experience of Nuremberg's Jews during the Third Reich.

For his part, mayor Urschlechter emphasised the overwhelmingly harmonious relationship between Jews and non-Jews in the city prior to 1933. In his words, 'they were loyal citizens; they engaged, thought and acted on behalf of the city and also sacrificed themselves when the fatherland called them in 1914–1918. They lived among us and consciously with us in the city community.'[31] Glaser, likewise, avoided mention of the widespread anti-Semitism present locally before 1933 in favour of underlining that 'in this city we, too, can be proud of a long series of men and women who worked persistently and successfully for harmonious co-existence with the Jewish citizens in both the private and the official sphere'.[32] It was, by implication, only the arrival of the external force of Nazism – in Glaser's words the 'forced entry [*Einbruch*] of the violent power of barbarism' – which brought this state of harmony to an abrupt end. Glaser was quick to point to another factor, that of the 'indifference

---

[29] StadtAN C 73 I/394, Aktenvermerk Stadtarchiv und Volksbücherei (undated, 1965).

[30] StadtAN C 73 I/394, Aktenvermerk Dr Glaser, 7.1.65.

[31] 'Schicksale jüdischer Mitbürger in Nürnberg', *Amtsblatt der Stadt Nürnberg*, 14.4.65.

[32] StadtAN C 73 I/394, Rede Hermann Glasers zur Eröffnung der Ausstellung 'Schicksale jüdischer Mitbürger 1850–1945'. On manifestations of anti-Semitism in the local political culture before 1933, see Anthony Kauders, *German Politics and the Jews. Düsseldorf and Nuremberg 1910–1933* (Oxford, 1996).

of the many who did not resist the state-conceived crimes', but this remark, while intended as a moral admonition of the majority, served only to understate again the degree of active involvement of ordinary citizens in the anti-Semitic policies and practices of the Nazi regime. There followed a somewhat contorted, nebulous passage of speech on the nature of the Third Reich in which the Nazis' crimes were described in terms of 'moral perversion' pursued with 'sadistic pleasure', while 'immanent evil' and the 'irruption of base demonism' were blamed for the destruction of the centuries-old pursuit of a cultured, humane social order. Here, Glaser focused his critique on petit-bourgeois conformism, both for its tolerance of the crimes of Nazism and for its willingness to pretend that 'nothing had happened'. In his view, such 'repression' was a positive sign that ordinary people were conscious of the wrongness of the Third Reich, but 'a society can never be restored to health by repression'.

Alongside this cultural and psychological account of the origins, nature and consequences of Nazism, Glaser did offer a more overtly political, ideological reading of the histories under consideration in the exhibition. As with the speeches marking the opening of the Auschwitz exhibition, however, Glaser's remarks were striking for the extent to which they eschewed a narrowly partisan, Social Democratic narrative in favour of one designed to appeal more generally to the politically and socially progressive elements in Nuremberg society. In his view, the exhibition showed above all how the 'great project of liberalism to create a humane social order was dismantled step by step, and how through anti-Semitism the dark ages of religious Jew-hatred re-emerged to force a progressive state structure and social order into anarchy'. The moral of this was that 'it is the task of a moral state and a moral social order to guarantee the shared harmony and co-operative existence of its citizens and to eradicate promptly every move to prevent a lived pluralism'. As in the case of the Auschwitz exhibition, the emphases in such a historical account served a present- and future-centred agenda of fostering democratic engagement among the citizenry, but it also privileged the maintenance of consensual historical narratives across the entire community over the enforcement of the local political and cultural hegemony of Social Democracy.

The emphasis on Nazism and the Holocaust as the product of the rejection of nineteenth-century liberalism was also strongly implied in the exhibition itself. After a very brief survey of the history of the Jews in Nuremberg from the twelfth century onwards, the exhibition started its main account in 1850.[33] Under the heading 'Co-existence under the Sign of Liberalism', the first full section of the exhibition detailed the gradual return of Jews to Nuremberg during the nineteenth century and the introduction of laws leading to their

---

[33] *Schicksal jüdischer Mitbürger in Nürnberg 1850–1945. Ausstellungskatalog mit Dokumentation bearbeitet von Stadtarchiv und Volksbücherei Nürnberg* (Nuremberg, 1965).

equal status during the emancipation era, before considering the flourishing of the community, the development of its institutions, the contributions of its members to public life, and the successful assimilation of the Jews into the political, economic and cultural fabric of the city more generally.

From here, the exhibition proceeded to its account of 'Persecution under National Socialism 1933–1945'. In its preliminary descriptions of 'Anti-Semitism in Nuremberg before 1933' it acknowledged – contrary to the more soothing implications of Glaser's opening speech – that 'modern anti-Semitism begins long before the persecution of the Jews' and that 'in Nuremberg as in the whole of the Reich there were anti-Jewish currents' before 1914.[34] Moreover, in its discussion of Hitler's rise to power, it went considerably further than the opening speeches in locating responsibility for anti-Semitic politics, arguing that 'Hitler was able to win his voters from the masses of the dissatisfied, who came above all from the bourgeoisie'.[35] There followed clear sections on the local boycotts in 1933, the exclusion of Jews from the professions, the development of schools policy, the Hitler Youth and the BdM – including references to local anti-Semitic teachers and pedagogues – and on aryanisation, the destruction of Nuremberg's syna-gogues and the deportation of Nuremberg's Jews during the war.

Backed up and illustrated with documents from a variety of sources, the exhibition made clear how the horrors of Nazi persecution and mass murder had been visited upon local Jewish citizens in familiar, local spaces. Yet, having alluded to the mass support enjoyed by the Nazi movement, the exhibition took a step firmly backwards when addressing the identities and the range of the perpetrators, and the extent of popular complicity in the crimes of the Third Reich. Alongside an emphasis on Julius Streicher and the *Stürmer* as evidence of a pathological anti-Semitism which had (implicitly) been the preserve of a few fanatics, the perpetrating agents were overwhelmingly referred to in such anonymising collective nouns as 'the *Gauleitung*', 'party functionaries' or 'the power holders'. Blame was attributed solely to party agencies, and not to the broader range of institutions of communal or civic life: in placing responsibility on party organs (which had been dissolved in 1945) rather than addressing the complicity of still extant institutions (which had enjoyed a substantial degree of personal and institutional continuity into the post-war years) such narratives thus served to emphasise the essential pastness of the Nazi era, and its fundamental separateness to the here and now in which the exhibition occurred. In this way, an exhibition which purported to confront troubling local histories of genocide served, in fact, to distance its viewers from the very histories being described.

[34] Ibid., 28.
[35] Ibid., 29.

This was compounded by the deployment of notions of agency which became increasingly nebulous as the account moved closer to events during the war itself. Once deportation became the theme, the text either abandoned any notion of specific agency or, most notably, switched to the passive voice. In its account of the decision-making process leading up to the Holocaust, 'one considered deportation to Madagascar'; by the time of the Wannsee Conference 'mass destruction was the announced goal of those responsible'; in phrases such as 'mass deportations were considered' any residual notion of agency was completely dissolved.[36]

Moreover, while the close geographical focus of the exhibition allowed examination of local experiences of Jewish suffering, it also served to foreclose discussion of the complicity of most local people in the Holocaust. The Holocaust was not, after all, something primarily perpetrated within the confines of this space: most of those Nuremberg citizens involved in mass murder had been so not in the city itself but in the multiple spaces of occupied Europe in which they had served as policemen, soldiers, or SS-men in the 'resettlement', mass shooting or deportation of foreign Jews. Rather than open up these troubling histories, the exhibition insisted, indeed, on the ignorance of ordinary local people during the Holocaust, claiming that 'if the measures against the Jews before the war had taken place in the complete open, the introduction and implementation of the destruction was hidden with the mantle of silence'.[37]

Rather than encourage the viewer to ponder his or her own complicity as a member of the perpetrating majority society, the exhibition therefore offered an account in which Nuremberg's citizens were murdered by an external regime and its local agents; in inviting the local viewer to identify the Jews as former fellow citizens and co-participants in a shared, mutually enriching communal life prior to 1933, rather than as victims of a widespread anti-Semitism which had helped Nazism to power in the first place, the viewer was permitted to see in the destruction of the Holocaust a process which had victimised *all* Nuremberg citizens, not just its Jewish minority.

The reach of the exhibition extended far beyond its actual visitors. Fifteen hundred copies of the catalogue were distributed not only to local schools, churches and civic dignitaries, but also to participants in the Nuremberg Conversations that were being held at the same time; some copies were also sent to former Jewish citizens with whom the city was now initiating contact. Moreover, public interest generated by the exhibition was such that the city council engaged the services of a local schoolteacher, Arnd Müller, to write a more comprehensive history of the Jews of Nuremberg from 1146 to 1945.

[36] Ibid., 37.
[37] Ibid., 37.

Despite the obstructiveness of conservative voices on the board of the foundation whose financial support the city council was seeking in order to publish the book – who expressed the fear that it might 'reawaken the reputation of Nuremberg as an anti-Semitic city' and accused it of offering 'manipulated history' – the book was eventually published in 1968.[38]

The Holocaust exhibitions of the 1960s thus demonstrated how, even twenty years after the war, local political and cultural elites faced difficulty in championing a critical historical pedagogy that focused directly on local structures of support and involvement in the singular crimes of the Third Reich; they underlined how, even as the Holocaust began to emerge as a subject of debate, the operations of a local memory culture still demanded that these elites restrict themselves to narratives which would not excessively challenge the post-fascist civic peace. In many respects, then, the exhibitions on the Third Reich and the Holocaust mirrored the local reportage in the 1960s on trials of Nazi-era crimes. The mere fact of their occurrence signalled that a shift in memory politics was under way. Moreover, they interacted with other manifestations of that shift to generate a series of debates and pedagogical impulses which helped, slowly, to shift the moral and political norms of post-war West German society. However, the narratives they projected mixed enlightenment with ongoing evasiveness. The meanings attached by civic opinion-leaders to those aspects of the past which were debated and engaged betrayed the workings of a memory culture in which, above all, a proclivity remained to see 'the city' either as an oasis of humanity before which the march of barbarism had been forced to halt, or itself as the actual victim of a regime which had been forced on the town from outside. Many other questions remained unanswered: the reason for this, of course, was that they remained unasked.

---

[38] Müller, *Geschichte der Juden*; for the obstructionism see StadtAN C 36 I/255, Aktennotiz, Stadtarchiv betr. Müller, Geschichte der Juden in Nürnberg (Vertraulich), 12.7.67.

Critiquing History, Creating Democracy?

The Nuremberg Conversations, 1965 to 1968

That the significance of the new wave of trials of Nazi-era crimes did not lie solely in the extent to which they propelled new, more critical narratives directly into the West German public sphere through the print and other media, but resided equally in the range of wider pedagogical and cultural initiatives they encouraged, is also shown by the example of the Nuremberg Conversations of the late 1960s. This intentionally informal nomenclature was applied to a series of annual four-day public symposia initiated by Hermann Glaser and the local cultural and educational authorities, and organised with the support of the Federal and Bavarian Offices for Political Education and Bavarian State Radio. Each year, around fifty academics, journalists and other prominent commentators from West Germany and abroad gathered at the invitation of the city to engage in interdisciplinary debate – both in camera and in public – over questions connecting Germany's past, present and future. As the timing of the first congress – April 1965 – and indeed the presence, among others, of Hesse Attorney General Fritz Bauer, suggest, it was the Auschwitz trial which provided a decisive stimulus for more general pedagogical initiatives; the references to the trial during the first congress show that, even if local media reportage of the trial itself was limited and distorted, the Frankfurt proceedings stimulated debate and action in a manner not achieved to the same extent by previous trials.

Such events also revealed the extent to which the emergence of a more critical discourse on the Nazi past was both symptom and cause of a wider process of liberalisation under way across West German democracy during the 1960s. The very format of the events, which, for all their usage of opening lectures and summary reports, foregrounded the notion of debate, dissent and dispute in an atmosphere of open exchange contained a clear didactic function, rooted in the desire to reclaim and reinvigorate traditions of rational criticism and independence of mind in the service of a 'second Enlightenment'. The constant attempt to focus on themes that allowed the discussion to proceed from critical engagement with Germany's past and present to prescriptions for the consolidation and improvement of West German democracy betrayed, similarly, a progressive desire to connect analysis with action – indeed, one of the annual Conversations took this as its overarching theme.[1]

At the same time, the echoes of the congresses across civil society showed that the emergence of a more critical discourse across the Federal Republic was not a simple top-down process whereby 'elite' political, judicial or pedagogical agendas were transmitted to local audiences. On the one hand, the practice of inviting local educationalists to semi-closed seminars with the international 'experts' and the holding of public symposia at which a local audience listened to expert discussion were designed to send impulses through the educational, cultural and political life of the city itself. On the other hand, the congresses also sent considerable impulses back into the culture of the Federal Republic as a whole: not only were they reported extensively in national and regional newspapers and other publications, but they were broadcast and discussed on the radio, giving them a much greater reach. Moreover, the publication of the lectures, reports and extracts from the podium discussions in an annual series of volumes created a permanent record of the congresses which could also be disseminated more widely.[2]

As was the case in other media, the content of the congresses revealed significant shifts in the manner in which the past was engaged in public in the 1960s. If some participants continued to indulge in the more nebulous formulations of German history inherited from the immediate post-war years, others were remarkable for the extent to which they were able to proffer far more critical accounts of Auschwitz and its causes. In lectures, podium discussions and seminar reports, audiences listened to interpretations of continuities in German history spanning both the years 1933 and 1945 which gave the lie to conventional wisdom regarding Nazism's status as an 'accident' or short-term aberration: historical accounts stressed, in various ways, the long-term roots of the catastrophe of 1933 in a manner which acted to publicise notions of a German 'Special Path' that were then gaining academic currency, while

---

[1] On the place of the Nuremberg Conversations in Hermann Glaser's broader agenda for cultural policy in Nuremberg, see Franziska Knöpfle, *Im Zeichen der 'Soziokultur'. Hermann Glaser und die kommunale Kulturpolitik in Nürnberg* (Nuremberg, 2007), 154–83. This book appeared after the completion of this study.

[2] For those of the congresses which fall within the temporal scope of this study, see Hermann Glaser (ed.), *Haltungen und Fehlhaltungen in Deutschland. Ein Tagungsbericht* (Freiburg, 1966); Hermann Glaser (ed.), *Aufklärung heute – Probleme der deutschen Gesellschaft. Ein Tagungsbericht* (Freiburg, 1967); Hermann Glaser (ed.), *Erkennen und Handeln – Gegenwart und Zukunft der deutschen Gesellschaft. Ein Tagungsbericht* (Freiburg, 1967); Hermann Glaser and Karl-Heinz Stahl (eds), *Opposition in der Bundesrepublik. Ein Tagungsbericht* (Freiburg, 1968).

during debates on the state of democracy in the Federal Republic criticisms were voiced concerning the extent of authoritarian inheritances from the Wilhelmine and Nazi eras.

What, however, was most significant about these discussions was the prominent platform they gave to voices which had hitherto been marginalised by the operations of memory politics in the city. The willingness of the city's cultural authorities to invite émigrés, refugees and foreigners to participate in debates on German history, politics and society testified to a new desire to embrace outside perspectives as part of the pursuit of a pluralist political culture. Most strikingly, the congresses included on their roster a number of prominent Holocaust survivors who were given free rein to voice their criticisms, marking a crucial re-centering of ethical sensibility – on the part of the progressive political establishment, if not necessarily of all – away from the imagined community of victims of the 1950s and towards a position willing to give voice to, and to listen to, the victims of Nazi genocide.

At the same time, the congresses – like the exhibitions of the 1960s – betrayed the presence of an ongoing need on the part of the local political and cultural establishment to find modes of discussing the past which did not challenge too directly the fragile civic consensus between the city's competing political traditions. There were, accordingly, limits to the criticism, or, rather, the congresses' remit tended to privilege some kinds of criticism over others. If the congresses were informed by the historical fact of Auschwitz, they were not, for the most part, centred on it. Accordingly, analysis of the historical specificities of the Holocaust was a marginal aspect of even the historically focused aspects of the congresses. Moreover, the intellectual framework and historical understandings that underpinned the rationale for the congresses offered few starting points for discussing issues of specifically local complicity in the crimes of the past, and thus for challenging the legitimacy of local political, economic or institutional elites. Discussions of the relative balance of rational and irrational forces in German history – of the competing presence of the 'Enlightened' and the 'Romantic' – inspired by the findings of literary criticism offered the possibility of diagnosing faults in Germany's development in the nineteenth century, but they did not engage with the extreme political divisions between bourgeoisie and working class that had been such a central dimension of the interwar crisis. Similarly, discussions of the presence of 'Hitler in us', drawn from social psychology or psychoanalysis, marked a welcome step forwards from the widespread insistence in the 1950s that Hitler had been the fault of someone else, but did little to locate institutional, social or political responsibility for Nazism more directly or accurately. In this way, the 'pedagogy of radical humanism' which informed the congresses again demonstrated – precisely in its construction of the legacies of Nazism as an educational, psychological and individual problem rather than as a political issue – the ongoing need to find ways of engaging with the past which could find acceptance within progressive bourgeois as well as Social Democrat circles, and thus transcend the historical fault lines in local society in a manner capable of preserving civic peace.

Hermann Glaser's commitment to pursuing historical education not for its own sake but in order to reinforce contemporary reforming agendas and, in particular, the wider process of democratisation of West German political culture, was made transparently evident in the invitations issued by the city's Schools and Culture Office to local schools to visit the two exhibitions on Auschwitz and the Jews of Nuremberg which were being mounted at the same time that the first Nuremberg Conversations were held. Here, the relevant official observed that 'the notion of "overcoming the past" [*Bewältigung der Vergangenheit*] has been rigorously debated in recent times', and stated that 'the past can only be remembered, while the present and future are there to be shaped'.[3] To this end, he insisted that ' "overcoming the past", as we understand it and in terms of what motivated us to mount the two exhibitions, resides in the will, gained through insight into the past, to work in our time for an ethical and democratic state and social order'. The purpose of looking at the past, according to the invitation, 'was to strengthen the old and the young in their efforts to be humane'.

Such an agenda was also clearly visible in the early proposals for the Nuremberg Conversations. In 1964, shortly after his appointment as head of the city's Schools and Culture Office, Glaser suggested a congress on 'the nature, origins and combating of prejudice'.[4] As even this initial concept suggested, Glaser was motivated by a reading of German history which combined interests in social psychology with a belief that Nazism had represented the triumph of irrational forces in German society and the abandonment of 'enlightened' values of humanity which he wished to reassert in the contemporary context. By the time Glaser had developed a fuller rationale for the congresses, these themes had crystallised even more clearly. Referring to Nuremberg's historical associations with Nazism as the overarching justification for mounting the gatherings, Glaser argued that 'the city of Nuremberg sees in this an obligation to engage to a greater degree than hitherto in the dismantling of false positions and false developments and to contribute in theory and practice through model efforts and institutions to the strengthening of democratic consciousness'.[5] To this

---

[3] StadtAN C 73 I/394, Schul- und Kulturreferat der Stadt Nürnberg, Rundschreiben 23 an die Direktorate der städtischen und staatlichen Schulen, 22.3.65.
[4] StadtAN C 73 I/394, Glaser an Urschlechter, 3.6.64.
[5] StadtAN C 73 I/799, Das Nürnberger Gespräch: Vorurteile, Leitbilder, politische Verantwortung (undated, 1965).

end, Glaser now proposed a series of congresses 'on sociological, politological, anthropological and similar problem fields' to which leading academics and commentators from around the world would be invited; in particular, they should discuss 'questions of the formation and combating of prejudices, the dangers and possibilities of role models in a free society, along with the possibilities of educating people towards political responsibility'.

As the title of the proposed first congress – 'Positions and False Positions . . .' or 'Stances and False Stances in Germany' (*Haltungen und Fehlhaltungen in Deutschland*) – implied, the aim was to generate conversations that focused simultaneously on political traditions, intellectual positions, mental dispositions and personal stances, and which drew on the interdisciplinary insights of a wide range of experts. The first congress was also intended firmly to link questions concerning the past to questions of the present, the rationale stating that 'at its core is the view that since the end of the eighteenth century certain false dispositions (in the form of a type of "German ideology") can be seen as a syndrome (of varying extent and strength) down to the most immediate present'. Specifically, Glaser sought to question how far the structuring presence of national patterns of ideological thinking (*nationale Ideologisierung*) and the corresponding 'ideological alienation from reality' were still there in West German society and what could be done to counter them. The implied continuity between the political culture of the Federal Republic and that of a previous era embodied in such assertions and, in particular, the accusation of a residual authoritarianism in contemporary West Germany, reflected the concerns of the new critical climate that was emerging in the 1960s, and underpinned the democratising agenda of the congresses. Such notions of continuity between the Third Reich and the post-war era marked a radical challenge to the shared wisdom concerning the relationship of the Federal Republic to the Nazi past that had prevailed in the 1950s.

The first congress was held in April 1965, to coincide with the Auschwitz and 'Jews of Nuremberg' exhibitions. Its fifty-nine overwhelmingly male participants included academics such as the historians Walther Hofer (Bern), Kurt Sontheimer (Berlin) and Fritz Stern (Columbia); political scientists such as Thomas Ellwein (Frankfurt), or the German literature specialist Hans Schwerte (Erlangen); journalists such as Fritz René Allemann, Dietrich Strothmann of *Die Zeit* and the Israeli journalist Shalom Ben-Chorin, who worked on the only Israeli German-language newspaper; they also included Holocaust survivor H.G. Adler, who had been interned in Theresienstadt, Auschwitz and Buchenwald, and former lecturer for the Central Association of German Citizens of Jewish Faith Eva Reichmann, who had fled to Great Britain in 1939 eventually to become the first post-war director of research at the Wiener Library. Underlining the connections between the trials of Nazi-era crimes and the wider critical discourse on the past that was emerging at this time, the other participants included Attorney General for Hesse Fritz Bauer and Henry Ormond, the lawyer and co-plaintiff in the Auschwitz trial.[6] The congress was opened with a public lecture by Walther Hofer, on 'Fatherland – Powerful Past, Fulfillable Future?'; the closed workshops focused on 'Ideological Stereotypes and Exemplary Models as Forms of Social Integration', 'Archetypes and Tabus in their Effects on the Social Structure' and 'Historical Interpretation and Self-Understanding in the Nineteenth and Twentieth Centuries'; the succession of evening podium discussions, meanwhile, which were open to the public at large, took as their themes, 'What does Auschwitz have to do with the "German Person"?', 'What Remained to Us? Two Hundred Years of German Cultural and Intellectual History', 'Germany – Revisited' and 'The Future of Democracy in Germany'. A closing public podium event on the final day heard summary reports from the three closed workshops and offered a plenary discussion on the theme of 'Prejudice – Role Models – Political Responsibility'.

The degree of critical tone in the lectures, papers and discussions varied, reflecting the nature of the mid-1960s as an extended moment of transition between, on the one hand, the customary inherited view of Nazism which regarded it as an aberration in an otherwise healthy history and, on the other, the new, more critical attitude which saw it as a culmination of problematic longer-term developments. Similarly, some papers and discussions made only marginal reference to the Holocaust, while others took it as the central, defining problem of modern German history. Some, especially those which took the longer historical perspective, were striking for the extent to which they avoided discussion of the awkward specificities, or gave an account of the history of intellectual currents that was disconnected from the ongoing competition for power between the conflicting interests in German society. Others, however, were more willing to consider the challenging questions of institutional and individual intent and agency in the recent German past.

The less radical voices in this context included Walther Hofer's opening lecture, which traced the vicissitudes of German national history and the difficulties of finding a stable modus vivendi in Germany's relationship with Europe before calling for the rediscovery of a positive, acceptable national identity rooted in a commitment to liberal institutions and the constitutional state. In his insistence that nationalism had been 'perverted' by the racist ideology of Nazism and his reference to the 'corruption of the national idea by National Socialism' he spoke for those who continued to assume that there was nothing inherently problematic in either nationalism or the longer historical trajectories of the German nation-state. Similarly, Hans Schwerte's

---

[6] For a full list of the participants see Glaser, *Haltungen und Fehlhaltungen*, 197–203; for the characteristics of the generation of intellectuals, journalists and activists who dominated the roster, see Hodenberg, *Konsens und Krise*, 229ff.; Moses, *German Intellectuals and the Nazi Past*.

summary of the findings of his workshop's discussion of ideological stereotypes confined itself to the uncontentious assertion that 'the Germans must
learn to deal with the so-called other, the so-called alien . . .' and that 'the
German must – like every other people – free himself from the generations-
long processes of deffamation . . . [that] so-and-so and so-and-so "is bad" by
nature, simply because of his nationality, race, colour, religion, confession,
because of his appearance and character. . . .'[7] Like much of the discussion at
the congress and in the published proceedings, it gave the impression that
recent German history had been characterised by an unfortunate excess of
prejudice, but offered no meaningful analysis of genocide. Moreover, while
the universalising emphasis of its rejection of prejudice in favour of humanity
was hard to dispute, it largely sidestepped the specific challenges the historical
fact of Auschwitz posed to an overwhelmingly German audience. (The great
irony, of course, was that, of all the participants, Hans Schwerte was in a
unique position to offer a much closer analysis: years later it transpired that
'Hans Schwerte' – by now Rector of the Technical University at Aachen – was
in fact the former SS man Hans Ernst Schneider, who had been a leading functionary of the SS-*Ahnenerbe* during the war and had assumed a false identity
after the collapse of the Third Reich.)[8]

Others, however, were at once more specific and more challenging, testifying to the greater prominence being gained by those who sought a more
rigorous debate about the origins and implications of Nazism. The summary
account to the public of the workshop on 'Historical Interpretation and Self-
Understanding in the Nineteenth and Twentieth Centuries', for example,
offered an open critique of the nationalist proclivities of the academic historical profession, the ease with which it accommodated itself to Nazism and its
willingness to provide the regime with legitimating narratives of German
history. Most indicative of the emergent new sensibility, however, and most
revealing of the extent to which the Frankfurt Auschwitz trial fed wider public
debate about the Nazi past, was the open podium discussion, 'What does
Auschwitz have to do with the "German Person"?' The participants in this
were Holocaust survivor H.G. Adler and Attorney General for Hesse Fritz
Bauer, the journalists Horst Krüger and Dietrich Strothmann, and the
academics Ernst Weymar and – ironically once more – Hans Schwerte.

Before a packed auditorium, in an atmosphere described by the *Nürnberger
Nachrichten* as 'gripping and enthralling', these individuals debated the implications of the Holocaust against the background of the ongoing trial.[9] The

---

[7] Glaser, *Haltungen und Fehlhaltungen*, 45.
[8] Helmut König, W. Kuhlmann, K. Schwabe (eds), *Vertuschte Vergangenheit. Der Fall Schwerte
und die NS-Vergangenheit der deutschen Hochschulen* (Munich, 1997).
[9] 'Herrenmenschen und ihre willfährigen Büttel', *Nürnberger Nachrichten*, 27.4.65.

perspectives were as varied as the participants. In direct contradiction of the image of Auschwitz as a sealed, separate space conveyed cumulatively by the trial proceedings, H.G. Adler insisted that while Auschwitz had been 'a "most extreme" camp, "extreme" in every sense', it had to be seen 'in the context of all the other concentration camps and also in context with the *Einsatzgruppen* and with the brutality of the Gestapo and the SS'.[10] Bauer, meanwhile, opined that while he saw the problem as one which affected all human beings, and not just Germans, it still demanded that those present 'see the Hitler in ourselves, in the German person and to question which elements in our history, perhaps, led to Auschwitz'.[11] Schwerte, for his part, discussing the issue of Germans' alleged propensity to follow orders as the product of an authoritarian political culture, argued that 'if one knows the ideology of the Germanic master race then one sees that this is no longer a question of duty for duty's sake, but the fulfilment of a quite specific sense of mission'. This implicit acknowledgement of the degree of voluntarist participation in Nazism born of ideological commitment was, again, a considerable departure from the insistence on the presence of totalitarian domination which had characterised the 1950s. There followed a discussion of the nature of the perpetrators currently in the dock in Frankfurt. Krüger sought to grapple with the challenge posed by the completely different mental and moral frameworks of the defendants, while Strothmann offered the provocative assertion that 'Auschwitz is theoretically possible in the whole world, but practically possible in Germany' because of the nature of German people, and claimed that 'no new type of German has emerged in the Auschwitz trial . . . it is an old German and a German who will always be there'.[12] Strothmann's essentialist, undifferentiated caricature was contradicted, in turn, by Weymar and by Fritz Bauer, who insisted that 'the accused people in the Auschwitz trial are all completely different people'.[13]

The significance of the discussion, in any case, lay less in its precise content than in the fact that it was taking place, in the identities of the participants, and in the modalities of the podium discussion format. Most obviously, the dimension of the Nazi past singularly absent from the dominant narratives of the 1950s – the Holocaust – was now the subject of extensive discussion at a public symposium. Furthermore, a civic memory culture whose operations had conspired to marginalise those voices that had sought to preserve Holocaust memory in the 1950s was now – through the offices of its senior cultural administrators – actively providing a public platform from which they could offer their perspectives. At the same time, a culture which had

[10] Glaser, *Haltungen und Fehlhaltungen*, 107.
[11] Ibid., 107.
[12] Ibid., 114–15.
[13] Ibid., 116.

privileged the pursuit of consensus in the 1950s was now seeking to promote debate, dissent and dialogue in the pursuit of a pluralist society with an engaged, active citizenry. Here, discussion of the failings of the past connected directly to critiques of the allegedly excessive conformism and veneration of order in contemporary society. It was, again, Fritz Bauer who made these connections most explicit when he argued that 'without the practice of daily resistance, of resistance against small wrongs, one is not in a position to practice the large-scale resistance, of which, unfortunately, too little use was made in the Third Reich . . . one of the demands must be that criticism and opposition do not appear as a crime, but precisely as the foundation for the struggle for human rights'.[14]

The responses to the congress were mixed. More than one organ commented positively on the considerable public interest generated by the event. The Protestant parish newsletter, for example, observed that 'anyone who knows the lethargy of people today, their unwillingness to engage with difficult or sensitive questions, and their talent for evading such embarrassing memories as those of Auschwitz and the role of German people in it was surprised to see just how many people attended the public lectures . . .'[15] The *Münchener Merkur* acknowledged that '[Glaser] and the Nuremberg public have shown that it is possible to mount something outside the state capital that even the last cultural congresses in Munich have not achieved: connecting serious work in small groups with public communication'.[16] The *Frankfurter Allgemeine Zeitung* observed that 'apart from one moment of hostile barracking in response to an – overly simplistic – remark concerning the relationship between desk perpetrators and the German mentality the public listened willingly and swallowed some bitter pills; there were many young people there'.[17]

Others focused, with varying degrees of cynicism, on the connections between the historical burdens of the city and the motivations for mounting the event. The *Nürnberger Nachrichten* made the most explicit connections, observing that 'the city of Nuremberg is setting out on a new path, in order to step out of the shadows of its past, and at the same time to benefit for the future. The largest scholarly congress within its walls of the post-war years . . . is intended to relieve the former "City of the Reich Party Rallies" of another piece of the political burden which was placed on it during twelve years of National Socialist tyranny.'[18] Meanwhile, its reporting of Hermann Glaser's

[14] Ibid., 118.
[15] 'Wo blieb die Theologie? Eindrücke und Gedanken eines christlichen Zuhörers beim Nürnberger Gespräch', *Nürnberger Evangelisches Gemeindeblatt*, 9.5.65.
[16] StadtAN C 73 I/799, Aus Pressekommentaren zum Nürnberger Gespräch, (undated, 1965).
[17] 'Grosswildjagd im ideologischen Dschungel', *Frankfurter Allgemeine Zeitung*, 5.5.65.
[18] 'Lehren für die Zukunft aus der Vergangenheit', *Nürnberger Nachrichten*, 24./25.4.65.

insistence that 'it is not a question of whitewashing the city' created the illusion of journalistic balance while making reference to an accusation that was clearly in the air. For the Social Democratic party newspaper *Vorwärts*, the subject matter was 'dry' and the participants had talked 'academic hot air'.[19] The *Frankfurter Allgemeine Zeitung* also complained, from its more conservative perspective, of conceptual fuzziness, opining that 'it is hard to say how many different norms past and present German false attitudes were measured against, as the yardsticks, which were often hidden beneath complicated terminology, remained untransparent'.[20] It was, indeed, in its discomfort with the multitude of perspectives on offer, as much as in its rejection of the allegedly undifferentiated critiques of German history at the congress, that its conservative perspective was betrayed.

The congress was also the focus of much criticism and hostility from bourgeois voices within the city council. In deliberations on the future of the congresses, CSU councillor Holzbauer complained that 'the overall theme was too general in our view and on more than one occasion encouraged the participants to offer superficial, one-sided and purely present-centred interpretations in a journalistic manner'. He continued that 'often, for example, it lacked clear conceptualisation, theses were formulated in a very one-sided manner, or blanket judgements were made without opportunity being given to promote opposing theses or to correct, for example, those remarks in the short papers of the working groups which appeared to contradict the findings of research'.[21] Beneath the more generalised accusation of absent scholarly niveau, however, lay a more overtly partisan complaint: as well as drawing its speakers from too narrow a range of disciplines, Holzbauer argued, the congress suffered from the fact that 'the set of speakers was also one-sided from a political and ideological standpoint . . . this congress was a gathering of overwhelmingly extreme left-orientated newspapermen and educationalists'.

Above all, in pointing to the perceived irony that former Jewish citizens and émigrés had had to perform the function of 'contradicting German participants who spoke from the spiritual no-man's-land in which they were unwilling or unable to identify with their own fatherland', Holzbauer reflected the extent to which strong residual national mentalities functioned as a barrier within some bourgeois circles to the self-critical, humanist dialogue which Glaser was seeking to foster. Likewise, FDP councillor Bibel's later wearied request in respect of plans for the 1966 congress that the organisers 'should try to ensure that the blame for all the wrongs in the world is not

---

[19] 'Gespräche in Nürnberg', *Vorwärts*, 12.5.65.
[20] 'Grosswildjagd im ideologischen Dschungel', *Frankfurter Allgemeine Zeitung*, 5.5.65.
[21] StadtAN C 85 III/47, Niederschrift über die 99. Sitzung des Stadtrates, 21.9.65.

always just dumped on the Germans' betrayed a defensiveness within bourgeois circles towards attempts at critical analysis, a defensiveness rooted in the fictitious assertion that such critical engagement had been ongoing for years and was no longer necessary, when it in fact was only just beginning to occur.[22]

Glaser and his co-protagonists were, ultimately, able to resist CSU attempts to place a curatory committee above him – a move evidently designed to influence the congresses in a less critical direction – and a series of subsequent congresses was held each year largely on the model of the first. In 1966 the theme was 'Enlightenment Today'; in 1967 'Cognition and Action'; in 1968 'Opposition in the Federal Republic' and in 1969 'Communication and Participation'. As Glaser's exposé for the 1966 congress made clear, the concept remained that of progress through dialectical exchange between the values of reason and humanism and the reactionary, irrational forces of nationalism. Citing Kant's famous pronouncement that 'Enlightenment is man's release from his self-incurred tutelage', and repeating the associated invocation to 'dare to know', Glaser argued that 'Enlightenment' referred not just to a historical epoch, but also to a constantly desirable state of being. In his words, 'tolerance in the social, religious and political spheres belonged to the watchwords of the Enlightenment. This meant the emancipation of suppressed minorities, the rise of suppressed classes and the overcoming of national barriers. Such a stance is also very necessary in and for our own time, in which world citizenship, pluralism, state citizenship and tolerance are often made impossible by a terrible, quite different reality.'[23]

As the 1966 theme – 'Enlightenment Today' – also made clear, the congresses were motivated by the desire to move from historical analysis to contemporary action: in the words of the exposé, 'While last year's congress was focused on engagement with the most recent past, with the origins and characteristics of National Socialism, this year's congress is focused entirely on the present, although of course historical references will be necessary.' The themes of the individual workshops and lectures did, indeed, become more present- and future-centred with each successive congress. By 1967 it was not just the full title of the congress – 'Cognition and Action – the Present and Future of German Society' – that indicated the fading historical focus of the events. Workshops on 'Science and Politics', 'The Task of Education in

---

[22] StadtAN C 73 I/410, Auszug aus der Niederschrift über die Sitzung des Schul- und Kulturausschusses vom 18.2.66. For further evidence of local conservative criticisms and opposition to the Nuremberg Conversations, see StadtAN C 73 I/410, Johannes Geiger (Junge Union) an Hermann Glaser, 25.4.65; Georg Holzbauer an Hermann Glaser, 1.2.66; S. Rost, 'Die CSU und das zweite Nürnberger Gespräch' in 'Junge Union Nürnberg' (April 1966).

[23] StadtAN C 73 I/410, Bemerkungen zum Thema des Nürnberger Gesprächs (undated, 1966).

Industrial Society' or 'Individual and Society', podium discussions on 'Concepts for a New Education' or 'Concepts for a New Bureaucracy', and seminars on 'The Citizen and the Parties', 'The Citizen and the Justice System', 'The Citizen and the Federal Armed Forces', 'The Citizen and the Churches' or 'The Citizen and the Press' showed the increasingly contemporary pedagogical agenda that underpinned the congresses.

Indeed, while the historical assumptions of the congresses continued to be shaped by notions of the German past as ongoing conflict between reason and romanticism, discussions at the congresses of romantic protest against modernity, democracy or post-national agendas increasingly centred on the contemporary challenge of the NPD as much as on the historical problem of Nazism itself.[24] Similarly, by 1968 it was the allegedly undemocratic situation caused by the presence in Bonn of the Great Coalition between the Christian Democratic Union of Germany (CDU) and SPD, rather than historical consideration of Nazism, which drove discussion of resistance, its necessity and possibility. The planning exposé for that year's congress argued that 'there is increasing concern at the lack of opposition and oppositional possibilities in the Federal Republic. The Great Coalition has made this question particularly clear in the parliamentary sphere'; it continued that 'in the realms of public and cultural life contradiction, conflict and controversy are often defamed as damaging or suppressed as unwanted. Extra-parliamentary forms of protest and opposition have become expressions of this disquiet over harmonisation in the interests of the establishment.'[25]

If explicitly historical themes were largely absent from the agendas of subsequent congresses, however, their deliberations were very much informed by historical assumptions concerning Nazism and the failings of Germany's democratic traditions. Moreover, the evolving political context of the mid- to late 1960s – shaped as it was by the rise of the NPD, the presence of the Great Coalition, the formulation of the emergency laws and the presence of an ex-Nazi party member as Chancellor of the Federal Republic – made the drawing of distinct boundaries between discussion of the present and discussion of the past next to impossible. At the same time, those lectures and contributions which did take historical themes as their focus testified to the evolution of a more stridently critical tone over the course of the mid- and late 1960s.

The extent to which progressive critical agendas at the time were shaped by an understanding of past and present forms of authoritarianism or illiberalism which drew little conceptual distinction between the two was shown, for example, by the opening lecture of the 1966 congress. While a year previously Walther Hofer had spoken in favour of drawing upon positive national tradition, Waldemar Besson, of the Institute of Political Science at the University of

---

[24] On the NPD see below, Chapter IV.4.
[25] LKAN Kd Nbg 140, Vorläufiges Exposé: Das Nürnberger Gespräch 1968 (undated).

Constance, offered a set of reflections on 'Germany between Romanticism and Rationalism' which argued before a broad public the outlines of the 'Special Path' thesis of German history that was then gaining ground among academics. Basing his critique of the German bourgeoisie's alleged historical inability to turn its economic power into political influence on Max Weber's analysis of Wilhelmine Germany offered in his 1895 Freiburg inaugural lecture, and on Werner Sombart's arguments that the German bourgeoisie had become 'feudalised' in the nineteenth century, he argued that 'it is not difficult to recognise that the arrested political emancipation of the German bourgeoisie in the nineteenth century marked the point at which the German special path compared to west Europe finally branched off'.[26] For Besson, however, this was not merely a historical problem, but also one of contemporary politics. From here, he offered the question: 'Let us ask . . . if we can still say today that the Federal Republic, the German state which re-emerged after 1945, has inherited the old conflicts and discrepancies, and that we have again today a socially modern but spiritually reactionary Germany.'[27] While it first seemed that, in comparison to the post-1918 years, West Germany had successfully embraced western liberal values, 'Today it appears to us that our assumptions of a secure democratic achievement were too optimistic.'[28] In Besson's view, West German political culture still suffered from a number of weaknesses, not least of which was the 'ongoing power of authoritarian values'.[29] This linked, in turn, to current debates surrounding reunification, the legality of the Munich Agreement of 1938 or the status of the Oder-Neisse line, debates that were 'marked by a dangerous irrationalism which can easily join up with a revisionist subcurrent and a nationalist irredenta'.[30]

If, meanwhile, developments had reached the point where local progressive cultural activists could mount an event such as the Nuremberg Conversations and provide a forum in which the past could be critically debated, the ongoing dynamic of this liberalising political culture and the more radical forms of protest politics it was starting to spawn were such that by 1967 even more challenging historical and contemporary viewpoints could be articulated.[31] In his lecture on 'Authority and Freedom', Holocaust survivor Jean Améry spoke openly of the 'immense majority of all Germans for whom a world collapsed on the announcement of Hitler's death' before calling for 'a radical change in relations of power and property' and the pursuit of freedom through the

---

[26] Glaser, *Aufklärung heute*, 17.
[27] Ibid., 21.
[28] Ibid., 25.
[29] Ibid., 27.
[30] Ibid., 30.
[31] On the emergence of a radical counter-public in the late 1960s, see Hodenberg, *Konsens und Krise*, 361–439.

'struggle against power and authority'.[32] Again, the offer of a platform to a concentration camp survivor on which to discuss the social and ideological consensus that had underpinned fascist rule in Germany marked a gesture unthinkable even at the start of the decade; the political arguments with which Améry's historical analysis were entwined showed how far memory politics were mutually implicated with the ideological ferment of the protest cultures of the 1960s more generally.[33]

That the Nuremberg Conversations quickly became an established feature of the local cultural landscape is shown by the overall attendances for the events, which rose from 4,400 in 1965 to 5,250 in 1968.[34] A more detailed breakdown of attendances for the 1966 congress gives a greater insight into the possible extent and nature of the impulses the congresses sent into local civil society. The evening lectures generated audiences of between 550 and 1,220, while the seminars achieved attendances between 20 and 80.[35] Of the 300 individuals who attended such seminars, 77 were teachers or lecturers, 34 came from other academically related professions and 78 were students; the remainder of the attendees was distributed, a handful at a time, between other liberal and caring professions, artists, journalists and a few blue- and white-collar workers and housewives.[36] In other words, while the lectures immediately reached a broader interested audience, the most likely impact of the seminars was through the initiatives developed subsequently within the local educational establishment and implemented over time.

From the late 1950s onwards, a clear shift had taken place in the memory culture of the Federal Republic, which reproduced itself, with local inflexions, in Nuremberg. In retrospect – if not necessarily at the time – this marked the onset of the decisive move away from a set of dominant narratives which privileged, in various ways, notions of German victimhood and marginalised the racial dimensions of the Nazi past. In some cases, the decisive impetus towards greater critical engagement with the crimes of the past was forced from outside; in other cases local actors collaborated with colleagues and institutions from outside of the city to ensure that the new critical impulses did not stop short of Nuremberg's city walls but echoed within them too; in yet other cases local memory activists launched initiatives that sent impulses back out into the wider culture of the Federal Republic.

This transition is only inadequately and incompletely described if one characterises it as a simple linear shift from 'silence' to 'noise' or from 'evasion' to

[32] Glaser, *Erkennen und Handeln*, 58–9.
[33] Gassert and Steinweis, *Coping with the Nazi Past*.
[34] LKAN Kd Nbg 140, Fünf Jahre Nürnberger Gespräch. Bilanz-Ende-Neuer Anfang, 11.4.69.
[35] StadtAN C 73 I/410, Statistik, Nürnberger Gespräch 1966 (undated, 1966).
[36] StadtAN C 73 I/410, Teilnehmer an den Seminaren nach Berufsgruppen (undated, 1966).

'confrontation'. As the trials of Nazi-era crimes showed, interest waxed and waned, while images of the perpetrators generated by the trials and their reportage offered ordinary citizens ample opportunity to demonise Nazi murderers and distance themselves from them. In the case of exhibitions, there was a similar tendency to stress the 'otherness' of the perpetrators relative to ordinary citizens, and to re-emphasise both the separateness of the spaces in which the crimes had been committed and the status of the local as a space in which decency and humanity were preserved. As the pedagogy of radical humanism pursued in the Nuremberg Conversations also amply demonstrated, local memory activists, including partisan political actors allied to the locally hegemonic SPD, continued to seek modes of engaging the Nazi past which demonstrated cognisance of the ethical problems Nazi-era crimes represented but which did not challenge too directly the fragile consensus forged in the 1950s. As local political and cultural elites responded to the unpalatable truths with which the new discourse challenged them – indeed, as they helped to push forward the new, critical discourse themselves – they continued to seek narrative frameworks through which the most explosive potential of the new impulses could be successfully contained.

What was also striking about the Nuremberg Conversations, finally, and most significant when assessing the nature and extent of their impact upon the memory culture of the city, was the extent to which their protagonists knew themselves to be acting in the face of resistance. In writing in the foreword to the published edition of the first congress of the need to question traditions and so find the way to a progressive future, Glaser acknowledged that 'whoever does this opens himself up increasingly to the reproach of national masochism. Some of the protagonists of the Restoration are developing – irrespective of the facts, and working with the usual falsifiers' methods – a campaign of defamation, in which they appeal implicitly to "healthy" national sentiment and characterise the "commotional overcoming of the past" [*Bewältigungsrummel*] as self-mutilation . . .'[37] Such comments reproduced themselves, indeed, in various forms across the local political culture in the 1960s, and were constantly voiced by those seeking to foster a more open discussion of the problematic Nazi past. In March 1965, for example, the Protestant parish newsletter reproduced remarks of State Bishop Hanns Lilje on the trials of Nazi-era crimes, the Statute of Limitations and justice which referred to 'the dangerous relativisation of the consciousness of right and wrong, still tangible today in the German people'.[38]

Such remarks were not merely rhetorical foils setting the authors' own arguments into contrapunctal relief. They were telling acknowledgements of

[37] Glaser, *Haltungen und Fehlhaltungen*, 8.
[38] 'Gerechtigkeit muß glaubwürdig sein', *Nürnberger Evangelisches Gemeindeblatt*, 7.3.65.

the many small resistances to the new impulses that were starting to resonate through Nuremberg's memory culture in the 1960s, and a reminder that the shifts in the public discourse on the past of the Federal Republic did not just happen of their own accord, but had to be pushed through in a constant succession of concrete efforts in local, specific contexts. They remind, simultaneously, that there were extensive cultural spaces into which the new discourse did not intrude, and numerous milieus in which the new impulses gained little, if any, traction. The ongoing presence of these forms the subject of the last section of this book.

IV

Nationalist Residues in a Decade of Flux

Old Responses, 1958 to 1968

IV. 1

The 'Victims of War' (i)
The Soldiers' Last Retreat

Just because things are not new it does not mean that they are not there. Despite the radical transformation of post-war West Germany's landscapes – from fields of ruins to flourishing cities – and despite the attendant transformation of most ordinary West German citizens' standards of living over the two decades following 1945, the impact of the war continued to be felt by large numbers of those citizens old enough to have been affected by it. Similarly, despite the new challenges which emerged in the 1960s to the fragile memory consensus as it had evolved over the 1950s, broad sections of the community continued to imagine their shared and individual pasts in a manner largely consistent with that developed in the previous decade.[1]

Such continuities were underpinned, at least in part, by residual hostility to Jews, by more general forms of national narcissism that prevented adequate contemplation of the sufferings of those seen as 'other', or by the persistence of less obviously ideological habits of stubbornness and indifference. But they were also rooted in the ongoing physical, psychological and emotional shocks of the war itself. In 1965, for example, twenty years after the end of the war, the *Kriegsopfer-Rundschau*, which was published in Nuremberg and had a strong local base, published the following reader's letter – from a war veteran from Ingolstadt – in which he shared his experience of being visited by a former comrade who, like him, had lost a foot during the war: 'When I complained that I constantly suffer from having one cold foot my comrade sent me to the Terme company in Ingolstadt. There they were immediately willing to sell me a single felt shoe! This is really the kind of accommodating attitude that one does not meet every day. Why should one always have to buy a pair of felt shoes

[1] On the longevity of modes of remembrance established during the 1950s, compare Thießen, 'Das Gedächtnis der Stadt', 193ff.

when one only needs one shoe ... I would be pleased if I can help some comrades with this tip.'[2] For all that certain shifts in the public discourse on the past encouraged *Heimkehrer* to reconsider the events in which they had participated, a missing limb such as this represented a constant mnemonic prompt, functioning as a strong counterweight to calls to think differently: the irreversible permanence of such an absence on the very body of the self translated into a fixity in the autobiographical imagination that defied emerging calls to consider oneself as a perpetrating agent of genocidal war.

Similarly, in October 1962, nearly seven years after the return of the last surviving prisoners of war from the Soviet Union had closed down the subject of the 'missing' as a prominent topic of concern, the *Kriegsopfer-Rundschau* published a letter from Hamburg asking, 'Who knows something of the fate of Alfred Hütt, born 9.1.1924 in Birkenmühle, East Prussia ... Missing since 10.10.1944 south-east of Warsaw', accompanying details of his military post numbers with the plaintiff plea that 'his father, now 80 years old, would much like to hear something of his son'.[3] Such letters remind us that, on the level of the individual family, memories of the war continued to be shaped by the experience of bereavement, or by the ongoing absence of news. The continued focus in both religious and secular organs on the creation of official war graves, both at home and abroad during the 1960s, suggests that desire for knowledge of the final resting place of loved ones, and the need to believe in an orderly burial, remained strong.[4] Indeed, relative prosperity now afforded some the possibility of undertaking journeys to such locations which the chaos and hardship of the immediate post-war years had rendered impossible, permitting the satisfaction of emotional need and the simultaneous re-enactment of the role of 'war victim'.[5]

At the same time as such 'war victims' were demonstrating their imperviousness to calls to remember the Holocaust, voices from within their milieu were calling with increasing intensity for ordinary West Germans to remember the war. In 1962, for example, in its reflections on the Day of National Mourning for

---

[2] *Kriegsopfer-Rundschau*, Aug./Sept. 1965.

[3] *Kriegsopfer-Rundschau*, October 1962.

[4] See, for example, 'Im Tode vereint', *Kriegsopfer-Rundschau*, Aug./Sept. 1965; on the inauguration of the German war cemetery at Costermano in Italy, see 'Heimatrecht in fremder Erde', *Kriegsopfer-Rundschau*, June 1967; 'Nach dem Schlaf wird die Nacht vorbei sein. Flug zu den Soldatengräbern in italienischer Erde', *Nürnberger Evangelisches Gemeindeblatt*, 20.10.61; 'In langen Reihen steh'n die Kreuze. Deutsche Kriegsgräber auf Sizilien und Sardinien', *Nürnberger Evangelisches Gemeindeblatt*, 18.11.62.

[5] More than 1,100 relatives 'from all parts of the Federal Republic' attended the inauguration of the Munich cemetery, for example ('Im Tode vereint'); in the case of Costermano, 'The more than 10,000 relatives who came to the inauguration in Costermano on 6 May 1967 found consolation in the certainty that their loved ones had found a dignified resting place here.' ('Heimatrecht in fremder Erde'); for the linking of narratives of tourist travel to the pursuit of emotional (and spiritual) peace, see 'Nach dem Schlaf'.

that year, the Protestant Church's newsletter stated that 'our generation has experienced terrible things; our young people can often not grasp that some of us still
suffer from this and become pensive on such a day'.[6] A space for such warnings
had already opened up in the 1950s, as commentators concerned at the alleged
superficiality of modern consumer life admonished those apparently given solely
to enjoying the pleasures of the moment to remember the difficulties faced by
those who had not made such an easy transition to peacetime. But in the 1960s
this space widened; for a while, the voices which filled it became perceptibly more
shrill. Underlying this was a growing perception among those who continued to
classify themselves as 'victims of war' of their own increasing marginality, both
demographically and politically. This sense of marginalisation, however exaggerated it may have been initially, was exacerbated by the challenges emerging in the
1960s to existing narratives of wartime sacrifice, narratives which were now
starting to appear as rather fragile artifices. Alongside the dialogue between
remembering and forgetting the Holocaust which was opening up in the 1960s,
therefore, a parallel set of arguments emerged which, far from focusing primarily on Jewish experiences, hardly featured Jews at all, and which turned, instead,
on the demands of one generation of Germans that their suffering and sacrifice
during the war be remembered by an increasingly ignorant, indifferent or downright hostile younger one.[7]

Both the continuities of this still widespread discourse of German war victimhood and its growing fragility and sense of marginality can be seen in the
activities of the war victims' and veterans' associations in the 1960s, as well as
in the memorials established to mark their suffering, which – paradoxically at
first sight – were just as numerous as in the previous decade. The *Heimkehrer*
and regimental associations, the disabled sports associations and the war
victims' associations constituted an interlocking milieu of political activism,
therapeutic support, sociability and reminiscence whose bonds were –
internal disputes notwithstanding – strengthened by their slow retreat from
public prominence; if the meeting of their demands for additional memorials
marked, on the surface, an apparent reinforcement of the existing memory
culture of the city, it also provided spaces in which surviving members of
this milieu could commemorate their dead in the face of an increasingly
indifferent wider public.

The activities of the Nuremberg branch of the BDKK, for example, remained
much the same in the 1960s as they had been in the 1950s, a change of name
to the League of German War Victims (Bund Deutscher Kriegsopfer – BDK)

---

[6] 'Versöhnung, Friede, Menschlichkeit', *Nürnberger Evangelisches Gemeindeblatt*, 18.11.62.
[7] On perceptions of generational difference among war veterans, see Kühne, ' "Kameradschaft" ',
526.

notwithstanding. It continued to report on developments relating to pensions and compensation for war victims, paying particular attention to the issues of war widows' and parents' pensions, in which it saw a particular injustice.[8] Its caseworkers continued to help members complete applications for pensions or pursue appeals against the welfare authorities. It continued to organise social events on occasions such as Mother's Day.[9] Its newspaper carried articles on the progress of the disabled sports association with which it was linked and on the development of prosthetic limb technology.[10] On occasion its members joined those of other chapters to celebrate the inauguration of a branch's new banner, or with other war veterans to participate in protest marches, including the major 1963 *Heimkehrer* protest march in Bonn.[11] Likewise, it continued its close association with the League for the Care of German War Graves. The League regularly attended its meetings, providing slide shows or films on the League's ongoing activities, which reaffirmed for the BDK's members that 'still today many thousands of fallen comrades cannot be located, so that their whereabouts remain unknown for their relatives'.[12] For the BDK's activists, the situation of such relatives demanded both the continued remembrance of the dead and the honouring of wartime bonds through help to surviving dependants in need; this help was construed as a higher moral act which renewed the spirit of soldierly sacrifice and comradeship as a positive ethical standard for peacetime. As the Nuremberg branch's welfare officer put it following a show mounted by the League for the Care of German War Graves in 1961, such reminders of the past were simultaneously a call 'that we participate in united fashion in the honouring of our fallen at the forthcoming Day of National Mourning', while 'precisely because of this it is our noblest task to help the relatives and current war victims'.[13]

In most respects, indeed, the language, self-image and self-display of the organisation remained the same. Its members continued to refer to one another as 'comrade'; in its use of the iron cross, steel helmet and oak leaves its letterhead remained beholden to a national-conservative visual idiom; its members regularly referred to the Day of National Mourning as Heroes' Remembrance Day; similarly, the official song of the national BDK organisation – emphasising as it did terms such as 'faith', 'nation', 'fatherland', 'comradeship', 'loyalty' and 'action'

[8] See, for example, StadtAN E 6/601/217, Mitgliederversammlung vom 3.3.61; 21. Ausschuss-sitzung vom 12.9.61; Mitgliederversammlung vom 9.11.61; 9. Ausschusssitzung, 8.6.65.
[9] StadtAN E 6/601/217, Minute, 8.5.59.
[10] See, for example, 'Sie gaben ein Beispiel für uns alle!', *Kriegsopfer-Rundschau*, Oct. 1962; 'Von der eisernen Hand des Götz von Berlichingen zur bioelektrischen Hilfe. Entwicklung moderner Prosthesen', *Kriegsopfer-Rundschau*, Nov. 1966.
[11] StadtAN E 6/601/217, Ausschusssitzung am 9.4.63; Ausschusssitzung, 14.5.63.
[12] StadtAN E 6/601/217, Mitgliederversammlung vom 9.11.61.
[13] StadtAN E 6/601/217, Mitgliederversammlung vom 9.11.61; in very similar vein, see also Mitgliederversammlung, 9.11.62 in the same file.

– drew on a lexicon of terms closely associated with national-conservative ideology and mentalities.[14]

The rhetoric accompanying its campaigning activism also adapted arguments familiar from the 1950s. By the late 1960s, it was, it is true, no longer foregrounding the suffering of its members in the war. Instead, it emphasised the shared successes of all in the achievement of reconstruction, rehearsing the standard myths of the post-war years regarding its causes: 'In the years following the complete collapse the Federal Republic of Germany has experienced an exceptional economic upswing, thanks not least to the industriousness and hard work of the German people.' Yet the peculiar claims which followed from this were recognisably the same as those made in the 1950s. As in the 1950s, the specific experience of the war victims in this shared history endowed a prior claim to assistance. For, while all had contributed to reconstruction, not all could enjoy its ameliorating benefits in the same way: 'The disabled and surviving relatives among our people from two world wars have helped, as far as it was in their power, to ensure that flourishing cities emerged once more from the fields of ruins and that the terrible traces of catastrophic destruction gradually fade. Those traces which the war has left on them, however, can no longer be obliterated. The emotional pain and the physical complaints, the loss of relatives and the loss of limbs and health cannot be overcome even in the face of economic flourishing and prosperity.' It continued, therefore, to base its claims to privileged recognition on the assertion that the suffering of the war victims was of a different moral quality. In its words, 'the sacrifice of the disabled and the surviving relatives was based not on serving one's own cause, but solely on service to the community. Every attempt to describe as "group interests" the welfare claim of the war victims, which is inextricably linked with their sacrifice of life and health, must be decisively opposed.'

In its assertions that 'recognition of the peculiar moral achievement of the soldier's sacrifice is the foundation of dignified welfare', the BDK demonstrated its awareness of the ongoing need to project conventional narratives of the soldiers' role in the Second World War if it was to press the claim for improved welfare rights successfully.[15] This went hand in hand with a continued proclivity to assert the soldiers' victim status in a manner which denied the more awkward dimensions of the war and the soldiers' agency within it. Meanwhile, critical juxtapositions of the welfare payments made to BDK members with those made to the victims of fascism continued to

[14] StadtAN E 6/601/49, '20 Jahre Bund Deutscher Kriegsopfer. Landesverband Bayern e.V.'; see also Kühne, 'Zwischen Vernichtungskrieg und Freizeitgesellschaft', 110.
[15] On the complex archaeology of this rhetoric see Greg Eghigian, 'Pain, Entitlement and Social Citizenship in Modern Germany' in Betts and Eghigian, *Pain and Prosperity*, 16–34.

imply a strongly relativising understanding of the different kinds of suffering endured in the Second World War. In 1962, for example, the chairman complained that 'a 30 per cent disabled war veteran receives a pension of 35 DM, in contrast to someone who is 30 per cent disabled as a result of an accident, who gets 86 DM for the same physical damage, while a victim of National Socialism gets for the same physical damage 126 DM!'[16]

In other respects, however, the rhetoric of the BDK took on a new quality in the 1960s, implicit in which was a recognition of the increasingly fragile purchase of its moral claims within the broader community. It bespoke a self-perception of the slow, but unmistakeable marginalisation of the war victims in the wider competition for public acknowledgement and the distribution of resource. If the relativising comparisons with the victims of Nazism betrayed a wilful blindness to the realities of Nazi genocide, other comparisons revealed a more inchoate moral anger rooted in the sense that changing social values were preventing recognition of their justified demands. At a meeting in 1962, for example, the chairman complained that 'in the last half year over half a billion Deutschmarks were saved from the war victims in the Federal budget. Against this there is always money for so-called foreign aid to underdeveloped countries – apparently at our expense too!'[17] At a similar meeting the welfare officer claimed indignantly that 'compared to the money spent on so-called development aid to Negro princes [*Negerfürsten*] our demands are really neither excessive nor unrestrained and our resentment and disappointment ought surely to be understandable and apprehensible!'[18] In similar vein the longstanding BDK functionary, Karl Langfritz, claimed in the *Kriegsopfer-Rundschau* that 'those who sacrificed life and health for the fatherland have gone from the shadows of the economic miracle to the shadows of the defence budget and international aid'.[19]

These criticisms, in turn, were wrapped up in a yet more general anger, the focus of which was more the Adenauer government than those other groups with whom the BDK activists compared themselves. Indeed, for all their occasional polemics against the victims of Nazism or the recipients of international aid, at the root of the BDK's shrill rhetoric lay not so much hostility to these other groups as bitterness at the perceived failure of the government to allow it to share adequately in the fruits of reconstruction. In meeting after meeting in the 1960s, its speakers asserted that 'we war victims have not participated in the economic miracle, but have come away empty-handed', or that 'we are still

---

[16] StadtAN E 6/601/217, Protokoll zur Generalversammlung vom 14.9.62; for a similar example see StadtAN E 6/601/217, Mitgliederversammlung am 13.9.63; see also Mitgliederversammlung am 8.11.1963.
[17] StadtAN E 6/601/217, Mitgliederversammlung am 29.6.62.
[18] StadtAN E 6/601/217, Protokoll zur Generalversammlung vom 14.9.62.
[19] 'Im Zeichen der Landeswahlen', *Kriegsopfer-Rundschau*, Oct 1962.

the ones who have been deceived'.[20] Such remarks embodied the tone of a populist anti-governmentalism of the Right for which 'Bonn' signified an uncaring government inhabited by politicians whose own comforts blinded them to the problems of war victims living in modest circumstances. The right-wing oppositionalism of the BDK's protest-driven politics, despite its claims to impartiality, was reflected in the fact that its chairman stood as a candidate for the *Gesamtdeutsche Partei* in Federal and state elections in the early 1960s.[21]

The frustrations evident in such anti-government polemics were compounded by a growing sense of the organisation's own decline from the early 1960s onwards. Internal disputes in the late 1950s had culminated in a split and had led to a loss of membership. While attendance at individual meetings fluctuated, the general pattern was one of declining participation in the 1960s. Although there were occasional complaints in the early 1960s of an inactive committee, the problem was, if anything, the opposite: one of a small group of committed activists ploughing on in the face of slow organisational decline.[22] The great majority of the 1,500 or so members of the Nuremberg branch were clearly entirely passive by this point. In his overview of the year's activities in 1960 the chairman recorded that 'the meetings were poorly attended'.[23] Similar criticisms were levelled in 1961 at members' failure to attend the city's commemorative ceremony on 2 January.[24] Around the same time, the welfare officer was complaining that 'even today it is a particularly fortunate thing if members can be found who are ready to volunteer to work unselfishly for their comrades and for their well-being';[25] shortly thereafter the same person bemoaned the 'sad fact of the general reluctance to turn up, especially on public occasions'.[26] This was apparently mirrored in a growing failure to impress upon the general public the concerns of the organisation: in 1962, for example, the annual Bavarian War Victims Collection produced – in the opinion of the chairman – a 'disgraceful' result.[27] Such adjectives reflected

---

[20] StadtAN E 6/601/217, Mitgliederversammlung vom 29.6.62; Mitgliederversammlung vom 9.11.61.
[21] StadtAN E 6/601/217, 20. Ausschusssitzung vom 8.8.61; Mitgliederversammlung 9.11.62. The *Gesamtdeutsche Partei* was formed in April 1961 as a shortlived fusion of the *Deutsche Partei* and the *Gesamtdeutsche Block*/BHE, both now fringe protest formations of the political Right. See Richard Stöss (ed.), *Parteienhandbuch. Die Parteien der Bundesrepublik Deutschland 1945–1980* (Opladen, 1984), vol. 2: *FDP bis WAV*, 1460–77.
[22] For complaints of inactivity see StadtAN E 6/601/217, 8. Ausschusssitzung am 5.9.60; for evidence of declining membership and attendance by the late 1960s, see StadtAN E 6/601/218, Niederschrift über die am 29.3.68 stattgefundene Vorstandssitzung der Ortsgruppe Nürnberg.
[23] StadtAN E 6/601/217, 12. Ausschusssitzung am 21.12.60.
[24] StadtAN E 6/601/217, 13. Ausschusssitzung vom 11.1.61.
[25] StadtAN E 6/601/217, 21. Ausschusssitzung vom 12.9.61.
[26] StadtAN E 6/601/217, Mitgliederversammlung vom 9.11.61.
[27] StadtAN E 6/601/217, Mitgliederversammlung vom 9.11.62.

the anger of frustrated expectation as much as the objective achievements of the collection itself, but testified all the more eloquently to the BDK's sense that it was not getting the attention it felt it legitimately deserved.

In the face of this decline, the BDK resorted all the more vociferously to demands that the war not be forgotten. In its *Kriegsopferjahrbuch* for 1960 an account of the bombing of Hamburg was subtitled 'produced as a serious warning for all those who today have already forgotten those terrible years and play frivolously with peace'.[28] Likewise, it justified its publication in 1964 of the account of a former prisoner of war in the Soviet Union with the assertion that 'this book does not wish to tear open wounds which are still far from healed. Rather, it aims to contribute to ensuring that the Passion of the German prisoners of war and thus also the tragic fate of the war victims does not fade all too early into oblivion in the wake of prosperity and comfortable satisfaction.'[29] In 1969, on the occasion of the twentieth anniversary of the organisation's creation, Bavarian CSU Minister President Alfons Goppel – regarded by the BDK as an ally – contributed a formal greeting to the celebratory brochure which lauded the work of the BDK especially because 'in our prosperous society more and more the inclination exists to downplay the selfless deployment in the war, rich in sacrifice, and to allow it to drift into oblivion'.[30]

Such admonitions could not, however, hold up the biological effects of time. If, in the 1950s, meetings were opened with a moment's silence in memory of the war dead, by the late 1960s they included a silence for recently deceased members too. Moreover, as time went on, the emphasis shifted in favour of the latter. In 1966, at a meeting of Mid-Franconian delegates, 'all delegates rose from their seats to remember the fallen and missing of both world wars, and the association members who had died in recent years'.[31] By 1969, the reverse was true: delegates at a similar event 'rose from their seats to remember those comrades who had died since the last regional committee meeting, and also the fallen and missing of both world wars'.[32]

What was true of the BDK also held true for the veterans' associations, although this manifested itself to varying degrees and produced very diverse surface effects. A largely similar retreat from public prominence over the 1960s can be seen in the case of the Association of Former Prisoners of War. Into the early and mid-1960s, the local newsletters of individual suburbs

---

[28] 'Der Tod schritt durch die Stadt', *Kriegsopferjahrbuch 1960*.
[29] 'Vorwort zum 17 Kriegsopferjahrbuch', *Kriegsopferjahrbuch 1964*.
[30] StadtAN E 6/601/49, '20 Jahre Bund Deutscher Kriegsopfer. Landesverband Bayern e.V.'
[31] StadtAN E 6/601/214, Bezirksverband Mittelfranken. Protokoll über die Bezirkstagung des BDK-Bezirkes Mittelfranken am 14.5.66.
[32] StadtAN E 6/601/214, Protokoll über die erweiterte Bezirksausschusssitzung des BDK-Bezirkes Mittelfranken, 30.8.69.

carried advertisements announcing the monthly meetings of the branch in that suburb.[33] In some instances, additional advertisements carried news of annual general meetings.[34] Yet in the mid-1960s the local newsletters generally ceased carrying such advertisements. If the dissolution of the milieu which sustained the association was a long, drawn-out process, it appears that the decline in interest had reached a stage where many suburbs could no longer sustain their own groups; at best, activity was concentrated in fewer larger sections. As with the BDK, an underlying biological logic accounted for some of the decline. More pertinently, the Association of Former Prisoners of War had lost much of its reason for existence following the return of the last prisoners of war in 1956; the absence of an ongoing focal point in the form of the remaining prisoners in the east deprived the organisation of much of its emotional cement. Although it continued to campaign for improved pensions and for compensation for particular groups of *Heimkehrer* hitherto excluded from welfare provision, significant further legislation was not to be expected for the great majority of former prisoners of war. If successive government measures had eroded the campaigning *raison d'être* of the association, meanwhile, the mere fact of shared military service or imprisonment provided insufficient unifying force for a veterans' movement whose members' war experiences had varied widely, and for whom there were more obvious institutional forums for reminiscence.

These were provided by the regimental associations, where the organisation of veterans into groups linked by shared experiences of particular military campaigns continued to provide the basis for a rhetoric of comradeship which had a more substantial basis in past shared experience than similar appeals from the Association of Former Prisoners of War. The activities of these associations varied. The Afrika-Korps Association, for example, continued to focus its commemorative acts on its hero Rommel, and to pursue welfare activities in his name on behalf of needy members. However, from the 1960s onwards its activities evolved into largely apolitical forms of sociability the emphases of which were, even more so than in the 1950s, on celebrations of *Fasching*, Father's Day or Christmas, or on walking trips, as much as on formalised wartime reminiscence. While its literature continued to expound the virtues of chivalry, sacrifice and love of people and fatherland, it emphasised that these included engagement on behalf of the democratic state and that the association had no political agendas.[35]

---

[33] See, for example, StadtAN C 85 I Abg. 94/A90, 'Alt-Mögeldorf: Monatsschrift für Geschichte und Belange Mögeldorfs', 10/1 (1962).
[34] StadtAN C 85 I Abg. 94/A89, 'Langwasser-Kurier: Nachrichtenblatt des Vorstadtvereins', 7/1 (1964).
[35] See, for example, StadtAN E 6/580/1, Chronik des Verbandes Deutsches Afrika-Korps e.V. 1951–1980; also Satzung des Verbandes Deutsches Afrika-Korps e.V. (1972) and Satzung der Rommelsozialwerk e.V. (1972).

A more strident public tone was adopted by the competing regimental associations of the former Infantry Regiment 21, whose relationship to one another had descended into bitter hostility by the 1960s.[36] This manifested itself in the holding of rival meetings; it also manifested itself in disputes over the appropriate siting of regiment-specific war memorials, of which a number were established in the 1960s. It is, indeed, in these regiment-specific war memorials that the complex mix of assertiveness and defensiveness that characterised the voices of the existing 'victim discourse' in the 1960s can best be seen. For, while the small wave of regimental memorials characterising the 1960s marked a superficial efflorescence of a veterans' commemoration culture, it simultaneously bore witness to the underlying process of retreat from public prominence, whereby commemorative acts hitherto performed and shared by a wider public were superseded by smaller, more introspective acts of commemoration participated in largely by the veterans themselves. While, on the surface, the regimental memorials appeared – through their focus on the German war dead – to mark a simple reassertion of the dominant victim discourse of the 1950s, their forms, inscriptions, iconographies and locations, as well as the practices of their usage in the 1960s, signalled the presence of underlying shifts in the public discourse on the past which were slowly eroding the narrative of German military sacrifice and its purchase.

An initial attempt to gain the city council's agreement to establish a memorial to the IR 21 was made in 1959 by one of the two competing regimental associations.[37] While the senior representatives of the FDP and the CSU argued in favour of acceding to the request, the Social Democrats were unenthusiastic. In part this reflected the deeper mental habits of a political tradition that remained suspicious of anything that might be associated with militarism. Yet this was not the main argument. Councillor Kaiser, speaking for the SPD fraction in the council, argued that 'it would be completely fatal if on the Day of National Mourning, for example, the official celebration took place at the memorial while on the other hand – because a plaque had now been put in the barracks [one of the proposed sites] – a further celebration was held by a group. I cannot enthuse about the idea that these celebrations take place among different groups.' Deputy mayor Haas, likewise, warned against the precedent such a plaque would set, arguing that 'if one group is allowed to erect a plaque do we have to assume that the second group of the 21ers will submit a similar request?' Opposition to a proliferation of sites, and

---

[36] See StadtAN C 85 III/397, Niederschrift über die 49. Sitzung des Ältestenrats, 8.5.64; C 85 III/399, Niederschrift über die 69. Sitzung des Ältestenrats, 22.4.66; Niederschrift über die 1. Sitzung des Ältestenrats, 10.6.66.
[37] StadtAN C 85 III/389, Niederschrift über die 55. Sitzung des Ältestenrates am 9.10.59.

the consequences of this, similarly underlay mayor Urschlechter's view that 'I do not think it expedient for such plaques to be distributed around the town, given that we have the monument in the *Luitpoldhain*.'

Attempts over the following years to mediate between the rival groups and to forge consensus over the desirability of one shared memorial, rather than a number of competing regimental monuments, reflected simultaneously an aesthetic objection to the proliferation of such sites, a desire to protect a spirit of piety towards the dead in the face of disputes which were becoming increasingly rancorous, and a forlorn attempt to foster peace between factions of an associational milieu for which the SPD felt at best modest sympathy. Above all, however, moves on the part of the mayor to resolve the conflict and thereby to counter the tendency towards the proliferation of memorials reflected Urschlechter's attempt – in his civic capacity as mayor rather than as a representative of the SPD – to protect the *Luitpoldhain*, the Day of National Mourning and the fragile commemorative consensus that had been built up around these from fragmenting under the challenge of a multitude of competing voices which were inimical to the unity-fostering and identity-endowing function of official acts of remembrance.[38]

Conflicting claims and competing demands were, nonetheless, part of the logic of a pluralist associational life; as those born of the distributional conflicts of the post-war era were smoothed, the workings of the more open, democratic political culture that was evolving in the 1960s ensured that others emerged. As the city council also ultimately recognised, it was not its task to mediate between rival factions or its right to silence the regimental groups' calls for recognition.[39] As a consequence, it agreed in 1966 to the establishment on the *Köpfleinsberg*, in the centre of the city, of a plaque in memory of the fallen and missing soldiers of IR 21, in accordance with one faction of the regimental association.[40]

The plaque itself bore a simple inscription: 'Infantry Regiment 21. To the honourable memory of the fallen and missing comrades of the Nuremberg House Regiment of the War of 1939–1945, and as a warning reminder to the living. Erected in the year 1966 by the regimental association of the IR 21 – the "twenty-oners" '. In its focus on the deaths of the soldiers rather than on their actions, and in its obvious lack of references to the specific political context of the war, it reproduced all the familiar silences of the monuments of the 1950s. The construction of the Second World War as an ordinary war was

---

[38] On the resistance of civic leaders to the fragmentation of the city as a cohesive memory space, see Derix, 'Der Umgang', 274ff.
[39] For the city council's reactions to these disputes see StadtAN C 85 III/399, Niederschrift über die 69. Sitzung des Ältestenrats, 22.4.66; Niederschrift über die 1. Sitzung des Ältestenrats, 10.6.66.
[40] StadtAN C 85 III/399, Beschluss des Ältestenrats, 22.4.66.

additionally reinforced by the site on which the plaque was mounted – on the *Siegessäule* ('Victory Column') erected to commemorate the Franco-Prussian War of 1870 and the subsequent creation of the German Reich. In using this column, to which had already been added a plaque marking Germany's colonial campaigns in China and Africa before the First World War, the IR 21's military campaigns of 1939 to 1945 were placed within a broader narrative of military tradition – itself, ironically, deeply problematic – which elided the differences between different wars and thereby refused acknowledgement of the peculiarities of the latter conflagration.

From the late 1950s and throughout the 1960s a series of similar regimental plaques was mounted on the external wall of the *Johanniskirche*, in the historic Johannis Cemetery to the north-west of the old city. All were highly simple plaques, commemorating the dead and missing of those regiments with a connection to Nuremberg or to its region, and consisting of inscriptions similar to those on the *Köpfleinsberg*. The plaque commemorating the IR 213, one of the 'daughter' regiments of the IR 21, was the first to be established, in 1958; its inscription read '1939–1945. To the fallen and missing of Infantry Regiment 213 of the Second World War in permanent memory. God will wipe away all tears'. With the exception of an iron cross at the head of the plaque and

15. Memorial to Infantry Regiment 213, *Johanniskirche*, Nuremberg (1958).

limited decorative leafing it contained no iconography or insignia, military or otherwise. Likewise, the plaque to IR 351, another 'daughter' regiment of IR 21, which was inaugurated in 1967, read 'to the fallen and missing comrades of the Franconian-Sudeten German Infantry Regiment 351 of the 183 Infantry Division in honourable memory', confining its use of visual imagery to an iron cross; a subsidiary plaque listed the other units in its division.

If the plaque to the 98th Infantry Division, meanwhile, made use of a very similar inscription – 'to the fallen and missing comrades of the Franconian-Sudeten German 98th Infantry Division in honourable memory 1939–1945' – its iconography, while similarly simple, contained a more multilayered set of meanings. At its base stood three crucifixes. On one level they recalled the field graves of soldiers, evoking the attendant pathos which surrounded such images. At the same time they echoed the insignia of the League for the Care of German War Graves, which continued to be part of the associational networks in which the veterans' groups operated. Yet they also had unmistakeable echoes of Calvary, intimating at religious narratives of death and transcendence. While the two secondary crucifixes suggested a more complex set of stories to those who contemplated the memorial's meanings, the most prominent crucifix, whose significance was much more firmly embedded in the cultural knowledge of the average citizen, told stories of innocent sacrifice, or of laying down one's life so that others might live. In the Cold War context of the 1960s, they suggested a narrative of death in defence of the homeland which fitted well with anti-Communist reworkings of the history of the war still prevalent across the political culture of the Federal Republic.[41]

This iconography thus contributed to the continued construction in the 1960s of German soldiers as innocent, noble or heroic victims rather than as perpetrators of a genocidal war of aggression, while the mounting of these plaques on a wall on which comparable monuments to Bavarian regiments had been placed in the interwar years similarly fostered an image of the continuity of healthy military tradition. Yet the obvious differences between those created after the First World War and those created after the Second World War simultaneously indicated an awareness that the verbal and visual idiom deployed to commemorate the earlier conflagration was in many respects inappropriate for the latter.

For one thing, the near-absence of military imagery in the memorials of the post-1945 period stood in stark contrast to those created in the interwar years, in which figurative representations of soldiers, sometimes on horseback, of steel helmets or of weapons were prominent. If the eschewing of visual

---

[41] For the ongoing presence of anti-Communist rhetoric in narratives of wartime sacrifice produced in the 1960s, see, for example, 'Wofür sind unsere Soldaten gefallen?' *Nürnberger Evangelisches Gemeindeblatt*, 17.11.63.

16. Memorial to Infantry Division 98, *Johanniskirche*, Nuremberg (1960s).

imagery suggests a general aesthetic shift away from figurative representation, then the particular absence of the military imagery that had been prominent hitherto bespeaks an awareness of the difficulty of finding the appropriate visual idiom to capture the peculiar histories of the Second World War. Similarly striking was the absence of political cause in the monuments to the Second World War when compared with those to the earlier war. The inscription of the Royal Bavarian *Chevauleger* Regiment, dedicated to the men 'who fell for Kaiser and Reich, King and Fatherland in the World War of 1914–1918', found no counterpart in the inscriptions to those who died in the Second World War. Such silences marked an act of dissociation of the soldiers' deaths from the broader cause for which they had been fighting, testifying implicitly to an awareness that this cause had been anything but honourable.[42] Similarly absent was the language of heroism present in some, although not all, of the First World War monuments: if the veterans' milieu was still not ready to acknowledge openly the historical fact of the genocide, there was clearly sufficient unspoken awareness that a resolutely nationalist idiom was no longer appropriate.

[42] Mosse, *Fallen Soldiers*, 216.

17. Memorial to the Royal Bavarian *Chevauleger* Regiment, *Johanniskirche* (1920s).

What was also striking was the egalitarianism of the monuments to the Second World War – whereas the interwar monuments distinguished between the numbers of officers, junior officers and other ranks who were killed, the monuments of the 1960s privileged the universal language of comradeship, referring, if at all, simply to 'the fallen and missing comrades'. If such linguistic shifts reflected in part the legacies of the Third Reich's levelling ideology of community, the foregrounding of notions of comradely remembrance also implied key distinctions of audience and ownership of the monuments. The First World War monuments were, in cases, explicitly funded by surviving members of the regiment together with the families of the fallen. But as their inscriptions sometimes suggested, their message was intended for a much wider audience. The inscription on the monument to the Royal Bavarian 8th Field Artillery Regiment, for example, closed expressing the hope that 'May Future Generations Never Forget its Acts', explicitly claiming a desire for broad resonance in doing so. The plaques of the 1960s, by contrast, were much more circumspect: their language of comradeship described not only the circle of those being remembered, but also, quite clearly, those doing the remembering. They marked spaces for an altogether more introspective ethos of remembrance in circles of veterans whose growing separateness from the wider community reinforced the increasingly inward-looking culture of their milieu. In this, they also distinguished themselves from the plaques erected in the 1950s in memory of the dead of the Second World War: whereas those of the 1950s listed the entire dead of the community, functioning as focal points for the articulation of grief shared by almost every family, those of the 1960s reflected the far more self-contained memory culture of a slowly dwindling band of veterans. Superficially, the veterans got their way in the 1960s. Underneath, however, they were becoming ever more marginal.

In one obvious respect – in their focus on the German war dead – the regimental monuments of the 1960s reflected the key factor which continued to determine who was regarded as worthy of inclusion among those to be remembered and who was not. For all the competitiveness of the various subsidiary memory cultures in the city, they had largely operated hitherto on the shared assumption that Germanness was a prerequisite for inclusion. Nascent attempts to integrate the Holocaust into public narratives of the war marked one challenge to this; the shift towards acknowledging the war dead of other combatant nations embodied another. However, national ways of thinking continued to act as a barrier to the commemorative embrace of the dead of other nations, especially the foreign victims of Nazi racism. Indeed, the complex interaction of acknowledgement and evasion that characterised the shifting culture of the 1960s, the ongoing presence of pregnant silence in the ostensible moves towards greater critical openness, and the residual presence of national mentalities learned in an earlier age were evident precisely in memory acts that marked an attempt to move beyond the ethnic narcissism which had so strongly shaped the memory culture of the 1950s.

A case in point was the issue of the graves of the thousands of Soviet prisoners of war in the South Cemetery. These had languished, apparently untended, throughout the 1950s in an area of the burial ground that had become a cultural 'dead space' for the majority community, its graves tended for a time only by residents of the Valka refugee camp. In an intimation of the slowly changing sensibilities of the early 1960s, the Protestant parish newsletter published an article to mark the 'Day of the Dead' in 1960 which, for the first time since 1945, made extensive reference to the presence of large numbers of Soviet graves in Nuremberg.[43] The author described how, upon leaving an event attended by 2,000 people, 'I once again walked past the gravestones of the Russian soldiers who died or starved somewhere in German camps between 1941 and 1945.' Contrasting the care given to German war victims' graves with those of the undecorated Soviet graves, he gently admonished the flock for its

---

[43] 'Gott vergißt nicht. Ungeschmückte russische Gräber', *Nürnberger Evangelisches Gemeindeblatt*, 27.11.60.

lack of interest: 'Not one of the two thousand thinks of them, and not one parish or one Protestant youth group.' If the very fact that such an article was published showed that voices were gradually emerging to demand that the ethnic narcissism of the dominant memory culture be overcome, the descriptions of popular indifference to the Soviet graves bore accurate witness to the fact that the history of foreign forced labour remained firmly excluded from all mainstream narratives of the Nazi past in local circulation at this point.

The shared assumption that the Soviet forced workers were excluded from those circles of the dead whom the city was obliged to remember underpinned moves within the city administration to dissolve the graves of the forced labourers in the South Cemetery in 1962. That the issue was addressed in the Law and Economics Committee of the city council underlines the fact that officials saw in this merely an issue of legal procedure, rather than one of moral probity; at the same time, the pragmatic arguments put forward by the relevant official betrayed not just the bureaucracy's own blindness to the ethical issues involved but also a clear sense of the moral frameworks with which the wider public continued to judge such matters. As the official emphasised, 'It relates to about 1,400 graves here in Nuremberg, which have not been properly cared for for years. This will damage the appearance of our cemeteries, unless they are cared for at the city's expense. The means for this are not, however, available. In any case, their slow, ongoing descent into disrepair will cause anger among the public.'[44]

Drawing on the public's perceived desire for neat, orderly cemeteries as justification, he requested that the graves be dissolved, so that they could be reused for other burials in coming years. While a certain bureaucratic logic underpinned the viewpoint of cemetery officials, deputy mayor Haas' support for this proposed act of erasure deployed comparisons with the neglect of German graves to justify a position which was clearly rooted in indifference: 'Haas asked if any relatives had ever paid any attention to the graves in the past. He pointed out that we as Germans also place emphasis on our graves which are located abroad not falling in disrepair, but that the eastern states had refused to care for the graves of Germans who were killed in the war.' The fact that many relatives of the Soviet victims – assuming they had survived the war themselves – might have no knowledge of the whereabouts of their loved ones, and the possibility that distance, poverty and the circumstances of the Cold War might make such care by Soviet relatives difficult, did not figure in his deliberations.

Other SPD members of the committee, however, displayed greater sensitivity. Councillor Bleistein, for example, opposed the suggestion, 'although

---

[44] StadtAN C 85 III/508, Niederschrift über die Sitzung des Rechts- und Wirtschaftsausschusses, 21.3.62.

he could understand why the administration would want to see the issue disposed of in this way'. In his view, 'this is after all a question of people who were deported from their homelands as a result of war and who were deployed as labour here . . . one should be a little more careful . . . and it ought to be entirely irrelevant to us whether it concerns the dead of the western or eastern spheres'. He proposed that, at the very least, the graves should be preserved in a space marked by a single cross or monument. The FDP representative, Bergold, while paying lip service to the arguments of piety put forward by Bleistein, maintained that the graves must gradually be dissolved 'to make room for new ones'. The remains, however, should be put into a collective grave and marked by a monument. The CSU concurred with this compromise proposal, which formed the basis of a decision to dissolve the individual graves and to place the exhumed remains in a collective grave 'to be cared for and maintained by the city of Nuremberg'.[45] A plan for the cemetery space was adopted in April 1963 and subsequently implemented.[46]

If the marking of the space which held the remains of the Soviet victims with a permanent memorial represented an ostensible victory for those Social

18. Memorial to Soviet forced workers, South Cemetery, Nuremberg (c. 1963).

[45] StadtAN C 85 III/508, Beschluss des Rechts- und Wirtschaftsausschusses, 21.3.62.
[46] StadtAN C 85 III/440, Niederschrift über die 54. Sitzung des Bauausschusses am 1.4.63.

Democratic voices opposed to the de facto obliteration of all memory of the forced workers' presence, the monument established was singularly evasive in its explication of its purpose. The city officials had been aware from the outset of the historical fate of the dead people concerned, bringing the issue to the attention of the relevant committees under the headings 'Dissolution of the Graves of Former Conscripted Foreign Workers' and 'Dissolution of the Graves of Forcibly Deported Foreign Workers'. They were, in other words, clearly aware that these had not been ordinary prisoners of war who had died of natural causes, wounds or the general hardships of war, but had been victims of Nazi policies. Yet, despite the warnings of another Social Democratic councillor at the original meeting of the Law and Economics Committee that 'one should be careful in the shaping of the memorial and not just downplay the fate of these deportees. This was actually a case of forced labourers, who were deported from their homeland to us. The plaques must also properly reflect the facts', the series of stone pillars erected to mark the graves studiously avoided all such reference.[47] When the monuments were erected, the 'forcibly deported foreign workers' – who had hailed from various Soviet states, including White Russia and the Ukraine – had been redescribed as 'Russian soldiers'. The assertion that these were the graves of ordinary soldiers denied the peculiarities of the barbaric racial exploitation and murder of the forced labour programme; the homogenising description of Soviet citizens of various national backgrounds as 'Russian', meanwhile, reproduced the ethnic arrogance of earlier generations' stereotyping gaze on the peoples of eastern Europe.

Moreover, if the monuments were far from honest in their identification of the victims, they were entirely silent on the historical context. The avoidance of all reference to their suffering was accompanied by an absence of any reference to its cause, to the nature of the perpetrating regime or to the identity of its perpetrating agents. Indeed, the failure to identify the perpetrating agents or structures – the civil agencies which had administered the forced labour programme, and above all the hundreds of local businesses, large and small, which had been complicit in their brutal exploitation – remained a blind spot in the local memory culture throughout the 1960s. If a consensus was hesitantly emerging in the 1960s that the foreign victims of the Third Reich, its racial barbarism and genocide deserved recognition, civic memory politics avoided all discussion of, or reference to, the identity of local perpetrators. This continued to rest on the apparent shared understanding that such a discussion would be too divisive. The preservation of the post-war civic peace forged around the fragile minimum victim consensus demanded that

[47] StadtAN C 85 III/508, Niederschrift über die Sitzung des Rechts- und Wirtschaftsausschusses, 21.3.62.

formulations of the identity of the perpetrators remained nebulous, or represented them as outsiders: if local society was now willing to begin to express through its civic culture the knowledge that there had been other dimensions to this war and other victims, it nevertheless continued to connive in the myth that they had been victims not of a regime in which the city, its institutions and inhabitants had participated, but victims of someone, or something, from somewhere else.

IV.2

The 'Victims of War' (ii)
The Expellees' Offensive

If the demographic shifts engendered by generational change contributed to the gradual fading of one set of 'war victim' voices in the memory culture of the city, another such set of shifts was partly behind the increasing prominence of other voices. Throughout the 1950s, but particularly from the mid-1950s onwards, the city experienced both an absolute and a relative increase in the number of refugees and expellees among the population, as the achievements of reconstruction enabled those previously consigned to rural poverty to move into urban communities. In 1950, the refugees and expellees accounted for 7 per cent of the population;[1] in 1954 this group – including those who had fled from the German Democratic Republic (GDR) – accounted for approximately 14 per cent.[2] By the early 1960s, the 100,000 refugees and expellees in the city comprised nearly one-quarter of the population.[3]

If nothing else, therefore, an underlying demographic and democratic logic demanded not only that civic authorities be seen to address the quotidian demands of this group, but also that they modify official narratives of war and defeat to include refugee and expellee suffering. Other factors, moreover, worked actively in the same direction. For one thing, the expellee associations had evolved by this point into highly prominent organisations, capable of mobilising considerable campaigning activism. Building on the networks of contacts and influence gained through participation in the refugee committees of the early post-war years, their leading functionaries had moved into influential positions in civil society from which they could intervene in the local memory culture to considerable effect. The head of the League of

[1] *Verwaltungsbericht der Stadt Nürnberg 1950*, 2.
[2] *Verwaltungsbericht der Stadt Nürnberg 1954*, 3.
[3] StadtAN C 85 III/396, Niederschrift über die 39. Sitzung des Ältestenrats, 28.6.63.

Expellees in Nuremberg, Josef Schmidt, for example, was simultaneously a member of the city council.[4] This was not a uniform process, and expellee organisations were no more immune from the possibility of decline than any other. The Homeland Association of East and West Prussians, for example, dissolved its Nuremberg chapter in April 1965.[5] Yet, overall, the 1960s were marked by a strengthening of the presence of the expellee groups in the associational life and civic culture of the city.

To these were added economic and political factors. The easing of distributional conflict in the wake of reconstruction led to a substantial decline in the anti-refugee rhetoric that had characterised the early post-war years, making it more possible for the indigenous population to acknowledge the suffering experienced by the expellees. For the expellees themselves, meanwhile, the establishment of the Berlin Wall in 1961 markedly altered the context in which their commemorative practices could unfold. If, in the 1950s, hopes of return were deemed to be sufficiently realistic for many not to feel the need to mark their experiences through memorials in Nuremberg, expellees' recognition of the harsh realities of division underlined by the events of 1961 provide part of the explanation for the initiation in the 1960s of moves to establish a permanent memorial to the expulsions in the city. While the onset of the détente era made reference to the expellee experience inexpedient at Federal level, therefore – leading, for example, to the cessation of Federal government-backed exhibitions on German culture in the east in the Germanic National Museum – economic, social and political factors worked on the local level towards an integration of expellee experience into the 'victim' narratives that had evolved in the 1950s.

At the same time, however, other factors ensured that some fault lines remained and that other new ones opened up. While the fact that some 18,000 of the 100,000 expellees in the city were members of organised expellee groups in the early 1960s testifies to the relatively high level of political–cultural consciousness and cohesion among the expellee population, the fact that over 80,000 remained outside the homeland associations reminds us that the great majority were not necessarily concerned with preserving their refugee identities, or the memory of the expulsions – at least not in this way.[6] The radicalisation of organised expellee rhetoric on reunification and foreign policy issues after 1961 may have exacerbated the gap between the minority of activists and the inactive majority further.[7] It certainly underlay the consistently cautious attitude of the

[4] StadtAN C 85 I Abg. 94/A43, Arbeitsgemeinschaft Bund der Vertriebenen und Flüchtlinge, 'Tag der Heimat 1965', 1.
[5] StadtAN C 22 VI/1618, Aktennotiz, Amt für öffentliche Ordnung, June 1965.
[6] On generational change and refugee memory politics, see Engelhardt, 'Generation und historisch-biographische Erfahrung', 331–58.
[7] Ahonen, *After the Expulsion*, 155ff.

local authorities towards organised expellee politics, especially at moments of heightened east–west tension such as the spring of 1968. If the 1960s marked an extended moment in which the expellee experience was integrated into the memory culture of the city, therefore – culminating in the establishment of a prominent memorial to the expulsions in 1968 – closer examination of local expellee politics during this decade underlines the fact that the modified 'victim' discourse that prevailed continued to mask divisions, tensions and rifts within a civil society in which an altogether more contested memory of Nazism and war existed just below the surface.

As in the 1950s, the expellees continued to be organised not into one, but into a number of associations. The League of Expellees still acted as an umbrella institution, pressing the city council on issues of shared concern to all expellees, regardless of their origins. Its emphasis remained on political activism and it continued to articulate overtly political demands, stating on the occasion of the Homeland Day of 1965 that its aim was to 'maintain the ethnic identity [*Volkstum*] of middle and eastern Germany and of the other expulsion zones spiritually, culturally and materially, for the whole of Germany in its undiminished substance' – a clear assertion of territorial claim over areas it continued to refer to as German, rather than Polish.[8]

For the most part, however, the focal point of organised expellee activity remained the individual homeland associations, which regularly held cultural events in Nuremberg throughout the 1960s. In some cases these were small gatherings arranged by the local chapters of the individual homeland associations, or meetings of relatively small homeland associations which united expellees from a particular town; at the other extreme, they could be very substantial meetings in which state-wide or even Federal gatherings of the homeland associations descended on Nuremberg for a weekend. The former included events such as the slide show mounted by the Association of Briegers, put on in Nuremberg in 1960 'to gather our fellow citizens of Brieg in remembrance of the fatherland of their birth after fifteen years of separation from our Silesian homeland'.[9] The latter included large-scale events such as a state gathering of the Bavarian section of the Pomeranian Homeland Association, which involved costume displays, the performance of native music and the recital of dialect poetry, through which Pomeranian culture was celebrated as the loss of territory was lamented. In mounting a 'flag procession of the German East, the South East and the indigenous people' they attempted on such occasions to

---

[8] StadtAN C 85 I Abg. 94/A43, Arbeitsgemeinschaft Bund der Vertriebenen und Flüchtlinge, 'Tag der Heimat 1965', 6.
[9] StadtAN C 73 I/481, Vereinigung der Brieger e.V. an Urschlechter, 1.4.60; for another example see C 51/299, Beschluss des Schul- und Kulturausschusses am 10.12.62.

mobilise traditions of local patriotism in their host community in support of their own identities and political claims; in the performance of songs such as 'Blessed are those who Suffer Persecution' nostalgic remembrance combined with the continued projection of a rhetoric of victimhood.[10]

The scale of these events was such that they indeed embraced indigenous participants and witnesses – the largest, for example the Sudeten German rally of 1964, were major events in the civic calendar the size of which assured them considerable public prominence. In the case of the 1964 rally, the Sudeten German Homeland Association – which had already held such events in Nuremberg in the 1950s – demanded not only a subvention of 50,000 DM but also, among other things, the flagging and lighting of buildings, the provision of schools and gymnasia as temporary quarters for participants, a camping place for 4,000 young people and the provision of an office in the city for some six months in advance of the event. The city authorities, for their part, were keen to oblige, overcoming the caution they had displayed in the 1950s. In mayor Urschlechter's words, the city should be willing to accept the request to host the gathering and to provide the facilities 'as through this a large circle of visitors will see the construction work in Nuremberg and the name of the city will be emphasised'.[11] If, in the 1950s, an element of mistrust had combined with fears concerning the city's incomplete reconstruction and a recent memory of large-scale rallies to foster nervousness, by the early 1960s the forces of economic pragmatism rendered the city much better disposed towards providing the expellees with a forum for the articulation of their demands.

While the cultural events of the homeland societies tended to strike a nostalgic note, their larger gatherings could also be accompanied by a variety of highly politicised rhetorics which argued, in one way or another, for the right of return. On the occasion of the Homeland Day of 1965, for example, the League of Expellees' accompanying brochure carried a large number of statements from differing homeland associations in which a number of themes recurred in various ways, revealing together the range of arguments for which the expellees continued to reach during this decade.

Some, especially the Sudeten German Homeland Association, struck a decidedly legalistic tone, repeating the Federal association's 1965 statement to the effect that 'we want to return to our homeland and to exercise our right to self-determination as free people, but not to live out our lives as a tolerated minority'.[12] For this group, claims of a 'right to homeland' – which were as legally nebulous as they were politically unrealistic – were grounded in reference

---

[10] StadtAN C 73 I/481, Landestreffen der Pommerschen Landsmannschaft in Bayern am Sonnabend/Sonntag, 25/26. Mai 1963 in den Messehallen.
[11] StadtAN C 85 III/396, Niederschrift über die 40. Sitzung des Ältestenrats, 13.9.63.
[12] StadtAN C 85 I/Abg. 94/A43, Arbeitsgemeinschaft Bund der Vertriebenen und Flüchtlinge, 'Tag der Heimat 1965', 35.

to Wilson's Fourteen Points and allusions to the Munich Agreement of 1938. In the case of the latter, the broader context of Hitler's aggressive foreign policy was not, of course, mentioned. Emphasising their status as the 'legally valid Sudeten German indigenous population', they embedded their specific claims in a wider set of demands for a 'free and peaceful Europe' – encoded in which was a virulently anti-Communist stance – and the international recognition of minority rights.

Anti-Communism, indeed, was central to nearly all of the homeland associations' statements. The climate of détente notwithstanding, hostility towards the Soviet Union and its client regimes in the east remained a mainstay of expellee rhetoric and provided for a strong degree of continuity in the ways in which the events of 1945 to 1946 were imagined within this group from the 1950s into the 1960s. The Thuringian Homeland Association, for example, noted that 'once more the Homeland Day is upon us, once again we see our beautiful homeland in the chains of Communist power behind the wall of shame'. Placing its faith in political initiatives towards the long-term goal of reunification, it asserted that, 'Until things have reached this point we will counter the destructive power of Ulbricht and his comrades whenever and wherever we can.'[13] Often wrapped up in such anti-Communist language was criticism of the indifference of those who did not get involved in the struggle. The Association of the Soviet Zone Refugees, for example, insisted that 'our demand is not comfortable, either for our western allies or for the Soviet occupation authority. It is not even comfortable for many federal citizens, who, twenty years after the end of the war, prosperity leads to close their eyes and hearts in the face of the need of our brothers and sisters in the zone'.[14] In their more nationalist incarnations, such as that offered by the Homeland Association of the Upper Silesians, claims such as these were embedded in a longer historical narrative of abandonment, or criticism of the failure of western Germans to support their fellow Germans in the 'population struggle' in the east.[15]

For those unable to make legalistic claims, however spurious, in the manner of the Sudeten German association, the right of return was justified in a number of ways. Those homeland associations focused on more eastern territories asserted the centrality of German cultural influence on the development of eastern Europe; those focused on 'central Germany' – that is, the territory of the German Democratic Republic – stressed the cultural contribution of those areas to the German nation with a view to underscoring the necessity of reunification. The Homeland Association of the East and West Prussians emphasised the status of East and West Prussia as the home of Herder, Kant and

[13] Ibid., 29.
[14] Ibid., 25.
[15] Ibid., 32–3.

Schopenhauer. While praising the eternal beauties of their homeland's natural landscape, the League of Silesians also stressed the peaceful cultural achievements of its 'poets, thinkers, researchers and inventors'.[16] Those associations focused on disparate areas of German settlement in the south-east, meanwhile, underlined the contribution of German culture in and from these places to the achievements of the German cultural nation more generally. The League of Danube Swabians, for example, emphasised that 'on his father's side Albrecht Dürer, one of the greatest artists of the German people, the most famous son of Nuremberg, hailed from south-east Europe' and offered a long list of writers, doctors and musicians, including Franz Liszt, in support of its claim that the region had made a great contribution to German culture.[17]

In such assertions of cultural achievement the homeland associations revealed the double-edged quality of much of their rhetoric. On the one hand, they sought to emphasise the positive contributions their ethnic groups had made in the regions from whence they came, as part of a broader strategy of disputing the legitimacy of the expulsions. On the other hand, emphasising their high levels of cultural achievement and the contributions they had made to German national culture served to foster acceptance on the part of an indigenous population sometimes given to looking down on those from further east, or, in the case of those who had settled in far-flung corners of Europe centuries ago, to disputing their claims to membership of the German nation. In doing so they implicitly acknowledged the ongoing presence of schisms between expellees and the indigenous population even as they sought to mobilise the latter behind languages of national solidarity.

Most narratives of German settlement in the east emphasised the centuries-old presence of the settler groups or the invited nature of the settlement. These, in turn, were wrapped up in accounts of inter-ethnic relations that represented the history of the German presence in the east as one of harmonious co-existence. The Homeland Association of Germans from Lithuania, for example – the representative of an ethnic German group that had just participated in genocidal massacres in the Second World War – conceded that there had been conflicts between the German ethnic group and the Lithuanian state over church policy but ventured that, despite this, 'The Germans in Lithuania always had a good neighbourly relationship with the Lithuanians, the Russians, Poles and Jews, living together in peaceful, hearty, and friendly fashion, in tolerance and respect for people, irrespective of their faith or nationality.'[18]

Others, however, told a more explicitly colonial story, linking their presence in the east to a Christian, and often specifically Protestant, cultural mission.

---

[16] Ibid., 30; 17.
[17] Ibid., 12–14.
[18] Ibid., 40.

This, in turn, could easily become infused with the language of self-defence. The Homeland Association of the Upper Silesians, for example, foregrounded the Annaberg mountain as a 'symbol of Christian basic stance and German sensibility'.[19] In doing so it deployed notions of settlement that were still overtly racialised and which drew strongly on the nationalist fervour of the borderland struggles of the interwar years. As the association put it, using language barely distinguishable from the Nazis' own version of history, 'The history of our homeland was always a struggle for Germandom, a struggle to remain in the great German fatherland, a struggle against the Mongol hordes storming from the east and later against the constant infiltration by Slavdom.'[20] Indeed, in its celebration of the German response to Polish insurgency in 1921 it openly deployed the egalitarian, populist language of national community favoured in the Third Reich: 'From all sides volunteers flooded to Upper Silesia to rescue and to protect German blood and German imperial soil. The student stood alongside the experienced soldier of the World War, the Bavarian alongside the Rhinelander. The German Self Protection League was formed from members of all estates and all tribes . . .'[21]

Each homeland association thus drew upon a shared repertoire of images, representations and rhetorical positions that combined anti-Communist sentiment, national ambition and the pursuit of return with a historical narrative of the German presence in the east which cast Germans as hapless victims of either history or of other ethnic groups, and which was silent on Germans' recent genocidal activities in the diverse spaces which together constituted 'the east'. In this they differed little from their public interventions of the 1950s.

What was striking about such literature in the 1960s, however, was not just the continuity of anti-Communist rhetoric or the ongoing insistence by the expellees themselves on the superiority of the German cultural mission in the east and its achievements. Equally notable was the fact that the indigenous victim groups were now contributing to such brochures. In its contribution, the Association of Former Prisoners of War continued to prefer, like the expellee groups, the nationalist language prevalent in conservative victim groups in the 1950s. It counselled that 'the reality of the current division of Germany speaks a very hard language, but love of the German fatherland is indivisible as the German fatherland itself. The history of a century, which hammered us together into a German nation, cannot be simply brushed aside with the penstrokes of diplomats, as was tried from Teheran to Potsdam.'[22] If

[19] Ibid., 32.
[20] Ibid., 32–3.
[21] Ibid., 33.
[22] Ibid., 9.

the expellees' offerings distinguished themselves in their evasive treatment of the wider circumstances of the war, meanwhile, the war victims' contribution stood out for the manner in which they erased the histories of post-war conflict between the expellees and the indigenous population. The BDK, for example, contributed passages comparing and eliding the fates of the two groups which belied the deep resentments towards expellees that had characterised the immediate aftermath of war: 'Love for the homeland and responsibility for the community of the people determined the ethic of soldierly sacrifice in two world wars. Wherever war victims and expellees find themselves together, they are linked by this feeling of love for the fatherland and belief in the reunification of our fatherland in peace and freedom.'[23] If the material hardships of the 1950s had underpinned a rhetoric of hostility, the marginalisation in the shadow of the 'economic miracle' sensed by the BDK was clearly leading it to pursue new alliances: 'He who has given the highest sacrifice of life and health for his people or had to leave his homeland due to inhumane force still feels how the wounds of the last great war are far from healed, despite prosperity and economic flourishing.' And, in pursuit of these new alliances, it was willing to indulge in straightforward falsification of the history of the post-war years: 'From shared bitter fate a comradely bond grew up between expellees and the victims of two world wars which should be visible above all on the Homeland Day.'

Even more striking, perhaps, were the lengths to which a civic leadership that had done little in the 1950s to acknowledge formally the suffering of the expellees was now willing to go to integrate the expellees' experiences into the dominant local narratives of German wartime suffering and post-war reconstruction success. In his foreword to the same Homeland Day brochure for 1965, for example, mayor Urschlechter wrote that 'this day has gradually acquired symbolic meaning for the sense of shared belonging and the engagement for one another which characterised the community of fate of the old and new citizens of Nuremberg forged in difficult years'.[24] By the mid-1960s, clearly, the demographic presence, organisational strength and level of economic and social integration of the expellees had reached a point at which their suffering could be – indeed had to be – integrated into official narratives of war. Statements such as these sidestepped the enormous antipathy towards the expellees which had existed in the immediate post-war years and accorded the expellee contribution a significance in the achievements of reconstruction that it simply had not had. Ignoring the fact that the overwhelming majority of the city's 100,000-strong expellee population had moved into the city from the

[23] Ibid., 9.
[24] Ibid., 3.

middle of the 1950s onwards, mayor Urschlechter nodded to the strength of their current presence by asserting that 'together they completed the work of reconstructing our city, in whose economic flourishing thousands of expellees also play a substantial part'.

Such remarks embodied present-centred fictions rather than truthful accounts of the past, and are to be read for their situational utility rather than their historical accuracy. They testify, therefore, to the considerable progress which had been made in integrating the expellees into Nuremberg society by the mid-1960s. At the same time, divisions remained. The positions adopted by the main political parties were also not uniform. While some SPD politicians, including deputy mayor Haas, appear to have embraced the reunification agenda, others, such as the young city councillor Willy Prölss, continued to foreground social welfare and social integration. In general, indeed, it was the CSU which showed most inclination to consider expellee affairs in their diplomatic, rather than social, dimensions, mirroring a set of shifts whereby organised expellee politics in Bavaria became gradually aligned with the political Right.[25]

Such realignments took place within a wider process of change in the political culture both of the city and of West Germany, through which the expellees' relations to the institutions of a pluralistic civil society were renegotiated over the course of the 1960s. That this sometimes cut across conventional political lines is shown by the evolving relationship of the expellees to conservative institutions such as the Protestant Church in Nuremberg. In the 1950s, the Protestant Church's attitude had been at best lukewarm. In a city such as this, with its very strong Protestant tradition, the arrival of the expellees was seen by the Church as sitting within a longer-term process of dissolving Protestant hegemony, induced by unfolding modernity, which it naturally regarded with unease. In 1960, for example, in an account of the recent history of the city and the Church, the Protestant parish newsletter relayed how 'the end of the war brought 90,000 expellees to our town; moreover, the pull of ever-increasing industrialisation relentlessly drew thousands into Nuremberg from the Upper Palatinate, and has long since contributed to a dilution of the Protestant character of the former Reich city'.[26] Despite the claims of this piece, again, a very small number of refugees had come into the city in the immediate post-war era; the fact that many of those who did come had, indeed, been Roman Catholics, doubtless explains why the Protestant Church had paid relatively little attention to the expellees in the 1950s, and

[25] See, for example, the comments of CSU councillor (and later Federal minister) Oscar Schneider in StadtAN C 85 III/396, Niederschrift über die Sitzung des Ältestenrats, 3.5.63.
[26] 'Nürnbergs Geschichte lebt!', *Nürnberger Evangelisches Gemeindeblatt*, 14.8.60.

why – unlike in some Roman Catholic churches – the expellee experience was not acknowledged in Protestant memorials to the war.[27]

The conservative, national traditions of the Protestant Church were such that, up to the turn of the decade, it continued to articulate the German claim on the eastern territories. Accordingly, the Protestant parish newsletter repeated uncritically the line of the Eastern Churches Committee, which represented the nineteen German Protestant churches of the east. In reflections on the role of the church in international relations published in 1960, for example, which addressed the contentious issue of the Oder-Neisse line, it argued that problems of inter-state relations could not be solved by violence, and that 'applied to the German situation, these considerations tell us: the recognition of the Oder-Neisse line, simply on the basis of the given situation, would represent the legalisation of a wrong and thus an infringement of a moral principle, the disregarding of which would call into question the permanence of a peace formed on this basis. Meeting a wrong with a wrong does not make a new right.'[28] Nonetheless, as the liberalising impulses resonating through West German political culture also began to manifest themselves in conservative institutions such as the Protestant Church, and as the changed diplomatic constellation created by the establishment of the Berlin Wall led more sober voices from all quarters to call for a more realistic stance on Germany's border issues, the relationship of organised expellee groups to the Protestant Church became more fractious.

The initial cause of this was the 1962 leaking of the so-called 'Tübingen Memorandum'.[29] Penned in 1961 by a number of leading Protestant thinkers, the discussion paper sought to stimulate debate on wide-ranging aspects of West German politics and society; however, the rancorous debate which followed its publication focused largely on its contentious suggestion that, in the interests of reconciliation, West Germany's intransigent position on the Oder-Neisse line be modified. Organised expellee groups had reacted angrily, labelling such suggestions 'treacherous' and in some cases demanding that calls for the renunciation of territorial claims be made a punishable offence. The Protestant Church, for its part, responded firmly to suggestions from within nationalist expellee circles that the authors of the memorandum sat in a continuum of treacherous behaviour with the July bomb plotters of 1944, accusing such expellee voices of adopting the perspective of the Nazis themselves and riposting that while 'accommodation with so-called realities is not

---

[27] On the attitudes of the Catholic Church to refugees see most recently Buscher, 'The Great Fear', 204–24.
[28] 'Neues Recht aus altem Unrecht?', *Nürnberger Evangelisches Gemeindeblatt*, 7.8.60.
[29] On the Tübingen Memorandum and its impact see Martin Greschat,' "Mehr Wahrheit in der Politik!" Das Tübinger Memorandum von 1961', *Vierteljahrshefte für Zeitgeschichte* 48 (2000), 491–513.

a good principle ... the absence of remorse in respect of a system which brought so much shame on the German name is a miserable, indeed reprehensible standpoint. Whoever says "Silesia" and means Hitler should not be allowed to speak for the expellees.'[30]

Such remarks are interesting if only because the embrace of the moral standpoint of the July 1944 resisters over that of the authority which they challenged marked a shift from the Church's position of the post-war years: as late as 1954, the then dean Julius Schieder had argued that 'I cannot abandon my conviction that it was a good thing for the German people that the assassination failed. One cannot make a rule out of this 20 July.'[31] They indicate again, therefore, how the culture of even the most conservative institutions was shifting in response to the liberalising impulses of the early 1960s. However, in rejecting the extreme nationalist rhetoric on the Oder-Neisse line in its comments on the Tübingen memorandum debate in 1962, the Protestant Church was disputing the tone, as much as the content, of the expellee position. The gap between expellee politics and the Church remained narrow; as such, this debate functioned as a mere forerunner to the much more tumultuous debates of 1965, especially concerning the Protestant Church's own memorandum on 'The Situation of the Expellees and the Relations of the German People to their Eastern Neighbours' of October 1965.[32]

In contrast to its position in 1960, the Protestant parish newsletter defended the call to political moderation and reason embodied in the October memorandum. Having adopted the essentially legalistic position of the expellee groups in 1960, it now re-emphasised the memorandum's argument that 'in efforts to find a sustainable reordering of the relationship to our eastern neighbours ... "the readiness for reconciliation, the recognition of mutual implication in guilt and the sober assessment of the world situation" must play as great a role as references to the legal position.'[33]

The numerous articles in subsequent newsletters engaging in the arguments proposed by the Church's opponents on the issue attested, meanwhile, to the strength of the reaction.[34] As such disputes showed, the relationship of

---

[30] 'Heimatrecht – aber nicht so!', *Nürnberger Evangelisches Gemeindeblatt*, 9.12.62.

[31] LKAN Kd Nbg 53, Schieder an Oberkirchenrat Koch, 22.1.54.

[32] On the background see Ahonen, *After the Expulsion*, 203–8.

[33] 'EKD wünscht sachliches Gespräch über Ostfragen', *Nürnberger Evangelisches Gemeindeblatt*, 7.11.65; see also the comments in 'Recht und Versöhnung in der deutschen Ostpolitik', *Nürnberger Evangelisches Gemeindeblatt*, 6.6.65.

[34] See, for example, 'Nach langem, schweren Weg ein gutes Ende', *Nürnberger Evangelisches Gemeindeblatt*, 14.11.65; 'Auflockerung der kirchlichen Fronten. Die westdeutschen Synodalen nahmen zur Vertriebenen-Denkschrift Stellung', *Nürnberger Evangelisches Gemeindeblatt*, 5.12.65; 'Auch Reden kann Gold sein. EKD-Synode zu Denkschrift und Ökumene', *Nürnberger Evangelisches Gemeindeblatt*, 3.4.66, and in the same issue 'Vertreibung und Versöhnung'; for an account of expellee responses see 'Heimatvertriebene greifen evangelische Kirche an', *Nürnberger Evangelisches Gemeindeblatt*, 11.9.66.

the expellees and their organisations to the indigenous population and to pre-existing institutions, both civil and ecclesiastical, remained complex; a dynamic of integration and acknowledgement of expellee suffering existed alongside both ongoing divisions and the emergence of new fissures in the civic culture of the city. Above all, the often aggressive rhetoric of a minority of expellee activists generated conflict with a wider society which was gradually moving towards acceptance of the loss of the eastern territories.

The simultaneous process of integrating the expellees and acknowledging their historical suffering on the one hand while maintaining a degree of distance towards organised expellee interest politics on the other was most visible in the protracted debates on the establishment of a memorial to the expulsions in the 1960s. In the 1950s, official debate on a memorial to the expulsions had been entirely absent. There were, it is true, public representations of the expulsions in the form of reliefs or murals depicting the events of 1945 to 1946 on individual houses. The narratives these embodied were conventional and predictable, with their decontextualising emphasis on German civilian suffering and their focus on the hardships endured by the nuclear family in flight; on occasion, they drew on a biblical iconography of exodus to make their point. However, it seems that these were mostly integrated into housing projects disproportionately inhabited by refugees – the mural relief (depicted opposite) was painted on to a building erected on or close to the site of a refugee camp, for example – so that their audience was disproportionately those who had experienced the expulsions, rather than the indigenous Nuremberg public.[35]

The discussions concerning an official memorial to the victims of the expulsions were initiated by the local League of Expellees in 1963. While there were minor divisions of opinion within the city authorities, a consensus quickly emerged that the city should be willing to establish a memorial in the 'Waffenhof' courtyard, in the city's historic walls. Such a location suited itself to the holding of commemorative rituals – the League of Expellees clearly worked on the assumption that it could fill a space which would accommodate up to 2,000 participants – and fitted the League's desire for a site which would not only lend itself to occasional events 'but would also remind the citizenry of the division of Germany'.[36] Although one official dissented, arguing that the location would better serve a memorial to the destruction of the old city on 2 January 1945, another argued that 'this question could be connected

---

[35] The image depicted here was on an apartment block now just outside Nuremberg, in neighbouring Fürth; it was obliterated during renovations in 2007.
[36] StadtAN C 85 III/440, Niederschrift über die Sitzung des Bauausschusses am 27.5.63; C 85 I Abg. 94/A43, Aktennotiz 13.12.63.

19(a-b). Reliefs, *Refugees, 1945* and *New Beginning, 1951,* Dr-Hermann-Luppe Platz, Nuremberg (early 1950s).

20. Mural, *Leyerstrasse* (now *Fürth*)(1953).

to the expellee memorial. Both could only complement one another', a further indication of how in the 1960s the expellee experience was gradually being integrated into the broader dominant 'victim' narrative of the city.[37]

The speed with which consensus was reached over the acceptability of the proposal in principle was more than matched, however, by the endless delays in turning it into practice – a process which lasted a full five years. For one thing, the search for an appropriate visual idiom prompted a rearticulation of divisions of opinion concerning the appropriate political response to the expellee problem. For another, the heterogeneity of the expellee community made the search for a unifying symbol problematic. According to mayor Urschlechter, 'one ought to choose a symbol of the German east for the memorial plaque with a corresponding inscription'. As councillor Buchner observed, however, 'If one or another symbol of the German east is sought there will be difficulties between the Silesians, Sudeten Germans and so on.'[38] At the same time, discussions within the city revealed the caution which continued to characterise attitudes towards the organised expellee groups. As SPD councillor Prölss made clear, part of the rationale for city involvement lay in the opportunity it afforded to domesticate the more intemperate expellee voices, and to ensure that the inflammatory potential of an ill-conceived memorial was avoided. On the one hand, as he argued, 'if one sees what role the homeland associations and the expellees play in public life then one has to say that almost all parties are obliged to make certain concessions'.[39] In the following meeting, however, he counselled that 'we should ensure that we have influence over the artistic form and if necessary over any text . . . one should proceed cautiously here and just include an indication that it is a memorial for the expellees'.[40] CSU councillor Schneider likewise opined that 'as far as the inscription is concerned it must be a short one and free from polemical intent or current slogans'.

More intractable than aesthetic concerns or issues of political tact, however, was the question of financing the memorial. The League of Expellees clearly assumed that the city would be willing to cover the bulk of the cost; indeed, in May 1964 it openly requested that the city council pay the full 25,000 DM cost of the monument.[41] The League's assumption in its initial 1963 negotiations that the monument would be ready for inauguration at the upcoming Sudeten German rally of 1964 likewise betrayed a certain presumptuousness on its part.[42]

[37] StadtAN C 85 I Abg. 94/A43, Ausschnitt aus dem Kurzprotokoll über die Referentenbesprechung, 18.2.64.
[38] StadtAN C 85 III/440, Niederschrift über die Sitzung des Bauausschusses am 27.5.63.
[39] StadtAN C 85 I Abg. 94/A43, Auszug aus der Niederschrift der Sitzung des Ältestenrats, 8.5.64.
[40] StadtAN C 85 I Abg. 94/A43, Auszug aus der Sitzung des Ältestenrats vom 24.9.65.
[41] StadtAN C 85 I Abg. 94/A43, Bund der Vertriebenen, Kreisgruppe Nürnberg/Vereinigte Landsmannschaften an Urschlechter, 6.5.64.
[42] StadtAN C 85 I Abg. 94/A43, Aktennotiz, 13.12.63.

This presumptuousness, however, was misplaced. The city council was willing to pay only half of the memorial's cost, up to a maximum of 12,500 DM, insisting that 'the other half must be contributed by the League of Expellees or its members'.[43] The League of Expellees responded with various ruses. It first tried to get the city to pay the first instalments of the memorial, before the League had raised its own contribution, with the clear aim of engineering the half-completion of the memorial, thus manoeuvring the city into a position where it would then feel obliged to complete the entire project.[44] When this failed, it instructed its sculptor to design a scaled-down model costing 15,000 DM, trying to retain the same 12,500 DM originally offered by the city.[45]

If the detail of such discussions represent little more than the arcane day-to-day manoeuvrings of local council affairs, they nonetheless reveal much about the nature of expellee politics in the city. Underlying the fact that the League of Expellees was forced to adopt these tactics was its inability to raise meaningful sums within the wider expellee population. While a minority of expellee activists were insistent upon the need for such a monument, their campaign clearly generated little resonance with the silent majority of Nuremberg's 'new citizens'. Despite leaflets insisting that 'we all have a duty to help ensure that an impressive and dignified monument reminding us of our dead is created', and that each expellee should contribute 'freely and from inner conviction, united in the idea that the memory of flight and expulsion should find a visible symbolic expression', the collection raised negligible sums.[46] In the words of Schmidt, the head of the League of Expellees, the results were 'modest';[47] in one city councillor's words, they were 'shameful'.[48] As Schmidt was forced to admit, the League of Expellees' campaign to establish a monument was in a 'hopeless' situation.[49]

In the event, it took a further three years – and additional financial concessions from the city council – before the memorial was finally unveiled, at a different point to that originally designated in the city walls, in 1968.[50] The absence of an archival trail allows no insight into the completion of the project, but it is clear that the League of Expellees had struggled to persuade

[43] StadtAN C 85 I Abg. 94/A43, Auszug aus der Niederschrift der Sitzung des Ältestenrats, 8.5.64; Beschluss des Ältestenrats, 8.5.64.
[44] StadtAN C 85 I Abg. 94/A43, Bund der Vertriebenen/Stadtrat Schmidt an Oberbürgermeister Urschlechter, 24.11.64.
[45] StadtAN C 85 I Abg. 94/A43, Bund der Vertriebenen, Kreisverband Nürnberg/Schmidt an Urschlechter, 24.7.65.
[46] StadtAN C 85 I Abg. 94/A43, Unser Mahnmal ersteht (flyer)(January 1965).
[47] StadtAN C 85 I Abg. 94/A43, Bund der Vertriebenen, Kreisverband Nürnberg/Schmidt an Urschlechter, 24.7.65.
[48] StadtAN C 85 I Abg. 94/A43, Auszug aus der Sitzung des Ältestenrats vom 24.9.65.
[49] StadtAN C 85 I Abg. 94/A43, Bund der Vertriebenen, Kreisverband Nürnberg/Schmidt an Urschlechter, 7.7.65.
[50] StadtAN C 85 I Abg. 94/A43, Aktennotiz Urschlechter, 14.3.68.

its wider constituency of the need for the monument. Much as the regimental monuments of the 1960s marked the last meaningful efflorescence of a veteran memory milieu in retreat, rather than the expression of an ingrained culture of military commemoration across the city's population, the protracted history of the expellee memorial project thus revealed the limits to which expellee activist concerns reflected those of the majority of expellees by this point. To this extent, the scepticism embodied in one city councillor's remark in 1963 – 'I would be interested to know how many real members this organisation actually represents and how many of the roughly 100,000 expellees in Nuremberg really feel represented by this league' – was well founded.[51] The fact that the League's leader, councillor Schmidt, represented the *Gesamtdeutsche Partei*, rather than the SPD or CSU, on the city council, also indicates the limits of the extent to which the expellee activists' politics reflected those of the wider expellee community, the majority of whom voted for the SPD or CSU.

Nonetheless, for all the council's dislike of aspects of the organised expellee groups' agendas, and for all the ongoing divisions between different elements of the expellee community, the League of Expellees had achieved its goal with the creation of the monument. With its establishment in 1968, the integration of the expellee experiences of 1945 to 1946 into the official local narrative of German wartime suffering reached its conclusion. This stood in stark contrast to the ongoing absence of a memorial in a non-Jewish public space to the victims of the Holocaust.

However, it would be wrong to juxtapose ongoing silence on the Holocaust in the memorial landscape of the city with the creation of the expellee monument in a manner which implied that the apparent perpetuation of the German 'victim' discourse was simply a direct reflection of the continuously narcissistic memory culture of a majority perpetrator community. The evidence surrounding discussions of a memorial to the murdered Jews is limited, but it is clear that the truth was, again, more complex. In 1958, the Society for Christian–Jewish Cooperation had suggested to the city council that plaques be established on the sites of the two former Nuremberg synagogues.[52] As already argued, the suggestion had found immediate acceptance among SPD, FDP and CSU representatives; it was agreed that plaques should be prepared in time for the anniversary of the 'Night of the Glass' in November 1959.[53] On this occasion, however, it had been the Jewish community leadership who had advised

[51] StadtAN C 85 III/396, Niederschrift über die Sitzung des Ältestenrats, 3.5.63.
[52] StadtAN C 85 III/388, Niederschrift über die 41. Sitzung des Ältestenrats, 21.11.58.
[53] StadtAN C 85 III/389, Niederschrift über die 45. Sitzung des Ältestenrats, 13.2.59.
[54] StadtAN C 85 III/389, Niederschrift über die Sitzung des Ältestenrats, 10.7.59.

against the establishment of the plaques.[54] When the issue was again raised in 1964, the city responded to the inquiry – an individual request – with the explanation that 'following extensive discussions, the Israelite community has decided to refrain from expressing such a wish'.[55] This response did not, in fact, imply that the Jewish community was still opposed to the establishment of a memorial. Rather, it reflected a view within the Jewish community that if such a memorial were to be established it should be initiated from within the community of former perpetrators, not from within the Jewish community itself.[56] In the event, a memorial was erected on the site of the synagogue on the *Hans-Sachs-Platz* in 1971.[57] In marking an act of physical vandalism and local violence rather than the fact of genocide, and in focusing on the persecution of the Jews of Nuremberg rather than on the continent-wide process of mass murder, the memorial mirrored the limitations of the nascent culture of Holocaust remembrance in the city; nonetheless, it reflected the substantial shifts that had taken place in the previous decade.

Compared to the 100,000 expellees in the city, the Jewish community – numbering some 200 people – remained tiny in the 1960s. Yet in the 1960s the suffering of both groups competed for acknowledgement in the transitional memory culture of the city. On the one hand, exhibitions on Auschwitz and war crimes trials were at the forefront of pushing a new sensibility towards the Holocaust in which at least some Germans were able to re-imagine the Germany of the past as an initiator, organiser and perpetrator of genocide rather than – or at least as well as – a victim of war. On the other hand, the overwhelming demographic advantage of the expellees, combined with the ready repertoire of victim stories that remained available to them in the 1960s, and the presence of an indigenous population more willing to accept them as part of the local population, meant that the expellees were at least as successful in placing their suffering upon the commemorative agendas of the city in that decade. If, in the long run, the 1960s marked the turning point in which the Holocaust began to attain a fuller place in the memory culture of the Federal Republic, in the short term it was the expellees, as much as the Jews, whose sufferings were formally acknowledged by the majority community in these years.

[55] StadtAN C 85 I Abg. 94/A44, Ausschnitt aus dem Kurzprotokoll über die Referentenbesprechung vom 21.7.64.
[56] I owe this insight to a former member of the Nuremberg Jewish community leadership.
[57] *Juden in Nürnberg. Geschichte der jüdischen Mitbürger vom Mittelalter bis zur Gegenwart* (Nuremberg, 1993), 64.

IV.3

Fading Personal Experience, Forging Public Meaning

Commemorations and Civic Identity Politics
in the 1960s

Many of the characteristics of the memory culture of the 1960s revealed by
examination of the landscapes of associational life and the ongoing acts of
memorialisation were also evident in the official commemorative practices of
the city. On the one hand, a strong element of continuity prevailed. This continuity was, first and foremost, one of form. The Day of National Mourning
continued to be held annually in November at the *Luitpoldhain* monument on
the former party rally grounds, while the 2 January commemorations of the
bombing of the city at the South Cemetery memorial evolved into an additional
annual event in the early 1960s. Surrounding these events was a strong degree
of rhetorical continuity, most obviously apparent in the highly repetitive
rehearsals of the customary victim narrative as it had evolved in the 1950s. This
reflected, in turn, continuities in the underlying ideological context – which
after as before 1961 was provided by the Cold War – and continuities in the local
political culture, in the form of ongoing Social Democratic domination of politics in the city. If nothing else, this translated into a strong element of continuity
in the ascription of meaning to the events of the war. Above all, commemoration remained largely self-centred. Alternately in the foreground were either
Nuremberg's citizens or those of the Federal Republic; where a collective was
deployed it was, similarly, either 'the city' or some variant of 'the German
nation'. Even when limited moves to acknowledge the Holocaust on such occasions were undertaken, they remained limited, vague and contested; civic
leaders continued largely to confine themselves to acknowledgement of the
persecution of Nuremberg's, or at best Germany's, Jews; at similar ceremonies
organised from within the community, rather than by the city council, there was
still no mention of Jews or the Holocaust whatsoever.

These continuities reflected the operations of an official memory culture
constrained by two factors. Firstly, the continued asymmetry between a

majority of the population which had supported, colluded in, or at the very least made convenient compromises with the Nazi regime, and a minority which had opposed or suffered under the same regime, was such that, given the underlying democratic logic of memory politics, civic authorities remained obliged to enunciate narratives agreeable to people still mostly unwilling to consider themselves as perpetrating agents of a genocidal war. Even if the workings of demographic change meant that this directly compromised section of the population was less sizeable than before, it was still sufficiently present to make it difficult for a mayor charged with speaking to and for the community as a whole to utter divisive or critical comments on commemorative occasions. Second, the need to maintain a minimum degree of civic consensus in a community in which real political divisions between the bourgeoisie and working class continued to manifest themselves in both material and ideological conflict militated against, not in favour, of the partisan expression of critical narratives of the Nazi past on occasions such as the Day of National Mourning.

In the case of officialdom, therefore, the usage of a consensual memory culture to bridge the social, political and ideological divisions of both past and present continued to preclude direct challenges to the sanctity of the victim discourse. For this reason, above all, there remained a marked unwillingness to identify former perpetrators, either as institutions or individuals. Where agency was acknowledged at all, it continued to be ascribed to 'the Nazi regime' or to 'the Nazis', rather than to the local party activists, civil servants, businessmen, police or medical professionals and many others who had sustained the regime in power or implemented its criminal acts. While limited progress was being made in acknowledging the historical fact of genocide and the suffering of its victims in the 1960s, consideration of the identities of the perpetrators and the political and moral challenges these might pose remained strictly off-limits in official memory politics: it remained too divisive a problem.

However, as closer examination of the histories of the Day of National Mourning and of the commemoration of the bombing also shows, things were gradually changing. The outcome of these changes was as yet unclear, again underlining that the 1960s marked a period of extended flux in the memory culture of the city which contained a number of possible outcomes. Some of these changes, clearly, reflected the gradual emergence of 'Holocaust awareness', but other processes under way were quite distinct from these and could certainly have evolved in similar ways irrespective of the genocide. Above all, the gap that was opening up between those for whom memory of the war was rooted in immediate experience – those for whom cultural narratives connected (or collided) with images within – and those with no direct personal experience of the war began to change the tone of commemorative activity.

This was discernible in new aspects of the rhetoric accompanying the ritual moments. On the one hand, the striking regularity with which official voices resorted to a highly visual language when speaking or writing on commemorative occasions indicates a shared recognition of the fact that many in the community continued to live with very vivid personal memories of appallingly violent experiences. On the 2 January commemorations of 1965, for example, the official city gazette referred to the 'dreadful images' (*Schreckensbilder*) left by the attacks;[1] in January 1962, mayor Urschlechter recounted how 'the fires and explosions raged through our city like furies and left in those who were able to avoid death a permanent image of horror and terror [*ein ständiges Bild des Grauens und Entsetzens*] that even nowadays on some occasions is present in the eye of those of our citizens who had to experience it'.[2] Clearly, the mayor could not know what such images were in individual cases, but neither were his regular references to visual imagery accidental: they testify to the fact that while the wider discourse on the war and Nazi past was slowly shifting in the 1960s, the memories of many in the population continued to be dominated by the recall of their own experiences of violence and destruction during the bombing raids.

On the other hand, a generation was slowly emerging for whom the war existed only in narratives communicated through public culture or oral transmission within the family or community. Again, the impact of this generational change was complex and uneven; the speed with which the transition occurred should not be overestimated. After all, young people in the 1960s who had not experienced the war as conscious individuals had still had ample opportunity to experience its effects: the childhoods of those in their early twenties in the mid-1960s had been characterised by hardship and hunger amidst the ruins. Moreover, the concentration of *Wehrmacht* casualties in the second half of the war, and particularly in 1944 to 1945, meant that many of those born during the war had endured the absence of a father when growing up; many others suffered from the effects of a disabled father. While intergenerational relationships in this era were constructed by the culture of a later period as overwhelmingly conflict-ridden, this was not always the case, and the impact of the war on German families was such that, presented with the obvious evidence of parental suffering, narratives of German victimhood could easily gain purchase with the first post-war generation too.[3]

---

[1] '2. Januar 1945: Mahnung und Vermächtnis', *Amtsblatt der Stadt Nürnberg*, 5.1.65.

[2] 'Gedenkfeier auf dem Südfriedhof', *Amtsblatt der Stadt Nürnberg*, 4.1.62.

[3] On the role of the family as the vector of shared narratives as opposed to site of memory conflict, and thus as a site of resistance to the new impulses, see Harald Welzer, 'Krieg der Generationen. Zur Tradierung von NS-Vergangenheit und Krieg in deutschen Familien' in Naumann, *Nachkrieg in Deutschland*, 552–71.

If the effects of generational change can easily be overestimated in the short term, however, a transition was nonetheless under way. One obvious sign of this transitional culture, which marked the end of what was in many respects a 'long 1950s' of remembrance, was the city's decision to make the 1965 commemorations of 2 January 1945 the last annual ceremony. Another was the increasingly formulaic character of the Day of National Mourning. Here, the regularity with which a variety of voices insisted that expressions of sorrow should be more than mere 'lip service' indicated a growing sense that the commemorations were in danger of becoming empty rituals performed as a matter of routinised obligation. While for some the impact of the war retained its immediacy and intensity, for others it was slowly losing its significance; while for some the experience of war remained central to their sense of self, for others it was part of cultural memory only. Even those who did wish to retain German suffering at the centre of narratives of war had to acknowledge that the forms in which the war was remembered had to change. Either way, differing responses to the war and to the modes of remembering it, as much as conflicting attitudes to the genocide against the Jews, were at the heart of fissures in the memory culture as the 1960s progressed.

The extent to which elements of continuity and intimations of change competed with each other around moments of formal commemoration in the 1960s can been seen by comparing the evolving responses of two differing conservative voices – the BDK and the Protestant Church. The language of the BDK, on the one hand, was characterised by a strong degree of continuity from the 1950s. Its representations of war and both past and present politics drew on all the familiar refrains of the post-war years. In its reflections on the Day of National Mourning – to which it continued to refer as 'Heroes Remembrance Day' – in 1966, it argued that war memorials to dead soldiers remained justified as 'the soldierly vocation was ever simple and without pathos and based on the sober foundations of strict obedience and loyal fulfilment of duty according to the oath, on a deep sense of responsibility to house and homestead, people and homeland'.[4] Rejecting the possibility that the soldiers' 'heroic struggle' had been meaningless, pointless or wrong, as some had falsely implied in the 'confused post-war years', it argued that 'the diplomatic developments after the Second World War alone, and not least that icy wind which blows over to us from the east and bears everything but the spirit of freedom have made clear the significance of this sacrifice in all its greatness'.

Such characterisations of the war as one of anti-Bolshevik defence drew on a familiar repertoire of Cold War refrains, but the BDK's reflections made equally clear that underlying the commemorative act remained a sense of

[4] 'Opfer der Toten, Wille zum Leben', *Kriegsopfer-Rundschau*, November 1966.

shared grief and mourning that had lost little of its immediacy in the milieu of which it was part. It was a reminder that, of the millions of bereaved wives and mothers, 'while some of them linger in spirit on a lonely hillock in a distant land, at a simple birch cross, and, despite their pain, find peace again, relatives of the missing are still consumed with anxious hope and wearing uncertainty'. These pathos-ridden remarks were part of a stock of images regularly deployed by the BDK in its continued campaigns, and part of the ongoing competition for moral capital pursued by the various victim groups in the 1960s, but they underline again that the BDK was part of an organisational milieu whose members were of a generation to have experienced the suffering of war first hand. This was equally true, obviously, of those of its members who had been at the front. Resorting to the same highly visual language used by mayor Urschlechter in the 1960s, it described how 'impressions and images which cannot be erased pass through our memory. Images from combat – from moments of need and danger, of fear and desperation, but also moments of dogged defiance and willingness to fight to the last.' Again, the recourse to such a visual language and the emphasis on the intensity of the original experience give no insight into the specific memories of any particular individuals or how they affected the person concerned. At the same time, such language was neither arbitrary nor accidental, and reflected the fact that for many of the war participants' generation the commemorative acts of post-war culture provoked the memory of great physical or emotional suffering, and that the meanings attached to these were relatively impervious to the challenges of whatever changes were taking place in the wider culture by this point.

Only in the late 1960s, indeed, did the Holocaust begin to find a modest place in the BDK's reflections on the Day of National Mourning. In 1968, for example, it made fleeting reference to 'the innocent victims murdered in the gas chambers'.[5] However, the increasing moves across the Federal Republic to integrate the Holocaust into the wider memory culture manifested themselves not so much in reflections on the murder of the Jews as in a reformulation of the BDK's pre-existing victim rhetoric in response. In the same piece in 1968, for example, it alluded to the sense of moral uncertainty engendered by the shifting memory politics of the 1960s, observing that 'we find ourselves with conflicting thoughts and feelings. On the one hand, we wish neither to devalue nor to suppress that which is deserving of respect and recognition. On the other, however, the truth demands that on the Day of National Mourning we also speak of the horrific side of the great bloodshed during the Second World War, which can only be described as a process of murder and being murdered. The number of those who did not fight as soldiers in battle, but

---

[5] 'Die Toten mahnen', *Kriegsopfer-Rundschau*, November 1968.

who merely became passive victims of a brutal mechanism of destruction, is, of course, not less than the men in the grey tunic.' Such references to the 'brutal mechanism of destruction' betrayed awareness of the increasing references across West German culture to the 'factory style' or 'industrial' mass murder which characterised much speaking and writing about Auschwitz. However, they were not born of an attempt to acknowledge the horrors of the Holocaust and to adjust the BDK's victim rhetoric accordingly. For, by the victims of this 'brutal mechanism of destruction', the BDK understood: 'the dead of the air wars, the victims of expulsion from the east, the victims among those left behind in the territories vacated by the German troops'. Far from marking an attempt to address the moral challenge of the Holocaust itself, therefore, reworking German civilian losses into the casualties of a machine-like war merely marked a reconfiguration of the BDK's relativising rhetoric concerning Jewish suffering.

Echoes of this relativising language can be seen in the parallels drawn by the Protestant Church between the different experiences of suffering it sought to acknowledge on the Day of National Mourning in 1962: 'Included in this are the women and men who died in emigration, as well as the children who died in the refugee trek, whose lives were ended by the war, just as it had similarly brought death to Jewish children a few years earlier.'[6] Yet the mere fact that the Protestant Church was acknowledging the suffering of Jews on the Day of National Mourning, together with the émigrés – who had been viewed with suspicion and hostility in conservative circles ten years earlier – shows that the memory culture was in flux, and that change was under way. Indeed, its account of the overall number of deaths of the war noted that 'half were civilians, victims of the bombing war, Jews, Poles, Russians, French, Dutch, Belgians and members of other peoples': for all its ongoing privileging of the comparatively few Germans killed in the air war compared to the 'Jews, Poles, Russians', the mere mention of the latter groups on such an occasion marked a shift towards contemplation of the war in the east and its consequences which had not occurred in any meaningful way in the 1950s. Why the Protestant Church should reflect changes in the wider memory culture from the early 1960s onwards in its reflections on the Day of National Mourning when the BDK was still failing to do so meaningfully in the late 1960s is, perhaps, explicable by differing rates of change in the leadership cadres of each institution – in the Protestant Church the nationalist-inclined generation of leaders such as Bavarian state bishop Hans Meiser and dean Julius Schieder had departed by the late 1950s, whereas in the BDK the same caste of increasingly elderly activists dominated in the 1960s. Either way, the different rates of

---

6 'Versöhnung, Friede, Menschlichkeit', *Nürnberger Evangelisches Gemeindeblatt*, 18.11.62.

change in each underline how progress was not simultaneous across civil society but occurred at different speeds in different institutions or agencies in this decade of transition.

The fact that change was beginning to manifest itself even in hitherto conservative institutions such as the Protestant Church on the Day of National Mourning in the early 1960s makes the continuity in the official ceremonies themselves all the more striking. These, after all, were largely shaped by the SPD and mayor Urschlechter – who, elsewhere, was pushing the new agenda of Holocaust awareness. Here, however, it was overwhelmingly continuity that prevailed. The annual ceremony, which continued to be dedicated to 'the victims of two world wars and of National Socialist tyranny', was held each year at the *Luitpoldhain* monument; the attendance list remained dominated by the same institutions and individuals that had provided the bulk of the official participants in the 1950s. Indeed, if anything, a larger list of veterans' and war victims' associations was represented in the 1960s than in the 1950s.[7] The choreography of the event remained very similar, centred as it was on speeches of the mayor alongside those of representatives of the Protestant and Roman Catholic churches, together with a wreath-laying ceremony; the accompanying music drew on a largely familiar canon of German secular and sacred pieces with the ubiquitous 'Song of the Good Comrade' accompanying the wreath-laying itself – again, much as it had done in the 1950s.[8]

Most obviously, mayor Urschlechter's speeches revealed a strong degree of continuity in content and tone when compared to those of his predecessors in the 1950s. Particularly striking, indeed, was the highly fixed quality both of the overall structure of his annual speeches and the individual turns of phrase contained therein. Year in, year out, his catalogue of German suffering rehearsed a familiar list – German soldiers, the victims of bombing, the victims of fascism – before moving on to a familiar set of conclusions – the need for peace, the need to provide for the relatives of the dead and the need to oppose atomic weapons. Throughout the 1960s, Urschlechter continued to contextualise this catalogue of German suffering within the wider history of the war, but not that of a continent-wide occupation or genocide, so that the main impression remained that of an ordinary war in which Germany had figured as an ordinary belligerent nation.

As in the 1950s, the decency of German soldierly sacrifice was foregrounded. In 1961, for example, he reflected that 'a feeling of responsibility,

---

[7] StadtAN C 85 I/167, Einladungskreis Volkstrauertag, 1964.
[8] StadtAN C 85 I/167, Einladungskarte: Volkstrauertag 1964; see also the accounts in the *Amtsblatt der Stadt Nürnberg* for the 1960s.

21. Day of National Mourning, *Luitpoldhain*, Nuremberg (1963).

soldierly sense of duty and a real sense of seriousness led them to be drawn to the fronts of this war';[9] in 1965, in a very similar formulation, he recounted how 'with a feeling of responsibility and deep seriousness, not with false hurrah-patriotism or even chauvinism, they went to the fronts of this war'.[10] And, as in the 1950s, the speeches elided the deaths of soldiers and civilians, foregrounding in particular those victims of the air raids killed in Nuremberg. The highly exact and specific references to local civilian casualties contrasted with exceptionally vague references to the Holocaust. If references to the 'millions of people who were eradicated by National Socialist tyranny as a result of a blind dictatorial ideology in the concentration camps, in the prisons and penitentiaries of the Third Reich' offered some acknowledgement of the scale and nature of the crimes, they remained highly nebulous and partial: above all, the enormity and variety of the spaces in which the crimes were committed, the large number of perpetrators involved, and the foreign-ness of the overwhelming majority of the victims remained blind spots. Indeed, for mayor Urschlechter, the true horror of the crime appeared to

---

[9] 'Gedenkfeier zum Volkstrauertag', *Amtsblatt der Stadt Nürnberg*, 23.11.61.
[10] 'Mit allen Kräften für den Frieden!' *Amtsblatt der Stadt Nürnberg*, 18.11.65.

reside specifically in the fact that the victims had been assimilated, productive citizens of Germany: 'How much thought and care precisely these people had given to the building of their country and to the flourishing of the German Reich, what pride they felt both in their civic responsibility and activity for the state and in their vocation as true citizens of our city, our country and fundamentally their homeland.'[11] In this way, acknowledgement of the crimes of the Nazis became a means not to address the issue of Germans as perpetrators, but to reformulate myths of local victimhood within a narrative of wartime suffering which remained overwhelmingly ethnocentric in its focus.

Where the mayor did break through the ethnocentric focus of his speeches to reflect upon the suffering endured by foreigners, it was in a manner which served to reassert the normality of the German war experience, and the mutuality of violence and suffering on each side. Building on moves to acknowledge the losses on the other side expressed on the Day of National Mourning since the late 1950s, he argued in 1961 that 'our thoughts go in this hour also to those who died for their homeland in both world wars on the other side, in that they gave their lives in fulfilment of their duty . . . in these ill-fated wars, which of course determine fates on both sides of the front'. In 1968, similarly, he emphasised the simultaneity of commemorative acts held not just across Germany but in other countries too, insisting that 'we gather before this memorial to our dead in exactly the same way as the other people of the world, be that in France, in the Netherlands, in Dennmark, in Czechoslovakia, in Russia, in the USA, in Finland or in a quiet mountain village in Austria'.[12] Such comments marked an increased willingness to think beyond the boundaries of the nation in contemplating the suffering brought by the war, but did so in a manner which was silent on the peculiar asymmetry of a war which had been characterised by imperialist aggression and genocidal destruction on the one side and national self-defence on the other.

There were, it is true, some differences between mayor Urschlechter's speeches in the 1960s and the official narratives on offer locally in the 1950s. In the first place, the growing prominence of the expellees within the city's population was mirrored in a new willingness to integrate reference to the expulsions into local commemorative acts. In 1961, for example, Urschlechter added that 'our thoughts at this hour also go to those people who, as a result of the events of the Second World War had to flee their homeland, in order to find sanctuary in our own Federal Republic of Germany, but who were unable to reach the security of this sanctuary as either violence or illness on this

[11] 'Gedenkfeier zum Volkstrauertag', *Amtsblatt der Stadt Nürnberg*, 23.11.61.
[12] 'Ein Appell zur Arbeit für den Frieden', *Amtsblatt der Stadt Nürnberg*, 21.11.68.

flight, on this path of suffering brought their life to an end'.[13] His 1964 speech, meanwhile, underlined further how the expellees' fate had become wrapped up in Cold War rhetoric locally: 'Our thoughts also turn to the women, men and children who lost their lives in the great refugee movements shortly before and after the end of the Second World War on the path of suffering of their flight. Included are those who, since then, were unable to reach the safe ground of our Federal Republic of Germany in flight from dictatorship to freedom and who had to bleed to death before the wall of shame or in the barbed wire obstacles and minefields.'[14]

Similarly, while a strong element of peace rhetoric, and particularly opposition to rearmament, had always characterised the speeches of successive post-war SPD mayors, Urschlechter's speeches in the 1960s were characterised by an increased willingness to make overtly political points.[15] In 1962 he reminded his audience that 'we live in an age of world-political tension' in which living standards had risen substantially but where on the other hand 'the threats which endanger the maintenance of these living standards, in the form of war scares and great catastrophes, are growing all the time', and that 'the days, one might even say the hours, of the conflict between East and West in the Cuba crisis lie only just weeks behind us, hours in which all of us, even some of the indifferent ones, became directly aware of the threatened danger of the destruction of human life and human existence'.[16] By 1967, the city's official record was reporting that Urschlechter 'showed the terrifying events of the wars, the loss of homes and work places, all the crimes and the death which the struggle between peoples brings with it, and remembered also the immense suffering being endured in Vietnam'.[17] By this point, specific commemoration of the events of the Second World War was giving way to the expression of a more generalised anti-war sensibility which, at times, had almost apocalyptic overtones: 'His remarks reflected the concerns caused by the arming of the great powers and described the terrible possibilities of technical development which space exploration made possible for warfare too. With these modern methods it was becoming possible to destroy the world in a few minutes.' Such remarks reflected the changed political climate of the late 1960s, but did little to sensitise their audience to Nazi crimes themselves.

Moreover, the increased willingness of Urschlechter to use the Day of National Mourning to make political comments about the present was more

[13] 'Gedenkfeier zum Volkstrauertag', *Amtsblatt der Stadt Nürnberg*, 23.11.61.
[14] 'Würdiger Totengedenkfeier am Ehrenmal', *Amtsblatt der Stadt Nürnberg*, 19.11.64; see also 'Mit allen Kräften für den Frieden!' *Amtsblatt der Stadt Nürnberg*, 18.11.65.
[15] On the presence of peace rhetoric in ceremonies held within Social Democratic local political cultures, compare Arnold, ' "In Quiet Remembrance"?', 120–4.
[16] 'Gedenkfeier zum Volkstrauertag', *Amtsblatt der Stadt Nürnberg*, 22.11.62.
[17] 'Ihr Tod mahnt uns an den Frieden', *Amtsblatt der Stadt Nürnberg*, 23.11.67.

than matched by his stubborn refusal to address the politics of the past. Repeatedly, mayor Urschlechter sidestepped the question of agency, responsibility or culpability for the crimes of Nazism. In 1961, he opined that 'this hour should not be burdened with the question of cause and guilt for things past'.[18] In the following year, in a move typical of SPD responses to Nazism and the war throughout the post-war period, he characterised glossing over questions of culpability as a positive contribution to the pursuit of peace, arguing, 'Let us not seek after cause and guilt for past things! Rather, in the years belonging to our generation, in which we live and are confronted with the decisive questions of co-existence in our world, let us move on from the past.'[19]

To what should one attribute this stubborn refusal to articulate clearly the issues of agency behind Nazi crimes, the patterns of involvement or the structures of responsibility behind the Nazi regime? In part this mode of speech, inherited by Urschlechter from the habits of his predecessors, reflected continuities in a local political culture dominated now as before by the SPD, and was characterised by rhetorical traditions that foregrounded the welfare needs, not moral dilemmas, of post-war society when seeking to define the most salient issues. To a lesser extent, it reflected the ongoing influence of the Cold War ideological framework. Yet, ultimately, the explanation lay elsewhere – in the peculiar function of official memory politics in the reconstitution of civil society in the post-war era. Its cause was alluded to in the reflections of the Protestant parish newsletter for the Day of National Mourning in 1962, which suggested that 'the Day of National Mourning pulls open wounds in our people which have still yet to heal. It may be hard for some resistance fighters to think today of fallen former political opponents; it may certainly be difficult for former soldiers to remember today the victims of a concentration camp; it may be even harder for young people today to connect all of these things that they have not experienced'.[20] On one level, the wounds to which the newsletter referred were clearly the wounds of war. On another, however, the Church's words suggest that it saw the wounds as also having been inflicted by the internecine struggle of domestic political division. For all the extent to which the achievements of reconstruction and the attendant prosperity had overcome the worst of the divisions of the early and mid-century years, divisions still remained. While the material shortages which had given post-war distributional conflict its intensity no longer pertained in such extreme form, the underlying political divisions that characterised life in an industrial city such as Nuremberg – divisions which had underpinned the conflicts of the 1920s, and which had been submerged, but not destroyed, by Nazism – were still there.

---

[18] 'Gedenkfeier zum Volkstrauertag', *Amtsblatt der Stadt Nürnberg*, 23.11.61.
[19] 'Gedenkfeier zum Volkstrauertag', *Amtsblatt der Stadt Nürnberg*, 22.11.62.
[20] 'Versöhnung, Friede, Menschlichkeit', *Nürnberger Evangelisches Gemeindeblatt*, 18.11.62.

Moreover, while SPD dominance of local politics was such that its mayors could use occasions such as the Day of National Mourning to voice their anti-atomic weapons agenda, the peculiar position of the mayor, with his formal obligation to speak for the entire community, continued to preclude the voicing of partisan histories. The ongoing need to maintain political consensus in a polity the operations of which demanded a greater degree of pragmatic cooperation than at supra-local level made it impossible to use the Day of National Mourning to challenge the dignitaries present with what amounted to accusations concerning their own pasts.

Something of the difficulty involved in challenging myths and voicing that which remained conveniently silent was demonstrated on the Day of National Mourning of 1961. Following the occasion, the commandant of the *Bundeswehr* garrison in Nuremberg wrote to mayor Urschlechter complaining that 'following your exemplary speech this year the representative of the Protestant Church found words which were out of place at this commemoration. I am not alone in this view and would like to assume that you were just as unpleasantly surprised by the comments of Pastor Dr Eichner as I was.'[21] The commandant's remark that 'soldiers who participate in an official capacity on such an occasion are obliged to consider whether their presence is tenable in the face of such remarks' suggests that the pastor had referred to involvement in war crimes of some kind. The commandant further requested that the mayor 'use his personal influence' to ensure that next time a representative 'who is equal to his task' is chosen to speak. Some months later the commandant wrote to the mayor again asking him, 'in the light of a discussion with Pastor Dr Eichner ... to consider my letter as unwritten'.[22] Nonetheless, it was noticeable that a different pastor spoke at the following year's event.

In terms of historical narratives, therefore, the dominant characteristic of the Day of National Mourning in the 1960s was one of continuity. Nascent moves to acknowledge the Holocaust or to integrate it into wider narratives of war and destruction notwithstanding, mayor Urschlechter's speeches signified the achievement of a kind of modus vivendi in local memory politics whereby the price of preserving civic peace was the avoidance of mentioning certain things. If the character of the Day of National Mourning was slowly changing, the significance of that change lay elsewhere. The narrative continuities that characterised the Day of National Mourning in the 1960s were accompanied by a clear sense that its function in civil society was gradually

[21] StadtAN C 85 I Abg. 94/A235, Standort-Kommandatur Nürnberg/Der Stadtkommandant an Oberbürgermeister Urschlechter, 21.11.61.
[22] StadtAN C 85 I Abg. 94/A235, Standort-Kommandatur Nürnberg/Der Stadtkommandant an Oberbürgermeister Urschlechter, 2.5.62.

shifting.[23] In November 1963, for example, the Protestant parish newsletter observed of the Day of National Mourning that '18 years after the bloody tragedy which broke out across our world it is not to be expected that the impact has the same undiminished strength of the first post-war years. For 20-year olds it is all already history, for the 30-year olds fading memory, and only for those now in their forties does the horror of those events still stand "unmastered" like an erratic block in their life'.[24]

For this church author, the apparently fading immediacy of the war was merely a foil to enable him to expound upon the 'real', immutable meanings of the Day of National Mourning – those to be found in biblical truths concerning life and death – but the piece nonetheless addressed a secular truth at the same time: the proportion of the population for whom the Day of National Mourning had immediate resonance, rooted in personal experience, was slowly but surely declining. Similarly, the BDK's claim on the occasion of the Day of National Mourning in 1962 that 'not lip-service at war monuments to the fallen, but real concern for the fate of the living is the yardstick for the thanks of the fatherland to the dead of two world wars' reflected, as ever, the rhetoric of its ongoing campaigns for material redress, but simultaneously touched upon an increasingly obvious fact of life as far as the day itself was concerned – its transformation into a formulaic ritual performed as a matter of routine obligation.[25] The Protestant Church publication openly suggested as much in 1963, asking whether the mourning referred to in the name of the day actually went on any more, or whether 'the whole thing has just become a formality which we fulfil with public commemorations, speeches of remembrance and services of mourning'.[26] Indeed, while on one level the continuities of official rhetoric surrounding the Day of National Mourning reflected wider continuities of political culture, the more mundane truth was that the highly repetitious speeches of the mayor also reflected the simple fact that a busy local dignitary, pressed for time, pulled the same prompt notes from his filing cabinet year after year to give a speech most people in the audience knew inside out from previous occasions.

How far the rhetoric of conservative institutions surrounding the propensity of young people to ignore the war reflected the reality of those people's attitudes is a moot point. The attendance figures, however, told their own story. In 1961, city officials recorded that the Day of National Mourning was 'very well-attended by the population';[27] in 1963, the 2–3,000 attendances

[23] On the evolving place of the Day of National Mourning in the 1960s see Assmann and Frevert, *Geschichtsvergessenheit, Geschichtsversessenheit,* 210–11.
[24] 'Volkstrauertag', *Nürnberger Evangelisches Gemeindeblatt,* 17.11.63.
[25] 'Zum Volkstrauertag 1962: Im Gedenken an die Toten!', *Kriegsopfer-Rundschau,* November 1962.
[26] 'Volkstrauertag', *Nürnberger Evangelisches Gemeindeblatt,* 17.11.63.
[27] 'Gedenkfeier zum Volkstrauertag', *Amtsblatt der Stadt Nürnberg,* 23.11.61.

planned for by the authorities were still the same as the late 1950s.[28] By 1967, however, the authorities were estimating that 1,500 would attend.[29] Even this adjustment proved incapable of keeping pace with reality, for, a year later, the authorities worked on the assumption that a mere 1,000 would turn up.[30]

The clear decline in attendance at the Day of National Mourning in the mid- and late 1960s suggests that something of a turning point had been reached in the memory culture of the city. The complexities of a transitional era in which certain formal and rhetorical continuities persisted in a culture undergoing a less obvious but more fundamental process of change are revealed to a greater extent, however, by the development of the commemoration of the events of 2 January 1945 in the 1960s.

The ceremony first held in 1959 at the South Cemetery to inaugurate the memorial to the victims of bombing became an annual event in the early 1960s. In its ritual forms and choreography it was similar to the Day of National Mourning. Like the November event, it consisted of the mayor laying a wreath before an assembly of dignitaries, politicians, officials, industrialists, foreign consuls and representatives of victim groups.[31] The day gained visibility beyond the circle of those who participated in the formal ceremony by virtue of the flying of flags on civic buildings and on other landmarks at half mast for the day. In 1965, on the occasion of the twentieth anniversary of the raid, the customary illumination of the city's historic buildings was stopped for one night.[32]

As on the Day of National Mourning, mayor Urschlechter's speech rehearsed a highly standardised account of the air raids, largely telescoped into the events of 2 January, in which the bombing attacks were torn not only from the wider context of Nazi ideological aggression, but from any meaningful discussion whatsoever of the overall dynamic of the war. Neither the industrial nature of the city nor its important symbolic function for the Nazi regime was mentioned when discussing Nuremberg as a target: rather, the city was represented as a passive site of civilian calm, whose citizens were returning to work 'after several days of festive and holiday peace' when they were interrupted by the raid.[33] The account of the air raid was followed

---

[28] StadtAN C 85 I Abg. 94/A235, Volkstrauertag 1963, Aktennotiz, 15.10.63.

[29] StadtAN C 85 I/167, Aktennotiz betr. Volkstrauertag 1967, 3.10.67.

[30] StadtAN C 85 I/167, Aktennotiz betr. Volkstrauertag 1968, 1.10.68.

[31] StadtAN C 85 I Abg. 94/A235, Aktennotiz betr. Gedenkfeier für die Opfer des Bombenkrieges, 2.1.63; Einladungskreis: Gedenkfeier am Glockenturm im Südfriedhof am 2.1.63.

[32] StadtAN C 85 I/167, Aktennotiz, 9.12.64.

[33] For the striking repetition of variants of this phrase each year see, for example, 'Gedenkfeier auf dem Südfriedhof', Amtsblatt der Stadt Nürnberg, 7.1.60; 'Gedenkfeier auf dem Südfriedhof', Amtsblatt der Stadt Nürnberg, 4.1.61; 'Gedenkfeier auf dem Südfriedhof', Amtsblatt der Stadt Nürnberg, 4.1.62.

by the customary calls for peace and expressions of opposition to atomic weapons.

The opposition both to the bombing of civilians as a military tool and to the development of atomic weapons was rooted, Urschlechter emphasised, in the experience of the city's own population. As on the Day of National Mourning, Urschlechter alluded to the continuing intensity of those memories in his accounts of the raids. However, even by the mid-1960s the truth was becoming more complex; the relationship between popular experience and civic memory more fragile and indirect. The original circumstances of 2 January 1945, combined with the substantial demographic effects of the post-war years, meant that a mere twenty years after the event, the proportion of citizens who had had first-hand experience of the 2 January raid was already, in fact, quite small. For a start, nearly one-quarter of the population was made up of expellees. Approximately one-fifth of the population, moreover, had been born since the war. Of those who had been registered as Nuremberg citizens in January 1945, some 40 per cent had already left the city in response to earlier raids and had thus not lived through the iconic attack. Of the remainder who had been in the city, approximately one-sixth had been foreign workers, the great majority of whom had left shortly after the war.[34] The demographic structure of the German population of Nuremberg in 1945 – which had consisted disproportionately of elderly people – meant that a significant proportion had died in the intervening years.[35] While it is idle to pursue a detailed calculation, a general estimate would suggest that perhaps one-quarter of the city's population in 1965 had had direct experience of 2 January 1945.

As was the case with the Day of National Mourning, attendance figures at the 2 January commemorations indicated their declining purchase within the population. In 1962, the official record noted that attendance 'was not so numerous as in previous years'.[36] While it claimed in the next year that 'a very considerable number of citizens attended', in 1964 it recorded 'hundreds' rather than the thousands seen at commemorations or prisoner of war vigils in the 1950s.[37] The city council responded by decreeing that the 1965 commemorations, held to mark the twentieth anniversary of the destruction of the old city, would be the last such annual event. A larger programme of events was held in that year, including an evening of speeches, readings and music in the city's new *Meistersingerhalle* venue, which culminated in a

[34] See Chapter I.7 above.
[35] For an overview of the impact of the bombing on the city's population structure, see Gregor, '*Schicksalsgemeinschaft?*', 1068–70.
[36] 'Gedenkfeier auf dem Südfriedhof', *Amtsblatt der Stadt Nürnberg*, 4.1.62.
[37] 'Gedenkfeier auf dem Südfriedhof', *Amtsblatt der Stadt Nürnberg*, 4.1.63; 'Gedenkfeier auf dem Südfriedhof', *Amtsblatt der Stadt Nürnberg*, 9.1.64.

performance of Mozart's Requiem.[38] After 1965, the city confined itself to the flying of flags at half mast and the placing of a wreath; the next major formal commemoration was on the twenty-fifth anniversary, in 1970.

In terms of mourning human losses, the cessation of the 2 January commemorations thus also points to the mid-1960s as marking the end of a transitional period in which a post-war memory culture dominated by the emotional shocks administered to ordinary Germans by the war finally faded. If the mid- to late 1950s marked the beginning of this transitional era, as the immediate impact of the war was overcome, the mid-1960s may be seen as marking its end. In the intervening years, the presence of new impulses that sought to foster a greater engagement with the Holocaust competed with the stubborn presence of a memory culture centred on German suffering which, if fading, still had considerable residual purchase.

In another key respect, however, the mid-1960s marked a transitional moment. By this point, it was increasingly apparent that 2 January 1945 had evolved into a focal point of local civic identity as much as a moment of shared mourning among those who had first-hand experience of the suffering it had caused. The extent to which this was the case was shown by the city's official account of the commemorations surrounding the twentieth anniversary of the attack. This led with an account of the damage to the buildings and historic monuments of the city rather than an account of the effects of the attack on the population, thus foregrounding the physical and cultural impact of the air raids rather than the human suffering they caused. In its words, 'twenty years ago, on 2 January 1945, the fury of war raged through Nuremberg in a singular rage of destruction. Within a few minutes numerous irreplaceable historic buildings and monuments fell to rubble and ash. The old city went up in flames; the property and possessions of the citizens were destroyed.' Only then did it remark: '1,829 people were killed, over 6,000 suffered heavy injuries . . .'[39] Thereafter, 2 January 1945 became a fixed reference point in the cultural memory and civic identity of the city, even as mourning of the human losses faded in intensity.

There again, it should be emphasised that this transition from a memory culture that reflected the emotional effects of war to a memory culture that formed part of a wider ongoing process of civic identity construction did not occur overnight, nor did the latter entirely supersede the former. Despite the scaling down of the city's official commemorations, private individuals and representatives of victim groups continued to congregate unofficially at the memorial to the victims of bombing for a number of years. In its anniversary

[38] '2 Januar 1945: Mahnung und Vermächtnis', *Amtsblatt der Stadt Nürnberg*, 5.1.65; C 85 I/167, Aktennotiz betr. Gedenktag 2 Januar, 4.1.65.
[39] '2 Januar 1945: Mahnung und Vermächtnis', *Amtsblatt der Stadt Nürnberg*, 5.1.65.

comments of January 1967, for example, the *Nürnberger Nachrichten* noted that, despite the absence of a formal ceremony, 'the visitors stood before the wreath-strewn monument for some minutes in silent communion with their unforgotten dead relatives'.[40] In the following year, similarly its report carried a picture of 'relatives of the victims who had gathered to remember at the memorial'.[41]

In many respects, therefore, the mid-1960s marked an era of transition in the memory culture of the city. As examination of the new impulses shows, the historical fact of the Holocaust was beginning to be addressed: both political leaders and sections of opinion-forming civil society had begun to pursue initiatives aimed at raising awareness of the genocide. Seen in the long perspective, such moves marked the decisive shift away from a culture of neglect or marginalisation. However, in the short term their strength and breadth was limited, and the permanency of their impact far from guaranteed; they were occurring in a wider situation of flux whose outcomes were still unclear. If the experiences of a hitherto excluded group were integrated into official narratives in the 1960s, it was arguably those of the expellees, not the Jews. Moreover, the 1960s were significant not so much for the extent to which the ethical focus of memory politics – which remained essentially narcissistic – changed, as for the fact that the nature of both commemorative acts and the wider memory culture in which they operated was in transition from one in which direct experience of suffering provided the underlying logic to the mourning process to one in which the past was increasingly being appropriated in the service of civic identity politics.

Perhaps the best indication that acts of commemoration remained self-centred in the 1960s, and the clearest insight into the difficulties faced by civic leaders in thinking beyond the idea that commemorative acts should focus on the majority community's own dead, is afforded by discussions in the 1960s over whether to include a speaker from the Jewish community at the Day of National Mourning. The initiative for this came from a Jewish resident, who wrote to mayor Urschlechter asking for a representative of the Jewish community to speak alongside the Protestant and Roman Catholic speakers. While the imminence of the 1963 event made this impossible, the mayor sought consensus from the main parties on how to deal with the issue for the subsequent year.[42]

The discussion in the city's Senior Council was instructive. Urschlechter, who had recently returned from his visit to Israel, was clearly unenthusiastic,

[40] 'Die Opfer sind unvergessen', *Nürnberger Nachrichten*, 3.1.67.
[41] 'Die Opfer sind nicht vergessen', *Nürnberger Nachrichten*, 3.1.68.
[42] StadtAN C 85 I Abg. 94/A 235, Urschlechter an Stadtratsfraktionen der SPD, CSU, FDP, 19.6.64.

stating that 'my impression is that in Israel more emphasis is placed on the fact that the years before 1945 should not be forgotten than on whether something externally visible is implemented', and that 'we will have to bear in mind the relative strength of the confessions'.[43] Such a position, which revealed a fundamental inability or unwillingness to engage with the facts of how the exclusionary violence of the Third Reich had impacted upon the minority Jewish community, was reinforced by deputy mayor Haas: 'I would like to warn against acceding to this wish, as other groups might then come along. After all, 98 per cent of the population belongs to the Christian faith. If we extend things here, then the Free Religious community will have to be catered for, then the Jehovah's Witnesses et cetera.' The CSU's representative, Oscar Schneider, concurred, insisting not only that 'the event has taken place in very dignified form hitherto' but also that 'the persecutees of the regime have been sufficiently remembered'. It was left to the young SPD fraction leader, Willy Prölss, the most consistently far-sighted councillor in these matters, to point out the glaringly obvious: 'Of course we only have a small Jewish community in our city. But the cause of this lies in the era of the thousand-year Reich.' Pointing out that the Jewish community had suffered the greatest damage, he encouraged the council to seek the views of the Jewish community itself.

The meeting's conclusion that participation of a Jewish representative should not be encouraged 'in order to avoid the remembrance ceremony becoming too long' indicated the ongoing presence of fundamental blind spots in the way in which the city's commemorative practices were conceived in the mid-1960s, but the response of the Jewish community leadership was equally instructive.[44] Declining the option to participate on the grounds that he had 'always participated in the remembrance ceremony at the *Luitpoldhain*', the chairman of the Jewish community at this time, Adolf Hamburger, was most concerned that the individual who had made the request be encouraged to articulate future such requests through the official community representatives.[45] Here, again, the Jewish community's priority was to control Jewish voices that it feared might disrupt the community's carefully crafted good relations with the city, or rebound negatively upon the tiny Jewish community as a whole.

As a result, official commemoration of Jewish suffering remained separate from the main civic events. Each year the mayor laid a wreath at the memorial in the new Jewish cemetery on the occasion of the anniversary of the

---

[43] StadtAN C 85 I Abg. 94/A 235, Auszug aus dem Niederschrift über die Sitzung des Ältestenrats vom 13.7.64 betr. Totengedenkfeier der Stadt Nürnberg am Volkstrauertag.
[44] StadtAN C 85 I Abg. 94/A 235, Beschluss des Ältestenrats vom 13.7.64.
[45] StadtAN C 85 I Abg. 94/A 235, Niederschrift über eine Besprechung mit dem Vorsitzenden der Israelitischen Kultusgemeinde, Herrn Hamburger, am 27.7.64.

Night of the Glass in November 1938.[46] If the gesture was well meant, it was also revealing of the ongoing failure of the civic leadership to grasp the dimensions of the Holocaust or the challenge it posed to customary commemorative politics. In laying a wreath 'in memory of the terrible events of the Night of Glass', the ceremony's focus on a moment of mob vandalism of German property in which scores of German Jews were killed – horrific as that occasion was – sidestepped the European-wide process of mass murder over years that had characterised the Holocaust. In laying it 'in memory of all Jewish fellow citizens' rather than simply 'all Jews' it revealed once more how, even as it tried to acknowledge the suffering of the Jews, the underlying logic of a local memory culture, largely focused on events that had occurred within the confines of its own community, struggled to make the appropriate connections between whatever suffering had occurred in the city and the unfathomable suffering brought about during the Second World War across the whole of Europe. For all the shifts that were occurring in the 1960s, the local framework of the civic memory culture remained a fundamental barrier to re-imagining the events of the war in a manner which embraced the historical enormity of the Holocaust.

---

[46] StadtAN C 85 I Abg. 94/A48, Aktennotiz betr. Kranzniederlegung für die jüdischen Opfer, 12.11.68.

The Fascist as 'Outsider'

Nuremberg, the Nazi Party Rallies
and the NPD

As consideration of interest group politics, memorial building and formal commemorative rituals shows, the 1960s represented an era of multi-dimensional flux in the memory politics of the Federal Republic as played out in local spaces. The changing material contexts provided by the achievements of reconstruction, the evolving political and ideological constellations provided by the domestic and international climate, the slow processes of liberalisation and democratisation of the political culture of the Federal Republic, the fading physical, mental and emotional shocks of the war, and the impact of demographic changes had combined to make challenges to the fragile memory consensus of the 1950s possible. While the racial dimensions of Nazi politics had established a place in the memory culture of the 1960s in a manner which marked a shift from that of the 1950s, the permanence of this was far from guaranteed; other histories continued to compete for acknowledgement, and other political, economic and demographic logics were such that they had as much chance of success as those pushed by interests seeking recognition of the Holocaust. Above all, even where the historical fact of genocide was being engaged and its significance debated, the elisions, distortions and silences remained highly evident.

The complexities of the transitional era of the 1960s are underlined further when one considers that, in addition to exhibiting locally symptoms of changes that were occurring across the Federal Republic, the city played host to an ongoing series of challenges and conflicts surrounding both the specific associations of the city with the Nazi regime and the physical legacies that regime had bequeathed. This was, indeed, precisely how the city administration imagined the problem: in 1958, in one of many discussions of what to do with the remains of the Nazi party rally grounds, the head of its Construction Office, Heinz Schmeissner, described the colossal, half-finished relic of the

Congress Hall as 'an unusual and difficult inheritance' from an 'unsympathetic testator'.[1] During the 1960s, however, an issue that had hitherto been dealt with by a dual approach – pragmatic use of its physical residues, pointed sidestepping of its political symbolism – gained in immediacy. Firstly, this was because the crumbling state of some of the relics gave succour to those who were critical of the absence of engagement with the crimes of the past; second, because the new impulses towards discussing the more problematic sides of the Nazi regime were manifesting themselves specifically in voices pointing to Nuremberg's particular historical burdens; and, third, because the absence of historically minded, politically aware engagement with the relics of Nazi rule from a democratic standpoint had left opportunities for others who wished to engage in the symbolic occupation of such ideologically, politically and morally charged spaces and to annex them once more in the pursuit of pernicious, xenophobic agendas.

As the sometimes tortuous pronunciations of prominent civic personalities such as mayor Urschlechter or Hermann Glaser on occasions such as the opening of exhibitions or the Nuremberg Conversations showed, awareness of the city's historic burdens provided a key framework within which the local memory culture evolved. Figures such as Urschlechter or Glaser constantly negotiated a balancing act between, on the one hand, seeking to ground the pursuit of democratic politics on the obvious warnings that local experience of recent history offered, while rejecting, on the other, the notion that the city and its people had been any more responsible than others for the catastrophe of Nazism. At the same time, efforts to re-forge an alternative political and cultural identity as a progressive city had to be constantly defended against accusations that officials were seeking to sanitise the city's reputation.

Politicians and officials were not the only ones to engage the question of how Nuremberg's historical relationship to Nazism should be represented. Rather, the changing engagement with specifically local histories of Nazi rule can be seen in the multiple and diverse items of popular literature generated in this period – in the myriad offerings of tourist histories, diary extracts, travel writings and general accounts published in the reconstruction years. Taken individually, of course, the narratives on offer in such texts have no greater claim to stand for what ordinary citizens or visitors knew or believed than those presented in any other form of text. Yet while each piece of writing offered a representation of Nuremberg's past which was peculiar to itself, telling nothing about how its readers engaged with its contents, such literature does, when considered as a whole, reproduce elements of narrative and mark

[1] StadtAN C 7 IX/740, Niederschrift über die 36. Sitzung des Stadtrats, 23.4.58.

shifts in representation that were simultaneously visible across other fields of activity and forms of text. More specifically, it also confirms insights suggested by examination of other elements of the peculiarly local discourse on a local set of stories and problems.

In many respects typical of the popular literary products of the mid- and late 1950s was the brochure *Nuremberg. A Guide Through the Old City* written on behalf of the city's tourist office by Wilhelm Schwemmer, the director of the city's art collection.[2] Focusing on the 'historic' monuments of the city centre, it oscillated ambiguously between acknowledging the extent of wartime damage – with a view to lauding the achievements of reconstruction – and denying its effects in order to assert the continuity, depth and strength of Nuremberg's cultural heritage. In its introduction it stated uncontroversially that 'the high praise previously given to the city of Nuremberg by many visitors has always been primarily focused on the splendid state of preservation of its monuments from older times', before observing that 'whoever had the opportunity to see Nuremberg in 1945 after the end of the war and wanders once more through the streets of the old town must be amazed at the immense work of reconstruction that has, above all, been invested in the buildings of artistic and cultural significance. Any contemplation of Nuremberg in this respect must start from the situation in 1945 in order to permit the correct judgement.'[3] Yet for the most part its subsequent account ignored the war, or glossed over its effects in brief and passing phrases that did little justice to the massive devastation it had brought. Rather than discuss the destruction of monuments during the war it focused on the age of the original building and on its function in the medieval or early modern era; where damage or destruction was acknowledged the book's emphasis was overwhelmingly on the faithful 'reconstruction' (*Wiederaufbau*) or 'restoration' (*Wiederherstellung*) of a copy or near likeness. Above all, in focusing on individual 'historic' monuments rather than on the wider process of rebuilding the old city – which had been extensively remodelled in line with modern commercial, traffic and sanitary needs, and to take account of demographic shifts towards suburban living – it implied that the post-1945 incarnation of the old city was almost indistinguishable, once reconstructed, from its pre-war form. Such programmatic intent was confirmed in the book's cover, which used a section of the Krell Altarpiece of *c.* 1480 from the *Lorenzkirche* containing the oldest known image of the Reich city. Ultimately, therefore, the book chose to gloss over the effects of the bombing on the city's historic skyline and landscape in favour of an emphasis on continuity with the

[2] Wilhelm Schwemmer, *Nürnberg. Ein Führer durch die Altstadt* (Nuremberg, 1956). References are to the second edition (1957).
[3] Ibid., 5–6.

medieval and early modern era. This was, in part, born of the book's intended function – as a publication designed to highlight Nuremberg's renewed attractiveness to tourists despite the events of the war – but it also testified to the ambivalence that continued to characterise many responses to the bombing in the mid-1950s.

At the other extreme, the journalist Fritz Nadler's near simultaneous publication in 1957 of *I Saw the Downfall of Nuremberg* – which reproduced diary extracts written by Nadler in 1945 – focused intensively on the destructiveness and suffering visited upon the city in 1945. Beginning with the events of 2 January, it continued through the battle for Nuremberg and into the hardships of the early occupation period.[4] As juxtaposition of Schwemmer's and Nadler's accounts shows, the mobilisation of histories of suffering and destruction in the service of the victim discourse – of which the latter's book was a part – sat in considerable tension with accounts of successful reconstruction the emphasis of which was on cultural continuity. Nadler's account also distinguished itself from Schwemmer's in its acknowledgement of the presence of the Nazi regime. Whereas in Schwemmer's account the war took place in an apparently politics-free space, Nadler's depicted the dying days of a regime full of unsympathetic Nazi party members. Yet it did so only to emphasise the tyranny visited upon the hapless citizens whose suffering was thereby compounded further. For all their differences, both texts reproduced the silences and absences familiar from other elements of the dominant memory culture of the 1950s, above all the complete lack of contextualisation of the city's martyrdom in the history of the regime's genocidal war of annihilation across Europe.

Above all, for all the passing references to Reich party rallies in Nadler's text, neither meaningfully engaged the challenge posed by Nuremberg's own historical associations with the Nazi regime. That challenge came from elsewhere – and, quite clearly, it initially came from outside. In 1966, for example, the travel magazine *Merian* devoted an issue to the city, carrying, as was its convention, a series of articles discussing life in the city and its attractions to the modern visitor. Some articles continued to ignore the recent past, to gloss over its effects, or to stress the continuities between the atmosphere of the contemporary city and that of its picturesque medieval counterpart. Friedrich Hagen, for example, an émigré who had left Nuremberg during the Nazi years, reproduced the familiar caricatures of a city with a particularly industrious, phlegmatic and sober population – a long-standing component of the cultural armoury of the city that was mobilised with insistent regularity in the post-war years to distance the population from all things excessive,

---

[4] Nadler, *Ich sah wie Nürnberg unterging.*

hysterical and radical, and thus implicitly to dissociate them from blame for the Nazi regime.[5] Others, however, were more critical, and reflected openly on the historical associations and burdens of the city.

The most obvious of these was a set of reflections on 'The Last Thirty Years' by the co-editor of the *Frankfurter Allgemeine Zeitung*, Nikolas Benckiser.[6] Referring to the destruction of Nuremberg and why it was so much more striking than that of many other cities, Benckiser openly remarked, 'Not for a moment in the days and months after 1945 could one forget that this pile of rubble that was Nuremberg was simultaneously the site of the deepest debasement for Germany: it was the city in which the hubris of the National Socialist leadership was to be displayed most sumptuously at the Reich party rallies, and precisely because of this it was to be chosen by the victorious allies for the deepest humiliation.'[7] As if pressing this wound was not enough, he followed his lengthy reflections on the party rallies and associated hysteria with a pointed reminder that those whose rubble existences after the war had allowed them to indulge in myths of victimhood had had previous histories which were not always those of the innocent bystander. Describing life in the post-war ruins he observed that 'when isolated impoverished figures scurried past, one wanted to ask oneself where this man or that woman had stood during those parades, whether they had worn a uniform, had been lined up in those columns, or had observed silently from their windows in civilian attire, perhaps against their will or with dark premonition in their hearts . . .'[8] The accusation of a forgetfulness that was highly self-interested and rooted in individuals' own compromised pasts mirrored, in Benckiser's account, the evasiveness shown by the city with regard to the relics of the Nazi regime: 'One speaks little of these memory traces. Hardly any of the German tourists, who omit nothing from the clockwork figures on the *Frauenkirche* to the *Bratwurstglöcklein*, is interested in seeing them; no travel guide is keen to point them out.'[9] The restoration of old monuments feted by Wilhelm Schwemmer a decade earlier was now the object of criticism: in Nuremberg, in Benckiser's opinion, 'forgetting the recent past is made almost too easy in favour of remembering the deeper past'.[10]

For at least some outsiders, therefore, the apparent refusal to address openly the issues raised by the city's recent, awkward past marked a profound lacuna

---

[5] Friedrich Hagen, 'Ich stand da ohne Worte', *Merian*, vol. 19, no. 8 (August, 1966), 4–9; for similar caricatures see Werner Schultheiss, *Kleine Geschichte Nürnbergs* (Nuremberg, 1966), pp.13–14. On the self-perception of the city as moderate and phlegmatic, see also Chapter II.4 above.

[6] Nikolas Benckiser, 'Die letzten dreißig Jahre', in ibid., 10–16. Benckiser had himself worked on the Nazi journal *Das Reich* before 1945. (Hodenberg, *Konsens und Krise*, 269.)

[7] Benckiser, 'Die letzten dreißig Jahre', 11–13.

[8] Ibid., 13.

[9] Ibid., 16.

[10] Ibid., 15–16.

in the memory politics of the town. Moreover, in asking what the city's bombed-out inhabitants had done during the preceding era Benckiser was suggesting that at least some ordinary citizens had been culpable participants in the Nazi project. Such challenges were being thrown down, again, in a climate in which the racist, genocidal dimensions of Nazi rule were beginning to be addressed by critically minded voices across the Federal Republic more generally. In the face of such challenges, the old strategies of denial and evasion, of simply ignoring the histories both of Nazi display and of Nazi persecution played out locally between 1933 and 1945 were clearly no longer adequate. Yet at the time that outsiders such as *Merian* were issuing their challenge, popular literary representations of Nuremberg and the Nazi past produced from within the city itself revealed that its historic associations with the Nazi regime lent themselves not so much to a more far-reaching, self-critical confrontation of the past but rather to the reformulation and reassertion of the powerful myths of ignorance, innocence and victimhood which had become so entrenched in the 1950s.

One such example was the widely disseminated *Short History of Nuremberg* published in 1966 by Werner Schultheiss, the head of the city's municipal archive.[11] Unlike the accounts written in the 1950s, it engaged openly in its closing sections with the city's historical links to the Nazi regime, embedding its remarks in a wider account of the Third Reich. Yet rather than reflect upon the political choices made by broad sections of the population of Nuremberg in the early 1930s, and in particular upon the fatal susceptibility of the city's bourgeoisie to the siren attractions of fascism, Schultheiss told a story in which blame lay firmly elsewhere. Both the crises of the 1920s and the 1930s and the movement to which they gave rise, Schultheiss made clear, came from outside. Rehearsing the mantras of the interwar Right, he insisted, firstly, that it was the 'dictated peace' of Versailles – rather than the economic and political bankruptcy of the Imperial regime – that had been to blame for the inflation and the subsequent impoverishment of sections of the middle class.[12] Similarly, the recovery and economic and cultural achievements of the 'golden years' were brought to an end by a Depression whose roots were foreign.[13]

In his account of the growth in Nazi support, moreover, Schultheiss – quite erroneously – ascribed the main blame to the unemployed: 'This unfortunate economic situation and the lack of government initiative gave the NSDAP and above all Julius Streicher the opportunity for an irresponsible propaganda which promised everything, to which broad circles of the population, above

[11] Schultheiss, *Kleine Geschichte Nürnbergs.*
[12] Ibid., 136.
[13] Ibid., 142.

all the many unemployed, fell victim.'[14] In his emphasis on voters 'falling victim' to Nazi propaganda, Schultheiss obviated the need to reflect upon the choices actively made by many ordinary citizens. In emphasising that Nazi success had been born of a moment of singular economic crisis which had mainly affected the working class he evaded the need for comment on the ideological proclivities, political ambitions and mental habits of broad sections of the German bourgeoisie that had formed the backbone of the fascist consensus. Above all, his emphasis on propaganda allowed silence on the integrative radical nationalism and racism which had been central to Nazism's mobilisation of mass support.

The evasiveness of such an account of the Nazi rise to power – which absolved the middle classes and elite interest groups of their central culpability – was mirrored in Schultheiss' narrative of the Nazi years. Rather than address the issues of widespread institutional, commercial and personal complicity in the 'aryanisation' of Jewish assets, for example, he ascribed this to a small clique of leading Nazis, relating how 'the circle around Streicher . . . shamelessly enriched itself on the confiscated property of Jewish citizens'.[15] The persecution of the Jews, meanwhile, took place out of the public eye. Schultheiss recorded the murder of many Nuremberg Jews, but his brief account insisted on the ignorance of most ordinary citizens: 'The majority and the most decisive of the Gestapo's activities did not impinge upon the public. Only the responsible offices, chance witnesses and neighbours knew that in 1942/3 the rest of the local Jews were shipped in three transports to camps in the east, where 1,626 Nuremberg Israelites met their deaths through gassing, disease and hunger.'[16] And just as ordinary citizens were entirely innocent of the persecution of the city's Jews, Schultheiss insisted that the city bore no responsibility for those aspects of the regime particularly associated with it. His perfunctory account of the Nazi party rallies, whose staging had been a joint enterprise involving the city council as well as outside agencies, asserted that 'Adolf Hitler officially branded Nuremberg the "City of the Reich Party Rallies" and wanted hereby to draw on the old tradition of the medieval *Reichstage* for his people and before foreigners. Enormous demonstrations and gatherings of the party formations and masses of people gathered together from all over Germany were to generate sympathy for the new regime.'[17] In this way, the Nazis were represented as outsiders who came to Nuremberg for one week in the year to parade and hear speeches before departing again, leaving the ordinary citizens of Nuremberg to get on with their daily lives. The collective innocence of the

[14] Ibid., 142.
[15] Ibid., 145.
[16] Ibid., 147.
[17] Ibid., 143.

city and its population were made explicit in Schultheiss' account of the Nuremberg Laws: 'In 1935 the so-called "Nuremberg Laws", which promulgated the disenfranchisement of Jewish fellow citizens, were decided at a rally specially convened in Nuremberg. In this way Nuremberg was discredited in the eyes of the world without its own involvement.'[18]

What pretended to be 'a scholarly exposition of the history of the city' and 'an objective source of information and a reference work for the historian, friend of history, the teacher and the resident' by a respected local archivist revealed itself in its treatment of the Nazi era, therefore, to be a highly partial account that systematically downplayed the widespread culpability of local institutions and individuals for the crimes of the Third Reich.[19] Above all, in focusing on certain aspects of the historical subject matter at the expense of others, it sidestepped the firm anchoring of the regime's local daily practices of domination and exclusion in the voluntarist participation of broad sections of the city's bourgeoisie.

Schultheiss' work was not an isolated case. As examination of Fritz Nadler's second volume of diary extracts, published in 1969 under the title *A City in Streicher's Shadow* reveals, Schultheiss' account was, if anything, the typical product of a local culture that still stubbornly refused to contemplate issues of local complicity in Nazi criminality and chose, instead, to draw upon all the cultural resources at its disposal to reassert its innocence in the face of new external challenges.

Unlike Schultheiss' supposedly 'objective' account, the authority of which lay in the scholarly credentials of its author, Nadler's account presented itself as a narrative of revelation of those things hidden to the population at the time, penned by a political outsider whose journalist status had given him privileged access to insider information. Its claims to importance lay in the sensationalising, and simultaneously exculpatory, assertion that 'few of the details contained in this documentary report were preserved for the post-war world by the newspapers of the era. The official city chronicle also gives only very limited information. The censor ensured that nothing was known.'[20] The 'Streicher's shadow' of the title functioned as a metaphor for Nazi tyranny, repressing the city and its population; the cover of the book, which depicted the city's historic skyline plunged into darkness – by what was clearly to be understood as Streicher's menacing presence – implied that the particularly vicious dimensions of Nazi rule associated with the city were to be the starting point not for the argument that Nuremberg was in need of greater confrontation of the past than elsewhere, but for the idea that the city itself had been

---

[18] Ibid., 144.
[19] Ibid., 7–8.
[20] Nadler, *Eine Stadt im Schatten Streichers*, 6.

uniquely victimised. Indeed, the use of the historic skyline, a long-standing focal point of local civic identity, to suggest the impact of Nazi oppressiveness, ensured that the peculiar histories of racism and persecution played out locally were invoked to reinforce local self-understandings of the collective 'Nuremberg' as embodying the antithesis of all things Nazi. In contrast to Schultheiss' distanced account of 'the Nurembergers' and 'their' history, Nadler narrated his account in a manner that implied close identity with a collective 'we' who simultaneously formed his subject and his readership, a 'we Nurembergers' defined, again, by common sense, moderacy and pragmatism who, when they were not figuring as its victims, observed the unfolding of Nazi power from the sidelines.

Like Schultheiss, however, Nadler lost no time in insisting that Julius Streicher was a foreign import to Nuremberg's political culture. In his foreword, he emphasised that 'it should first be underlined that the "Leader of the Franconians", Julius Streicher . . . was actually neither born in Nuremberg nor of Franconian descent. He was born in the non-Franconian location of Fleinshausen . . .'[21] Nadler also depicted Nazi affairs in a manner which juxtaposed local Nuremberg bystanders with the politics of a regime that came – quite literally – from outside. Depicting a meeting on the main market place (the then *Adolf-Hitler-Platz*) which marked the prelude to the destruction of the main synagogue on the *Hans-Sachs-Platz* in August 1938, he noted how 'already in the morning hours around 40,000 heavy boots pounded the paving stones of Nuremberg: storm formations of the SA, functionaries, sections of the *Werkvolk* [*sic*], of the Hitler Youth and the BdM girls; neither were those of the Women's Organisation missing. They streamed towards the city centre, flowing together from the suburbs, from the east, south, west and north, in radial form. Many Nurembergers were astonished at these marching columns.'[22]

In common with his own earlier publication, the bulk of Nadler's book focused on German wartime suffering – in this case between the defeat at Stalingrad and the end of 1944, at which point in time his first book had begun its story. Unlike the 1957 volume, which had been all but silent on the racial crimes of the Nazis, it opened with a lengthy account of the destruction of Nuremberg's main synagogue. Yet, while this in itself symbolised a key shift in the focal points of popular historical writing in the era, the silences characterising Schultheiss' treatment of this subject were all too evident in Nadler's writing too. Like Schultheiss, Nadler foregrounded the ignorance of the local civilian population; like Schultheiss, Nadler insisted that the beneficiaries of Nazi corruption and expropriation were limited to a few.[23]

[21] Ibid., 5.
[22] Ibid., 8.
[23] Ibid., 29.

The bulk of the population, meanwhile, according to Nadler, exhibited the famed moderacy which made them apparently immune to the blandishments of the Nazi regime. Such traits were particularly in evidence in locals' treatment of the forced foreign workers during the war. In contrast to his 1957 publication, in which forced workers had figured only as illegitimate plunderers at the end of the war, the 1969 volume distinguished itself by a tangible shift in the identification of victimhood: by this point, forced workers featured as hapless victims of the Third Reich and as deserving of the reader's sympathy. Such a shift testified to the slow change of attitudes that had enabled the memorials to the Soviet prisoners of war to be established in the South Cemetery a few years earlier. Yet this apparent embrace of the forced workers' fate served, in turn, to reassert the distinctions between the Nazi regime, which was depicted as brutal and tyrannical, and the Nuremberg citizens, who figured as humane allies of forced workers with whom they were in the same boat. Noting, for example, newspaper announcements forbidding citizens to give food, coupons or money to prisoners of war deployed in rubble clearance, Nadler's diary extract observed that 'such threats do not work, however. Most Nurembergers think in more humane fashion. Where prisoners of war help to clear up, people mostly give them – despite the ban – a piece of bread, a couple of potatoes or a plate of soup, even though the donors are hungry themselves.'[24] Similarly, he recounted in another extract (on foreign workers who rode the trams in the city) how 'one can often observe that quite poorly clothed passengers get on who do not say a word and simply give their destination – "town park" – to the conductor. They do not wish to reveal their native language. Sometimes, however, the conductor notices he has given a ticket to a foreigner. But nowhere does it say that passengers have to show their birth certificates. There were actually conductors like this in Nuremberg!'[25]

What was, finally, striking about Nadler's account was his depiction of Nazis. Not only did the peculiarly vicious figure of Streicher lend itself easily to a representation of the Nazi regime in which a few fanatics terrorised the entire population, but the focus on the demolition of the synagogue as a symbol of Nazi criminality led to an emphasis on the 'mob' dimensions of Nazi brutality perpetrated by the SA, rather than the more ordered, bureaucratic mechanisms of exclusion and destruction managed by the civilian administrative and policing apparatus and the largely bourgeois occupants of posts in these institutions. While leading party members were characterised as low-life, sub-intelligent perverts who lacked awareness of bourgeois manners and conventions, and thus, by implication, came from outside of the mainstream of respectable society, the perpetrators of Nazism's impulsive violence were represented as 'boorish louts'

[24] Ibid., 118.
[25] Ibid., 132; see also 184.

(*Rabauken*) and 'columns of thugs' (*Schlägerkolonnen*), who 'ransacked like Vandals'.[26] The compulsiveness of the image of the Nazis as a lumpenproletarian mob was no doubt enforced by Streicher's own position as a representative of the radical, populist, crude 'old fighter' element of the Nazi movement, but the focus on the SA perpetrator type over that embodied in the representatives of bourgeois administrative, institutional and commercial life performed a more general function: in focusing on Nazi-specific formations as the agents of its criminality, the inherent 'pastness' of the perpetrators, rather than their continued presence within the multitude of civic institutions that had survived Nazi rule, was underlined. This was, in other words, a mode of talking about the past that underlined precisely the implication that it was all very much in the past, and not in any way a challenge for the present. In this way, again, the presence and identity of local perpetrators of Nazi crimes who had now been reintegrated into the fabric of bourgeois social life in the city could be conveniently sidestepped.

For the city authorities, meanwhile, the issue of local associations with Nazi Germany was not merely one of sanitising the city's reputation, important as this continued to be. The party rally grounds represented a set of physical objects and spaces demanding constant attention. Occupying a massive area on the south-east side of the city, they consisted of a disparate collection of monumental buildings, decaying barrack complexes, marching arenas and in-between spaces with little coherence or obvious alternative overall function. Some elements offered the possibility of pragmatic re-usage and even commercial exploitation; some represented major maintenance challenges with all the attendant costs; in the case of the massive Congress Hall the relics represented a genuinely unprecedented dilemma. The Congress Hall was too big and solid to dismantle, yet it was incomplete, and unusable for any imaginable single purpose, precisely because of its size. The knowledge of its original intended purpose remained, even if it was mostly unspoken. It stood as an embarrassing but seemingly immutable reminder of an awkward past.

In the immediate post-war years the usage of the various barrack complexes had been determined by the depth of the welfare crisis, the exceptional shortages of accommodation and the constant presence of people in transit. The SA camp had been used as the internment camp for Nazi party activists before being turned over for refugee accommodation; part of it had become the Valka camp. Over the course of the 1950s and 1960s these spaces were gradually transformed into permanent residential housing. The SS camp had been used as a displaced persons camp. A considerable area had been used by the US army as a base, while the *Grosse Strasse* marching strip had been used by US forces as a runway. Other areas had been restored to parkland. The original

[26] Ibid., 15; 145.

Luitpoldhain First World War monument had been reappropriated as a democratic memory space by the city council, while the rest of the *Luitpoldarena* had been dismantled in 1959 to 1960. In the immediately adjacent space the completion of the *Meistersingerhalle* concert hall in 1963 symbolised the city council's ongoing attempts to associate the city with alternative historical and cultural traditions. The Zeppelin Tribune, meanwhile, was utilised for motor sports events, for political demonstrations (such as large homeland associations rallies) or for religious gatherings – the American evangelical preacher Billy Graham spoke from it in 1963, for example. The adjacent Zeppelin field, again, was used by the US army for sporting purposes.[27] If practical necessity governed both immediate usages and the gradual evolution of the appearance of the rally ground landscapes over the 1950s, it is clear, moreover, that the slow process of erasure to which this inevitably gave rise was not entirely unwelcome. Reflecting on the transformation of the disparate elements of the site by 1958, the head of the city's Construction Office, Heinz Schmeissner, related that 'it is a pleasing fact that we have been able to lay out the large open area as a public park; the last remains of the *Luitpoldarena* are being removed; the excavation pit has disappeared, for which we have the "silver lake". The towers in the "March Field" will have to give way to the commuter town of Langwasser. The Zeppelin arena . . . is more or less ready.'[28]

A particular challenge, however, was posed by the enormous Congress Hall, which was the subject of repeated discussion in the city council in the 1950s and 1960s. In the words of mayor Urschlechter, the question was 'whether the torso should be dismantled, should be allowed to crumble as a kind of Pompeii, or whether it should be given over to usage'. In the immediate post-war years it was, indeed, used for a number of practical purposes. It hosted a 1949 building exhibition, an exhibition in 1950 to mark the 900th anniversary of the city, and a number of smaller events, and was also used as a storage depot.[29] From the mid-1950s, as thoughts turned from the immediate welfare priorities of the post-war era to longer-term planning issues, various proposals for a permanent transformation were considered – most notably the questions of roofing the space and of turning it into a soccer stadium.[30] These ideas failed in the face of the intractable technical and financial challenges they posed.

---

[27] This summary is taken from the excellent overview provided in Eckart Dietzfelbinger, *Der Umgang der Stadt Nürnberg mit dem früheren Reichsparteitagsgelände* (Nuremberg, 1990); for an overview see also Reichel, *Politik mit der Erinnerung*, 52–9.

[28] StadtAN C 7 IX/740, Niederschrift über die 36. Sitzung des Stadtrats, 23.4.58.

[29] Dietzfelbinger, *Umgang*, 13–15, 23–24.

[30] See, for example, StadtAN C 29/332, Brochure: Vorschläge über Verwendungsmöglichkeiten der ehemaligen Kongresshalle, Hauptamt für Hochbauwesen, Nürnberg, August 1955; StadtAN C 7 IX/740, Niederschrift über die 36. Sitzung des Stadtrats, 23.4.58; Niederschrift über die Sitzung des Stadtrats am 7.5.58; C 7 IX/744, Niederschrift über die Sitzung des Stadtrats am 15.7.59; C 85 III/23, Niederschrift über die 32. Sitzung des Stadtrats, 14.3.62.

Such discussions reflected a broad consensus across the city council that purely pragmatic criteria should govern future usage. Indeed, discussions in the 1950s and 1960s were characterised by a near-complete absence of historical sensibility regarding the issue. When mayor Urschlechter claimed in a council discussion in 1958 that 'we have approached matters from a deep feeling of responsibility' it is clear that the responsibility he had in mind was to the local taxpayer and to the need to raise the city's profile as a tourist and conference destination. He continued: 'A year ago there was a discussion concerning the holding of a Protestant Church congress in Nuremberg and we were shocked not to be able to offer that which the state capital [Munich] is able to offer. If the project were there the Protestant Church congress would have come here, and we would also have a Catholic Church congress in Nuremberg and other things. This is the motor which moves us to ask you to reach a decision.'[31] Throughout the 1960s there was no meaningful movement on the issue; not until the remaining relics of the party rally grounds were given protected monument status by the Bavarian government in 1973 was the city council forced to begin slowly to contemplate the historical and moral dimensions of the challenge posed by the buildings.[32]

By the mid-1960s there were thus few signs that a new sensibility concerning the historical significance of the relics was emerging. While the size and solidity of the Congress Hall were such that dismantling it was not a realistic option, the poor original construction of the Zeppelin Tribune was such that it was becoming unstable and dangerous. As a result, mayor Urschlechter sanctioned the partial demolition of the structure in 1967.[33] Similarly, in 1966 and 1967 eleven colossal square towers on the 'March Field' were demolished to make way for ongoing residential construction.[34]

Yet it would be incorrect to suggest that the city council suffered from a complete inability to contemplate the significance of the historically loaded spaces in its charge. Neither was it unaware of the problematic meanings attached by some to a set of sites that could easily be misappropriated for pernicious ideological ends. On the contrary, it remained acutely sensitive to the issue. In 1968, for example, on the occasion of a discussion concerning the proposal to hold the Sudeten German Homeland Association's 1969 rally in the city, SPD fraction leader Willy Prölss reminded us that, although the city council had not been its organiser, 'It cannot be overlooked that the last Sudeten German rally had unpleasant side effects for the city too, and

[31] StadtAN C 7 IX/740, Niederschrift über die 36. Sitzung des Stadtrats, 23.4.58.
[32] Dietzfelbinger, Umgang, 25.
[33] StadtAN C 85 III/457, Niederschrift über die 20. Sitzung des Bauausschusses am 16.5.67.
[34] Dietzfelbinger, Umgang, 9.

produced a worldwide echo, but of an overwhelmingly negative nature.' As he explained, 'Our problem is that Nuremberg is historically loaded territory, for the Sudeten German Homeland Association as well ... speeches on the Nuremberg *Hauptmarkt* are judged differently to the same speeches on the *Königsplatz* in Munich.'[35] While the meeting agreed to host the rally, there was agreement as to the sentiment of Prölss's suggestion that 'the historical past of this city should be very clearly pointed out to these gentlemen and they should bear this in mind when making their public speeches'.

The historical associations of both the *Hauptmarkt* – previously the *Adolf-Hitler-Platz* – and the former party rally grounds became a particularly acute problem from the mid-1960s onwards with the emergence of the neo-nationalist NPD.[36] In the March 1966 local elections the NPD won three seats on the city council.[37] At least one of its councillors, Eberhard Engelhardt, had a long history of moving in extreme right-wing circles – in 1952 he had acted as a lawyer in defence of the neo-Nazi Socialist Reich Party.[38] In the Bavarian state elections of November 1966 the party not only gained 7.4 per cent of the votes across the state, but 13.1 per cent in Nuremberg in particular. Moreover, beyond the political challenge to the mainstream democratic parties represented by such results, the NPD repeatedly engaged in the symbolic occupation of Nuremberg's historically problematic spaces in a manner which provocatively implied that it saw itself as standing in a direct continuum with the NSDAP. On three occasions from 1966 to 1968 the NPD held mass gatherings in the city's main conference venue, the *Messehalle*; during the election campaigns of 1966 it mounted demonstrations on the *Hauptmarkt*; in renting the *Meistersingerhalle* for a mass gathering in 1965 it was consciously holding a meeting on the terrain of the original Nazi party rallies, within throwing distance of the *Luitpoldhain* memorial and in the shadow of the Congress Hall.

From within civil society protest was led by a broad coalition of the Extra-Parliamentary Opposition (APO), the trade unions and former victims of fascism.[39] In the case of the former, this protest against neo-fascist potentials

---

[35] StadtAN C 85 III/401, Niederschrift über die 23. Sitzung des Ältestenrats, 11.10.68.
[36] For the following details see the chronicles in Walter Bauer (ed.), *Nachrichten aus der Provinz. 1968 und die APO in Nürnberg* (Nuremberg, 1998), and Bauer and Mahlert, *Kennen Sie das andere Nürnberg?*
[37] For contemporary accounts of the emergence of the NPD see Hans Maier and Hermann Bott, *Die NPD. Struktur und Ideologie einer 'nationalen Rechtspartei'* (Munich, 2nd edn, 1968); Lutz Niethammer, *Angepaßter Faschismus. Politischer Praxis der NPD* (Frankfurt/Main, 1969); also Horst Schmollinger, 'Die Nationaldemokratische Partei Deutschlands' in Stöss, *Parteienhandbuch*, 1922–94.
[38] StadtAN C 29/312 Eberhard Engelhardt (Rechtsanwalt) an Amtsgericht Nürnberg, 4.8.52; Aktennotiz des Polizeipräsidenten Stahl betr. Klage des Rechtsanwalts Eberhard Engelhardt, 27.8.52.
[39] On the APO see Karl A. Otto, *Vom Ostermarsch zum APO. Geschichte der ausserparlamentarischen Opposition in der Bundesrepublik 1960–1970* (Frankfurt/Main, 1970); Thomas, *Protest Movements*.

coagulated with a broader critique of perceived authoritarian continuities embodied, most obviously, in the 'Great Coalition' Federal government of CDU and SPD, and in the proposed Emergency Laws, which were regarded by many in the mid- and late 1960s as an assault on democracy reminiscent of the legislation of 1933. The student element of the APO mounted a series of protests against the NPD's presence from the mid-1960s onwards. However, the numbers it was able to mobilise were mostly limited. Moreover, the infla-tionary definitions of 'fascist' with which it operated – in particular its elision of 'Fascist' as an ideological descriptor and 'fascist' as a general term of abuse – were such that it drew little, if any, meaningful distinction between the NPD and the CSU, or the bourgeois forces the latter represented; as a result, it did as much to obscure understanding of the political phenomena it sought to oppose as it did to promote it. Much more significant was the broader opposi-tion of the trade unions, which were able to mobilise thousands of supporters for counter-demonstrations or other protests, and which drew on the deep-seated anti-fascist reflex present in the organised labour traditions of the city. This itself drew on memories of anti-fascist struggle in the 1920s and 1930s and of persecution and repression in the subsequent years of Nazi rule; it was the same anti-fascist reflex that had underpinned working-class criticisms of the inadequacies of denazification in the late 1940s and which had been the vehicle of a working-class counter-memory in the 1950s.

22. Anti-NPD demonstration (1967).

Within the mainstream democratic parties on the city council, meanwhile, there was strong consensus on the need to combat the NPD and its provocative activities in the city. Following the local elections of 1966 the SPD, FDP and CSU all announced their refusal to engage in any form of political cooperation with the party.[40] Upon convening the new council they immediately activated a mechanism in the council's statutes permitting the reduction of membership of the council's committees from fifteen to thirteen. As a result of this, the NPD was denied the one representative on each committee to which it would otherwise have been entitled. While the main parties insisted that this move was based purely on the realisation, gained through previous experience, that committees of fifteen were too unwieldy and ineffective, it was transparently obvious that this was a politically driven move designed to keep NPD influence on civic affairs to a minimum.[41]

Much more problematic for the city council was the issue of the NPD's symbolic appropriation of Nuremberg as a site for its gatherings. The second half of the 1960s witnessed protracted debates and legal disputes – the latter usually won by the NPD – concerning the council's right to refuse usage of public venues that it partly owned. The legal advice the council received confirmed its own awareness that there was little it could do to prevent constitutionally admissible parties from hiring venues dedicated for public pursuits.[42] It feared that refusal to allow use of the *Meistersingerhalle* before the 1966 local elections would constitute illegal obstruction of electioneering and enable the NPD to dispute the subsequent results.[43] Moreover, even the representative of the FDP – a party notorious in the post-war years for its silent tolerance of former Nazi party members – felt moved to observe that 'I don't want to say that I mistrust the judges in Munich, but they do come from an era which did not entirely fail to leave its political mark on them in the past'.[44] Such remarks acknowledged the awkward truth that the strong continuities from the Nazi to post-war era in a profession noted for its nationalist and authoritarian proclivities translated into a dilemma of realpolitik for city officials seeking to use the ostensibly neutral structures of Federal and state law to push back NPD influence.

While most recognised the weak legal grounds for the refusal of use of facilities, however, politicians from across the democratic spectrum argued on

[40] StadtAN C 85 III/55, Eberhard Engelhardt, Rudolf Böhland, Lothar Thilke an Oberbürgermeister der Stadt Nürnberg, 12.5.66.

[41] StadtAN C 85 III/55, Niederschrift über die 3. Sitzung des Stadtrats, 15.6.66.

[42] StadtAN C 85 III/518, Niederschrift über die 84. Sitzung des Rechts- und Wirtschaftsausschusses, 9.2.66; for mayor Urschlechter's pessimistic evaluations of the legal room for manoeuvre, see C 85 III / 400, Niederschrift über die außerordentliche Sitzung des Ältestenrats, 9.5.67.

[43] StadtAN C 85 III/518, Niederschrift über die 84. Sitzung des Rechts- und Wirtschaftsausschusses, 9.2.66.

[44] StadtAN C 85 III/52, Niederschrift über die 108. Sitzung des Stadtrats am 16.2.66.

numerous occasions that the attempt to block the NPD should be made nonetheless, for reasons of political symbolism and ethical necessity. As councillor Lippert (FDP) argued in respect of the proposal to break an already extant contract allowing the NPD to use the *Messehalle* in May 1967, 'We are morally in the right and we must try everything to prevent this event on moral grounds. A Reich party rally in association with the name of the city of Nuremberg is just completely impossible.'[45] The SPD, in particular, argued on political, rather than legalistic grounds. Deputy mayor Haas opined in the Legal Committee discussion of February 1966 that legal means should be tried, however unpromising, 'in order that we do not belong to those of whom it is later maybe said that they faced this issue without putting up a struggle'.[46] Likewise, in subsequent discussions in full council session, Willy Prölss argued that 'I recognise that this case has to be handled by the legal people purely according to legal principles, but for us, at least in my fraction, it is also an issue of making a political demonstration.'[47]

In May 1967, finally, the city council elected to make the symbolic gesture of refusing the NPD entry to the *Messehalle*, despite the fact that its management had previously entered into a formal binding contract to permit it to do so.[48] The legal justifications it offered, it knew, were spurious; indeed, subsequent proceedings found in the NPD's favour. However, in the immediate short term the desired effect was achieved, in that a symbolic exclusion of the NPD had occurred; the holding of a mass demonstration of 6,000 protestors opposite the *Messehalle* under the auspices of the trade unions, at which mayor Urschlechter spoke on behalf of 'democratic Nuremberg', provided evidence of wider opposition to radical nationalist politics in the city.

Both the firm commitment which drove the opposition of the mainstream parties to the NPD and the visceral anti-fascism of the trade union-led wider protest movement were expressions of a democratic sensibility that was now far more deeply embedded in the political culture of the city than the radical nationalist proclivities of a minority. Yet even in its discussions of the political and moral necessity of resistance the city council – including its most progressive and historically aware members – revealed the continued lacunae in the memory culture of the city. For one thing, it was clear that, as was so often the case, concern for the reputation of the city, as much as a desire to dispute the ideological positions of the NPD, underlay much of the commitment to resist. Moreover, insofar as the opposition was rooted in the genuine anti-fascist reflex that characterised left-wing politics in the city in particular, it was

[45] StadtAN C 85 III/400, Niederschrift über die außerordentliche Sitzung des Ältestenrats, 9.5.67.
[46] StadtAN C 85 III/52, Niederschrift über die 84. Sitzung des Rechts- und Wirtschaftsausschusses, 9.2.66.
[47] StadtAN C 85 III/52, Niederschrift über die 108. Sitzung des Stadtrats am 16.2.66.
[48] StadtAN C 85 III/400, Niederschrift über die außerordentliche Sitzung des Ältestenrats, 9.5.67.

23. Empty *Messehalle* following barring of NPD (1967).

a reflex born of the knowledge that Nazism had brought untold destruction not to Europe, but to Nuremberg itself. As such, debates on the NPD in the 1960s, like so many other debates, marked a process whereby the city and its political and cultural arbiters reformulated their myths of local victimhood by imagining themselves in innocent opposition to, not complicity with, the crimes of the past.

This was shown, most obviously, in the declaration issued by the mainstream parties to mark the refusal of entry of the NPD to the *Messehalle* in May 1967.[49] Announcing that all those represented by the democratic majority were fully committed to the constitutional system of the Federal Republic, it called upon all citizens to 'combat the beginnings! Radicalism and fanaticism have given rise to an unsurpassable amount of suffering, need, persecution and misery in the political life of our people', and called upon 'the German and international public to recognise that the Nuremberg population has nothing to do with the revival of a dangerous nationalism and political fanaticism which is contrary to German interests'. Instead, it insisted that the political values of Nuremberg and its population were those of democracy, Christianity, humanism and tolerance.

If its rejection of racism offered a nod to the genocidal crimes of the regime, however, the suffering on which it focused overwhelmingly in justifying its anti-fascist stance was, as ever, that of ordinary Germans. Its opening statement of historical background referred to 'radical and fanatic hatred of foreign races and peoples', but foregrounded as the consequence of this not the mass murder of millions of the citizens of Europe but the fact that 'the German Reich was destroyed and divided and the German people were damaged in the most terrible and enduring fashion'. In particular, 'these politics, which went against divine and human law, also led to the downfall of the city of Nuremberg in the flames of the Second World War and left the population of Nuremberg an enormous field of ruins in which irreplaceable cultural and material values were buried'. Rather than contemplate the possibility that many tens of thousands of Nuremberg citizens had played their part in sustaining the fascist and racist consensus that had unleashed the war, and drawing its moral argument from that insight, the declaration drew the conclusion that its democratically minded citizens must stand together 'if they are not once again to fall victim to blind nationalists, intolerant racists or thoughtless seducers'.

Once again, then, the inhabitants of Nuremberg were depicted as having been victim to nationalism and racism – rather than the nationalists and racists themselves. Even as they sought to resist new manifestations of fascist extremism, the city councillors were thus unable to puncture a stubbornly narcissistic memory culture that refused acknowledgement of the central truth: that Nazism had been a political phenomenon which had gained considerable traction in the local political culture, had successfully mobilised wide sections of the local population in pursuit of its radical nationalist and imperialist agendas, and had co-opted large numbers of local people in the implementation of unspeakable crimes.

Conclusion

War and the circumstances of defeat administered a massive, multi-dimensional and unprecedented shock to German society. The collapse of the German army in the east in the summer of 1944 not only precipitated the eventual collapse of the German Reich, its government and institutions, but also led to spiralling military losses, culminating in the enormous losses of the winter of 1944 to 1945. The demographic impact of this was felt by millions of German families; the circumstances of many soldiers' deaths – and, above all, the fact that many were simply recorded as 'missing' – also ensured that it remained a live political, social and cultural issue, as well as a focal point of intense emotional anxiety, for many years after the war. The simultaneous intensification of the allied air raids in the last year of the war brought massive destruction of Germany's cities and infrastructure and levels of civilian suffering which eclipsed even the severe hardship endured by Germans in the First World War. The landscapes of rubble bequeathed by these air raids ensured that millions of Germans lived in at best deeply straitened circumstances for many years after the war. The expulsion of millions of ethnic Germans from the east and their forced propulsion into West German communities struggling to rebuild themselves added not only an additional material burden to overcome but also an additional experience of violence for both the expellees and their host communities to seek to comprehend.

These interlocking experiences of violence and suffering came in the wake of the collapse of a regime of barbaric destructiveness that had mobilised millions of Germans in pursuit of its murderous campaigns of imperialism and genocide. Even as they sought to comprehend the suffering they were now experiencing, many – although, it bears repeating, not all – ordinary Germans thus lived with the knowledge of what they had done, witnessed or at least tacitly sanctioned, and of the untold suffering this had brought to millions of others across the whole of occupied Europe, and indeed in Germany itself.

Finding a language with which to narrate these experiences, to express this knowledge, and to confront these actions was, arguably, a near-insurmountable task. Various vocabularies were available. These were, in part, shaped by the Cold War context in which post-war Germany memory cultures evolved. Yet equally if not more important in furnishing ordinary Germans with the words to describe their experiences, were the vocabularies and rhetorical traditions inherited from a previous era: as often as not it was an older set of languages for which they reached. In Nuremberg this manifested itself most clearly in the prevalence of a strong Social Democratic idiom in the city's official memory culture; particularly striking, also, was the extent to which the strongly Protestant traditions of the city shaped the dominant narratives within broad sectors of society. As these key examples demonstrate, the memory culture of the city was shaped both by secular and religious ways of seeing and thinking: scholars of mid-century Germany ignore the presence of the latter in the mental landscapes even of urban communities with strongly progressive traditions at their peril.

As German society recovered from the disorientating shock of war its members slowly began to make sense of their experiences – to order them into amenable narratives. The silences in those narratives were complex. In some cases they reflected political or ideological expediency. In others they reflected the self-centredness of a culture which had undergone such a massive shock that its members were collectively unable to think beyond their own suffering or to connect it to that they had inflicted upon others. Even as the local memory culture of the city evolved from its initial strong emphasis on German victimhood to a position where some were able and willing to begin to contemplate the murder of the Jews, its core characteristic remained its essentially narcissistic focus. Yet in other cases the silences were more profound again, and reflected the fact that much that had happened in the Nazi era defied description: for many years after the war there was nothing meaningful to say.

In forging an official culture of commemoration of the past, city officials not only faced the difficult task of ascribing positive meaning to unfathomably shocking and shameful events, but also that of offering meaningful narratives that could command consensus across the rifts of a highly divided, conflict-ridden society. In the immediate post-war period a generalised rhetoric of victimhood served not only to relativise the murderous crimes committed by Germans against Jews, foreigners and other victims of Nazism, but also to mask and bridge the schisms between different war victim communities within German society itself. Re-founding a workable political community at local level also meant embracing a shared vocabulary of victimhood – and a corresponding 'grammar of exculpation' – which could command consensus across the divides of a city that hosted competing political traditions.[1] In the context of mid-century German history it bears repeating that these traditions had stood in a state of near-civil war in 1932 to 1933; indeed, members of one tradition – the nationalist one – had been responsible for the widespread persecution and murder of the other, working class one within recent living memory. On a local level, the task of replacing a dictatorship with a democracy was, effectively, one of re-forging a workable culture of political civility in a community whose competing traditions had, until very recently, existed in a relationship of fratricidal hatred.

As West Germany recovered from the war, the 'victim discourse' which had come to predominate in the 1950s became gradually less compelling. As the political culture of the Federal Republic became progressively more liberal the virtues of consensus were challenged by those who saw merit in conflict, debate, argument and criticism. The varied, often unconnected, demands emanating from an ever-increasing range of voices that West German society consider the genodical, and not just the military, dimensions of the last war echoed positively in at least some spheres of a civil society that was undergoing significant cultural change. If the defeat of 1945 and attendant constitutional democratisation had marked the establishment of a Republic based on anti-Nazi legal and political norms, it took the democratisation of West Germany's political culture, which occurred from the late 1950s onwards, to ensure that active contemplation of the genocidal crimes of the past became part of the Federal Republic's critical self-understanding.

The extent to which this had occurred by the end of the 1960s should not, however, be overestimated: the activists who pushed through this shift in the focus of West German memory did so in the face of considerable opposition in a climate in which nationalist residues were still strong. Moreover, the peculiar challenge a more critical memory culture posed to the fragile civic peace constructed at a local level in the 1950s was such that key issues remained too thorny and hence unspoken: above all, the ongoing presence within the city's bourgeois elites of former perpetrators of, and accomplices to, the crimes of Nazism made a partisan politics of memory impossible to Social Democratic powerholders charged with speaking for the community as a whole. Instead, both the city's powerholders and the diverse arbiters of local cultural life co-opted peculiarly local histories of Nazism – those symbolised by the crumbling architectural relics of the regime – into exculpatory narratives in which the city figured as 'victim' not only of the war – because of the impact of allied bombing – but also, because of its use as a backdrop for the party rallies, as a victim of Nazism itself. In this way the physical relics of

---

[1] The phrase is Jeffrey Olick's: Olick, *In the House of the Hangman*, 212.

Nazism did not so much foster critical self-contemplation as contribute to containing the challenges the nascent culture of Holocaust remembrance posed to the civic peace so carefully created in the 1950s. The local functioned as a key site of resistance to the implications of the more critical memory culture that was emerging in the 1960s because it was here that the key unpalatable truth – that ordinary, local people in ordinary, local communities had participated in the machinery of persecution and murder – was most challenging.

For all its limitations, though, a shift had occurred, a shift which, in hindsight, turned out to be the decisive turn in the development of the memory culture of the Federal Republic. Do the temporal delay between the end of the war and the emergence of a critical memory culture on the one hand, and the connections between the emergence of that culture and the wider process of liberalisation of the Federal Republic from the late 1950s onwards on the other offer starting points for thinking about the relationship between political transitions, the overcoming of fratricidal and genocidal conflict, and the forging of cultures of reflection and self-criticism in other contexts? If the example of West Germany tells us anything, it is that it may be asking too much to insist that members of war-torn communities reflect immediately upon the implications of the violence they have visited upon others, however obviously barbaric that violence may have been. Rather, the case gives grounds for hoping that, if a dictatorial regime, however violent, can be successfully supplanted by a vibrant democratic political culture, those same citizens may, with time, begin to ponder those crimes and think critically about them for themselves.

Primary Sources

Stadtarchiv Nuremberg

C 7 I	Hauptregistratur
C 7 IX	Stadtratsprotokolle
C 22 VI	Vereinsrecht
C 28	Wirtschafts- und Ernährungsamt
C 29	Dir.A
C 34	Städtische Museen
C 36	Stadtarchiv
C 40	Ausgleichsamt
C 51	Kulturverwaltungsamt
C 73 I	Schul- und Kulturreferat
C 85 I	Bürgermeisteramt
C 85 III	Bürgermeisteramt
E 6	Vereine
F 2	Stadtchronik
F 5	Quellen und Forschungen zur Geschichte Nürnbergs
F 6	OMGBY

Germanisches Nationalmuseum Nuremberg

Uncatalogued files

Landeskirchlichesarchiv Nuremberg

Diakonisches Werk
Kreisdekan Nürnberg

Printed Primary Sources

Amtsblatt der Stadt Nürnberg
Frankfurter Allgemeine Zeitung
Fränkische Tagespost
Jahresberichte des Germanischen Nationalmuseums
Kriegsopferjahrbuch
Kriegsopfer-Rundschau
Merian
Neue Zeitung
Newsweek
Nürnberger Evangelisches Gemeindeblatt
Nürnberger Nachrichten
Nürnberger Zeitung
Siebenbürgischer Zeitung
Süddeutsche Zeitung
Verwaltungsberichte der Stadt Nürnberg
Vorwärts

Index

Aachen, 287
Adenauer, Konrad, 121, 169, 221, 228, 233, 255, 304
Adler, H.G., 285ff.
Adolf-Hitler-Platz, 363, 370
Africa, 310
Afrika-Korps Association, 144–6, 307
Aid Service for Prisoners of War and the Missing, 79
Air raids, 1ff., 21, 25–9, 38, 51ff.
and memorials, 1–5, 6, 161, 175–82
victims of, 7, 11, 15, 21, 36, 55, 86, 162, 175, 197, 199, 203, 360
commemoration of, 203–7, 212, 336–9, 342–3, 349–52
Aktion Sühnezeichen, 239, 243
Albania, 81
Allgemeine Wochenzeitung der Juden in Deutschland, 238
Allied Control Council, 80, 138
Allemann, Fritz René, 285
Altdorf, 130
American military government, 114, 125–8, 154, 156, 166, 209–10
establishment of control, 26–7
and expellees, 38, 41, 47, 149
and denazification, 56, 91–3, 96, 99–101
and returning soldiers, 65, 67
and DPs, 105–8
and concentration camp survivors, 108–10
Améry, Jean, 293
Anti-Communism, 37, 128, 339

and memory politics, 6, 19, 118, 121ff., 227–8, 311
former soldiers and, 67
missing soldiers and, 81–2
of Protestant Church, 100
of military government, 109
and victims of fascism, 158
expellees and, 220, 227–8, 323, 325
Anti-Semitism, 66, 113, 116–18, 272, 299; *see also* Jews; Holocaust
of Protestant Church, 100, 129, 237
opposition to, 232, 236–8, 255
in Nuremberg, 276–80
Aronsfeld, Caesar, 276
Aryanisation, 116, 278, 361
Associated East German Homeland Associations, 221
Association of the Bavarian War Blind, 196
Association of Briegers, 321
Association of Democratic Resistance Fighters and Persecutees' Organisations of North Bavaria, 157
Association of Former Prisoners of War (VdH), 142–3, 148, 168–9, 191, 195–6, 306–7, 325
Association of the Former 98th Infantry Division, 70
Association of the Persecutees of the Nazi Regime (VVN), 111, 157–8, 173, 190, 199
Association of the Soviet Zone Refugees, 323
Augsburg, 145, 267
Auschwitz, 239, 244, 248, 251, 259ff., 341
Austria, 344